Lecture Notes in Computer Science 3986

Commenced Publication in 1973
Founding and Former Series Editors:
Gerhard Goos, Juris Hartmanis, and Jan van Leeuwen

T0226207

Ketil Stølen   William H. Winsborough
Fabio Martinelli   Fabio Massacci (Eds.)

Trust
Management

4th International Conference, iTrust 2006
Pisa, Italy, May 16-19, 2006
Proceedings

 Springer

Volume Editors

Ketil Stølen
SINTEF ICT
P.O. Box 124, Blindern, 0314 Oslo, Norway
E-mail: Ketil.Stolen@sintef.no

William H. Winsborough
University of Texas at San Antonio
Dept. of Computer Science, One UTSA Circle
San Antonio, TX 78249-1644, USA
E-mail: wwinsborough@acm.org

Fabio Martinelli
Istituto di Informatica e Telematica - IIT
National Research Council - C.N.R., Pisa Research Area
Via G. Moruzzi 1, Pisa, Italy
E-mail: fabio.martinelli@iit.cnr.it

Fabio Massacci
Università di Trento
Facoltà di Ingegneria
Via Mesiano 77, Trento, Italy
E-mail: fabio.massacci@unitn.it

Library of Congress Control Number: 2006925250

CR Subject Classification (1998): H.4, H.3, H.5.3, C.2.4, I.2.11, K.4.3-2, K.5

LNCS Sublibrary: SL 3 – Information Systems and Application, incl. Internet/Web and HCI

ISSN   0302-9743
ISBN-10   3-540-34295-8 Springer Berlin Heidelberg New York
ISBN-13   978-3-540-34295-3 Springer Berlin Heidelberg New York

Springer is a part of Springer Science+Business Media

springer.com

© Springer-Verlag Berlin Heidelberg 2006
Printed in Germany

Typesetting: Camera-ready by author, data conversion by Scientific Publishing Services, Chennai, India
Printed on acid-free paper   SPIN: 11755593   06/3142   5 4 3 2 1 0

Preface

This volume constitutes the proceedings of the 4th International Conference on Trust Management, held in Pisa, Italy during 16–19 May 2006. The conference followed successful International Conferences in Crete in 2003, Oxford in 2004 and Paris in 2005. The first three conferences were organized by iTrust, which was a working group funded as a thematic network by the Future and Emerging Technologies (FET) unit of the Information Society Technologies (IST) program of the European Union.

The purpose of the iTrust working group was to provide a forum for cross-disciplinary investigation of the applications of trust as a means of increasing security, building confidence and facilitating collaboration in dynamic open systems.

The aim of the iTrust conference series is to provide a common forum, bringing together researchers from different academic branches, such as the technology-oriented disciplines, law, social sciences and philosophy, in order to develop a deeper and more fundamental understanding of the issues and challenges in the area of trust management in dynamic open systems.

The response to this conference was excellent; from the 88 papers submitted to the conference, we selected 30 full papers for presentation. The program also included one keynote address, given by Cristiano Castelfranchi; an industrial panel; 7 technology demonstrations; and a full day of tutorials.

The running of an international conference requires an immense effort from all parties involved. We would like to thank the people who served on the Program Committee and the Organizing Committee for their hard work. In particular, we would like to thank the people at the Institute for Informatics and Telematics at the Italian National Research Council for handling the logistics for the conference.

May 2006
Ketil Stølen
William H. Winsborough

Organization

General Chairs

Fabio Martinelli
Fabio Massacci

Program Co-chairs

Ketil Stølen
William H. Winsborough

Demonstration Chairs

Yücel Karabulut
Stephane Lo Presti

Organizing Committee

Adriana Lazzaroni
Beatrice Lami

Program Committee

Eliza Bertino
Jon Bing
Jeremy Bryans
L. Jean Camp
Cristiano Castelfranchi
David Chadwick
Andrew Charlesworth
David Crocker
Mark Roger Dibben
Theo Dimitrakos
Dag Elgesem
Sandro Etalle
Rino Falcone
Sonja Grabner-Kräuter
Peter Herrmann

Valerie Issarny
Christian D. Jensen
Andrew Jones
Audun Jøsang
Yücel Karabulut
Paul Kearney
Heiko Krumm
Ninghui Li
Javier Lopez
Volkmar Lotz
Stephen Marsh
Refik Molva
Mogens Nielsen
Christos Nikolaou
Paddy Nixon
Anja Oskamp
Siani Pearson
Stephane Lo Presti
Jens Riegelsberger
Babak Sadighi
Pierangela Samarati
Giovanni Sartor
Simon Shiu
Paulo Pinheiro da Silva
Luca Simoncini
Cecilia Magnusson Sjöberg
Yao-Hua Tan
Sotirios Terzis
Dimitris Tsigos
Andrew Twigg
Stephen Weeks
Emily M. Weitzenböck
Marianne Winslett

External Reviewers

Adrian Baldwin
Yolanta Beres
Damiano Bolzoni
Gustav Boström
Folker den Braber
Michael Brinkløv
Liqun Chen
Marcin Czenko
Marnix Dekker

Table of Contents

Invited Talks

Why We Need a Non-reductionist Approach to Trust
Cristiano Castelfranchi 1

Full Papers

Dynamic Trust Federation in Grids
*Mehran Ahsant, Mike Surridge, Thomas Leonard, Ananth Krishna,
Olle Mulmo* 3

Being Trusted in a Social Network: Trust as Relational Capital
Cristiano Castelfranchi, Rino Falcone, Francesca Marzo 19

A Requirements-Driven Trust Framework for Secure Interoperation in
Open Environments
Suroop Mohan Chandran, Korporn Panyim, James B.D. Joshi 33

Normative Structures in Trust Management
Dag Elgesem 48

Gathering Experience in Trust-Based Interactions
Colin English, Sotirios Terzis 62

Multilateral Decisions for Collaborative Defense Against Unsolicited
Bulk E-mail
Noria Foukia, Li Zhou, Clifford Neuman 77

Generating Predictive Movie Recommendations from Trust in Social
Networks
Jennifer Golbeck 93

Temporal Logic-Based Specification and Verification of Trust Models
Peter Herrmann 105

Modelling Trade and Trust Across Cultures
*Gert Jan Hofstede, Catholijn M. Jonker, Sebastiaan Meijer,
Tim Verwaart* 120

Estimating the Relative Trustworthiness of Information Sources in
Security Solution Evaluation
Siv Hilde Houmb, Indrakshi Ray, Indrajit Ray 135

Trust-Based Route Selection in Dynamic Source Routing
Christian D. Jensen, Paul O Connell 150

Implementing Credential Networks
Jacek Jonczy, Rolf Haenni 164

Exploring Different Types of Trust Propagation
Audun Jøsang, Stephen Marsh, Simon Pope 179

PathTrust: A Trust-Based Reputation Service for Virtual Organization
Formation
*Florian Kerschbaum, Jochen Haller, Yücel Karabulut,
Philip Robinson* 193

A Versatile Approach to Combining Trust Values for Making Binary
Decisions
Tomas Klos, Han La Poutré..................................... 206

Jiminy: A Scalable Incentive-Based Architecture for Improving Rating
Quality
*Evangelos Kotsovinos, Petros Zerfos, Nischal M. Piratla,
Niall Cameron, Sachin Agarwal*.................................. 221

Virtual Fingerprinting as a Foundation for Reputation in Open Systems
Adam J. Lee, Marianne Winslett 236

Towards Automated Evaluation of Trust Constraints
Siani Pearson 252

Provision of Trusted Identity Management Using Trust Credentials
Siani Pearson, Marco Casassa Mont 267

Acceptance of Voting Technology: Between Confidence and Trust
Wolter Pieters.. 283

B-Trust: Bayesian Trust Framework for Pervasive Computing
Daniele Quercia, Stephen Hailes, Licia Capra 298

TATA: Towards Anonymous Trusted Authentication
Daniele Quercia, Stephen Hailes, Licia Capra 313

The Design, Generation, and Utilisation of a Semantically Rich
Personalised Model of Trust
    Karl Quinn, Declan O'Sullivan, Dave Lewis, Vincent P. Wade 324

A Trust Assignment Model Based on Alternate Actions Payoff
    Vidyaraman Sankaranarayanan, Shambhu Upadhyaya 339

Privacy, Reputation, and Trust: Some Implications for Data Protection
    Giovanni Sartor 354

A Reputation-Based System for Confidentiality Modeling in
Peer-to-Peer Networks
    Christoph Sorge, Martina Zitterbart 367

Robust Reputations for Peer-to-Peer Marketplaces
    Jonathan Traupman, Robert Wilensky 382

From Theory to Practice: Forgiveness as a Mechanism to Repair
Conflicts in CMC
    Asimina Vasalou, Jeremy Pitt, Guillaume Piolle 397

A Novel Protocol for Communicating Reputation in P2P Networks
    Kouki Yonezawa 412

A Scalable Probabilistic Approach to Trust Evaluation
    Xiaoqing Zheng, Zhaohui Wu, Huajun Chen, Yuxin Mao 423

Demonstration Overviews

The Agent Reputation and Trust (ART) Testbed
    Karen K. Fullam, Tomas Klos, Guillaume Muller,
    Jordi Sabater-Mir, K. Suzanne Barber, Laurent Vercouter 439

Trust Establishment in Emergency Case
    Laurent Gomez, Ulrich Jansen 443

Evaluating Trust and Authenticity with CAUTION
    Jacek Jonczy 449

Using Jiminy for Run-Time User Classification Based on Rating
Behaviour
    Evangelos Kotsovinos, Petros Zerfos, Nischal M. Piratla,
    Niall Cameron 454

Traust: A Trust Negotiation Based Authorization Service
  Adam J. Lee, Marianne Winslett, Jim Basney, Von Welch 458

The Interactive Cooperation Tournament: How to Identify
Opportunities for Selfish Behavior of Computational Entities
  Philipp Obreiter, Birgitta König-Ries 463

eTVRA, a Threat, Vulnerability and Risk Assessment Tool for eEurope
  Judith E.Y. Rossebø, Scott Cadzow, Paul Sijben 467

Author Index 473

Why We Need a Non-reductionist Approach to Trust

Cristiano Castelfranchi

Institute of Cognitive Sciences and Technologies, National Research Council,
via San Martino della Battaglia 44, 00185 - Roma Italy,
69042 Heidelberg, Germany
cristiano.castelfranchi@istc.cnr.it

Abstract. I will underline the real complexity of trust (not for mere theoretical purposes but for advanced applications), and I will criticize some of those reductionist view of Trust. I will illustrate: how trust can be a disposition, but also is an 'evaluation', and also a 'prediction' or better an 'expectation'; and how it is a 'decision' and an 'action', and 'counting on' (relying) and 'depending on' somebody; and which is the link with uncertainty and risk taking (fear and hope); how it creates social relationships; how it is a dynamic phenomenon with loop-effects; how it derives from several sources.

1 Introduction

Trust is a major problem in IT:

- in HCI and especially in computer-mediated interaction on the web (for in searching for reliable information, in e-commerce, e-communities, virtual organizations, e-democracy,....);
- in human-autonomous-agents interaction, both with software agents (personal assistants, mediating agents,..) and with robots;
- in Agent-Agent interaction and in MAS, in particular in partner selection and in negotiation and commitment.

There are natural tendencies to reduce the theory and the implementation of trust to the specific practical aspects needed in each application, without a real perception of the complexity of the phenomenon. On the contrary:

- Trust is a very complex construct, with many interdependent dimensions; and
- too simplified approaches will not be really adequate for building and managing trust in virtual social reality and with artificial intelligences.

I will underline the real complexity of trust (not for mere theoretical purposes but for advanced applications), and I will criticize some of those reductionist view of Trust.

I will illustrate: how trust can be a disposition, but also is an 'evaluation', and also a 'prediction' or better an 'expectation'; and how it is a 'decision' and an 'action', and 'counting on' (relying) and 'depending on' somebody; and which is the link with uncertainty and risk taking (fear and hope); how it creates social relationships; how it is a dynamic phenomenon with loop-effects; how it derives from several sources.

K. Stølen et al. (Eds.): iTrust 2006, LNCS 3986, pp. 1–2, 2006.

Then I will argue:

- why trust built on a theory of Dependence and of Autonomy, and which is the relationship between (bilaterally adjustable) autonomy and the degrees of trust;
- why trust cannot be reduced to the frequency of a given behavior and requires 'causal attribution' and a model of the 'kripta' (hidden, mental) feature determining the certainty and the quality of the expected behavior;
- why trust cannot be just reduced to subjective probability; and why a simple 'number' is not enough for managing trust;
- why trust cannot just be based on 'norms' and and their respect;
- why it is not true that where there are contracts and laws there is no longer trust;
- why trust has not (only) to do with cooperation (as economists assume);
- why we need a non simplistic theory of Trust 'transmission' beyond its pseudo-transitivity;
- why failure and disappointment do not necessarily decrease trust;
- why trust has to do with knowledge sharing and management;
- why we have to build trust on various sources not only on direct experience and reputation;
- why we cannot reduce trust to safety and security, since on the one side what matters is first of all the 'perceived' safety, and, on the other side, building a trust environment and atmosphere and trustworthy agents is one basis for safety.

Dynamic Trust Federation in Grids

Mehran Ahsant[1], Mike Surridge[2], Thomas Leonard[2],
Ananth Krishna[2], and Olle Mulmo[1]

[1] Center for Parallel Computers, Royal Institute of Technology, Stockholm, Sweden
{mehrana, mulmo}@pdc.kth.se
[2] IT-Innovation Center, University of Southampton, Southampton, UK
{ms, tal, ak}@it-innovation.soton.ac.uk

Abstract. Grids are becoming economically viable and productive tools. They provide a way of utilizing a vast array of linked resources such as computing systems, databases and services online within Virtual Organizations (VO). However, today's Grid architectures are not capable of supporting dynamic, agile federation across multiple administrative domains and the main barrier, which hinders dynamic federation over short time scales is security. Federating security and trust is one of the most significant architectural issues in Grids. Existing relevant standards and specifications can be used to federate security services, but do not directly address the dynamic extension of business trust relationships into the digital domain. In this paper we describe an experiment which highlights those challenging architectural issues and forms the basis of an approach that combines a dynamic trust federation and a dynamic authorization mechanism for addressing dynamic security trust federation in Grids. The experiment made with the prototype described in this paper is used in the NextGRID[1] project to define the requirements of next generation Grid architectures adapted to business application needs.

1 Introduction

A Grid is a form of distributed computing infrastructure that involves coordinating and sharing resources across Virtual Organizations that may be dynamic and geographically distributed[20]. The long-term future of the Grid will be to provide dynamic aggregations of resources, provided as services between businesses, which can be exploited by end-users and application developers to solve complex, multi-faceted problems across virtual organizations and business communities. To fulfill this vision, we need architectures and detailed mechanisms for bringing together arbitrary Grid-based resources, along with other resources such as conventional web-services, web-based information sources and people, in a highly dynamic yet manageable way. At present, this is not possible: it takes a lot of time and effort to implement such a collaboration using current technology.

---

[1] The work presented in this paper has been supported by NextGRID project, a project funded by the European Commission's IST programme of the 6th Framework Programme (contract number 511563).

K. Stølen et al. (Eds.): iTrust 2006, LNCS 3986, pp. 3–18, 2006.

The NextGRID project [2] aims to define the architecture for next generation Grids, and addressing this need for highly dynamic federation is one of its main design goals.

Federating security and trust is one of the most significant architectural issues in Grids. Basic Grid security is based on well-developed mechanisms drawing from a wealth of off-the-shelf technology and standards, and work is now underway to address Grid scalability issues and support policy-based access control. However, trust (i.e. dependency) relationships may be expressed in different ways by each service, and the infrastructure may itself impose additional dependencies (e.g. through certificate proxy mechanisms).

In this paper, we focus on the architectural needs of Grid security to support dynamic federation of trust between Grid services running under different Grid (or non-Grid) infrastructure according to different binding models and policies. We examine relevant off-the-shelf components, standards and specifications including WS-Trust and WS-Federation to federate security services in a usage scenario in the Grid. We describe an experiment to test their use to federate trust between heterogeneous security mechanisms in a business relationship. We analyse this experiment to show that available standards cannot directly address the dynamic extension of business trust relationships into the digital domain. We show that it is possible by *combining* a trust federation mechanism and dynamic authorization to enable dynamic federation of resources based on a short-term, rapidly formed business relationship. We ultimately provide an experimental prototype to evaluate our approach by using a real example scenario based on rapid outsourcing of computation to a service provider in order to meet a deadline, based only on commonplace business-to-business trust mechanisms. This paper is structured as follows: in section 2 we describe the shortcomings of supporting dynamic Federation in Grids and we will mention why security and trust are the main barriers in this regard. In section 3, we give a Grid usage scenario that allows us to focus on dynamic aspects of Federation in Grids for our experiment. Section 4 introduces off-the-shelf components: GRIA and STS that we use as the starting point for our experiment. Based on these components, an experimental design will be provided in section 5. In section 6, we give an overview of WS-trust and WS-Federation as the current existing relevant specifications and in section 7, we analyse the architectural and standardisation challenges for addressing dynamic trust federation. Section 8 describes our approach to tackling architectural issues. Conclusion and future work are described in section 9.

2   Dynamic Trust Federation and Grids

Today's Grid architectures are not capable of supporting dynamic, agile federation across multiple administrative domains. Federation is possible if all parties use the same software, but to set it up is expensive and time consuming, and thus it is only occasionally cost-beneficial. It is reasonable to ask the question: why has the Grid so far failed to deliver the ability to federate resources in a cost-effective fashion dynamically? We believe there are two main reasons for this:

- Dynamic federation is a holistic property of Grids, but Grid architectures have been formulated in a fragmented way by specialized working groups (e.g. those of the Global Grid Forum [19]).
- Previous Grid visions such as those from the Globus team [20], although en compassing dynamic federation are too high level or too specific to scientific collaboration scenarios, with insufficient attention to business trust.

It is not possible today for different organizations running different Grid infrastructure to support even static federations. For example the GRIP project showed that some level of interoperability is possible between Globus and UNI-CORE, but that there were fundamental incompatibilities in the security architecture and resource descriptions [21] used by each system. Moreover, it is hard for domains to interact and federate resources even if they run the same Grid infrastructure. The complex negotiations needed to establish certification across multiple sites, establish access rights, open firewalls and then maintain software compatibility are well known and documented [22, 23].

Establishing trust relationships, and using them to facilitate resource sharing is one of the most challenging issues in Grids. Dynamic trust establishment and interoperability across multiple and heterogeneous organizational boundaries introduce nontrivial security architectural requirements. The main challenge is to ensure that:

- Trust formation across organizational boundaries is subject to due diligence, usually carried out by humans in their business frame of reference.
- Trust exploitation (enabling resource sharing on commercial or non-commercial terms) is then automated, so the benefits of a decision to trust can be realized very rapidly.

Current Grids do not support automation, so the number of human decisions needed is large, and federation takes a long time. Current Grids also do not support convenient trust scoping mechanisms, so a decision to trust an actor may involve placing complete trust in them, so the due diligence process is often arduous and time-consuming.

The OGSA v1 document [1] describes a range of security components to support access control and identity mapping for VOs. However, all are based on the existence of services established by the VO to support the necessary interactions (e.g. credential translation and centralized access control policy administration and implementation). These mechanisms assume that a VO is well-established, already fully-trusted by all participants, and has its own (trusted) resources to support the required services. We cannot make pre-assumptions about VO lifecycle or trust relationships between a VO and participating domains. Instead, we must support dynamic evolution of both VO and the trust relationships they are built upon, in a much more flexible way than before, in minutes rather than months, and with minimal (ideally zero) overheads and shared infrastructure [8].

3   A Grid Usage Scenario

To provide a focus for our work we have chosen a scenario for which the required application technology is already available from the GRIA project [6]. This allowed us to focus on the dynamic trust federation and access control issues for our experiment.

KINO is a leading producer of high-quality video content based in Athens. In the course of their business, KINO has a need to perform high-definition 3D digital video rendering calculations, taking "virtual" 3D scenes and characters and generating high-quality video sequences from them. However, this facility is only needed for a small subset of their work, so KINO cannot justify buying a large computational cluster to run such computationally intensive calculations. We assume that an animator is working on a high-definition video rendering job for a customer. On the day before the deadline, he realizes that there is not enough time to complete the rendering computations needed using the in-house systems available to him. However, he learns of the existence of some GRIA services for rendering high-definition video, operated by GRIA service providers, and capable of providing the level of computational power required on a commercial basis. (We do not concern ourselves here with how the animator finds out about these services, but focus on the trust federation challenges of using them). The animator tells his supervisor, and they agree that they should outsource the rendering jobs to meet their deadline. To do this, the supervisor must set up an account with one or more service providers, so the animator can submit rendering jobs to them. To meet the deadline, everything must be set up and the jobs submitted by the end of the day, so the animator can collect the output and assemble the final video in the morning. The problem is that the GRIA services require that account holders and users be authenticated via X.509 certificates. However, KINO operates a Kerberos (e.g. Active Directory) domain, and does not have a relationship with a third party certification authority. To get certificates from a trusted third party such as Verisign will take far too long – the only solution is to establish a dynamic VO between itself and at least one service provider.

4   Background

4.1   GRIA

GRIA [6] is a Web Service grid middleware created by the University of Southampton and NTUA in the GRIA project, based on components developed by them in GRIA, in the EC GEMSS [17] and UK e-Science Comb-e-Chem [7] projects. The GRIA middleware was tested using two industrial applications, one of which was KINO's high-definition video rendering application. GRIA uses secure off the shelf web services technology and it is designed for business users by supporting B2B functions and easy-to-use APIs. It can easily support legacy applications.

Unlike more "traditional" Grids, GRIA was designed from the outset to support commercial service provision between businesses [7], by supporting conventional B2B procurement processes. The security infrastructure of GRIA is designed to support and enforce these processes, so that nobody can use GRIA services without first agreeing to pay the service provider. The procedure for using GRIA services is summarized in Figure 1:

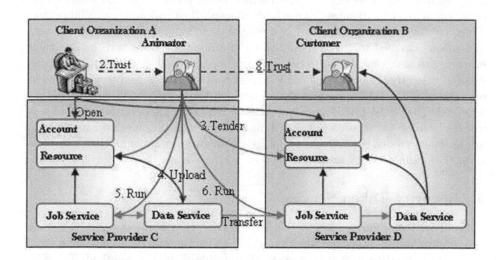

Fig. 1. GRIA usage procedure

Each GRIA service provider has an account service and a resource allocation service, as well as services to store and transfer data files and execute jobs to process these data files. The procedure for using GRIA services is as follows:

1. Account Establishment: First, the supervisor must open an account with the service provider, providing evidence of creditworthiness (e.g. a credit card number) to their account service. If the details are accepted, the service provider will assign an account with a credit limit, to which the supervisor can control access.
2. Resource Allocation: The animator must then allocate resources using the service provider's resource allocation service. This is only possible if the animator has access to an account (the one controlled by their supervisor), to which the resource allocation will be billed.
3. Data Transfer: To transfer data, the animator has to set up a data store using the data service. The animator can only do this if he/she has a resource allocation from which to assign the necessary resources (maximum storage and data transfer volume).
4. Data Processing: To process data, the animator has to set up a job using the job service. This also requires a resource allocation from which to assign the necessary resources (processing time and power). Once the job has been set up, the animator can specify which data stores the job should use for input and output, and subsequently start the job.

5. Data Retrieval: Once the job has finished, the animator can retrieve results from the specified output data store(s), or enable access so their customer can do so.

As indicated in Figure 1, it is not necessary for the same person to carry out all these steps. Each service provides methods that allow the primary user to enable access to a (fixed) subset of methods to a specified colleague or collaborator. Thus, the supervisor in Figure 1 can enable their animator to initiate resource allocations charged to the account, and the animator can in turn enable their customer to have read access to the computational output. This feature is implemented using dynamically updatable access control lists, linked to management operations of the GRIA services through which the corresponding resources are accessed. The GRIA middleware was a convenient starting point for these experiments because (a) it already has a dynamic authorization mechanism, and (b) applications needed for KINO's scenario are already available as GRIA services from the original GRIA project.

5   Security Token Service

A Security Token Service (STS) is a Web Service that issues security tokens as defined by the WS-Trust specification [11]. This service can be used when a security token is not in a format or syntax understandable by the recipient. The STS can exchange the token for another that is comprehensible in recipient domain. For example, if the user holds a Kerberos ticket asserting his identity, but the target service needs an X.509 certificate, the Kerberos ticket can be presented to an STS, which will issue the holder with an equivalent X.509 certificate asserting the same identity.

The STS developed for this experiment was specifically focused on Kerberos-PKI interoperability, converting identity tokens only, but is architecturally open and able to handle attributes other than identity and other token formats such as SAML[13] . Our STS implementation is based on a Kerberised Certification Authority (KCA), which issues short-lived user certificates based on the user's Kerberos identity. The KCA has its own certificate signing key, and a long-lived, self-signed CA certificate, which is not widely known. A relying party must trust the KCA's own certificate in order to verify user certificates issued by it. Thus, the KCA does not directly address the problem of establishing trust between domains. It does however provide a good starting point for experiments involving identity mapping and trust federation between domains including a translation between different authentication mechanisms.

6   Experimental Design

In the KINO application scenario described earlier, we assume that the KINO end users are authenticated via Kerberos, while the GRIA service provider requires X.509 authentication. Other, more complex scenarios involving peer-to-peer interactions between Kerberos domains are also possible, but these are not explored in this paper. We used an STS that can be used to convert identity credentials between Kerberos and X.509 representations, and GRIA dynamic authorization to support dynamic extension of trust between the two users and the service provider through dynamic policy updates reflecting the new trust relationship. The two KINO users will use these capabilities to perform the following tasks:

1. The supervisor will open an account with a GRIA service provider, using a credit card to establish KINO's creditworthiness. To do this, the supervisor must present an X.509 certificate, which they get from the STS.
2. The supervisor will enable access to the account for the animator, allowing him to charge work to the account. To do this, the supervisor must specify the identity of the animator granted access to the account.
3. The animator will then allocate resources and submit their rendering jobs. To do this, the animator must present an X.509 certificate, which they get from the STS.
4. The following day the animator will retrieve the rendered video and compose it with other sequences to create the finished commercial.
5. Later the supervisor will receive a statement of jobs and charges to their credit card, giving the details of the user(s) who ran these jobs.

For simplicity, we consider only a single service provider even though it is obviously possible to use the same approach with multiple service providers, at least in a B2B service grid like GRIA. We assume that the credit card used by the supervisor is acceptable to the service provider (up to some credit limit), and that the supervisor is willing to trust the animator to decide how much rendering computation is needed (within that limit) and to submit the jobs. Thus, the three parties (supervisor, animator and service provider) are willing to trust each other sufficiently for the above scenario to be implemented. Our goals are therefore to conduct experiments to answer the following questions:

1. How can the service provider translate business trust (in the creditworthiness of the KINO supervisor) into a trusted digital authentication mechanism based on KINO's "self-signed" certification mechanism?
2. How can the supervisor dynamically authorize the animator to use this trust relationship and access the service provider's rendering service?
3. How can the service provider be sure the animator is the person who the supervisor intends should have access to his account?
4. When the supervisor gets their statement, how can they recognize that the correct person has been running jobs on their account?

Finally, in answering these questions, we also want to establish how these things can be achieved using current and proposed standards, and where (if at all) those standards cannot meet our needs.

7   Review of Standards and Specifications

7.1   WS-Trust

WS-Trust [11] defines a protocol by which web services in different trust domains can exchange security tokens for use in the WS-Security header of SOAP messages [10]. Clients use the WS-Trust protocols to obtain security tokens from Security Token Services. WS-Trust is highly relevant to the question of how to obtain an X.509 certificate for accessing a web service based on a Kerberos-authenticated identity indeed this is a scenario commonly used to illustrate how WS-Trust works.

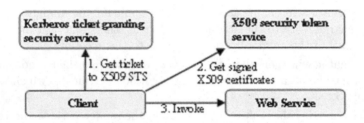

Fig. 2. WS-Trust example using Kerberos and X509

In this example, a client presents a Kerberos ticket granting ticket (obtained when the user logged in to the Kerberos domain) to a ticket granting service, and gets back a Kerberos ticket for an X.509 security token signing service, from which it can obtain a signed X.509 certificate for presentation (e.g. in the WS-Security header) to the target service. WS-Trust defines how the tokens are exchanged (steps 1 and 2 above). However, WS-Trust does not actually provide any mechanisms to manage trust between domains, and only describes token exchange between entities that already trust each other.

7.2   WS-Federation

WS-Federation [12] describes how to use WS-Trust, WS-Security and WS-Policy together to provide federation between security domains. It gives a number of scenarios, starting with a simple example involving two domains, as shown in Figure 3.

In this scenario, a client from domain A authenticates itself to its own organisation's Identity Provider (a type of security token service). To use the service in domain B, it needs a different token that will be trusted by that organization. WS-Federation describes the pattern of WS-Trust exchanges needed for this and many other scenarios. However, WS-Federation does not define any standard way to establish this trust relationship dynamically.

According to the specification:

> "The following topics are outside the scope of this document:
> 1: Definition of message security or trust establishment/verification protocols..."

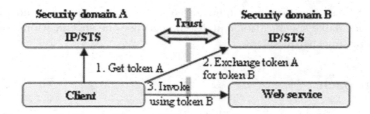

Fig. 3. Usage of WS-Federation between two security domains

Thus, trust relationships must already exist between the WS-Trust token services in a WS-Federation exchange, as indicated in Figure 3. Although these two specifications describe the message exchanges needed, they do not solve the problem of dynamic trust and security federation.

8 Architectural and Standardization Challenges

The standards and specifications described above cover many aspects of building a secure grid spanning multiple security domains over a public network. However, they leave four major questions unanswered from a Grid architecture and standards perspective.

Our experiments were designed to answer these questions, as indicated in Figure 4:

1. How can the security token service guarantee the identity or other attributes of users (the authentication problem)?
2. How does the security token service know what tokens to issue to a user with a given set of home domain attributes (the mapping problem)?
3. How can the web service validate tokens issued by the security token service (the trust problem)?
4. How does the web service know how to interpret the security token issued tokens (the policy problem)?

Fig. 4. Key architectural challenges

Some of these questions are unanswered because it is not clear how best to apply the available specifications, and some because the specifications explicitly avoid addressing the question.

9 Approach

In practice, the four questions highlighted above are clearly related. For example, the access control policy used by the target web service specifies the attributes (tokens) required by a user in order to gain access to the service. This policy in effect defines how the web service will interpret tokens presented to it. The mapping used by the security token service to issue tokens to authenticated users must therefore be consistent with the access policy of the target web service.

Thus the web service can only trust the security token service if the mapping used *IS* consistent with its access policy, *AND* it has a way to digitally verify that tokens claimed to have been issued by the security token service are genuine, *AND* the security token service has accurate information about users when applying its mapping to decide what tokens it can issue.

For example, suppose the web service policy is such that a user identified as *goodguy@kino.gr* can access the service. This implies that security token service will only issue a certificate in this name to a KINO user if they are supposed to be able to access the service. The mapping might be done as in the following:

- supervisor → *goodguy@kino.gr.*
- animator → *goodguy@kino.gr.*
- cameraman → *badboy@kino.gr.*

This would be fine if the intention is that the supervisor and animator can access the service but the cameraman cannot. If we now want the cameraman to have access, we can:

- change the internal identity authentication mechanism so the cameraman can authenticate themselves to the security token service as "animator".
- change the security token service mapping so that a user authenticated as "cameraman" can get a certificate in the name of *goodguy@kino.gr.*
- ask the web service provide to change their access policy so *badboy@kino.gr* can also have access to the service.

This is why we decided to combine dynamic access control and trust (attribute) federation and mapping mechanisms and investigate them together. In dynamic security these aspects must remain consistent, so treating them separately will neglect some possible scenarios, and may even be dangerous. Conversely, using them together gives us more options to solve the trust and security federation problems.

Clearly, relationships (1) and (3) in Figure 4 represent critical points in our investigation, since they are the points where one has to validate some action by a remote user. The obvious solution is to co-locate two of the services so that one of these relationships operates within a single trust domain. The normal approach is to co-locate the security token service and the target web service, suggested by Figure 3. This makes it easy to define the meaning of tokens (in terms of the access rights associated with them), and to digitally verify them at the target service. However, when users from a new domain wish to use the service, one must dynamically update the mapping used by the security token service (taking account of the attributes that might be presented by the new users), and create a new digital authentication path (1) between the new user domain and the security token service. Our approach was therefore to place the security token service in the same domain as the client, co-locating the security token service and the user authentication service. This makes it easy to establish the authentication relationship (1) from Figure 5 and it means the mapping used by the security token service only needs to handle user attributes from one domain. (It also makes it easy to implement the security token service in a Kerberos domain). Then instead of updating the mapping in the security token service, we can use the dynamic authorization mechanism from GRIA to allow trusted users on the client side to amend the access control policy (restricted to the resource they control) in terms of the X.509 security tokens issued by the STS.

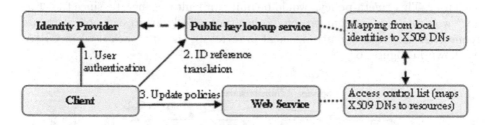

Fig. 5. Dynamic authorization in GRIA

There are still some practical problems to be solved, one of which is shown in Figure 5 to tell the web service (step 3) that a new user is to be authorized, we need to know what (mapped) token that user would have got from the security token service. We therefore need a second service for translating user attributes based on the same mapping. Since the STS is a kinds of CA that issues X.509 identity certificates, the translation service must provide a way to look up the X.509 certificate that would be issued to a specified user. Note that this second service does not sign a public key presented by the requester, as the requester would then be able to claim the attributes specified in the returned token. The token simply allows the requesters to refer to another user's identity in a way that can be recognized later by the target service.

9.1 Dynamic Authorization

Dynamic authorization is only needed at the service provider, following the pattern of Figure 5 . In our experiment, we relied on the existing GRIA process-based access control (PBAC) dynamic authorization system, but we did consider how this might be used in combination with more generic trust mapping facilities in future. One interesting point is that the dynamic authorization functions are provided by methods of the target service (e.g. *enableAccess, disableAccess* on the account service, *enableRead, enableWrite* on the data service, etc). This makes sense, because:

– The access policy should refer to capabilities of the service, so dynamic update options available must also be related to capabilities of the service; and
– Access to the dynamic update options should also be regulated by the same dynamic policy, so the full trust lifecycle can be supported in a single architectural mechanism.

It would be possible to provide a generic "dynamic authorization" WSDL port type, using a standard method for requesting more access policy amendments. However, any user who was allowed to access this method would be able to request any policy amendment (not just enabling *badboy@kino.gr* to access their account). One would then need a further, more complex authorization policy regulating what kinds of dynamic policy amendments could be requested by each user. This "meta-policy" would be quite difficult to generate, since the "target" would be a constraint on some other (potentially arbitrary) policy update request. A more sensible arrangement is to retain the approach used in GRIA, as shown in Figure 6.

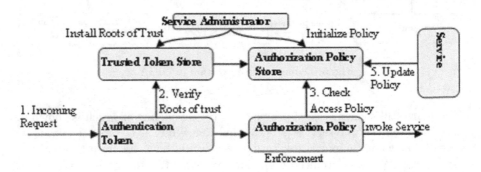

Fig. 6. Dynamic authorization infrastructure

In this approach, the interfaces to the dynamic policy store (3) and (5) should only be accessible to the service provider, so it is not essential that they be standardised, though it would be advantageous for service implementation portability. There are several candidate specifications for checking policy (3) including XACML [25], and IETF Generic AAA [14], but these do not explicitly address dynamic policy updating mechanisms. Obviously, when performing operations like *enableAccess*, the client must specify the scope of the policy change. In GRIA, this is done by sending a context identifier specifying what is to be made accessible (e.g. an account code), as well as a reference token relating to the colleague or collaborator who should be added to the access control list for that context. This approach can also be applied to WSRF resources, and use SAML tokens or X.509 attribute certificates to indicating more general role-based policy updates, of course.

10   Implementation and Technical Validation

A proof-of-concept implementation of this prototype has been provided for both: the client (Kerberos) side and server (X.509) side. The components that client side contains are: a GRIA client application and middleware, able to send authenticated requests to use GRIA services, A STS, that can supply signed X.509 identity tokens in response to GRIA client and a Public Key Certificate service that can supply X.509 certificates (but not the private keys) for any user in the Kerberos domain.

Having located all the trust (attribute) mapping technology on the client side (inside the client Kerberos domain), the only components we need on the server side would be a set of GRIA services for managing accounts and resource allocations, and for transferring and processing data. To validate the modified GRIA implementation, we ran tests between a prospective client in a Kerberos domain (at KTH) and a GRIA service provider established at IT-Innovation. A GRIA client application for rendering was released to KTH, and used to run rendering calculations at IT Innovation.

The system worked exactly as expected. A user at KTH was unable to access the GRIA services initially, but he was able to apply for an account. When the service administrator at IT Innovation approved the account, the service became capable of authenticating credentials issued by the STS inside the KTH domain. The user at KTH was then able to use the account and delegate to colleagues authenticated in the same way, so they could allocate resources and run jobs. The main lessons learned in conducting these tests were as follows:

Previously untrusted users can open accounts, and become trusted if the service provider's checks show that the business risks are acceptable. However, the service provider will then accept connections from other users that have X.509 credentials from the same source as the new user. For example, if a school teacher opened an account using the school's corporate credit card, their students would then be able to make connections to the GRIA service as well. Only the original account holder would be added to the authorization policy of the service, so requests from the students would be rejected unless explicitly authorized by the teacher. However, in principle it would be better to impose some authorization checks at the transport layer as well as the service layer to reduce risks of attack by "malicious colleagues".

Trusted users cannot delegate access rights to users from a currently untrusted Kerberos domain. It is clear that this could be supported by allowing a trusted user to specify a new token source as well as the attributes of their intended delegate. The problem is that it would then be a remote (though trusted) user, rather than a service provider, who approved a decision to trust a new token source. The new user's rights would be tightly specified, but again there could be a risk of "malicious colleague" attack, so service providers may prefer not to delegate such decisions to customers.

Adding the client's STS certificate to the service provider's trust store once business trust is established provides for an efficient implementation. One could use a call-back token authentication mechanism (as in Shibboleth [24]), but that adds an overhead to each subsequent call to the service by the newly trusted user. Note that in a conventional X.509 configuration, a call-back would be needed to check the Certificate Revocation List for the remote user. However, the STS issues short-lived tokens, so the risks associated with infrequent updates of the CRL are much lower than in a conventional PKI. The remote server has to be certified by a "well known" CA that the client already trusts, or else the client cannot risk passing any sensitive information to it. In our test scenario, the supervisor passes a credit card number (or other evidence of creditworthiness) to the GRIA service, so he must be able to authenticate it even if the service cannot at that stage authenticate him except through the validity of the card number. Thus, it is necessary to hold a set of "well known" CA certificates in a trust store, while simultaneously updating the client's key pair and associated certificate. It is not normally appropriate to attempt to use simultaneous bidirectional trust propagation at least not using the mechanisms tried here.

11   Conclusion and Future Work

Dynamic resource federation is an obvious requirement of next generation Grid architecture, to address the need for short-term virtualization of business relationships to address transient opportunities and deliver short-term goals. Our studies have been based on a practical (if small scale) scenario from KINO, which is driven by a transient, short-term business need. The main barrier to dynamic federation over short time scales in such scenarios is security. We have examined relevant standards and specifications including WS-Security, WS-Trust, WS-Federation and other WS specifications. These can be used to federate security services, but do not directly address the dynamic extension of business trust relationships into the digital domain.

Our analysis of specifications shows that dynamic trust federation and dynamic authorization (access control) are intimately coupled aspects of dynamic security federation on the Grid. The mechanisms used to federate trust (i.e. authenticate attributes and tokens) are quite different from those needed to enforce access control policies. However, both aspects must be consistent, and in a dynamic federation scenario, this means they need to be changed through some concerted procedure. On the other hand, the fact that dynamic federation can be achieved through a combination of the two mechanisms offers a wider range of options for implementing federation mechanisms. Our analysis suggests that trust (e.g. identity) mapping should normally be performed by the domain in which the identity (or other) attributes are assigned to users, while the consequences are defined in the target domain by using dynamic authorisation mechanisms to update the policy for the target service. This is not the pattern traditionally seen in WS-Federation, but uses the same specifications.

We developed an experimental Grid prototype based on trust mapping technology used by KTH (STS) and a Business-to-Business Grid middleware (GRIA) that includes dynamic authorization support. The experimental prototype shows that by combining trust federation and dynamic authorization, one can enable dynamic federation of resources based on a short-term, rapidly formed business relationship.

The next step will be to formalize the architectural concepts used to achieve this as part of the NextGRID next generation Grid architecture. A more general reference implementation of these concepts is now being produced within the NextGRID project, and will be made available to the community and incorporated in a future release of the GRIA middleware, and possibly other NextGRID compatible Grid middleware in future.

References

1. The Open Grid Services Architecture. V1.0 July 2004. Feb. 2005, $< http : //www. gridforum.org >$
2. EC IST Project 511563: The Next Generation Grid. Sep. 2004, $< http : //www. nextgrid.org >$
3. The NextGRID Architecture Straw Man. Sep. 2004, $< http : //www.nextgrid. org >$
4. Derrick J Brashear, Ken Hornstein, Johan Ihren, et al: Heimdal Kerberos 5, Feb. 2005, $< http : //www.pdc.kth.se/heimdal/heimdal.html >$
5. Chris Kaler, et al: Web Services Security X.509 Certificate Token Profile, 1st March 2004. Feb. 2005, $< http : //docs.oasis - open.org/wss/2004/01/oasis - 200401 - wss - x509 - token - profile - 1.0.pdf >$
6. EC Project IST-2001-33240 Grid Resources for Industrial Applications. Apr. 2005 $< http : //www.gria.org for the current GRIA middleware version >$
7. Surridge, M., Taylor, S. J. and Marvin, D. J.: Grid Resources for Industrial Applications. In Proceedings of 2004 IEEE International Conference on Web Services. San Diego, USA. (2004) pages pp. 402-409
8. Surridge, M., Taylor, S. J., De Roure, D and Zaluska, E. J.: Experiences with GRIA - Industrial applications on a web services Grid. In Proceedings of 1st IEEE Conference on e-Science and Grid Computing, Melbourne, Australia, Dec 2005.
9. RFC3820, Apr. 2005, $< http : //www.ietf.org/rfc/rfc3820.txt >$
10. Chris Kaler: Web Services Security (WS-Security) v1.0,April 2002, Apr. 2005, $<http : //www - 106.ibm.com/developerworks/webservices/library/ws - secure/>$
11. Steve Anderson, Jeff Bohren, et al.:Web Services Trust Language (WS-Trust) v1.1, May 2004, Apr. 2005, $< http : //www - 106.ibm.com/developerworks/ webservices/library/ws - trust >$
12. Chris Kaler and Anthony Nadalin: Web Services Federation Language (WS-Federation), July 2003, Apr. 2005,
$< http : //www-106.ibm.com/developerworks/webservices/library/ws-fed/ >$
13. Frank Cohen: Debunking SAML myths and misunderstandings,IBM developerWorks, 08 July 2003, Apr. 2005, $<http : //www - 106.ibm.com/developerworks/ xml/library/x - samlmyth.html>$

14. The IETF has published generic AAA specifications as RFC2903 (architecture) and RFC2904 (framework).Apr 2005, $< http : //www.ietf.org/rfc/rfc2903.txt$ $andhttp : //www.ietf.org/rfc/rfc2904.txt >$

15. IETF draft, PKIX, Apr. 2005, $< http : //www.ietf.org/internet-drafts/draft-ietf - pkix - certstore - http - 08.txt >$

16. GEMSS project, Apr. 2005, $< http : //www.gemss.de >$

17. Comb-e-Chem project, Apr. 2005, $< http : //www.comb - e - chem.org >$

18. D. De Roure et al: The semantic Grid: a future e-Science infrastructure. 2002, Apr. 2005, $< http : //www.semanticgrid.org/documents/semgrid - journal/ semgrid - journal.pdf >$

19. The Global Grid Forum, Apr. 2005, $< http : //www.gridforum.org >$

20. I. Foster, C. Kesselman, S. Tuecke.: The Anatomy of the Grid: Enabling Scalable Virtual Organizations, Apr. 2005, $< http : //www.globus.org/research/ papers/anatomy.pdf >$

21. J. Brooke, K. Garwood and C. Goble: Interoperability of Grid Resource Descriptions: A Semantic Approach, APr. 2005, $< http : //www.semanticgrid.org/ GGF/ggf9/john/ >$

22. TERENA Task Force on Authentication, Authorisation Coordination for Europe, Feb. 2005, $< http : //www.terena.nl/tech/task - forces/tf - aace/ >$

23. V Welch: Globus Toolkit Firewall Requirements, Apr. 2005, $< http : //www. globus.org/security/v2.0/firewalls.html >$

24. Scott Cantor, Steven Carmody, Marlena.Erdos, et al.:Shibboleth v 1.2.1, Feb. 2005, $< http : //shibboleth.internet2.edu/shibboleth - documents.html >$

25. Tim Moses: eXtensible Access Control Markup Language (XACML) Version 2.0 draft 04, Dec. 2004, Apr 2005, $< http : //www.oasis - open.org/committees/ xacml >$

Being Trusted in a Social Network: Trust as Relational Capital[*]

Cristiano Castelfranchi, Rino Falcone, and Francesca Marzo

Istituto di Scienze e Tecnologie della Cognizione – CNR – Roma
{r.falcone, c.castelfranchi, francesca.marzo}@istc.cnr.it

Abstract. Trust can be viewed as an instrument both for an agent selecting the right partners in order to achieve its own goals (the point of view of the trustier), and for an agent of being selected from other potential partners (the point of view of the trustee) in order to establish with them a cooperation/ collaboration and to take advantage from the accumulated trust. In our previous works we focused our main attention on the first point of view. In this paper we will analyze trust as the agents' *relational capital*. Starting from the classical dependence network (in which needs, goals, abilities and resources are distributed among the agents) with potential partners, we introduce the analysis of what it means for an agent to be trusted and how this condition could be strategically used from it for achieving its own goals, that is, why it represents a form of power. Although there is a big interest in literature about 'social capital' and its powerful effects on the wellbeing of both societies and individuals, often it is not clear enough what is it the object under analysis. Individual trust capital (relational capital) and collective trust capital not only should be disentangled, but their relations are quite complicated and even conflicting. To overcome this gap, we propose a study that first attempts to understand what trust is as *capital of individuals*. In which sense "trust" is a capital. How this capital is built, managed and saved. In particular, how this capital is the result of the others' beliefs and goals. Then we aim to analytically study the cognitive dynamics of this object.

1 Introduction

In multi-agent systems trust is a growing field of analysis and research and ways to calculate it have already been introduced to enhance studies on commercial partnership, strategic choice, and on coalition formation. In particular, in almost all the present approaches the focus is on the trustier and on the ways for evaluating the trustworthiness of other possible trustees. In fact, there are no so many studies and analyses about the model of *being trusted*. Also our socio-cognitive model of trust (1, 2) was about the cognitive ingredients for trusting something or somebody, and how trust affects decision, which are the sources and the basis for trusting, and so on; we never modeled what does it means to be trusted (with the exception of the work on

---

[*] This paper has been founded by the European Project **MindRACES** (*from Reactive to Anticipatory Cognitive Embodied Systems*): Contract Number: FP6-511931.

K. Stølen et al. (Eds.): iTrust 2006, LNCS 3986, pp. 19–32, 2006.
© Springer-Verlag Berlin Heidelberg 2006

trust dynamics (3) in which the focus was on the reciprocation and potential influences on the trustworthiness) and why it is important.

In this paper we address this point, analyzing what it means that trust represents a strategic resource for agents that are trusted, proposing a model of 'trust as a capital' for individuals and suggesting the implication for strategic action that can be performed. Our thesis is that to be trusted:

i)   increases the chance to be requested or accepted as a partner for exchange or cooperation;

ii)   improves the 'price', the contract that the agent can obtain[1].

The need of this new point of view derives directly from the fact that in multi-agent systems it is strategically important not only to know who is trusted by who and how much, but also to understand how being trusted can be used by the trustee.

It has been already shown that using different levels of trust represents an advantage in performing some tasks such as task allocation or partners' choice. Therefore, having "trust" as a cognitive parameter in agents' decision making can lead to better (more efficient, faster etc.) solutions than proceeding driven by other kind of calculation such as probabilistic or statistical ones. This study already represented an innovation since usually trust has been studied as an effect rather than a factor that causes the developing of social network and their maintenance or structural changing.

In order to improve this approach and to better understand dynamics of social networks, now we propose a study of what happens on the other side of the two-way trust relationship, focusing on the trustee, in particular on a cognitive trustee. Our aim is an analytical study of what it means to be trusted. The idea of taking the other point of view is particularly important if we consider the amount of studies in social science that connect trust with social capital related issues. Our claims are:

-    to be trusted usually is an *advantage for the trustee* (agent Ag_i); more precisely received trust is a capital that can be invested, and that requires decisions and costs to be cumulated;
-    it is possible *to measure this capital*, which is relational, that is depends on a position in a network of relationships;
-    trust *has different sources*: personal experience that the other agents have with Ag_i; circulating reputation of Ag_i; Ag_i belongingness to certain groups or categories; the signs and the impressions that Ag_i is able to produce;
-    the value of this capital is *context dependent* (for example, market dependent) and dynamic;
-    received trust strongly affects the '*negotiation power*' of Ag_i that cannot simply be derived from the "dependence bilateral relationships".

Although there is a big interest in literature about 'social capital' and its powerful effects on the wellbeing of *both societies and individuals*, often it is not clear enough

---

[1] This point in particular, does not necessary imply and does not mean that a deceiving trustee would have surely an individual advantage. This misinterpretation is a typical point of view coming from domains like commerce and exchange in which trust is considered just as an instrument for solving questions like Prisoner Dilemma problems. In fact, we are interested to model trust in more general domains and contexts: for example, in strict cooperation in which a deceiving trustee jeopardizes its own interests and goals.

what is it the object under analysis. To overcome this lack, we propose a study that first attempts to understand trust as capital of individuals. How is it possible to say that "trust" is a capital? How is this capital built, managed and saved? Then we aim to analytically study the cognitive dynamics of this object, with a particular focus on how they depend on beliefs and goals.

2 Trust and Relational Capital

Social Capital (4, 5, 6, 7) can be seen as a multidimensional concept and can be studied in its relation both with social norms and shared values and with networks of interpersonal relations. While in the former case studies about conventions and collective attribution of meanings can be useful to understand how social capital can be a capital for the society, in the latter, one of the basic issues that need to be studied is how it can happen that networks of relations can be built, which ways they develop, and how they can both influence individual behaviours and be considered as an individual capital (22).

We also would like to underline that social capital is an ambiguous concept. By social a lot of scholars mean in fact 'collective', some richness, advantage of any for the collective; something that favors cooperation, and so on. On the contrary, we assume here (as a first step) an individualistic perspective, considering the advantages of the trusted agent, not the advantages for the community, and distinguishing between 'relational capital' (8) and the more ambiguous and extended notion of 'social capital'. The individual (or organization) Ag_i could use its capital of trust, for *anti-social* purposes. Although the idea of a clear distinction of the two levels is not completely new in literature, usually relational capital is addressed in relation with meta-cognitive aspects of human capital (23) rather than being studied through an analysis of its own cognitive mechanisms.

In particular, we would like underline that there is no advantage to use social capital at individual level because the two interpretation of it (social and relational) are not only ambiguous but also contradictory. Social capital at individual level (relational capital) could be in conflict with the collective capital: for example, for an individual is better to monopolize trust, while for the community it is better to distribute it among the several individuals.

In economic literature the term "capital" refers to a commodity itself used in the production of other goods and services: it is, then, seen as a human-made input created to permit increased production in the future. The adjective "social" is instead used to claim that a particular capital not only exists in social relationships but also consists in some kind of relationships between economical subjects. It is clear that for the capital goods metaphor to be useful, the transformative ability of social relationships to become a capital must be taken seriously. This means that *we need to find out what is the competitive advantage not simply of being part of a network, but more precisely of being trusted in that network.*

The additional value of trusting has been shown as a crucial argument in decision making and in particular in choice of relying on somebody else for achieving specific goals included in the plans of the agents. In these studies trust has been analysed as valuation of the other and expectations on it, and it has been shown how these characteristics and mechanisms, being part of the decision process at the cognitive level, represent an advantage both for the society in terms of realizing cooperation among its actors and for the trustier in terms of efficiency of choices of delegation and reliance (9).

Changing the point of view, we now want to focus on the trusted agent (the trustee). What does imply to be trusted for the trustee? As we said, the intuitive answer could be that:

i)   the *probability to be chosen* for exchange or for partnership will grow;
ii)   the *negotiation power* of that agent will increase.

However, to account for this it is necessary to rethink the whole theory of negotiation power based on dependence (10,11,12,13).

Try to build a theory of dependence including trust does not mean to base the theory of social capital on dependence, but to admit that the existent theory of dependence network and the consequent theory of social power is not enough without the consideration of trust. What we need, then, is a comprehensive theory of trust from the point of view of the trusted agent, in order to find out the elements that, once added to the theory of dependence, can explain the *individual social power in a network*, on one hand, and, the *social capital meant as a capital for the society,* in a second phase.

Once a quantitative notion of the value of a given agent is formulated calculating on *how much the agent is valued by other agents in a given market for a given task*, we can say that this trust-dependent value is a real capital. It consists of all the relationships that are possible for the agent in a given market and, together with the possible relationships in other markets, it is the so-called *relational capital* of that agent. It differs from simple relationships in given networks, which are a bigger set, since it only consists of those relationships the agent has with those who not only need it but have a good attitude toward it and, therefore, who are willing to have it as a partner.

How much the agent is appreciated and requested? How many potential partners depends on Ag_i and would search for Ag_i as partner? How many partners would be at disposal for Ag_i's proposals of partnership, and what "negotiation power" would Ag_i have with them?

These relationships form a capital because (as any other capital) it is the result of investments and it is costly cumulated in order to be invested and utilized. In a certain sense it represents a strategic tool to be competitive, and, as it happens with other capitals such as the financial one, it is sometimes even more important than the good which is sold (being it either a service or a material good). For example when Ag_i decides of not keeping a promise to Ag_j, it knows that Ag_j's trust in Ag_i will decrease: is this convenient for future relationships with Ag_j? Will Ag_i need counting on Ag_j in future? Or, is this move convenient for reputation and other relationships?

For all these raising questions it is very important to study how it is possible for the agent to cumulate this capital without deteriorating or waste it: since the relational capital can make the agent win the competition even when the good it offers is not the best compared with substitutive goods offered in the market, it should be shown quantitatively what this means and what kind of dynamical relationships exist between quality of offered good and relational capital. This is in fact the same problem present in the *Iterated Prisoner Dilemma*, where the agents have to consider the future potential exchanges with other agents (before cheating for their own benefits). In other, and more general, terms the relational and reputational capital of an agent is more valued than its immediate reward.

3 Cognitive Model of Being Trusted

3.1 Objective and Subjective Dependence

Before considering trust from this new perspective, let us underline a very important point, which will be useful for this work.

The theory of trust and the theory of dependence are not independent from each other. Not only because – as we modelled (1, 2), before deciding to actively trust somebody, to rely on it (Ag_i), one (Ag_j) has to be dependent on Ag_i: Ag_j needs an action or a resource of Ag_i (at least Ag_j has to believe so). But also because *objective* dependence relationships (10) that are the basis of adaptive social interactions, are not enough for predicting them. *Subjective* dependence is needed (that is, the dependence relationships that the agents know or at least believe), but is not sufficient; then, it is necessary to consider two beliefs: (i) the belief of being dependent, of needing the other, (ii) the belief of the trustworthiness of the other, of the possibility of counting upon it. If I wouldn't not feel dependent on, I couldn't rely on the other.

The theory of dependence includes in fact two types of dependences:

(1) the *objective dependence*, which says who needs whom for what in a given society (although perhaps ignoring this). This dependence has already the power of establishing certain asymmetric relationships in a potential market, and it determines the actual success or failure of the reliance and transaction;

(2) the *subjective (believed) dependence*, which says who is believed to be needed by who. This dependence is what determines relationships in a real market and settles on the negotiation power; but it might be illusory and wrong, and one might rely upon unable agents, while even being autonomously able to do as needed.

More Formally, let $Agt=\{Ag_1,..,Ag_n\}$ a set of *agents*; we can associate to each agent $Ag_i \in Agt$:

-   a set of *goals* $G_i=\{g_{i_1},..,g_{i_q}\}$;
-   a set of *actions* $Az_i=\{\alpha_{i_1},.., \alpha_{i_z}\}$; these are the elementary actions that Ag_i is able to perform;
-   a set of plans $\Pi=\{p_{i_1},..,p_{i_s}\}$; the Ag_i's plan library: the set of rules/prescriptions for aggregating the actions; and
-   a set of *resources* $R_i=\{r_{i_1},..,r_{i_m}\}$.

The achievement/maintenance of each goal needs actions/plans/resources. Then, we can define the *dependence relationship* between two agents (Ag_j and Ag_i) with respect a goal g_{jk}, as: *Obj-Dependence* (Ag_j, Ag_i, g_{jk}) and say that:

An agent Ag_j has an Objective Dependence Relationship with agent Ag_i with respect to a goal g_{jk} if for achieving g_{jk} are necessary actions, plans and/or resources that are owned by Ag_i and not owned by Ag_j.

More in general, Ag_j has an Objective Dependence Relationship with Ag_i if for achieving at least one of its goals $g_{jk} \in G_j$, are necessary actions, plans and/or resources that are owned by Ag_i and not owned by Ag_j.

As in (12) we can introduce the *unilateral, reciprocal, mutual* and *indirect* dependence (see Figure 1). In very short and simplified terms, we can say that the difference between reciprocal and mutual is that the former is on different goals while the latter is on the same goal.

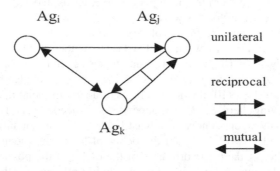

Fig. 1

If the world knowledge would be perfect for all the agents, the above described objective dependence would be a common belief about the real state of the world. In fact, the important relationship is the network of dependence *believed by each agent*. In other words, we cannot only *associate* to each agent a set of goals, actions, plans and resources, but we have to evaluate these sets as believed by each agent (the subjective point of view), also considering that they would be partial, different from each others, sometime wrong, and so on. In more practical terms, each agent will have a different (subjective) representation of the dependence network as exemplified in Figure 1. So, we introduce the Bel_kG_z that means the Goal set of Ag_z believed by Ag_k. The same for Bel_kAz_z, $Bel_k\Pi_z$, and Bel_kR_z. That is to say that the dependence relationships should be re-modulated on the basis of the agent subjective interpretation.

We introduce the *Subj-Dependence(Ag_j, Ag_i, g_{jk})* that represents the Ag_j's point of view with respect to its dependence relationships.

In a first approximation each agent should correctly believe the sets it has, while it could mismatch the sets of other agents.

We define *Dependence-Network(Agt,t)* the set of dependence relationships (both subjective and objective) among the agents included in *Agt* set at the time *t*. Each agent $Ag_j \in Agt$ must have at least one dependence relation with another agent in *Agt*.

3.2 Dependence and Negotiation Power

Given a *Dependence-Network(Agt,t)*, we define *Objective Potential for Negotiation* of $Ag_j \in Agt$ about a goal of own g_{jk} -and call it *OPN(Ag_j, g_{jk})*- the following function.

$$OPN(Ag_j, g_{jk}) = f(\sum_{i=1}^{n} \frac{1}{1+p_{ki}})$$

Where: f is in general a function that preserves monotonicity (we will omit this kind of functions in the next formulas); n represents the number of agents in Agt set that have a dependence relation with Ag_j with respect to g_{jk} (this dependence relation should be either reciprocal or mutual: in other words, there should also be an action, plan, or resource owned by Ag_j that is necessary for some goal of Ag_i); p_{ki} is the number of agents in Agt that are competitors with the Ag_j on the same actions/plans/ resources owened by Ag_i (useful for g_{jk}) in a not compatible way (Ag_i is not able to satisfy at the same time all the agents).

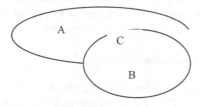

Fig. 2

In Figure 2 we show the objective dependence of Ag_j: A represents the set of agents who depend from Ag_j for something (actions, plans, resources), B represents the set of agents from which Ag_j depends for achieving an own specific goal g_{jk}. The intersection between A and B (part C) is the set of agents with whom Ag_j could potentially negotiate for achieving support for g_{jk}. The greater the overlap the greater the *negotiation power* of Ag_j in that context. In other and more simple words, *the more the agents being at the same time depending and depended upon Ag_j, the greater the negotiation power of Ag_j.*

However, the negotiation power of Ag_j also depends on the possible alternatives that its potential partners have: the few alternatives to Ag_j they have, the greater its negotiation power (see below).

We can define the *Subjective Potential for Negotiation* of $Ag_j \in Agt$ about an its own goal g_{jk}-and call it $SPN(Ag_j, g_{jk})$- the following function:

$$SPN(Ag_j, g_{jk}) = \sum_{i=1}^{n} \frac{1}{1 + p_{ki}}$$

Where we have the same meanings as for the previous formula but now *we make reference to the believed* (by Ag_j) *dependence relations* (not necessarily true in the world): in particular both n (the number of direct dependences) and p (the indirect, competitive dependences) are believed.

Analogously, we can interpret Figure 2 as the set of believed relationships (by Ag_j) among the agents. In this case we have the subjective point of view.

It is also possible to introduce a modulation factor (m) that takes into account the special kind of dependence: reciprocal ($x=r$), mutual ($x=mu$):

$$SPN(Ag_j, g_{jk}) = \sum_{i=1}^{n} \frac{m_x}{1 + p_{ki}} \qquad \text{with } 0 < m_x < 1$$

Usually, we can say that $m_{mu} \geq m_r$.

More in general, we can say that the *Subjective Potential for Negotiation* of $Ag_j \in Agt$ about the whole set of its own goals (G_j) in the *Dependence-Network(Agt,t)* is:

$$SPN(Ag_j, G_j) = \frac{1}{s}\sum_{k=1}^{s}\sum_{i=1}^{ns}\frac{m_x}{1+p_{ki}}$$

Where s is the number of goals of Ag_j, and ns is the number of other agents in the set Agt, that have a dependence relation with Ag_j with respect to the goal g_{jk}. p_{ki} is the number of agents in Agt that are competitors with the Ag_j on the same actions/plans/ resources owened by Ag_i (useful for g_{jk}) in a not compatible way. In words, the global subjective potential for negotiation of an agent in a dependence network with respect of all its own goals is the sum of the believed terms above showed[2].

3.3   The Trust Role in Dependence Network

Before taking into account the trustee's point of view we would like to introduce into the dependence network also the trust relationships. In fact, *although it is important to consider dependence relationship between agents in a society, there will be not exchange in the market if there is not trust to enforce these connections.* Considering the analogy with the Figure 2, we will have now a representation as given in Figure 3 (where D includes the set of agents that Ag_j considers trustworthy for achieving g_{jk}).

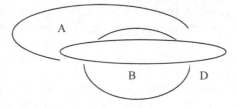

Fig. 3

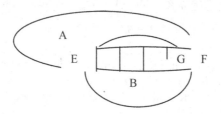

Fig. 4

---

[2] An interesting problem is that an agent could be a competitor towards itself for achieving its own goals; for example:

1) Ag_j needs action α_r both for g_s and g_t and there is only an agent in Agt that has α_r but is unable to provide two times the action α_r.
2) Ag_j needs action α_r for g_r and α_s for g_s and for both the actions α_r and α_s it depends only from Ag_i that can provide only an action.

We have now a new subset (showed outlined in Figure 4) containing the potential agents for negotiation. The analysis of the part E, F and G will result in: part E includes agents who depend form Ag_j, who are trusted but on different tasks; part F includes agents not depending from Ag_j and trusted on different tasks; part G includes agents trusted for the achievement of the goal g_{jk} but not depending from Ag_j.

Not only the decision to trust presupposes a belief of being dependent, but notice that a dependence belief (*BelDep*) implies on the other side a piece of Trust (as modelled in (1,2)). In fact *to believe to be dependent means*:

- (*BelDep-1*) to believe not to be able to perform action α and to achieve goal g; and
- (*BelDep-2*) to believe that Ag_i is *able* and in condition to achieve g, to perform α.

Notice that (*BelDep-2*) is precisely one component of Trust in our analysis: the *positive evaluation* of Ag_i as competent, able, skilled, and so on. However, the other fundamental component of trust as evaluation is lacking: reliability, trustworthiness: Ag_i really intends to do, is persistent, is loyal, is benevolent, etc. Thus he will really do what Ag_j needs.

Given the basic role played by "believed networks of dependence", established by a believed relationship of dependence based on a belief of dependence, and given that this latter is one of the basic ingredient of trust as a mental object, we can claim that this overlap between theories is the crucial issue and our aim is namely to study it deeply.

So introducing also in the *Subjective Potential for Negotiation* (of $Ag_j \in Agt$ about an its own goal g_{jk}) the basic beliefs about trust (1,2) we have:

$$SPN(Ag_j, g_{jk}) = \sum_{i=1}^{n} \frac{Do(Bel_j(A_i)) * Do(Bel_j(W_i))}{1 + p_{ki}}$$

Where: $m_{mu} = m_r = 1$; $Do(Bel_j(A_i))$ is the degree of (believed by Ag_j) ability (with respect of the goal g_k) of the agent Ag_i; $Do(Bel_j(W_i))$ is the degree of (believed by Ag_j) willingness (with respect the goal g_k) of the agent Ag_i. We do not consider here the possible relations between the values of $Do(Bel_j(A_i))$ and $Do(Bel_j(W_i))$ with the p_{ki} variable. $1 \geq Do(Bel_j(A_i)), Do(Bel_j(W_i)) \geq 0$.

Let us, now, explicitly recall what are the cognitive ingredients of trust and *reformulate them from the point of view of the trusted agent*. In order to do this, it is necessary to limit the set of trusted entities. It has in fact been argued that trust is a mental attitude, a decision and a behavior that only a cognitive agent endowed with both goals and beliefs can have, make and perform. But it has been also underlined, that the entity that is trusted is not necessarily a cognitive agent. When a cognitive agent trusts another cognitive agent, we talk about social trust.

We consider that the set of actions, plans and resources owned/available by an agent can be useful for achieving a set of tasks ($\tau_1, ..., \tau_r$).

We take now the *point of view of the trustee agent in the dependence network*: therefore *we present a cognitive theory of trust as a capital*, which is, in our view, a good starting point to include this concept in the issue of negotiation power. *That is to say that if somebody is potentially strongly needed by other agents, but it is not trusted, its negotiation power does not improve.*

We call the *Subjective Trust Capital* of $Ag_i \in Agt$ about a specific task τ_k, the function:

$$STC(Ag_i, \tau_k) = \sum_{j=1}^{n} Do(Bel_j(A_{ik})) * Do(Bel_j(W_{ik}))$$

Where n is the number of agents need the task τ_k. Ag_j, $Ag_i \in Agt$.

Do(Bel$_{ji}$ (A$_{ik}$)) means the A$_j$'s degree of belief (believed by A$_i$) with respect the A$_i$'s ability about the task τ_k.

Do(Bel$_{ji}$ (W$_{ik}$)) means the A$_j$'s degree of belief (believed by A$_i$) with respect the A$_i$'s willingness about the task τ_k.

In words, the cumulated trust capital of an agent Ag_i with respect of a specific task τ_k, is the sum (on all the agents needing that specific task in the network dependence) of the corresponding abilities and willingness believed by each dependent agent. The subjectivity consists in the fact that both the network dependence and the believed abilities and willingness are believed by (are the point of view of) the agent Ag_i.

We call *Degree of Trust* of the Agent Ag_j on the agent Ag_i about the task τ_k ($DoT(Ag_j Ag_i \tau_k)$):

$$\mathrm{DoT}(Ag_j Ag_i \tau_k) = Do(Bel_j(A_{ik})) * Do(Bel_j(W_{ik}))$$

Analogously, we can also call the self-trust of the agent Ag_i about the task τ_k we can write:

$$ST(Ag_i, \tau_k) = Do(Bel_i(A_{ik})) * Do(Bel_i(W_{ik}))$$

From the comparison between $STC(Ag_i, \tau_k)$, $DoT(Ag_j Ag_i \tau_k)$ and $ST(Ag_i, \tau_k)$ a set of interesting actions and decision are taken from the agents (we will see in the next paragraph).

Starting from the Trust Capital we would like evaluate the usable part of this trust capital. In this sense, we introduce the *Subjective Usable Trust Capital* of $Ag_i \in Agt$ about an its own task τ_k as:

$$SUTC(Ag_i, \tau_k) = \sum_{j=1}^{n} \frac{Do(Bel_{ji}(A_{ik})) * Do(Bel_{ji}(W_{ik}))}{1 + p_{kj}}$$

where p_{kj} is (following the Ag_i's belief about the beliefs of Ag_j) the number of other agents in the dependence network that can achieve the same task with a trust value comparable with the one of Ag_i. We have two *comparable trust values* when the difference between them is in a range under a given threshold that could be considered meaningless with respect to the achievement of the task.

4   Dynamics of Relational Capital

What has not been considered enough in organization theory is the fact that the *relational capital* is peculiar in its being crucially based on beliefs: again, what makes relationships become a capital is not simply the structure of the networks (who "sees" whom and how clearly) but the *levels of trust which characterizes the links in the networks* (who trusts whom and how much). Since trust is based on beliefs – including, as we said, also the believed dependence (who needs whom) – it should be clear that *relational capital is a form of capital, which can be manipulated by manipulating beliefs.*

Thanks to a structural theory of what kind of beliefs are involved it is possible not only to answer some very important questions about agents' power in network but also to understand the dynamical aspects of relational capital. In addition, it is possible to study what a difference between trustee's beliefs and others' expectations on her implies in terms of both reactive and strategic actions performed by the trustee.

4.1 Increasing, Decreasing, and Transferring

For what concerns the dynamic aspects of this kind of capital, it is possible to make hypotheses on how it can increase or how it can be wasted, depending on how each of the basic beliefs involved in trust are manipulated.

First, let us consider what kind of strategies can be performed to enforce the other's dependence beliefs and in particular his beliefs about agent's competence.

i) Ag_i can make the other agent dependent on him by making the other lacking some resource or skill (or at least inducing the other to *believe* so).

ii) Ag_i can make the other agent dependent on him by activating or inducing in it a given goal (need, desire) on which the other is not autonomous (14) (or it believes so).

iii) Since dependence beliefs are strictly related with the possibility of the others to see the agent in the network and to know her ability in performing useful tasks, the goal of the agent who wants to improve her own relational capital will be to *signaling* her presence and her skills (15,16,17). While to show her presence she might have to shift her position (either physically or figuratively like, for instance, changing her field), to communicate her skills she might have to hold and show something that can be used as a signal (such as certificate, social status etc.). This implies, in her plan of actions, several and necessary sub-goals to make a signal. This sub-goals are costly to be reached and the cost the agent has to pay to reach them can be taken as the evidence for the signals to be credible (of course without considering cheating in building signals). It is important to underline that using these signals often implies the participation of a third subject in the process of building trust as a capital: a third part which must be trusted (2). We would say the more the third part is trusted in the society, the more expensive will be for the agent to acquire signals to show, and the more these signals will work in increasing the agent's relational capital. We will see later how this is related with the process of transferring trust from an agent to another (building reputation).

Obviously also Ag_i's *previous performances* are 'signals' of trustworthiness. And this information is also provided by the circulating *reputation* of Ag_i (18, 19).

In formal terms, we can say that Ag_i has to work for increasing:

$$Do(Bel_j(A_i)) \text{ and consequently } Do(Bel_{ji}(A_i)).$$

iv) Alternatively, Ag_i could work for reducing the believed (by Ag_j) value of ability of each of the possible competitors of Ag_i (in number of p_{kj}) on that specific task τ_k.

Let us now consider how willingness beliefs can be manipulated. In order to do so, consider the particular strategy performed to gain the other's good attitude through gifts (20). It is true that the expected reaction will be of reciprocation, but this is not enough. While giving a gift the agent knows that the other will be more inclined to reciprocate, but she also knows that her action can be interpreted as a sign of the good willingness she has: since she has given something without being asked, the other is driven to believe that the agent will not cheat on him. Then, the real strategy can be played on trust, sometimes totally and sometimes only partially – this will basically depend on specific roles of agents involved.

Again in formal terms, we can say that Ag_i has to work for increasing:

$Do(Bel_j(W_i))$ and as a consequence $Do(Bel_{ji}(W_i))$. Alternatively, it could work for reducing the believed (by Ag_j) value of willingness of each of the possible competitors of Ag_i (in number of p_{kj}) on that specific task τ_k.

An important consideration we have to do is that a dependence network is mainly based on the set of actions, plans and resources owned by the agents and necessary for achieving the agents' goals (we considered a set of tasks each agent is able to achieve). The interesting thing is that the dependence network is modified by the dynamics of the agents' goals, from their variations, from the emergency of new ones, from the disappearance of old ones, from the increasing request of a subset of them, and so on (21). On this basis changing the role of each agent in the dependence network, it changes in fact the trust capital of the agents.

Relational capital can also circulated inside a given society. If somebody has a good reputation and is trusted by somebody else, she can be sure this reputation will pass and transfer to other actors – and this is always considered in marketing strategies of making voice circulate. What is not clear yet is how these phenomena work. But when trust on an agent circulates, it is strategically important for the agent to know very well how this happens and in which ways (not only figurate) trust begin to expand and keep on doing it. In fact, not all the ways are the same: it is possible that being trusted by a particular agent can mean that she just has one more agent in her relational capital, but gaining the trust of another agent can be very useful to her and exponentially increase her capital thanks to the strategic role or position of this other agent. That said, it should be clear the importance of understanding if and how much an agent is able to manage this potentiality of her capital.

Basically, here also, the role of agents involved play a crucial part: for this reason it is necessary for agent to know the multiplicative factor represented by the recognized and trusted evaluator in the society. It is not necessarily true, in fact, that when somebody trusts somebody else and this latter trusts a third one, the first one will trust the third one: the crucial question is "which role the first recognizes to the second". If the second one is trusted as an evaluator by the first one, than she can trust the third one for specific goals.

Usually how well these transitive process works depends on what kind of broad-casting and how many links the valuator has as well as on how much she is trusted in each of those links, so, basically, it recursively depends on the valuator's relational capital.

4.2 Strategic Behavior of the Trustee

Until now we just have considered trust as something quantitatively changeable, but we did not talk about subjective difference in the way trust is perceived by the two parts of the relationship. Nevertheless, to be realistic, we must take into account the fact that *there is often a difference between how the others actually trust an agent and what that agent believes about that*; and also between this (believed trust of others on her) and the level of trustworthiness that agent perceives in herself. Since being able is not necessarily the cause of trust: it can be the case of a diffuse atmosphere that makes the others to trust the agent although the agent has not all the characteristics to be trusted.

In fact, these subjective aspects of trust are fundamental in the process of managing this capital, since it can be possible that there is the capital but the agent does not know to have it. Can be possible to use the relational capital even if who uses it is not aware of having it?

At the base of the possible discrepancy in subjective valuation of trustworthiness there is the perception of how much an agent feels herself trustworthy in a given task and the valuation that agent makes about how much the others trust her for that task.

In addition, this perception can change and become closer to the objective level while the task is performed: the agent can either find out of being more or less trustworthy than what he believed, or realize that the others' perception was wrong (either positively or negatively). All this factors must be taken into account and studied together with the different components of trust, in order to build hypotheses on strategic actions that the agent will perform to cope with her relational capital.

Then, we must consider what can be implied by these *discrepancies* in terms of strategic actions: how they can be individuated and valued? How the trusted agent will react when aware of them?

She can either try to acquire competences in order to reduce the gap between others' valuation and her own one, or exploiting the existence of this discrepancy, taking advantage economically of the reputation over her capability and counting on the others' scarce ability of monitoring and testing her real skills.

5 Conclusions

As we said, individual trust capital (relational capital) and collective trust capital not only should be disentangled, but their relations are quite complicated and even conflicting. In fact, since the individual is in competition with the other individuals, he has a better position when trust is not uniformly distributed (everybody trusts everybody), but when he enjoys some form of concentration of trust (an oligopoly position in the trust network); on the contrary the collective social capital could do better with a generalized trust among the members of the collectivity.

References

[1] Castelfranchi C., Falcone R., Principles of trust for MAS: cognitive anatomy, social importance, and quantification, *Proceedings of the International Conference of Multi-Agent Systems (ICMAS'98)*, pp. 72–79, Paris, July, 1998.

[2]   Falcone R., Castelfranchi C., (2001). Social Trust: A Cognitive Approach, in *Trust and Deception in Virtual Societies* by Castelfranchi C. and Yao-Hua Tan (eds), Kluwer Academic Publishers, pp. 55–90.

[3]   Falcone R., Castelfranchi C. (2001), The socio-cognitive dynamics of trust: does trust create trust? In *Trust in Cyber-societies: Integrating the Human and Artificial Perspectives* R. Falcone, M. Singh, and Y. Tan (Eds.), LNAI 2246 Springer. pp. 55–72.

[4]   Bourdieu, P. 1983: Forms of capital. In: Richards, J. C. ed. Handbook of theory and research for the sociology of education, New York, Greenwood Press.

[5]   Coleman, J. C. 1988: Social capital in the creation of human capital. American Journal of Sociology 94: S95–S120.

[6]   Putnam, R. D. 1993: Making democracy work. Civic traditions in modern Italy. Princeton NJ, Princeton University Press.

[7]   Putnam, R. D. 2000: Bowling alone. The collapse and revival of American community. New York, Simon and Schuster.

[8]   Granovetter, M. (1973). The strength of weak ties. American Journal of Sociology, 78, 1360–1380.

[9]   Castelfranchi, C., Falcone, R., (1998) Towards a Theory of Delegation for Agent-based Systems, *Robotics and Autonomous Systems*, Special issue on Multi-Agent Rationality, Elsevier Editor, Vol 24, Nos 3–4, , pp.141–157.

[10] Castelfranchi C., and Conte R., The Dynamics of Dependence Networks and Power Relations in Open Multi-Agent Systems. In Proc. COOP'96 – Second International Conference on the Design of Cooperative Systems, Juan-les-Pins, France, June, 12-14. INRIA Sophia-Antipolis, 1996. Pp. 125–137.

[11] Sichman, J, R. Conte, C. Castelfranchi, Y. Demazeau. A social reasoning mechanism based on dependence networks. In *Proceedings of the 11th ECAI*, 1994.

[12] Castelfranchi, C., Miceli, M. e Cesta, A., Dependence relations among autonomous agents. In E. Werner, Y. Demazeau (Eds), *Decentralized A. I. - 3*, pp. 215–227, North Holland, Amsterdam, 1992.

[13] Conte, R. e Castelfranchi, C. (1996) Simulating multi-agent interdependencies. A two-way approach to the micro-macro link. In U. Mueller & K. Troitzsch (eds) *Microsimulation and the social science*. Berlin, Springer Verlag, Lecture Notes in Economics.

[14] Castelfranchi, C. Falcone R. (2003), From Automaticity to Autonomy: The Frontier of Artificial Agents, in Hexmoor H, Castelfranchi, C., and Falcone R. (Eds), Agent Autonomy, Kluwer Publisher, pp.103–136.

[15] Schelling, T., *The Strategy of Conflict*. Cambridge, Harvard University Press, 1960.

[16] Spece, M. 1973 Job market signaling. *Quarterly Journal of Economics*, 87, 296–332.

[17] R. Bliege Bird & E. Alden Smith "Signaling Theory, Strategic Interaction, and Symbolic Capital", *Current Antropology*, vol. 46, n. 2. April 2005.

[18] R. Conte and M. Paolucci, Reputation in Artificial Societies. Social Beliefs for Social Order. Kluwer 2002.

[19] A. Jøsang and R. Ismail. *The Beta Reputation System*. In the proceedings of the 15th Bled Conference on Electronic Commerce, Bled, Slovenia, 17–19 June 2002.

[20] Cialdini, R. B. 1990: Influence et manipulation, Paris, First.

[21] Pollack, M., Plans as complex mental attitudes in Cohen, P.R., Morgan, J. and Pollack, M.E. (eds), *Intentions in Communication*, MIT press, USA, pp. 77–103, 1990.

[22] Nan Lin 2001: Building a Network Theory of Social Capital, In Nan Lin, K. Cook, and R. Burt (Eds), *Social Capital: Theory and Research*, Somerset NJ, Aldine Transaction.

[23] Glaeser, E.L., Laibson D., Scheinkman J.A., and Soutter C.L., 2000: Measuring Trust, *The Quarterly Journal of Economics*, 115: 811–46.

A Requirements-Driven Trust Framework for Secure Interoperation in Open Environments

Suroop Mohan Chandran, Korporn Panyim, and James B.D. Joshi

Department of Information Sciences and Telecommunications,
University of Pittsburgh
smc44@pitt.edu, kop1@pitt.edu, jjoshi@mail.sis.pitt.edu

Abstract. A key challenge in emerging multi-domain open environments is the need to establish trust-based, loosely coupled partnerships between previously unknown domains. An efficient trust framework is essential to facilitate trust negotiation based on the service requirements of the partner domains. While several trust mechanisms have been proposed, none address the issue of integrating the trust mechanisms with the process of integrating access control policies of partner domains to facilitate secure interoperation. In this paper, we propose a requirements-driven trust framework for secure interoperation in open environments. Our framework tightly integrates game-theory based trust negotiation with service negotiation, and policy mapping to ensure secure interoperation.

1 Introduction

In emerging application environments, loosely coupled entities typically collaborate to provide unified solutions. This has led to the development of service-based applications like Web Services, P2P and Grid applications. Business organizations and commercial entities are now moving towards service-based applications to provide integrated solutions with reusable components [21]. The components themselves may be distributed and only Internet-accessible [22]. Typically, services distribution is managed in a centralized manner, either through some service-broker or some public directory [23]. Typically, in such cases, even trust establishment and management is centralized. But with emerging applications, service requirement specification and provision requires a distributed framework. In such cases, recognizing service requirements and composing services that can satisfy these requirements, becomes quite complex. Furthermore, establishing secure interoperation is crucial because of the variety of requirements and the possibility of many domains interoperating in a collaborative framework. Establishment of trust in such environments is the first significant step to establishing secure interoperation. Trust must be negotiated to satisfy the security requirements of all the domains involved. This is done by the disclosure of sensitive information such as credentials, policies, context of service use etc. A trust framework should address all of the above issues.

Several trust negotiation mechanisms have been proposed in the literature including *Trust-Serv* [1], *TrustBuilder* [2], *H-Trust* [4], *Trust-X* [3] and others [5, 6, 7, 8, 9]. Earlier work has addressed the issue of trust negotiation and trust establishment

K. Stølen et al. (Eds.): iTrust 2006, LNCS 3986, pp. 33–47, 2006.

separately. But none of these frameworks have used negotiation and trust computation together. The level of trust to be established is inherently linked to service requirements. These methods fail in the following aspects: (1) primarily based on the client-server interaction model, (2) based on credential exchange and do not handle credential types, and (3) do not consider service requirements as a factor in trust negotiation or establishment.

In this paper, we propose a requirements-based trust framework to support integrated trust and service negotiation, policy mapping, and a ticketing mechanism for fast cross domain accesses. The proposed framework includes the trust sustenance and evolution components. Following are the key contributions of the paper:

- Trust negotiation is driven by service requirements. It supports bi-directional negotiation of service and context requirements.
- Trust negotiation involves establishing agreeable *trust levels* and *trust token types* to facilitate mapping of policy elements for secure interoperation. Once negotiation is done, *trust tokens* are used for authentication and *trust tickets* are generated to support fast authorized accesses for agreed-upon services under the given context.

The rest of this paper is organized as follows: In section 2, we present related work. In section 3, we present the proposed trust framework. In section 4, the details of service and trust negotiation are presented. In section 5, we discuss the issues behind trust sustenance and evolution and some naïve solutions to the problem.

2 Related Work

The notion of trust among interoperating domains has been loosely divided into two types– negotiation of trust based on credentials and establishing trust based on peer-measured values such as reputation and ranking. Existing work on trust negotiation focuses on the negotiation of credentials, with little focus on the generic requirements of secure interoperation, such as in *Trust-Serv* [1], *TrustBuilder* [2], *H-Trust* [4], *Trust-X* [3], and others [5, 6, 7, 8, 9]. *Trust-Serv* is a model-driven framework that uses state machines to represent and determine credential exchanges for access to resources [1]. Both *TrustBuilder* and *Trust-X* use credential disclosure trees and negotiation strategies to facilitate protection of credential information during negotiation. *TrustBuilder* defines families of disclosure trees to facilitate negotiation between entities that have different disclosure trees for the same resource [2]. The *Trust-X* system introduces the notion of *trust ticket* for efficient negotiation [3], which has been adopted in our framework.

Decentralized systems typically use trust negotiation based on peer reviews and reputations. *HTrust* defines functions to establish, sustain and evolve trust based on entity behavior history [4]. Work in [5] defines a trust establishment and sustenance framework for peer to peer systems using reputation as a basis for trust establishment. Reputation is distributed across peers through the formation of peer grids or p-grids. The notion of sustenance is based on the concept of complaints, where peers can make complaints regarding other peers to reduce their rank among other peers [7]. A certainty factor can be calculated to quantify the belief (and/or disbelief) a peer has on another peer [6]. Another reputation-based model calculates the reputation for every session based on the number of authentic responses to a query, where authentic responses are defined as original documents matching the query [12]. An approach similar to the reputation-based approaches is taken by [13] for Grid systems, where a trust index is calculated using fuzzy logic, based on the success rate of a job and the defense capability of the domain. A trust index is also calculated as a function of the direct relationship between the domains and the reputation of the target domain. The direct trust relationship is itself a function of the trust level assigned by the domain through interactions and the temporal decay of that trust level [14]. A privacy-enhanced reputation based method can be used to attach a trust value to an entity based on certain events, but these events cannot be traced back from the trust value [15]. A hybrid approach can also be taken, as in [16], where reputation and negotiation is mixed by negotiation of trust tokens between the interoperating domains and the domains confirming the trustworthiness of these tokens through security/trust agents. Similar to the reputation approach is the recommender approach [17, 18].

These systems do not satisfy all the requirements for peer-to-peer trust negotiation and also are not flexible in terms of their credential exchange technique. Our framework is suited for a distributed environment where trust is negotiated based on the service requirements of each domain involved. We introduce trust token types (discussed in Section 4), for establishing a generic security requirement, but still allow negotiation of trust based on the acceptability of different trust token types. Further, we also consider negotiation of trust integrated with service negotiation, such that different trust levels are established for different services exchanged. Trust levels are computed based on a variety of direct and indirect factors, which we shall discuss in Section 4.

3 The Proposed Requirements-Driven Trust Framework

The proposed trust framework, as shown in Figure 1, is composed of two principle modules – the requirements-based *Trust Establishment* (TE) module and the Trust Sustenance and Evolution (TSE) module, which are briefly overviewed below.

3.1 Requirements-Based Trust Establishment

Trust establishment involves establishing the services that will be exchanged between the interoperating domains and establishing a negotiated trust level for service access.

Service/Context Negotiation. A service requesting domain will publish its requirements, but it is not necessary that there exists a domain that can exactly satisfy these requirements. Even if there is one, it may not be able to provide them all. Under such circumstances, services and their contexts may need to be negotiated to converge on a set of service requirements that can be satisfactorily provided by the other domain.

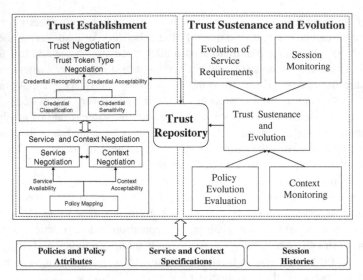

Fig. 1. The proposed Requirements-driven Trust Framework

Trust Negotiation. Trust negotiation involves negotiation of the set of trust tokens that need to be disclosed based on the trust token type required for service access. *Trust token types* are sets of attributes and their allowed range of values, while *trust tokens* represents any set of digital certificates that collectively can show that all the *TT* attributes have values from the specific range. For instance, a trust token type may indicate the requirement for proof of *age* to be above 18. Digital credentials that form valid trust tokens may include *Passport, university ID* or *Driver's License*. The negotiation phase establishes which of these credentials could be used as trust tokens. Note that credential certificates used as tokens may have attributes with varying *protection requirements*.

A key result of the negotiation and trust establishment phase is the mapping of the policies in domains if each provides a service to the other, or within the provider domain. Our proposed trust framework assumes that the individual domains employ GTRBAC policies. The fine-grained service requests are represented as a set of abstract permissions that a particular role within the requesting domain needs to access in the provider domain. Our preliminary work on integration of GTRBAC policies reported in [26] is currently used in the proposed framework. The policy mapping facilitates mapping in presence of timing constraints and hybrid hierarchies. We have also extended the GTRBAC model for location-based access control, in LoT-RBAC [28], and the same policy mapping techniques now be used for secure interoperation in mobile environments as well. A brief overview of the policy mapping process is presented in Section 4.1.

3.2   Trust Sustenance and Evolution

Trust sustenance refers to maintaining trust levels when domain characteristics change during the period of interoperation. Trust evolution refers to the change in trust levels because of changes in domain characteristics.

Evolution of Service Requirements. During a session, a new service requirement can arise or some services may no longer be required. Since trust is requirements-based, evolution of service requirements may trigger a decision on whether to sustain the trust value or re-evaluate, or even renegotiate. Changes in trust values could also be used to renegotiate services; for instance, to reduce the set of accesses given originally.

Context Monitoring. In highly dynamic environments, context changes are inevitable. Since trust levels are context-dependant, it is important to monitor the changes in the context and consequently sustain or calculate the changes to the trust level.

Policy Evolution Evaluation. Changes in policies could cause service usage/provision to be affected (like change in contextual constraints on services), leading to either trust re-evaluation or re-negotiation. Policy mapping will be particularly affected.

Session Monitoring. Anomalous and malicious behavior should be tracked and immediately recognized, so that trust levels can be changed based on the behavior of the other domain. This is a run-time decision on trust sustenance or evolution.

Trust sustenance is usually associated with changes in domain characteristics that are not very significant and can be handled to gracefully end interoperation. Some examples of these changes are change of context, policy changes causing conflict in access resolution, etc. Trust evolution is usually associated with more significant changes, like complete change of context, or access to highly sensitive information. In such cases, trust threshold levels are recomputed and if necessary, trust is renegotiated.

4 Requirements-Based Trust Establishment

A distinct feature of our framework is the negotiation and establishment of trust based on the service requirements of the interoperating domains. Next, we briefly discuss how service requests are made and the need for policy mapping for service negotiation.

4.1 Service Requests and Policy Mapping

Typically, service requests are made by member entities of a domain (like users that have assumed certain roles). The requests are usually access to resources and can have a context associated with them. We assume abstract permissions. Following definition captures the generalization of a service request [26]:

Definition 1 (**Service Request**): *A requesting domain d_x's service request is defined as:*

$$d_x.SR = <\{r_1, (P_{11}, C_{11}), ..., (P_{1n}, C_{1n})\}, ..., \{r_n, (P_{n1}, C_{n1}), ..., (P_{nn}, C_{nn})\}>$$

where r_i is a role in domain d_x, P_{ij} is the jth permission set requested by r_i in context C_{ij}

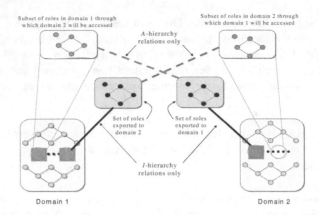

Fig. 2. Role Mapping and Secure Interoperation in GTRBAC-based systems [26]

The roles $\{r_1, .., r_n\}$ may or may not be regular roles in the domain but could also be special roles created by the local policy for interoperation management. The service provider domain will then determine if the service can be provided by doing a preliminary policy mapping, where roles $\{r_1, ..., r_n\}$ are mapped to some local roles for access to the requested permissions. The mapping is done by looking up which roles in the role hierarchy are authorized for the requested permissions. Based on hierarchy structures and permission-role assignments, roles may be exported for use by other domains as such or by creating temporary roles in the hierarchy. Export roles are created specifically for the purpose of interoperation. For details on policy mapping for secure interoperation please refer to [26]. with explanation of the use of Inheritance-only, Activation-only and Inheritance and Figure 2 shows how policy mapping is done in GTRBAC-based systems.

4.2 Services and Trust

In general, the interoperating domains try to negotiate what services they require and can provide, in order to match each other's service requirements. If any domain provides services worth less than it received, then it can pay some incentive to the domain that provided more services. Such service requirements-driven service negotiation can be seen in practical applications and should be facilitated to support ad hoc partnerships between a pair of domains. Various cost factors may play a significant role as to how the negotiation may proceed.

Definition 2 (**Service Negotiation Parameters**): *Let d_x and d_y be service domains such that services requested by each are satisfied by the other after negotiation. Then we define the parameters for negotiation as shown in Table 1.*

Definition 3 (**Service Negotiation Convergence**): *We say that the negotiation between d_x and d_y converges when the following condition holds for both d_x and d_y:*

$$c \leq b + i$$

Table 1. Cost parameters for trust negotiation

$m_{d_x}^{d_y}$	Cost incurred to d_y for policy mapping, to satisfy requirements of d_x ($d_x.SR$)
$r_{d_x}^{d_y}$	Cost incurred to d_y for resources used by d_x when using services provided by d_y (as per $d_x.SR$)
$i_{d_x}^{d_y}$	Incentives that d_y may receive (or lose) in the interoperation
$c_{d_x}^{d_y}$	Cost incurred by d_y for providing services to satisfy $d_x.SR$: $c_{d_x}^{d_y} = m_{d_x}^{d_y} + r_{d_x}^{d_y}$
$b_{d_x}^{d_y}$	Benefits for d_y when using service provided by d_x (as per $d_y.SR$)

Ideally, the cost incurred to a domain during interoperation should be less than the benefits and incentives it gets. Note that the condition for convergence may never occur as internal constraints on the services required or provided may restrict further negotiation. In such a situation, secure and desirable interoperation may not be possible.

Trust negotiation is carried out simultaneously with service negotiation to enable establishment of interoperation. Typically, if two domains (say d_x and d_y) are involved in interoperation through exchange of services, each domain requests the other to disclose some information of a certain type as proof of trustworthiness. We introduce the notion of *trust token type* that indicates a set of attributes and the range of values they should be constrained to. Formally we define them as follows:

Definition **4** (**Trust Token Type, Trust Token**): *Let TT and T denote a trust token type and a trust token, respectively. Further, let $A=\{ a_1,...,a_n \}$ be a generic set of attributes, Dom (a_i) be the evaluation domain of attribute a_i , and $A_1 \subseteq A$. Then,*

- *$TT = (A_1, VS)$, where $VS=\{V_1,...., V_{|A|}\}$ such that $V_i \subseteq Dom (a_i)$.*
- *$T = (A_1, V)$, where $v_i \in V$ is such that $v_i \in V_i \subseteq Dom (a_i)$ $(i = 1.. |A|)$;*

Further, a trust token T is said to satisfy *a trust token type TT (denoted as $T \equiv TT$) if the following conditions hold:*

- *$\forall a_i \in TT.A, V_i \in TT.VS, [v_i \in T.V_i \wedge v_i \in V_i]$*

The service-provider domains demand the disclosure of credentials that verify a set of trust token types. Some typical examples of trust token types are ({*age*}, {greater than 18}) and ({*nationality, residence*}, {*US and US Minor Islands, Pennsylvania*}). Credentials are digitally signed endorsements of some attributes of an entity. They are basically attribute certificates, as specified in [27]. A trust token is constructed by selecting a set of *candidate credentials* that collectively satisfy the trust token type. It is possible that only a subset of the attributes endorsed by each credential is needed to satisfy the trust token type. Formally a trust token can be defined as follows:

Definition 5 (Certificates for Trust Token): *Let TT be a trust token type, CA_i be certification authority, and $C=\{ Cert_{CA_1} (A_1), ..., Cert_{CA_n} (A_n)\}$ be such that*

- *each element of C at least has one unique a ∈ TT.A*
- *the attribute set over all elements of C ⊆ TT.A.*

Then $C_{CA}^{TT.A}$ represents a trust token generated by projecting over attribute set TT.A. of C and then certified by CA. If $C_{CA}^{TT.A} \equiv TT$, then $C_{CA}^{TT.A}$ is a valid trust token for TT. Note that n = 1 is possible in which case the certificate either exactly represents a trust token or a projection over its attributes is needed to generate a trust token.

As per the definition, a trust token may need to be generated dynamically to satisfy the required trust token type. The requesting domain may decide to generate such an on-the-fly trust token using the credentials he has by creating a third party certified certificate (CA is a third party). In such a case trust factor will relate to who certifies the trust toke. For instance, a military personnel may have certificates given to him by the military department and may contain many sensitive attributes and while interacting with a private agency may decide to have the military agency certify his token to satisfy the trust token type required by the public agency. It is possible that the CA is the provider himself. In such a case, to satisfy the trust token type, the requester may simply submit a set of credential certificates. An issue here is the protection requirements of the attributes in the certificates that are not required. Exposure of such is a risk that the requester may take based on the trust that it has on the provider and should be incorporated in the trust computation. For the military personnel in our example earlier, exposure of such attributes to the private agency may not be an option at all.

Trust Factors. Prior to negotiation, the interoperating domains also compute $tr_{S,C}^{d_y \to d_x}$, which denotes the trust d_x has with regards to d_y for services defined by S in contexts C. As we shall see later in this section, this is a value that is used to compute the payoff of a negotiation strategy. The computation of the overall trust values is the weighted sum of the *recommended* trust and *direct* trust values [14]. It is possible that a domain does not have both these values for another domain. The direct trust variables are *historical satisfaction level* (h) and *risk* (rk). Here, h indicates the cumulative level of satisfaction that a domain has had for another domain on their previous interactions and is computed based on session histories and older h values. Variable rk captures risks associated with the desired interoperation. An example is the risk of too many claimed trust tokens being invalid. Another risk is that of services promised but not provided. The historical satisfaction level is also affected by the result of the verification of trust tokens in the earlier sessions. That is, if a domain presents valid trust tokens, then in interoperation, during actual cross domain accesses, the historical satisfaction level will not be negatively affected. The sustenance of the direct trust is based on a family of functions, and can typically be a time-decaying value [14]. Recommended trust is determined by the recommendation value $r_{S,C}^{d_R \to d_y}$ and the trust level for the recommender [16, 17, 20], denoted by $tr_{S,C}^{d_x \to d_y}$, where d_R is the recommending domain, and d_R is the recommender.

Recommended trust can also be a result of a chain of recommendations, where each recommender assigns a trust value for the previous recommender [16].

The parameters that affect the trust relationship are context and the service specifications. Earlier works have found the dependence of trust on contextual parameters like time and location [14, 19]. With respect to temporal context, it is different from time decay of trust, because time decay only shows trust value changing over some time, while temporal context for trust refers to the trust levels at different instances of time. Trust is also specific to service specifications for a particular session – for different services being provided (or requested) the trust levels may be different.

***Definition* 6 (Trust Level):** *Let S and C be the services provided by d_y and the corresponding contexts of interoperation. The trust level $tr_{S,C}^{d_y \to d_x}$ that d_y has on d_x, for services S in contexts C, is defined in Table 2 follows.*

Table 2. Trust level computation

$tr_{S,C}^{d_y \to d_x} =$ $(\alpha \times dtr_{S,C}^{d_y \to d_x}) + (\beta \times rtr_{S,C}^{d_y \to d_x})$	• $\alpha, \beta, \gamma, \delta, \psi, \lambda$ and ε are weights • α is typically greater than β, as direct trust is usually more influential than recommended trust. • Very often α is a result of a time-decay function which represents the degradation in the trust for a domain, due to the lack of interaction.
$dtr_{S,C}^{d_y \to d_x} =$ $(\gamma \times h_{S,C}^{d_y \to d_x}) - (\delta \times rk_{S,C}^{d_y \to d_x})$	• $h_{S,C}^{d_y \to d_x}$ is the historical satisfaction level that d_y has for d_x • $h_{S,C}^{d_y \to d_x}$ is bound by the previous risk levels as follows: $h_{S,C}^{d_y \to d_x} = \eta \times rk_{S,C}^{d_y \to d_x}$, where $0 \leq \eta \leq 1$
$rtr_{S,C}^{d_y \to d_x} =$ $(\psi \times tr_{R,C}^{d_y \to d_R}) + (\lambda \times r_{S,C}^{d_R \to d_x})$	• $rk_{S,C}^{d_y \to d_x}$ is the *risk* • $r_{S,C}^{d_R \to d_x}$ is the recommendation given by d_R for domain d_x.

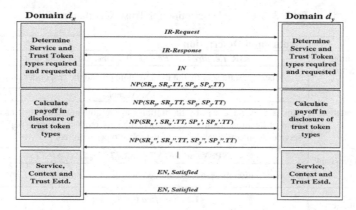

Fig. 3. Protocol for Service, Context and Trust Negotiation

$rk_{S,C}^{d_y \to d_x}$ is a complex parameter with a simple quantification done by computing a value from previous validations of trust tokens of the same type from the same domain. $tr_{S,C}^{d_y \to d_x}$ is computed for two purposes – (*i*) primarily to compute the payoff that is determined for each negotiation strategy, described later in this section; or (*ii*) to set a threshold (minimum) level on the trust that a domain must establish with the other. This facilitates trust token negotiation as well.

4.3 Negotiation Protocol

Negotiation between the domains is done to determine the services required/available and to establish trust, based on the trust tokens. Negotiation of services and associated trust tokens is done simultaneously as can be seen from Figure 3, which describes a protocol for negotiation of services and trust tokens. Note that, simultaneously, even context of service is also negotiated. The messages exchanged by the domains are given in Table 3.

To determine the convergence point of the negotiation, we take the game-theoretic approach of defining payoffs for different strategies. Here trust tokens are strategies,

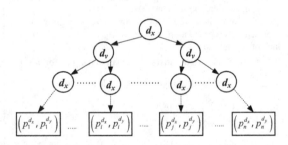

- Negotiation Tree = {*V, E*}
  V={*Root, Non-Leafs, Leafs*}
- The domains alternate every level of the tree.
- *Root*: Requesting Domain
- *Edges*: Strategy execution by a domain at the previous level
- *Non-Leafs*: State of Negotiation after previous domain's strategy
- *Leaf Nodes*: Payoff for a sequence of strategies

Fig. 4. The negotiation tree

Table 3. Message Description for Trust Negotiation

Message	Syntax and Description
Interoperation Request/Response (**IR**)	<**IR**, *Required (or Provided), Name, Service, Context*>
	Such messages are sent by the initiator domain and the responder domains
Initiate Negotiation (**IN**)	<**IN**, *Accept*>
	This is a message sent by the initiator to the domain(s) which it has selected from a set of domains that responded to its request, to start negotiation of services, context of service and trust token types required.
Negotiation Proposal (**NP**)	<**NP**, *Name, SR, SR.C, SR.TT, Sp, SP.C, SP.TT*>
	The negotiation messages exchanged between the domains
End Negotiation (**EN**)	<**EN**, *Satisfied (or Not Satisfied)*>
	This message is sent to end the negotiation either in satisfaction or disapproval

and each trust token has a different overall protection requirement. Based on the choice of trust tokens for disclosure, corresponding domains have gains (or losses). The payoff for each domain is the linear sum of the payoffs from services and trust token negotiations respectively.

The trust token negotiation payoff is the difference between the trust level established and the protection level required of the trust tokens disclosed, as given below:

$$\phi'_{ij}\,(\,p_i^{d_x},p_j^{d_y}) = ((tr_{S,C}^{d_x \to d_y}\text{-}ProtLevel(d_x.T_i)),\,(tr_{S,C}^{d_y \to d_x}\text{-}ProtLevel(d_y.T_j))),$$

The service negotiation payoff is the difference between the benefits from usage of services and the losses incurred through service exchange and service provision.

$$\phi''_{ij}(\,p_i^{d_x},p_j^{d_y}) = (\,b_{d_y}^{d_x} - c_{d_y}^{d_x} \; - \; i_{d_y}^{d_x},b_{d_x}^{d_y} - c_{d_x}^{d_y} \; - \; i_{d_x}^{d_y}\,)$$

Thus the overall negotiation payoff is given as:

$$\phi_{ij}(\,p_i^{d_x},p_j^{d_y}) \; = \; \phi'_{ij}\,(\,p_i^{d_x},p_j^{d_y}) + \phi''_{ij}(\,p_i^{d_x},p_j^{d_y})$$

The negotiation is essentially modeled as a negotiation tree. The different strategies used by the domains are the disclosure of different trust tokens that satisfy the other domain's requirements but have different protection requirements. It is reasonable to assume that protection requirement of a trust token is directly related to trust level desired. For instance, a passport is a more trustworthy proof of age, but it also contains more sensitive details. Traversal of the tree represents negotiation exchanges between the domains. Each domain computes the payoffs at the leaf nodes and selects a set of *candidate payoffs*. Using a goal-driven approach (goal being any of the candidate payoffs), the domains negotiate the payoffs. Ideally, both domains select the same candidate payoffs, because in game-theory-based negotiation, strategies are selected that optimize payoff for both parties. The candidate payoff values are selected through empirical studies. Consequently, backtracking is also facilitated in the negotiation – if say d_y proposes a set of services and trust tokens that would lead to poor payoff for say d_x, then d_x will reject the proposal and d_y will have to go back and try another proposal. The negotiation tree structure is given in Figure 4.

Figure 5 shows the flowcharts for service and trust token negotiation, for both atheservice requester and provider. For service provision, the domain checks the availability of those services before determining the trust token type(s) required for each service. The domain may reject the request message if required service is not available. If the requested service is available, the domain determines the trust token types required. The domain grants interoperation of requested services if the trust tokens, claimed to match the trust token types, are satisfactory, otherwise it determines a new set of trust tokens required for the next round of negotiation. For service requests, the domain checks if the set of services from the provider is enough. If so, then the domain checks the availability of trust tokens matching the trust token type requested from the other domain. The domain may reject the service request, if it does not possess trust tokens of the requested type. Otherwise, it determines the set of trust tokens to disclose, that has the best payoff for both domains. We believe that although the open environment is assumed, most trust-based relations may be established well before there is any access of resources.

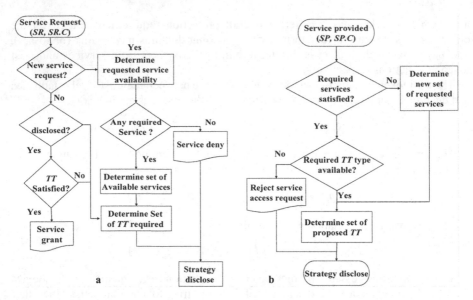

Fig. 5. a. Service and Trust Token Disclosure for Service Provider; b. Service and Trust Token Disclosure for Service Requester

The time between the trust establishment and resource access can be long enough to make some trust-tokens become invalid. In earlier systems, this would lead to re-negotiation of credentials [1, 2, 3]. But in our model, we would only renegotiate the one trust-token type in case the peer might actually have a trust token with different protection requirements associated with credential attributes. Thus, when the *StudentID* is proved invalid, E_2 asks for another trust token type, and the customer discloses the possession of *StateID* which is then accepted, with the same trust level and same set of privileges.

Trust Ticket. One enhancement to the system is the use of a *trust ticket*. The *trust ticket* can be used to by pass the trust token validation process. By disclosing a trust ticket, a domain can access a set of requested services indicated in a trust ticket. Service provider issues a trust ticket for each successful interoperation. Trust tickets offer the flexibility in future interoperations, since a set of services and context indicated in the ticket may be a part of service requests in other interoperations. The trust ticket issued to service requester is encrypted by an established session key k_s to ensure integrity of the ticket.

The data structure of a trust ticket is shown in Figure 6. The detail of the trust ticket is as follow: Trust ticket identifier is stored in *Ticket ID*. The *Ticket Issuer* indicates domain, which issued the ticket and *Ticket Holder* indicates the domain or

Ticket ID	Services	Trust Token ID	Ticket Issuer	Ticket Holder	Lifetime	Shared Secret

Fig. 6. Trust Ticket data fields

a specific users that uses the ticket. A set of service identifiers associated to a ticket is specified in *Services*. *Lifetime* is an expiration time of the trust ticket. A random number, *Shared Secret* increases with each of multiple accesses. Validity of the ticket is specified in *Lifetime*. The *Lifetime* indicates the time-interval that the ticket is valid, which is usually not greater than duration of interoperation session. It is essential to ensure that valid duration of trust ticket is no longer than all lifetime of all certificates associated with the ticket.

During subsequent accesses, trust tickets can now be used instead of the trust token which requires credential validation. Once negotiation of services and trust token types succeeds, service provider creates a trust ticket to service requester. Both domains establish a session key k_s for encryption of trust ticket used between both parties. Service provider domain evaluates the trust ticket by checking validity of the trust ticket and all associated certificates. If the ticket and all the certificates are valid, the credential validation process grants access to the requested services without actual credential validation. The trust ticket is encrypted by established shared secret key k_s to guarantee privacy and integrity of the ticket. Requester domain uses *Shared Secret* value as a counter to keep track of number of service accessing by increasing *Shared Secret* value by one each time he accesses the resource.

4.4 Implementation

We have implemented a very basic *proof of concept* system to ensure that the framework works. The implementation involves each domain running three Java threads – a Peer, Recommender and Certifier. Peers request services amongst each other and credentials. The proposed negotiation trees are created for the prototype. We are currently working on a full-fledged implementation along with integration with an access-control framework based on the location and time based RBAC model (LoT-RBAC [28]).

5 Conclusions and Future Work

We introduced the notion of requirements-based trust negotiation to induce more effective trust negotiation and establishment. We have used the notion of trust token types to abstract the requirements of a domain to establish trust. Some concepts that we have touched upon in our work (like protection requirements of trust tokens and risk) are out of scope of our discussion, because of which we have not elaborated on their computation. But these are important to the trust negotiation and trust framework, and we are currently exploring methods of good estimations of these values. We have also used the game-theoretic approach for disclosure strategy selection and shown flowcharts for strategy selection based on payoffs. Computation of the set of potential payoffs is still complex and we are currently working on efficient search and computation algorithms for these. We have also briefly addressed the issues of trust sustenance and evolution, but the decision to perform either under the given conditions is empirically determined. We are currently working on the implementation of this framework and will obtain empirical results for trust evaluation and sustenance.

Acknowledgement. This research has been supported by the US National Science Foundation award IIS-0545912. We thank the anonymous reviewers for their helpful comments.

References

1. Skogsrud, H., Benatallah, B., Casati, F., "Model Driven Trust Negotiation for Web Services", IEEE Internet Computing, November-December 2003, Pages 45–52.
2. Yu, T., Winslett, M., Seamons, K. E., "Supporting Structured Credentials and Sensitive Policies through Interoperable Strategies for Automated Trust Negotiation", ACM Transactions in Information Systems Security, Vol. 6, No.1, February 2003, Pages 1–42.
3. Bertino, E., Ferrari, E., Squicciarani, A.C., "Trust-X: A Peer to Peer Framework for Trust Establishment", IEEE Transactions on Knowledge and Data Engineering, Vol. 16, No. 7, July 2004, Pages 827–842
4. Capra, L., "Engineering Human Trust in Mobile System Collaborations", in Proceedings of ACM SIGSOFT/FSE-12, Pages 107–116, Oct 31-Nov 6, 2004, Newport Beach, CA
5. Aberer, K., Despotovic, Z., "Managing Trust in a Peer-2-Peer Information System", in Proceedings of ACM CIKM'01, Pages 310–317, November 5-10, 2001, Atlanta, GA
6. Xianliang, H. M. L., Chuan, Z.-x-Z., "A trust model of P2P system based on confirmation theory", ACM SIGOPS Operating Systems Review, Volume 39, Issue 1 (January 2005), Pages: 56–62
7. Gupta, M., Judge, P., Ammar, M., "A Reputation System for Peer-to-Peer Networks", in Proceedings of *NOSSDAV'03,* June 1–3, 2003, Monterey, California, USA.
8. Damiani, E., di Vimercati, S. de C., Paraboschi, S., Samarati, P., Violante, F., "A Reputation-Based Approach for Choosing Reliable Resources in Peer-to-Peer Networks", CCS'02, November 18–22, 2002, Washington, DC, USA.
9. Ye, S., Makedon, F., Ford, J., "Collaborative Automated Trust Negotiation in Peer-to-Peer Systems", in Proceedings of the Fourth International Conference on Peer-to-Peer Computing, 2004. 25–27 Aug. 2004 Page(s):108–115
10. Khedr, M., Karmouch, A., "Negotiating context Information in Context-Aware Systems", IEEE Intelligent Systems, Volume 19, Issue 6, Nov-Dec 2004 Page(s):21–29
11. Ryutov, T., Zhou, L., Neuman, C., Leithead, T., Seamons, K. E., "Adaptive Trust Negotiation and Access Control", in Proceedings of SACMAT 2005, June 1–3, 2005, Stockholm, Sweden, Page(s): 139–146
12. Marti, S., Garcia-Molina, H., "Identity-Crisis: Anonymity vs. Reputation in P2P Systems", in Proceedings of The Third International Conference on Peer-to-Peer Computing, 2003. (P2P 2003). 1–3 Sept. 2003 Page(s):134–141
13. Song, S., Hwang, K., Macwan, M., "Fuzzy Trust Integration for Security Enforcement in Grid Computing," in Proceedings of IFIP International Symposium on Network and Parallel Computing (NPC-2004), Wuhan, China. Oct. 18–20, 2004. pp. 9–21.
14. Azzedin, F., Maheswaran, M., "Towards Trust-Aware Resource Management in Grid Computing Systems", in Proceedings of the 2nd IEEE/ACM International Symposium on Cluster Computing and the Grid (CCGRID'02), 18–21 Aug. 2002, Page(s):47–54
15. Bussard, L., Roudier, Y., Molva, R., "Untraceable Secret Credentials: Trust Establishment with Privacy", in Proceedings of the Second IEEE Annual Conference on Pervasive Computing and Communications Workshops (PERCOMW '04), 14–17 March 2004 Page(s):122–126

16. Au, R., Looi, M., Ashley, P., "Automated Cross-organisational Trust Establishment on Extranets", in Proceedings of Workshop on Information Technology for Virtual Enterprises, 2001. ITVE 2001, 29-30 Jan. 2001 Page(s):3–11

17. O'Donovan, J., Smyth, B., "Trust in Recommender Systems", in Proceedings of IUI'05, January 9–12, 2005, San Diego, California, Page(s): 167–174

18. Shand, B., Dimmock, N., Bacon, J., "Trust for Ubiquitous, Transparent Collaboration", Wireless Networks 10, 711–721, 2004, Kluwer Academic Publishers.

19. Manchala, D. W., "E-Commerce Trust Metrics and Models", Internet Computing, IEEE Volume 4, Issue 2, March-April 2000 Page(s):36–44

20. Daskapan, S., Vree, W. G., Eldin, A. A., "Trust Metrics for survivable security systems", in Proceedings of IEEE International Conference on Systems, Man and Cybernetics, 2003. Volume 4, 5-8 Oct. 2003 Page(s):3128–3135

21. Patrick, P., "Impact of SoA on Enterprie Information Archietctures", Proceedings of *SIGMOD 2005*, June 14–16, 2005, Baltimore, Maryland, USA.

22. Benatallah, B., Dumas, M., Fauvet, M.-C., Rabhi, F. A., Sheng, Q.-Z., "Overview of some Patterns for Architecting and Managing services", ACM SIGecom Exchanges, Vol. 3, No. 3, August 2002, Pages 9–16.

23. Baresi, L., Heckel, R., Thone, S., Varro, D., "Modeling and Validation of Service-Oriented Architectures: Application vs. Style", Proceedings of *ESEC/FSE'03,* September 1–5, 2003, Helsinki, Finland.

24. Joshi, J.B.D., Bhatti, R., Bertino, E., Ghafoor, A., "Access-control language for Multidomain environments", IEEE Internet Computing, Volume 8, Issue 6, Nov.-Dec. 2004 Page(s):40–50

25. Joshi, J.B.D.; Bertino, E.; Latif, U.; Ghafoor, A., "A generalized temporal role-based access control model"**,** IEEE Transactions on Knowledge and Data Engineering, Volume 17, Issue 1, Jan 2005 Page(s):4–23

26. Piromruen, S., Joshi, J. B. D., "An RBAC Framework for Time Constrained Secure Interoperation in Multi-domain Environment," in Proceedings of IEEE Workshop on Object-oriented Real-time Databases (WORDS-2005), 2005.

27. Farrell, S., Housley, R., "An Internet Attribute Certificate Profile for Authorization", RFC 3281, April 2002.

28. Mohan Chandran, S., Joshi, J. B. D., "LoT-RBAC : A Location and Time-based RBAC Model", Proceedings of 6th International Conference on Web Information Systems Engineering, November 20–22, 2005, New York City, NY.

Normative Structures in Trust Management

Dag Elgesem

Department of information science and media studies,
University of Bergen, Norway
dag.elgesem@uib.no

Abstract. The modelling of trust for the purpose of trust management gives rise
to a puzzle that opens up fundamental questions concerning the relationship
between trust and calculative reason as the basis for cooperation. It is argued
that, ironically, trust management seem not to maximise trust but, instead, to
reduce the need for trust. This conclusion is used to argue that the normative
aspects of trust must be given a central role in the modelling of trust and trust
management. The following question is addressed: What can an agent R infer
about the future actions of another agent E, if R assumes that E is trustworthy?
It is suggested that a generalised version of Barwise and Seligman's theory of
information flow can be used to model the role of normative structures in
reasoning in trust relationships. Implications for trust management are discussed.

1 The Puzzle of Trust Management

What is it that trust management is supposed to achieve? It is uncontroversial, I
believe, to claim that the ultimate goal is to enable the development of mutually
beneficial cooperation. It is natural to suggest, furthermore, that the role of trust
management is to maximise trust between the parties and thereby provide a basis for
cooperation to develop. But this further suggestion creates problems. Empirical
evidence shows, I will argue, that rather than increasing trust, trust management will
have the effect of reducing the need for trust. Hence, trust is not maximised after all.
There is no reason to believe, however, that trust management does not support the
development of cooperation. This is the puzzle, then: how can trust management
provide the basis for cooperation without maximising trust?

2 Does Trust Management Maximize Trust?

As a starting point for the discussion of this puzzle, consider first the perspective on
trust management provided by Jøsang et. al. (2005). On their definition, which
expresses a representative view, trust management is:

> "[t]he activity of creating systems and methods that allow relying parties
> to make assessments and decisions regarding the dependability of potential
> transactions involving risk, and that also allow players and system owners to
> increase and correctly represent the reliability of themselves and their
> systems." (Jøsang et al 2005: 96)

K. Stølen et al. (Eds.): iTrust 2006, LNCS 3986, pp. 48–61, 2006.

The essence of trust management, on this definition, is to provide a better informational basis for analysing the risks and benefits of the transaction. Typical examples would be the collection of relevant information about the reputation of the other party or the systematic analysis of my own experiences from previous encounters with her, and the communication of my own policies in situations of this kind. The same understanding of the point of trust management emerges from the survey of trust management provided by Rouhaama et al. (2005)

The aim of trust management must be to facilitate beneficial cooperation and to avoid interactions that are not beneficial. Secondly, trust is often an important basis for cooperation. This idea is found in much of the trust literature, for example in the influential account of Marsh and Dibben (2005). They define trust as "the belief (or measure of it) that a person (the trustee) will act in the best interest of another (the truster) in a given situation, even when controls are unavailable and it may not be in the trustee's best interest to do so." (Marsh and Dibben 2005: 19) The definition is far from clear, but the many questions that it raises need not concern us here. The main point is that they view trust as a belief that can be measured, and that they use this to formulate a rule which says, roughly, that if the degree of trust is greater than a certain cooperation threshold, then the agent will cooperate.

Marsh and Dibben do not discuss trust management explicitly and they are used here only to exemplify a typical view of the positive relationship between trust and cooperation. A further, natural suggestion, not made by Marsh and Dibben, would be that the function of trust management is, at least in part, to *maximise* trust. To see why this is a plausible idea, let us distinguish the perspective of the truster and that of the trustee. From the perspective of the *truster*, trust management would be, following the definition of Jøsang et al. above, to determine the trustworthiness of the trustee. This could have the negative result that the he was not trustworthy. In this case there cannot be an increase in trust. But in the case the other party is judged to be trustworthy, with the aid of reputation mechanisms for example, one could perhaps think that the truster's trust in the trustee would increase. Conversely, if we consider trust management from the perspective of the trustee, a natural suggestion would be that he could raise the trustor's level of trust in him by communicating trustworthiness. This is an idea that seem to be involved in what we might call this the marketing perspective on trust management, i.e. marketing efforts to induce trust in potential customers (for an example, see Cheskin 1999). It is not clear, however, whether this marketing perspective should be considered to be part of the scientific study of trust management. The majority of contributions to the field seem to as its starting point the perspective of the prospective truster. In the discussion below I will also focus on trust management only from the perspective of the truster.

3   The Growth of Trust in Social Structures

My claim, now, is that trust management does not promote cooperation by increasing trust. I have two arguments to support this claim, one empirical and one theoretical. The empirical argument draws on experiments on trust and cooperation done by Kollock (1994) and Molm, Takahashi and Peterson (2000). Kollock studied the development of trust under conditions of varying degrees of uncertainty. The contrast between the two types of situations that he simulates in his experiments can be illustrated by the markets for rubber and markets for rice. The market for rubber is characterized by a high level of uncertainty, Kollock explains.

> Rubber is an interesting commodity in that at the time of sale it is impossible to determine its quality. It is not until months later, after extensive processing, that the buyer can determine whether the grower took the extra time and expense to insure high-quality crop. Within this situation the buyers are not motivated to pay a high price for goods of unknown quality and the growers are not motivated to produce high quality goods as there is no simple, objective way of displaying the care they took. The participants are faced with a type of Prisoner's Dilemma that is the result of asymmetric information. Furthermore, there is no regulatory agency to monitor and sanction the actions of each exchange partner. (Kollock 1993: 314)

Still, in this market buyer and sellers have been able to develop a stable pattern of cooperation, because "they have abandoned the anonymous exchange of the market for personal, long-term exchange relationships between particular buyers and sellers. Within this framework it is possible for the growers to establish reputation for fairness and trustworthiness." (Kollock 1993: 314)

In contrast to the market for rubber, the market for rice is characterised by low uncertainty, because "[u]nlike rubber, the quality of rice can be ascertained directly and at essentially no cost by rubbing a few grains of together between blocks of wood." (Kollock 1993: 315). In the word of Popkin, who has described this market, it is "what Adam Smith thought all capitalism was like – information easily and readily ascertainable, easy switching of buyers, little reason for loyalty to any marketer or buyer." (cited in Kollock 1993: 315). For this reason there is in this market little need for trust, and "the need for commitment and the concern over reputation will be lower." (Kollock 1993: 315)

Kollock studied experimentally the development of trust within situations with respectively very high and very low uncertainty, to investigate the ideas that exchange under uncertainty leads to the development of trust while exchange under certainty does not. There is not space here to go into the details of the experimental setup, the measurements for trust and commitment or a detailed analysis of the results. What is of importance to the present discussion is that Kollock found the following hypotheses confirmed:

(1) "Commitment will be greater in the uncertain-quality condition"

(2) "Subjects will be more likely to report staying with an exchange partner even though they could get a better price else in the uncertain-quality condition"

(3) "Subjects will rate their partners as significantly more trustworthy in the uncertain-quality condition." (Kollock 1993: 327)

The explanation for these results is that under conditions of uncertainty, traders are given the opportunity to show their trustworthiness in practice. And this proof of trustworthiness generates trust in the other party. "Thus, the development of high levels of trust requires more than just ongoing interaction. Some level of risk must also be present so that there is a *test* of trust." (Kollock 1993:319). If the situation is "correspondent" in the sense that the interaction is based on a recognition of mutual interest, there is no risk of defection and hence no test of trustworthiness. "The implication is that trust is likely to be higher among actors who manage to establish successful exchange relations in such situations as the rubber market (where information asymmetries introduce significant risks), as opposed to actors in situations similar to the rice market (where more information is available and the risks are significantly lower). Of course, risk creates a breeding ground not only for trust but for exploitation as well." (Kollock 1993: 319)

Kollock's study give support to the idea that more information – i.e. reduced uncertainty - goes together with less need for trust and that therefore less trust is developed. This result is relevant to the understanding of what goes on in trust management. Trust management is precisely the use of techniques for the provision of more information relevant to the assessment of the reliability of the trustee, hence to reduce uncertainty. This suggests that it is perhaps not plausible to claim that the trust management maximises trust as the basis for cooperation. Rather, it is more plausible to claim that trust can management facilitates the development of beneficial cooperation by reducing the need for trust.

4 Trust, Assurance and Contracting

This conclusion is also supported by empirical studies of the relationship between trust and negotiated exchange, as compared to development of trust in relationships where exchange occurs without negotiation before the exchange. Like Kollock, Molm et al. (2000) are conducting experiments to test their prediction, which in their case is the classical proposition of exchange theory "that trust is more likely to develop between partners when exchange occurs without explicit negotiations of binding agreements. Under these conditions, the risk and uncertainty of exchange provide the opportunity for partners to demonstrate their trustworthiness." (Molm et al 2000:1396) Their approached is based on a distinction between expectation of behaviour based on *trust* and expectations based on *assurance*. When trust is involved, there are "expectations of benign behaviour based on inference a partner's personal traits and intentions", while there is assurance when we the exchange partner has "expectations based .. on knowledge of an incentive structure that encourages benign behaviour." (Molm et al 2000: 1397) Their central claim is that exchanges under binding agreement provide assurance, while reciprocal exchanges generate trust among the parties.

Like Kollock's study, the result of the experiment was that trust is developed primarily when the trustworthiness of the partners are tested in practice. And, again, this seems to be relevant to the understanding of the role of trust management. Assuming that negotiation is a form of trust management, the study supports the claim that the function of trust management could not be to generate more trust, but instead to reduce the need for trust. Molm et.al make the observation that "ironically, the very mechanisms that were created to reduce risk in transactions – the negotiation of terms and strictly binding agreements – have the unintended consequence of reducing trust in relationships." (Molm et al 2000: 1398) This observation is relevant also to the discussion here because, first, negotiated agreement will be part of trust management in some case, and, secondly, because it makes plausible the more general claim that mechanisms to reduce risk in transactions will tend to reduce the need for trust.

It is not part of my claim here that trust management has negative effects on cooperation. On the contrary, I assume that trust management often will result in cooperation that would not otherwise develop. My claim is only that trust management does not provide the basis for cooperation by raising the level of trust, but, instead, by providing a better basis for calculative reason. Consequently, I also believe that the studies discussed above shows the need for taking seriously the relationship between trust and calculative reason in the theory of trust.[1] I will return to this in my discussion of trust below.

5 Trust and Calculativeness

Williamson (1993) has addressed this issue from the perspective of transaction cost economics. One of his claims is that "Calculative trust is a contradiction in terms." (Williamson 1993: 463) Furthermore, he claims that the notion of trust is redundant in the understanding of commercial transactions in a society with economic institutions. Williamson believes that "trust" is a notion that is needed primarily to describe personal relations. In impersonal transactions, Williams argues, only calculative reasoning is needed. Calculativeness is defined as a situation where "the affected parties (1) are aware of the range of possible outcomes and their associated probabilities, (2) take cost-effective actions to mitigate hazards and enhance benefits, (3) proceed with the transaction only if expected net gains can be projected, and, (4) if X can complete the transaction with any of several Ys, the transaction is assigned to that Y for which the largest net gain can be projected." (Williamsson 1993: 467) He then goes on to show that all of the relevant examples offered as examples of trust based transactions in the contribution to the classical volume Gambetta (1988)[2], can be fully explained as exercises of calculativeness. Drawing on the central assumptions of transaction cost economics, bounded rationality and opportunism, Williamson then concludes that there is no need to bring in the notion of trust at all in order to "describe commercial exchange for which cost-effective safeguards have been devised in support of more efficient exchange." (Williamson 1993: 463)

There is no need for the present purposes to go into a discussion of this general claim of Williamson's that the concept of trust is redundant in the explanation of market transactions. The aim of trust management is to provide the basis for reasoning about what exchanges to enter into in a specific situation, not to explain afterwards why the transaction took place, and for this purpose the notion of trust is clearly useful. The interest of Williamson's discussion in our context is the way he clarifies the distinction between trust and calculative rationality. This is again relevant to the understanding of trust management, I believe, because it seems clear that the implicit ideal of trust management as it is presented in the literature, is to provide the basis for the application of calculative reasoning in the sense Williamson identifies.

---

[1] Note that I do not suggest that this is something to regret, or that calculative reasoning gives an inferior basis for cooperation.

2

The suggestion, once again, is that trust management should be seen not to aim to increase trust, but, instead, to make possible the use of calculative reasoning and thereby reduce the need for trust.

The discussion shows that a satisfactory account of trust should clarify the relationship between trust and calculative reasoning and to provide an explanation of what constitutes trust in contrast to expectations on the basis of calculative reasoning. In the next section I will sketch the elements of such an account.

6 Trust as a Normative Notion

In most definitions trust is construed as a form of expectation concerning the behaviour of others. Gambetta's (1988)[3] influential definition is an example:

> Trust (or, symmetrically, distrust) is a particular level of the subjective probability with which an agent assesses that another agent or group will perform a particular action, both before he can monitor such an action (or independently of his capacity ever to be able to monitor it) and in a context in which it affects his own action.

Many more examples could be given, and we already saw above that Dibben et al defined trust in a similar fashion. One problem that immediately arises with definitions of trust as expectation arises from the discussion of the results of Kollock and others. Drawing on this work, I have been arguing that cooperation based on trust should be distinguished from cooperation based on calculation. The difference in question is a difference in the sources of motivation to cooperate. Hence, in both cases there are expectations about the cooperativeness of the other party, but the basis for these expectations are importantly different: trust in the one case and calculation of interests in the other. However, by defining trust as expectation or subjective probability this difference is simply left out of view. This is problematic because this distinction, if I am right, is crucial to the understanding of trust and trust management.

The element that is missing from these theories of trust and trust management, in my view, is recognition of the fact that trust is a *normative* notion. My suggestion is not that trust is a normative notion in the sense that people trust others because they ought to trust them. There are perhaps social norms that prescribe trust in some situations, but this is not what is relevant here. And there certainly are social norms that prescribe trustworthiness in certain situations: to keep our promises for example. But my point is not that trust is normative in the sense that there are norms of trustworthiness. My point is conceptual: trust is a normative notion in the sense that an essential ingredient in all cases of trust and trustworthiness is the existence of a set of norms that provide the motivation to cooperate. People are said to be trusting or trustworthy in virtue of being motivated to cooperate by mutually recognised norms.

To illustrate the suggestion, consider the development of trust and cooperation in the market for rubber as analysed by Kollock (1993), discussed above. The analysis was that trust developed over time as a result of successful tests of trustworthiness and that this was the basis for stable and mutually beneficial cooperation over time.

---

[3] Can We Trust Trust, in Gambetta 1988, p. 217.

One intuitively plausible description of what happened here is, I think, that norms of truthfulness and cooperativeness evolved in this process between the parties. Furthermore, it seems clear from Kollock's description that they were motivated by these norms in their cooperation. My conceptual suggestion, to repeat, is that what distinguishes this cooperation as a relationship based on trust, in contrast to a relation of cooperation based on calculativeness, is precisely the role that mutually recognised norms play as motivating factors.

7 Modelling Trust

The question, now, is how the norms that motivates in trusting relationships should be modelled. An account of trust which to some extent takes into consideration the normative dimension is the theory of Bacharach and Gambetta (2001a, 2001b) on trust in signs. They argue that the theory of should focus on the second order question of how to detect whether a signal claiming that the trustee is trustworthy, is trustworthy. They start by making a distinction between the "raw payoffs" and "all-in payoffs" of the truster and the trustee. Assume, for example, that the trust problem for the trustor is whether to give up personal information to a web site or not. The problem is that he will do this only if he believes that the web site will protect the information and not use it to spam him later on. Bacharach and Gambetta use pairs of payoff structures to characterize the basic trust game. For the trustor the structure of the payoff would be like in table 1 and the payoff of the trustee would be as in table 2.[4]

Table 1

Raw payoff structure of trustor		Possible actions of website	
		Protect information	Sell and spam
Possible actions of visitor (truster)	Give up information	3	-3
	Not give information	0	0

Table 2

Raw payoff structûre of trustee		Possible actions of website	
		Protect information	Sell and spam
Possible actions of visitor (truster)	Give up information	1	4
	Not give information	0	0

These are the raw payoff structures of the two players in the sense that this is their evaluation of the outcomes from the egoistic perspective of each player. However, the payoff could look different if a larger set of considerations are brought in, for example the relevant privacy norms. If the trustee is committed to privacy norms, such as the rule that information should only be used in a way that is compatible with the purpose to which the subject has consented, his preferences and payoffs might be more like in table 3.

---

[4] The tables are variants of those used by Bacharach and Gambetta (1999). Of course, only the relevant size of the rewards in the structures is relevant.

Table 3

All-in payoff structure of trustee with norms		Possible actions of website	
		Protect information	Sell and spam
Possible actions of visitor (truster)	Give up information	3	-4
	Not give information	0	0

There can be many reasons why the all-in payoffs of the trustee are different from her raw payoff, Bacharach and Gambetta observes. "Some of these take the form of reasons the trustee has to choose B [to cooperate]. One such reason, is his very belief that the truster is trusting him. Another class of reasons [..] include general moral principles supporting altruistic behaviour, and context specific norms, such as those which govern teamwork. [...] From a game theoretic standpoint, all these properties have the effect of transforming the trustee's raw payoffs." (2001a: 6-7) This is an interesting move which brings in the important role of norms in the analysis of trust.

Bacharach and Gambetta then go on to define trust: "in a basic trust game, the truster trusts the trustee E if R expects E to choose B [e.g. to respect the user's privacy]. " (2001a: 5) Using the notion of trust, they define the trustee to be trustworthy in this case: "if E believes R trusts him, E chooses B". (2001a: 5)

Two comments are in order. As mentioned already, I think the important distinction between trust and calculativeness is left out by defining trust in terms of 'expectations'. Furthermore, I believe it is to put things backwards to define trustworthiness on the basis of trust. It might be right that a trustworthy person can be relied on to follow the rule suggested in the definition. It seems strange to say that this is the *meaning* of trustworthiness. Rather, in my view the natural thing would be, on the contrary, to say that to trust someone is to believe that they are trustworthy.[5]

Bachrach and Gambetta focus in their theory on the second order problem of detecting whether the trustee's *signal* that he is trustworthy, is trustworthy. The problem is that it would be profitable for cynical websites, for example, to claim that they are respecting their visitor's privacy in order to trick people into trusting behaviour, and then exploit their trust for their own benefit. Bacharach and Gambetta develop a very sophisticated theory of trust in signs, and analyse this second order problem as a signalling game. This is a contribution of great relevance to trust management, I believe, but I will not go into this part of their theory. I will however adopt their distinction between raw payoffs and transformed all-in payoffs as part of an analysis of trust and trustworthiness to be developed below.

One widely shared intuition is that trust involves risk. A great virtue of the approach of Bacharach and Gambetta is that they can give a very sophisticated analysis of the risk aspect of a situation involving trust. By making the distinction between the two payoff structures, we can see that the problem of risk arises at two levels. First, there is the question of the risk in the sense of the potential gains and losses in the two payoffs. Second, there is the question of how great the risk is that the trustee will not cooperate. This distinction is in my view an important contribution to the characterization of situations involving trust.

---

[5] The point that trustworthiness is basic is also argued at length by Hardin (2002) chapter 2.

On the basis of this framework we can account for several conceptual relation-ships. First, let us say that an agent E is *trustworthy* if his actions are governed by the mutually recognised norms, and that another agent R *trust* E if R believes that E is trustworthy. By characterizing trust in this way we can get a possible explanation of how norms enter into the motivation of a trusting agent: trust involves the belief that the acts of the trustee will be governed by mutually recognised norms. This account also gives a possible explanation of the difference between cooperation based on calculativeness and on trust. Note that on this model the trustor can infer the intentions of the trustee in two different ways, either directly via the constraints or via knowledge about the all-in payoff structure of the trustee. With cooperation based on calculativeness the trustee's intention is inferred by considerations of his all-in payoff structure, I suggest, while in cooperation based on trust the intentions are inferred based on the normative constraints alone. I emphasize, however, that I believe that there are mixed cases and that actions can be governed both by norms and rationality.

Molm et al (2000), discussed above, contrasted trust with *assurance*, where assurance was understood as a situation where the parties cooperated on the basis of a negotiated contract. In exchange based on contract, Molm et al argued, there was little need for trust and, consequently, little by way of trust was developed. On the present account, the reason why trust is not involved here is that the parties cooperate on the basis of their raw payoff structures.

A trust relation, on the present account, is characterized by cooperation on the basis of mutually recognized norms. A number of objections could be made to this suggestion. Let me address only one. It could be argued that people follow norms only to avoid social sanctions and that normative behaviour, therefore, is just another form of rational, maximizing behaviour.[6] But this is not plausible, I think. There are many situations where people follow norms even though the risk of negative sanctions is nil. For most people trustworthiness is the default even towards strangers they will not meet again. I do believe, however, that norm following is sustained by guilt and other emotional reactions. But this does not make norm following calculative, in my view. It is not plausible to claim that people are always trustworthy only to avoid feeling guilty. Jon Elster makes the distinction I am concerned with here in a slightly different way. He argues that the crucial difference is that rational action is concerned with outcomes while norms are not outcome-oriented. "Rationality says: if you want to achieve Y, do X. By contrast, I define social norms by the feature that they are *not outcome oriented*." (Elster 1989: 99). My suggestion is that relations of trust are governed by norms in this sense.

These considerations show, in my view, the fruitfulness of drawing the distinction between raw payoff structures and normatively transformed payoff structures in the characterization of situations involving trustworthiness and trust. At this point it is important to distinguish two questions. The first question is: how do we as potential trusters determine whether the other party is trustworthy? This is the question Bacharach and Gambetta pursues. But there is another question that is also important: What can the potential truster R infer about the future actions of the other agent E, if R *assumes* that E is trustworthy? To this question I now turn.

---

[6] This objection was raised by one of the anonymous referees.

8 Using Norms to Reason About the Actions of Trustworthy Agents

The notion of normative constraints on action has an important role to play in situations involving trust, I have argued. I will now try to make this notion more precise by discussion how these constraints can be modelled as information structures in the sense of Barwise and Seligman (1996).[7] The suggestion here is that norms play the role of information structures in the reasoning about what the other party will do, assuming that he is trustworthy. I argue for this by way of showing how such reasoning can be represented in the theory of information flow by Barwise and Seligman (1996).

In Barwise and Seligman's approach, the notion of a *classification* is central, a notion that is borrowed from formal concept analysis where classifications have been studied extensively.[8] Paraphrasing Barwise and Seligman, a classification is a triple $\mathbf{R} = \langle R, \Sigma_R, \models_R \rangle$ where R is a set of objects to be classified (the tokens of the classification), Σ_R is a set of types used to classify the objects in R, and $\models_R$ is a binary relation on R and Σ_R that says which tokens are of which type.

To make the suggestion more concrete and also to illustrate the approach of Barwise and Seligman, consider the following example – inspired by the game discussed above. Suppose we have three classifications R, N, and E, of the possible actions of the truster R, the interaction prescribed by the norms N, and the possible actions of the trustee E. Suppose the tokens of these three classifications are as follows:

Truster R		Norms N		Trustee E	
Tokens	Types	Tokens	Types	Tokens	Types
r_c	*Send*	n_c	*Cooperate*	e_c	*Protect*
r_d	*Skip*	n_d	*Defection*	e_d	*Spam*

For simplicity we assume that there are only two tokens and two types in each classification with the first type classifying the first token and the second type classifying the second token. In a more realistic modelling we would have a set of tokens – intuitively sets of actions at different times - classified as being of type *Send*, or the type *Skip*, etc. and also much richer sets of types. But for the purpose of exemplification it is better to keep it simple.

To model the information relationship between the classifications, and hence the flow of information in the system, Barwise and Seligman use the idea of an *infomorphism*. Using the classifications in our example, an infomorphism is defined a mapping between two classifications $R \leftrightarrows N$ defined in the following way. Intuitively, an infomorphism consists of two functions, one from the type of R to the types of N, and one from the tokens of N to the tokens of R. These functions satisfy the following constraints.

Definition. If $\mathbf{R} = \langle R, \Sigma_R, \models_R \rangle$ and $\mathbf{N} = \langle N, \Sigma_N, \models_N \rangle$ are classifications then an *infomorphism* is a pair $f = \langle f^{type}, f_{token} \rangle$ of functions $f^{type}: \Sigma_R \rightarrow \Sigma_N$ and $f_{token}: N \rightarrow R$ and satisfying the following biconditional, where ρ is a type in the classification $\mathbf{R}$:

---

[7] The following is basically an exposition of Chapter 2 of Barwise of Seligman (1996). But the idea to apply the framework to reasoning about norms is however – as far as I know - new.

[8] See B. Ganter and Wille (1998).

$$f_{token} (n)|=_R \rho \quad \text{iff} \quad n \models_N f^{type} (\rho)$$

This is "the fundamental property of infomorphisms" in the theory. The point of the construction is to formulate in a precise manner the idea that information flows in virtue of systematic connections between classifications of parts of a system. Informally, the idea is that "[i]t is by virtue of regularities among connections that information about some components of a distributed system carries information about other components." (1996: 35)

Let us now define the information relationships between the three classifications in our example.[9] The idea is to give a simplified model of a normative system. The core of the system is the set of norms to which the two actors relate their actions. The point of the example, furthermore, is to see how it is possible to reason about the actions of the agents via the norms. Let us therefore use the classification **N** as the central element in the system and the two classifications **R** and **E** have relations of infomorphism to this core as depicted in this diagram. The arrows that run into **N** are supposed to stand for the functions on types and the arrows that run from **N** represent the functions on tokens.

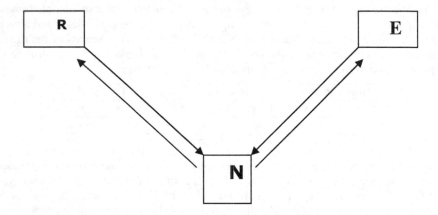

Let us now define the functions for the two infomorphisms. Call the function connecting the classifications **R** and **N** for f, and the function connecting the classifications **E** and **N** for g.

f^{type}	f_{token}	g^{type}	g_{token}
f^{type} (*Send*) = *Cooperate*	$f_{token} (n_c) = r_c$	g^{type} (*Protect*) = *Cooperate*	$g_{token} (n_c) = e_c$
f^{type} (*Skip*) = *Defection*	$f_{token} (n_d) = r_d$	g^{type} (*Spam*) = *Defection*	$g_{token} (n_d) = e_d$

We can now see that the functions f and g are infomorphisms from the classifications **R** and **E** respectively into the classification **N** that satisfy the fundamental biconditional.

The next step is to see what logical structure this gives rise to. The notion of entailment is in the theory of Barwise and Seligman formulated as a relation between sets of types:

---

[9] Again, this is in parallel to the discussion in Barwise and Seligman (1996: 37 ff).

Definition. Let **A** be a classification and let $\langle \Gamma, \Delta \rangle$ be a sequent of **A**. A token $\underline{a}$ of **A** satisfies $\langle \Gamma, \Delta \rangle$ provided that if $\underline{a}$ is of type α for every α element in Γ then $\underline{a}$ is of type α for some α element in Δ. We say that Γ entails Δ in **A**, written $\Gamma \vdash_A \Delta$, if every token $\underline{a}$ of **A** satisfies $\langle \Gamma, \Delta \rangle$. If $\Gamma \vdash_A \Delta$ then the pair $\langle \Gamma, \Delta \rangle$ is called a constraint supported by the classification **A**.

If we return to our example, we see that our classifications do not give rise to any interesting constraints on their own. We only have constraints of the form

$$\{Send, Skip\} \vdash_R \qquad \text{- i.e. no token satisfies both types.}$$

What we are after, however, is the possibility of making inferences about the actions of the agents on the basis of the norms. Let us construct therefore a new infomorphism from the sum of the classifications **R** and **E** into the classification **N**. This infomorphism is characterized by the function $h = f + g$. This new function again can be applied to tokens and types. Applied to tokens n, $h(n) = \langle f(n), g(n) \rangle$. And applied to types from R we use f^{type}, and applied to types from E we use g^{type}.

With this construction we can be said to reason about some aspects of the actions of agents on the basis of the norms, because we get constraints like this:

$$h(Send) \vdash_N h(Protect)$$

We do not, however, in general get this:

$$Send \vdash_{R+E} Protect$$

- i.e. we cannot infer *Protect* from *Send* on the basis of **R** + **E**, but we can infer this on the basis of the normative classification **N** taken as the core of the normative system in question. The reason this last constraint does not hold is that the sum of classifications **R** + **E** takes pairs of tokens from each classifications as their tokens and not every such pair will in general satisfy the constraint.[10]

This is but one example, of course, but I do think it shows that this is an interesting approach to the reasoning about the actions of a trustworthy agent. The point of the exercise was to suggest how we in the theory of information flow as developed by Barwise and Seligman can find an approach to the reasoning abut trustworthiness on the basis of knowledge of the norms.

I am of course not the first to suggest that we should focus on the role of norms in the reasoning about properties of trustworthy agents. One interesting proposal is due to Jones and Firozobadi (2001). The core of their proposal, coarsely put, is the analysis of what it is for an agent's communicative acts to be trustworthy. In their analysis, the normative element pertains to the assumption that the conditions of the communicative channel are *ideal*. This ideal is understood as "the conditions under which the signalling system concerned is in an optimal state qua (declarative) signalling system".[11] And what they call "the governing rule" of their analysis of the reliability of a signal is defined s:

$$E_a m \Rightarrow_s O_s p$$

---

[10] For the details of the properties of this so called *local logic* see Barwise and Seligman (1996) pp. 38–39.

[11] Jones and Firozobadi (2001: 164).

This says, roughly, that the agent a's bringing about of the signal m in institutional context S under optimal conditions will count as p. This then provides the basis for a characterization of what it is for an agent to trust a trustworthy agent's signalling act. The analysis is based on two assumptions that I believe are fundamentally correct. The first is that trustworthiness involves the appeal to a normative ideal to which the trustee is judged to subscribe. The second idea underlying Jones and Firozobadi's account is that trustworthiness is the fundamental concept and that trust and related notions should be defined on this basis. I fully share both assumptions. The approach is different from the one discussed above in the sense that in Jones and Firozobadi's account the role of the norms as information structures are not made explicit into the analysis.

9 Conclusion

The discussion above has brought out four ideas.

1. The studies of Kollock and others showed the need for a characterization of the difference between calculativeness and trust. This difference should be explained at the level of motivation for cooperation.
2. Trust is a normative notion and norms play a central role as motivations to cooperate in situations involving trust.
3. The distinction between the agent's raw payoff and his all-in payoff, transformed by norms, is a central aspect of situations involving trust.
4. The role of norms in reasoning about a trustworthy agent can be modelled as systems of constraints and connections between constraints, where norms are analysed as information structures in the sense of Barwise and Seligman's theory of information flow.

The main argument of the paper has been that the notion of a norm has to be brought into the characterization of trust and n the modelling of the reasoning about trustworthiness. Furthermore, I have argued that this will give a better account of trust, trustworthiness and related notions. This also has implications for trust management which should, if my argument is correct, focus more on the role of norms than has previously been the case.

References

Bacharach, M. and D.Gambetta. 2001a. Trust As Type Detection. In *Trust and Deception in Virtual Societies*, edited by Christiano Castelfranchi and Yao-Hua Tan. Kluwer.

Bacharach, M. and D. Gambetta. 2001b.Trust in Signs. In *Trust in Society*, edited by Karen S. Cook. Russel Sage, pp. 148–184.

Barwise J. and J. Seligman. 1996. *Information flow. The Logic of Distributed Systems.* Cambridge University Press.

Cheskin. 1999. eCommerce Trust. Report from the consultant firm Cheskin, downloaded from www.cheskin.com at 18.02.06

Elster, J. 1989. Social Norms and Economic *Theory. Journal of Economic Perspectives.* Vol. **3**. No. 4. Fall., pp. 99–117.

Ganter, B. and R.Wille. 1998. *Formal Concept Analysis: Mathematical Foundations*, Springer.

Russell Hardin. 2002. *Trust and trustworthiness*. Sage.

Gambetta, D. 1988. *Trust: Making and Braking Cooperative Relations*. Basil Blackwell.

Jones A.J.I. and B. S. Firozobadi. 2001. On the Characterization of a Trusting Agent – Aspects of a Formal Approach. In *Trust and Deception in Virtual Societies*, edited by Christiano Castelfranchi and Yao-Hua Tan. Kluwer.

Jøsang, C. Keser and T. Dimitrakos. 2005. Can We Manage Trust?, in *Trust Management*. Edited by Peter Herrmann, Valerie Issarny and Simon Shui, pp. 93–107. Springer.

Kollock, P. 1994. The Emergence of Exchange Structures: An Experimental Study of Uncertainty, Commitment, and Trust. *The American Journal of Sociology*, Vol. **100**, no. 2, 313–345.

S. Marsh and M. R. Dibben. 2005. Trust, Untrust, Distrust and Mistrust – An Exploration of the Dark(er) Side. In Trust Management. Edited by Peter Herrmann, Valerie Issarny and Simon Shui, pp. 17–32. Springer.

Molm, L.D. et a: 2000. Risk and Trust in Social Exchange: An Experimental Test of a Classical Proposition. *American Journal of Sociology*, Vol. **105**, no. 5. Pages 1396–1427.

Rouhaama, S. and L. Kutvonen. 2005. Survey of trust management, in Trust Management. Edited by Peter Herrmann, Valerie Issarny and Simon Shui, pp. 77–92. Springer.

Ullman-Margalit, E. 2004. Trust, Distrust, and In Between. In *Distrust*, edited by Russell Hardin. Sage.

Williamson, O. Calculativeness, 1993. Trust, and Economic Organizations". *Journal of Law and Economics*, vol. **XXXVI** (April).

Gathering Experience in Trust-Based Interactions

Colin English and Sotirios Terzis

University of Strathclyde,
Department of Computer and Information Sciences
Firstname.Lastname@cis.strath.ac.uk

Abstract. Evidence based trust management, where automated decision making is supported through collection of evidence about the trustworthiness of entities from a variety of sources, has gained popularity in recent years. So far work in this area has primarily focussed on schemes for combining evidence from potentially unreliable sources (recommenders) with the aim of improving the quality of decision making. The large body of literature on reputation systems is testament to this. At the same time, little consideration has been given to the actual gathering of useful and detailed experiential evidence. Most proposed systems use quite simplistic representations for experiences, and mechanisms where high level feedback is provided by users. Consequently, these systems provide limited support for automated decision making. In this paper we build upon our previous work in trust-based interaction modelling and we present an interaction monitor that enables automated collection of detailed interaction evidence. The monitor is a prototype implementation of our generic interaction monitoring architecture that combines well understood rule engine and event management technology. This paper also describes a distributed file server scenario, in order to demonstrate our interaction model and monitor. Finally, the paper presents some preliminary results of a simulation-based evaluation of our monitor in the context of the distributed file server scenario.

1 Introduction

Trust management is emerging as a promising technology for facilitating collaboration with entities in environments where traditional security paradigms cannot be enforced due to lack of centralised control and incomplete knowledge of the environment. In particular, evidence-based trust management attempts to mitigate the risks inherent in interactions lacking concrete security assurances by gathering evidence to support trusting decision making.

Studying the literature on evidence based trust management highlights that most systems focus on sharing evidence and opinions among peers and combining this evidence to make trust decisions (e.g. [10]). However, the means to gather personal experiential evidence is often lacking. The systems that provide such functionality tend to use simple representations of experience, such as a numeric rating (e.g. [1]). To support an expressive trust model for decision making in complex interactions, it becomes more important to get detailed feedback upon which to base future decisions. Additionally, many systems rely on the user to provide feedback (e.g. [14]). Even in commercial systems, such as EBay the user provides very simple feedback ratings. However, many

K. Stølen et al. (Eds.): iTrust 2006, LNCS 3986, pp. 62–76, 2006.

interaction decisions that might benefit from trust management techniques will take place in the absence of a user. Even with the user present, it may not be appropriate or convenient to require them to provide feedback. This introduces a requirement for feedback to be largely automated.

This work builds upon our earlier work in trust management [5], which defined a trust model [11] that recognises the strong link between personal observations and trust. The model views an interaction as a set of possible outcomes, based of a set of observable events within the interaction, which is organised in an event structure (see [11] for details). Computations can be defined over interaction outcome histories to derive a trust value for a specific entity. In conjunction with information on the costs of the possible outcomes, a trust value enables the evaluation of risk in an interaction to facilitate a decision process [13]. In [4], we defined an interaction model that extended this trust model to capture more detailed observations about generic interactions and their associated costs. An application developer can instantiate this model for a specific type of interaction to define a set of observations that may be made either directly or indirectly about the behaviour of a trustee. The observations are defined to represent the aspects of the interaction type that the developer deems relevant to a trusting decision. The model is event based, facilitating the automated gathering of objective evidence for subjective evaluation in a decision process. The same paper presented initial steps towards automating this evidence gathering, introducing a preliminary architecture for a generic monitor that could be used to follow interactions based on the model.

In this paper, we advance our previous work by refining the monitor architecture and examining the use of existing reactive technologies to provide an implementation of the architecture. After briefly outlining the interaction model in section 2, we describe the requirements for the monitor in section 3, followed by a refined monitor architecture in section 4. These refinements were the result of a more thorough investigation of the technologies used in the monitor and the instantiation of the model for specific application scenarios. In section 5 we present a prototype implementation of the architecture. In section 6 we present a preliminary evaluation of the prototype. This is based on a particular instantiation of the interaction model for a file server scenario (presented in section 6.1), which forms the basis for a simulation platform outlined in section 6.2. This simulation platform and the prototype monitor provide a basis for our evaluation, some preliminary results of which are presented in section 6.3. The paper concludes and looks to the future in section 7.

2   The Interaction Model

Our interaction model provides a number of extensions to the trust model in [11] that allow more detailed observations to be made about the state of an interaction in order to fully support a trust-based decision process. The focus of our model remains on observable events that capture a variety of aspects of the interaction. The events of the model can be further decomposed into a set of *trust events* (E_T) and a set of *cost events* (E_C). The trust events are those which capture the aspects of an interaction that reflect the trustee's behaviour in some way and hence something relevant to its trustworthiness (e.g. a file server's integrity). This set takes the form of an event structure. The cost events are added to the model in order to represent an occurrence of something that affects the costs associated with outcomes rather than the outcomes themselves. Thus we may also capture the dynamism of interaction progression from a cost perspective. To increase the flexibility of the trust events, we can further subdivide E_T into *directly observable events* and *quantified events*. While the former represent aspects of an interaction that can be expressed through single event instances, some aspects require the more abstract notion of quantified events, which are single logical events under which a series of low level observations can be aggregated, to form a *measure* of the quantified event (e.g. the latency measure of a file server). The low level observations are referred to as *measure events*. The relationship between the main event types can be seen in figure 1. Measure events are not shown, as although observable as single event instances, they are not part of the trust event structure, merely incorporated into an outcome via the measures of quantified events.

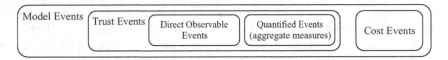

Fig. 1. Event Type Relationships

Modelling a particular type of interaction involves identifying the above sets of observable events for the set of outcomes. Through these event sets, we have means of representing the state of an interaction from start to finish. Experience thus represents objective evidence which can be evaluated subjectively for trust decision making, such that we can differentiate fact and opinion. The feedback loses no information and can be as detailed as the specified interaction model. Furthermore, feedback can be provided throughout an interaction rather than at its conclusion, which can be useful in adjusting our trust opinions in a timely fashion. The model is described in more detail in [3].

3   The Monitor Requirements

The monitor is designed to operate as a service on a single device that can monitor interactions for a number of that device's applications. We have chosen to co-locate the monitor with the client application as this provides some privacy within the context of a single user's machine. In cases where the monitor needs to run on a resource constrained device, it could run in a proxy configuration providing access to an external service on a more powerful machine, in a manner transparent to the application.

From the interaction model described above, the natural separation of trust and cost events provides us with a means of separately representing the *trust-state* and *cost-state* of an interaction. All events from E_T seen so far in an interaction represent its trust-state. The cost-state is represented by a mapping from the possible outcomes to the currently associated costs and the set of events from E_C seen so far. Together, these states give us the *interaction-state*, which can be used to provide detailed feedback at any point during an interaction. The two main issues that arise for the monitor here are how to collect the events that contribute to the interaction state and when to pass the collected information back to the client application.

3.1 Event Communication

Even though the monitor and application may exist on the same machine, it is likely that the sources of many events will be remote. As we may have event sources external to both the monitor and client application, we can see three categories of interaction model events emerge. These are events internal to the client application, those external to the application yet from the trustee and those external to both, perhaps from some separate service. Event (or messaging) systems provide a form of asynchronous messaging that allows the monitor to be decoupled from event sources, while supporting many different event systems via plug-ins and maintaining the generic qualities of the monitor.

Features of individual event systems vary widely. A major factor is the connection model communication is based on. A single central event broker is inappropriate for distributed and heterogeneous event sources and prone to failure. Hierarchically distributed event servers or an even more decentralised peer-to-peer (P2P) network is preferable. Most event systems support both *point-to-point* (PTP) or *publish/subscribe* (pub/sub) messaging. PTP messaging uses dedicated queues and is suitable for internal client and trustee events, where the client can inform the monitor on how to subscribe to the particular source. However, events from an external service will generally be global rather than interaction specific in scope, such as cost events that affect more than one application. These events fit more appropriately with a pub/sub paradigm which allows for many-to-many event communication where the the subscriber does not need to know the specific source. Whether PTP or pub/sub is used, the client application must tell the monitor how and where to subscribe to event sources.

Our event system requirements also include the ability for the source to push events to a consumer rather than have the consumer periodically request notifications, in order that they be received in a timely fashion. The event notifications must permit parameters to incorporate any pertinent information about the event itself. Reliability of event notification is closely linked to the fault tolerance of the underlying connection model and its network protocols. However, many systems also offer some form of message persistence like store and forward or polling. Best effort delivery is likely to be the limit of our reliability guarantee for the monitor in general, as the monitor has little or no control over the measures the sources employ. Finally, security measures are important to ensure the privacy of generated events.

3.2 Provision of Feedback

Through the interaction model and a suitable event system, we have the means to both gather and represent interaction-state. We therefore need some means to reason over it in order to provide relevant feedback when required. At the end of an interaction, it is clear that we should pass all collected evidence to the application in order to update the interaction history with the new outcome and provide the best support for decision making possible. However, there may be some scenarios in which we would like either periodic updates during an interaction, or even notification of certain states that we deem important in order to take action and minimise damage. Furthermore, prompt feedback spanning across the ongoing interactions can provide the most up to date relevant evidence for decisions. We need to be able to communicate to the monitor the desired feedback and when to deliver it. Therefore, we use a rule-engine-based architecture whereby the application can specify rules about feedback and the monitor can reason over the state to meet the needs of a particular client.

We use a particular type of rule, called *Event Condition Action Rules* (ECA rules). ECA rule engines have been commonly used in active databases [12] for a number of years, but are now coming into more widespread use through decoupling them from specific database systems to make more generic reasoning engines [2]. ECA rules express an action to execute when some combination of events is witnessed, provided that a boolean condition holds true. These rules are the natural choice given that we have an event based interaction model to provide triggers for the rules and values from event counts, parameters and outcome costs for use in conditions. The client can define a set of these rules and communicate them to the monitor, such that it can provide feedback as defined in the action part of a rule. It should be clear that the monitor therefore need not understand the semantics of the events, rather just match patterns as defined in the rules. It is up to the definer of a specific rule to specify meaningful feedback for itself, which might take the form of a pertinent message or reports of current interaction-state.

The features of different existing ECA engines vary a great deal. A good framework for evaluating the range of functionalities can be found in [12]. For our purposes, it is mainly important to ensure that the engine provides for the kind of rules that are useful given the interaction model. For example, the operators permissible for event combinations and conditions is important. This will include primarily logical set combinations for events, and arithmetic functions and comparisons for the value based conditions. The engine must support parameterised events such that the associated values can be of use in conditions. The primary consideration for rule actions is that the communication mechanism for reporting feedback can be called upon. The mechanism may be either synchronous or asynchronous, as we can use the same inter-process mechanism used for the monitor's management API to provide callbacks, or use the event communication mechanism to send a feedback message. A further useful feature would be the ability to have rules generate events upon which other rules could be triggered, commonly referred to as the *cycle policy* of the engine. This would allow the monitor itself to generate events for chaining or even blocking other rules as specified by the rule set definer. In section 5 we will describe how our prototype monitor incorporates the functionality outlined here.

4   The Monitor Architecture

With the above considerations in mind, we can go on to describe an architecture for a monitor, which operates as a self-contained software component to enable it to be used in a generic fashion across a range of applications. In [4], we described our preliminary architecture, which has now been refined. The refined high-level architecture can be seen in figure 2.

The architecture highlights the responsibilities of the different components and the interfaces between them and the management API of the monitor. In this section we will highlight the major changes from the previous architecture in [4]. The monitor is itself constructed from various components. Firstly, an Event Manager (EM) is responsible for subscribing to all events. The EM has been refined to clarify its responsibility for translating events for further processing. The Interaction-state Store (IS) component maintains trust and cost-state in working memory, accessible to the final major component, the ECA Rule Engine (RE), which has been refined based on investigations into rule engine implementations. These monitor components are not visible to the application, which interacts with the monitor mainly via its public API for management purposes.

The monitor API has been made more concrete in the new architecture, as can be seen in figure 2. The API provides the means by which an application can register itself and its interaction model, via the `register(appSetUp,responseQ)` method. To initiate monitor ing of a particular interaction, the `initialize(xnSetUp,rules)` method can be called. Via the `updateCS(CostTable)` method, an application can explicitly define costs to associate with an interaction's outcomes, perhaps triggered by feedback when the monitor receives a cost event. This is appropriate when the application has some complex means of determining what certain events mean in terms of costs it will incur. However, in many cases, the application will be abe to define a set of rules for cost updates which incorporate functions to alter the costs directly on the monitor.

The EM exposes a `subscribe(sources)` method for the monitor to forward subscription details from the API's `subscribe(sources)` method. The Subscriber subcomponent of the EM is responsible for creating and maintaining PTP and pub/sub connections to event sources based on this information. All event notifications are time-stamped[1] and passed to the Transformation Adapter (TA), which then translates them from the source format into that used in the IS and RE. The Subscriber and TA can be extended via plug-ins for new event systems. The EM also provides feedback through the messaging system when the RE calls the `notifyApp(feedback,responseQ)` method as a rule action. The EM calls the IS's `add(e)` method to pass all event notifications into storage.

The IS represents the working memory for the RE, providing access to the relevant elements of interaction-state for rules. Sets of events and cost tables are stored and updated for each ongoing interaction. When an interaction's final outcome has been fed back to the application, the events of that outcome may be removed from the IS. The `updateCS(costTable)` method provides the means for the costs of a specific interaction's outcomes to be updated from the application. The methods `query(e_set)` and `query(expr)` allow the components of the RE to query the state of particular interactions for rule evaluation. Finally, the IS is also responsible for notifying the RE of new events via its `notify(e)` method.

Finally, we come to the reactive component of the monitor, the ECA Rule Engine (RE), consisting of a number of decoupled sub-components. The Rule Manager (RM)

---

[1] The notifications are timestamped in the EM when observed as remote clocks cannot be relied upon for consistent time.

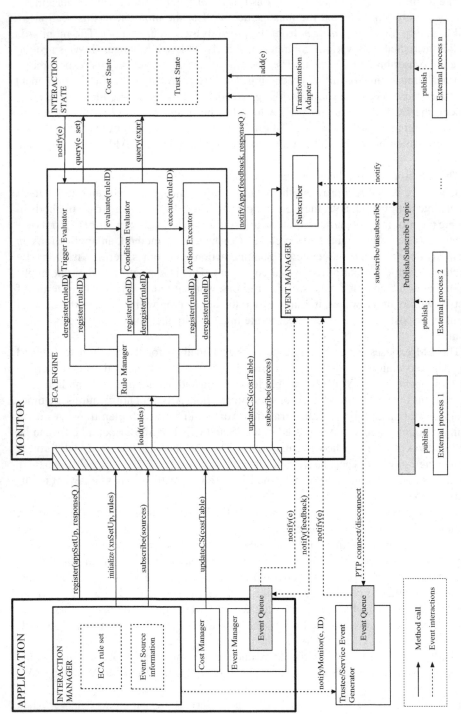

Fig. 2. The Monitor Architecture

manages rule activation, execution, scheduling and represents the state of each active rule. Rules are registered via the `load(rules)` method and propagated to the relevant component. The RM maintains state for the event trigger part of rules, to be processed and updated by the Trigger Evaluator (TE) as notifications of events are received through its `notify(e)` method. Trigger state can be seen as a tree structure of logical primitive event combinations, the expressiveness of which depends on the rule language. When the root of the tree becomes true, the `evaluate(ruleID)` method of the Condition Evaluator (CE) is called automatically. The CE is then responsible for evaluating the boolean expression in the condition part of the rule by querying the IS. Again the operators supported in the boolean expression depends on the rule language. If the condition is true, the CE calls the `execute(ruleID)` method of the Action Executor (AE), which schedules relevant rule's action for execution. The `notifyApp(feedback, responseQ)` method of the EM is commonly called by the action of a rule to pass relevant feedback as message through the appropriate event system. The message is defined in the rule and should contain all pertinent information.

The application component in figure 2 just outlines the type of components that the application might have, but this will be up to the developer of the application.

5   A Prototype Monitor

A prototype monitor has been developed for the evaluation of the architecture and interaction model. It was implemented in Java to take advantage of available class libraries and technologies for the two main functional aspects of the monitor; the ECA rule engine and the event system. The monitor exports an RMI remote interface for the application to interaction with, in accordance with the monitor architecture. The monitor runs as a single thread which enables single-point logging of interaction events as seen by the event manager, for the purpose of interaction trace replay and testing of different rule sets.

A myriad of rule engines are available (e.g. [7, 9]), which offer varied functionality. Having examined a range of such technologies, we chose the Java Expert System Shell (Jess) [6] to implement the ECA rule engine as it is very well documented and supported, with a large user community. It provides very good integration with Java, ranging from applications written purely in Java code to mainly Jess code simply launched through a Java application. The Jess Shell can also be used as a Java scripting environment to aid in rapid prototyping. As everything we reason over must be available in working memory, we have in effect combined the IS and RE into one component, the *ECA Engine*, which instantiates the Jess inference engine. Jess uses the Rete algorithm [6], in which rules have state modelled internally in a manner similar to the complex event tree mentioned in section 4. A Rete network is built from single input fact nodes and two input join nodes. The fact nodes represent patterns and the join nodes represent a number of *conditional elements* such as logical combinations of facts. Rete shares nodes across the set of rules for more efficient processing. A rule is executed once for each matching set of facts. Furthermore, queries over working memory can be defined and run under direct program control to process collections of facts. Jess is not explicitly designed for ECA rules, rather for inference in applications such as Expert

Systems. However, ECA rules can be modelled by asserting facts for events and specifying conditions using *test* conditional elements that may contain arbitrary boolean expressions written in the Jess language. Furthermore, it is possible to define functions in Jess code to extend the functionality/operator set. Similar functions can be defined to perform the necessary actions, expressed on the left hand side of the rules.

5.1   Coding the Generic Interaction Model in Jess

Before we can assert facts into working memory to represent interaction-state, we must define templates for the facts in accordance with our interaction model. Thus the generic interaction model is defined in the monitor by running a batch file of template definitions through the instantiated Jess engine. An *interaction* template is defined with fields to store interaction, application and trustee IDs along with the queue-name to which feedback should be sent. A *measure* template allows for temporary storage of measure events until they are assigned to the relevant quantified events at the end of an interaction. An *outcome-cost* template allows a cost to be associated with a specific outcome for a specific interaction. An *event* template is defined with fields to link asserted event facts to a specific interaction and store a timestamp. This basic event template is further extended to a *trust-event* template and *cost-event* template, which themselves are further extended to produce *measure-event, direct-observable-event, quantified-event* templates etc. This extension mechanism is also the means by which a specific application's interaction model is defined. New specific event templates extend the basic event templates to give a hierarchy of event types (see the examples in section 6.1). This enables useful queries to be expressed over the working memory that allow, for example, all events relating to a particular trustee to be processed in some way. We have defined a basic set of queries over the templates of the generic interaction model, including queries over specific application templates based on template names.

```
(defquery find-xn-named-events
   (declare (variables ?xn ?name))
   ?ev <- (event (xnID ?xn))
   (test (eq ((?ev getDeftemplate) getBaseName) ?name)))
```

The results of queries can be iterated over and processed to provide useful functionality for test clauses (i.e. rule conditions). We therefore further define a set of generic functions that may be used in test clauses or for feedback actions. This set includes functions to determine the maximum/minimum/average/total value of a particular field from a collection of facts and functions to extract particular facts or values amongst others. An important function *notify-xn-app* is defined for rule actions, which calls a java method in the monitor from the Jess engine to return a feedback string via the response queue for a specified interaction.

```
(deffunction notify-xn-app (?xnID ?string)
   ((fetch MONITOR) notifyApp
      (get-specific-interaction-response-queue ?xnID) ?string))
```

In effect these queries and functions extend the expressivity of the rule language, so to be of use they must be defined in the working memory before rules can be defined that use them. In fact, a developer can also define new functions for use in test clauses, to be supplied as part of the interaction set up phase.

5.2   Implementing the Event Manager

The other major component for the monitor is the Event Manager, implemented to enable plug-in event systems via an extension of a MessengerLayer interface. For the monitor prototype, we wished to use a decentralised system, preferably with a P2P connection model. Furthermore, we felt a standards based approach that supported both PTP and pub/sub would be beneficial, to show that a number of implementations of such a standard could easily be supported. For these reasons, we sought an appropriate implementation of the Java Messaging Service (JMS)interfaces which provide a standard for asynchronous event communication in the Java language. Various implementations (or *JMS providers*) available which support a P2P connection model, but we decided to use MantaRay [8] as it provides its P2P functionality through a self-contained transport layer implemented over either TCP or SSH and HTTP, with the necessary discovery protocols. Furthermore, it implements persistence through a store and forward mechanism and has highly configurable logging mechanisms.

The plug-in built for MantaRay sets up the necessary JMS connections to the transport layer for both queue (PTP) and topic (pub/sub) based messaging. It manages collections of message senders, receivers, publishers and subscribers and facilitates the sending and publishing of events via method calls. Finally it acts as a message listener, passing any notifications onto the Transformation Adapter component. The messages received must be in the form of JMS Map messages in the prototype as these enable name-value mapping for event parameters. This is to simplify the Transformation Adapter of the plug-in to have only one input format which it must translate into Jess assertions. To enable translation, the application must supply the adapter with template objects for all event types in its interaction model. These templates define which event parameters are strings or numbers, ensuring correct assertion strings can be built for execution in the Jess engine.

6   Monitor Evaluation

Before presenting the evaluation of the monitor and interaction model, it is important to discuss the performance of the Jess and MantaRay technologies that form the basis of the monitor. As the Rete algorithm upon which Jess is based maintains rule state and only updates changes, its complexity is something like $O(R'F'^{P'})$ where R' is a number less than R the current number of rules, F' is the number of facts that have changed and P' is a number between 1 and the average number of patterns per rule [6]. Furthermore, the performance of a Rete-based system also depends on the number of partial matches generated by the rules, so badly written rules may exhibit poor performance. Performance of join computations for each rule can be tweaked to trade off memory usage against speed of computation. The usual messaging system performance tests include scalability for destinations (topics and queues), publishers and subscribers in terms of number of messages per second throughput. MantaRay's P2P architecture removes the concern over destination load as the destinations can be hosted on individual peers. The performance of MantaRay depends on logging levels, persistence mechanism choice and transport layer protocol. MantaRay supports database or file persistence, with file persistence offering far superior throughput. Using file persistence in a single queue or topic, with minimal logging and TCP connections, message rates between 6000 to 7000 per second have been reported in online discussion fora. It is also worth mentioning that MantaRay is a lightweight solution; the transport layer may need only 3 MB hard disk space.

Based on the above performance analysis, it is evident that these technologies, while suitable for deployment on laptop devices, are too heavy-weight for resource constrained devices such as PDAs. This could however be overcome using a proxy configuration to a more powerful machine. As the event sources can implement the queues and (for this scenario at least) the event notification rate is likely to be well within the above bounds, scalability is no problem for MantaRay. Furthermore, (at least with sensible rules) Jess can provide prompt feedback.

For evaluation of our monitor and interaction model we decided to follow a simulation based approach, as this provides the necessary control over the environment for varied experimentation. Simulation also has the benefit of being able to run a number of experiments in a short time and removes the possibility of incurring real world damage from running tests on a real implementation. Our approach involves simulation of a number of application scenarios. So far we have concentrated on a distributed file server scenario which we will outline below.

6.1   File Server Scenario

In our file server scenario, many users can subscribe to host files on many different distributed file servers for a specific duration. This is an interesting scenario from the point of view of the client trusting the server, as there is a rich set of clearly defined aspects of server behaviour that can be witnessed and the interaction has a duration that allows for continuous feedback. Furthermore, a number of interactions may be ongoing at any one point in time (even with the same server), thus prompt feedback from one interaction may be useful for decisions on others. First we define the trust events that reflect aspects of server behaviour in terms of the outcome of an interaction. The specific aspects used will depend on what the application developer deems important for decision making. The aspects we have chosen are the *availability* of the server, the *latency* of access, how well it protects the *integrity* of the hosted file, and how well it maintains the *confidentiality* of the file.

From this set of aspects, the developer can define the set of events that represent an outcome. The availability and latency aspects require quantified events to be defined, with an associated measure, as the individual measure events that reflect these aspects can be repeated. We model the other aspects as direct observable events. For example, we assume that the integrity of a file is either maintained throughout or not, although a different view could have been taken here to incorporate degrees of damage. We assume that we can only directly observe a breach of confidentiality, as we can never say for sure that confidentiality was maintained. Furthermore, we model whether the interaction lasted the full duration or the file was removed early. We thus define the following trust event and cost event types by extending the basic interaction model event types from section 5:

- **availability-qe** with associated measure events **available-me** and **unavailable-me** one of which is seen for any attempt to access the server.
- **latency-qe** with associated measure event **latency-me** with a *latency parameter*.
- **integrity-undermined-event** and **integrity-maintained-event** are conflicting; one must always occur in an outcome.
- **confidentiality-breached-event** may or may not occur for any specific interaction.
- **host-event** and **not-host-event** are conflicting; no other events are seen if not-host-event is received for an interaction.
- **bad-xnend-event** and **good-xnend-event** are conflicting; one must be seen to signify the end of an interaction.
- **cxn-cost-changed-event** has a *cxn-cost-change parameter* to represent the change in connection costs when changing, for example, from a broadband connection to dail-up.
- **file-update-event** has a *file-value-change parameter* to show the effects, for example, of updating a file with critical data.

As a Jess code example, consider the following which shows the extension of a generic cost event to give the `file-value-event` template:

```
(deftemplate cost-event extends event
  (slot appID (default "GLOBAL"))
  (slot xnID (default "GLOBAL"))
  (slot trusteeID (default "GLOBAL")))

(deftemplate file-update-event extends cost-event
  (slot file-value-change))
```

The event definitions described here, which capture the interaction model for an application, are passed to the monitor when the application registers with the monitor, via a batch file of Jess code. This file also contains other set up information, including the definition of an **fs-interaction** fact that extends the basic interaction fact to include a fileID and file-value, and **latency-measure** and **availability-measure** facts that extend the basic measure fact to link the relevant measure events to the relevant quantified events. The final part of this file contains rules triggered on the cost events to update the outcome costs. Once this file has run, a rule set for feedback can be defined.

6.2 The Simulation

Based on the file server scenario described in section 6.1, we have developed a simulation environment to provide an experimental platform for the evaluation of the monitor prototype. The simulation (outlined in more detail in [3]) comprises an application component and a file server component that can be instantiated on a number of remote machines, to provide a realistic environment in which to test the monitor and interaction model. Both the application component and the file servers are JMS enabled through individual Mantaray transport layers. Queues are used for communicating most events for privacy, with only the global `cxn-cost-changed-events` passed via topics. The file server exports an RMI interface for file hosting and subsequent file operations from which server behaviour can be observed (see figure 3).

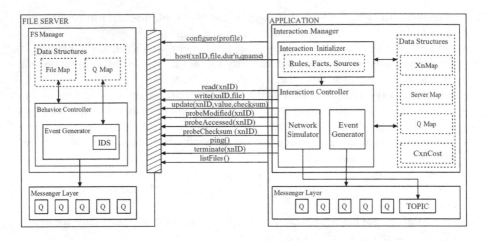

Fig. 3. The File Server and Application

In order to keep the file servers lightweight for the simulation, we define file objects rather than create real files for storage. These encapsulate the file's ID, a file value, an integrity checksum and last modified and accessed timestamps. File servers store these file objects and perform a number of actions upon them based on a *behavioural profile* configured through the interface. This profile influences server behaviour on each aspect of latency, availability, integrity and confidentiality. The *Behavioural Controller* component uses these profiles to determine thresholds for certain behaviours, continually iterating over the currently hosted files and acting upon them in a number of ways. This includes generating `confidentiality-breach-events` and `integrity-undermined-events` for an interaction via the *Event Generator*, simulating an intrusion detection system (IDS) and disk corruption notifications. The Behaviour Controller can also alter a file's checksum, value or timestamps without generating an event, leaving the application to discover faults as a result of later method calls. Further to this, latency profiles influence the amount of delay added to operations to simulate a slow or overloaded server and availability profiles influence the chance of an `UnavailableException` being thrown by remote methods.

All the events defined in the file server interaction model may also be generated by the application based on the results of file operations when compared to a local file store. Once the application's *Interaction Initialiser* has hosted a file and initiated monitoring for the interaction, the *Interaction Controller* is responsible for iteratively executing file actions in the set of current interactions. To enable events to be generated from file operations, it provides wrapper methods around each of the remote method calls such that the relevant return values can be compared to the local store. The relevant JMS map messages are generated and sent to the monitor queue. Common wrapper functionality includes recording the time delay for a method call in order to generate a `latency-me` from any successful access. This means an `available-me` can be generated, but wrappers also catch `UnavailableExceptions` in order to generate `unavailable-mes`. The wrapper methods also update local storage as necessary based on return values from RMI calls. Additionally, each wrapper method also calls the *Network Simulator* subcomponent to simulate how the current network type will affect the call. This component periodically changes to a new random connection type, selecting from dail-up modem, broadband, LAN or WLAN, each of which introduces different network delays and changes the application's connection cost. This change triggers a `cxn-cost-changed-event`, which is global rather than belonging to a specific interaction and is thus published to a topic rather than queue. The connection cost, along with the value of a new file and hosting costs allows newly initialised interactions to be assigned realistic outcome-costs at start up.

6.3   Preliminary Results

The file server scenario has the scope, duration and complexity to permit a variety of interesting experiments to be defined. To give a taste of the kind of experiments, we consider a situation where feedback is desired when the integrity of any file from the application is undermined on a server. In this case, feedback tells the application to terminate all of its interactions with this server. We can express such a rule in the Jess language, using our generic functions as follows:

```
(defrule preliminary-experiment (integrity-undermined-event
  (appID "fileserverapplication")(xnID ?xn)(trusteeID ?server))
  => (notify-xn-app ?xn (str-cat "TERMINATE-ALL:" ?server)))
```

To evaluate the usefulness of this rule, the simulation models a storage fault that gradually propagates through the server affecting more and more files on the way. The server does not notify of any of the integrity breaches and the application must do so when it discovers the problem. The evaluation compares the number of files corrupted on file server when no rule is specified, then runs a trace replay with the rule to determine how many files were saved by early removal, one file at a time. The experiment is run with 100 files at different speeds of corruption propagation, the averages number of corrupted files from 5 runs at each speed seen in figure 4.

As can be seen, the number of files saved is is proportional to the frequency of corruption, and in each case around 84% of files were saved, with around 35% of the corruptions occurring after the first termination call.

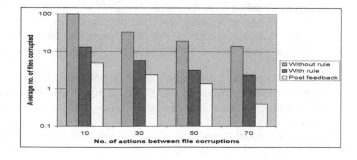

Fig. 4. File corruption experimental results

7 Conclusions and Future Work

We have presented our model of interaction, a monitor architecture and a prototype implementation. Together these support detailed evidence collection during trust-based interactions and can guide a decision process by providing useful, relevant, detailed feedback promptly and in an automated manner. While the model requires the developer to put in more effort to define a particular type of interaction up front, this alleviates the burden on the user at runtime to provide detailed feedback. Our evaluation is still in the preliminary stages, but as seen in section 4, our monitor can provide useful and prompt feedback. We intend to continue validating the monitor using more rules in the file server scenario and also using other scenarios within a more realistic context.

References

1. A. Abdul-Rahman and S. Hailes. Supporting trust in virtual communities. In *Proceedings of the 33rd Hawaii International Conference on System Sciences-Volume 6*. IEEE Computer Society Press, January 2000.
2. Mariano Cilia, Christof Bornhovd, and Alejandro P. Buchmann. Moving active functionality from centralized to open distributed heterogeneous environments. In *CoopIS '01: Proceedings of the 9th International Conference on Cooperative Information Systems*, pages 195–210. Springer-Verlag, 2001.
3. Colin English and Sotirios Terzis. Monitoring interactions between trusting entities *A Simulation-based Analysis*. Technical Report 02 (to appear), University of Strathclyde, Computer and Information Sciences, December 2005.
4. Colin English, Sotirios Terzis, and Paddy Nixon. Towards self-protecting ubiquitous systems: monitoring trust-based interactions. *Personal and Ubiquitous Computing*, November 2005.
5. V. Cahill et al. Using Trust for Secure Collaboration in Uncertain Environments. In *Pervasive Computing Magazine*, volume 2, pages 52–61. IEEE Computer Society Press, 2003.
6. Ernest Friedman-Hill. *Jess in Action*. Manning Publications, 2003.
7. The Mandarax Project Homepage. http://mandarax.sourceforge.net/.
8. The Mantaray Project Homepage. http://www.mantamq.org/.
9. The RuleCore System Homepage. http://www.rulecore.com/.
10. Adun Jøsang, Elizabeth Gray, and Michael Kinateder. Analysing topologies of transitive trust. In Theo Dimitrakos and Fabio Martielli, editors, *Proceedings of the Workshop on Formal Aspects of Security and Trust (FAST2003) at FM2003*, volume TR-10/2003 of *IIT Technical Reports*, pages 9–22, Pisa, Italy, September 2003.
11. Mogens Nielsen and Karl Krukow. On the formal modelling of trust in reputation-based systems. In J. Karhumki, H. Maurer, G. Paun, and G. Rozenberg, editors, *Theory is Forever: Essays Dedicated to Arto Salomaa*, volume 3113 of *LNCS*, pages 192–204. Springer, 2004.
12. Norman Paton and Oscar Diaz. Active database systems. *ACM Computing Surveys*, 31: 63–103, March 1999.
13. Sotirios Terzis, Waleed Wagealla, Colin English, and Paddy Nixon. Trust lifecycle management in a global computing environment. In C. Priami and P. Quaglia, editors, *Post-Proceedings of the Global Computing 2004 Workshop*, volume 3267 of *LNCS*, Roveretto, Italy, 2004. Springer.
14. Li Xiong and Ling Liu. A reputation-based trust model for peer-to-peer ecommerce communities. In *Proceedings of the 4th ACM conference on Electronic commerce*, pages 228–229, San Diego, CA, USA, 2003. ACM Press.

Multilateral Decisions for Collaborative Defense Against Unsolicited Bulk E-mail

Noria Foukia[*], Li Zhou, and Clifford Neuman

Information Science Department University of Otago, Dunedin,
Box 56 Dunedin, Otago - New-Zealand
nfoukia@infoscience.otago.ac.nz
Information Sciences Institute University of Southern California (USC),
4676 Admiralty Way, Marina del Rey, California 90292-6695 USA
{zhou, bcn}@isi.edu

Abstract. Current anti-spam tools focus on filtering incoming e-mails. The scope of these tools is limited to local administrative domains. With such limited information, it is difficult to make accurate spam control decisions. We observe that sending servers process more information on their outgoing e-mail traffic than receiving servers do on their incoming traffic. Better spam control can be achieved if e-mail servers collaborate with one another by checking both outgoing and incoming traffic. However, the control of outgoing traffic provides little direct benefit to the sending server. Servers in different administrative domains presently have little incentive to improve spam control on other receiving servers, which hampers a move toward cross-domain collaboration. We propose a collaborative framework in which spam control decisions are drawn from the data aggregated within a group of e-mail servers across different administrative domains. The collaboration provides incentive for outgoing spam control. The servers that contribute to the control of outgoing spam are rewarded, while traffic restriction is imposed on the irresponsible servers. A Federated Security Context (FSC) is established to enable transparent negotiation of multilateral decisions among the group of collaborators without common trust. Information from trusted collaborators counts more for one's final decision compared to information from untrustworthy servers. The FSC mitigates potential threats of fake information from malicious servers. The collaborative approach to spam control is more efficient than a decision in isolation, providing dynamic identification and adaptive restriction to spam generators.

1   Introduction and Motivation

Unsolicited Bulk E-mail (UBE), also called junk e-mail or spam, has a significant negative impact on the Internet. It wastes the time of users and administrators and consumes significant storage, communication, and computational resources. Many anti-spam techniques such as spam filters [6] and blacklists [15] are employed by

---

[*] The first two authors, Noria Foukia and Li Zhou, are placed in alphabetical order.

K. Stølen et al. (Eds.): iTrust 2006, LNCS 3986, pp. 77–92, 2006.
© Springer-Verlag Berlin Heidelberg 2006

e-mail users and e-mail servers to avoid the receipt of UBE. Although these tools are capable of identifying and eliminating some UBE, significant deficiencies remain.

This paper discusses a peer-to-peer approach for collaborative defensive strategies against UBE where e-mail servers in different administrative domains establish a collaboration to block unsolicited e-mail. Each server determines a local view of spam control by examining what it has recently received. Then, these local views are exchanged among collaborative servers and aggregated to form global views. Finally, decisions on spam control are made on the basis of these global views. Our framework supports mutual and dynamic actions to restrict servers that generate large amounts of unsolicited e-mail, while rewarding the E-mail Service Providers (ESPs) that are responsible and efficient with regards to outgoing spam control. Restrictions are taken by reducing the flow of e-mail traffic coming from irresponsible ESPs whereas ESPs that reduce their volume of outgoing unsolicited e-mails will gradually regain higher traffic as the reward. Consequently, all entities have the incentive to improve their outgoing spam control in order to avoid the restrictions imposed by the collaborating server network.

Moreover, in our proposed framework, the collaborative group of ESPs can extend across administrative domains and cooperate securely in spite of the general absence of common trust among ESPs. Each collaborator aggregates its system-wide information independently, according to how much it trusts the others. Information from trusted collaborators counts more towards the final decision, while information from untrustworthy servers contributes less to the final decision, so that potential threats of fake information from malicious servers are mitigated. This arrangement is based on the establishment of a Federated Security Context (FSC), which is designed to enable transparent negotiation of multilateral decisions among a group of potentially skeptical collaborators.

Experienced spam generators circumvent current anti-spam tools and spam is still pervasive in "inboxes" worldwide. Typically, spam generators seek open relays on the Internet. In these open relays the Simple Mail Transfer Protocol (SMTP) service is not configured to prevent unauthorized users from sending e-mail. The original design of SMTP [16][1][2] assumed that all users were trustworthy and required no sender authentication. Consequently, in both research and commercial environments there are millions of open SMTP servers that "spammers" can use as intermediate servers to conceal their real identities.

One widely-used solution to use of these open relays is the publication of blacklists of verified spam sources. Many organizations subscribe to these blacklists, refusing e-mail from listed sources. Unfortunately, the use of blacklists for rejecting e-mail is problematic because legitimate e-mail sent or relayed by the listed sites are also rejected. Even relay only mail from their own domain may occasionally be used by zombie machines within the ESP's own network. In addition, if a blacklist has not been updated to reinstate an ESP, mail from that ESP may be wrongly rejected. In this situation, it is not desirable to definitively blacklist these ESPs. There exists a dilemma here; If such ESPs are blacklisted, good e-mail traffic is also blocked; yet, if their responsibility for sending or forwarding spam traffic is not questioned, they have no incentive to control spam behavior. This dilemma reveals the difficulties and challenges in existing spam control techniques and the necessity to make more accurate anti-spam decisions. We think that better spam control can be achieved if e-mail servers collaborate to check both outgoing and incoming traffic and our collaborative defensive framework can assist in such collaboration.

In the following section we elaborate on the incentives and provide design for performing collaborative e-mail control. We discuss the need for collaborative defense based on today's e-mail patterns. In section 3 we describe our collaborative defense framework. We explain how a Federated Security Context Agent (FSCA) transparently negotiates the multilateral decisions in Section 4. Section 5 presents the demonstration scenario of the collaborative defense against UBE. Section 6 presents the approach simulation and section 7 discusses related works.

2 Why Collaborative Defense?

2.1 Difficulties and Challenges to Existing Spam Control

Today, we use the following two filtering methods for spam control:

- The first method uses tools to analyze patterns in the content of the e-mail and an automatic analyzer to evaluate the spam suspicion of each e-mail. If the suspicion rate is higher than a certain threshold, the e-mail is considered as spam, can be rejected and the sender added to the local blacklist of the e-mail server.
- The second method uses public blacklists to block IP addresses, e-mail accounts or e-mail servers that are known to generate or relay spam. E-mail servers can refuse any e-mail originating from servers listed on well known public blacklists [15].

Nevertheless, apparent deficiencies remain with these two methods:

- **Accuracy:** If the filter does not integrate changes made by the new tools used to generate spam, this leads to false negatives and false positives[1]. Blacklisting open relays that also deliver legitimate e-mails increases the number of false positives.
- **Impersonation:** An experienced spam generator can also easily bypass the blacklist mechanism by stealing legitimate e-mail accounts or forging headers of messages.
- **Evasion:** The elusive nature of spam [10] makes it difficult to identify with existing methods. Thus, experienced spam generators find ways to circumvent the filter by padding conjunctive symbols in sensitive keywords, by intentional misspelling of keywords, etc. They scatter e-mail messages by automatically creating many different public e-mail accounts or by using the many different open relays.
- **Dependence:** Blacklists represent a constrained solution imposed by a third party and the system does not adapt to criteria based on individual choices made by ESPs.
- **Length of Correction:** When an open relay has been blacklisted and its operator closes the relay, the process of removing the relay is often slow. Sometimes there is no way to appeal a removal in spite of the operator's goodwill [17].

---

[1] A false positive occurs when a legitimate e-mail is wrongly blocked by a spam filter. A false negative occurs when spam is wrongly placed in the user's mailbox.

2.2   The Merit of Collaborative Spam Identification

The building of a collaborative framework where a community of ESPs cooperate with each other to identify spam presents several advantages:

- **Reciprocal:** Spam is better identified by a collaboration of ESPs than by any ESP in isolation. Since a spam generator may dispatch its bulk e-mail to many ESPs, the spam control information from one ESP may contribute to the protection against similar spam traffic on the other ESPs. Collaboration allows ESPs to benefit from the varying tools, experiences and knowledge of other ESPs.
- **Dynamic:** Because ESPs would cooperate dynamically to control spam behavior, a burst of spam traffic is controlled in real-time. This is a control not available via public blacklisting that only provides long-term spam control. Furthermore, the collaborative framework allows partial and temporary filtering of suspected ESPs, thus mitigating the damage to legitimate e-mail traffic.
- **Adaptive:** Once a spam source is identified, the framework would not simply block all its e-mail traffic and blacklist it indefinitely. Instead, a sending ESP that is suspicious is immediately notified of its suspicious behavior by the other collaborative servers and it is granted a minimum credit to control its outgoing traffic. By decreasing the spam it sends, a suspected ESP can regain its reputation among the other servers and thus, has an incentive to improve its behavior.

2.3   Collaborative Restriction and Incentives for Outgoing Spam Control

Today, many e-mail server administrators still believe that allowing some spam to go out causes little harm to outgoing e-mail servers. However, not employing additional spam controls on outgoing e-mail causes inconvenience to the users. The direct victims of spam are the users and the servers who receive spam, not the users who deliver spam. The receiver suffers from the additional load placed on the server resources and the waste of time and money caused by spam. Thus, in practice, it is hard to push every server administrator to take partial altruistic responsibility unless we can introduce an incentive to make most e-mail servers more responsible for their traffic. The problem is very similar to the prisoner's dilemma in game theory [4][5]. If a majority of the servers employ spam control on outgoing e-mail, the overall quality of service is improved. Yet, if only some individual servers employ it, they incur the cost of identifying suspicious ESPs but do not receive the same benefit from other potential collaborators. To avoid the prisoner's dilemma, the one who makes the most contribution to the others by controlling outgoing spam needs to be rewarded, while the one who is irresponsible needs to be put at a disadvantage so that all ESPs have the same level of incentive to improve the control on outgoing e-mails.

Sending ESPs are in a better position to apply spam control to outgoing e-mails. Compared to incoming ESPs, they have more adequate information, such as the history record of respective e-mail accounts, to distinguish spam and spam generators from legitimate senders. If we think in terms of collaboration, the collaborative restrictions are a good incentive to push the ESP to apply better outgoing spam control. If we restrict the spam sources and reward responsible servers, collaborative actions performed by a group of servers are more objective and efficient than isolated actions and push ESPs to control their outgoing traffic.

Our proposed framework outlines the "how" and "why" of a collaborative design. The servers usually lie in different administrative domains and do not have common trust among each other. Instead, they evaluate the trust in one another on a case-by-case basis. If a high volume of incoming spam e-mails is detected by a server, that ESP will notify all the collaborative servers. As a restriction, they will cooperatively decrease the quota on the number of e-mails they can accept during each time span from the server generating spam. The collaborative network will temporarily also reject the excessive amount of e-mails with relatively higher spam suspicion.

A potential problem with this system is having legitimate e-mail rejected at the receiving server when the quota is reached. An option to mitigate this issue is to impose the resolution of temporal Human Interactive Proof (HIP) [19] or Computational Proof by the sender as suggested by Goodman et al. [18]. Senders who are real legitimate users can choose to pay the cost of resolving the proof. For spammers such an expensive burden of proof will act as a deterrent.

The more spam a server allows to go out, the more serious restrictions it will encounter from the collaborative network. The only way for a server to gain back its corresponding quota is to improve the spam control on its outgoing traffic in a responsible and timely manner.

3   The Collaborative Defense Framework

The collaborative defense framework for the particular case of the e-mail service is composed of three levels: (1) The e-mail service and the SMTP protocol for the exchange of the e-mails among the servers.

(2) The server-specific Local Delivery Policies (LDP) that specify the conditions to accept a message from another server and the conditions to deliver a message to a user. These policies are evaluated based on different factors which are: a) Originator of the message. b) Destination of the message. c) Content of the message. d) Current state of the e-mail server. e) History record of each sender and trust rate on each e-mail server. f) User preference. g) Suspicion value attributed to the message. The decision is taken from various security mechanisms such as the use of blacklists and/or whitelists, Intrusion Detection Systems (IDS), spam, worm and anti-virus filters. If the policies are local and specific to each e-mail server, the final decisions should integrate the more recent evaluation of the other collaborating servers. This is provided by the third level.

(3) The collaborative defense negotiation level that governs the decisions and actions taken from negotiation with the other servers and establishes a federated security context among the community of servers. Each server will integrate the other servers' part of the negotiation according to the level of trust granted to each collaborating server. The result of each negotiation is integrated locally as updates of the parameters evaluated by the LDP.

More precisely, in the third level a Federated Security Context Agent (FSCA) integrates the collaborative negotiation in the local decisions taken by each ESP. Figure 1 explains how a decision is made under the collaborative defense framework for UBE detection. When a request for a message arrives from a sending server (1), it is

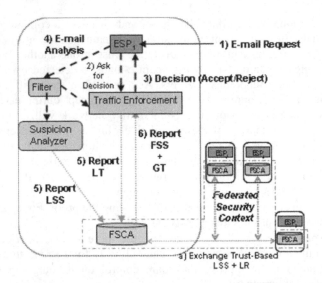

Fig. 1. The Collaborative Defense Framework

reported to the traffic enforcement level for decision making (2). The counter of in-coming e-mails from the sending server is increased and the decision is made accord-ing to the restrictions imposed on this sending server evaluated by the LDP (3). In our case, restrictions are imposed in terms of traffic quota. If the quota is exceeded, the e-mail request is rejected. Otherwise the e-mail is analyzed (4) by the local security mechanisms and the corresponding spam suspicion value is computed by SpamAssas-sin [6] and accumulated with previous suspicion values of incoming e-mails received from the same server for a predefined period of time. Periodically the local FSCA receives the Local Spam Suspicion (LSS) from the analyzer and the Local Traffic Rate (LT) of incoming e-mails from the traffic enforcement level (5) and exchanges these values with the other FSCAs (a). Each FSCA integrates these values to compute a Federated Spam Suspicion (FSS) and the Global Traffic Rate (GT) of all e-mail messages sent from the same server to the others for the last period of time (a detailed explanation of the variable integration is given in Section 5).

Both, FSS and GT are returned to the traffic enforcement level (6). They will be used to impose e-mail traffic restrictions to misbehaving servers and also to dynamically adjust the threshold value over which SpamAssassin considers the message as spam.

4   Federated Security Context Agent (FSCA)

The FSCA is designed to transparently negotiate multilateral decisions among a group of collaborating entities without global trust. The FSCA fits an environment where a number of independently administrated entities need to share and aggregate informa-tion to strengthen their security protection. However, one cannot fully trust others and use the information presented by others without imposing any constraint. Instead, each entity aggregates the information on the basis of how much one can trust the other, which is defined by the trust rate.

4.1 Trust-Based Security Variable

In our collaborative spam control framework, email servers share information for multilateral spam control decisions. However, since the ESPs in a collaborative group may extend across many administrative domains, no global trust exists among the collaborators. Other collaborators may make improper judgments, or even be malicious. We can not unconditionally adopt the information from the others. To reconcile the conflict between the need for collaboration and the absence of common trust, we originate a design of a trust-based security variable (TSV) which integrates the trust relationships into the sharing of the FSC.

From each server's point of view, the TSV looks similar to a variable in programming language. Nevertheless, the underlying mechanism of TSV is distinct. A TSV is globally shared among a collaborating group of servers. Every collaborator keeps two separate interface values for each TSV: **TSV-shared** and **TSV-federated**. TSV-shared reflects ones local view and TSV-federated reflects a federated view over the whole system. The underlying communication among the collaborators and the integration of the trust relationship are made transparent.

The maintenance of the trust-based security variable (TSV) consists of three phases:

- **Variable Proposing:** First, every collaborator proposes its own share to the TSV, which is called TSV-shared. Update operation only takes effect on its local TSV-shared so that different collaborator may keep different value as its TSV-shared.
- **Variable Exchange:** Secondly, the TSV-shared will be dynamically exchanged among the collaborators, so that every collaborator can obtain all recent values of TSV-shared from other collaborators.
- **Variable Integration:** Finally, each collaborator will integrate the collection of TSV-shared values into its own TSV-federated. Again, the values of TSV-federated may vary from host to host. The integration of TSV depends on two factors:

  (a) **Integration Algorithm:** Each type of the TSV defines its respective algorithm for the variable integration (the details are given in section 4.3).
  (b) **Trust Relationship:** Each collaborator keeps its respective trust relationship, which defines how much one can trust the other collaborators.

4.2 Trust Rates

The trust relationship takes a significant role in the negotiation of multilateral security decisions. According to the respective relationship of how much one can trust the other collaborators, each entity may derive its different view on the same TSV. In our framework, the magnitude of how much a collaborator X trusts another collaborator Y is defined by the **trust rate**: TR_{XY}. It is a decimal value in range [0.0, 1.0]. The more you trust someone, the higher is the value of the trust rate. In the following, we brief the three ways to derive trust rates:

1) **Empirical Assignment:** every user assigns empirical trust rates to other users, domains, or institutional groups that she knows. The trust rates on unknown collaborators are initialized as 0.0.

2) **Indirect Derivation:** When collaborator X has no direct empirical trust on Y, we can still use the following propagation algorithm (*Formula 1*) to derive the user X's trust rate on Y and the algorithm can be applied recursively.

$$TR_{XY} = \max_{Z \in M} (TR_{XZ} \times TR_{ZY}) \qquad M = \{Z \mid TR_{XZ} \neq 0 \wedge TR_{ZY} \neq 0\} \qquad (1)$$

3) **Dynamic Rectification:** The trust relationship can be adjusted in real-time on the basis of each entity's past experiences.

4.3 Integration Algorithms

Since trust-based security variables serve various data types and various functionalities, the FSCA supports many different types of the TSV. Each TSV type defines its own integration algorithm. In our collaborative spam control system, we mainly use two TSV types: *Confined-Global-Quota* and *Trust-Weighted-Average*. The *Confined-Global-Quota* is used to enforce each e-mail server with a quota on the e-mail traffic rate in total throughout the collaborative group (*Section 5, formula 7 and formula 9*). The *Trust-Weight-Average* is used to draw the average of spam suspicion rate and history reputation rate by each e-mail server. Both types of TSV are calculated on the basis of trust rates.

• Confined Global Quota

The integration algorithm in *Confined-Global-Quota* adds up every collaborator's local value (TSV-shared) to a total value (TSV-federated), and then check if the total value exceeds its corresponding global quota or not. However, we do not fully trust all our collaborating ESPs. Some collaborator, with the purpose of blacklisting an e-mail sender maliciously, may claim a faked TSV-shared with a large value (equal to or larger than the global quota). If all the other collaborating ESPs unconditionally accept this false claim and believe that the victim user has exceeded his quota, then the victim e-mail sender may be blacklisted on all the collaborators although she did nothing wrong. By using the *Confined-Global-Quota*, one does not unconditionally accept the values of TSV-shared from the other collaborators. Instead, an upper limit of the TSV-shared is assigned to each collaborator. The upper limit that one has on each collaborator is derived from the product of the global quota and the trust rate on the collaborator. The less you can trust a collaborator, the smaller is the upper limit. When some collaborator proposes a TSV-shared that is beyond its upper limit, the integration algorithm only counts the upper limit value into its local TSV-federated. Thus, for each collaborator H, we can calculate its TSV-federated as follow:

$$TSV^{federated}(H) = \sum_{K = all\ collaborators} \min(TSV^{shared}(K), TR_{HK} \times Quota^{Global}) \qquad (2)$$

• Trust-Weighted-Average

The integration algorithm in *Trust-Weighted-Average* calculates an average value (TSV-federated) from the local values (TSV-shared) of all the collaborators throughout the system. Again, to confine the potential threat from malicious collaborating ESPs, the aggregation of the average value (TSV-federated) is weighted by the trust rates. The more we can trust a collaborator, the more portion of its TSV-shared value will be integrated into our own TSV-federated value. On the other hand, the

TSV-shared values from less trusted collaborators contribute less to the TSV-federated value so that the potential threats from it are contained. If a collaborator does not have any value evaluated on this TSV, the integration algorithm will not count their null TSV-shared values. Thus, for each collaborator H, we have the following integration algorithm for *Trust-Weighed-Average*:

$$TSV^{federated}(H) = \frac{\sum_{K \in M} TSV^{shared}(H) \times TR_{HK}}{\sum_{K \in M} TR_{HK}} \quad M = \{K \mid TSV^{shared}(K) \neq null\} \quad (3)$$

For a TSV of type *Combined-Global-Quota* or *Trust-Weighted-Average*, every collaborator may derive different TSV-federated values according to the different trust rates on others, so that each collaborating ESP respectively draws its own view.

5 Scenario

In this scenario, a group of collaborative e-mail servers: $C=\{ESP_1, ESP_2,...,ESP_N\}$ use FSCA to setup a collaborative environment for the spam control. Each entity (ESP_X) defines a trust rate TR_{XY} on every other collaborator (ESP_Y): 0.0 represents no trust and 1.0 represents full trust. The practice of collaborative spam control includes four major phases: local spam evaluation, federated spam evaluation, restrictions imposed from the collaboration, and countermeasures.

• Local Spam Evaluation

In the first phase, each e-mail server evaluates its local spam suspicion on all other servers with which it communicates. Each server can customize its own application [6] and configuration to evaluate the spam suspicion on the basis of keyword filtering, pattern recognition, etc. On server ESP_X, we name the repository of incoming e-mails from ESP_Y as E_{XY}. For each e-mail $e \in E_{XY}$, it checks the content of e-mail e and evaluates a spam suspicion value S_e on e. S_e ranges from *0.0* (no suspicion) to *1.0* (confirmed spam). We split the axis of time into spans in length of t (typically, $t=1$ minute) and label the spans with a serial number. At the end of each time span K, we accumulate the suspicion rates of all e-mails that come from ESP_Y to ESP_X during this time span:

$$AS_{XY}(K) = \sum S_e \{e \mid e \in E_{XY} \wedge now - t < T(e) \leq now\} \quad (4)$$

Furthermore, ESP_X derives its local spam suspicion rate on server ESP_Y after the time span K, $LSS_{XY}(K)$. The coefficient λ (between 0.0 and 1.0) is introduced to make the local suspicion rate time-digressive, so that spam suspicions from more recent e-mail messages will count more into LSS than older spam suspicions.

$$LSS_{XY}(K) = \sum_{p=0,K} AS_{XY}(p) \cdot \lambda^{K-p} = AS_{XY}(K) + LSS_{XY}(K-1) \cdot \lambda \quad (5)$$

• Federated Spam Suspicion

In the second phase, the N collaborative servers exchange their local suspicion rates and integrate their respective federated spam suspicion rates. The value of federated spam suspicion highly depends on how much one can trust another. The higher value is the trust rate TR_{XY}, the greater portion of local spam suspicion on ESP_Y will be integrated into the federated spam suspicion on ESP_X. Formula 6 calculates ESP_X's federated spam suspicion on ESP_Y.

$$FSS_{XY}(K) = (\sum\nolimits_{Z \in C} LSS_{ZY}(K) \cdot TR_{XZ}) / (\sum\nolimits_{Z \in C} TR_{XZ}) \qquad (6)$$

• **Imposing Collaborative Restriction**

The collaborative servers restrict the server they suspect, ESP_Y, by imposing local and global quotas on the volume of e-mail traffic that ESP_Y can send in each time span, and cut off the exceeded part by rejecting the e-mail sending requests from that suspect server. We have three predefined parameters. The maximum local quota (MLQ_{XY}) defines the maximum rate of incoming e-mail that ESP_X can accept from ESP_Y. The maximum global quota (MGQ_Y) confines the overall rate of incoming e-mail from ESP_Y to the entire collaborative group. The blacklist threshold (BT_Y), determines that when the federated spam suspicion of ESP_Y is beyond the threshold BT_Y, all traffic from ESP_Y should be rejected. If no spam comes from ESP_Y, we assign MLQ_{XY} and MGQ_{XY} as the local and global quota on ESP_Y. As suspicious unsolicited e-mail messages from ESP_Y are identified and the federated spam suspicion rate rises, we should reduce the local quota and global quota on ESP_Y as a penalty. So, the actual local quota (LQ) and global quota (GQ) are decreasing functions of the federated spam suspicion (Figure 2).

$$LQ_{XY} = \begin{cases} MLQ_{XY} - FSS_{XY} \cdot MLQ / BT_Y & as\ 0 \le FSS_{XY} < BT_Y \\ 0 & as\ FSS_{XY} \ge BT_Y \end{cases} \qquad (7)$$

$$GQ_{XY} = \begin{cases} MGQ_{XY} - FSS_{XY} \cdot MGQ / BT_Y & as\ 0 \le FSS_{XY} < BT_Y \\ 0 & as\ FSS_{XY} \ge BT_Y \end{cases}$$

In addition, a counter is maintained to track the volume of incoming e-mails from every e-mail server during the past time t, which is called the Local Traffic Rate (LT).

$$LT_{XT} = sizeof(\{e \mid e \in E_{XY} \wedge now - t < T(e) \le now\}) \qquad (8)$$

The FSCAs periodically exchange their local traffic rates with one another. Each FSCA independently aggregates its overall count of incoming e-mail throughout the entire collaborative group according to the trust rate. As it is described in section 4.3, for the *Confined-Global-Quota* the TSV integration algorithm cuts down each local traffic rate with a threshold which is proportional to the corresponding trust rate, and sum up these tailored values into each server's Global Traffic Rate (GT). This mechanism can mitigate potential negative effects of global quota imposition if a collaborator maliciously claims a fake high rate to impede the regular traffic of other e-mail servers.

$$GT_{XY} = \sum\nolimits_{Z \in C} \min(LT_{ZY}, GQ_{XY} \cdot TR_{XZ}) \quad C = all\ collaborators \qquad (9)$$

Each time an e-mail request comes in, the e-mail server should query its local e-mail agent for inspection. Only after the inspector verifies that the LT is below the current local quota ($LT_{X\ Y} \le LQ_{XY}$) and the GT does not exceed the current global quota ($GT_{XY} \le GQ_{XY}$), will the e-mail be processed. Otherwise, when either LT or GT exceeds the corresponding quotas, ESP_X should directly reject the surplus and send back an alert of spam control to ESP_Y.

$$Decision = \begin{cases} accepted & as\ LT_{XY} \leq LQ_{XY}\ and\ GT_{XY} \leq GQ_{XY} \\ rejected & as\ LT_{XY} > LQ_{XY}\ or\ GT_{XY} > GQ_{XY} \end{cases} \quad (10)$$

As Figure 2 shows, during the dynamic process of spam control, the e-mail agent may encounter three possible circumstances. If both local and global quotas are met, ESP_Y is in the "white area", which means all e-mail requests from ESP_Y are accepted and passed to the spam filter. As LT or GT has exceeded the corresponding quota, ESP_Y enters the "gray area", which means some of the e-mail requests will be rejected to cut off the surplus traffic rate. Finally, if spam keeps coming in from ESP_Y and the FSS_{XY} rises beyond the blacklist threshold (BT_Y), ESP_Y falls into the "black area" and all the e-mail requests from ESP_Y are rejected.

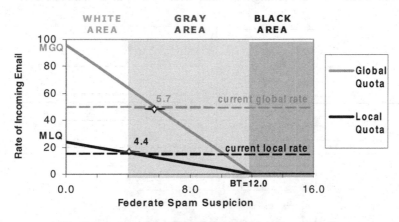

Fig. 2. How Local and Global Quotas Shape E-mail Traffic

• Countermeasures

In the last phase, when ESP_Y perceives that its outgoing e-mails are rejected by the other servers because of spam control, it can autonomously decide how to cope with the penalty. If no countermeasure is taken and spam keeps going out, the quotas that are imposed will be tightened more and more until eventually ESP_Y is blacklisted completely. In contrast, after proper countermeasures (such as demanding temporary SMTP authentication, filtering outgoing e-mails with higher spam suspicions) are taken and the volume of outgoing unsolicited e-mails is reduced, the quotas that are imposed on ESP_Y will gradually recover to higher values as a reward for taking countermeasures. Since spam suspicion rates are time-digressive and as time elapses, the records in the past count for less and less. Even if ESP_Y falls into the blacklist, after its outgoing spam control is improved, it will gradually come back to the gray area and then to the white area.

6 Approach Simulation

To assess our approach we implemented the FSCA on different nodes (machines). The FSCA is implemented using the Otago Agent Platform (OPAL) [22]. Opal is a highly modular FIPA-compliant [23] platform for the development of a Multi-Agent System (MAS) where agents can cooperate by exchanging messages. The tests involve four collaborating nodes (ESPs). Each node sends e-mail messages to the other nodes at random intervals between 1 and 5 seconds. An e-mail can have a spam suspicion between 1 (lowest) and 10 (highest). TR for all nodes is fixed to 0.5. LSS and LT are exchanged every minute.

Two servers (server A and server B) send e-mails with random spam suspicions, i.e. simulating no control of outgoing messages (spam suspicion randomly varies between 1 and 10). Another server (server C) is sending only messages (spam suspicion < 4), and the last one (server D) sends only bad messages (spam suspicion > 7). D might deliberately spam, or might be taken over by an attacker and abused.

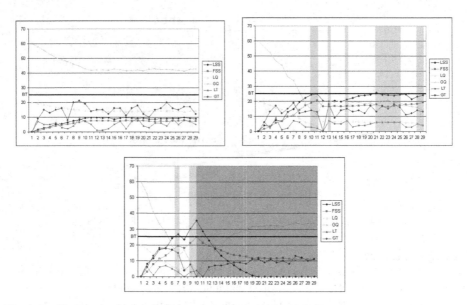

Fig. 3. Traffic Received by A *(Axis Y)* sent by B (top-left) - Received by A sent by C (top-right) - Received by A sent by D (bottom) during 29 sec *(Axis X)*

Figures 3 show *(Axis Y)* the LSS, FSS, LT, GT, LQ and GQ computed by A for the traffic received by the other three nodes during 29 seconds *(Axis X)* of the test:

- Figure 3 (top-left) shows the result of traffic coming from C: C sends only good messages. The local traffic rate always stays under local quota, and global traffic rate always stays under global quota. Therefore C is always in the white area.
- Figure 3 (top-right) shows the result of the traffic coming from B: B has no outgoing spam control and goes sometimes into the grey area, where its e-mail traffic is limited.

- Figure 3 (bottom) shows the result of the traffic coming from *D*: *D* spams *A* all the time. It goes into the grey area for a short time, before going above the black-list threshold and being blacklisted (black area).

In these tests, the MLQ is set to 20 and the MGQ is set to 60 for each node, as 60 would be the maximum of messages a node could send out if it was sending every second. The blacklist threshold is set to 25 (it was chosen seeing that the highest possible FSS obtained for the test was 55).

The graphs show clearly how the FSS influences LQ and GQ and how the different areas are reached depending on the behaviour of the sending servers *B*, *C* or *D*.

7 Related Work

Work related to defensive collaboration of both spam and Denial of Service (DoS) attacks exhibit similar characteristics and are described below.

The Defensive Cooperative Overlay Mesh [7] is a peer-to-peer distributed framework allowing exchange of information and services between largely distributed nodes for Distributed DoS (DDoS) defense. A tree propagating the DDoS alert is built from victim to collaborating nodes of the peer network that forward any traffic to the victim. The nodes cooperate to limit the rate of the DDoS traffic through the tree.

The Cossack [8] architecture allows coordination among defense software components called watchdogs. Watchdogs located at different edge networks of the Internet fight DDoS attacks. When an attack is in progress the watchdog close to the victim notices the increase of the network traffic and multicasts the alert to other watchdogs. In the Defensive Cooperative Overlay Mesh [7] and Cossack [8], a collaborative detection system constrains the network which is the source of the attack to perform better control of outgoing traffic. Both systems [7][8] use a static trust relationship between collaborators, rather than a dynamic one that evolves during the collaboration.

Kaushik et al. [9] propose an architecture to encourage beneficial behavior of e-mail providers by providing better quality of service to good senders and discouraging bad senders. Alternate policies enable the e-mail receiving server to specify to the sending server what it considers to be abusive mail. The collaboration is only bilateral and does not involve other servers. Damiani et al. [10] describe a peer-to-peer approach for spam filtering. Several e-mail servers attached to the same super-peer server send reports about new spam detected. In case of suspicion, e-mail servers query the super-peer to determine whether a message (digest) has been reported as spam by other servers or by other super-peers. The super-peer transmits all similar digests to the requesting server. The requesting server takes its final decision based on a confidence value that measures the propensity of a digest to be spam and a reputation associated with the server which reported the spam. The collaboration is only used to exchange digests and does not push servers to block their outgoing spam. Razor [11], Cloudmark [14] and SmartScreen [13] operate in a manner similar to [10]. The Distributed Checksum Clearinghouse (CDD) [12] uses distributed open servers to maintain a database of message checksums sent by clients (mail users or ESPs).

Clients make decisions about spam based on how many instances of the same messages have been reported. The scheme is subject to false positives if many fake reports of the same message are intentionally sent by a malicious client. Compared to [10], [11], and [12] our approach operates at a higher level, not basing decisions on individual messages. The FSC for multilateral decisions allows dynamic integration of collaborators' opinions mitigated by the trust granted to each one of them, limiting the impact of false positives or negatives.

Goodman et al. [18] present three techniques with initial cost (money, computation and HIP), on outgoing e-mail, each designed to impose a minimum cost on legitimate users and to be too costly for spammers. Goodman et al. [18] show that not every message needs to be charged to discourage spammers. But the average cost for the spammer during the lifetime of an account needs to exceed his profit. For that, the techniques impose limited initial costs and stop charging until a complaint is received. When the sending server receives a complaint, it temporarily terminates the account. This is a sufficient discouragement for spam generators because of the cost of a new account.

Jung and Sit [20] present an empirical study of spam traffic and the use of blacklists. It shows that blacklists are quantitatively related to one another by analyzing how many spam generators appear in the seven main blacklists and concludes that correlated blacklists should be considered to estimate that a host is a spam generator. This can be dynamically provided through the collaboration between blacklist servers.

8 Conclusion

This paper presented a framework for collaborative defense against Unsolicited Bulk E-mail based on multilateral decision making among e-mail servers and on the trust relationships among them. We argued that the collaboration provides better protection because of the three principles: (1) Reciprocity: the means employed at one ESP can contribute to the protection at another ESP. (2) Dynamics: supports control of spam in real-time and deals with temporary bursts of traffic. (3) Adaptive restriction: restricted ESPs regain reputation by controlling their outgoing spam. Temporary application of restrictions decrease the damage to legitimate users.

Collaborative actions performed by a group of servers are more objective and efficient than isolated actions. Collaborative traffic restrictions are applied to spam generators and collaborative rewards are applied to responsible ESPs, providing ESPs an incentive to improve their outgoing spam control. The collaboration is provided using a Federated Security Context (FSC) where a Federated Security Context Agent (FSCA) [21][3], transparently negotiates the multilateral decisions among ESPs. Each ESP aggregates the information on the basis of how much it trusts the other and the final decision made by the FSCA, mitigating the effect of false claims from malicious ESPs.

The collaboration between ESPs was tested using OPAL agents acting on behalf of e-mail servers located at different network nodes. The paper presented preliminary results of the effect of the FSS on the traffic limitation.

Acknowledgement

This research was supported by funding from the National Science Foundation under grants no. CCR-0325951 and ACI-0325409. The views and conclusions contained herein are those of the authors and should not be interpreted as representing the official policies or endorsement of the funding agencies. Figures and descriptions were provided by the authors and are used with permission. This research was also supported by the Swiss National Research Foundation under the funding of the Post-Doc scholarship: PBGE2-102311.

References

1. RFC 2554 – SMTP Service Extension for Authentication
2. RFC 3207 – SMTP Service Extension for Secure SMTP over Transport Layer Security
3. Zhou, L., Neuman, C.: Negotiation of Multilateral Security Decisions for Grid Computing. Technical Report TR 2004-15, October 8, 2004
4. Nash, J. F.: Non-Cooperative Games. The Annals of Mathematics, Second Series, vol. 54, no. 2, pp. 286-295, September 1951
5. Poundstone, W.: Prisoner's Dilemma: John von Neumann, Game Theory, and the Puzzle of the Bomb. Oxford University Press, Oxford, UK, 1993
6. SpamAssassin, http://spamassassin.apache.org
7. Mirkovic, J., Robinson, M., Reiher, P.: Alliance Formation for DDoS Defense. In Proceedings of the 2003 Workshop on New Security Paradigms, Ascona, Switzerland, 2003
8. Papadopoulos, C., Lindell, R., Mhreinger, J., Hussain, A., Govindan, R.: COSSACK, Co-ordinated Suppression of Simultaneous Attacks. DARPA Information Survivability Conference and Exposition, Washington, DC, USA, 2003
9. Kaushik, S., Ammann, P., Wijesekera, D., Winsborough, W., Ritchtey, R.: A Policy Driven Approach for E-mail Services. Fifth IEEE International Workshop on Policies for Distributed Systems and Networks (POLICY'04), New York, USA, 2004
10. Damiani, E., De Capitani di Vimercati, S., Paraboschi, S., Samarati, P.: A P2P-Based Collaborative Spam Detection and Filtering. The Fourth IEEE International Conference on P2P Computing, Zurich, Switzerland, August 24-27, 2004
11. Razor: http://razor.sourceforge.net/
12. Distributed Checksum Clearinghouse: http://www.rhyolite.com/anti-spam/dcc/
13. SmartScreen, http://www.microsoft.com/presspass/press/. Microsoft Adds New Spam Filtering Technology Across E-Mail Platforms, November 17, 2003
14. Cloudmark: http://www.cloudmark.com/
15. Distributed Sender Blackhole List, http://www.dsbl.org
16. Postel, J.: Simple Mail Transfer Protocol. RFC 821 Internet Engineering Task Force, 1982
17. Jacob, P.: The Spam Problem: Moving Beyond RBLs
    http://theory.whirlycott.com/~phil/antispam/rbl-bad/rbl-bad.html, January 3, 2003
18. Goodman, J., Rounthwaite, R.: Stopping Outgoing Spam. ACM Conference on Electronic Commerce, New York, 2004
19. Naor, M., Verification of a Human in the Loop or Identification via the Turing Test, Manuscript 1996. http://www.wisdom.weizmann.ac.il/~naor/
20. Jung, J., Sit, E.: An Empirical Study of Spam traffic and the Use of DNS Black Lists. Internet Measurement Conference, Taormina, Italy, 2004

21. Zhou, L., Neuman, C.: Establishing Agreements in Dynamic Virtual Organizations, IEEE SECOVAL Workshop of SECURECOMM 2005, Athens, Greece, September 5-9, 2005
22. Nowostawski, M., Purvis, M., and Cranefield, S.: OPAL A Multi-level Infrastructure for Agent-Oriented Development. In Proceedings of the First International Joint Conference on Autonomous Agents and Multi-Agent Systems (AAMAS 2002), ACM Press (2002) pp.88-89, 2002
23. FIPA. Foundation For Intelligent Physical Agents (FIPA): FIPA 2000 Specifications. http://www.fipa.org/specifications/index.html

Generating Predictive Movie Recommendations from Trust in Social Networks

Jennifer Golbeck

University of Maryland, College Park, 8400 Baltimore Avenue,
College Park, Maryland 20740
golbeck@cs.umd.edu

Abstract. Social networks are growing in number and size, with hundreds of millions of user accounts among them. One added benefit of these networks is that they allow users to encode more information about their relationships than just stating who they know. In this work, we are particularly interested in trust relationships, and how they can be used in designing interfaces. In this paper, we present FilmTrust, a website that uses trust in web-based social networks to create predictive movie recommendations. Using the FilmTrust system as a foundation, we show that these recommendations are more accurate than other techniques when the user's opinions about a film are divergent from the average. We discuss this technique both as an application of social network analysis, as well as how it suggests other analyses that can be performed to help improve collaborative filtering algorithms of all types.

1 Introduction

Web-based social networks are growing in size and number every day. A website that maintains a comprehensive list of these networks shows 140 networks with well over 200,000,000 user accounts among them.[1] Users spend hours maintaining personal information, blog entries, and lists of social contacts. The benefit of this time investment is vague. While a small percentage of these networks are dedicated to building business contacts, most are for entertainment purposes.

While entertainment may motivate users to maintain a presence in these web-based social networks, there is great potential to utilize the social data for enhancing end user applications. Since the networks are web-based, the information is largely publicly available. Many of these networks are beginning to output their members' profiles using FOAF, a Semantic Web vocabulary for representing social networks, means that the data is not only available but easily readable by applications.

One space that these social networks can be integrated into applications is in creating interfaces that act "intelligently" with respect to the user's social connections. This can be further refined by looking at specific features of social relationships. Nearly half of the social networks found in the aforementioned list provide some means for users to add information about their relationships with others.

---

[1] http://trust.mindswap.org/

K. Stølen et al. (Eds.): iTrust 2006, LNCS 3986, pp. 93–104, 2006.

This could include the type of relationship (e.g. "friend", "sibling", "co-worker", etc.), the strength of the relationship (e.g. "acquaintance", "good friend", "best friend", etc.), or how much the users trust the people they know. Our research is specifically focused on this trust relationship because it has many features that make it ideal for integrating into socially intelligent interfaces.

Specifically, we are will use social trust as the basis for a recommender system. For this technique to be successful, there must be a correlation between trust and user similarity. Abdul-Rahman and Hailes [1] showed that in a predefined context, such as movies, users develop social connections with people who have similar preferences. These results were extended in work by Ziegler and Lausen [2] that showed a correlation between trust and user similarity in an empirical study of a real online community.

Furthermore, there is evidence to support that users will prefer systems with recommendations that rely on social networks and trust relationships over similarity measures commonly used for making recommendations. Research has shown that people prefer recommendations from friends to those made by recommender systems [3] and that users prefer recommendations from systems they trust [4]. By producing recommendations through the use of trust in social networks, both of those user preferences are addressed. Recommendations come through a network of friends, and are based on the explicit trust expressed by the user.

In this paper, we present FilmTrust, a website that integrates web-based social network- king into a movie recommender system. We begin with a description of the FilmTrust website, followed by an analysis of its features. TidalTrust, a trust inference algorithm, is used as the basis for generating predictive ratings personalized for each user. The accuracy of the recommended ratings is shown to outperform both a simple average rating and the ratings produced by a common correlation-based collaborative filtering algorithm. Theoretically and through a small user study, some evidence is also developed that supports a user benefit from ordering reviews based on the users' trust preferences.

2 Background and Related Work

Recommender systems help users identify items of interest. These recommendations are generally made in two ways: by calculating the similarity between items and recommending items related to those in which the user has expressed interest, or by calculating the similarity between users in the system and recommending items that are liked by similar users. This latter method is also known as collaborative filtering.

Collaborative filtering has been applied in many contexts, and FilmTrust is not the first to attempt to make predictive recommendations about movies. MovieLens [5], Recommendz [6], and Film-Conseil [7] are just a few of the websites that implement recommender systems in the context of films.

Herlocker, et al. [8] present an excellent overview of the goals, datasets, and algorithms of collaborative filtering systems. However, FilmTrust is unlike the approach taken in many collaborative filtering recommender systems in that its goal is not to present a list of good items to users; rather, the recommendations are generated to suggest how much a given user may be interested in an item that the user already found. For this to work, there must be a measure of how closely the item is related to the user's preferences.

Before making any computations with trust in social networks, it is vitally important to know what trust is. Social trust depends on a host of factors which cannot be easily modeled in a computational system. Past experience with a person and with their friends, opinions of the actions a person has taken, psychological factors impacted by a lifetime of history and events (most completely unrelated to the person we are deciding to trust or not trust), rumor, influence by others' opinions, and motives to gain something extra by extending trust are just a few of these factors. For trust to be used as a rating between people in social networks, the definition must be focused and simplified. We adopt this as the definition of trust for our work: trust in a person is a commitment to an action based on a belief that the future actions of that person will lead to a good outcome. The action and commitment does not have to be significant. We could say Alice trusts Bob regarding movies if she chooses to watch a film (commits to an action) that Bob recommends (based on her belief that Bob will not waste her time).

Other work has touched on trust in recommender systems, including [9] and [10]. These works address the use of trust within systems where the set of commonly rated items between users is sparse. That situation leads to a breakdown in correlation-based recommender system algorithms, and their work explores how incorporating even simple binary trust relationships can increase the coverage and thus the number of recommendations that can be made.

3   Experimental Platform: The FilmTrust Website

The FilmTrust system, at http://trust.mindswap.org/FilmTrust, is a website that combines a web-based social network and a movie rating and review system. It's membership forms the basis for our investigation.

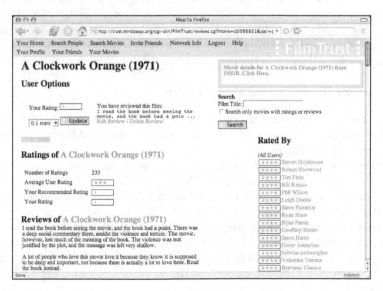

Fig. 1. A user's view of the page for "A Clockwork Orange," where the recommended rating matches the user's rating, even though the average is quite different

3.1 Social Networking with FilmTrust

The social networking component of the website allows users to maintain a list of friends who are also in the network. Our system requires users to provide a trust rating for each person they add as a friend. When creating a trust rating on the site, users are advised to rate how much they trust their friend about movies. Users are advised to consider trust in this context: "...if the person were to have rented a movie to watch, how likely it is that you would want to see that film."

In the FilmTrust network, relationships can be one-way, so users can see who they have listed as friends, and vice versa . If trust ratings are visible to everyone, users can be discouraged from giving accurate ratings for fear of offending or upsetting people by giving them low ratings. Because honest trust ratings are important to the function of the system, these values are kept private and shown only to the user who assigned them.

3.2 Movie Features

The other features of the website are movie ratings and reviews. Users can choose any film and rate it on a scale of a half star to four stars. They can also write free-text reviews about movies.

Social networks meet movie information on the "Ratings and Reviews" page shown in Figure 1. Users are shown two ratings for each movie. The first is the simple average of all ratings given to the film. The "Recommended Rating" uses the inferred trust values, computed with TidalTrust on the social network, for the users who rated the film as weights to calculate a weighted average rating. Because the inferred trust values reflect how much the user should trust the opinions of the person rating the movie, the weighted average of movie ratings should reflect the user's opinion. If the user has an opinion that is different from the average, the rating calculated from trusted friends – who should have similar opinions – should reflect that difference. Similarly, if a movie has multiple reviews, they are sorted according to the inferred trust rating of the author. This presents the reviews authored by the most trusted people first to assist the user in finding information that will be most relevant.

3.3 Computing Recommended Movie Ratings

One of the features of the FilmTrust site that uses the social network is the "Recommended Rating" feature. As Figure 1 shows, users will see this in addition to the average rating given to a particular movie.

The "Recommended Rating" is personalized using the trust values (direct or inferred) that the user has the people who have rated the film (the raters). If a user Alice has directly assigned a trust rating to another user, Bob, then the trust value is known. If Alice has not rated Bob, we need to infer how much she might trust him. Trust inference systems are a growing area of interest. In this application, we utilize TidalTrust, a breadth first search-based algorithm that outputs an inferred trust value by finding paths form Alice to Bob and composing the trust values found along those paths. Details of that algorithm are beyond the scope of this paper, but can be found in [11] and [12].

To compute the recommended movie rating, the FilmTrust system first searches for raters who the user knows directly. If there are no direct connections from the user to any raters, the system moves one step out to find connections from the user to raters of path length 2. This process repeats until a path is found. The opinion of all raters at that depth are considered. Then, using TidalTrust, the trust value is calculated for each rater at the given depth. Once every rater has been given an inferred trust value, only the ones with the highest trust values will be selected; this is done by simply finding the maximum trust value calculated for each of the raters at the selected depth, and choosing all of the raters for which that maximum value was calculated. Finally, once the raters have been selected, their ratings for the movie (in number of stars) are averaged. For the set of selected nodes S, the recommended rating r from node s to movie m is the average of the movie ratings from nodes in S weighted by the trust value t from s to each node:

$$r_{sm} = \frac{\sum_{i \in S} t_{si} r_{im}}{\sum_{i \in S} t_{si}}$$

This average is rounded to the nearest half-star, and that value becomes the "Recommended Rating" that is personalized for each user.

As a simple example, consider the following:

- Alice trusts Bob 9
- Alice trusts Chuck 3
- Bob rates the movie "Jaws" with 4 stars
- Chuck rates the movie "Jaws" with 2 stars

Then Alice's recommended rating for "Jaws" is calculated as follows:

$$\frac{t_{Alice \to Bob} * r_{Bob \to Jaws} + t_{Alice \to Chuck} r_{Chuck-Jaws}}{t_{Alice \to Bob} + t_{Alice \to Chuck}} = \frac{9*4 + 3*2}{9+3} = \frac{42}{12} = 3.5$$

4 Experimental Setup and Design

We are interested in knowing if the trust-based movie ratings offer a benefit to the users, and if so, in what instances. To check this, we used the data users have entered into the FilmTrust system.

4.1 Experimental Setup and Design

The FilmTrust user base was used as the foundation for our experiments. When joining the network, members were informed that their participation was part of a research project, and they consented to allow their data to be used within experiments. The system has just over 500 members.

Members were invited by friends who were already members and also found out about the website from postings in movie related forums. There is a strong Semantic Web component to the website (social network and movie information is all published in RDF), so members were frequently recruited from this circle of interest. Subjects ranged in age from 14 to 79, with an average age of 32. Subjects were 29% female and 71% male.

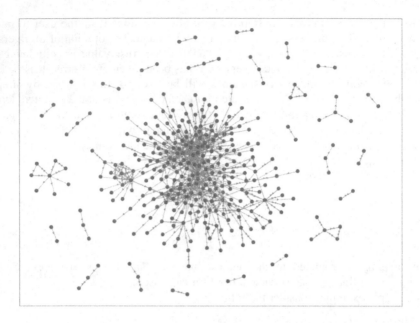

Fig. 2. A visualization of the FilmTrust social network

FilmTrust users have created approximately 11,250 ratings and movie reviews for 1,250 different movies. For each movie, the average rating was computed as the simple average of all the ratings assigned to the film. To ensure that a common set of movies were rated, users were asked during the registration process to assign ratings to any movies they had seen the top 50 films AFI Top 100 Films list [13].

Not all of these members are connected into the social network. Approximately 150 of the 500 members do not have any social connections. Their participation is limited to entering data about movies. Of the members who are participating in the social network, most are connected into a strong central core, with a scattering of small groups. A spring-embedded visualization of the social network structure is shown in Figure 2.

4.2 Experimental Results

To determine the effectiveness of the recommended ratings, we compare to see how closely they resemble the actual ratings a user has assigned to a film. We use the absolute difference between the recommended rating and actual rating as our measure. In this analysis, we also compare the user's rating with the average rating for the movie, and with a recommended rating generated by an automatic collaborative filtering (ACF) algorithm. There are many ACF algorithms, and one that has been well tested, and which is used here, is the classic user-to-user nearest neighbor prediction algorithm based on Pearson Correlation [5]. If the trust-based method of calculating ratings is best, the difference between the personalized rating and the user's actual rating should be significantly smaller than the difference between the actual rating and the average rating. We label these measures as follows:

- ∂r – the absolute difference between the user's rating and the trust-based recommended rating
- ∂a – the absolute difference between the user's rating and the average rating
- ∂cf – the absolute difference between the user's rating and the recommended rating from the collaborative filtering algorithm

Because the recommended ratings rely on using the trust values in the social network, we were only able to make this comparison for users with social connections, approximately 350 of the 500 total users. For each user, we selected each movie and computed the ∂ values. In the end, we made comparisons for a total of 1152 movies.

On first analysis, it did not appear that that the trust-based ratings that utilized the social network were any more accurate than average. The difference between the actual rating and the recommended rating (∂r) was not statistically different than the difference between the user's actual rating and the average rating (∂a). The difference between a user's actual rating of a film and the ACF calculated rating (∂cf) also was not better than ∂a in the general case. A close look at the data suggested why. Most of the time, the majority of users actual ratings are close to the average. This is most likely due to the fact that the users in the FilmTrust system had all rated the AFI Top 50 movies, which received disproportionately high ratings. A random sampling of movies showed that about 50% of all ratings were within the range of the mean +/- a half star (the smallest possible increment). For users who gave these near-mean rating, a personalized rating could not offer much benefit over the average.

However, one of our initial motivations for creating the trust-based recommended ratings was to help people who disagree with the average. In those cases, the personalized rating should give the user a better recommendation, because we expect the people they trust will have tastes similar to their own [10].

To see this effect, ∂a, ∂cf, and ∂r were calculated with various minimum thresholds on the ∂a value; that is, the user's rating had to be at least ∂a stars different from the average rating. If the recommended ratings do not offer a benefit over the average rating, the ∂r values will increase at the same rate the ∂a values do. The experiment was conducted by limiting ∂a in increments of 0.5. The first set of comparisons was taken with no threshold, where the difference between ∂a and ∂r was not significant. As the minimum ∂a value was raised it selected a smaller group of user-film pairs where the users made ratings that differed increasingly with the average. Obviously, we expect the average ∂a value will increase by about 0.5 at each increment, and that it will be somewhat higher than the minimum threshold. The real question is how the ∂r will be impacted. If it increases at the same rate, then the recommended ratings do not offer much benefit over the simple average. If it increases at a slower rate, that means that, as the user strays from the average, the recommended rating more closely reflects their opinions. Figure 3 illustrates the results of these comparisons.

Notice that the ∂a value increases about as expected. The ∂r, however, is clearly increasing at a slower rate than ∂a. At each step, as the lower threshold for ∂a is increased by 0.5, ∂r increases by an average of less than 0.1. A two-tailed t-test shows that at each step where the minimum ∂a threshold is greater than or equal to 0.5, the recommended rating is significantly closer to the user's actual rating than the average

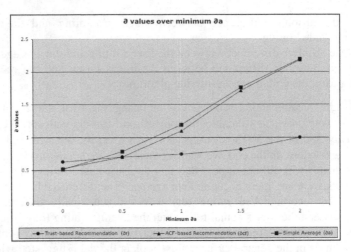

Fig. 3. The increase in ∂ as the minimum ∂a is increased. Notice that the ACF-based recommendation (∂cf) closely follows the average (∂a). The more accurate Trust-based recommendation (∂r) significantly outperforms both other methods.

rating is, with $p<0.01$. For about 25% of the ratings assigned, $\partial a<0.5$, and the user's ratings are about the same as the mean. For the other 75% of the ratings, $\partial a>0.5$, and the recommended rating significantly outperforms the average.

As is shown in Figure 3, ∂cf closely follows ∂a. For $\partial a<1$, there was no significant difference between the accuracy of the ACF ratings and the trust-based recommended rating. However, when the gap between the actual rating and the average increases, for $\partial a>=1$, the trust-based recommendation outperforms the ACF as well as the average, with $p<0.01$. Because the ACF algorithm is only capturing overall correlation, it is tracking the average because most users' ratings are close to the average.

Figure 1 illustrates one of the examples where the recommended value reflects the user's tastes. "A Clockwork Orange" is one of the films in the database that has a strong collective of users who hated the movie, even though the average rating was 3 stars and many users gave it a full 4-star rating. For the user shown, $\partial a=2.5$ – a very high value – while the recommended rating exactly matches the user's low rating of 0.5 stars. These are precisely the type of cases that the recommended rating is designed to address.

Thus, when the user's rating of a movie is different than the average rating, it is likely that the recommended rating will more closely reflect the user's tastes. When the user has different tastes than the population at large, the recommended rating reflects that. When the user has tastes that align with the mean, the recommended rating also aligns with the mean. Based on these findings, the recommended ratings should be useful when people have never seen a movie. Since they accurately reflect the users' opinions of movies they have already. Because the rating is personalized, originating from a social network, it is also in line with other results [3,4] that show users prefer recommendations from friends and trusted systems.

One potential drawback to creating recommendations based solely on relationships in the social network is that a recommendation cannot be calculated when there are no paths from the user to any people who have rated a movie. This case is rare, though, because as long as just one path can be found, a recommendation can be made. In the FilmTrust network, when the user has made at least one social connection, a recommendation can be made for 95% of the user-movie pairs.

In addition, the quality of results is dependent on users assigning accurate trust values to people in the system. If the trust ratings become too noisy, they cease to be an effective grounds for making recommendations. The FilmTrust system is still relatively small compared to other social networks, which can have tens of thousands up to millions of members. It remains to be seen how well this technique will work on larger networks. We have not yet been given access to trust values in some of the larger networks, and that analysis will be necessary to verify that user behavior will support our approach.

4.3 Presenting Ordered Reviews

In addition to presenting personalized ratings, the experience of reading reviews is also personalized. The reviews are presented to the user in order of the trust value of the author, with the reviews from the most trustworthy people appearing at the top, and those from the least trustworthy at the bottom. The expectation is that the most relevant reviews will come from more trusted users, and thus they will be shown first.

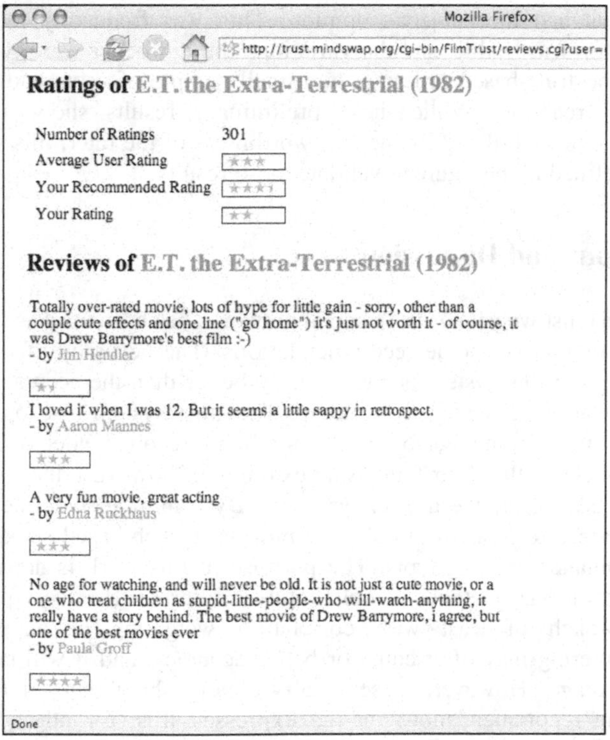

Fig. 4. Reviews of "E.T." sorted according to the trust value that the user has for each author. Note that the ratings of the ordering also corresponds to how closely the reviewers' ratings of the film correspond with the user's rating, even though that was not considered in choosing the ordering.

For example, Figure 4 shows the reviews of "E.T." ordered for a user. The reviews from more trusted people appear at the top of the list, and less trust people are further down. Notice that the user's rating is 2 stars. Even though the reviewers' rating were not considered in the ordering, they are ordered as well; the reviewers with ratings that most closely match the user's rating are shown first, and the reviews further down in the list are different from the user. This supports the premise that ordering reviews by trust rating will show users the opinions more relevant to their own perspective first.

Unlike the personalized ratings, measuring the accuracy of the review sort is not possible without requiring users to list the order in which they suggest the reviews appear. Without performing that sort of analysis, much of the evidence presented so far supports this ordering. That definition also supports the ordering of reviews. Trust with respect to movies means that the user believes that the trusted person will give good and useful information about the movies. The analysis also suggests that more trusted individuals will give more accurate information. It was shown there that trust correlates with the accuracy of ratings. Reviews will be written in line with ratings (i.e. a user will not give a high rating to a movie and then write a poor review of it), and since ratings from highly trusted users are more accurate, it follows that reviews should also be more accurate.

A small pilot study with 9 subjects was run on the FilmTrust network. Subjects were shown the reviews for a movie and asked to order them according to how closely they matched the subject's opinion. This was frequently identical to the ordering based on trust value, and the variations the did occur were typically small. When shown the trust-based ordering, our small sample of users had a universally strong positive reaction. While these preliminary results show a strong user preference for reviews ordered by the trustworthiness of the rater, this study must be extended and refined in the future to validate these results.

5   Conclusions and Discussion

Within the FilmTrust website, trust in social networks has been used as the foundation for generating predictive movie recommendations, The accuracy of the trust-based predictive ratings in this system is significantly better than the accuracy of a simple average of the ratings assigned to a movie. The trust system also outperforms the recommended ratings from a Person-correlation based recommender system.

Overall, we believe that FilmTrust is an example of how trust and social networks can be exploited to refine the user experience. By using the social network data in computations, the efforts users are already putting to web-based socializing can be harnessed to enhance existing tools. The purpose of this work is not necessarily to replace more traditional methods of collaborative filtering. It is very possible that a combined approach of trust with correlation weighting or another form of collaborative filtering may offer equal or better accuracy, and it will certainly allow for higher coverage. However, these results clearly show that, in the FilmTrust network, basing recommendations on the expressed trust for other people in the network offers significant benefits for accuracy.

There are many future steps for both refining this work and taking it in future direct-ions. One step is to do a deeper comparison with the most advanced collaborative filtering algorithms. We have chosen a common, basic algorithm for comparison in this study. Since our goal was not to out perform collaborative filtering techniques, but rather to show that the trust-based recommendations were useful,

One current project we have underway is investigating how users assign trust in social networks. The results presented here show that it is not merely correlation of opinions; if that were the case, we would have seen equivalent performance between the trust-based recommendations and the collaborative filtering recommendations. We believe that users assign trust based more on agreement on outliers, rather than on overall agreement. For example, say Bob and Alice both hated the "Lord of the Rings" movies, loved "From Justin to Kelly" , but otherwise had a large variation in movies about which they are less enthusiastic. We believe that they may trust each other more than they would trust someone with a higher overall correlation but who disagreed about "Lord of the Rings" and "From Justin to Kelly". Understanding which features of user profiles correlate to higher trust values will give social insight, but it also suggests how different features of profile similarity can be incorporated into collaborative filtering algorithms to improve their accuracy even when social networks are unavailable.

Acknowledgements

This work, conducted at the Maryland Information and Network Dynamics Laboratory Semantic Web Agents Project, was funded by Fujitsu Laboratories of America -- College Park, Lockheed Martin Advanced Technology Laboratory, NTT Corp., Kevric Corp., SAIC, the National Science Foundation, the National Geospatial-Intelligence Agency, DARPA, US Army Research Laboratory, NIST, and other DoD sources.

References

1. Abdul-Rahman, A. and Hailes, S. 2000. Supporting trust in virtual communities. In Proceedings of the 33rd Hawaii International Conference on System Sciences. Maui, HW, USA.
2. Ziegler, Cai-Nicolas, Georg Lausen (2004) Analyzing Correlation Between Trust and User Similarity in Online Communities" Proceedings of Second International Conference on Trust Management, 2004.
3. Sinha, R., and Swearingen, K. (2001) "Comparing recommendations made by online systems and friends." In Proceedings of the DELOS-NSF Workshop on Personalization and Recommender Systems in Digital Libraries Dublin, Ireland.
4. Swearingen, K. and R. Sinha. (2001) "Beyond algorithms: An HCI perspective on recommender systems," Proceedings of the ACM SIGIR 2001 Workshop on Recommender Systems, New Orleans, Louisiana.
5. Herlocker , Jonathan L., Joseph A. Konstan , John Riedl, Explaining collaborative filtering recommendations, Proceedings of the 2000 ACM conference on Computer supported cooperative work, p.241-250, December 2000, Philadelphia, Pennsylvania, United States.

6. Garden, Matthew, and Gregory Dudek (2005) Semantic feedback for hybrid recommendations in Recommendz. Proceedings of the IEEE International Conference on e-Technology, e-Commerce, and e-Service (EEE05), Hong Kong, China, March 2005.
7. Perny, P. and J. D. Zucker. Preference-based Search and Machine Learning for Collaborative Filtering: the "Film-Conseil" recommender system. Information, Interaction , Intelligence, 1(1):9-48, 2001.
8. Herlocker , Jonathan L., Joseph A. Konstan , Loren G. Terveen , John T. Riedl, (2004) Evaluating collaborative filtering recommender systems, ACM Transactions on Information Systems (TOIS), v.22 n.1, p.5-53, January 2004.
9. Massa, P., P. Avesani. 2004. Trust-aware Collaborative Filtering for Recommender Systems. In Proceedings of the International Conference on Cooperative Information Systems (CoopIS) 2004.
10. Massa, P., B. Bhattacharjee. 2004. Using Trust in Recommender Systems: an Experimental Analysis. In Proceedings of iTrust 2004 International Conference.
11. Golbeck, Jennifer. 2005. Computing and Applying Trust in Web-Based Social Networks, Ph.D. Dissertation, University of Maryland, College Park.
12. Golbeck, Jennifer. 2005. Personalizing Applications through Integration of Inferred Trust Values in Semantic Web-Based Social Networks. Proceedings of Semantic Network Analysis Workshop. Galway, Ireland.
13. American Film Institute, "100 Years, 100 Movies" http://www.afi.com/tvevents/100years/ movies.aspx

Temporal Logic-Based Specification and Verification of Trust Models

Peter Herrmann

Norwegian University of Science and Technology (NTNU),
Telematics Department, 7491 Trondheim, Norway
herrmann@item.ntnu.no

Abstract. Mutual trust is essential in performing economical transactions. In modern internet-based businesses, however, traditional trust gaining mechanisms cannot be used and new ways to build trust between e-business partners have to be found. In consequence, a lot of models describing trust and the mechanisms to build it were developed. Unfortunately, most of these models neither provide the right formalism to model relevant aspects of the trust gaining process (e.g., context and time of a trust-related interaction), nor do they allow refinement proofs verifying that a trust management tool implements a certain trust model. Therefore, we propose the temporal logic-based specification and verification technique cTLA which provides a formalism enabling to model context- and time-related aspects of a trust building process. Moreover, cTLA facilitates formal refinement proofs. In this paper, we discuss the application of cTLA to describe trust purposes by means of simple example systems which are used to decide about the application of certain policies based on the reputation of a party. In particular, we introduce a basic and a refined reputation system and sketch the proof that the refined system is a correct realization of the simple one.

1 Introduction

Since the very beginnings of mankind, trust is an essential ingredient for human cooperation. In a society based on the division of labor, people often are willing to rely on others, even though they might face negative consequences. According to McKnight and Chervany [1], however, this is exactly the definition of trust. Ways to build trust include personal experience with the party, one relies on, recommendation by third parties as well as the reduction of the negative consequences in the case of unfounded trust (e.g., by using an insurance covering financial losses in case of malicious behavior of a trusted party).

These traditional trust gaining mechanisms, however, can hardly be applied in modern internet-based businesses. Here, one performs transactions on an ad-hoc basis with often changing anonymous partners living in other countries with different legal systems. Thus, it is difficult to gain any personal experience about transaction partners and trustworthy third persons which can give meaningful recommendation are also hardly available. Furthermore, suing for ones personal

K. Stølen et al. (Eds.): iTrust 2006, LNCS 3986, pp. 105–119, 2006.

rights in another legal system is stressful. Many security mechanisms are also only of limited benefit in an electronic environment providing ad hoc cooperations between anonymous parties. For example, it is tedious to use a password-based authentication system with proof of identity and exchange of passwords if the user wants to perform a business transaction only once. Instead, a party needs mechanisms to foster the building of well-founded trust to its partner based, for instance, on recommendations by trustworthy third parties or by the partner's reputation. The creation of this kind of mechanisms is a goal followed up by the Trust Management research discipline.

To support the trust building process by a computer, one has to find suitable representations of trust, so-called trust values (cf. [2, 3]). Moreover, one needs mechanisms to compute the trust values in a way that the natural way to build up trust is modeled fairly realistically. Thus, these mechanisms should be able to consider experiences and recommendations of computer users to compute suitable trust values. As pointed out by Falcone and Castelfranchi [4], new trust is influenced by already existing trust in rather complex ways which should also be reflected by a trust value computation mechanism. Furthermore, the mechanism has to consider the context in which building of trust takes place (cf. [1, 5]). Relevant aspects of a trust context are according to Jøsang et al. [6] the utility of possible outcomes, environmental factors (e.g, law enforcement, contracts, security mechanisms) as well as the risk attitude of the trusting party.

Another important aspect of a trust building mechanism is time. Falcone and Castelfranchi, for instance, call in [4] trust a very dynamic phenomenon evolving in time and having a history. Likewise, a Cheskin Research study [7] examining trust concepts of e-commerce sites describes trust as "function of time and specific formal characteristics of sites". Also Mezzetti [8] states that trust values may be changed in the course of time. He considers recent events more relevant than older events for building trust, "since obsolete information is not considered to accurately describe more recent behaviors".

In between, several trust models describing formats for trust values as well as trust building mechanisms were proposed (cf. Sec. 2). Some of these models focus on the description of relevant aspects of the human trust building process per se which may be viewed from a rather formal mathematical or philosophical perspective (e.g. [9, 10]) as well as from a more sociological-cognitive view (e.g. [5, 8, 11]). Other models are devoted to computer-implementable solutions fostering the gaining of the trust [12, 13, 14]. While these approaches offer a variety of very useful concepts to specify and compute the generation of trust, most of them, however, miss the sufficient formalism to model all relevant aspects of trust building including context and time. Moreover, they do not allow to carry out deduction proofs that an implementation of a trust management system fulfills a trust model and particular trust properties. For this reason, we propose the temporal logic cTLA (compositional Temporal Logic of Actions [15]) as a method to model and to verify trust mechanisms. cTLA is based on Lamport's Temporal Logic of Actions (TLA, [16]). It supports the modular description of processes which, in contrast to TLA, can be coupled to system models both in a resource-oriented and a constraint-oriented specification style (cf. [17]). In a resource-oriented style a process describes a physical system resource in its entirety, while processes in the constraint-oriented style model certain functional properties of a system which may be realized by several cooperating resources. This specification style facilitates system descriptions by composing models of the various system constraints which reflects the logical connections and dependencies of a system very well. cTLA also enables the description of continuous flows [18]. Thus, it is possible to model the dynamic trust building process as a continuous process which is influenced by discrete events (e.g., the selection of an access policy based on positive or negative valuations of a party).

The composition of cTLA processes to a system has the character of superposition (cf. [19]) guaranteeing that all relevant properties of a process or a subsystem are also properties of the systems embedding it [15]. Therefore, one can simplify formal deduction proofs of properties by considering only a subsystem guaranteeing the property to be verified. In combination with the constraint-oriented specification style, one can define often very small subsystems which can easily been proven to realize a certain property. Thus, the structuring of a verification process into relatively simple proof steps is supported.

All-in-all, we consider cTLA as a suitable method to model complex context- and time-dependent trust building mechanisms since it facilitates the description of various context-relevant aspects by separate constraint-oriented modes which also makes the refinement proofs simpler. Yet, we do not intend to create a completely new trust model but adapt existing approaches like Jøsang's Subjective Logic [9] or Mezzetti's work [8] to cTLA.

In the remainder, we discuss several trust models (Sec. 2) followed by an introduction to cTLA (Sec. 3). Thereafter we will point out the specification of trust management systems by means of two example systems. A more abstract system introduced in Sec. 4 describes a simple reputation system collecting good and bad experiences based on which one of two policies is selected. In Sec. 5 we introduce a refined system collecting the experiences from two separate users which have to be combined in a fair manner. Afterwards, in Sec. 6 we sketch the carrying out of refinement proofs in cTLA by outlining the verification that the more complex system correctly implements the more abstract one. The cTLA processes and proofs can also be looked at in the WWW (URL: http://www.item.ntnu.no/~herrmann/specs/trust).

2   Trust Model Survey

Trust is a rather complex human emotion and the models describing it tend to be complex as well. To reduce the complexity, however, most models consider only certain aspects of trust building. A class of trust models specifies relevant issues of trust very realistically without being devoted directly to implementation purposes. These models tend to be relatively formal and describe trust gaining from a mathematical-philosophical or from a sociological-cognitive perspective.

An approach to describe trust by uncertain probabilities is Jøsang's Subjective Logic [9] which is introduced to more detail in Sec. 4. Here, a trust value is modeled by a so-called opinion which consists of three values modeling the belief resp. disbelief in the honesty of a party as well as the uncertainty about it. Operators of the logic enable various combinations of trust values. Unfortunately, it does not allow to model time-dependent behavior yet. In contrast, Jones and Firozabadi [10] use a modal logic of action to describe that a party a receiving a piece of information by a party b has to decide based on b's credibility if the information is true. The trust gaining processes are modeled in a rather descriptive way and can hardly be realized on a computer.

Falcone and Castelfranchi [5, 11] provide an extensive model to describe trust building from a sociological and cognitive-psychological view. Their so-called Socio-Cognitive Model of Trust considers various forms of social dependence between parties which lead to different forms of beliefs (i.e., ability/competence, disposition/availability, unharmfulness, opportunity and danger beliefs). Mezzetti [8] defined a simpler model consisting of a set of rules which specify the building of trust from experience and recommendations based on aspects like competence, willingness, and dependence. This model reflects time aspects of experiences and uses a decay function.

Other approaches concentrate more on the realization of trust values and trust building mechanisms on computers. An early approach to integrate trust issues into software emerges from the field of access control. Since traditional access control models are not adequate for the Internet with its many fluctuating participants, so-called credential-based systems like PolicyMaker, REFEREE or KeyNote were designed (cf. [12]). Parties interested to access a resource have to pass credentials to the resource provider stating that the credential issuer considers the credential owner as trustworthy. Based on his own trust in the recommendations of the credential issuer, the resource owner decides to provide access. Another framework for trust-based policies was developed by Grandison and Sloman [13]. It enables descriptions of trust policies by means of Prolog statements which may be evaluated in order to support trust-based decisions about granting access to certain resources. Abdul-Rahman and Hailes [14] designed a trust management system enabling to rate experiences with a party by different values. The trust in recommendations of a party is computed by comparing the difference between the values of a recommendation and the later evaluation of the recommended party. Later recommendations of the recommender are adapted by adding this difference, the so-called semantic distance.

Of these interesting and innovative models we consider Jøsang's Subjective Logic, the formalization of Falcone's and Castelfranchi's Socio-Cognitive Model of Trust, Mezzetti's work as well as the more practical-oriented approaches as well suited to be integrated into our cTLA-based approach. One may even think to combine different models in order to get a better description of the actual building of trust. For instance, a combination of different approaches is used in our example models in which we combine elements of Jøsang's Subjective Logic [9] with a decay function similar to that proposed by Mezzetti (cf. [8]).

3   cTLA

TLA [16] is a linear time temporal logic describing properties of state transition systems by means of often lengthy and complex canonical formulas. To provide a better understanding of specifications, in contrast, cTLA [15, 18] omits the canonical parts of TLA formulas. It is oriented at programming languages and introduces the notion of processes. A specification is structured into modular definitions of process types. An instantiation of a process type forms a process which either has the form of a simple process or that of a process composition. Simple processes, which directly refer to state transition systems, are used to model single system resources or system constraints.

Fig. 1 depicts the example of a simple process type used to model a part of our example trust systems. The header declares the process type name (e.g., *Policy-Decider* and generic module parameters (e.g., *beliefThreshold*). These parameters facilitate the modeling of similar but not identical processes by a single process type specification. The part headed by the keyword *CONSTANTS* enables the definition of constant expressions (e.g., the record type *TrustValues*).

The process type body defines the state transition system. The state space is specified by state variables (e.g., *policy*) and the subset of initial states is modeled by the predicate *INIT*. Moreover, the body contains actions. An action (e.g., *retrievePolicy*) is a predicate on pairs of current and next states and specifies a set of state transitions. The state variables referring to the current state are noted in simple form (e.g., *policy*) while variables describing the successor state occur in the primed form (e.g., *policy'*). An action may have action parameters enabling to specify different actions by a single representation. The disjunction of the actions forms the next state relation of the process. In the course of time, a process may perform action steps (i.e., it changes its state in accordance with an action) or stuttering steps (i.e., it does not change its state while the environment performs a state transition).

```
PROCESS PolicyDecider (beliefThreshold : real;
                       disbeliefThreshold : real)
CONSTANTS
  TrustValues ≜ [[ b : real; d : real; u : real ]] ;
BODY
  VARIABLES
    policy : {"lowTrust","highTrust"};
  INIT ≜ policy = "lowTrust";
  ACTIONS
    retrievePolicy (p : {"lowTrust", "highTrust"}) ≜
      p = policy ∧ policy' = policy;
    CONT (INPUT i : TrustValues) ≜
      policy' = IF i.b ≥ beliefThreshold ∧ i.d ≤ disbeliefThreshold
               THEN "highTrust" ELSE "lowTrust";
END
```

Fig. 1. cTLA Process Type *Policy Decider*

Following [21], real-time is represented by means of a real-valued state variable *now* which is incremented lively by a clock action *tick* in non-constant intervals. Unlike other variables, which are private in exactly one process, *now* can be read by all processes of a system. Additional real-time constructs specify minimum waiting times and maximum reaction times for actions.

Continuous properties of a process are expressed by means of the special action type *CONT*. The *CONT*-actions of all processes modeling a system and the *tick*-action of the clock occur simultaneously. A *CONT*-action specifies difference equations and, since an execution corresponds to a very small time step, continuous behavior is approximated well. In the difference equations, we express the time steps by *now'-now*. The inputs and outputs of continuous processes are modeled by action parameters. In Fig. 1, the variable *policy* is set according to the *IF-THEN-ELSE*-statement depending on the input value i.

Systems and subsystems are described as compositions of concurrent process instances. The coupling of the processes is specified by synchronously executed process actions while, with exception of *now*, the process variables are encapsulated and cannot be read or modified by other processes. In consequence, a system state is the vector of the process variables. The system transitions are modeled by system actions and each process contributes to a system action by either exactly one process action or a stuttering step. Therefore a system action is a conjunction of process actions and process stuttering steps. Fig. 2 shows an example of a system specification. In the part *PROCESSES*, the processes of the system are listed as instantiations of process types (e.g., process E of the type *TrustValueEngine* and process *PD* of the process type *PolicyDecider* depicted in Fig. 1). In addition, the instantiations of the module parameters are listed (e.g., the module parameters *beliefThreshold* and *disbeliefThreshold* of process *PD* are replaced by the values 0.99 resp. 0).

```
PROCESS OneUserReputationSystem
CONSTANTS
   TrustValues ≙ [[ b : real; d : real; u : real ]];
PROCESSES
   E  : TrustValueEngine(0.01,0.04,0.001,0.004);
   PD : PolicyDecider(0.99,0);
ACTIONS
   reportGoodExperience ≙
     E.reportGoodExperience ∧ PD.stutter;

   reportBadExperience ≙
     E.reportBadExperience ∧ PD.stutter;

   retrievePolicy (p : {"lowTrust", "highTrust"}) ≙
     PD.retrievePolicy(p) ∧ E.stutter;

   CONT (OUTPUT o : TrustValues) ≙
     E.CONT(; o) ∧ PD.CONT(o; );
END
```

Fig. 2. System *One User Reputation System*

In the part headed by *ACTIONS*, the system actions are defined as conjunctions of process actions and stuttering steps. For instance, the system action *retrievePolicy* models that process *PD* performs its process action *retrievePolicy* while *E* carries out a stuttering step.

4   Simple Trust Management Model

We introduce the application of cTLA to specify trust models by means of two example systems. The first trust management model describes a very simple reputation-based policy decision system. In particular, users report positive and negative experience reports about a party in question from which trust values are computed. Based on the trust values, the system selects one out of two trust-based policies to be used, for instance, to decide about granting access to a resource. The system specification is a composition of two cTLA processes. One of them models the collection of experience reports and the computation of the trust values while the other specifies the trust policy selection.

The specification and computation of the trust values is based on Jøsang's Subjective Logic [9]. There, trust values are described as so-called opinions which are triples of real values b, d and u in the range between 0 and 1. b and d state the belief resp. disbelief in a party while u describes uncertainty. Thus, one can distinguish if the lack of trust results from malicious experience or from missing knowledge about a party. Since a trust value fulfills the constraint $b + d + u = 1$, it can be modeled by a point in the so-called opinion triangle (cf. Fig. 3). A trust value stating a high degree of uncertainty is described by a point close to the top of the triangle while points on the right or left bottom state great belief resp. disbelief based on a lot of experience with a party.

Trust values are used to describe both the direct trust in a party itself and the trust in the recommendation of a party about another one. Jøsang and Knapskog introduce the following metric [20] to compute trust values from the number p of positive valuations and n of negative valuations of the party in question:

$$b = \tfrac{p}{p+n+1} \qquad d = \tfrac{n}{p+n+1} \qquad u = \tfrac{1}{p+n+1} \qquad (1)$$

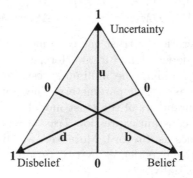

Fig. 3. Opinion Triangle (taken from [20])

```
PROCESS TrustValueEngine (pDMin, pDMax, nDMin, nDMax : real)
CONSTANTS
  TrustValues ≜ [[ b : real; d : real; u : real ]] ;
BODY
  VARIABLES
    p : real; n : real;
  INIT ≜ p = 0 ∧ n = 0;
  ACTIONS
    reportGoodExperience ≜
      p' = p + 1 ∧ n' = n;
    reportBadExperience ≜
      n' = n + 1 ∧ p' = p;
    CONT (OUTPUT o : TrustValues) ≜
      o = [[ b ↦ p / (1 + p + n); d ↦ n / (1 + p + n);
             u ↦ 1 / (1 + p + n) ]] ∧
      p' ≤ max(0,p - (now'-now) · pDMin) ∧
      p' ≥ max(0,p - (now'-now) · pDMax) ∧
      n' ≤ max(0,n - (now'-now) · nDMin) ∧
      n' ≥ max(0,n - (now'-now) · nDMax);
END
```

Fig. 4. Process Type *Trust Value Engine*

Unfortunately, this metric does not reflect the time when an experience report was handed over. In reality, the trust resp. distrust in a party is definitely higher if it is based on more recent experience in comparison to older impressions which leads to a higher degree of uncertainty (cf. e.g., [5]). Therefore, we combine the trust value-computation metric with a decay function reducing the numbers p of positive and n of negative experience reports in the cause of time. In order to model the decay per time-unit in a flexible way, we do not describe it by a fixed function but enforce that it has to stay within certain borders. Therefore we define four values *pDMin*, *pDMax*, *nDMin* and *pDMax* describing the minimum resp. maximum decay rates of positive and negative valuations as stated in the following formula[1]:

$$p - \Delta t \cdot pDMax \le p' \le p - \Delta t \cdot pDMin$$
$$n - \Delta t \cdot nDMax \le n' \le n - \Delta t \cdot nDMin \tag{2}$$

The time-related generation of trust values is modeled by the cTLA process type *TrustValueEngine* depicted in Fig. 4. Here, the values *pDMin*, *pDMax*, *nDMin* and *pDMax* determining the minimum resp. maximum decays of the experiences are specified as module parameters. Therefore a user can adapt the decay values to the requirements of the trust model modeled by the particular cTLA specification. The constant expression *TrustValues* defines the three tuple used to model trust values as a record. Moreover, we specify the numbers p of positive resp. n of negative experiences by two variables of the type *real* which both carry the value 0 initially.

---

[1] Following the cTLA style, p' and n' refer to the next state.

The state changes modeled by instances of this process type are specified by means of two atomic actions describing discrete steps and the special action *CONT* defining continuous behavior. The action *reportGoodExperience* models the reception of a positive valuation. It increments the variable p by 1 while n remains unchanged. In similar, the action *reportBadExperience* describes the submission of a negative experience report resulting in an increment of n by 1. As discussed in the introduction, we consider the computation of the trust values and the "forgetting" of older experience reports as a continuous process. Therefore the corresponding behavior is specified by the action *CONT* modeling very small time steps *now'-now* (cf. Sec. 3). The action contains an output parameter o describing the current trust value which may be used as an input for other cTLA processes. The calculation of o from the variables p and n according to the metric introduced in formula 1 is described by the first conjunct of the action. The other conjuncts model the decay of p and n by the inequations listed in formula 2. Since neither p nor n must get values below 0, we added the function *max* to the inequations.

The selection of a low trust resp. a high trust policy based on the current trust value is specified by the cTLA process type *PolicyDecider* listed in Fig. 1. The policy selection is guided by two thresholds *beliefThreshold* and *disbeliefThreshold* which are introduced by means of module parameters. The variable *policy* describes the currently active policy. Initially it is set to *"lowTrust"* stating that in the first state the low trust policy is active. The action *retrievePolicy* enables external cTLA processes to read the current policy. It contains a parameter p describing the current value of the variable *policy* which is not changed by the action. The adjustment of the currently active policy based on the trust value is a continuous process and therefore modeled by the action *CONT*. We assume that the high trust policy is only available if the belief element b of the current trust value, which is modeled by the import parameter i, is not lower than *beliefThreshold* while the disbelief element d must not exceed *disbeliefThreshold*.

The example system is modeled by the process type *OneUserReputation System* depicted in Fig. 2. It consists of instances E of the process type *TrustValueEngine* and *PD* of *PolicyDecider*. The module parameters of E are instantiated in a way that the decay limits of positive experiences are 0.01 and 0.04 while those of the negative experiences are 0.001 resp. 0.004. Thus, a positive experience is "forgotten" in between 25 and 100 time units while a negative one is lost after between 250 and 1000 time units[2]. The parameter instantiations of *PD* state that the high trust policy is only used if the belief b in the current trust value is at least 0.99 while the disbelief has to be 0. Thus, one needs at least 99 positive but no negative valuations to run the high trust policy.

The couplings of the process actions to system actions are straightforward. The system actions *reportGoodExperience* and *reportBadExperience* are conjunctions of the corresponding process actions of E and stuttering steps of *PD* while *retrievePolicy* is coupled the other way round. The interaction between the two

---

[2] These settings do not reflect well-founded experience about trust gaining processes but are only used to exemplify the application of cTLA.

process instances is basically an exchange of the current trust value which is modeled by the coupling of the two process actions $CONT$ where the output parameter of action $E.CONT$ and the input parameter of $PD.CONT$ are identical. In consequence, in the system action $CONT$, the parameters of both process actions are set to the system action parameter o.

5 Refined Trust Management Model

The simple trust management model introduced above includes only one single trust value engine and, thus, does not distinguish whether the experience reports are submitted by one or more users. In contrast, the model introduced below uses two trust value engines in order to distinguish between two separate sources for valuations. Thus, two trust values ω_1 and ω_2 are created and have to be combined to a third trust value ω in order to determine the active trust policy. An adequate means to compute ω fairly from ω_1 and ω_2 is the consensus operator $\oplus$ introduced in Jøsang's Subjective Logic [9]. If $\omega_1 = (b_1, d_1, u_1)$ and $\omega_2 = (b_2, d_2, u_2)$ are two trust values stating trust in a party based on two separate sources, one can describe by this operator a consensus of these two opinions. The operator is specified by the formula

$$\omega = \omega_1 \oplus \omega_2 \,\hat{=}\, ((b_1 u_2 + b_2 u_1)/\kappa, (d_1 u_2 + d_2 u_1)/\kappa, (u_1 u_2)/\kappa) \qquad (3)$$

in which κ is defined as $u_1 + u_2 - u_1 u_2$. Since the consensus-operator is commutative and associative, it can be used to combine trust values from various sources.

The operator is specified by the cTLA process type $ConsensusOperator$ listed in Fig. 5. Since the process type models only stateless behavior, it does not contain variables. The action $CONT$ specifies formula 3 in which the operands are specified by the input parameters $i1$ and $i2$ while the result corresponds to the output parameter o. The LET-IN-construct enables the definition of constant expressions (e.g., κ) in the LET-section which can be used in the formula listed behind the keyword IN.

```
PROCESS ConsensusOperator
CONSTANTS
   TrustValues ≜ [[ b : real; d : real; u : real ]];
BODY
   INIT ≜ True;
   ACTIONS
      CONT (INPUT i1, i2 : TrustValues; OUTPUT o : TrustValues) ≜
         LET κ ≜ i1.u + i2.u - i1.u · i2.u;
         IN o = [[ b ↦ (i1.b · i2.u + i2.b · i1.u) / κ;
                   d ↦ (i1.d · i2.u + i2.d · i1.u) / κ;
                   u ↦ (i1.u · i2.u) / κ ]];
END
```

Fig. 5. Process Type *Consensus Operator*

```
PROCESS TwoUserReputationSystem
CONSTANTS
  TrustValues ≜ [[ b : real; d : real; u : real ]] ;
PROCESSES
  E1 : TrustValueEngine(0.01,0.02,0.001,0.002);
  E2 : TrustValueEngine(0.01,0.02,0.001,0.002);
  CO : ConsensusOperator;
  PD : PolicyDecider(0.99,0);
ACTIONS
  reportGoodExperience1 ≜
    E1.reportGoodExperience ∧ E2.stutter ∧ CO.stutter ∧ PD.stutter;
  reportGoodExperience2 ≜
    E2.reportGoodExperience ∧ E1.stutter ∧ CO.stutter ∧ PD.stutter;
  reportBadExperience1 ≜
    E1.reportBadExperience ∧ E2.stutter ∧ CO.stutter ∧ PD.stutter;
  reportBadExperience2 ≜
    E2.reportBadExperience ∧ E1.stutter ∧ CO.stutter ∧ PD.stutter;
  retrievePolicy (p : {"lowTrust", "highTrust"}) ≜
    PD.retrievePolicy(p) ∧ E1.stutter ∧ E2.stutter ∧ CO.stutter;
  CONT (OUTPUT o1, o2, o : TrustValues) ≜
    E1.CONT(; o1) ∧ E2.CONT(; o2) ∧ CO.CONT(o1, o2; o) ∧ PD.CONT(o; );
END
```

Fig. 6. System *Two User Reputation System*

The refined system is modeled by the cTLA process type *TwoUserReputation-System* depicted in Fig. 6. The system contains two trust value engines specified by the processes *E1* and *E2*. In contrast to the simple system in Sec. 4, the engines uses maximum decay rates of only 0.02 resp. 0.002. Thus, a positive experience is lost not before 50 and a negative one not before 500 time units passed. The system also contains a process *CO* modeling the consensus operator. Finally, we use a policy decider which is modeled by the process *PD* and uses the same parameter instantiations as in the simple system.

Due to the use of two trust value engines, the system specification defines each two actions to model the reception of positive resp. negative experiences. Moreover, it declares an action to retrieve trust policies and the action *CONT* defining the continuous trust value computation. Here, the outputs *o1* and *o2* of the trust value engines are the operands of the consensus operator. The result *o* of this operator forms the input of the policy decider. Thus, we model that the active trust policy is determined based on the experience reports of both trust value engines, the generated trust values of which are combined by means of the consensus operator.

6 Example Proof

Due to the superposition property of cTLA, we can reduce a cTLA refinement proof, that a more detailed system T implements a more abstract system O, to some relatively simple proof steps. At first, we verify that each process of O is implied by a subsystem of T. At second, we prove that the processes of T and O are consistently coupled which, however, profits significantly from the other proof steps. Thus, the verification, that an instance T of process type *Two User Reputation System* (cf. Fig. 6) implies an instance O of *One User Reputation System* (cf. Fig. 2) can be reduced to the following proof steps:

1. A subsystem $\widehat{T}$ of T implies the process E of O.
2. The process PD of T implies the process PD of O.
3. The actions of the processes in T are coupled in consistence with those in O.

The subsystem $\widehat{T}$ used in the first proof step consists of the processes and action couplings of *Two User Reputation System* with the exception of the process PD. In consequence, we omitted the system action *retrievePolicy* and the other system actions include the same conjuncts as their counterparts in *Two User-Reputation System* except for those referring to PD.

A problem of the proof $\widehat{T} \Rightarrow O.E$ is that $\widehat{T}$ and $O.E$ contain different state types. Therefore we define a so-called refinement mapping (i.e., a function mapping the state space of $\widehat{T}$ to that of $O.E$ which has to contain some side properties to be proven below; cf. [22]). Here, we define the refinement mapping by the following formulas:

$$O.E.p \mathrel{\widehat{=}} T.E1.p + T.E2.p \qquad O.E.n \mathrel{\widehat{=}} T.E1.n + T.E2.n \tag{4}$$

Thus, the numbers of positive and negative valuations in the simple model corresponds to the sum of the numbers of experience reports stored by the two trust value engines in the refined model. Now we can start to carry out the first proof step, for which we have to verify that the initial states of $\widehat{T}$ are mapped to initial states of $O.E$ and that each action of $\widehat{T}$ implies either an action of $O.E$ or a stuttering step.

The first proof $\widehat{T}.INIT \Rightarrow O.E.INIT$ is merely trivial since $\widehat{T}.INIT$ implies $T.E1.p = 0 \wedge T.E1.n = 0 \wedge T.E2.p = 0 \wedge T.E2.n = 0$ which according to the refinement mapping in formula 4 implies $O.E.p = 0 \wedge O.E.n = 0$. This, however, is exactly the definition of $O.E.INIT$.

At next, we verify that the action $\widehat{T}.reportGoodExperience1$ implies $O.E.reportGoodExperience$. From $\widehat{T}.reportGoodExperience1$ we can infer $T.E1.p' = T.E1.p + 1$ while all other variables do not change their values. Due to the refinement mapping, however, $O.E.p' = O.E.p + 1 \wedge O.E.n' = O.E.n$ holds which implies $O.E.reportGoodExperience$. Similarly, we can prove that $\widehat{T}.reportGoodExperience2$ implements $O.E.reportGoodExperience$ and that the two actions, modeling reception of negative experience reports in $\widehat{T}$, imply $O.E.reportBadExperience$.

In the next step[3], which is the most complex of the overall proof, we verify that the action $CONT$ of $\widehat{T}$ implies $O.E.CONT$ (i.e., $\forall o1, o2, o \in TrustValues :$

---

[3] The semicolons in the action parameter sections state that $o1$, $o2$ and o are output parameters.

$\widehat{T}.CONT(; o1, o2, o) \Rightarrow O.E.CONT(; o))$. In particular, we prove for each conjunct of $O.E.CONT$ that it is fulfilled by $\widehat{T}.CONT$. To verify the first conjunct of $O.E.CONT$, we prove firstly that $\widehat{T}.CONT$ implies the setting of the record element $o.b$ (i.e., $o.b = O.E.p/(1 + O.E.p + O.E.n)$). For clarity, we use in this proof the two auxiliary constants $\lambda_1 = 1 + \widehat{T}.E1.p + \widehat{T}.E1.n$ and $\lambda_2 = 1 + \widehat{T}.E2.p + \widehat{T}.E2.n$. From $\widehat{T}.CONT$, we can infer the following formulas:

$$o1.b = \frac{\widehat{T}.E1.p}{\lambda_1} \qquad o2.b = \frac{\widehat{T}.E2.p}{\lambda_2} \qquad o.b = \frac{o1.b \cdot o2.u + o2.b \cdot o1.u}{o1.u + o2.u - o1.u \cdot o2.u} \qquad (5)$$

By inserting the first two of these formulas into the third one, we get the following result:

$$o.b = \frac{\frac{\widehat{T}.E1.p}{\lambda_1} \cdot \frac{1}{\lambda_2} + \frac{\widehat{T}.E2.p}{\lambda_2} \cdot \frac{1}{\lambda_1}}{\frac{1}{\lambda_1} + \frac{1}{\lambda_2} - \frac{1}{\lambda_1 \lambda_2}} = \frac{\widehat{T}.E1.p + \widehat{T}.E2.p}{\lambda_1 + \lambda_2 - 1} \qquad (6)$$

By application of the refinement mapping in formula 4 we can, however, infer that the right term of formula 6 implies $o.b = O.E.p/(1 + O.E.p + O.E.n)$ which was the goal of this partial proof. In a very similar way, we can also prove that $\widehat{T}$ implies the settings of $o.d$ and $o.u$ which guarantees that the first conjunct of $O.E.CONT$ is correctly implemented by $\widehat{T}$.

To verify the four other conjuncts of $O.E.CONT$ describing the decay of the variables $O.E.p$ and $O.E.n$, we use the following inequations which can easily be proven by means of a case separation:

$$\forall a, b, k \in real : a, b, k \geq 0 \Rightarrow$$
$$max(0, a + b - 2k) \leq max(0, a - k) + max(0, b - k) \leq max(0, a + b - k) \qquad (7)$$

To prove, for instance, the third conjunct of $O.E.CONT$, we use the fact that $\widehat{T}.CONT$ implies both $\widehat{T}.E1.p' \geq max(0, \widehat{T}.E1.p - (now' - now) \cdot 0.02)$ and $\widehat{T}.E2.p' \geq max(0, \widehat{T}.E2.p - (now' - now) \cdot 0.02)$. By a simple invariant proof, we can show that both $\widehat{T}.E1.p$ and $\widehat{T}.E2.p$ are never smaller than 0. Therefore we can apply the left inequation of formula 7 and verify that $\widehat{T}.E1.p' + \widehat{T}.E2.p' \geq max(0, \widehat{T}.E1.p + \widehat{T}.E2.p - (now' - now) \cdot 0.04)$ holds. According to the refinement mapping, this corresponds to the conjunct to be proven. Likewise, we verify the remaining conjuncts of $O.E.CONT$ finishing the formal proof $\widehat{T}.CONT \Rightarrow O.E.CONT$. Thus, we now achieved the first proof step $\widehat{T} \Rightarrow O.E$ entirely.

The second proof step stating $T.PD \Rightarrow O.PD$ is very simple since both $T.PD$ and $O.PD$ use the same module parameter instantiation. Therefore, the two cTLA process instances are identical and $T.PD$ implies $O.PD$ trivially.

The third proof step states that the actions of the two systems are being consistently coupled. A consistent coupling is guaranteed if the process actions participating in a system action of T are mapped to process actions all being coupled to the same system action of O. This verification, however, is also merely trivial since we can apply the intermediate results of the first two proof steps. A sketch of the complete proof is listed on the WWW (URL: http://www.item.ntnu.no/~herrmann/specs/trust).

7 Concluding Remarks

We introduced the use of the temporal logic cTLA to specify trust models and to perform refinement proofs. We can also apply cTLA to specify more detailed specifications of computer implementations and to verify that the realizations fulfill the trust models. For instance, the trust model with two users can be refined to a model which does not specify continuous behavior. Here, the actions *CONT* are replaced by repeatedly executed discrete system actions which compute the decay of the experience numbers and calculate the trust values based on the time-step since the last execution. The cTLA processes of the implementation and the refinement proof can be retrieved from our web page.

Due to the compositionality of cTLA, specifications can be designed and refinement proofs can be carried out in a quite simple way. Nevertheless, one can facilitate the use of cTLA even more by using so-called specification frameworks [15]. Here, cTLA process types describing aspects of a certain application domain are collected in repositories. The framework user creates system specifications by taking suitable process types from the framework, instantiating their module parameters and composing them to a system model. Moreover, a specification framework contains repositories of theorems. A theorem is proven by the framework designer and states that an instance of a cTLA framework process type is fulfilled by a certain subsystem consisting of other framework process instances. The framework user can reduce a refinement proof into proof steps which correspond directly to the framework theorems. Thus, the verification effort is reduced to some simple checks guaranteeing that a certain theorem can be applied in a particular proof. These checks can be automated and tool support is available. cTLA-based specification frameworks were realized for telecommunication protocols [15], hazard analysis of hybrid technical systems [18] and security proofs of component-structured software [23]. Another framework to describe trust-based systems and trust models is under development.

References

1. McKnight, D.H., Chervany, N.L.: The Meanings of Trust. Working Paper Series 96–04, University of Minnesota — Carlson School of Management (1996)
2. Gambetta, D.: Can We Trust Trust? In Gambetta, D., ed.: Trust: Making and Breaking Cooperative Relations. Basil Blackwell (1990) 213–238
3. Jøsang, A.: The right type of trust for distributed systems. In: Proc. UCLA New Security Paradigms Workshop, Lake Arrowhead, ACM (1996) 119–131
4. Falcone, R., Castelfranchi, C.: The socio-cognitive dynamics of trust: Does trust create trust? In Falcone, R. et al., eds.: Proc. 4th Workshop on Agents — Trust in Cyber-Societies. LNCS 2246, Barcelona, Springer-Verlag (2001) 55–72
5. Falcone, R., Castelfranchi, C.: Social Trust: A Cognitive Approach. In Castelfranchi, C., Tan, Y.H., eds.: Trust and Deception in Virtual Societies. Kluwer Academic Publishers (2001) 55–90
6. Jøsang, A., Keser, C., Dimitrakos, T.: Can We Manage Trust? In Herrmann, P. et al., eds.: Proc. 3rd International Conference on Trust Management (iTrust 2005). LNCS 3477, Paris, Springer-Verlag (2005) 93–107

7. Cheskin Research and Studio Archetype/Sapient: eCommerce Trust Study. (1999)
8. Mezzetti, N.: A Socially Inspired Reputation Model. In Katsikas, S.K. et al., eds.: 1st European Workshop on Public Key Infrastructure (EuroPKI 2004). LNCS 3093, Samos Island, Springer-Verlag (2004) 191–204
9. Jøsang, A.: A Logic for Uncertain Probabilities. International Journal of Uncertainty, Fuzziness and Knowledge-Based Systems **9** (2001) 279–311
10. Jones, A.J.I., Firozabadi, B.S.: On the Characterisation of a Trusting Agent — Aspects of a Formal Approach. In Castelfranchi, C., Tan, Y.H., eds.: Trust and Deception in Virtual Societies. Kluwer Academic Publishers (2001) 157–168
11. Falcone, R., Pezzulo, G., Castelfranchi, C.: A Fuzzy Approach to a Belief-Based Trust Computation. In: AAMAS 2002 International Workshop on Trust, Reputation, and Security. LNCS 2631, Bologna, Springer-Verlag (2003)
12. Blaze, M., Feigenbaum, J., Lacy, J.: Decentralized Trust Management. In: Proc. 17th Symposium on Security and Privacy, Oakland, IEEE (1996) 164–173
13. Grandison, T., Sloman, M.: Specifying and Analysing Trust for Internet Applications. In: Proc. 2nd IFIP Conference on E-Commerce, E-Business & E-Government (I3E), Lisbon, Kluwer Academic Publisher (2002) 145–157
14. Abdul-Rahman, A., Hailes, S.: Supporting Trust in Virtual Communities. In: Proc. 33rd Hawaii International Conference. Volume 6., Maui, Hawaii, IEEE Computer Society Press (2000)
15. Herrmann, P., Krumm, H.: A Framework for Modeling Transfer Protocols. Computer Networks **34** (2000) 317–337
16. Lamport, L.: Specifying Systems. Addison-Wesley (2002)
17. Vissers, C.A., Scollo, G., van Sinderen, M.: Architecture and specification style in formal descriptions of distributed systems. In Agarwal, S., Sabnani, K., eds.: Proc. 8th IFIP International Conference on Protocol Specification, Testing and Verification (PSTV'88), Elsevier (1988) 189–204
18. Herrmann, P., Krumm, H.: A Framework for the Hazard Analysis of Chemical Plants. In: Proc. 11th IEEE International Symposium on Computer-Aided Control System Design (CACSD2000), Anchorage, IEEE CSS, Omnipress (2000) 35–41
19. Kurki-Suonio, R.: A Practical Theory of Reactive Systems — Incremental Modeling of Dynamic Behaviors. Springer-Verlag (2005)
20. Jøsang, A., Knapskog, S.J.: A metric for trusted systems. In: Proc. 21st National Security Conference, NSA (1998)
21. Abadi, M., Lamport, L.: An old-fashioned recipe for real time. In de Bakker et al., eds.: Real-Time: Theory in Practice. LNCS 600, Springer-Verlag (1991)
22. Abadi, M., Lamport, L.: The Existence of Refinement Mappings. Theoretical Computer Science **82** (1991) 253–284
23. Herrmann, P.: Formal Security Policy Verification of Distributed Component-Structured Software. In König, H. et al., eds.: Proc. 23rd IFIP International Conference on Formal Techniques for Networked and Distributed Systems (FORTE'2003). LNCS 2767, Berlin, Springer-Verlag (2003) 257–272

Modelling Trade and Trust Across Cultures

Gert Jan Hofstede[1], Catholijn M. Jonker[2], Sebastiaan Meijer[1],
and Tim Verwaart[1]

[1] Wageningen University, P.O. Box 9109, 6700 HB Wageningen,
The Netherlands
{Gertjan.Hofstede, Sebastiaan.Meijer,
Tim.Verwaart}@wur.nl
[2] Radboud Universiteit Nijmegen, Montessorilaan 3, Nijmegen,
The Netherlands
C.Jonker@nici.ru.nl

Abstract. Misunderstandings arise in international trade due to difference in cultural background of trade partners. Trust and the role it plays in trade are influenced by culture. Considering that trade always involves working on the relationship with the trade partner, understanding the behaviour of the other is of the essence. This paper proposes to involve cultural dimensions in the modelling of trust in trade situations. A case study is presented to show a conceptualisation of trust with respect to the cultural dimension of performance orientation versus cooperation orientation.

1 Introduction

"High quality! Traced and guaranteed!" Thus yells an American middleman in a session of the Trust and Tracing Game [1]. The man is buying and selling envelopes that have an invisible quality attribute. They can be either high quality or low quality, and of course the first variant fetches a better price. But why is he having his products traced up front? The producer he buys from knows the hidden quality of each envelope, and if the middle man trusted him he could save himself the tracing cost.

The answer has to do with trust. The middle man may or may not trust his provider, but he expects that no buyer will trust *him* to be sincere about the quality of his pretended high-quality envelopes unless he has them traced. So he makes the best of a cost factor and he uses the act of tracing as a marketing device.

The same game, played with Dutch participants, yields a different network. The game's pace tends to be slower and some negotiations are prolonged. Nobody traces anybody else, until the game leader reveals that consumers have been cheated and are stuck with low quality after having paid for high quality. This induces some tracing in the next round, but not much. By having his purchase traced, a Dutch buyer would indicate distrust of the seller, and that is not done. The seller himself would never think of tracing up front, because that would be throwing away money in vain, and he expects to be trusted anyhow.

K. Stølen et al. (Eds.): iTrust 2006, LNCS 3986, pp. 120–134, 2006.

We have been witness to the above events. In miniature, they mirror the unwritten rules of the game of real trade in the US and the Netherlands. The same game with the same explicit rules yields very different behaviour of the trade network because the hidden rules and assumptions differ.

Agent models of trade networks have been around for some years. The behaviour in an agent model is an emergent property resulting from the behaviour of all the agents. The role of the agents' preferences in such a model is not too hard to represent. But can we also incorporate the unwritten rules and expectations of culture? That is the subject of this paper.

The context of this study is research into social aspects of food supply chains and networks, as introduced in [2]. That research aims to increase insight in human behaviour in trade relations, with the goal to design efficient institutional environments for production and distribution of food, meeting high standards of to consumer satisfaction, health, food safety, and social responsibility. Especially for food with its potential hidden contaminations that can lead to severe health effects, trust is a key research item [3]. But this preliminary study abstracts from the food context and applies to any trade situation in which the products have hidden quality attributes. Human simulation games are used in combination with multi-agent simulations, to develop models for the role of trust in supply networks, by iteratively implementing models in multi-agent simulations, comparing simulation results with human simulations, and refining the models [4]. As illustrated by the example in the beginning of this section, observations of human games indicate that culture cannot be ignored.

Models of player's behaviour in simulation games entail models for deciding about agent's intentions, based on agent's beliefs and desires. According to March [5], decision making processes may be rational or rule following. Rational decision making aims to maximize a utility function. In rule following decision making, a decision maker classifies the situation and its own role in it; subsequently, she applies rules to answer the question: what is appropriate for a person like me to do in a situation like this? Human decision making processes often have both rational and rule-following aspects. Rule-following decision making can be seen as imposing moral boundaries on acceptable outcomes of rational decision making. It can also be seen as consolidated experience or an evolutionary outcome of rational decision making [5].

It is an interesting question to ask if artificial agents like human decision makers should apply both types of decision making. Agents that are designed to outperform people in rational decision making processes by use of superior computation power can probably do without rule-following. Agents that are designed to simulate human behaviour in some way will probably need to apply both processes of decision making simultaneously, although it may not strictly be necessary to follow equal procedures to get sufficiently resembling results. Especially in simulations that aim to increase understanding of human decision making, simulation of human rules is a sine qua non. This implies that the latter kind of agents must have cultural scripts.

Both a decision maker's desires (goals of the decision making) and its procedures for decision making are culture-dependent in several ways. First, the priority of goals depends on culture; for instance "maximize personal wealth" may have priority over "maintain pleasant interpersonal relations". Second, preferences for rational versus rule following procedures differ across cultures; e.g. in collectivistic cultures with large power distance, following the rules is more appropriate then in individualistic cultures with little power distance where rational decision making will prevail. Third, if a rule following procedure is chosen, the rules depend on culture. Fourth, a decision may be interpreted offensive by an opponent having adifferent cultural background. Also, the appropriate reaction to inappropriate behaviour differs across cultures.

The focus of this paper is on the relation between culture and trust in human trade networks. We abstract from personality and select a single dimension of culture as a modelling case. The next sections describe the background of culture theory, the background of trust literature used for the case study, the Trust and Tracing Game, a case study of modelling a dimension of culture, its application to the Trust and Tracing Game, and conclusions.

2 Culture and Trust

Culture is what distinguishes one group of people from another [6]. This implies that culture is not an attribute of individual people, unlike personality characteristics. It is an attribute of a group that manifests itself through the behaviours of its members.

For a trading situation, culture of the trader will manifest itself in four ways. First, culture filters observation. It determines the salience of clues about the acceptability of trade partners and their proposals. Second, culture sets norms for what constitutes an appropriate partner or offer. Third, it sets expectations for the context of the transactions, e.g. the enforceability of regulations and the possible sanctions in case of breach of the rules. Fourth, it sets norms for the kind of action that is appropriate given the other three, and in particular, the difference between the actual situation and the desired situation.

Our US middle man, for instance, sees as acceptable a trade partner who has his products traced so that quality is out in the open. He will be keen to observe any offer of untraced high-quality goods and to distrust the one offering it. He expects his clients to think in the same way, and in order to be deemed respectable, he has traces performed himself. It also helps that he expects heavy-handed punishment in case of infringement of explicit laws.

Our Dutch trader, on the other hand, likes trade partners who are forgiving and friendly and who place implicit trust in one another's good intentions. He will perceive it when somebody asks for a trace and label that person as distrustful. In order not to be thought distrustful himself, he will not trace until proven wrong, and if proven wrong he will try to avoid the bad guy, or most likely (if it is the first offence) ask the cheater to be honest the next transaction and sell for a low price to make up the losses from the cheated transaction.

What is it that makes these two traders behave in such different ways? It could be their personalities, or their experiences, or it could be the way they were brought up, in other words: their culture. It turns out that in terms of culture, the USA and the Netherlands are unusually easily comparable, because they are rather alike but for one aspect. Culture at the national level is concerned with five big issues of social life: hierarchy, identity, cooperation-performance orientation, the unknown, and the gratification of needs. Hofstede and Hofstede [6] conceptualize each of these issues as a bipolar continuum ranging from about 0 to about 100: from small to large power distance, from collectivist to individualist, from cooperation oriented to performance oriented, from weak to strong uncertainty avoidance, and from short-term to long-term orientation. As figure 1 shows, the Netherlands and the USA differ considerably on the Cooperation-Performance orientation dimension and little on the other four. Incidentally, this is not to say that culture only occurs at a national level – but the national averages in these two countries happen to differ. Of course, every individual is unique, and many subgroups with their own culture exist within any country.

In this article, we shall abstract from the real world in an important way. We shall describe agents as if the dimension of performance orientation were the only one. This is a deliberate choice, but it should be borne in mind that in reality, behaviour is always the outcome of a mix of factors: all elements of one's culture, all elements of one's personality and all contextual and historical coincidences.

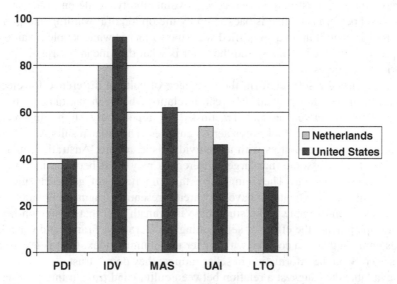

Fig. 1. The cultures of the Netherlands and the USA compared (PDI = Power Distance index, IDV = Individualism index, MAS = Masculinity index, also called the cooperation-performance orientation index, UAI = Uncertainty avoidance index, LTO = Long-term orientation index)

What does the dimension of performance orientation indicate? Let us describe the two extremes – more extreme in fact than any real-world culture – to give the big idea. Performance oriented cultures are cultures in which people are expected to place value on measurable performance criteria such as size, speed and quantity. Money is good and rich people are admired. Life is conceptualized as a series of contests and winning is paramount while losing is a disaster. Implicit trust is low; if you get cheated upon it is your own fault and you are a loser. If you do good, you also do it in a large way. If you commit crimes, they are large ones, not petty ones. Big is beautiful in everything.

Cooperation oriented cultures are the opposite. Winners are at risk of awakening feelings of jealousy. Small is beautiful, implicit trust is high, and cheaters are looked down upon. Yet small-scale cheating occurs a lot because society is permissive, and punishments are low or, in the case of small misdemeanours, you may be forgiven. Good intentions are more important than good performance.

These two descriptions are stereotyped extremes. Yet citizens from either of these two countries who have been exposed to the other one's culture probably recognize quite a bit of them. And because the Netherlands and the USA also have quite many contacts in actual business life, the comparison is meaningful in the real world.

The meaning of trust across cultures is related to this dimension of culture. In fact, the statement 'Most people can be trusted' was one of the constituents of the dimension in Hofstede's original research. In cooperation-oriented cultures, people agree with it more. Since then, many others have investigated the variations of the meaning of the concept across cultures. See e.g. chapter 8 in [3] for a discussion of the dynamics of trust and transparency across cultures, and [7] for a conceptualization of trust and a literature review. This latter article distinguishes *intrinsic trust* from *enforceable trust*. Intrinsic trust is trust that accepts vulnerability, while enforceable trust is trust in good performance that is backed up by the option of rewarding and punishing the trustee. To sum it up in a simplified way: the former is what people mean by trust in cooperation oriented cultures, and the latter is what they mean by trust in performance oriented cultures.

Some published results confirm the relevance of cultural difference for electronic trade, for instance Huang et al. [8] report relations between nationality, trust and internet adoption. Jarvenpaa and Tractinsky [9] report only slight differences in consumer trust in on-line bookstores across cultures. The latter results were based on observations in three countries with an individualistic culture: Australia, Finland and Israel. The authors assume that larger differences may exist between individualistic and collectivistic nations. They emphasize the importance of gathering more data. However, only few publications have appeared, presenting fragmented data of only a few countries. An example is the study by Vishwanath [10] that relates on-line auction participation and the effect of seller ratings in Germany, France and Canada. His findings confirm that in a country with higher masculinity index, trust is less relevant: bidders do rely on the information in seller ratings; they do not trust.

All available data suggest a relation between culture and trust in internet participation. However, available data are insufficient for foundation of cross-cultural models of consumer trust that can be used for agent design. Development of well-founded trust models incorporating culture requires empirical, preferably experimental, data.

3   Agent Based Simulations of Trust and Trade

Castelfranchi and Falcone proposed a model of trust that can serve as a basis for agent based simulations [11, 12]. The main issues in their model are:

- Trust is at the same time: a mental attitude towards another agent, a decision to rely on another agent, and a behaviour that entails a relation with another agent.
- Trust consists of beliefs about another agent's competence and willingness to fulfil some task. Willingness arises from a complex of motivations.
- A condition for trust is the belief that it is better to rely on the trustee than not.
- The decision to trust may be influenced by environmental factors: opportunities, obstacles, adversities, and interferences.

- In the decision whether to trust or not, an agent weights and prioritises the above influences and compares the result with a threshold of acceptable risk. Weight factors, priorities and risk threshold depend on context and agent's personality.

Although the authors do not relate trust with culture, their model offers opportunities to do so. When viewing trust as a mental attitude towards another agent, an agent's cultural background and the cultural context will influence its valuation of the motivations to trust. When viewing trust as an intention to rely on an agent, the criteria, priorities, and weight factors for the decision process reflect cultural background.

Trust models can be put into operation in a testbed. A recently proposed approach is the ART testbed architecture [13]. The authors propose a software architecture for testing and comparing reputation and trust models, either in experimentation or in competition mode. The testbed provides relative performance indicators for reputation and trust models. The testbed offers a java environment where researchers can implement java methods to implement the models. Thus, it can test any model with any cultural script in any cultural or cross-cultural setting. However, the testbed approach is not related to data from real human cultures.

Jonker et al. [4] present an approach to interrelate multi-agent simulations and human simulation games in order to validate and refine trust models, especially with respect to different cultural and institutional settings. The game focuses on the role of trust in supply chains with asymmetrical information about product quality between sellers and buyers. Playing this game with people from different countries showed different development of patterns of trust and co-operation between cultures. The approach is effective in producing empirical data. As it requires multiple game sessions of several hours with some twenty players, it is very time-consuming. This is the necessary cost of a controlled way to acquire empirical data for model formulation, parameter estimation and model validation in multi-agent systems.

Simpler experiments, e.g. those presented by Jonker et al. [14], could be used to compare isolated aspects of trust across cultures. The paper presents a method for measuring the effect of sequences of positive experiences and disappointments on the level of trust. Results are acquired from a single cultural setting. It would be interesting to compare dynamics of trust across cultures using this experimental approach.

Partner selection is a special point of attention in trade models, especially in multi-agent simulations. Partner selection starts with models for partner preference. Models based on experience with regard to negotiation success are describeded by, for instance, Tesfatsion [15] and Munroe and Luck [16]. Sen et al. [17] present a model for players that anticipate their opponents selecting partners based on experience. However, none of these models explicitly represents cultural dimensions.

4 Trust and Tracing Game

The Trust and Tracing [1] game for human players is a research tool for supply chain and network studies. This tool places the choice between relying on trust versus spending money on complete information in trade environments at the core of a social simulation game. The game is used both as a data gathering tool about the role of reputation and trust in various types of business networks, and as a tool to make participants reflect on their own daily experiences in their respective jobs.

In the game sellers of a commodity have more information about the quality of the goods than buyers, as quality is invisible and only known by the producers. This leads to information asymmetry and the opportunity for deceit. Meijer and Hofstede [1] describe the dilemma similar to the well-known Prisoners Dilemma in the so-called Trader's Predicament.

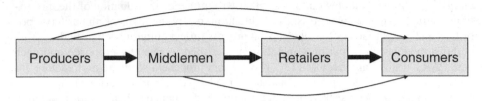

Fig. 2. Supply network configuration

In the human Trust and Tracing game 12 to 25 participants play roles in a supply network. There are producers, middlemen, retailers and consumers (see Figure 2). The producers receive an initial amount of goods. The good traded is a sealed envelope that comes in 3 different types (colours) and each of the types in two qualities (high and low). The quality is invisible, as it is hidden in the sealed envelope. Producers know which envelopes are high quality and which are low. The only person in the game allowed to open an envelope is the tracing agency. Table 1 specifies satisfaction values of each good for a consumer (utility).

Table 1. Consumer satisfaction value by the type and quality

Quality	Type		
	Blue	Red	Yellow
Low	1	2	3
High	2	6	12

An agent buying a high quality envelope takes a risk, as he cannot know the real quality. The buyer can check afterwards by doing a trace at the tracing agency, but this costs money. Tracing is cheaper early on in the network than for consumers. When consumers prefer traced goods (certified high quality) it would be economical to let a middleman do the trace and sell the traced product throughout the network along with the certificate. Successful deception is beneficial for a seller as he receives an additional income. (The difference between the price of a high and that of a low-quality product) However, if the deception is discovered the cheater has to pay a fine. Resellers of cheated products who did not check the quality themselves have to pay a smaller "ignorance" fine.

In the case study a situation is considered in which two traders meet for the first time and know nothing about each other. Trader P is very much performance oriented, trader C is the opposite, i.e., cooperation oriented. The traders negotiate about one envelop, said to contain a high quality commodity. The profile of trader P is such that he is willing to trade for a final price of about Q. The profile of trader C is such that he is willing to trade for a final price of about Q. Given that Q is an acceptable price, everything is set in such a way that a deal is possible if the negotiations are performed in an acceptable manner, acceptable that is to the other party.

5 Modelling Cooperation- Versus Performance Orientation

The dimension of performance orientation versus cooperation orientation has its effect on the way people will behave in the Trust and Tracing Game. In this section this effect is described informally and then (partially) specified formally as prodcution rules).

A performance oriented trader is interested in fast trades, with as many goods as possible in one trade. This trader is rather impatient, and if bids are too far off from his profile, he will walk away quickly. The performance oriented trader always traces the goods after buying, since he expects the possibility of deception. He sticks to the contract of the deal, and will deceive the trade partner to the limits of the contract without any compunction. As a consequence, the performance oriented trader sees no problems in dealing again with a trader that conned him in the past: "It's all in the game". Each subsequent negotiation will be dealt with without taking past trustworthiness into account. Each new contract will be set up from scratch. The trader learns from mistakes to make sure that the contract will not lead to new and uncomfortable surprises on his side.

A cooperation oriented trader is interested in the relationship with the trade partner, building trust is important, the amount of goods is not of the most interest. The trader is also interested in negotiating about one envelope only, because the relationship built during that negotiation might pay off in future negotiations. Given the interest in the relationship with the trade partner, a first negotiation with a trade partner will take time that is willingly spent by the trader. During such negotiations, the trader appreciates a negotiation process in which both partners show a willingness to accommodate the other over time. Past negotiations do play an important role in subsequent negotiations. The trader is perfectly willing to see the current negotiation as a kind of continuation of the previous one. If the trade is about the same commodity, the trader will start the negotiation from the deal of the last one. If the other accepts, then the deal can be made in one round and in seconds, whereas the first deal might have taken a lot of rounds and lots of time. In principle, the cooperation oriented trader does not trace, since in his mind this would constitute ostentation of distrust. If conned, then the cooperation oriented trader will avoid the conman if possible, or give him one more chance. In the human games we observed that he then asks for a very good new deal to reaffirm the relationship. In the application of the rules to the setting described in Section 4, the following simplifications are made. The cooperation oriented trader C is content in a first ever trade with another trader T, if negotiation takes 5 rounds before a deal is found, and over the rounds T tries to accommodate C. A bad negotiation is one that is not satisfying. A performance oriented trader P is content in a first ever trade with another trader T, if negotiation is successful and fast (at most 2 rounds), and both P and T showed steadfastness in their bidding. Trader P respects and appreciates steadfastness in T and will show the same behaviour towards T. For trader P a satisfying negotiation is one that is short (at most 2 rounds) and in which both traders show steadfastness.

Both trader P and trader C prefer reaching a deal after a satisfying negotiation over a deal that was reached on the basis of a bad negotiation. Not reaching a deal after a satisfying negotiation is better than having no deal after a bad negotiation. Bear in mind that the traders differ strongly in what is considered a satisfying negotiation. Furthermore, note that their cultural scripting will also lead them to behave differently during the negotiations. Trader P might very well walk away (no deal) as soon as he receives a first bid of trader C that is very far off price Q. Whereas trader C might be put off by the steadfastness of trader P, and certainly by his walking away after few rounds. However, C will be forgiving and willing to negotiate with P one more time, although C will trust P less and avoid risk in the next deal.

Some essential parts of the specification are presented in the remainder of this section; more can be found in Appendix A, and a full specification can be obtained from the authors. The specifications are formulated as production rules.

The cultural dimension has performance orientation at one extreme of the spectrum, and cooperation orientation at the other. This dimension is modelled by one value, indicated by the function named pc_orientation. A value of 0 corresponds to extreme cooperation orientation, whereas value 1 corresponds to extreme performance orientation. A personality factor is used to account for individual differences in decision making.

```
(1)    If cultural_script_contains(pc_orientation(F: Real))
          And minimum_utility(M: Real)
          And personality_factor(impatience, I: Real)
       Then impatience_factor(F: Real * (I: Real + 0.5))
          And preferred_relative_deal_size(F: Real)
          And allowed_relative_gap_size(F: Real)
          And cut_off_value(M: Real * F: Real);
```

At each moment during the negotiation the trader can decide to cut off the negotiations without a deal, or to accept the opponent's last offer (deal), or to continue with the negotiations. The other party can of course also take the initiative to accept the deal of the trader or to cut off the negotiations without a deal. A deal corresponds to a contract that stipulates the conditions of the sale. His decisions after a negotiation has ended in a deal depend on the role that the trader is playing. As a seller, he has to decide whether or not to cheat upon his trade partner. This aspect is not considered in this paper, see [18] for a model on cheating in the Trust and Tracing Game. If the agent is a buyer, he has to decide whether or not to trace the commodities sold to him. Aspects of the negotiation process determine whether or not he changes his opinion of his trade partner. A change in opinion is regulated by change factors (values between 0 and 1). The change factors (big and small) and their dynamics are part of the personality profile of the trader, and not further elaborated here. The negotiations in the Trust and Tracing Game have a closed character, therefore, both negotiation partners only have their own utility function to evaluate both own bids and those of the negotiation partner. In reality many factors influence decisions to continue negiation, to trust or deceive a trade partner, etc. Where not all of the factors can be included in the model, random factors between 0 and 1 are used to obtain a more natural variability in behaviour.

Rule 2 describes that the trader will stop the negotiation if he considers the starting points of the bidding as too far apart. The impatience factor influences the decision; the higher F, the sooner the trader will stop for this reason.

(2)   If impatience_factor(F: Real)
        And current_negotiation(T: Trader, X: Integer, L: Commodity_List)
        And current_round(X: Integer)
        And others_bid_utility_in_round(U: Real, X: Integer)
        And cut_off_value(C: Real)
        And U: Real < C: Real
        And random(0, 1, S: Real)
        And 0.5 < S: Real * (F: Real + 0.5)
    Then stop_negotiation(T: Trader, X: Integer, L: Commodity_List, gap);

The lower the impatience factor, the higher the probability that the trader will stop the negotiation if progress is slow:

(3)   If impatience_factor(F: Real)
        And current_negotiation(T: Trader, X: Integer, L: Commodity_List)
        And current_round(X: Integer)
        And progress_in_bids(X: Integer – 3, X: Integer, P: Real)
        And minimal_progress_value(M: Real)
        And P: real < M: Real
        And random(0, 1, S: Real)
        And 0.5 < S: Real * (1.5 - F: Real)
    Then stop_negotiation(T: Trader, X: Integer, L: Commodity_List, no_accom);

Rule 4 is an example of using a random factor to obtain more natural behavior. The rule updates the acceptability of the negotiation partner. The impatience factor influences the decision whether or not a change is made. If a decision is made for change, the size of the change depends on the change factor, which is part of the agent's personality profile.

(4)   If stop_negotiation(T: Trader, X: Integer, L: Commodity_List, gap)
        And impatience_factor(F: Real)   And acceptability(T: Trader, R: Real)
        And change_factor(B: Real, big_change)   And random(0, 1, S: Real)
        And 0.5 < S: Real * (F: Real + 0.5)
    Then new_acceptability(T: Trader, R: Real * B: Real) ;

Rule 5 describes the effect of a negotiation in which the other partner did not accommodate our trader. The smaller the impatience factor, the more the acceptability will decrease; the bigger the impatience factor, the more the acceptability will increase (see rule 1 for the relation of impatience with culture and personality). The turning point is at 0.5 at which no change occurs. Normalisation functions can be added to maintain the acceptability value between 0 and 1, however, they are left out for reasons of transparency.

(5)   If stop_negotiation(T: Trader, X: Integer, L: Commodity_List, no_accom)
        And impatience_factor(F: Real)
        And acceptability(T: Trader, R: Real)
    Then new_acceptability(T: Trader, R: Real * (F: Real + 0.5));

A buyer that is rather performance oriented will almost always trace the deal. Other aspects that play a role are his personality profile (for this example, only risk-attitude is taken into account) and the trustworthiness of the other party. Notice, that for a performance oriented trader the issue of trust is not that important as it is for cooperation oriented traders. The changes he makes to partner's trustworthiness are small, thus impact of trust on the next item is related to his initial trust in people. For the cooperation oriented trader, trust is important. Thus, for the cooperation oriented trader, the trust he has in others has a higher impact on his decision to trace or not.

```
(6)   If cultural_script_contains(pc_orientation(F: Real))
         And deal_in_round(T: Trader, B: Bid, X: Integer)
         And my_role(buyer)
         And personality_factor(risk_attitude, I: Real)
         And trustworthiness(T: Trader, H: Real)
         And random(0, 1, S: Real)
         And 0.5 < S: Real * (F: Real – H: Real – I: Real + 1.5)
      Then to_be_traced(B: Bid);
```

Rules 7-10 model the opposite effects of the length of a negotiation on performance oriented and cooperation oriented traders. The p-round boundary used in rule 7 is the number of rounds that a performance oriented trader typically allows before cutting off. The c-round boundary is the number of rounds a cooperation oriented trader would minimally prefer in negotiation with a trader he has no experience with. The p-round boundary could, for example, be set to 2 and the c-round boundary to 5.

```
(7)   /* performance oriented trader appreciates a fast deal */
      If deal_in_round(T: Trader, B: Bid, X: Integer)
         And impatience_factor(F: Real)                And p_round_boundary(A: Integer)
         And F: Real > 0.5                             And X: Integer ≤ A: Integer
         And change_factor(I: Real, big_change) And acceptability(T: Trader, R: Real)
      Then new_acceptability(T: Trader, R: Real * I: Real * (F: Real + 0.5) );

(8)   /* performance oriented trader dislikes long negotiation */
      If deal_in_round(T: Trader, B: Bid, X: Integer)
         And impatience_factor(F: Real)                And F: Real > 0.5
         And change_factor(D: Real, big_change)        And p_round_boundary(A: Integer)
         And X: Integer > A: Integer                   And acceptability(T: Trader, R: Real)
      Then new_acceptability(T: Trader, R: Real * D: Real);
```

A cooperation oriented trader appreciates a first long negotiation, even if it ends without a deal. To get a big increment, given change factors between 0 and 1, the change factor is mirrored in the line x=1, thus the factor 2 – I: Real.

```
(9)   If stop_negotiation(T: Trader, B: Bid, X: Integer, W: Reason)
         And number_of_earlier_negotiations_with(0, T: Trader)
         And not W: Reason = no_accom              And impatience_factor(F: Real)
         And F: Real < 0.5                         And acceptability(T: Trader, H: Real)
         And change_factor(I: Real, big_change)    And c_round_boundary(A: Integer)
         And X: Integer > A: Integer
      Then new_acceptability(T: Trader, H: Real * (2 - I: Real) );
```

A cooperation oriented trader dislikes a first short negotiation, even if it ended in a deal. Note that earlier rules can intensify this effect if during the negotiation the other party made no accommodations in his direction.

```
(10)  If stop_negotiation(T: Trader, B: Bid, X: Integer, W: Reason)
         And number_of_earlier_negotiations_with(0, T: Trader)
         And impatience_factor(F: Real)            And F: Real < 0.5
         And change_factor(D: Real, big_change)    And c_round_boundary(A: Integer)
         And X: Integer < A: Integer               And acceptability(T: Trader, H: Real)
      Then new_acceptability(T: Trader, H: Real * I: Real);
```

The trader compares different negotiation options as offered by other traders. These offers can be made to him on the initiative of the other trader, or on his request.

(11) If offered(T: Trader, X: Integer, L: Commodity_List)
        And my_wish_list(L': Commodity_List)
        And subset_of(L: Commodity_List, L': Commodity_List)
        Then possible_negotiation_with(T: Trader, X: Integer, L: Commodity_List);

Traders choose their trade partners on the basis of their acceptability value. As can be seen from the rules above, the performance oriented trader directly updates the acceptability value in many of these rules. The cooperation oriented trader decides mostly on trust, and only slightly updates the acceptability value directly. However, the cooperation oriented trader also chooses a trade partner on the basis of the acceptability values. In general, the acceptability value of a trade partner is an accumulation of several factors: effects as described by the rules above, personality traits, and other cultural dimensions. In this paper the only aspect modelled is the following. For the cooperation oriented trader the trustworthiness of the partner has a higher impact on the computated value of acceptability than for the performance oriented trader. Furthermore, the acceptability value used to determine new trade partners is recalculated after all negotiations have finished.

(12) If cultural_script_contains(pc_orientation(F: Real))
        And no_ongoing_negotiations
        And acceptability(T: Trader, R: Real)
        And trustworthiness(T: Trader, H: Real)
        Then new_acceptability(T: Trader, F: Real * R: Real + (1 – F: Real) * H:Real);

6   Application of the Model in the Trust and Tracing Game

Consider a performance oriented buyer P (pc_orientation 0.9) and cooperation oriented seller C (pc_orientation 0.1). The traders meet each other for the first time and start a negotiation about 1 envelope. Both traders have in mind to trade for a price of about 10 euro. The (relevant parts of the) profiles for the players are:

	Player C	Player P
Minimum utility	0.7	0.7
Personality factor impatience	0.4	0.6
Impatience factor	0.09	0.99
Cut off value	0.07	0.63
Minimal progress	0.1	0.01

In the first round P offers 9 euro for a high quality red commodity, and C replies with a bid including 16 euro and high quality. The utility of C's bid in the eyes of P is 0.6, which is below the cut-off value of 0.7. Now P has to decide whether he will continue or stop. Let us assume that P decides to continue (only rule 2 would apply, but assume the random factor determines otherwise), and bids 9 euro in the second round for high quality. C responds with 14 euro for high quality (none of the stopping rules apply). The utility is 0.62 which is again below P's cut-off value. We assume that P decides to continue the negotiation again (assume rule 2 randomly discarded), and he offers 10 for high quality in the third round. C continues and responds with 12 euro and low quality. P's utility for that bid is 0.5, again below his cut-off value. We assume that this time P decides to stop the negotiation (rule 2). P evaluates the process using the "gap" rule (4), and considerably lowers the acceptability of C. C uses the "no_accom" rule (5) and considerably lowers the acceptability of P. A shame because the prices they had in mind allowed for reaching a deal, but this behaviour is in conformity with the culture scripts.

7 Conclusion

Trade situations in the real world can be better understood by taking into account the cultural background of the traders. Concepts like trust and honesty do not mean the same in different cultures, nor do practical aspects such as cheating, negotiation time and good relationships. To be able to model and test agents with culture scripts a comparable data set from real world trade is needed. The Trust and Tracing game provides a conceptualisation of trust in a well-defined laboratory trade environment to compare artificial agent behaviour with.

This case study models one of the culture dimensions of Hofstede, that of cooperation-orientation versus performance orientation. This dimension is obviously related to the meaning of trust. Although singling out one dimension is a deliberate distortion of reality, there is a look-alike real-world case. American and Dutch cultures are alike on all dimensions but this one and thus provide a good analogy.

The culture scripts of performance and cooperation oriented agents presented use the four ways in which a culture manifests itself: culture filters observation, culture sets norms for what constitutes an appropriate partner or offer, it sets expectations for the context of the transactions, and it sets norms for the kind of action that is appropriate given the other three.

This paper advocates the incorporation of culture scripts in the modelling of trade and associated aspects such as trust. As an example, the paper presents a model of the effects of the Cooperation-Performance orientation index of the culture scripts in the models of trustworthiness and acceptability of trade partners in negotiation settings. An application of the model to an extreme setting of performance orientated versus cooperation oriented traders shows the expected behaviour as sketched in Section 2.

Future research should test our scripts against data from human games to validate the approach and find plausible values for the parameters in the models. Then the model can be extended to take into account other dimensions of culture as well, increasing validity.

References

1. S. Meijer and G.J. Hofstede. The Trust and Tracing game. In: *Proc. of the IFIP WG 5.7 SIG experimental learning workshop.* Aalborg, Denmark (May 2003).
2. T. Camps, P. Diederen, G.J. Hofstede, B. Vos (Eds.). *The emerging world of chain and networks.* Reed Business Information (2004).
3. G.J. Hofstede, L. Spaans, H. Schepers, J. Trienekens, A. Beulens (Eds.). *Hide or confide: the dilemma of transparency.* Reed Business Information (2004).

4. C.M. Jonker, S. Meijer, D. Tykhonov, T. Verwaart. Multi-agent Model of Trust in a Human Game. In: P. Mathieu, B. Beaufils, O. Brandouy (Eds.). *Artificial Economics, LNMES* 564 (2005) 91-102.
5. J.G.. March. *A Primer on Decision Making: How Decisions Happen.* Free Press (1994).
6. G.Hofstede and G.J.Hofstede. *Cultures and Organizations: Software of the Mind, Third Millennium* Edition. McGraw-Hill (2005).
7. G.J. Hofstede Intrinsic and enforceable trust: a research agenda. In: *Proceedings of the 99th European Seminar of the EAAE* (2006, forthcoming).
8. H. Huang, C. Keser, J. Leland, J. Shachat. Trust, the Internet and Digital Divide. *IBM Systems Journal*, 42, 3 (2003) 507-518.
9. S.L. Jarvenpaa and N. Tractinsky. Consumer Trust in an Internet Store: A Cross-Cultural Validation. *JCMC* 5(2) (December 1999).
10. A. Vishwanath. Manifestations of interpersonal trust in online interaction. A cross-cultural study comparing the differential utilization of seller ratings by eBay participants in Canada, France, and Germany. *New Media and Society* 6(2) (2004) 85-101.
11. C. Castelfranchi. Trust Mediation in Knowledge Management and Sharing. In: C. Jensen, S. Poslad, T. Dimitrakos (Eds.). *Trust management, LNCS* 2995 (2004) 304-318.
12. C. Castelfranchi and R. Falcone. Principles of Trust for MAS: Cognitive Anatomy, Social Importance and Quantification. In: *Proc. of ICMAS'98*, AAAI press (1998).
13. K..K. Fullam, T.B. Klos, G. Muller, J. Sabater, Z. Topol, K.S. Barber, J.S. Rosenschein, L. Vercouter. The Agent Reputation an Trust (ART) Testbed Architecture. *8th Workshop "Trust in Agent Societies" at AAMAS,05,* Utrecht, The Netherlands (July 2005).
14. C.M. Jonker, J.J.P. Schalken, J. Theeuwes, J. Treur. Human Experiments in Trust Dynamics. *Trust management, LNCS* 2995 (2004) 206-220.
15. L. Tesfatsion. A Trade Network Game with Endogeneous Partner Selection. In: H. M. Amman, B. Rustem, A. B. Whinston (Eds.), *Computational Approaches to Economic Problems,* Kluwer (1997) 249-269.
16. S. Munroe, M. Luck. Balancing Conflict and Cost in the Selection of Negotiation Opponents. *1st Int. Workshop on Rational Robust and Secure Negotiations in MAS. " at AAMAS,05,* Utrecht, The Netherlands (2005).
17. S. Sen, S. Saha, D. Banerjee. Trust-Based Contracting. *8th Workshop "Trust in Agent Societies" at AAMAS,05,* Utrecht, The Netherlands (July 2005).
18. C.M. Jonker, S. Meijer, D. Tykhonov, T. Verwaart. Modeling and Simulation of Selling and Deceit for the Trust and Tracing Game. *8th Workshop "Trust in Agent Societies" at AAMAS,05,* Utrecht, The Netherlands (July 2005).

Appendix A. Additional Parts of the Formal Specification

If a trader feels he has no more room to accommodate the other party, then he will stop the negotiations.

```
(13)  /* stop: no more room */
      If current_negotiation(T: Trader, X: Integer, L: Commodity_List)
        And current_round(X: Integer)
        And my_bid_utility_in_round(U: Real, X: Integer -1)
        And minimum_utility(M: Real)
        And U: Real - M: Real < 0.01
      Then stop_negotiation(T: Trader, X: Integer, L: Commodity_List, no_more_room);
```

If the trader has decided to stop the negotiation because his minimal utility was reached, then he also checks the progress made during the whole negotiation process.

Apparently, the negotiation originally did not stop for this reason, so this rule only affects the acceptability and trustworthiness once.

(14) If stop_negotiation(T: Trader, X: Integer, L: Commodity_List, no_more_room)
        And progress_in_bids(1, X: Integer, P: Real)
        And minimal_progress_value(M: Real)
        And P: real < M: Real
      Then stop_negotiation(T: Trader, X: Integer, L: Commodity_List, no_accom);

In negotiations the trader can accept the current bid of the other party if the utilities (according to his own function) of that bid and his own last bid are close enough. This notion of close enough is formalised by the acceptable_utility_gap.

(15) If current_negotiation(T: Trader, X: Integer, L: Commodity_List)
        And current_round(X: Integer)
        And others_bid_utility_in_round(U: Real, X: Integer)
        And my_bid_utility_in_round(U': Real, X: Integer)
        And acceptable_utility_gap(R: Real)
        And I U: Real – U': Real I ≤ R: Real
      Then stop_negotiation(T: Trader, X: Integer, accept_offer);

(16) If current_negotiation(T: Trader, X: Integer, L: Commodity_List)
        And current_round(X: Integer)
        And other_accepted_my_bid_in_round(T: Trader, B: Bid, X: Integer)
      Then stop_negotiation(T: Trader, X: Integer, my_offer_accepted)
        And deal_in_round(T: Trader, B: Bid, X: Integer);

(17) If stop_negotiation(T: Trader, X: Integer, accept_offer)
        And other_bid_in_round(B: Bid, X: Integer)
      Then deal_in_round(T: Trader, B: Bid, X: Integer);

Once the acceptability of the traders is determined, and the current negotiations have all stopped, new trade partners can be identified.

(18) If no_ongoing_negotiations   And acceptability(T: Trader, R: Real)
        And acceptability(T': Trader, R': Real)   And R: Real > R': Real
      Then more_acceptable_with_diff(T: Trader, T': Trader, IR: Real – R': RealI);

(19) If no_ongoing_negotiations   And acceptability(T: Trader, R: Real)
        And acceptability(T': Trader, R': Real)   And R: Real < R': Real
      Then more_acceptable_with_diff(T': Trader, T: Trader, IR: Real – R': RealI);

(20) If no_ongoing_negotiations
        And possible_negotiation_with(T: Trader, X: Integer, L: Commodity_List)
        And possible_negotiation_with(T': Trader, X': Integer, L': Commodity_List)
        And more_acceptable_with_diff(T: Trader, T': Trader, R: Real)
        And allowed_acceptability_difference(Epsilon: Real)
        And R: Real > Epsilon: Real
      Then to_be_ignored(T': Trader, X': Integer, L': Commodity_List);

(21) If no_ongoing_negotiations   And preferred_relative_deal_size(F: Real)
        And max_deal_size(M: Integer)   And P: Real = M: Integer * F: Real
        And possible_negotiation_with(T: Trader, X: Integer, L: Commodity_List)
        And possible_negotiation_with(T': Trader, X': Integer, L': Commodity_List)
        And I X: Integer – P: Real I < I X': Integer – P: RealI
        And acceptability_difference(T: Trader, T': Trader, R: Real)
        And allowed_acceptability_difference(Epsilon: Real)
        And R: Real < Epsilon: Real
      Then to_be_ignored(T': Trader, X': Integer, L': Commodity_List);

Estimating the Relative Trustworthiness of Information Sources in Security Solution Evaluation

Siv Hilde Houmb[1], Indrakshi Ray[2], and Indrajit Ray[2]

[1] Department of Computer Science,
Norwegian University of Science and Technology,
Sem Sælands Vei 7-9, NO-7491 Trondheim, Norway
sivhoumb@idi.ntnu.no
[2] Computer Science Department, Colorado State University,
601 S. Howes Street, Fort Collins, CO 80523-1873, USA
{iray, indrajit}@CS.colostate.EDU

Abstract. When evaluating alternative security solutions, such as security mechanism, security protocols etc., "hard" data or information is rarely available, and one have to relay on the opinions of domain experts. Log-files from IDS, Firewalls and honeypots might also be used. However, such source are most often only used in an "penetrate and patch" strategy, meaning that system administrators, security experts or similar surveillance the network and initiate appropriate reactions to the actions observed. Such sources refers to real-time information, but might also be used in a more preventive manner by combining it with the opinions provided by the domain experts. To appropriately combine the information from such various sources the notion of trust is used. Trust represents the degree to which a particular information source can be trusted to provide accurate and correct information, and is measured as information source relative trustworthiness. In this paper we show how to assign this relative trustworthiness using two trust variables; (1) knowledge level and (2) level of expertise.

1   Introduction

Achieving the correct level of security in an application depends not only on the security level, but also on the time-to-market (TTM) and budget constraints imposed upon the system. This advocates the need for evaluating alternative security solutions. The security standard ISO 15408:1999 Common Criteria for Information Technology Security Evaluation [7] supports the evaluation of security solutions through a hierarchy of evaluation assurance levels (EAL). These levels and associated guidelines takes an evaluator through activities assessing the security level of a security solution. Risk management standards, such as the Australian/New Zealand standard for Risk Management AS/NZS 4360:2004 [1] and its companion guideline standard HB 436:2004 Risk Management Guidelines [2], evaluate security solutions through a set of risk treatment assessment

K. Stølen et al. (Eds.): iTrust 2006, LNCS 3986, pp. 135–149, 2006.
© Springer-Verlag Berlin Heidelberg 2006

activities. However, in most cases both security standards and risk management standards relies heavily on subjective assessment by one or few assessors. Rather than having an assessor interpret information, it would be beneficial to directly make use of information from various information sources when doing security solution evaluation. Such an approach would not only simplify the process of security solution evaluation, but would also provide technique that aid evaluators by offering a way to structurally combine the large amount of information that such evaluations include.

Because the information that are available in security solution evaluations are both subjective and experience or empirical, aggregation techniques that can handle information of various degrees of uncertainty is needed. This paper describes a trust-based performance strategy for aggregating various information using information sources' relative trustworthiness. This relative trustworthiness is an expression of the ability of an information source to provide accurate information, and is assessed by examining its past and expected future performance. The expected future performance is determine by examining to what degree the knowledge and expertise level of an information source is in accordance to that required for the problem in question. Expected future performance is evaluated by looking at the currently perceived performance of an information source using the two trust variables; (1) knowledge level and (2) level of expertise.

The paper describes how to determine the information source relative trustworthiness using the two trust variables. The approach is demonstrated by an example that determines the relative trustworthiness for four domain experts and a honeypot.

The paper is organised as following. Section 2 provides a brief description of potential information sources that might be used in security solution evaluations. Section 3 describes how to determine the information source relative trustworthiness using the two trust variables. Section 4 demonstrate how to use the approach described in Section 3. Section 5 puts the work into context and Section 6 conclude the paper with some pointers to future directions.

2   Information Sources for Security Solution Effect Evaluation

Information sources can be both active and passive entities, and their relative trustworthiness vary depending on the problem being assessed. When evaluating security solutions there are two main categories of information sources available; directly and indirectly observable sources. Directly observable or empirical and experience sources are sources that either have access to empirical information or that have directly observed a phenomena. Such sources have not been biased by human opinions, meaning that the source has gained knowledge and experience by observing actual events. Indirectly observable or interpreted sources includes sources that have indirectly observed a phenomena, such as subjective expert judgments or other types of interpreted information.

Commonly used directly observable information source are real-time information sources, such as Intrusion Detection Systems (IDS), log-files from firewalls, internet gateways (routers) and honeypots [16]. Other directly observable sources are company experience repositories, public experience repositories, domain knowledge, recommendations (best practices) and related standards. Examples of public repositories are the quarterly reports from Senter for Informasjonssikkerhet (SIS) in Norway, incident and security reports and white papers from CERT, NIST, NSA and CSO, reports from the Honeynet-project [17] and other attack trend reports.

For security solution evaluation two types of indirectly observable sources are commonly used; subjective expert judgment and interpreted expert information. In subjective expert judgment the experts have directly gained knowledge and experience that they use when providing information. Interpreted expert information refers to events observed by a third party, such as another expert or a directly observable source, and given as a recommendation. In such cases, the expert interprets the information given by other sources before providing the information.

3 Determining Information Source Relative Trustworthiness

Determining information source relative trustworthiness, in the trust-based performance approach for aggregating information for security solution evaluation, is done using two trust variables: (1) knowledge level and (2) level of expertise. Before describing the trust variables and explain how they are used to determine information source relative trustworthiness, we look into what is meant by the notion of trust.

The definition of trust and distrust used in the trust-based performance aggregation approach is modified from Ray and Chakraborty (2005) [15].

Trust is the firm belief in the competence of an information source *to provide accurate and correct information* within a specific context.

Distrust is the firm belief in the incompetence of an information source *to provide accurate and correct information* within a specific context.

As can be seen by the definitions, trust is specified in relation to a particular context and might exist in some situations and not in others, as described in the *x*Trust framework by Branchaud and Flinn (2004) [4]. Trust context describes the environment, purpose, assumptions and validity of a trust relationship. The way the trust context is specified might include a variety of variables, as well as vary from case to case depending on the trust purpose, as discussed in [4]. We will not elaborate more on the trust context in this paper, but rather assume that the trust context is specified in such a way that the available information can be combined. However, the reader should note that information from different information sources cannot directly be combined in situations where the trust context differs.

A trust relationship is usually established for some purpose between an truster A and a trustee B, and are valid in a particular time frame. A trust relationship is furthermore established under some assumptions, for a particular case in a particular environment. However, when determining the relative trustworthiness of information sources it is the information source's ability that is measured, and not an external entity's degree of trust in the information source.

3.1   Knowledge Level

The trust variable *knowledge level* are used to determine the level of domain knowledge of an information source, which is measured in terms of *knowledge score*. Knowledge in this context covers facts and experience that an information source has obtain in some way, most often through either education or professional work situations. The level of knowledge is clearly a subjective measure and should therefore be assessed not only by the information source itself, but also by the evaluator or a third party that has sufficient overview of both the education and work experience for the information source, as well as being sufficiently aware of the purpose of the information that the information source is providing.

The relative knowledge score for an information source are determined by establishing a general domain relation model, specify the knowledge domain relation model for the information source and then comparing this model with the general knowledge domain model. Estimating the relative weight from the comparison might be done in a variety of ways. In the example in Section 4 we use a score-based approach that are fairly simple, but that makes it easy to observe the effects of changing any of the domain models. The knowledge score is denoted K_i, where i represent information source number i.

Figure 1 shows a general reference knowledge domain model consisting of four domains. This domain model describes which knowledge domains that are relevant when evaluating security solutions, as well as specify the internal relations or relative weight/importance between the knowledge domains. In Section 4 we give an example of a reference knowledge domain model, information source knowledge domain models and how to compare the two models to derive at the knowledge score.

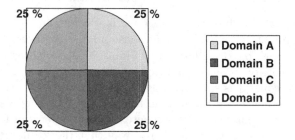

Fig. 1. General reference knowledge domain model

As mentioned earlier, each knowledge domain have a particular importance w_{imp} and coverage c_{cov} for the security solution evaluation being performed. Both the importance and coverage weights might be assigned by any of the involved stakeholders, standards, regulations, the evaluator or similar. The knowledge domain importance is modelled as the one-dimensional array $w_{imp} = [w(1), ...w(j), ..., w(m)]$, where w_j represent the importance weight for knowledge domain j, which stores these knowledge domain importance weights. The coverage is similarly modelled as the one-dimensional array $c_{cov} = [c(1), ..., c(j), ..., c(m)]$. The values of these arrays might be specified in the trust context or given during the evaluation process. It is often hard to assign $w(j)$ and $c_{(j)}$ before the stakeholders or evaluator have gained sufficient overview of the involved knowledge domains.

The importance and coverage weight for knowledge domains are part of the knowledge domain relative score model, which are used to compute the knowledge score for the knowledge domain involved in the security solution evaluation. The knowledge score is determined using (3), which multiplies each knowledge domain importance weight, derived using (1), with the coverage for each knowledge domain, derived using (2). The results are then normalised over the set of knowledge domains in (5) using the knowledge domain normalisation factor $f_{knowledge}$ derived in (4).

Knowledge domain relative score model is used to derive the relative score for each knowledge domain involved in a particular security solution evaluation.

$$w_{imp} = [w(1), ..., w(j), ..., w(m)] \tag{1}$$

$$c_{cov} = [c(1), ..., c(j), ..., c(m)] \tag{2}$$

$$P_{Kscore}(K(j)) = \sum\nolimits_{j=1}^{m} \frac{c(j) \times w(j)}{m} \tag{3}$$

$$f_{knowledge} = \frac{1}{\sum_{j}^{m} K(j)} \tag{4}$$

$$P_{relativeKscore}(K(j)) = f_{knowledge} \times K(j) \tag{5}$$

The subjective nature of assessing knowledge has some problems, such as e.g. that it requires a large amount of experience on the abilities of an information source for a third party to assess its knowledge domains accurately. We are therefore working on establishing a set of calibration variables for the level of knowledge variable. Calibration variables in this context could e.g. be in terms of several questions targeting the same issue, but formulated in such a way that their answers would contradict if not answered accurately enough. This is a well known method used during interrogations in crime investigation.

3.2   Level of Expertise

The second trust variable, *level of expertise*, are used to determine the relative level of expertise for an information source in relation to a particular security

Table 1. Example seed/calibration variables for determining the *level of expertise*

Variables	Categories
level of expertise	low, medium and high
age	under 20, 20-25, 25-30, 30-40, 40-50, over 50
years of relevant education	1 year, 2 years, Bsc, Msc, PhD, other
years of education others	1 year, 2 years, Bsc, Msc, PhD, other
years of experience from industry	1-3 years, 5 years, 5-10 years, 10-15 years, over 15 years
years of experience from academia	1-3 years, 5 years, 5-10 years, 10-15 years, over 15 years
role experience	database, network management, developer, designer, security management and decision maker

solution evaluation. As for *knowledge level*, the level of expertise is measured in terms of a score, in this case called *expertise score*. This expertise score is determined based on seed/calibration variables, which are assessed using a information source level of expertise questionnaire. Table 1 shows an example questionnaire containing an example set of seed/calibration variables. The associated categories for each of the seed/calibration variables are used to determine, in addition to the knowledge level, the relative trustworthiness for an information source. The reader should note that the categories used in this paper serves the purpose of being an example. The demonstration of its use is given in the example described in Section 4.

To determine the weight that should be given to each of the seed/calibration variables, the relative importance of each of the variables for the security evaluation being performed need to be determined. The relative importance for the calibration variables are modelled as the one-dimensional array $w_{imp} = [w(1), \ldots, w(k), \ldots, w(l)]$, where $w(k)$ refers to calibration variable for determining level of expertise number k and l is the number of calibration variables, as described in (6). Importance in this context relates to how essential or critical a particular calibration variable are for the ability of the information source to provide accurate and correct information. These importance weight might be provided as part of the trust context, but are also often provided during the security solution evaluation. The values might also be updated whenever new information becomes available.

During an security solution evaluation appropriate values for the calibration variables for each information source is provide. Because these variables are used to describe the information source, the values might be provided either by the information source or by a third party. Third party, in this context, does not refers to some other entity providing recommendation on a particular entity, as described in [15], but are represent knowledge and experience related to the information source. These values are then inserted into the calibration variable value array, which is modelled as the one-dimensional array

$c_{exp} = [c(1), \ldots, c(k), \ldots, c(l)]$, where $c(k)$ refers to the provide value for calibration variable number k and l is the number of calibration variables, as described in (7).

The calibration variable score for an information source is then determined using (8), which multiplies each calibration variable importance weight from (6) with the belonging value from (7). The results are then normalised over the set of calibration variables in (10) using the knowledge domain normalisation factor $f_{experience}$ derived in (9).

Expertise level relative score model is used to derive the relative score for each seed/calibration variable from the level of expertise questionnaire used in a particular security solution evaluation.

$$w_{imp} = [w(1), \ldots, w(k), \ldots, w(l)] \qquad (6)$$

$$c_{exp} = [c(1), \ldots, c(k), \ldots, c(l)] \qquad (7)$$

$$P_{Escore}(E(k)) = \sum_{k=1}^{l} \frac{c(k) \times w(k)}{l} \qquad (8)$$

$$f_{expertise} = \frac{1}{\sum_{k}^{l} E(k)} \qquad (9)$$

$$P_{relativeKscore}(E(k)) = f_{expertise} \times E(k) \qquad (10)$$

As for the level of knowledge variable, estimating an information source's level of expertise also have a high risk of bias. However, in this case one use a set of calibration variables, rather than a subjective evaluation, to estimate the level. This still does not represent an "objective" assessment because the relations between these variables is not always modelled accurately (and in this case, not at all). Aspects that might be of importance is to examine if their are any difference in relative importance between *years of experience from industry* and *years of experience from academia*. E.g. does one year from the industry have more influence on the expertise level than one year in academia, or visa versa. Another important aspect is to look into how the different age groups assess their own perceived *level of expertise*. These issues are part of an controlled experiment that we are currently performing.

3.3 Estimating Information Source Relative Trustworthiness

The result from the two trust variables; the knowledge and expertise score, is combined when estimating the information source relative trustworthiness using the estimate relative IS trustworthiness model. The initial trustworthiness is computed by the initial trustworthiness function $T(i)$, where i refers to information source number i and n is the number of information sources. This initial weight is derived by combining the relative knowledge and experience score for information source i. ε is the error function, which is used to neutralise any over and underestimation, and represent the models ability to capture experience gained on the use of the information source i. We will not elaborate more on this, but merely make the reader aware that this issue is handled in other parts of the trust-based performance aggregation approach. More information on the problem of under and overestimation or elicitation of expert judgments in general can be found in e.g. Cooke (1991) [9], Goossens et al. (2000) [11], Cooke Cooke and Slijkhuis (2003) [8] and similar sources.

After deriving the trustworthiness weight for each information source in (11), the weights need to be normalised. Normalisation is done in (12) and the relative trustworthiness normalisation factor $f_{relativeTrustw}$ is derived. The initial trustworthiness weights for each information source is then updated in (13).

Estimate relative IS trustworthiness model is used to combine the knowledge and expertise score such that the information source relative trustworthiness is derived.

$$T(i) = \sum_{j=1}^{m} \left(P_{relativeKscore}(j) \times K(j) \right) + \sum_{k=1}^{l} \left(P_{relativeEscore}(k) \times E(k) \right) - \varepsilon$$
(11)

$$f_{relativeTrustw} = \frac{1}{\sum_{i=1}^{n} T(i)}$$
(12)

$$T_{Trustw}(i) = T(i) \times f_{relativeTrustw}$$
(13)

$$T_{relativeTrustw}(i) = \frac{1}{\sum_{i=1}^{n} T_{Trustw}(i)}$$
(14)

Because the relative weight are normalised, trustworthiness is expressed with values in the range $[0, 1]$. The value 0 means no trustworthiness. Values close to 0 expresses little trustworthiness and values close to 1 describe high trustworthiness. Unknown trustworthiness can also be expressed, but is not covered here. However, the symbol $\perp$ is used to express such situations.

Whenever using the relative trustworthiness weight to evaluate a security solution, the relative trustworthiness weights are first combined with the information each of the information sources has provided, and then normalised over the number of information sources.

4   Example of Determining Information Source Relative Trustworthiness in Security Solution Evaluation

We use a .Net e-commerce system to demonstrate how to derive the relative trustworthiness for information sources using the two trust variables. The information sources included in this example are the directly observable information source log-files from a honeypot and four domain experts, which are indirectly observable or interpreted information sources.

Consider the login service of the .NET e-commerce platform prototype developed by the EU-project ACTIVE [10]. To access any of the services in the platform users must login. Users login using a web browser on their local machine. The browser communicates with a web server unencrypted over the Internet using the http protocol. For more details on the login mechanism the reader is referred to Houmb et al. (2005) [12].

Typical security threats for such a login service are different types of denial of service (DoS) attacks, such as TCP SYN flooding [6] and IP spoofing attacks [5].

A potential security solution for these type of attacks is a patch to the network stack software that keeps track of the state of sessions. This is done by first sending a cookie to the client, and then removing the pending connection. If the client does not respond within a short period of time, the cookie expires and the client must re-start the request for a connection. If the client responds in time, the SYN-ACK message is sent and the connection is set up. Adding the cookie message makes it unlikely that an attacker can respond in time to continue setting up the connection. The cookie will expire on the server, and the connection attempt is closed. If the client address has been spoofed the client will not respond in any event.

Another security solution for these two DoS attacks is a filtering mechanism, which is depicted in Figures 2 and 3. The filtering mechanism has an outbound and inbound part that checks the source address, srcAddr, against a set of accepted source IP addresses stored in internalNetAddr. Rather than adding control through the additional cookie, the filtering mechanism is implemented on the server side (usually on a firewall or an internet router) and configured to block unauthorised connection attempts.

To evaluate these two security solutions the directly observable source real-time data from a honeypot and the indirectly observable information source expert opinions from 18 domain experts were used. The honeypot was set up to reflect the configuration of the .NET e-commerce platform (Windows NT 4.0 operating system and IIS 4.0). As a second layer of logging the Intrusion Detection System (IDS) Snort were used. For more information on the honeypot and its configuration the reader is referred to Østvang (2003) [14]. The group of

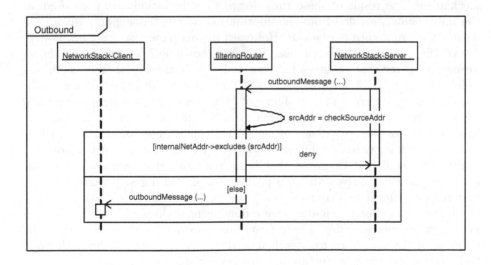

Fig. 2. Filter mechanism outbound

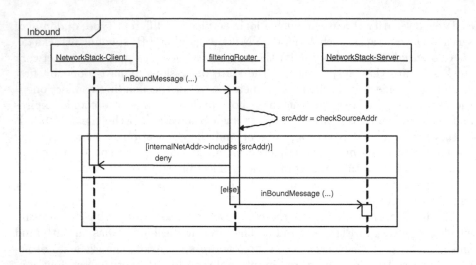

Fig. 3. Filter mechanism inbound

experts used were undergraduate students at Norwegian University of Science and Technology. Further information on the collection of expert judgments is provided in Houmb et al. (2004) [13].

For the honeypot information source only the connection attempts to TCP port 80, which is intended for the web server, were considered. Logging was done for the same amount of time, 24 hours, for the three different configurations: (a) system without any security solutions, (b) system with the patch to the network stack software; the cookie solution and (c) system with the filtering mechanism. The result of these three logging configurations are then used, as the information provided from the information source "honeypot", when evaluating the two security solutions. However, in this paper we focus on how to derive the relative trustworthiness. Because "honeypot" is an observable information source that observes fact, we assign to it the initial trustworthiness weight $T_{honeypot} = 1''$ according to (13). The value 1 indicates that the evaluator has complete trust in the ability of "honeypot" to provide accurate and correct information on number of DoS attacks. This means that the evaluator has a set of positive experience of using "honeypot". For information on how to derive such an trust weight the reader is referred to Ray and Chakraborty (2004) [15]. It should be noted that honeypots and IDSs are subject to the problem of false positives and the problem of simulating sufficiently realistic system environment and use.

Elicitation of expert judgments were done using a simple knowledge and expertise score questionnaire. The information provided on each expert for the variables in the questionnaire was then used to derive the knowledge and expertise score as described in Section 3.1 and Section 3.2. Due to space restrictions only the judgment from 4 of the 18 experts are included. For discussion on problems and possible biases related to the procedure of collecting expert judgment

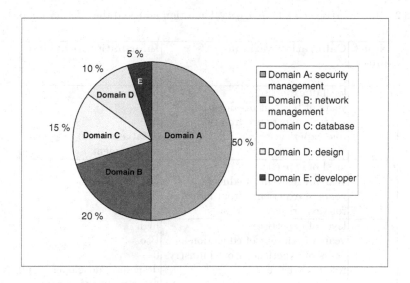

Fig. 4. The reference knowledge domain relation model for the example

the reader is referred to Cooke (1991) [9] and Goossens et al. (2000) [11] and similar sources.

As described in Section 3.1 the knowledge score for an information source is determined by comparing the information source knowledge domain models with the reference knowledge domain model. The reference knowledge domain model is created by identifying the relevant knowledge domains and assessing their internal relative importance. Here the relevant knowledge domains are; security management, design, network manager, database and developer. Figure 4 shows the four knowledge domains and their internal relative importance. For demonstrational purpose the focus is put on the result of the identification, rather than discussing techniques that can be used to identify these knowledge domains.

In this example a domain expert, one of the authors, that was not part of the expert judgment panel, performed the identification based on prior experience in the domain of secure system development. Due to the subjective nature of this assessment potential biases need to be assessed. We are currently working on establishing alternative and more "objective" techniques for knowledge domain identification.

The knowledge domains coverage for each expert is: 80 percentages on security management and 15 percentage on database for expert 4. 100 percentages on database for expert 6. 60 percentages for design, 30 percentages on developer and 10 percentages for security management for expert 15. 100 percentages on developer for expert 18. The knowledge level for each expert is computed using the knowledge domain relative score model from Section 3.1 and (11) from the estimate relative IS trustworthiness model.

Table 2. The expertise and knowledge level questionnaire and the information provided

Expert number	Calibration variable	Information provided
4	level of expertise years of relevant of education years of experience from industry role experience	medium Bsc 0 database and security management
6	level of expertise years of relevant of education years of experience from industry role experience	low Bsc 0 database
15	level of expertise years of relevant of education years of experience from industry role experience	high Bsc 0 designer, developer and security management
18	level of expertise years of relevant of education years of experience from industry role experience	low Bsc 0.5 developer

For expert 4, 6, 15 and 18 the initial knowledge score $K(4)$, $K(6)$, $K(15)$ and $K(18)$ are (the values are divided by 100 to make the computation more tractable):

$$P_{Kscore}(K(4)) = (50 \times 85) + (15 \times 15) = 4475/100 \approx 45$$
$$P_{Kscore}(K(6)) = (100 \times 1) = 1500/100 = 15$$
$$P_{Kscore}(K(15)) = (60 \times 10) + (30 \times 5) + (10 \times 50) = 1250/100 \approx 13$$
$$P_{Kscore}(K(18)) = (100 \times 5) = 500/100 = 5$$

Normalising the result is done using (4) to derive the normalisation factor $f_{knowledge}$ and (5) to update the knowledge scores. Using (4) gives $f_{knowledge}$ = 0.013 and the updated approximated knowledge scores are: $K_{relativeKscore}$ (4) = 0.6, $K_{relativeKscore}(6)$ = 0.2, $K_{relativeKscore}(15)$ = 0.19 and $K_{relativeKscore}(18) = 0.01$.

The level of expertise for each information source are derived using the calibration variables in Table 2. In this example we use three of the seed/calibration variables to determine level of expertise; *level of experience, years of relevant education* and *years of experience from industry*. For the calibration variable *level of experience* the importance weights using (6) are $w_{imp}(low) = 0.2$, $w_{imp}(medium) = 0.5$ and $w_{imp}(high) = 1.0$. For the calibration variable *years of relevant education* the importance weight are $w_{imp}(Bsc) = 0.2$. For the calibration variable *years of experience from industry* the importance weight is $w_{imp}(per_y ear) = 0.2$ for each year of industrial experience.

Using (8) the initial expertise level scores $P_{Escore}(E(k))$ are derived: $P_{Escore}(E(4)) = 0.5$, $P_{Escore}(E(6)) = 0.2$, $P_{Escore}(E(15)) = 1.0$ and $P_{Escore}(E(18)) = 0.02$.

These initial expertise level scores are then normalised by first determining the expertise level normalisation factor using (9), which gives $f_{expertise} = 0.6$. Then the expertise level scores are updated in (10), which gives the approximate scores $P_{Escore}(E(4)) = 0.3$, $P_{Escore}(E(6)) = 0.19$, $P_{Escore}(E(15)) = 0.6$ and $P_{Escore}(E(18)) = 0.01$.

Finally, we use the estimation relative IS trustworthiness model to derive the information source relative trustworthiness. In this model one first determine the initial trustworthiness using (11), which gives the approximated values: $T(honeypot) = 1.0$, $T(4) = 0.2$, $T(6) = 0.04$, $T(15) = 0.1$ and $T(18) = 0.01$. The second step in the model is to find the relative trustworthiness normalisation factor using (12), and the third step is to derive the initial information source relative trustworthiness using (13) and normalising the result in (14). This gives $f_{relativTrustw} = 0.7$. The resulting trustworthiness score for the information source "honeypot" is $T_{relatveTrustw}(honeypot) = 0.7$. The resulting trustworthiness score for expert 4, 6, 15 and 18 are: $T_{relatveTrustw}(expert4) = 0.1$, $T_{relatveTrustw}(expert6) = 0.1$, $T_{relatveTrustw}(expert15) = 0.1$ and $T_{relatveTrustw}(expert18) = 0.0$.

As can be seen by the result, these information source relative trustworthiness reflects the information provided on each source's knowledge domains and level of expertise. E.g. expert 1 has two knowledge domains where one of the domains is security management, which are assigned a high level of importance. Expert 1 also has medium level of expertise. It is therefore reasonable that expert 1 are given a higher trustworthiness score than expert 18, because expert 18 have a low level of expertise and one knowledge domain for which are given a low level of importance. As also can be seen by the result, we are not able to distinguish between expert 4, 6 and 15. This is also reasonable taking into account that their knowledge domains and level of expertise combined equals out the differences.

In security solution evaluation these information source relative trustworthiness weights are combined with the information each of the sources provide, which in this example gives the estimated security solution effect.

5   Related Work

There exist a variety of trust models. However, many of these models are designed for establishing trust relationships between entities for exchange of particular information in an distributed setting, such as e.g. encryption keys or session keys. In these cases trust is measured using binary entities, such as total trust or no trust. Example of more flexible trust models is the vector trust model developed by Ray and Chakraborty [15], ^{X} Trust developed by Branchaud and Flin [4] and the BBK metric developed by Beth, Borcherding and Klein [3].

However, our work does not concern entities that engage in information exchange in distributed networks or other system environments. The relative trustworthiness in our model relates to information sources providing information in security solution evaluation. The information sources are mostly domain experts of some kind, and the trustworthiness is not a measure of the value of the trust relationship between a truster and some trustee, as describe in [15], but between the trustees by examine their level of knowledge and experience related to the security solutions that are being evaluated. One might use any other trust model to derive the relative measures of trust. We have, however, focused on capturing how an evaluator works when assessing security targets, such at what kind of information are being used, how are the information being used etc., and therefore our model can be used to aid such processes.

6   Conclusion

The paper describes how to derive information source relative trustworthiness for security solution evaluation. The relative trustworthiness for each information source is determined using the two trust variables (1) knowledge level and (2) level of expertise. An information source's knowledge level is measured using a knowledge score, while the level of expertise is measure using a expertise score.

It is important to note, however, that the derived relative trustworthiness of information sources still merely represent the combination of domain knowledge and human interpretation of what is important to take into consideration in a particular security solution evaluation. This means that the construction of the knowledge domain models and the assessment of the level of expertise are critical for the correctness of the results.

Further work includes implementing the approach using Bayesian Belief Networks (BBN). BBN handle large scale conditional probability computations and allows for reason under uncertainty. More information the reader is referred to Houmb et al. (2005) [12].

References

1. Australian/New Zealand Standards. AS/NZS 4360:2004 Risk Management, 2004.
2. Australian/New Zealand Standards. HB 436:2004 Risk Management Guidelines – Companion to AS/NZS 4360:2004, 2004.
3. T. Beth, M. Borcherding, and B. Klein. Valuation of trust in open networks. In *Proceedings of ESORICS 94*, November 1994.
4. M. Branchaud and S. Flinn. xTrust: A Scalable Trust Management Infrastructure. In *Proceedings of the Second Annual Conference on Privacy, Security and Trust (PST 2004)*, pages 207–218, October 14-15 2004.
5. CERT Advisory CA-1995-01.   IP Spoofing Attacks and Hijacked Terminal   Connections,   September   1997.   CERT   Coordination   Centre, http://www.cert.org/advisories/CA-1995-01.html.
6. CERT Advisory CA-1996-21. TCP SYN flooding and IP spoofing attacks, November 2000. CERT Coordination Centre, http://www.cert.org/advisories/CA-1996-21.html.

7. ISO 15408:1999 Common Criteria for Information Technology Security Evaluation. Version 2.1, CCIMB–99–031, CCIMB-99-032, CCIMB-99-033, August 1999.
8. R.M. Cooke and K.A. Slijkhuis. Expert Judgment in the Uncertainty Analysis of Dike Ring Failure Frequency. *Case Studies in Reliability and Maintenance*, pages 331–350, 2003.
9. Roger M. Cooke. *Experts in Uncertainty: Opinion and Subjective Probability in Science.* Oxford University Press", 1991.
10. EU Project EP-27046-ACTIVE. EP-27046-ACTIVE, Final Prototype and User Manual, D4.2.2, Ver. 2.0, 2001-02-22., 2001.
11. L.H.J. Goossens, F.T. Harper, B.C.P. Kraan, and H. Metivier. Expert Judgement for a Probabilistic Accident Consequence Uncertainty Analysis. *Radiation Protection and Dosimetry*, 90(3):295–303, 2000.
12. S. H. Houmb, G. Georg, R. France, J. Bieman, and J. Jürjens. Cost-Benefit Trade-Off Analysis using BBN for Aspect-Oriented Risk-Driven Development. In *Proceedings of Tenth IEEE International Conference on Engineering of Complex Computer Systems (ICECCS 2005), Shanghai, China*, pages 195–204, June 2005.
13. S. H. Houmb, O. A. Johnsen, and T. Stalhane. Combining Disparate Information Sources when Quantifying Security Risks. In *1st Symposium on Risk Management and Cyber-Informatics (RMCI'04)*, July 2004.
14. M. E. Østvang. The honeynet project, Phase 1: Installing and tuning Honeyd using LIDS, 2003. Project assignment, Norwegian University of Science and Technology.
15. I. Ray and S. Chakraborty. A Vector Model of Trust for Developing Trustworthy Systems. In P. Samarati, P. Ryan, D. Gollmann, and R. Molva, editors, *Proceedings of the 9th European Symposium on Research in Computer Security (ESORICS 2005)*, pages 260–275, 13–15 September 2004.
16. L. Spitzner. *Honeypot – tracking hackers.* Addison-Wesley, 2003.
17. The Honeynet Project. The web page for The Honeynet Project. http://www.honeynet.org/. Accessed 27 November 2005.

Trust-Based Route Selection in Dynamic Source Routing

Christian D. Jensen[1] and Paul O Connell[2]

[1] Informatics & Mathematical Modeling,
Technical University of Denmark
Christian.Jensen@imm.dtu.dk
[2] Department of Computer Science,
Trinity College Dublin

Abstract. Unlike traditional mobile wireless networks, ad hoc networks do not rely on any fixed infrastructure. Nodes rely on each other to route packets to other mobile nodes or toward stationary nodes that may act as a gateway to a fixed network. Mobile nodes are generally assumed to participate as routers in the mobile wireless network. However, blindly trusting all other nodes to respect the routing protocol exposes the local node to a wide variety of vulnerabilities. Traditional security mechanisms rely on either the authenticated identity of the requesting principal or some form of credentials that authorise the client to perform certain actions. Generally, these mechanisms require some underlying infrastructure, e.g., a public key infrastructure (PKI). However, we cannot assume such infrastructures to be in place in an ad hoc network. In this paper we propose an extension to an existing ad hoc routing protocols, which selects the route based on a local evaluation of the trustworthiness of all known intermediary nodes (routers) on the route to the destination. We have implemented this mechanism in an existing ad hoc routing protocol, and we show how trust can be built from previous experience and how trust can be used to avoid routing packets through unreliable nodes.

1 Introduction

The notion of an ad hoc network is a new paradigm that allows hosts (called nodes) to communicate without relying on a predefined infrastructure to keep the network connected. Most nodes are assumed to be mobile and communication is generally assumed to be wireless. This means that traditional routing protocols are inadequate for ad hoc networks and a number of new routing protocols have been proposed for such networks [1, 2, 3, 4, 5]. Ad hoc networks are collaborative in the sense that each node is assumed to relay packet for other nodes that will in turn relay their packets. Thus, all nodes in an ad hoc network form part of the network's routing infrastructure. The mobility of nodes in an ad hoc network, means that both the population and the topology of the network can be highly dynamic.

In traditional networks, such as the Internet, routers within the central parts of the networks are owned and managed by a few well-known operators. These operators are generally assumed to be trustworthy, and this assumption is mostly justified since their entire business hinges on the preservation of this image of trustworthiness. However, this assumption no longer holds in ad hoc network, where all nodes may belong to users

K. Stølen et al. (Eds.): iTrust 2006, LNCS 3986, pp. 150–163, 2006.

from different organisations and where all nodes may be called upon to route packets for other nodes. Malfunctioning or malicious nodes may disrupt the routing protocol by distributing false routing information to other nodes or by not performing the routing correctly themselves, thereby disrupting service in an area of the ad hoc network. In this paper, we propose a novel security mechanism, for ad hoc routing protocols, that addresses this issue by allowing autonomous nodes to identify and avoid malfunctioning or malicious routers.

Sending packets in an ad hoc network, where the majority of routers[1] may be unknown, entails a certain element of risk and requires the sending node to trust those routers to deliver the packet to the final destination. Since a node may initially know nothing about any other router, this challenge is not unlike the challenge faced by human beings confronted with unexpected or unknown interactions with each other. Human society has developed the mechanism of trust to overcome initial suspicion and gradually evolve privileges. Trust has enabled collaboration amongst humans for thousands of years, so modelling route selection on the notion of trust offers an obvious approach to addressing the security requirements faced by secure routing in ad hoc networks.

We propose a trust-based route selection mechanism where the sending node evaluates the trustworthiness of all known routers on the route to the destination, in order to select which route to use. The freedom of choice depends on the number of available routes and the sending node's knowledge of the routers involved. If a single route exists, the sending node has no choice but to use that route and hope for the best; if, however, multiple routes exist, the sending node may select the route according to some route selection strategy. Different selection strategies may be used: one is to maximise the average trustworthiness of the known routers, possibly considering the ratio between the trustworthiness and the length of the route, another is to avoid untrusted routers, preferring unknown routers over untrusted ones, and a third is to prefer routes through known routers, regardless of their trustworthiness, in order to increase the predictability of the routing protocol. This list is non exhaustive and the experiments reported in this paper focus mainly on the first of these strategies.

We have implemented trust-based route selection as an extension to the dynamic source routing (DSR) protocol [4, 6]. In DSR, all routers on the path from source to destination are enumerated in the packet by the sending node, each router simply forward the packet to the next router in the list, so the sending node knows the identity of all involved routers.

Initially all routers are unknown and a random route is selected. However, every acknowledged packet will increase the sending node's trust in all the routers in the path to the destination, while every retransmission decreases the trust in all the routers, because it is impossible for the sender to know where the problem occurred. The route to the destination is re-calculated if it becomes too unreliable, but the information about all routers is retained since new routes may pass through some of the same routers. This means that trust-based route selection is self-configuring, an important property in ad hoc networks.

---

[1] Routers are simply other nodes in the network, so we use the two terms interchangeably in this paper.

Unlike existing security mechanisms based on a public key infrastructure (PKI) [7, 8] or incentive based schemes based on payments [9, 10], trust-based dynamic source routing does not rely on a trusted third party to certify keys or sell/redeem tokens. Instead, we only need the ability to recognise trustworthy routers. This means that we can "anonymously" identify routers by their public-key as long as they use the same private-key every time they sign a message.

The rest of this paper is organised in the following way: Section 2 presents related work on security in ad hoc networks, Section 3 presents an overview of the Dynamic Source Routing protocol and shows how to incorporate trust in the selection of routes. Section 4 describes our implementation while Section 5 describes the evaluation of our prototype. Section 6 presents directions for our future work and our conclusions are presented in Section 7.

2   Related Work

Trust-based dynamic source routing combine ideas from two active fields of research, namely ad hoc networks and trust management systems. An overview of related work in each of these areas is presented in the following.

2.1   Ad Hoc Networks

Existing work on security in wireless ad hoc networks has largely focused on two main areas: authentication (including key-management) and routing security. The role of authentication is to ensure that the receiving node is the intended recipient, while routing security ensures that messages reach the receiving node.

Authentication in wireless ad hoc networks cannot rely on traditional infrastructure rich solutions, e.g., certificate based authentication using a public key infrastructure. Instead, authentication is either based on a shared secret which is established using a *location-limited channel* [11, 12, 13, 14, 15] or based on a distributed key-management mechanism [5, 16, 17]. Other approaches include *entity recognition* [18] where nodes are recognised without verifying their identity and cryptographically binding public-keys to the network address of nodes in the network [19, 20].

Routing security has received less attention than authentication, but we have identified two proposals that are related to the mechanism presented in this paper.

Marti et al. [21] investigate the ability to identify misbehaving nodes in mobile ad hoc networks. They focus on DSR and propose a mechanism based on the ability of most network interfaces to enter "promiscuous mode" where all received packets are forwarded to the network layer. This enables each node to monitor whether the next node in the source route relays the packet as intended and to report misbehaving nodes back to the sender. This assumes that radio coverage is symmetric, which limits the stations' ability to manage their transmission power independently. Moreover, the authors themselves identify the inability of their mechanism to deal with Byzantine behaviour such as collusion and framing.

The CONFIDANT protocol [22] extends the simple mechanism defined by Marti et al. The protocol relies on feedback (ALARMS) from trusted nodes (friends) in the network. Whenever a node observes that a router does not forward a packet, it sends a ALARM to all its friends and the sender of the packet, warning them about the misbehaving node. Relying on feedback from trusted entities reduces the problem of one node framing another node, but selection of these trusted nodes remain an unsolved problem. In fact, "the reputation system is based on negative experience", so there is no way to bootstrap the system. Trust-based DSR complements the CONFIDANT protocol by providing a mechanism to establish initial trust among nodes in the network.

2.2 Trust Management in Distributed Systems

Research on security in large-scale open network infrastructures, such as the Internet, has exposed implicit assumptions about trust in existing security infrastructures.

Recent research in computer security, attempts to incorporate trust as an explicit component of the security model through trust management systems [23, 24, 25]. However, these trust management systems may help decide whether sufficient trust exists for a given principal to perform a given action, but they ignore the dynamic properties of trust, i.e., how trust is initially formed, and how trust evolves during the life-time of the participating entities.

Trust has also been investigated in the context of public key infrastructures, which lead to the development of such notions as "a trusted path" [26] between certificate authorities in separate administrative domains, a "web-of-trust" among peer-to-peer users [27] and a probabilistic model for reasoning about the benevolence and competence of key servers [28]. Certificate authorities and key distribution centres are supposed to be well-known entities that can be equally trusted by a large community (like a notary), so this research has been limited to the static properties of trust. In general, this research has developed detailed knowledge in a very limited area.

3 Trust-Based Dynamic Source Routing

We have extended the dynamic source routing (DSR) protocol with a route selection strategy based on an evaluation of the trustworthiness of all known nodes on the route to the destination. We chose DSR, because the sending node has to know about all nodes on the route to the destination, so trust-based route selection will be particularly effective in this protocol. However, we believe that trust-based route selection can be added to any ad hoc routing protocol, where the sender is offered the choice of multiple routes to the destination.

3.1 Dynamic Source Routing

Nodes in mobile networks have a finite communication range. For a given node, a subset of all the nodes is expected to be within range. Sending data to one of these nodes is relatively simple, since packets can be routed directly. However, sending data to nodes further removed, involves enlisting the help of intermediate nodes to relay the packet. Dynamic source routing is one of many routing protocols for ad hoc networks that address the problem of relaying packets to remote nodes. We refer the reader to the literature [4, 6] for a more comprehensive description of DSR.

Overview. The dynamic source routing protocol relies on source routing to relay packets from source to destination in an ad hoc network. It establishes these routes on demand, i.e., whenever they are needed to forward a packet to a new destination. Dynamic source routing relies on two separate protocols to dynamically discover new routes and to maintain routes to a dynamic set of remote nodes.

Route Discovery. The *route discovery* procedure involves broadcasting a *route request* to all nodes within communication range. Each such request contains the address of the requesting node and an identifier for the destination node. The request is relayed from each node to all of its neighbouring nodes, continually building a record of the route taken, until such time as it arrives at its destination. Upon doing so, the destination node reverses the recorded route and sends it back to the initiator of the request in the form of a *route reply*. The initiator can now use this route to send packets to any node along the route. The request initiator can receive multiple replies, each one specifying a different route to the same destination. It can use any one of them as the route of choice for sending data to a node along that route.

Route Maintenance. In the route maintenance protocol, every router waits for an acknowledgement from its successor in the route. Routers report unacknowledged packets back to the sending node, so that it may prune the source route at that point and repeat the route discovery procedure.

3.2   Routing Security in DSR

The security characteristics of ad hoc networks are very different from traditional fixed networks. The absence of a fixed/trusted infrastructure means that routers cannot rely on information from trusted servers, such as certificate authorities [11]. Therefore, every node must autonomously decide which route to use to send a packet to a given destination. Moreover, although certificate authorities can sometimes be used to establish the identity of another node, this identity conveys no *a priori* information about the likely behaviour of that node. Therefore, identity alone cannot be used for route selection decisions. This fact excludes the use of most security mechanisms currently in use on the Internet.

Protocol Vulnerabilities. We have identified the following vulnerabilities in the dynamic source routing protocol:

Corrupting the route request packet
   A malicious router can disrupt the dynamic source routing protocol by corrupting the router list in the route request packet, e.g., by adding a non-existing router to the list or removing an existing router from the list.
Spoofing route replies
   A malicious router may send a route reply back to the sending node, pretending that it was the last hop before the destination. It could then pretend to be the destination, or disrupt communication by not relaying the packet; this would result in a black hole [29].

Corrupting payload of relayed packets

A malicious router may try to compromise the confidentiality and the integrity of any packet that it is relaying. It may also perform traffic analysis and try to learn about the location of remote nodes. These problems also exist in fixed networks and a large number of solutions have been proposed. Moreover, these vulnerabilities are not specifically related to the routing protocol, so we do not consider them further in this paper.

Security Goals. As shown above, a malicious router has two ways of disrupting the routing protocol, either by diverting packets in the wrong direction or by attracting and ignoring packets.

Since we cannot assume *a priori* knowledge about the other routers, we cannot expect to completely avoid routing though untrustworthy nodes. Instead, we require the ability to detect malicious or malfunctioning routers and to route packets through alternative routes once such routers have been identified.

3.3   Trust-Based Dynamic Source Routing

In order to accommodate trust-based route selection in DSR, we have to extend DSR with functions that establish and maintain trust in other nodes and modify DSR to include a trust evaluation of all known routers when selecting the source route. These modifications are described in the following sections.

Trust-Based Route Discovery. Dynamic source routing returns a list of routers that should be included as a source route in the header of the packet. We need to recognise these nodes in order to find them in the trust management system and correctly assign a trust value to them. We have modified the route discovery mechanism of DSR, so that every router includes a signed hash value of the source route in the packet that it receives along with its own public-key and its IP-address in the relayed route request message. Thus, the destination node signs the complete source route, which is then returned in the route reply message. This prevents a router from selectively corrupting the route; either all of the routers from a certain point in the preceeding route are removed from the list or none of them.

The sending node adds a signed hash of the source route to every packet, in order to prevent intermediate nodes from corrupting the source route. This signature is only generated once for every source route. However, including the signed hash in every packet may introduce an unacceptable overhead for some applications, e.g., telephony, so we propose that this extension is made optional.

The addition of public-keys and signatures to every entry in the route request message introduces a substantial overhead in the protocol. However, this overhead is mostly confined to the route request message, which we believe to be acceptable. Moreover, the public-keys can be omitted from the route request message and instead obtained through a direct peer-to-peer key-exchange protocol between the sender and every node on the route to the receiver. The sender start by exchanging keys with the first node in the source route. Once this node's signature has been verified, it can be used to relay packets to exchange keys with the second node in the source route, etc.

Trust Formation. There is three basic ways to establish trust in an unknown entity, these are in order of decreasing reliability: personal experience, recommendations and reputation. Personal experience is gained when a node is trusted and it either honours or betrays this trust. It is important to balance risk and trust when building personal experience. A recommendation is a signed assessment of another node's trustworthiness. It is used to introduce a node to other nodes that trust the node that signed the recommendation, thereby accelerating the trust formation process. It is important to note that a recommendation can be issued by any node in the system and that routers make autonomous decisions about whether they trust this recommendation or not, i.e., we do not need a PKI to issue recommendations. This mechanism is similar to the *web-of-trust* in PGP [27]. A node's reputation is a summary of all other nodes' trust in that node. This summary is generated from a combination of recommendations from other, possibly unknown, nodes and from direct observations that a node can make, e.g., if all other nodes route their traffic through a particular node, that node gets a good reputation and it is probably trustworthy.

In order to build personal experience, a node must be able to observe the behaviour of other nodes, i.e., determine the behaviour of other nodes through observable system events. In trust-based routing, the observable event is whether the packet reaches its destination or not, which requires the receiving node to send acknowledgements back to the sender. In order to prevent intermediate nodes from forging acknowledgements, we require the receiving node to sign all acknowledgements. However, we do not need to acknowledge every packet, as long as the sender receives periodic feedback from the receiver. This reduces the overhead of acknowledgements when streaming audio or video across UDP.

Building personal experience is slow at first, when all nodes are unknown, but all packets pass through routers within the range of the sending node, so these nodes will appear in most source routes. Experience gained from routing through these nodes, is then used in subsequent route discoveries, so the trust evaluation process becomes faster and faster as more nodes are known, and untrustworthy nodes can be avoided.

Trust Management. The trust management process deals with maintaining and comparing trust information about other nodes. In order to reduce storage requirements and facilitate comparisons of trustworthiness, routers summarise their observations about other routers into a single value, known as the trust value, for a particular router. Trust values fall in the range [0,1] with the value 0.5 representing an unknown node. Routers with high trust values are assumed to be more trustworthy than routers with low trust values, so trust values can be compared directly by the trust-based route selection strategy.

The trust management system is also responsible for managing the trust life cycle, i.e., initial trust formation, updating trust values based on experience and expiring nodes that are no longer used. Trust that is not maintained through continuous interactions will slowly erode until information about the node can be removed from the trust management system. The delay until a node is removed depends on its trust value at the last interaction. Nodes with very high or very low trust values will remain in the system longer than nodes that are already close to the initial trust value of 0.5. The trust management system can also attribute different weights to experience, recommendations and reputation based on the context and the disposition of the node.

Route Selection. The route selection strategy calculates an aggregate trust value for each of the possible source routes to the destination. These aggregate values are then compared and the optimal source route is selected. The optimality of a particular route selection depends on the context; so different selection criteria may be used by different devices and in different environments.

Stimulating Collaboration. Trust-Based DSR is primarily designed to identify and avoid misbehaving routers. However, we believe that it could also be used to stimulate collaboration among nodes, if routers primarily forward packets from nodes that they trust, e.g., by only forwarding route requests from nodes with a minimum trust value. This means that routers that reliably forward packets from other nodes have a greater probability of getting their own packets forwarded by those same nodes.

3.4   Security Analysis

The sending node can only detect disruption to the routing protocol, by observing that its packets do not reach the intended destination, i.e., it does not receive acknowledgements.

Since none of the other nodes are a priori trusted, the sending node cannot know which router malfunctioned; its only option is to try with another source route. If the second route fails as well, a third route is tried and if that succeeds, there is a high probability that the malfunctioning router belongs to the intersection of the two malfunctioning source routes. The more alternative routes are being used, the more precisely we will be able to pinpoint the malfunctioning router. However, the main goal of the proposed mechanism is not to identify misbehaving routers, so once a reliable source route is found, this route will be used for all subsequent packets, which give reliable routers the opportunity to increase their trust value.

One of the fundamental problems in ad hoc networks is that we cannot assume the presence of a certificate authority, so nodes cannot be reliably authenticated. This means that every node has the ability to change its identity (IP-address and public-key) at will, e.g., immediately after misbehaving. In order to mitigate this risk, the sending node records the time when it first learns of another node; the age of a node's entry in the trust management system can then be taken into account when the trust values are calculated.

4   Implementation

We have implemented a DSR simulator in Java, which allows us to experiment with trust-based route selection in our extension to the dynamic source route protocol.

4.1   Overview

The architecture of our trust-based dynamic source routing system is shown in Figure 1.

The extended functionality of trust-based dynamic source routing has been added as a layer between the application and the DSR protocol. This layer consists of a trust management system and two components that interact directly with the DSR protocol and with each other through the trust management system. These components are described in greater detail in the following.

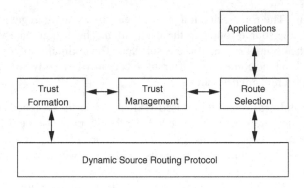

Fig. 1. Trust-based dynamic source routing architecture

4.2   Trust Formation

We dynamically assign a simple numerical trust value to all nodes that we encounter. This value lies in the interval [0,1], where 0 designates an unreliable node and 1 designates a node that reliably forwards all packets. We assume no prior knowledge about the surrounding nodes, so initially all routers have a trust value of 0.5. The trust formation component updates the trust values, in the trust management system, every time a packet is routed through the node. If the packet reaches its destination safely, the trust values of all routers on the route are incremented by a fixed amount; otherwise their trust values are decremented with the same amount. The trust management system ensures that the trust values remain within the specified interval.

4.3   Trust Management

We have implemented a simple trust management system, where a trust value is associated with every node that forms part of the source route. If the node is already known, the current trust value is used; otherwise the default value for unknown nodes is used.

4.4   Route Selection

DSR normally returns a number of routes to the route selection component after sending a route request. The route selection component stores all routes for analysis and selection. For each source route, the route selection component calculates the average trust value for that route and divides it by the number of intermediary nodes, thus favouring shorter routes.

Then, the route with the highest overall value is selected and used for subsequent attempts to send data to that route's destination. If the route fails, the trust-based dynamic source route selection algorithm is restarted.

5   Evaluation

We have used our simulator to evaluate the trust-based source routing protocol using a network consisting of 9 nodes. The topology of the network is shown in Figure 2.

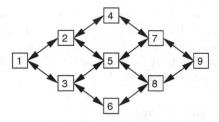

Fig. 2. 9-node network used in the evaluation

While this configuration may appear overly simplistic, it includes all relevant features. In particular, it allows us to examine the benefits of multiple independent paths from sender to receiver and the effects of misbehaviour in some nodes on the trust value of well behaved nodes in the neighbourhood.

The behaviour of each node in the network is configurable and the probability that a router works reliably ranges between 1 (forward all packets correctly) to 0 (corrupt every packet). The main goal of this evaluation is to show that the trust based DSR system correctly identify and avoid untrustworthy nodes.

5.1 Identification of Untrustworthy Nodes

The goal of the initial experiment is to demonstrate that a sending node can identify an untrustworthy node. The simulator is configured so that nodes 4 and 5 corrupt all packets that are routed through them, but all other nodes forward their packet correctly. We sent groups of 5 packets from node 1 to each of the nodes 9, 8 and 7. The trust values of node 1, for each of the nodes in the different routes, are shown in Figure 3.

It can be seen that node 4 is immediately found to be untrustworthy, and that nodes 3, 6 and 8 are identified as trustworthy. It can be seen that later in the experiment node 5 is singled out as being the least trustworthy. In fact, nodes 4 and 5 are equally

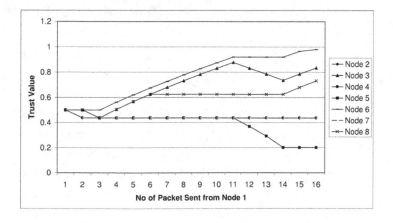

Fig. 3. Change of Node 1's trust values

untrustworthy; we simply have more experience with the untrustworthiness of node 5. The trust values for nodes 2 and 7 are identical to that of node 4, so they are unfairly viewed as being untrustworthy because of their proximity to nodes 4 and 5. An experiment in which packets are sent to all nodes in the network should allow nodes 2 and 7 to be disassociated from nodes 4 and 5.

5.2   Selection of Most Trustworthy Route

The goal of the second experiment is to demonstrate the behaviour of the route selection algorithm and show how it reacts to the trustworthiness of nodes in the network. The same nine-node topology was used, but nodes 4 and 5 have been configured to route 50% of the packets correctly. The experiment monitors the behaviour of the route selection algorithm when 20 packets are passed between nodes 1 and 9. The results of the experiment are shown on Figure 4.

A number of observations can be made from the graph about trust-based route selection. Initially, all nodes have the same trust value (0.5), so route length becomes the determining factor for route selection and the longer routes are avoided. The routes are broken into three groups, which reflect the 3 possible route lengths.

Initially route [1,2,4,7,9] is selected, but node 4 immediately drops the packet. All routes containing these nodes are decremented, the longer routes are able to absorb this reduction more, and so their trust values do not fall at the same rate. The next route selected by the sending node is route [1,3,5,8,9], which initially behaves well but then begins to drop packets. We see a reduction in its trust value from packet 6 to 13. Eventually route [1,3,6,8,9] is selected; this route delivers all packets correctly.

This experiment shows how trust-based route selection adapts to changes in the environment (the reliability of nodes 4 and 5) by discarding unreliable routes. Moreover, it indicates how trust-based route selection will eventually identify a reliable route, if such a route exists, and send all packets using that route. Finally, it shows that, although

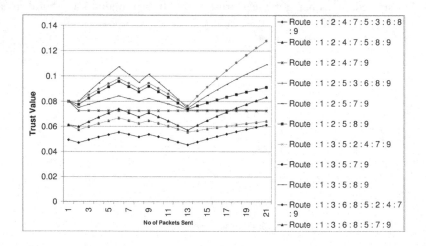

Fig. 4. The change in the route trust value over the number of packets sent

the unreliability of node 5 unfairly devalues the trust value of node 3, the final selection of a reliable route through node 3 eventually revalues this trust value.

6 Future Work

The implementation of trust-based routing, presented in this paper, allows us to expand our work in a number of ways. First, we would like to conduct further experiments with a combination of different route selection strategies, e.g., completely avoiding routes where the trust value of one of the routers is below a certain low watermark. Second, we would like to integrate a recommendation mechanism similar to the CONFIDANT protocol [22]. Third, we plan to extend our implementation with a more comprehensive trust management system (e.g., by replacing our simple trust management system with KeyNote [24]). Fourth, we plan to further investigate the issue of representing and maintaining trust in the form of scalar trust values. Finally we wish to extend our investigation of appropriate feed back mechanisms for building personal experience, in order to determine what events the nodes in the system should monitor.

The sending node's trust value for another router, summarises the sending node's experience with the other router's ability to deliver packets correctly to the destination. It can therefore be considered a subjective measurement of the other node's quality of service and the aggregate value for a particular route may be used to anticipate the quality of service of that particular route. We would like to further investigate the use of trust values for quality of service assessments.

7 Conclusions

Ad hoc networks have unique security characteristics. The fundamental assumption that nothing can be assumed about the underlying infrastructure excludes the use of authentication servers and certificate authorities, which means that existing identity based or credential based security mechanisms cannot be used. We have introduced a mechanism that evaluates the trustworthiness of other nodes based on past experience. The mechanism compares the aggregate values of the trustworthiness of all the routers on alternative routes, in order to select the route with the highest probability of delivery.

Trust-Based route selection represents a radical new approach to computer and network security, where sensitive operations are performed on the basis of trust rather than identity. This facilitates collaboration among nodes in environments that cannot rely on a common trusted third party (certificate authority), such as ad hoc networks.

Our evaluation has shown that trust-based route selection is able to identify a subset of all routers, which contains the unreliable nodes. We have also shown that trust-based routing is able to adapt to changes in the trustworthiness (reliability) of certain nodes. We therefore believe that an evaluation of the trustworthiness of other routers should be an important parameter for route selection in ad hoc networks.

References

1. G. Pei, M. Gerla, and X. Hong, "LANMAR: Landmark routing for large scale wireless ad hoc networks with group mobility," in *Proceedings of IEEE/ACM MobiHOC 2000*, Boston, MA, U.S.A., August 2000, pp. 11–18.
2. G. Pei, M. Gerla, and T.-W. Chen, "Fisheye state routing: A routing scheme for ad hoc wireless networks," in *Proceedings of the IEEE International Conference on Communications*, New Orleans, LA, U.S.A., June 2000, pp. 70–74.
3. C. Perkins and E. Royer, "Ad hoc on-demand distance vector routing," in *Proceedings of the 2nd IEEE Workshop on Mobile Computing Systems and Applications*, New Orleans, LA, U.S.A., February 1999, pp. 90–100.
4. D. Johnson and D. Maltz, "Dynamic source routing in ad hoc wireless networks," in *Mobile Computing*, T. Imielinski and H. Korth, Eds. Kluwer Academic Publishers, 1996.
5. Z. Haas and M. Pearlman, "The zone routing protocol (zrp) for ad hoc networks," Internet-draft, IETF MANET Working Group, June 1999.
6. D. Johnson, D. Maltz, Y.-C. Hu, and J. Jetcheva, "The dynamic source routing protocol for mobile ad hoc networks," Internet-draft, IETF MANET Working Group, March 2001.
7. D. Harkins and D. Carrel, "The internet key exchange (IKE)," Request for comments (RFC), IETF – Network Working Group, November 1998.
8. Telecommunication Standardization Sector of ITU, *Information Technology — Opens Systems Interconnection — The Directory: Authentication Framework*, Number X.509 in ITU–T Recomandation. International Telecomunication Union, November 1993, Standard international ISO/IEC 9594–8 : 1995 (E).
9. L. Buttyán and J.-P. Hubaux, "Nuglets: a virtual currency to stimulate cooperation in self-organized mobile ad hoc networks," Technical Report DSC/2001/001, Department of Communication Systems, Swiss Federal Institute of Technology, Lausanne, 2001.
10. M. Peirce and D. O'Mahony, "Flexible real-time payment methods for mobile communications," *IEEE Personal Communications*, vol. 6, no. 6, pp. 44–55, December 1999.
11. F. Stajano and R. Anderson, "The resurrecting duckling: Security issues for ad-hoc wireless networks," in *Security Protocols: 7th International Workshop*, Cambridge, U.K., April 1999.
12. N. Asokan and P. Ginzboorg, "Key agreement in ad hoc networks," *Computer Communications*, vol. 23, pp. 1627–1637, 2000.
13. D. Balfanz, D. Smetters, P. Stewart, and H. Wong, "Talking to strangers: Authentication in ad hoc wireless networks," in *Proceedings of the 9th Annual Network and Distributed System Security Symposium (NDSS)*, 2002.
14. S. Capkun, J-P. Hubaux, and L. Buttyán, "Mobility helps security in ad hoc networks," in *Proceedings of the 4th ACM International Symposium on Mobile Ad Hoc Networking and Computing (MobiHOC'02)*, Annapolis, U.S.A., June 2003.
15. B. Lehane, L. Doyle, and D. O'Mahony, "Shared rsa key generation in a mobile adhoc network," in *Proceedings of IEEE 2003 MILCOM Conference*, October 2003.
16. J. Kong, P. Zerfos, H. Luo, S. Lu, and L. Zang, "Providing robust and ubiquitous security support for mobile ad hoc networks," in *Proceedings of the 9th International Conference on Network Protocols (ICNP'01)*, November 2001.
17. S. Capkun, L. Buttyán, and J. Hubaux, "Self-organized public-key management for mobile ad hoc networks," *IEEE Transactions on Mobile Computing*, vol. 2, no. 1, 2003.
18. J-M. Seigneur, S. Farrell, C. Jensen, E. Gray, and Y. Chen, "End-to-end trust in pervasive computing starts with recognition," in *Proceedings of the First International Conference on Security in Pervasive Computing*, Boppard, Germany, March 2003., Springer Verlag (LNCS 2802).

19. G. O'Shea and M. Roe, "Child-proof authentication for mipv6 (cam)," *ACM Computer Communication Review*, vol. 32, no. 2, pp. 4–8, 2001.
20. G. Montenegro and C. Castellucia, "Statistically unique and cryptographically verifiable (sucv) identifiers and addresses," in *Proceedings of the 9th Annual Network and Distributed System Security Symposium (NDSS'02)*, San Diego, U.S.A., February 2002.
21. S. Marti, T. Giuli, K. Lai, and M. Baker, "Mitigating routing misbehavior in mobile ad hoc networks," in *Proceedings of the Sixth IEEE/ACM Conference on Mobile Computing and Networks*, 2000, pp. 255–265.
22. S. Buchegger and J.-Y. Le Boudec, "Performance analysis of the confidant protocol: Cooperation of nodes - fairness in distributed ad-hoc networks," Technical Report IC/2002/01, Swiss Federal Institute of Technology, Lausanne, January 2002.
23. M. Blaze, J. Feigenbaum, and J. Lacy, "Decentralised trust management," in *Proceedings of the 1996 IEEE Symposium on Security and Privacy*, May 1996, pp. 164–173.
24. M. Blaze, J. Feigenbaum, J. Ioannidis, and A. Keromytis, "The KeyNote trust management system – version 2," RFC 2704, Internet Engineering Task Force, 1999.
25. Y.-H. Chu, J. Feigenbaum, B. LaMacchia, P. Resnick, and M. Strauss, "REFEREE: Trust management for web applications," *World Wide Web Journal*, , no. 2, 1997.
26. J. Kohl and C. Neuman, "The kerberos network authentication service (V5)," RFC 1510, Internet Engineering Task Force, 1993.
27. S. Garfinkel, *PGP: Pretty Good Privacy*, O'Reilly & Associates, Inc., 1995.
28. U. Maurer, "Modelling a public-key infrastructure," in *Proceedings of the 1996 European Symposium on Research in Computer Security*, 1996, pp. 325–350.
29. F. Wang, B. Vetter, and S. Wu, "Secure routing protocols: Theory and practice," Tech. Rep., North Carolina State University, 1997.

Implementing Credential Networks

Jacek Jonczy and Rolf Haenni

University of Berne,
Institute of Computer Science and Applied Mathematics,
CH-3012 Berne, Switzerland
{jonczy, haenni}@iam.unibe.ch
http://www.iam.unibe.ch/~run

Abstract. Credential networks have recently been introduced as a general model for distributed authenticity and trust management in open networks. This paper focuses on issues related to the implementation of credential networks. It presents a system called CAUTION, which consists of a simple language to define credential networks and an underlying machinery to perform the evaluation. The paper also describes the necessary algorithms in further details.[1]

1 Introduction

Managing trust in large open networks is an emerging topic in different areas such as electronic commerce, public-key cryptography, peer-to-peer technologies, the Semantic Web, and many more. Two principal trust problems arise from the fact that network participants generally do not know each other in person. The first one is related to the *identity* and the second one to the *reliability* of an unknown network participant. We will refer to them as the problems of judging somebody's *authenticity* and *trustworthiness*, respectively.

The common approach to establish (indirect) trust between two unrelated participants is through (direct) trust statements from intermediate participants. Following [1], such statements are called *credentials*. To prevent forgeries, they are required to be digitally signed. There is a distinction between *positive*, *negative*, and *mixed* credentials. A credential referring to somebody's authenticity is called *certificate* (if it is positive) or *revocation* (if it is negative). Similarly, a credential referring to somebody's trustworthiness is called *recommendation* (if it is positive) or *discredit* (if it is negative). *Ratings* are corresponding mixed credentials used for both authenticity and trustworthiness.

In the general (decentralized) case, all network participants are allowed to issue credentials. The resulting collection defines a *credential network*. This is the basis for the derivation of indirect trust. The problem is thus to *evaluate* a given credential network.

---

[1] This research is supported by the Swiss National Science Foundation, project no. PP002–102652, and the Hasler Foundation, project no. 2042. Furthermore, we would like to acknowledge the helpful comments of Michael Wachter.

K. Stølen et al. (Eds.): iTrust 2006, LNCS 3986, pp. 164–178, 2006.

The evaluation method proposed in [1] makes use of the theory of *probabilistic argumentation*. This is a theory of uncertain reasoning which comes up with a pair of values called *degree of support* and *degree of possibility* [2, 3]. These are *probabilities of provability*, which are derived from corresponding sets of *arguments* and *counter-arguments*. In a credential network, arguments and counter-arguments correspond to chains of credentials between the two participants. An algorithm to find these (minimal) chains is described in [1], but it is restricted to positive credentials.

The most important roots of our approach are PGP's web of trust [4] and the deterministic PKI model of Maurer [5]. The latter stands out because of the soundness and clarity of its formalism, however, does not include negative evidence at all. His model has been readopted in [6] and recently extended in [7] by including time issues, revocations, and other things. Another closely related approach is Jøsang's Certification Algebra [8], which is very general in many respects (e.g. opinions as pieces of evidence), but the evaluation mechanism is somehow limited since it may be applied to a certain class of network scenarios only. Other important formal trust models include [9, 10, 11, 12]. Various other approaches for trust and authenticity management have been proposed, e.g. in the areas of e-commerce, reputation systems, and peer-to-peer networks.

This paper is a continuation of [1]. Its contribution is twofold. First, it presents a system called CAUTION, which consists of a simple language to define credential networks and an underlying machinery to perform the evaluation. Second, it describes the necessary algorithms for the general case of positive, negative, and mixed credentials. These are the two main parts of the paper, see Section 3 and 4, respectively. Section 2 gives a short formal introduction to credential networks, Section 5 presents an example, and Section 6 finally concludes the paper.

2   Credential Networks

The model proposed in [1] deals with the particular view of a participant or *user* X_0 of a distributed network. $\mathcal{U}$ denotes the set of other network users in which X_0 is interested in, and $\mathcal{U}_0 = \{X_0\} \cup \mathcal{U}$ is the set of all users including X_0. In the context of a corresponding credential network, X_0 is called *owner*.

From the perspective of X_0, the problem is to judge whether another network user $Y \in \mathcal{U}$ is *authentic* and/or *trustworthy*. To formally describe this, [1] suggests to use two propositions Aut_Y and $Trust_Y$, which are either true or false. Intuitively, Aut_Y means that the available information about Y's identity is authentic. This usually requires a corresponding public key K_Y to belong to user Y [5]. It is assumed that Aut_{X_0} is implicitly true.

The intuition of $Trust_Y$ is that Y behaves in a reliable way. Since there are many different things Y may do (offer a service, issue credentials, etc.), it is possible that Y is reliable in doing one thing but not the other. In this paper, we adopt the simplifying assumption of [1] and use $Trust_Y$ as a general proposition about anything Y may do. Again, it is assumed that $Trust_{X_0}$ is implicitly true.

If we assume that $Y \in \mathcal{U}$ is unknown to X_0, then there is no direct or explicit way of proving the truth or falsity of Aut_Y or $Trust_Y$. The judgment of X_0 must therefore rely upon statements about Y's authenticity and trustworthiness issued by third parties, i.e. by other users $X \in \mathcal{U} \backslash \{Y\}$ of the network. Examples of such statements are:

- *"I am 90% sure that Y is trustworthy."*
- *"I know that Y is not the one she/he claims to be."*
- *"on a scale between 0 and 10, I would rate Y's trustworthiness with 7."*

If statements like this are digitally signed, they are called *credentials*. Note that the use of digital signatures is an important security requirement [1]. A credential is always issued by a user $X \in \mathcal{U}_0$, the *issuer*, and concerns another user $Y \in \mathcal{U}_0$, the *recipient*. Figure 1a depicts a set of credentials as a graph for $\mathcal{U}_0 = \{A, B, C, D\}$. Different arrows represent different credential types (see following subsection).

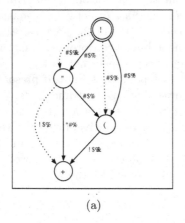

(a)

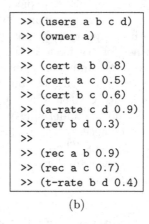

```
>> (users a b c d)
>> (owner a)
>>
>> (cert a b 0.8)
>> (cert a c 0.5)
>> (cert b c 0.6)
>> (a-rate c d 0.9)
>> (rev b d 0.3)
>>
>> (rec a b 0.9)
>> (rec a c 0.7)
>> (t-rate b d 0.4)
```

(b)

Fig. 1. (a) An example of a credential network. Nodes represent users, the owner being emphasized by a double circle. An arrow from X to Y denotes a credential issued by X for Y. (b) Corresponding CAUTION commands, producing the network shown in (a).

2.1 Credentials

There is a general distinction between two *classes* T and A of credentials, depending on whether it is a statement about the trustworthiness or the authenticity of the recipient. The convention is to denote A-credentials issued by X for Y by A_{XY} and T-credentials by T_{XY}. Note that the owner X_0 may as well issue and receive credentials, and issuing self-credentials A_{XX} or T_{XX} is not prohibited.

In addition to the two classes A and T, there is another distinction between three different *signs* $+$, $-$, and $\pm$ for *positive*, *negative*, and *mixed* credentials, respectively. The intuitive idea here is that the issuer of a credential may either want to make a positive or a negative statement about the authenticity or trustworthiness of another network user. A mixed statement can be seen as a *rating*. The combination of classes and signs yields six different credential types:

		Class A	Class T
	+	Certificate	Recommendation
Sign	−	Revocation	Discredit
	±	Authenticity Rating	Trust Rating

Another feature of the model allows the issuer of a credential, by assigning a value $\pi \in [0,1]$, to specify the *weight* of the credential. $\pi = 0$ and $\pi = 1$ are the two extreme cases of minimal and maximal weight, respectively. Formally, a credential is a 5-tuple

$$C = (class, sign, issuer, recipient, weight) \tag{1}$$

with $class \in \{\mathsf{T}, \mathsf{A}\}$, $issuer \in \mathcal{U}_0$, $recipient \in \mathcal{U}_0$, $sign \in \{+, -, \pm\}$, and $weight \in [0,1]$. To distinguish between the two classes, and to make the formal notation more compact, the convention in [1] is to denote A-credentials by

$$A^{sign,weight}_{issuer,recipient} = (\mathsf{A}, sign, issuer, recipient, weight) \tag{2}$$

and T-credentials by

$$T^{sign,weight}_{issuer,recipient} = (\mathsf{T}, sign, issuer, recipient, weight). \tag{3}$$

Sets of A- and T-credentials are denoted by $\mathcal{A}$ and $\mathcal{T}$, respectively. A *credential network* $\mathcal{N}$ owned by user X_0 is defined as a 4-tuple

$$\mathcal{N} = (\mathcal{U}_0, X_0, \mathcal{A}, \mathcal{T}). \tag{4}$$

For a pair of users $X, Y \in \mathcal{U}_0$, each set $\mathcal{A}$ and $\mathcal{T}$ is restricted to include at most one credential $A_{XY} \in \mathcal{A}$ and $T_{XY} \in \mathcal{T}$, respectively. Note that this does not exclude cases in which the sets $\mathcal{A}$ and $\mathcal{T}$ both include a credential between the same issuer X and recipient Y. In other words, X may issue at most one A-credential for Y, but at the same time, X may also issue (at most) one T-credential for Y.

An example of a simple credential network is shown Fig. 1a. It is specified by $\mathcal{U}_0 = \{A, B, C, D\}$, $X_0 = A$, and

$$\mathcal{A} = \{A^{+0.8}_{AB}, A^{+0.6}_{AC}, A^{+0.5}_{BC}, A^{-0.3}_{BD}, A^{\pm0.9}_{CD}\}, \quad \mathcal{T} = \{T^{+0.9}_{AB}, T^{+0.7}_{AC}, T^{\pm0.4}_{BD}\}.$$

Solid arrows are A-credentials, and dotted arrows denote T-credentials. The sign and number attached to an arrow indicate the sign and the weight of the credential.

2.2 Evaluation

For a given credential network, the question that arises now is how to evaluate it. On the basis of the evidence encoded in the network, and with respect to a particular user $X \in \mathcal{U}$, the primary goal is to quantitatively judge the authenticity (of a given public key) and the trustworthiness of X. The judgment should return corresponding values on a continuous scale between 0 and 1. The owner of the credential network may then use this information to decide whether a public key or a service is accepted or not.

The approach proposed in [1] is to translate the credential network into a *probabilistic argumentation system* [2,3]. The main part of a probabilistic argumentation system is a set Σ of propositional sentences describing the available knowledge. The idea thus is to express a given credential network by logical sentences, like in Maurer's model [5].

To illustrate the translation, consider the case of a certificate $A_{XY}^{+\pi} \in \mathcal{A}$. Let A_{XY}^+ be the proposition representing the event that the certificate $A_{XY}^{+\pi}$ holds. Since X may only be partially confident in A_{XY}^+, one can think of it as a random event with a given prior probability $p(A_{XY}^+) = \pi$. In order to use $A_{XY}^{+\pi}$ to logically prove Aut_Y, it is necessary that Aut_X, $Trust_X$, and A_{XY}^+ all happen to be true at the same time. As Maurer pointed out in [5], this can expressed by the logical rule $Aut_X \wedge Trust_X \wedge A_{XY}^+ \rightarrow Aut_Y$. The following table shows the corresponding logical rules for all six credential types [1].

Certificates	Recommendations
(C) $Aut_X \wedge Trust_X \wedge A_{XY}^+ \rightarrow Aut_Y$	(R) $Aut_X \wedge Trust_X \wedge T_{XY}^+ \rightarrow Trust_Y$
Revocations	Discredits
(V) $Aut_X \wedge Trust_X \wedge A_{XY}^- \rightarrow \neg Aut_Y$	(D) $Aut_X \wedge Trust_X \wedge T_{XY}^- \rightarrow \neg Trust_Y$
Authenticity Ratings	Trust Ratings
(CV) $Aut_X \wedge Trust_X \rightarrow (A_{XY}^\pm \leftrightarrow Aut_Y)$	(RD) $Aut_X \wedge Trust_X \rightarrow (T_{XY}^\pm \leftrightarrow Trust_Y)$

The logical rule for a particular credential $C \in \mathcal{A} \cup \mathcal{T}$ is denoted by $\gamma(C)$, i.e. $\Sigma = \{\gamma(C) : C \in \mathcal{A} \cup \mathcal{T}\} \cup \{Aut_{X_0}, Trust_{X_0}\}$ is set of propositional sentences representing a credential network. This is the basis for the evaluation, which consists of two parts. In the first *qualitative* part, the problem consists in finding the sets $Args(Aut_X)$ and $Args(Trust_X)$ of arguments and the sets $Args(\neg Aut_X)$ and $Args(\neg Trust_X)$ of counter-arguments, for which the hypotheses Aut_X and $Trust_X$ become true respectively false. Corresponding sets of minimal arguments $args(Aut_X) = \mu(Args(Aut_X))$ are obtained by applying the minimisation operator μ. Arguments and counter-arguments correspond to chains of credentials between the owner and the participant under consideration. For more details on this we refer to [1]. The necessary algorithms to compute these sets are described in Subsection 4.2.

The second *quantitative* part of the evaluation consists in computing the probabilistic weights of these arguments and counter-arguments. The resulting *degrees of support* $dsp(Aut_X)$ and $dsp(Trust_X)$ are the probabilities that Aut_X respectively $Trust_X$ are supported by arguments. Similarly, the *degrees of possibility* $dps(Aut_X)$ and $dps(Trust_X)$ are the probabilities that $\neg Aut_X$ respectively $\neg Trust_X$ are not supported by arguments, thus the probabilities that Aut_X respectively $Trust_X$ remain possible.

To decide whether to accept or reject the propositions $Trust_X$ and Aut_X of a user X, the owner may define a threshold $\lambda \in [0,1]$ in order to accept

Aut_X whenever $dsp(Aut_X) \geq \lambda$ and $Trust_X$ whenever $dsp(Trust_X) \geq \lambda$. Note that not accepting a hypothesis is not necessarily a reason to reject it. For this, it may be necessary to define another threshold $\eta \in [0,1]$, for which Aut_X is rejected if $dps(Aut_X) \leq \eta$ and similarly for $Trust_X$. Note that $\eta < \lambda$ is a necessary condition to exclude the case of simultaneously accepting and rejecting a hypothesis. If a hypothesis is neither accepted nor rejected, it means that the available information is insufficient to make a decision, i.e. more credentials are needed. This second part of the evaluation will be further discussed in Section 5.

3   The System CAUTION

This section is devoted to a system called CAUTION, which allows the specification, evaluation, and visualization of credential networks.[2] The name CAUTION is is an abbreviation for credential-based authenticity and trust in open networks. The system consists of the following three main components:

I. A description language for the specification of credential networks. The language also contains query commands to start the evaluation and print out the results.

II. A set of algorithms to perform the qualitative and quantitative evaluation with respect to a specified credential network.

III. A visualization environment to obtain a graphical representation of the network.

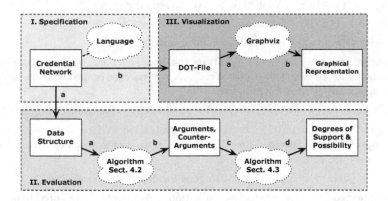

Fig. 2. The CAUTION framework: components and workflow

The structure of the CAUTION system with its main components and workflows is depicted in Fig. 2. An example of a network specification is given in Fig. 1(b). The corresponding graphical representation is depicted in Fig. 1(a). Examples of queries with corresponding outputs will be shown in the course of the paper.

---

[2] Consider the CAUTION website at *http://www.iam.unibe.ch/~run/trust.html*.

The CAUTION language is a simple description language designed for the specification and evaluation of credential networks. There is a distinction between commands for general credentials between two arbitrary users and commands for credentials issued by the owner. The latter may be considered as special cases of the former. The CAUTION language is implemented as a set of Common Lisp macros, i.e. it can easily be executed or integrated in any Common Lisp compatible environment. The following self-explanatory list shows all available CAUTION commands.

(users $<X_1>$ ... $<X_n>$) ::= Creates n new users $X_1, \ldots, X_n$.

(owner $<X>$) ::= Specifies the owner of the network. User X must already exist.

(cert $<X>$ $<Y>$ [$<\pi>$]) ::= Specifies a certificate issued by user X. The recipient is user Y, and π is the (optional) weight of the certificate. If no weight is given, the default weight $\pi = 1$ is assumed. The users X and Y must already exist.

(rec $<X>$ $<Y>$ [$<\pi>$]) ::= Analogous for recommendations.

(rev $<X>$ $<Y>$ [$<\pi>$]) ::= Analogous for revocations.

(dis $<X>$ $<Y>$ [$<\pi>$]) ::= Analogous for discredits.

(a-rate $<X>$ $<Y>$ [$<\pi>$]) ::= Analogous for authenticity ratings.

(t-rate $<Y>$ $<Y>$ [$<\pi>$]) ::= Analogous for trust ratings.

(aut $<Y>$ [$<\pi>$]) ::= Specifies a certificate issued by the owner. The recipient is user Y, and π is the (optional) weight of the certificate. If no weight is given, the default weight $\pi = 1$ is assumed. The users X and Y must already exist. This is an abbreviation for (cert $<X>$ $<Y>$ [$<\pi>$]), where X denotes the owner.

(trust $<Y>$ [$<\pi>$]) ::= Analogous for recommendations.

(negaut $<Y>$ [$<\pi>$]) ::= Analogous for revocations.

(distrust $<Y>$ [$<\pi>$]) ::= Analogous for discredits.

(show-args [$<X_1>$ ... $<X_n>$]) ::= Starts the evaluation and outputs the sets of arguments for each specified user $X_1, \ldots, X_n$. If no user is specified, the sets of arguments are printed for all users.

(show-counter-args [$<X_1>$ ... $<X_n>$]) ::= Analogous for counter-arguments.

(show-dsp [$<x_1>$ ... $<x_n>$]) ::= Starts the evaluation and outputs the degrees of support for each specified user $X_1, \ldots, X_n$. If no user is specified, the degrees of support are printed for all users.

(show-dps [$<x_1>$ ... $<x_n>$]) ::= Analogous for degrees of possibility.

(show-accepted $<\lambda>$) ::= Starts the evaluation and outputs all accepted hypotheses according to the specified threshold λ.

(show-rejected $<\eta>$) ::= Analogous for rejected hypotheses.

The starting point for both the evaluation and visualization is a credential network specified with the aid of the CAUTION language. The execution of the corresponding CAUTION commands produces two types of output: an internal

Common Lisp data structure (step Ia) and a DOT-file[3] (step Ib). Both types of output include all the relevant network data.

The internal data structure is the input for the algorithms to compute the sets of (minimal) arguments and counter-arguments for Aut_X and $Trust_X$ and all specified network users $X \in \mathcal{U}_0$ (steps IIa and IIb). These algorithms will be further discussed in Section 4.2. The sets of arguments and counter-arguments are then the inputs for the algorithms to compute corresponding degrees of support and possibility (steps IIc and IId). Section 4.3 describes a sampling technique to perform this step.

The above-mentioned DOT-file is the interface to the GRAPHVIZ[3] software (step IIIa), which renders the credential network as a directed and weighted multigraph (step IIIb). Several output formats such as PDF or JPEG are supported. The picture in Fig. 1a is an output example generated by GRAPHVIZ.

4   Algorithms

This section is devoted to the main computational problem related to credential networks, namely the problem of finding sets of (minimal) arguments and counter-arguments. General argument finding algorithms are well documented in the literature [3, 13, 14], but the goal here is a special purpose algorithm for the particular type of probabilistic argumentation system obtained from a credential network. This is the main part of this section and the topic of the first two subsections. The last subsection discusses an approach to compute degrees of support and possibility by *Importance Sampling* [16], which is an improvement of the classical Monte-Carlo method.

4.1   General Idea

In Section 2.1, we have seen how to express the meaning of credentials by logical rules [1, 5]. Since the rules for ratings are logically equivalent to corresponding pairs of rules for simple credentials, we only have to deal with the four rules (C), (R), (V), and (D). In these cases, the conjunction on the left hand side of the implication is a sufficient condition for the literal on the right hand side. This means that any combination of arguments for the propositions on the left hand side is an argument for the literal on the right hand side. This is the basic idea of the algorithm described in [1], but it is restricted to positive credentials.

In the general case, it is necessary to consider all logically equivalent rules of the same form, i.e. with a conjunction of literals on the left hand side and a single literal on the right hand side of the implication. In this way, we obtain four different versions for each of the above-mentioned rules. Since we are interested in arguments and counter-arguments for Aut_X and $Trust_X$, only the ones with Aut_X, $\neg Aut_X$, $Trust_X$, and $\neg Trust$ on the right hand side are important. The remaining twelve rules are shown in the following table:

---

[3] DOT is a description language for the specification of arbitrary graphs and GRAPHVIZ is the corresponding rendering tool. See http://www.graphviz.org for details.

Certificates	Recommendations
(C1) $Aut_X \wedge Trust_X \wedge A_{XY}^+ \rightarrow Aut_Y$	(R1) $Aut_X \wedge Trust_X \wedge T_{XY}^+ \rightarrow Trust_Y$
(C2) $Aut_X \wedge \neg Aut_Y \wedge A_{XY}^+ \rightarrow \neg Trust_X$	(R2) $Aut_X \wedge \neg Trust_Y \wedge T_{XY}^+ \rightarrow \neg Trust_X$
(C3) $Trust_X \wedge \neg Aut_Y \wedge A_{XY}^+ \rightarrow \neg Aut_X$	(R3) $Trust_X \wedge \neg Trust_Y \wedge T_{XY}^+ \rightarrow \neg Aut_X$

Revocations	Discredits
(V1) $Aut_X \wedge Trust_X \wedge A_{XY}^- \rightarrow \neg Aut_Y$	(D1) $Aut_X \wedge Trust_X \wedge T_{XY}^- \rightarrow \neg Trust_Y$
(V2) $Aut_X \wedge Aut_Y \wedge A_{XY}^- \rightarrow \neg Trust_X$	(D2) $Aut_X \wedge Trust_Y \wedge T_{XY}^- \rightarrow \neg Trust_X$
(V3) $Trust_X \wedge Aut_Y \wedge A_{XY}^- \rightarrow \neg Aut_X$	(D3) $Trust_X \wedge Trust_Y \wedge T_{XY}^- \rightarrow \neg Aut_X$

Of course, the above-mentioned basic idea is applicable to all twelve cases, i.e. any combination of arguments for the propositions on the left hand side of such a rule is an argument for the literal on the right hand side. Consider now all four cases of certificates, recommendations, revocations, and discredits with the corresponding rules (C1) to (C3), (R1) to (R3), (V1) to (V3), and (D1) to (D3). This leads us to the following theorems:

Theorem C. Let $A_{XY}^+ \in \mathcal{A}$ be a certificate issued by user X for user Y. If $\alpha_X \in Args(Aut_X)$, $\bar{\alpha}_Y \in Args(\neg Aut_Y)$, and $\beta_X \in Args(Trust_X)$, it follows:

1. $\alpha_X \wedge \beta_X \wedge A_{XY}^+ \in Args(Aut_Y)$.
2. $\alpha_X \wedge \bar{\alpha}_Y \wedge A_{XY}^+ \in Args(\neg Trust_X)$.
3. $\beta_X \wedge \bar{\alpha}_Y \wedge A_{XY}^+ \in Args(\neg Aut_X)$.

Theorem R. Let $T_{XY}^+ \in \mathcal{T}$ be a recommendation issued by user X for user Y. If $\alpha_X \in Args(Aut_X)$, $\beta_X \in Args(Trust_X)$, and $\bar{\beta}_Y \in Args(\neg Trust_Y)$, it follows:

1. $\alpha_X \wedge \beta_X \wedge T_{XY}^+ \in Args(Trust_Y)$.
2. $\alpha_X \wedge \bar{\beta}_Y \wedge T_{XY}^+ \in Args(\neg Trust_X)$.
3. $\beta_X \wedge \bar{\beta}_Y \wedge T_{XY}^+ \in Args(\neg Aut_X)$.

Theorem V. Let $A_{XY}^- \in \mathcal{A}$ be a revocation issued by user X for user Y. If $\alpha_X \in Args(Aut_X)$, $\beta_X \in Args(Trust_X)$, and $\alpha_Y \in Args(Aut_Y)$, it follows:

1. $\alpha_X \wedge \beta_X \wedge A_{XY}^- \in Args(\neg Aut_Y)$.
2. $\alpha_X \wedge \alpha_Y \wedge A_{XY}^- \in Args(\neg Trust_X)$.
3. $\beta_X \wedge \alpha_Y \wedge A_{XY}^- \in Args(\neg Aut_X)$.

Theorem D. Let $T_{XY}^- \in \mathcal{A}$ a discredit issued by user X for user Y. If $\alpha_X \in Args(Aut_X)$, $\beta_X \in Args(Trust_X)$, and $\beta_Y \in Args(Trust_Y)$, it follows:

1. $\alpha_X \wedge \beta_X \wedge T_{XY}^- \in Args(\neg Trust_Y)$.
2. $\alpha_X \wedge \beta_Y \wedge T_{XY}^- \in Args(\neg Trust_X)$.
3. $\beta_X \wedge \beta_Y \wedge T_{XY}^- \in Args(\neg Aut_X)$.

The four theorems C, R, V, and D form the computational basis for the algorithms discussed in the next subsection. Formal proofs are given in [15].

In the presence of counter-arguments, it is also necessary to compute sets of possible *conflicts* [3]. With respect to a credential network, computing conflicts is a rather trivial issue (see [15]), which will not be further discussed here.

4.2   Computing Arguments

We are now in a position to discuss the algorithm for the computation of the sets of (minimal) arguments and counter-arguments. The discussion will be based on the following notational conventions. Sets of users receiving a credential C from X will be denoted by $\mathcal{U}_{X \rightarrow}^{A^+}$ (if C is a certificate), $\mathcal{U}_{X \rightarrow}^{T^+}$ (if C is a recommendation), $\mathcal{U}_{X \rightarrow}^{A^-}$ (if C is a revocation), and $\mathcal{U}_{X \rightarrow}^{T^-}$ (if C is a discredit). Similarly, sets of users issuing a credential C for X are written as $\mathcal{U}_{X \leftarrow}^{A^+}$ (if C is a certificate), $\mathcal{U}_{X \leftarrow}^{T^+}$ (if C is a recommendation), $\mathcal{U}_{X \leftarrow}^{A^-}$ (if C is a revocation), and $\mathcal{U}_{X \leftarrow}^{T^-}$ (if C is a discredit). The initially empty sets of arguments will be denoted by $args^*(Aut_X)$, $args^*(Trust_X)$, $args^*(\neg Aut_X)$, and $args^*(\neg Trust_X)$. Finally $args^*(\bot)$ denotes the set of conflicts.

The idea now is to generalize the simple algorithm proposed in [1] to the case of positive and negative credentials. This means that the two recursive procedures addPosAutArg(α,X) and addPosTrustArg(α,X), on which the algorithm in [1] is based, need to be extended and accompanied by two additional procedures addNegAutArg(α,X) and addNegTrustArg(α,X).

a) Arguments. Let us first have a look at the extended versions of the procedures addPosAutArg(α,X) and addPosTrustArg(α,X). In the following, we will describe the former procedure in detail.

The idea of the algorithm is to incrementally fill up the sets $args^*(Aut_X)$ and $args^*(Trust_X)$ according to the theorems C, R, V, and D described in the last subsection. Each recursive call means to add a new argument α to the current set of arguments. At the beginning (line 3), the new argument α is checked for minimality with respect to the current set $args^*(Aut_X)$. If it is not minimal, the procedure stops. If α is minimal, it is added to $args^*(Aut_X)$ and other non-minimal arguments are deleted (line 4). According to the twelve logical rules and the corresponding theorems, the new argument α generates then a cascade of recursive calls (line 6 downward). Note that Aut_X or Aut_Y appears ten times as a positive literal on the left hand side of the twelve logical rules, i.e. addPosAutArg(α,X) includes ten recursive calls. For example, line 6 and 7 in the procedure correspond to the statements (1) and (2) of Theorem C. The situation in the case of addPosTrustArg(α,X) is analogous. On the left hand side of the twelve logical rules, $Trust_X$ or $Trust_Y$ appears ten times as a positive literal, i.e. addPosTrustArg(α,X) contains ten recursive calls as well. The duality between addPosAutArg(α,X), which is shown below, and addPosTrustArg(α,X) is obvious. This allows us to abstain from showing the procedure addPosTrustArg(α,X) explicitly. For more details we refer to [15].

```
 1  procedure addPosAutArg(α, X)
 2  begin
 3  │  if not ∃ α' ∈ args*(Aut_X) such that α' ⊂ α then
 4  │  │  set args*(Aut_X) to μ(args*(Aut_X) ∪ {α})
 5  │  │  for Y ∈ 𝒰_{X→}^{A+} do
 6  │  │  │  for β_X ∈ args*(Trust_X) do addPosAutArg(α ∧ β_X ∧ A_{XY}^+, Y)
 7  │  │  │  for ᾱ_Y ∈ args*(¬Aut_Y) do addNegTrustArg(α ∧ ᾱ_Y ∧ A_{XY}^+, X)
 8  │  │  end
 9  │  │  for Y ∈ 𝒰_{X→}^{T+} do
10  │  │  │  for β_X ∈ args*(Trust_X) do addPosTrustArg(α ∧ β_X ∧ T_{XY}^+, Y)
11  │  │  │  for β̄_Y ∈ args*(¬Trust_Y) do addNegTrustArg(α ∧ β̄_Y ∧ T_{XY}^+, X)
12  │  │  end
13  │  │  for Y ∈ 𝒰_{X→}^{A−} do
14  │  │  │  for β_X ∈ args*(Trust_X) do addNegAutArg(α ∧ β_X ∧ A_{XY}^-, Y)
15  │  │  │  for α_Y ∈ args*(Aut_Y) do addNegTrustArg(α ∧ α_Y ∧ A_{XY}^-, X)
16  │  │  end
17  │  │  for Y ∈ 𝒰_{X→}^{T−} do
18  │  │  │  for β_X ∈ args*(Trust_X) do addNegTrustArg(α ∧ β_X ∧ T_{XY}^-, Y)
19  │  │  │  for β_Y ∈ args*(Trust_Y) do addNegTrustArg(α ∧ β_Y ∧ T_{XY}^-, X)
20  │  │  end
21  │  │  for Y ∈ 𝒰_{X←}^{A−} do
22  │  │  │  for α_Y ∈ args*(Aut_Y) do addNegTrustArg(α ∧ α_Y ∧ A_{YX}^-, Y)
23  │  │  │  for β_Y ∈ args*(Trust_Y) do addNegAutArg(α ∧ β_Y ∧ A_{YX}^-, Y)
24  │  │  end
25  │  end
26  end
```

b) Counter-Arguments. The corresponding procedures responsible for computing counter-arguments follow the same scheme, but they are considerably simpler. This is due to the fact that Aut_Y appears only in the conditions of (C2) and (C3) as a negative literal. Similarly, $Trust_Y$ appears only in the conditions of (R2) and (R3) as a negative literal. Both procedures addNegAutArg(α,X) and addNegTrustArg(α,X) are thus limited to two recursive calls only. In the case of addNegAutArg(α,X), the procedure looks as follows:

```
 1  procedure addNegAutArg(α, X)
 2  begin
 3  │  if not ∃ α' ∈ args*(¬Aut_X) such that α' ⊂ α then
 4  │  │  set args*(¬Aut_X) to μ(args*(¬Aut_X) ∪ {α})
 5  │  │  for Y ∈ 𝒰_{X←}^{A+} do
 6  │  │  │  for α_Y ∈ args*(Aut_Y) do addNegTrustArg(α ∧ α_Y ∧ A_{YX}^+, Y)
 7  │  │  │  for β_Y ∈ args*(Trust_Y) do addNegAutArg(α ∧ β_Y ∧ A_{YX}^+, Y)
 8  │  │  end
 9  │  end
10  end
```

Again, since `addNegTrustArg`(α,X) is fully analogous to `addNegAutArg`(α,X), we abstain from showing it explicitly.

c) Main Procedure. The main procedure `computeArgs` begins with the initialisation of the sets of arguments and counter-arguments to the empty set. The recursive computation of the arguments starts by adding the empty argument $\top$ (the one that is always true) to the sets $args^*(Aut_{X_0})$ and $args^*(Trust_{X_0})$. This reflects the assumption that X_0 is implicitly authentic and trustworthy. The two initial calls are therefore `addPosAutArg`$(\top, X_0)$ and `addPosTrustArg`$(\top, X_0)$. Finally, the conflicts are computed and added to each argument set in order to complete the computation. This step is performed by calling the procedure `addConflicts`, which is a very simple one (see [15] for further details). Once the computation terminates, the procedure returns the sets of minimal arguments for all users $X \in \mathcal{U}_0$ in the credential network. We will see in Section 5 how the sample network of Fig. 1 is evaluated within the CAUTION environment.

```
 1  function computeArgs()
 2  begin
 3      for X ∈ U₀, h ∈ {Autₓ, Trustₓ, ¬Autₓ, ¬Trustₓ, ⊥} do
 4          | set args*(h) to ∅
 5      end
 6      do addPosAutArg(⊤, X₀)
 7      do addPosTrustArg(⊤, X₀)
 8      do addConflicts(args*(⊥))
 9      return {args*(h) : h ∈ {Autₓ, Trustₓ, ¬Autₓ, ¬Trustₓ, ⊥}, X ∈ U₀}
10  end
```

4.3 Computing Degrees of Support and Possibility

Once the sets of minimal arguments have been computed, we can proceed with the quantitative evaluation, thus the computation of degrees of support and possibility for a hypothesis of interest. The problem is to calculate the probabilities of the argument sets $args(h)$, which means to compute the probability of a DNF, a problem that is known to be a hard. The alternative we propose is to approximate the exact solution by applying a technique called *importance sampling* [16].

The algorithm `computeProb` follows a general setting with m ordered, non-exclusive events $E_1, ..., E_m \subseteq U$ (universe) with associated probabilities $p_1, ..., p_m$. The problem is to estimate the probability of the union $E = E_1 \cup ... \cup E_n$. The main idea is the following: instead of sampling uniformly from U, we concentrate on the sets of interest E_i and thus sample uniformly from E. Applying this setting to our problem means to choose an argument $\alpha_i \in args(h)$ according to its probability $p(\alpha_i)$ and then to choose (uniformly) a random sample compatible with α_i. The trial is successful if the sample is not contained in another argument α_j, $j < i$. This procedure is repeated N times. The ratio of successful trials to the total number of trials, multiplied with the sum of probabilities of all involved arguments, gives an estimate for the probability of the entire argument set under consideration. The general algorithm is shown below.

```
 1 function computeProb({E₁,...,Eₘ},{p₁,...,pₘ},N)
 2 begin
 3     set success to 0
 4     for k from 1 to N do
 5         select i randomly with probability pᵢ/∑ᵢ₌₁ᵐ pᵢ
 6         select x ∈ Eᵢ uniformly at random
 7         if ∄ j < i such that x ∈ Eⱼ then set success to success + 1
 8     end
 9     return success/N · ∑ᵢ₌₁ᵐ pᵢ
10 end
```

5   Example

Consider again the credential network of Fig. 1. With respect to user D, there are some arguments and counter-arguments for both Aut_D and $Trust_D$. The following output box shows the arguments obtained by calling (show-args d) and the counter-arguments by calling (show-counter-args d) in the CAUTION environment. Each numbered line denotes a minimal (counter-) argument.

```
>> (show-args d)
USER: D
  args(Aut_D):
     0: ((CERT A C) (CERT C D) (REC A C))
     1: ((CERT A B) (CERT B C) (CERT C D) (REC A B) (REC A C))
  args(Trust_D):
     0: ((CERT A B) (CERT B C) (CERT C D) (REV B D) (REC A B) (REC A C))
     1: ((CERT A B) (CERT A C) (CERT C D) (REV B D) (REC A B) (REC A C))
     2: ((CERT A B) (REC A B) (REC B D))
>> (show-counter-args d)
USER: D
  counter-args(Aut_D):
     0: ((CERT A C) (REC A C) (REV C D))
     1: ((CERT A B) (REV B D) (REC A B))
     2: ((CERT A B) (CERT B C) (REC A B) (REC A C) (REV C D))
  counter-args(Trust_D):
     0: ((CERT A B) (CERT B C) (CERT C D) (REV B D) (REC A B) (REC A C))
     1: ((CERT A B) (CERT A C) (CERT C D) (REV B D) (REC A B) (REC A C))
     2: ((CERT A B) (REC A B) (DIS B D))
```

Assume now that the corresponding degrees of support and possibility have been calculated for the hypotheses Aut_X and $Trust_X$, for all network users $X \in \{A, B, C, D\}$, as shown in the table below. Suppose now the owner A uses two thresholds, namely $\lambda = 0.7$ for accepting a hypothesis and $\eta = 0.6$ for rejecting it. In this case, the hypotheses Aut_B and $Trust_B$ are accepted. The owner may thus consider user B as being trustworthy as well as authentic. A himself receives of course maximal support for both, authenticity and trust, therefore Aut_A and $Trust_A$ are accepted too. On the other hand, only $Trust_D$ is rejected because its degree of possibility is below the threshold. All other hypotheses are left open. In the following table, the values of all accepted and rejected hypotheses are emphasised in bold. In the output box next to it, the values for user D are shown, as returned by the corresponding CAUTION commands.

	A	B	C	D
$dsp(Aut_X)$	**1.000**	**0.776**	0.681	0.384
$dps(Aut_X)$	1.000	0.969	0.969	0.837
$dsp(Trust_X)$	**1.000**	**0.888**	0.663	0.274
$dps(Trust_X)$	1.000	0.986	0.948	**0.589**

```
>> (show-dsp d)
USER: D
   dsp(Aut_D) = 0.384
   dsp(Trust_D) = 0.274
>> (show-dps d)
USER: D
   dps(Aut_D) = 0.837
   dps(Trust_D) = 0.589
```

In Fig. 3(a), pairs of degree of support and degree of possibility are depicted as points in the *opinion triangle* [8]. The right corner stands for $dsp = 1$ (max. support), the left corner stands for $dps = 0$ (min. support), and the top corner means $dps - dsp = 1$ (max. ignorance). The two thresholds are values on the unit interval between *Rejection* and *Acceptance*. Figure 3(b) shows all accepted and rejected hypotheses as returned by the corresponding CAUTION commands.

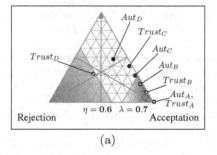

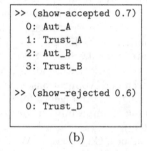

(a)   (b)

Fig. 3. (a) Hypotheses lying within the left subtraingle are rejected, those lying within the right subtraingle are accepted, and the remaining hypotheses are left open. (b) Output of the commands `show-accepted` and `show-rejected`.

6   Conclusion

This paper presents expressive algorithms for the computation of measures for the quantification of user trust as well as public key authenticity in open networks. The recently introduced concept of credential networks serves as the underlying formal model. The algorithms proposed in this paper work for arbitrary credential networks, i.e. where all types of credentials are involved. The resulting degrees of support and possibility state to what extent a user should be regarded as being authentic and trustworthy. A second contribution of this paper is the introduction of the CAUTION system, which provides an interactive environment used for the specification, evaluation, and visualisation of a credential network. Arbitrary networks can be described and evaluated by means of a simple description and query language. Future work will concentrate on a more differentiated trust model. Another goal is to speed up the necessary probability calculation using more efficient data structures.

References

1. Jonczy, J., Haenni, R.: Credential networks: a general model for distributed trust and authenticity management. In PST'05: 3rd Annual Conference on Privacy, Security and Trust, St. Andrews, Canada (2005) 101–112
2. Haenni, R.: Towards a unifying theory of logical and probabilistic reasoning. In ISIPTA'05, 4th International Symposium on Imprecise Probabilities and Their Applications, Pittsburgh, USA (2005) 193–202
3. Haenni, R., Kohlas, J., Lehmann, N.: Probabilistic argumentation systems. In Gabbay, D.M., Smets, P., eds.: Handbook of Defeasible Reasoning and Uncertainty Management Systems. Volume 5: Algorithms for Uncertainty and Defeasible Reasoning. Kluwer Academic Publishers, Dordrecht, Netherlands (2000) 221–288
4. Zimmermann, P.R.: PGP User's Guide Volume 2: Special Topics. (1994)
5. Maurer, U.: Modelling a public-key infrastructure. In Bertino, E., Kurth, H., Martella, G., Montolivo, E., eds.: ESORICS, European Symposium on Research in Computer Security. LNCS 1146, Springer (1996) 324–350
6. Kohlas, R., Maurer, U.: Confidence valuation in a public-key infrastructure based on uncertain evidence. In Imai, H., Zheng, Y., eds.: PKC'2000, Third International Workshop on Practice and Theory in Public Key Cryptography. LNCS 1751, Melbourne, Australia, Springer (2000) 93–112
7. Marchesini, J., Smith, S.W.: Modeling public key infrastructures in the real world. In Chadwick, D., Zhao, G., eds.: EuroPKI'04, 2nd European PKI Workshop: Research and Applications. LNCS 3545, Canterbury, U.K., Springer (2005) 118–134
8. Jøsang, A.: An algebra for assessing trust in certification chains. In: NDSS'99: 6th Annual Symposium on Network and Distributed System Security, San Diego, USA (1999)
9. Mahoney, G., Myrvold, W., Shoja, G.C.: Generic reliability trust model. In Ghorbani, A., Marsh, S., eds.: PST'05: 3rd Annual Conference on Privacy, Security and Trust, St. Andrews, Canada (2005) 113–120
10. Beth, T., Borcherding, M., Klein, B.: Valuation of trust in open networks. In: ESORICS'94, 3rd European Symposium on Research in Computer Security. LNCS 875, Springer (1994) 3–18
11. Blaze, M., Feigenbaum, J., Ioannidis, J., Keromytis, A.D.: The role of trust management in distributed systems security. In: Secure Internet Programming: Security Issues for Mobile and Distributed Objects. Springer, London, U.K. (1999) 185–210
12. Reiter, M.K., Stubblebine, S.G.: Authentication metric analysis and design. ACM Transactions on Information and System Security **2**(2) (1999) 138–158
13. Haenni, R.: Cost-bounded argumentation. International Journal of Approximate Reasoning **26**(2) (2001) 101–127
14. Haenni, R.: Anytime argumentative and abductive reasoning. Soft Computing – A Fusion of Foundations, Methodologies and Applications **8**(2) (2003) 142–149
15. Jonczy, J.: Kredentialnetze: ein allgemeines Modell für den Umgang mit Vertrauen und Authentizität in verteilten Netzwerken. Master's thesis, University of Fribourg, Switzerland (2005)
16. Motwani, R., Raghavan, P.: Randomized Algorithms. Cambridge University Press (1995)

Exploring Different Types of Trust Propagation

Audun Jøsang[1], Stephen Marsh[2], and Simon Pope[3]

[1] Queensland University of Technology,
Brisbane, Australia
a.josang@qut.edu.au
[2] National Research Council,
Fredericton, Canada
Stephen.Marsh@nrc-cnrc.gc.ca
[3] Defence Science and Technology Organisation,
Adelaide, Australia
Simon.Pope@dsto.defence.gov.au

Abstract. Trust propagation is the principle by which new trust relationships can be derived from pre-existing trust relationship. Trust transitivity is the most explicit form of trust propagation, meaning for example that if Alice trusts Bob, and Bob trusts Claire, then by transitivity, Alice will also trust Claire. This assumes that Bob recommends Claire to Alice. Trust fusion is also an important element in trust propagation, meaning that Alice can combine Bob's recommendation with her own personal experience in dealing with Claire, or with other recommendations about Claire, in order to derive a more reliable measure of trust in Claire. These simple principles, which are essential for human interaction in business and everyday life, manifests itself in many different forms. This paper investigates possible formal models that can be implemented using belief reasoning based on subjective logic. With good formal models, the principles of trust propagation can be ported to online communities of people, organisations and software agents, with the purpose of enhancing the quality of those communities.

1 Introduction

Trust is a phenomenon that only exists among living species equipped with advanced cognitive faculties. One usually considers the appreciation of trust to be a purely human characteristic, but it would be arrogant to exclude animals. When assuming that software agents can equipped with capabilities to reason about trust, risk assessment and decision making, one can talk about artificial trust. There is a rapidly growing growing literature on this topic [2, 3, 12, 19].

What humans perceive through their senses is a more or less distorted version of a reality which they assume exists. A considerable part of human science consists of modelling aspects of the world for the purpose of understanding, prediction and control. When trying to make statements about the assumed world, we actually make statements about the subjective perceived world. However, most reasoning models are designed for the assumed reality, not for the perceived reality.

A quite different approach would be to design a reasoning model for the perceived world. A key component of such a model is to include uncertainty resulting from partial

K. Stølen et al. (Eds.): iTrust 2006, LNCS 3986, pp. 179–192, 2006.
© Springer-Verlag Berlin Heidelberg 2006

ignorance. Several alternative calculi and logics which include degrees of uncertainty have been proposed and with some success applied to practical problems [4, 20]. The problem with many of the proposals has been that the calculi diverge considerably from standard probability calculus and therefore have received relatively little acceptance. A second key component of a model for the perceived world is to accept the fact that every belief is individual.

Subjective logic, which will be described here, takes both the uncertainty and individuality of beliefs into account while still being compatible with standard logic and probability calculus. The migration from the assumed towards the perceived world is achieved by adding an uncertainty dimension to the single valued probability measure, and by taking the individuality of beliefs into account.

A distinction can be made between interpreting trust as a belief about the reliability of an object, and as a decision to depend on an object [14]. In this paper, trust is interpreted in the former sense, as a belief about reliability. As a calculus of beliefs, subjective logic can therefore be used for trust reasoning. Although this model can never be perfect, and able to reflect all the nuances of trust, it can be shown to respect the main intuitive properties of trust and trust propagation.

As soon as one attempts to perform computations with input parameters in the form of subjective trust measures, parameter dependence becomes a major issue. If Alice for example wants to know whether tomorrow will be sunny, she can ask her friends, and if they all say it will be sunny she will start believing the same. However, her friends might all have based their opinions on the same weather-forecast, so their opinions are dependent, and in that case, asking only one of them would be sufficient. It would in fact be wrong of Alice to take all her friends' opinions into account as being independent, because it would strengthen her opinion without any good reason. Being able to identify cases of dependent opinions is therefore important, but alas difficult.

2   Trust Modeling with Subjective Logic

Subjective logic is a belief calculus specifically developed for modeling trust relationships. In subjective logic, beliefs are represented on binary state spaces, where each of the two possible states can consist of sub-states. Belief functions on binary state spaces are called *subjective opinions* and are formally expressed in the form of an ordered tuple $\omega_x^A = (b, d, u, a)$, where b, d, and u represent belief, disbelief and uncertainty respectively where $b, d, u \in [0, 1]$ and $b + d + u = 1$. The base rate parameter $a \in [0, 1]$ represents the base rate probability in the absence of evidence, and is used for computing an opinion's probability expectation value $\mathrm{E}(\omega_x^A) = b + au$, meaning that a determines how uncertainty shall contribute to $\mathrm{E}(\omega_x^A)$. A subjective opinion is interpreted as an agent A's belief in the truth of statement x. Ownership of an opinion is represented as a superscript so that for example A's opinion about x is denoted as ω_x^A.

Subjective opinions are equivalent to beta PDFs (probability density functions) denoted by beta (α, β) [1]. The beta class of density functions express probability density over the same binary event spaces as for subjective opinions, and this is also the basis for their equivalence.

Let r and s express the number of positive and negative past observations respectively, and let a express the *a priori* or base rate, then α and β can be determined as:

$$\alpha = r + 2a , \qquad \beta = s + 2(1 - a) . \tag{1}$$

The following bijective mapping between the opinion parameters and the beta PDF parameters can be determined analytically [5, 17].

$$\begin{cases} b_x = r/(r + s + 2) \\ d_x = s/(r + s + 2) \\ u_x = 2/(r + s + 2) \\ a_x = \text{base rate of } x \end{cases} \Longleftrightarrow \begin{cases} r = 2b_x/u_x \\ s = 2d_x/u_x \\ 1 = b_x + d_x + u_x \\ a = \text{base rate of } x \end{cases} \tag{2}$$

Without evidence, the base rate alone determines the probability distribution. As more evidence becomes available, the influence of the base rate diminishes, until the evidence alone determines the probability distribution. In order to separate between base rate and evidence in the beta PDF, we define the *augmented beta PDF* notation below.

Definition 1 (Augmented Beta PDF Notation). *Let the* a priori *beta PDF as a function of the base rate* a, *without evidence, be expressed as* $\text{beta}(2a, \ 2(1 - a))$. *Let the* a posteriori *beta PDF with positive evidence* r *and negative evidence* s *be expressed as* $\text{beta}(r + 2a, \ s + 2(1 - a))$. *The augmented beta PDF with the 3 parameters* (r, s, a) *is then simply written as* $\varphi(r, s, a)$, *defined by:*

$$\varphi(r, s, a) = \text{beta}(r + 2a, \ s + 2(1 - a)) . \tag{3}$$

Opinions can be mapped into the interior of an equal-sided triangle, and augmented beta PDFs can be visualised as 2D plots, as illustrated in Fig.1.

Fig.1 illustrates the example of a subjective opinion $\omega_x = (0.7, \ 0.1, \ 0.2, \ 0.5)$, and the corresponding equivalent augmented beta PDF $\varphi(7, 1, \frac{1}{2})$.

The fact that subjective logic is compatible with binary logic and probability calculus means that whenever corresponding operators exist in probability calculus, the probability expectation value $E(\omega)$ of an opinion ω that has been derived with subjective

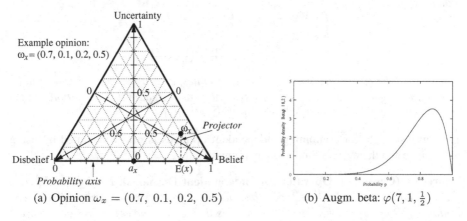

(a) Opinion $\omega_x = (0.7, \ 0.1, \ 0.2, \ 0.5)$ \qquad (b) Augm. beta: $\varphi(7, 1, \frac{1}{2})$

Fig. 1. Example equivalent subjective opinion and beta PDF

logic, is always equal to the probability value that would have been derived had simple probability calculus been applied. Similarly, whenever corresponding binary logic operators exist, an absolute opinion (i.e. equivalent to binary logic TRUE or FALSE) derived with subjective logic, is always equal to the truth value that can be derived with binary logic.

Subjective logic has a sound mathematical basis and is compatible with binary logic and traditional Bayesian analysis. Subjective logic defines a rich set of operators for combining subjective opinions in various ways [5, 6, 7, 8, 9, 10, 11, 12, 15, 16, 18]. Some operators represent generalisations of binary logic and probability calculus, whereas others are unique to belief calculus because they depend on belief ownership. With belief ownership it is possible to explicitly express that different agents have different opinions about the same issue.

The advantage of subjective logic over probability calculus and binary logic is its ability to explicitly express and take advantage of ignorance and belief ownership. Subjective logic can be applied to all situations where probability calculus can be applied, and to many situations where probability calculus fails precisely because it can not capture degrees of ignorance. Subjective opinions can be interpreted as probability density functions, making subjective logic a simple and efficient calculus for probability density functions. An online demonstration of subjective logic can be accessed at: http://www.fit.qut.edu.au/~josang/sl/.

3   Trust Fusion

3.1   Fusion of Independent Trust

This operator is most naturally expressed in the evidence space, so we will define it there first and subsequently map it over to the opinion space.

Definition 2 (Consensus Operator for Independent Beta PDFs). *Let* $\varphi(r_x^A, s_x^A, a_x^A)$ *and* $\varphi(r_x^B, s_x^B, a_x^B)$ *be two augmented beta PDFs respectively held by the agents A and B regarding the trustworthiness of x. The augmented beta PDF* $\varphi(r_x^{A\diamond B}, s_x^{A\diamond B}, a_x^{A\diamond B})$ *defined by*

$$\begin{cases} r_x^{A\diamond B} = r_x^A + r_x^B \\ s_x^{A\diamond B} = s_x^A + s_x^B \\ a_x^{A\diamond B} = \frac{a_x^A(r_x^B+s_x^B)+a_x^B(r_x^A+s_x^A)}{r_x^A+r_x^B+s_x^A+s_x^B} \end{cases}$$

is then called the consensus of A's and B's estimates, as if it was an estimate held by an imaginary agent $[A, B]$. By using the symbol $\oplus$ to designate this operation, we get $\varphi(r_x^{A\diamond B}, s_x^{A\diamond B}, a_x^{A\diamond B}) = \varphi(r_x^A, s_x^A, a_x^A) \oplus \varphi(r_x^B, s_x^B, a_x^B)$.

The consensus rule for combining independent opinions is easily obtained by using Def.2 above and the evidence-opinion mapping of Eq.(2).

Theorem 1 (Consensus Operator for Independent Opinions). *Let* $\omega_x^A = (b_x^A, d_x^A, u_x^A, a_x^A)$ *and* $\omega_x^B = (b_x^B, d_x^B, u_x^B, a_x^B)$ *be trust in x from A and B respectively. The opinion* $\omega_x^{A\diamond B} = (b_x^{A\diamond B}, d_x^{A\diamond B}, u_x^{A\diamond B}, a_x^{A\diamond B})$ *is then called the consensus between ω_x^A and ω_x^B, denoting the trust that an imaginary agent $[A, B]$ would have in x, as if* *that agent represented both A and B. In case of Bayesian (totally certain) opinions, their relative weight can be defined as $\gamma^{A/B} = \lim(u_x^B/u_x^A)$.*

Case I:
$$u_x^A + u_x^B - u_x^A u_x^B \neq 0$$

$$\begin{cases} b_x^{A\diamond B} = \dfrac{b_x^A u_x^B + b_x^B u_x^A}{u_x^A + u_x^B - u_x^A u_x^B} \\[3mm] d_x^{A\diamond B} = \dfrac{d_x^A u_x^B + d_x^B u_x^A}{u_x^A + u_x^B - u_x^A u_x^B} \\[3mm] u_x^{A\diamond B} = \dfrac{u_x^A u_x^B}{u_x^A + u_x^B - u_x^A u_x^B} \\[3mm] a_x^{A\diamond B} = \dfrac{a_x^A u_x^B + a_x^B u_x^A - (a_x^A + a_x^B)u_x^A u_x^B}{u_x^A + u_x^B - 2u_x^A u_x^B} \end{cases}$$

Case II:
$$u_x^A + u_x^B - u_x^A u_x^B = 0$$

$$\begin{cases} b_x^{A\diamond B} = \dfrac{(\gamma^{A/B}\, b_x^A + b_x^B)}{(\gamma^{A/B}+1)} \\[3mm] d_x^{A\diamond B} = \dfrac{(\gamma^{A/B}\, d_x^A + d_x^B)}{(\gamma^{A/B}+1)} \\[3mm] u_x^{A\diamond B} = 0 \\[3mm] a_x^{A\diamond B} = \dfrac{\gamma^{A/B}\, a_x^A + a_x^B}{\gamma^{A/B}+1} \end{cases}$$

By using the symbol '⊕' to designate this operator, we can write $\omega_x^{A\diamond B} = \omega_x^A \oplus \omega_x^B$.

It can be shown that ⊕ is both commutative and associative which means that the order in which opinions are combined has no importance. Opinion independence must be assured, which obviously translates into not allowing an entity's opinion to be counted more than once.

The effect of independent consensus is to reduce uncertainty. For example the case where several witnesses give consistent testimony should amplify the judge's opinion, and that is exactly what the operator does. Consensus between an infinite number of not totally uncertain (i.e. $u < 1$) opinions would necessarily produce a consensus opinion with $u = 0$. Fig.2 illustrates an example of applying the consensus operator for independent opinions where $\omega_x^A = \{0.8, 0.1, 0.1, a\}$ and $\omega_x^B = \{0.1, 0.8, 0.1, a\}$, so that $\omega_x^{A\diamond B} = \omega_x^A \oplus \omega_x^B = \{0.47, 0.47, 0.06, a\}$.

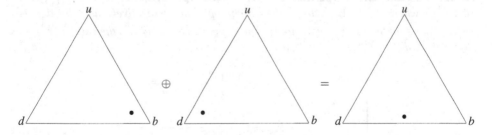

Fig. 2. Example of applying the consensus operator for fusing independent trust

3.2 Fusion of Dependent Trust

Assume two agents A and B having simultaneously observed the same process. Because their observations are identical, their respective opinions will necessarily be dependent, and a consensus according to Def.2 would be meaningless.

If the two observers have made exactly the same observations, and their estimates are equal, it is sufficient to take only one of the estimates into account. However, although two observers witness the same phenomenon, it is possible (indeed, likely) that they record and interpret it differently. The observers may have started and ended the observations at slightly different times, one of them may have missed or misinterpreted some of the events, resulting in varying, but still dependent opinions.

We will define a consensus rule for dependent beta PDFs based on the average of recorded positive and negative observations. Let two dependent augmented beta PDFs be $\varphi(r_x^A, s_x^A, a_x^A)$ and $\varphi(r_x^B, s_x^B, a_x^B)$, then we define the consensus estimate by the average of their parameters as $\varphi(\frac{r_x^A + r_x^B}{2}, \frac{s_x^A + s_x^B}{2}, \frac{a_x^A + a_x^B}{2})$. The general expression for the consensus between n dependent augmented beta PDFs can be defined as follows:

Definition 3 (Consensus Operator for Dependent Beta PDFs). *Let* $\varphi(r_x^{A_i}, s_x^{A_i}, a_x^{A_i})$, *where* $i \in [1, n]$, *be* n *dependent augmented beta PDFs respectively held by the agents* $A_1, ..., A_n$ *about the proposition* x. *The depended consensus beta PDF is then* $\varphi(r_x^{A_1 \diamondsuit ... \diamondsuit A_n}, s_x^{A_1 \diamondsuit ... \diamondsuit A_n}, a_x^{A_1 \diamondsuit ... \diamondsuit A_n})$, *where:*

$$
\begin{cases}
r_x^{A_1 \diamondsuit ... \diamondsuit A_n} = \frac{\sum_1^n r_x^{A_i}}{n} \\[3mm]
s_x^{A_1 \diamondsuit ... \diamondsuit A_n} = \frac{\sum_1^n s_x^{A_i}}{n} \\[3mm]
a_x^{A_1 \diamondsuit ... \diamondsuit A_n} = \frac{\sum_1^n a_x^{A_i}}{n}
\end{cases}
$$

By using the symbol $\oplus$ *to designate this operation, we get*
$$\varphi(r_x^{A_1 \diamondsuit ... \diamondsuit A_n}, s_x^{A_1 \diamondsuit ... \diamondsuit A_n}, a_x^{A_1 \diamondsuit ... \diamondsuit A_n}) = \varphi(r_x^{A_1}, s_x^{A_1}, a_x^{A_1}) \oplus ... \oplus \varphi(r_x^{A_n}, s_x^{A_n}, a_x^{A_n}). \quad \square$$

The corresponding consensus operator is obtained by applying Eq.(2) to Def.3.

Theorem 2 (Consensus Operator for Dependent Opinions). *Let* $\omega_x^{A_i} = \{b_x^{A_i}, d_x^{A_i}, u_x^{A_i}, a_x^{A_i}\}$ *where* $i \in [1, n]$, *be* n *dependent opinions respectively held by agents* $A_1, ..., A_n$ *about the same proposition* x. *The depended consensus is then* $\omega_x^{A_1 \diamondsuit ... \diamondsuit A_n} = \{b_x^{A_1 \diamondsuit ... \diamondsuit A_n}, d_x^{A_1 \diamondsuit ... \diamondsuit A_n}, u_x^{A_1 \diamondsuit ... \diamondsuit A_n}, a_x^{A_1 \diamondsuit ... \diamondsuit A_n}\}$, *where:*

$$
\begin{cases}
b_x^{A_1 \diamondsuit ... \diamondsuit A_n} = \frac{\sum_1^n (b_x^{A_i}/u_x^{A_i})}{\sum_1^n (b_x^{A_i}/u_x^{A_i}) + \sum_1^n (d_x^{A_i}/u_x^{A_i}) + n} \\[4mm]
d_x^{A_1 \diamondsuit ... \diamondsuit A_n} = \frac{\sum_1^n (d_x^{A_i}/u_x^{A_i})}{\sum_1^n (b_x^{A_i}/u_x^{A_i}) + \sum_1^n (d_x^{A_i}/u_x^{A_i}) + n} \\[4mm]
u_x^{A_1 \diamondsuit ... \diamondsuit A_n} = \frac{n}{\sum_1^n (b_x^{A_i}/u_x^{A_i}) + \sum_1^n (d_x^{A_i}/u_x^{A_i}) + n} \\[4mm]
a_x^{A_1 \diamondsuit ... \diamondsuit A_n} = \frac{\sum_1^n a_x^{A_i}}{n}
\end{cases}
$$

where all the $u_x^{A_i}$ *are different from zero. By using the symbol* $\oplus$ *to designate this operation, we get* $\omega_x^{A_1 \diamondsuit ... \diamondsuit A_n} = \omega_x^{A_1} \oplus ... \oplus \omega_x^{A_n}$.

The $\oplus$ operator is both commutative and associative. The effect of the dependent consensus operator is to produce an opinion which is based on an average of positive and an average of negative evidence. Fig.3 illustrates an example of applying the consensus operator for dependent opinions where $\omega_x^A = \{0.8, 0.1, 0.1, a\}$ and $\omega_x^B = \{0.1, 0.8, 0.1, a\}$, so that $\omega_x^{A \diamond B} = \omega_x^A \oplus \omega_x^B = \{0.45, \ 0.45, \ 0.10, \ a\}$.

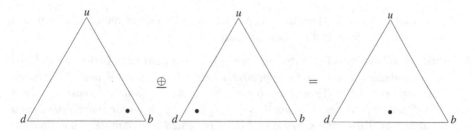

Fig. 3. Example of applying the consensus operator for dependent opinions

3.3   Fusion of Trust Under Partial Dependence

Let two agents A and B observed the same process during two partially overlapping periods. If it is known exactly which events were observed by both, one of the agents can simply dismiss these observations, and their opinions will be independent. However, it may not always be possible to determine which observations are identical.

Fig.4 illustrates a situation of partly dependent observations. Assuming that the fraction of overlapping observations is known, the dependent and the independent parts of their observations can be estimated, so that a consensus operator can be defined [13].

In the figure, $\omega_x^{Ai(B)}$ and $\omega_x^{Bi(A)}$ represent the independent parts of A and B's opinions, whereas $\omega_x^{Ad(B)}$ and $\omega_x^{Bd(A)}$ represent their dependent parts.

Let φ_x^A's fraction of dependence with φ_x^B and vice versa be represented by the dependence factors $\lambda_x^{Ad(B)}$ and $\lambda_x^{Bd(A)}$. The dependent and independent augmented betas can then be defined as a function of the dependence factors.

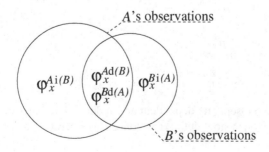

Fig. 4. Beta PDFs based on partly dependent observations

$$\varphi_x^{Ai(B)} : \begin{cases} r_x^{Ai(B)} = r_x^A(1 - \lambda_x^{Ad(B)}) \\ s_x^{Ai(B)} = s_x^A(1 - \lambda_x^{Ad(B)}) \end{cases} \qquad \varphi_x^{Bi(A)} : \begin{cases} r_x^{Bi(A)} = r_x^B(1 - \lambda_x^{Bd(A)}) \\ s_x^{Bi(A)} = s_x^B(1 - \lambda_x^{Bd(A)}) \end{cases}$$

$$\varphi_x^{Ad(B)} : \begin{cases} r_x^{Ad(B)} = r_x^A \lambda_x^{Ad(B)} \\ s_x^{Ad(B)} = s_x^A \lambda_x^{Ad(B)} \end{cases} \qquad \varphi_x^{Bd(A)} : \begin{cases} r_x^{Bd(A)} = r_x^B \lambda_x^{Bd(A)} \\ s_x^{Bd(A)} = s_x^B \lambda_x^{Bd(A)} \end{cases}$$

$$(4)$$

The cumulative fusion of partially dependent beta PDFs can then be defined as a function of the dependent and independent parts.

Definition 4 (Consensus Operator for Partially Dependent Beta PDFs). *Let φ_x^A and φ_x^B be two augmented beta PDFs respectively held by the agents A and B regarding the trustworthiness of x. We will use the symbol $\widetilde{\oplus}$ to designate consensus between partially dependent augmented betas. As before $\oplus$ is the operator for entirely dependent augmented betas. The consensus of A and B's augmented betas can then be written as:*

$$\varphi_x^A \widetilde{\oplus} \varphi_x^B = \varphi_x^{A\widetilde{\delta}B}$$
$$= \varphi_x^{(Ad(B)\underline{\delta}Bd(A))\diamond Ai(B)\diamond Bi(A)} \qquad (5)$$
$$= (\varphi_x^{Ad(B)} \underline{\oplus} \varphi_x^{Bd(A)}) \oplus \varphi_x^{Ai(B)} \oplus \varphi_x^{Bi(A)}$$

The equivalent representation of dependent and independent opinions can be obtained by using Eq.(4) and the evidence-opinion mapping Eq.(2). The reciprocal dependence factors are as before denoted by $\lambda^{Ad(B)}$ and $\lambda^{Bd(A)}$.

$$\omega_x^{Ai(B)} : \begin{cases} b_x^{Ai(B)} = b_x^A \mu_x^{Ai(B)} \\ d_x^{Ai(B)} = d_x^A \mu_x^{Ai(B)} \\ u_x^{Ai(B)} = u_x^A \mu_x^{Ai(B)} / (1 - \lambda_x^{Ad(B)}) \end{cases} \qquad \mu_x^{Ai(B)} = \frac{1 - \lambda_x^{Ad(B)}}{(1 - \lambda_x^{Ad(B)})(b_x^A + d_x^A) + u_x^A}$$

$$\omega_x^{Ad(B)} : \begin{cases} b_x^{Ad(B)} = b_x^A \mu_x^{Ad(B)} \\ d_x^{Ad(B)} = d_x^A \mu_x^{Ad(B)} \\ u_x^{Ad(B)} = u_x^A \mu_x^{Ad(B)} / \lambda_x^{Ad(B)} \end{cases} \qquad \mu_x^{Ad(B)} = \frac{\lambda_x^{Ad(B)}}{\lambda_x^{Ad(B)}(b_x^A + d_x^A) + u_x^A}$$

$$\omega_x^{Bi(A)} : \begin{cases} b_x^{Bi(A)} = b_x^B \mu_x^{Bi(A)} \\ d_x^{Bi(A)} = d_x^B \mu_x^{Bi(A)} \\ u_x^{Bi(A)} = u_x^B \mu_x^{Bi(A)} / (1 - \lambda_x^{Bd(A)}) \end{cases} \qquad \mu_x^{Bi(A)} = \frac{1 - \lambda_x^{Bd(A)}}{(1 - \lambda_x^{Bd(A)})(b_x^B + d_x^B) + u_x^B}$$

$$\omega_x^{Bd(A)} : \begin{cases} b_x^{Bd(A)} = b_x^B \mu_x^{Bd(A)} \\ d_x^{Bd(A)} = d_x^B \mu_x^{Bd(A)} \\ u_x^{Bd(A)} = u_x^B \mu_x^{Bd(A)} / \lambda_x^{Bd(A)} \end{cases} \qquad \mu_x^{Bd(A)} = \frac{\lambda_x^{Bd(A)}}{\lambda_x^{Bd(A)}(b_x^B + d_x^B) + u_x^B}$$

$$(6)$$

Having specified the separate dependent and independent parts of two partially dependent opinions, we can now define the consensus operator for partially dependent opinions.

Theorem 3 (Consensus Operator for Partially Dependent Opinions). *Let A and B have the partially dependent opinions ω_x^A and ω_x^B respectively, about the same* *proposition x, and let their dependent and independent parts be expressed according to Eq.(6). We will use the symbol $\widetilde{\oplus}$ to designate consensus between partially dependent opinions. As before $\underline{\oplus}$ is the operator for entirely dependent opinions. The consensus of A and B's opinions can then be written as:*

$$\omega_x^A \widetilde{\oplus} \omega_x^B = \omega_x^{A\widetilde{\diamond}B}$$
$$= \omega_x^{(\mathrm{Ad}(B)\underline{\diamond}\mathrm{Bd}(A))\diamond\mathrm{Ai}(B)\diamond\mathrm{Bi}(A)}$$
$$= \left(\omega_x^{\mathrm{Ad}(B)} \underline{\oplus} \omega_x^{\mathrm{Bd}(A)}\right) \oplus \omega_x^{\mathrm{Ai}(B)} \oplus \omega_x^{\mathrm{Bi}(A)} \tag{7}$$

It is easy to prove that for any opinion ω_x^A with a dependence factor $\lambda_x^{\mathrm{Ad}(B)}$ to any other opinion ω_x^B the following equality holds:

$$\omega_x^A = \omega_x^{\mathrm{Ai}(B)} \oplus \omega_x^{\mathrm{Ad}(B)} \tag{8}$$

4 Trust Transitivity

Assume two agents A and B where A trusts B, and B believes that proposition x is true. Then by transitivity, agent A will also believe that proposition x is true. This assumes that B recommends x to A. In our approach, trust and belief are formally expressed as opinions. The transitive linking of these two opinions consists of discounting B's opinion about x by A's opinion about B, in order to derive A's opinion about x. This principle is illustrated in Fig.5 below. The solid arrows represent initial direct trust, and the dotted arrow represents derived indirect trust.

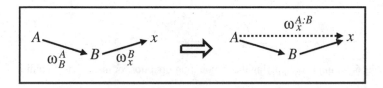

Fig. 5. Principle of the discounting operator

Trust transitivity, as trust itself, is a human mental phenomenon, so there is no such thing as objective transitivity, and trust transitivity therefore lends itself to different interpretations. We see two main difficulties. The first is related to the effect of A disbelieving that B will give a good advice. What does this exactly mean? We will give two different interpretations and definitions. The second difficulty relates to the effect of base rate trust in a transitive path. We will briefly examine this, and provide the definition of a base rate sensitive discounting operator as an alternative to the two previous which are base rate insensitive.

4.1 Uncertainty Favouring Trust Transitivity

A's disbelief in the recommending agent B means that A thinks that B ignores the truth value of x. As a result A also ignores the truth value of x.

Definition 5 (Uncertainty Favouring Discounting). *Let A, B and be two agents where A's opinion about B's recommendations is expressed as $\omega_B^A = \{b_B^A, d_B^A, u_B^A, a_B^A\}$, and let x be a proposition where B's opinion about x is recommended to A with the opinion $\omega_x^B = \{b_x^B, d_x^B, u_x^B, a_x^B\}$. Let $\omega_x^{A:B} = \{b_x^{A:B}, d_x^{A:B}, u_x^{A:B}, a_x^{A:B}\}$ be the opinion such that:*

$$\begin{cases} b_x^{A:B} = b_B^A b_x^B \\ d_x^{A:B} = b_B^A d_x^B \\ u_x^{A:B} = d_B^A + u_B^A + b_B^A u_x^B \\ a_x^{A:B} = a_x^B \end{cases}$$

then $\omega_x^{A:B}$ is called the uncertainty favouring discounted opinion of A. By using the symbol $\otimes$ to designate this operation, we get $\omega_x^{A:B} = \omega_B^A \otimes \omega_x^B$. □

It is easy to prove that this operator is associative but not commutative. This means that the combination of opinions can start in either end of the path, and that the order in which opinions are combined is significant. In a path with more than one recommending entity, opinion independence must be assumed, which for example translates into not allowing the same entity to appear more than once in a transitive path. Fig.6 illustrates an example of applying the discounting operator for independent opinions, where $\omega_B^A = \{0.1, 0.8, 0.1\}$ discounts $\omega_x^B = \{0.8, 0.1, 0.1\}$ to produce $\omega_x^{A:B} = \{0.08, 0.01, 0.91\}$.

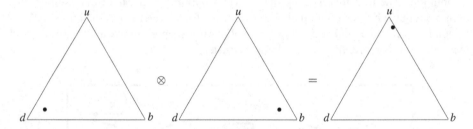

Fig. 6. Example of applying the discounting operator for independent opinions

4.2 Opposite Belief Favouring

A's disbelief in the recommending agent B means that A thinks that B consistently recommends the opposite of his real opinion about the truth value of x. As a result, A not only disbelieves in x to the degree that B recommends belief, but she also believes in x to the degree that B recommends disbelief in x, because the combination of two disbeliefs results in belief in this case.

Definition 6 (Opposite Belief Favouring Discounting). *Let A, B and be two agents where A's opinion about B's recommendations is expressed as $\omega_B^A = \{b_B^A, d_B^A, u_B^A, a_B^A\}$, and let x be a proposition where B's opinion about x is recommended to A as the opinion $\omega_x^B = \{b_x^B, d_x^B, u_x^B, a_x^B\}$. Let $\omega_x^{A:B} = \{b_x^{A:B}, d_x^{A:B}, u_x^{A:B}, a_x^{A:B}\}$ be the opinion such that:*

$$\begin{cases} b_x^{A:B} = b_B^A b_x^B + d_B^A d_x^B \\ d_x^{A:B} = b_B^A d_x^B + d_B^A b_x^B \\ u_x^{A:B} = u_B^A + (b_B^A + d_B^A)u_x^B \\ a_x^{A:B} = a_x^B \end{cases}$$

then $\omega_x^{A:B}$ is called the opposite belief favouring discounted recommendation from B to A. By using the symbol $\otimes$ to designate this operation, we get $\omega_x^{A:B} = \omega_B^A \otimes \omega_x^B$.   □

This operator models the principle that *"your enemy's enemy is your friend"*. That might be the case in some situations, and the operator should only be applied when the situation makes it plausible. It is doubtful whether it is meaningful to model more than two arcs in a transitive path with this principle. In other words, it is doubtful whether the enemy of your enemy's enemy necessarily is your enemy too.

4.3 Base Rate Sensitive Transitivity

In the transitivity operators defined in Sec.4.1 and Sec.4.2 above, a_B^A had no influence on the discounting of of the recommended (b_x^B, d_x^B, u_x^B) parameters. This can seem counterintuitive in many cases such as in the example described next.

Imagine a stranger coming to a town which is know for its citizens being honest. The stranger is looking for a car mechanic, and asks the first person he meets to direct him to a good car mechanic. The stranger receives the reply that there are two car mechanics in town, David and Eric, where David is cheap but does not always do quality work, and Eric might be a bit more expensive, but he always does a perfect job.

Translated into the formalism of subjective logic, the stranger has no other info about the person he asks than the base rate that the citizens in the town are honest. The stranger is thus ignorant, but the expectation value of a good advice is still very high. Without taking a_B^A into account, the result of the definitions above would be that the stranger is completely ignorant about which if the mechanics is the best.

An intuitive approach would then be to let the expectation value of the stranger's trust in the recommender be the discounting factor for the recommended (b_x^B, d_x^B) parameters.

Definition 7 (Base Rate Sensitive Discounting). *The base rate sensitive discounting of a belief $\omega_x^B = (b_x^B, d_x^B, u_x^B, a_x^B)$ by a belief $\omega_B^A = (b_B^A, d_B^A, u_B^A, a_B^A)$ produces the transitive belief $\omega_x^{A\diamond B} = (b_x^{A\diamond B}, d_x^{A\diamond B}, u_x^{A\diamond B}, a_x^{A\diamond B})$ where*

$$\begin{cases} b_x^{A\diamond B} = \mathrm{E}(\omega_B^A)b_x^B \\ d_x^{A\diamond B} = \mathrm{E}(\omega_B^A)d_x^B \\ u_x^{A\diamond B} = 1 + \mathrm{E}(\omega_B^A)u_x^B - \mathrm{E}(\omega_B^A) \\ a_x^{A\diamond B} = a_x^B \end{cases} \tag{9}$$

where the probability expectation value $\mathrm{E}(\omega_B^A) = b_B^A + a_B^A u_B^A$.

However this operator must be applied with care. Assume again the town of honest citizens, and let let the stranger A have the opinion $\omega_B^A = (0,\ 0,\ 1,\ 0.99)$ about the first person B she meets, i.e. the opinion has no basis in evidence other than a very high base rate defined by $a_B^A = 0.99$. If the person B now recommends to A the opinion $\omega_x^B = (1,\ 0,\ 0,\ a)$, then, according to the base rate sensitive discounting operator of Def.7, A will have the belief $\omega_x^{A:B} = (0.99,\ 0,\ 0.01,\ a)$ in x. In other words, the highly certain belief $\omega_x^{A:B}$ is derived on the basis of the highly uncertain belief ω_B^A, which can seem counterintuitive. This potential problem could be amplified as the trust path gets longer. A safety principle could therefore be to only apply the base rate sensitive discounting to the last transitive link.

There might be other principles that better reflect human intuition for trust transitivity, but we will leave this question to future research. It would be fair to say that the base rate insensitive discounting operator of Def.5 is safe and conservative, and that the base rate sensitive discounting operator of Def.7 can be more intuitive in some situations, but must be applied with care.

5   Mass Hysteria

One of the strengths of this work is in its analytical capabilities. As an example, consider how mass hysteria can be caused by people not being aware of dependence between opinions. Let for example person A recommend an opinion about a particular statement x to a group of other persons. Without being aware of the fact that the opinion came from the same origin, these persons can recommend their opinions to each other as illustrated in Fig.7.

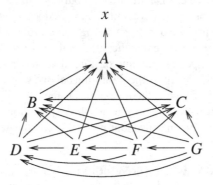

Fig. 7. The principle of mass hysteria

The arrows represent trust so that for example $B \longrightarrow A$ can be interpreted as saying that B trusts A to recommend an opinion about statement x. The actual recommendation goes, of course, in the opposite direction to the arrows in Fig.7.

It can be seen that A recommends an opinion about x to 6 other agents, and that G receives 6 recommendations in all. If G assumes the recommended opinions to be independent and takes the consensus between them, his opinion can become abnormally strong and in fact even stronger than A's opinion.

As a numerical example, let A's opinion ω_x^A about x as well as the agents' opinions about each other (ω_A^B, ω_A^C, ω_B^C, ω_A^D, ω_B^D, ω_C^D, ω_A^E, ω_B^E, ω_C^E, ω_D^E, ω_A^F, ω_B^F, ω_C^F, ω_D^F, ω_E^F, ω_A^G, ω_B^G, ω_C^G, ω_D^G, ω_E^G, ω_F^G) all have the same value given by $(0.7, 0.1, 0.2, a)$.

In this example, we will apply the consensus operator for *independent* beliefs to illustrate the effect of unknown dependence. We also apply the uncertainty favouring discounting operator which does not take base rates into account.

Taking all the possible recommendations of Fig.7 into account creates a relatively complex trust graph, and a rather long notation. In order to reduce the size of the notation, the transitivity symbol ":" will simply be omitted, and the cumulative fusion symbol ◇ will simply be written as ",". Analysing the whole graph of dependent paths, as if they were independent, will then produce:

$$\omega_x \begin{pmatrix} GA, \ GBA, \ GCA, \ GCBA, \ GDA, \ GDBA, \ GDCA, \ GDCBA, \ GEA, GEBA, GECA, \\ GECBA, \ GEDA, GEDBA, \ GEDCA, \ GEDCBA, \ GFA, \ GFBA, \ GFCA, \ GFCBA, \\ GFDA, \ GFDBA, \ GFDCA, \ GFDCBA, \ GFEA, \ GFEBA, \ GFECA, \ GFECBA, \\ GFEDA, \ GFEDBA, \ GFEDCA, \ GFEDCBA \end{pmatrix} = (0.76, 0.11, 0.13, a)$$

For comparison, if G only took the recommendation from A into account (as he should), his derived opinion would be $\omega_x^{G:A} = \{0.49, \ 0.07, \ 0.44, \ a\}$.

In real situations it is possible for recommended opinions to return to their originator through feedback loops, resulting in even more exaggerated beliefs. When this process continues, an environment of self amplifying opinions, and thereby hysteria, is created.

6   Conclusion

Subjective logic is a belief calculus which takes into account the fact that perceptions about the world always are subjective. This translates into using a belief model that can express degrees of uncertainty about probability estimates, and we use the term *opinion* to denote such subjective beliefs. In addition, ownership of opinions is assigned to particular agents in order to reflect the fact that opinions always are individual. The operators of subjective logic use opinions about the truth of propositions as input parameters, and produce an opinion about the truth of a proposition as output parameter.

In this paper, trust is interpreted as a belief about reliability, and we have shown how subjective logic can be used for trust reasoning. Although this model can never be perfect, and able to reflect all the nuances of trust, it can be shown to respect the main and intuitive properties of trust and trust propagation.

One difficulty with applying subjective logic is that trust and beliefs can be dependent without people being aware of it, in which case the calculus will produce "wrong" results. Our example illustrated how dependent opinions can influence peoples opinions without any objective reason, and even cause hysteria. In order to avoid this problem we introduced operators for belief and trust fusion that explicitly take dependence into account. This makes it possible to models real world situations involving dependent beliefs more realistically.

Another difficulty is to find a sound and intuitive operator for trust transitivity. This problem comes from the fact that trust transitivity is a psychosocial phenomenon that can not be objectively observed and modelled in traditional statistical or probabilistic terms. We have proposed possible alternative models to the traditional and conservative uncertainty favouring transitivity operator of subjective logic. However, we feel that more research and experiments are needed in order to determine optimal principles of modelling trust transitivity. It might also be the case that no single transitivity operator is suitable for all situations, and that particular situations will require specially designed transitivity operators.

References

1. M.H. DeGroot and M.J. Schervish. *Probability and Statistics (3rd Edition)*. Addison-Wesley, 2001.
2. Li Ding and Timothy Finin. Weaving the Web of Belief into the Semantic Web. In *Proceedings of the 13th International World Wide Web Conference*, New York, May 2004.
3. K.K Fullam et al. The Agent Reputation and Trust (ART) Testbed Architecture. In *Proceedings of the 8th Int. Workshop on Trust in Agent Societies (at AAMAS'05)*. ACM, 2005.
4. A. Hunter. *Uncertainty in information systems*. McGraw-Hill, London, 1996.
5. A. Jøsang. A Logic for Uncertain Probabilities. *International Journal of Uncertainty, Fuzziness and Knowledge-Based Systems*, 9(3):279–311, June 2001.
6. A. Jøsang. Subjective Evidential Reasoning. In *Proceedings of the International Conference on Information Processing and Management of Uncertainty (IPMU2002)*, Annecy, France, July 2002.
7. A. Jøsang. The Consensus Operator for Combining Beliefs. *Artificial Intelligence Journal*, 142(1–2):157–170, October 2002.
8. A. Jøsang, D. Bradley, and S.J. Knapskog. Belief-Based Risk Analysis. In *Proceedings of the Australasian Information Security Workshop (AISW)*, Dunedin, January 2004.
9. A. Jøsang, M. Daniel, and P. Vannoorenberghe. Strategies for Combining Conflicting Dogmatic Beliefs. In Xuezhi Wang, editor, *Proceedings of the 6th International Conference on Information Fusion*, 2003.
10. A. Jøsang, E. Gray, and M. Kinateder. Simplification and Analysis of Transitive Trust Networks (in press, accepted May 2005). *Web Intelligence and Agent Systems*, 00(00):00–00, 2006.
11. A. Jøsang, R. Hayward, and S. Pope. Trust Network Analysis with Subjective Logic. In *Proceedings of the 29th Australasian Computer Science Conference (ACSC2006), CRPIT Volume 48*, Hobart, Australia, January 2006.
12. A. Jøsang, R. Ismail, and C. Boyd. A Survey of Trust and Reputation Systems for Online Service Provision (in press, accepted June 2005). *Decision Support Systems*, 00(00):00–00, 2006.
13. A. Jøsang and S.J. Knapskog. A Metric for Trusted Systems (full paper). In *Proceedings of the 21st National Information Systems Security Conference*. NSA, October 1998.
14. A. Jøsang and S. Lo Presti. Analysing the Relationship Between Risk and Trust. In T. Dimitrakos, editor, *Proceedings of the Second International Conference on Trust Management (iTrust)*, Oxford, March 2004.
15. A. Jøsang and D. McAnally. Multiplication and Comultiplication of Beliefs. *International Journal of Approximate Reasoning*, 38(1):19–51, 2004.
16. A. Jøsang and S. Pope. Semantic Constraints for Trust Tansitivity. In S. Hartmann and M. Stumptner, editors, *Proceedings of the Asia-Pacific Conference of Conceptual Modelling (APCCM) (Volume 43 of Conferences in Research and Practice in Information Technology)*, Newcastle, Australia, February 2005.
17. A. Jøsang and S. Pope. Normalising the Consensus Operator for Belief Fusion. In *Proceedings of the International Conference on Information Processing and Management of Uncertainty (IPMU2006)*, Paris, July 2006.
18. A. Jøsang, S. Pope, and M. Daniel. Conditional deduction under uncertainty. In *Proceedings of the 8th European Conference on Symbolic and Quantitative Approaches to Reasoning with Uncertainty (ECSQARU 2005)*, 2005.
19. S. Marsh. *Formalising Trust as a Computational Concept*. PhD thesis, University of Stirling, 1994.
20. A. Motro and Ph. Smets. *Uncertainty management in information systems: from needs to solutions*. Kluwer, Boston, 1997.

PathTrust: A Trust-Based Reputation Service for Virtual Organization Formation

Florian Kerschbaum, Jochen Haller, Yücel Karabulut, and Philip Robinson

SAP Research, CEC Karlsruhe, Germany
{florian.kerschbaum, jochen.haller, yuecel.karabulut,
philip.robinson}@sap.com

Abstract. Virtual Organizations enable new forms of collaboration for businesses in a networked society. During their formation business partners are selected on an as-needed basis. We consider the problem of using a reputation system to enhance the member selection in Virtual Organizations. The paper identifies the requirements for and the benefits of using a reputation system for this task. We identify attacks and analyze their impact and threat to using reputation systems. Based on these findings we propose the use of a specific model of reputation different from the prevalent models of reputation. The major contribution of this paper is an algorithm (called PathTrust) in this model that exploits the graph of relationships among the participants. It strongly emphasizes the transitive model of trust in a web of trust. We evaluate its performance, especially under attack, and show that it provides a clear advantage in the design of a Virtual Organization infrastructure.

1 Introduction

We consider the problem of member selection in Virtual Organizations (VO). A VO is understood as a temporary coalition of geographically dispersed individuals, groups, enterprise units or entire organizations that pool resources, facilities, and information to achieve common business objectives. The partners in a VO enjoy equal status and are dependent upon electronic connections (ICT infrastructure) for the co-ordination of their activities [1]. This concept of VOs is advocated as a promising model for e-activities and it is strongly supported by the European Union Sixth Framework Program. Each VO has an initiator who is responsible for creating and managing the VO. The VO management function can be performed by a group of persons delegated by the VO initiator. A person becomes a VO initiator when he notifies the system of his intention to create a VO.

A VO has a lifecycle which is a state model, which we have adopted from [15] and extended [12]:

1. *Identification*: the preparatory phase of a VO, where the initiator specifies required business roles (e.g. storage provider or data analyzer in a Collaborative Engineering scenario), high-level work units and interactions in what is referred to as the "Collaboration Definition" (CD) and defines control requirements [4].

K. Stølen et al. (Eds.): iTrust 2006, LNCS 3986, pp. 193–205, 2006.
© Springer-Verlag Berlin Heidelberg 2006

2. *Formation*: the phase of the VO where members are discovered, selected and assigned to fulfilling the identified service requirements derived from the CD. There is therefore a period of negotiation between the initiator and members that concludes with these agreements being signed by the relevant interacting parties.
3. *Operation*: the Collaboration Definition is enacted and the end-points of the role assignments (i.e which are selected VO members) interact and exchange messages, documents and production information. Operation also has the implicit sub-state "dormant" when all members are inactive due to some technical or contractual exception that needs to be handled.
4. *Dissolution*: the final phase of the VO, where the business objective specified in the CD is met, or some technical or contractual violation occurs that invalidates the existence of the VO.

The focus of the paper is on the Formation phase and, especially, member selection during this phase. In the Formation phase the initiator has to perform following actions:

1. *Query*: the initiator sends a query containing keywords derived from the roles in the CD to a public registry and receives a list of candidates that have previously registered.
2. *Invitation*: the initiator contacts the candidates, informs them of his intention to form a VO and invites them to play a specific role. He sends them the partner profile detailing the expectations derived from the CD.
3. *Negotiation*: the initiator engages in negotiation about contractual terms with the candidates that have expressed interest in joining the VO. The initiator can negotiate with multiple candidates in parallel and pause or resume a negotiation to achieve the best result possible.
4. *Selection*: The initiator chooses the best-suited candidate and assigns him a role in the VO. The chosen candidate now becomes a member of the VO and other candidates are finally rejected.

If we expect a VO initiator to use a reputation system for member selection, it has to provide a benefit for him. There is likely no direct monetary benefit in using the reputation system rather he is likely to receive better service (or in general performance) by using a high reputable provider. So, one expectation would be that the overall number of positive transactions increases when using a reputation service for member selection.

The second benefit of using a reputation system arises when the initiator has to deal with unknown parties. Their business record may be unknown to the initiator and a reputation system can help establish trust. In our model one would then expect that a certain percentage of reputation values is based on the transitive trust evaluation.

We consider the question what kind of reputation system can support the selection of members for the VO. First, the initiator can invite only candidates whose reputation is above a certain threshold. The threshold can be fixed or adaptive to the candidates found (e.g. the ten best reputation values). Second, the initiator can choose from the set of candidates based on reputation. There are many other differentiating factors for candidates, such as price or delivery time, which must be considered in this decision, but reputation can be used as another weighted component in this mix or it can be used to make the final decision among a group of equally well-suited candidates.

The degree of influence reputation has varies with the selection method, but in any case: the higher the reputation the more likely a candidate is to be selected. And a higher selection ratio means more business and more profit. This implies that there is an incentive for attacking the reputation system, such that the attacker's reputation increases. A reputation system suitable for member selection needs to be resistant against this kind of attack.

We present a model of reputation that is derived from the way business partners are currently selected and differs from most other models of reputation, as discussed in the related work section. It is particular well-suited to withstand attacks from participants trying to increase their reputation. We present an algorithm that implements this model in our framework of VOs and evaluate its performance.

The paper is organized as follows: the next section reviews related work, section 3 presents our model of reputation and system architecture. Section 4 analyzes the attacks and outlines the design requirements on a reputation system for member selection. We then present in section 5 the design of our algorithm and show its evaluation in section 6. The last section concludes the paper.

2   Related Work

From a productive use perspective, reputation systems already play a role in several online businesses, such as eBay or Amazon. As in the work presented in this paper, business in those communities exhibits a transactional behavior and the partner selection for transactions is supported by reputation systems. Since the transactions are real business transactions involving money transfer, their reputations systems were subject of several published vulnerability and attack analysis [1][5][11]. Especially Resnick et al. in [11] classified the most common forms of attacks on reputation systems like badmouthing, liars or collusion attacks. They also put an emphasis on initial values, what kind of reputation value is initially assigned to a newly arriving entity without available prior knowledge or history. Josang et al. in [5] provide a quite exhaustive survey of reputation systems in industry and academic research. They also address the previously mentioned attacks for particular reputation systems. Bolton's analysis in [1] revealed that most productive reputation systems are susceptible to fraudulent behavior, for instance cheaters and liars in an eMarketplace. Addressing this particular issue of liars, Padovan et al. [9] and Sen et al. [14] present reputation systems which try to counteract fraudulent behavior or provide an augmented decision process. The work we present in this paper is rather changing the internal reputation mechanism/algorithm than working around a vulnerable system. An experimental evaluation of reputation systems was done in [13]. Many attacks, including fake transactions have been considered, but their main draw-back was the model of reputation that only considered global reputation values. We have designed a reputation algorithm that uses personalized reputation ratings and can show that it significantly performs better against this very important attack.

For Peer-to-Peer (P2P) networks several reputation algorithms have been proposed. These algorithms are related to ours, but usually need to consider different kind of attacks as they occur in real P2P networks. The algorithm proposed in [8] implicitly uses a personalized model of reputation, but is simpler than ours due to the restriction that it needs to be computed in a distributed fashion. The EigenTrust algorithm suggested in [7] is a global reputation system, but explicitly builds on the notion of a web of trust by computing the global reputation from the entire matrix of ratings. It has been evaluated against attacks in P2P networks and furthermore in [13]. It is based on Google's PageRank algorithm and therefore has a well established basis. We use it as our reference to compare against. A personalization of EigenTrust has been attempted in [3] by applying an extension for PageRank to EigenTrust, but the personalization is very limited. A related approach has been followed in [10], but the reputation is not feed-back based.

A reputation algorithm for eCommerce P2P networks has been suggested in [18]. It is a global reputation algorithm, but uses the reputation of the rater in a restricted fashion without explicit reference to a web of trust. It has been evaluated against some attacks, but not fake transactions. In [19] a reputation algorithm also for electronic marketplaces is described that exploits the graph for properties of the ratings to compute a personalized reputation. The algorithm itself uses all paths instead of our maximum-weight path which deteriorates in cyclic, fully connected graphs like ours and, most importantly, is not evaluated (or has any new design properties) to resist attacks from fake transactions. The Beta reputation system by Josang et al. [5] tries to predict future performance based on a statistical approach. It follows the global model of reputation and is suggested for eCommerce applications. In [17] it has very successfully been made resistant to the related attack of unfair ratings, but a brute-force attack of fake transactions has not yet been evaluated.

Voss suggests the use of reputation for VOs [16], but does not detail its suggestions, nor evaluates the threats that are derived from the suggested uses. The main contribution of the paper, an algorithm to privately leave feed-back ratings, is unrelated to our contribution.

3   Model of Reputation

In the non-electronic business world business partners are selected based on personal relationships. A business owner has experience of interacting with his partners and therefore bases his trust in them performing business transactions as expected on this experience. The more (positive) experience he has with a partner, the more trust he usually places in that partner. In a highly dynamic, electronic, geographically dispersed environment such as VOs it is difficult to form such personal relationships. Often one is confronted to make choices among candidates with which one has no previous experience. The reputation system can help form trust in such candidates. We view such relationships as the combination of previous performance and recommendation trust, since we believe that an established positive relationship will foster honesty in future recommendations and vice-versa.

In most reputation systems [7][13][18] reputation is scalar value $R(A)$ for each participant A that is a global ranking of the participants. Our reputation model views the system as a web of trust relationships, such as the personal relationships formed by the business owners. Reputation is the relation of a participant A wishing to engage in business with participant B: $R(A, B)$. It is a two-variable function of the two participants, i.e. two participants A and C may have very different views R(A, B) and R(C, B) of B's reputation.

The idea of using a web of trust is not new and many other reputation system involve the relationships of the participant in the computation of the reputation []. Our algorithm operates directly on the trust relationships and combines transitive trust (as in e.g. certificates or PGP keys) with a reputation rating: If a participant A trusts participant B (with a certain rating) and participant B trusts participant C (with a certain rating), then participant A trusts participant C (with a rating as a function of the other two ratings). One can also compare our algorithm to a recommender system. In some sense, B recommends C to A in the example above. It is also necessary to evaluate this model of reputation and its specific algorithm under the attacks important in its intended area of use (here selection of members for VOs).

This model of reputation (using the trust relationships amongst the participants) particularly lends itself to resistance against the attack of faking positive feedback. A group of attackers collaborate in order to boost their reputation rating by leaving false, positive feed-back for each other. In our model of reputation this will only strengthen the trust relationship among themselves, but not necessarily strengthen the path from an honest inquirer to the attacker, such that the reputation from the honest inquirer's point of view should remain unaffected. We test this hypothesis in the evaluation section of our algorithm.

The trust relationship between two participants is formed based on the past experience they had with each other. A participant leaves a feed-back rating after each transaction and these ratings are accumulated to a relationship value. The reputation R(A, B) can therefore also be seen as a function of all ratings left in the system, i.e. the ratings are the only input to form the pairs of reputations.

Another benefit of exploiting established relationships in member selection is the formation of long-term relationships. By relying on positive past experience well-performing members are likely to be selected again and business networks of participants can form. Such networks have the benefit that they can exploit further long-term optimization of business processes by investing in infrastructure and business process adaptation technology rather than just the short-term satisfaction of a common (temporary) business objective.

4 System Architecture

Underlying each VO there is an Enterprise Network Infrastructure (EN). This infrastructure provides basic services, such as registration and notification. It also provides the reputation service.

Each participant of a VO must first register with the EN in order to be eligible for membership status in a VO. He must present some credential (e.g. an entry in local administration's business registry) in order to obtain membership status in the EN. Each VO in turn is registered with the EN, as well. The set of registered participants is queried for candidates for a role in a VO during Formation phase. This service is also provided by the EN.

The reputation service is a centralized service offered by the EN. We anticipate there being one reputation service for all VOs, but different EN providers might choose to allow competing reputation services to cater for different needs and preferences. In the dissolution phase of each VO all members leave feed-back ratings with the reputation server for the other members with whom they have completed transactions. Each such rating can be authenticated to be associated with a specific VO and one cannot leave unsubstantiated feed-back. Nevertheless it is difficult for the EN provider to verify that a business transaction has taken place and an attacker can create fake VOs and leave feed-back for these with the reputation server, i.e. it is still possible for an attacker to create fake transactions.

Since each EN participant needs to register with some real-world credential in order to obtain EN member status, the multiple identities attack on the reputation system, where a participant always starts with a new identity once he has ruined his reputation of the old one, is sufficiently deterred, if not impossible.

Since the reputation service is central, it has access to all ratings and can do its computation locally instead of distributed, preventing difficulties in the reliability of the computation and the overhead of communication cost. Each query just sends the two parties (A and B) to the reputation service, which does a local trusted computation and returns the result.

5   Analysis of Attacks and Design Requirements

5.1   Analysis of Attacks

As described in the introduction the use of reputation in member selection can provide substantial gains to participants with high reputation, it is therefore necessary to prevent attacks that raise reputation.

The first attack we consider on the reputation system is the creation of fake transactions with positive feed-back. In most reputation systems this clearly raises the expected reputation of the participants the positive feed-back was left for. It therefore has the potential to increase profit when reputation is used for member selection and the attack is very critical. We evaluate the performance of our algorithm under this attack in section 6. A potential mitigation of this attack is to collect fees for every transaction that are supposed to capture the additional profit gained by the fake transactions, but the more vulnerable a reputation system is to this attack, the higher the fees have to be. A built-in resistance to this attack allows the fees to be lower covering the costs of the transaction rather than being used as a deterrence to create fake transactions. We don't consider using the value of the transaction in the reputation a useful deterrence of this kind of attack as suggested in [18], since the value of the transaction can be faked as well. Even if combined with fees, the attacker then can just replace several small fake transactions with one big one or vice-versa. Also the value of the transaction might be confidential in several business cases.

An attack on the overall system rather than on the reputation system itself is to consistently deliver bad performances. This attack is commonly considered for reputation systems in P2P networks, since it is actively being pursued in many real P2P networks. We do not consider this attack here, since we do not believe that any successful business model can be built on consistently performing badly. Differently from P2P networks, we do not see a motivation for this attack in our scenario and therefore ignore it in our evaluation. We consider however subtle differences in well performing participants, which are supposed to be highlighted by the reputation system.

A third attack is to leave false or no feed-back at all. First, currently methods are being researched in the TrustCoM[1] project that leave feed-back automatically and, second, leaving no or false feed-back has an immediate negative impact on the participant's own feed-back left by the partner. If a participant is allowed to change his feed-back he is capable of reacting to such actions by the business partner, even after he has left feed-back. Since in our setting it is in the attacker's best interest to raise (and not lower) his reputation this attack seems unlikely and we do not evaluate its impact.

There have been "successful" fake business attacks where the attacker offered some services, engaged in many business transactions, collected payments, but never delivered the goods or services. One could imagine the attacker exploiting the reputation service to lure customers to his business. This corresponds to the erratic or changing behavior attack considered in other reputation systems. Luckily there are some economic deterring factors to using reputation for this kind of attack, besides the "legal deterrence" of prosecution. First, building reputation can be a slow process and requires real (successful) transactions. Therefore the attacker would be required to at least set up a minimal real business which is, of course, associated with the initial investments. Second, there are many other differentiating factors, such as prices or advertisement, which can attract customers to a business that work much faster than building a good reputation. We opt for the "legal deterrence" and leave this attack as a whole to the authorities.

The last attack on the reputation system is to create new identities every time one's reputation drops below a certain threshold. This attack is prevented in our system by requiring a real-world credential (such as an entry into local administration's business registry) to enter the system. Furthermore, the attacker always starts out with an initial reputation that is lower than the one of established successful businesses leaving him at a competitive disadvantage.

5.2 Design Requirements

Besides attacks on the system and the reputation system there are other scenarios that a reputation system might have to deal with. A business' reputation might be subject to a rapid decline, e.g. if it has entered an insolvency process. Such participants should not be selected as members in a VO, but it is very difficult to represent this scenario using a reputation system, since reaction would need to be immediate and harsh (upon the first indication of such circumstances). Such harsh action often invites another kind of attack where the attacker leaves false feed-back in order to eliminate a competitor (similar to spreading false rumors). Although, one can design for such cases, e.g. using authorization for very negative feed-back, we didn't and would like to see such cases handled outside the scope of the reputation system, since they only provide means for an "emergency" case.

---

[1] www.eu-trustcom.com

Another important aspect for a B2B system, such as the VOs, is to support growth. The system will need to start slowly and continuously attract more and more participants. New participants need to be able to enter the market. We believe that VO system offers sufficient differentiating factors for business to be able to enter established markets and build good reputation. Furthermore, new services are offered all the time and allow business to build a good reputation that can be transferred to markets of established services in order to enter those markets as well.

6 Algorithm

Based on our model of reputation, the requirements and attacks, we designed an algorithm for a reputation system used for member selection, called *PathTrust*. As described earlier, the input to PathTrust is the set of all ratings. For each transaction in the system, the user of a service can leave feed-back for the provider. A feed-back rating r is a binary value, either positive or negative. Let *pos[i, j]* be the number of positive feed-back ratings left by participants i for participant j and *neg[i, j]* be the negative ones.

PathTrust sees the system as fully connected graph with edges between all participants registered with the EN. Each edge c_{ij} is a function of *pos[i, j]* and *neg[i, j]*:

$$c_{ij} = \max\left(0.001, \frac{pos[i, j] - \max\left(1, \sum_{k=0}^{n} pos[i, k] \middle/ \sum_{k=0}^{n} neg[i, k]\right) \cdot neg[i, j]}{\sum_{k=0}^{n} \left(pos[i, k] + neg[i, k]\right)}\right)$$

We lower-bound the system to the interval by *0.001* and normalize each edge by the number of total transaction a participant has performed, thereby limiting the weight to the interval *[0.001, 1]*. This provides a relative measure of trust for the participant in another participant (compared to his overall experience), but prevents comparison between edges from different participants. It allows us nevertheless to interpret the weight in our path-searching algorithm as a probability value. The lower bound allows our selection algorithm to choose edges with no experience, even if there are edges with experience from that participant. We weight negative feed-backs by the ratio between positive and negative feed-backs a participant has given to allow the algorithm to react even to fine-grained performance differences. This normalizes average performances to the lowest possible rating. If a ratio is not defined, because the denominator is zero, we default to the other option of the max operation.

We define the weight of a path $<i,j,k>$ from participant i to participant k via participant j as: $w_{<i,j,k>} = c_{ij} \cdot c_{jk}$. Upon receiving a query $R(A,B)$ for reputation of B from A PathTrust computes the path with the maximum weight from A to B. Since $0 < c_{ij} \leq 1$ (and therefore each path weight is constantly decreasing), we can do this simply using Dijkstra's shortest path algorithm. The maximum path weight is returned as the reputation for $R(A,B)$.

The algorithm fully exploits the graph properties of the system, and therefore should provide the required resistance against fake transactions. An attacker generating fake (positive) transactions just increases the weight of the edges with his colluders, but no trust relationship is formed with the other participants. Therefore the path between the honest participants and attackers is only strengthened if they engage in real (positive) transaction with each other. We evaluate the algorithms performance against this attack in the next section. Nevertheless the algorithm can form indirect paths based on transitive trust between participants allowing successfully querying the reputation of participants with whom there is no prior experience.

The algorithm supports the growth of the system for providers as described in the previous section, but the first query of an initiator will return equal reputations for every other participant. This applies to the very first query only, and therefore an initiator entering the system should be offered to choose a small set (one is actually enough) of trusted business partners. The value $pos[\cdot,\cdot]$ will be initialized to 1 for these participants simulating one positive transaction. The first query will then return the trust of those trusted partners. Over time as the initiator engages in more and more transactions the influence of the initial choice will be marginal. If an initiator is entering the system for the purpose of engaging in a specific transaction, this step can be replaced by the first transaction.

7 Evaluation

We ran several simulations to evaluate the performance of our proposed algorithm for VO member selection. The design of the experiments and their results are described in this section.

First, we need to describe how we intend the reputation system to be used for member selection. The service registry returns to the initiator a list of candidates from which the initiator chooses one (after negotiation). In our experiments we do not model negotiation or other differentiating factor between candidates, such as price. We assume that all candidates offer similar conditions and propose the weighted reputation selection algorithm: Let Φ be the set of candidates and let I be the initiator, then for each candidate $C \in \Phi$ the probability that she is chosen is

$$p(C) = \frac{R(I,C)}{\sum_{A \in \Phi} R(I,A)}$$

This approach supports our notion that reputation is a soft criterion for choosing candidates, since it is probabilistic and allows lower ranked candidates to be selected as well, e.g. they could have differentiated using additional services, such as payment options or price.

Besides the actual algorithm we proposed a specific model of reputation that views reputation as a function of the inquirer and the queried. We argued that this model provides inherent benefits in attack resistance compared to models that see reputation as a function of the queried only. We therefore compare our algorithm to the EigenTrust [7] algorithm. The EigenTrust algorithm also works on the web of trust, since it uses the rater's reputation in computing the final reputation. Nevertheless it still adheres to the model that reputation is a global function (i.e. equal for every inquirer). Furthermore it has performed well in studies of such algorithms [13].

We used 1000 participants (nodes in the graph) in our test bed. 30 services were available to initiators and each participant offers 3 services. The providers for a service were uniformly chosen from the set of participants, i.e. there are 100 providers for each service.

We then simulated the formation of a VO. Each VO has an initiator which has the need for a specific service. The initiator was uniformly chosen among all participants and the requested service uniformly among all services. The initiator then queries the registry for all available providers of that service and chooses a business partner using the weighted selection algorithm explained above. Each such transaction has a value associated with it. The value was chosen uniformly from the domain [1, 100] and given to the initiator. It represents the profit the service provider makes when being chosen for that VO. We did not simulate the profit of the initiator since the inception of the VO is random. The goal of each participant is to maximize its profit and since so far all choices are random, the means to achieve that is to boost reputation which has a direct impact on the probability being chosen for a VO. This models the situation and risk we have been discussing for choosing VO members using the reputation service.

We divided the simulation into rounds. During each round 100 VOs where formed in parallel and there were 100 rounds, i.e. we simulated 10000 transactions per test run. The reported numbers are averages of 3 test runs.

7.1 Resistance Against Fake Transaction

Our first test was to create fake transactions and see if the profit of cheaters increases compared to honest participants. Each cheater created one false transaction per round,

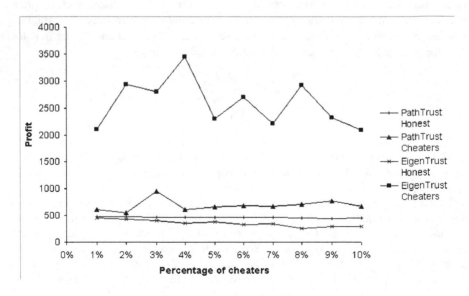

Fig. 1. Resistance to cheating

i.e. about 10 fake transactions per 1 real transaction. He always chose an assigned collaborator for the fake transaction and its value does not count towards the accumulated profit. In general, each transaction was positively rated, whether it was real or fake.

The results are summarized in Fig. 1. We increased the percentage of cheaters from 1% to 10% and depicted the average profit a cheater and an honest participant makes. From the graph we can see that EigenTrust is clearly more vulnerable to this kind of attack than PathTrust, since the average profit of a cheater in EigenTrust exceeds the one in PathTrust up to a factor of 5.6. From these numbers we can conclude that transaction fees that consume the additional profit of a cheater would need to be 10 times higher in EigenTrust consuming 47% of the profit of an honest participant compared to 4.8% using PathTrust.

7.2 Percentage of Positive Transactions

Our second test is supposed to measure the impact of the reputation system on overall system performance. A reputation value is supposed to predict the performance of a participant. It therefore should help choose the best provider for a given service. Besides acquiring trust in unknown candidates this is a further benefit for the initiator. We divided the set of participants into two: good performers which provide good service in 99% of the transactions and not-so-good performers which provide good service in 95% of the transactions. This reflects our view that all businesses need to achieve a reasonable level of performance to be successful and it makes it difficult for the reputation system to operate on those small differences. There were 100 bad performers, i.e. 10% of the participants. This implies that the expected average percentage of good performances of all transactions is 98.6% when using a random choice of VO members (i.e. no reputation system at all). An improvement over this number indicates an advantage of using this reputation system, i.e. the higher this number the better the reputation system. Even if the reputation system managed to separate the two groups completely and only chose good performers, the percentage of good performances would be 99%. So the possible improvement from using a reputation system in this scenario is small and even small improvements are difficult to achieve.

The results of this experiment are summarized in Fig. 2. We increased the percentage of bad performers that cheated using fake transactions attack as above from 0% to 100%. We thought that bad performers might be particularly inclined to conceal their disadvantage by resorting to cheating. No additional (good performing) cheaters were introduced. The graph depicts the percentage of good transactions given the percentage of cheaters. We can see that the EigenTrust algorithm looses its advantage over random choice once we introduce cheating. Furthermore, we see that this loss is much lower in the PathTrust, but still it looses its advantage to random choice suggesting that cheating annihilates one of the benefits of using a reputation system. We therefore suggest using transaction fees to deter cheating (which can be much lower in the PathTrust algorithm than in the EigenTrust algorithm as discussed in the previous section) and then both systems provide nearly the same benefit in performance gain to the initiator.

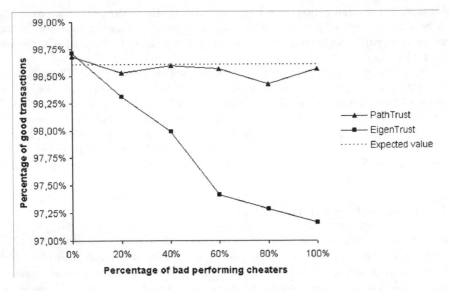

Fig. 2. System performance

8 Conclusion

We evaluated the requirements for a reputation system to be used for VO member selection. We identified threats and attacks that can be used against the whole system and the use of the reputation system in particular. Based on these findings we developed a model to be used for reputation system for VO member selection that seems particularly well suited to resist the major threats. Then we built a new reputation algorithm in this model and evaluated its performance in a simulation of VO formation against a chosen candidate from the prevalent model of reputation. The evaluation shows that our algorithm provides clear benefits in the presence of attacks. It is therefore beneficial to the operators of a VO infrastructure while preserving the advantages of using a reputation system to the users of that system, the VO initiators.

Currently, a VO infrastructure is being developed by the TrustCoM project that is supposed to be made available for use by business. It would be a great enhancement to this work to study the use and impact of a reputation system and the PathTrust reputation algorithm in particular in a real-world system.

References

[1] G. Bolton, E. Katok, and A. Ockenfels. How Effective are Online Reputation Mechanisms? Technical Report 2002-25, Max Planck Institute of Economics, Strategic Interaction Group, 2002. Available at http://ideas.repec.org/p/esi/discus/2002-25.html.

[2] R. Bultje, and J. van Wijk. Taxonomy of Virtual Organizations, Based on Definitions, Characteristics and Typology. VOnet Newsletter 2(3), 1998.

[3] P. Chirita, W. Nejdl, M. Schlosser, and O. Scurtu. Personalized Reputation Management in P2P Networks. Proceedings of the Trust, Security and Reputation Workshop, 2004.

[4] J. Haller, Y. Karabulut, and P. Robinson. Security Controls in Collaborative Business Processes. Proceedings of the 6th IFIP Working Conference on Virtual Enterprises, 2005.

[5] A. Josang, and R. Ismail. The Beta Reputation System. Proceedings of the 15th Bled Conference on Electronic Commerce, 2002.

[6] Josang, R. Ismail, and C. Boyd. A survey of trust and reputation systems for online service provision. (to appear) Decision Support Systems, 2005. Available at http://security. dstc.edu.au/papers/JIB2005-DSS.pdf.

[7] S. Kamvar, M. Schlosser, and H. Garcia-Molina. The EigenTrust Algorithm for Reputation Management in P2P Networks. Proceedings of the Twelfth International World Wide Web Conference, 2003.

[8] S. Marti, and H. Garcia-Molina. Limited reputation sharing in P2P systems. Proceedings of the 5th ACM conference on Electronic commerce, 2004.

[9] Padovan, S. Sackmann, T. Eymann, and I. Pippow. Prototype for an Agent-based Secure Electronic Marketplace including Reputation Tracking Mechanisms. Technical Report 0204002, Economics Working Paper Archive, 2002. Available at http://ideas.repec.org/p/wpa/wuwpco/0204002.html.

[10] J. Pujol, R. Sangüesa, and J. Delgado. Extracting Reputation in Multi Agent Systems by Means of Social Network Topology. Proceedings of the first international joint conference on Autonomous agents and multiagent systems, 2002.

[11] P. Resnick, K. Kuwabara, R. Zeckhauser, and E. Friedman. Reputation Systems. Communications of the ACM 43(12), 2000.

[12] P. Robinson, Y. Karabulut, and J. Haller. Dynamic Virtual Organization Management for Service Oriented Enterprise Applications. Proceedings of the 1st International Conference on Collaborative Computing, 2005.

[13] A. Schlosser, M. Voss, and L. Brückner. Comparing and Evaluating Metrics for Reputation Systems by Simulation. Proceedings of the IEEE Workshop on Reputation in Agent Societies, 2004.

[14] S. Sen, and N. Sajja. Robustness of reputation-based trust: boolean case. Proceedings of the first international joint conference on Autonomous agents and multiagent systems, 2002.

[15] T. Strader, F. Lin, and M. Shaw. Information Structure for electronic virtual organization management, Decision Support Systems 23, 1998.

[16] M. Voss, and W. Wiesemann. Using Reputation Systems to Cope with Trust Problems in Virtual Organizations. Proceedings of the 3rd International Workshop on Security in Information Systems, 2005.

[17] A. Whitby, A. Josang, and J. Indulska. Filtering Out Unfair Ratings in Bayesian Reputation Systems. The Icfain Journal of Management Research, 4(2), 2005.

[18] L. Xiong, and L. Liu. A Reputation-Based Trust Model for Peer-to-Peer eCommerce Communities. Proceedings of the IEEE Conference on E-Commerce, 2003.

[19] G. Zacharia, A. Moukas, and P. Maes. Collaborative Reputation Mechanisms in Electronic Marketplaces. Proceedings of the 32nd Hawaii International Conference on System Sciences, 1999.

A Versatile Approach to Combining Trust Values for Making Binary Decisions*

Tomas Klos[1],** and Han La Poutré[1,2]

[1] Dutch National Research Institute for Mathematics and Computer Science (CWI)
P.O. Box 94079, NL-1090 GB Amsterdam, The Netherlands
[2] Faculty of Technology Management, Technical University of Eindhoven
tomas.klos@cwi.nl
http://homepages.cwi.nl/~tomas/

Abstract. In open multi-agent systems, agents typically need to rely on others for the provision of information or the delivery of resources. However, since different agents' capabilities, goals and intentions do not necessarily agree with each other, trust can not be taken for granted in the sense that an agent can not always be expected to be willing and able to perform optimally from a focal agent's point of view. Instead, the focal agent has to form and update beliefs about other agents' capabilities and intentions. Many different approaches, models and techniques have been used for this purpose in the past, which generate trust and reputation values. In this paper, employing one particularly popular trust model, we focus on the way an agent may use such trust values in trust-based decision-making about the value of a binary variable.

We use computer simulation experiments to assess the relative efficacy of a variety of decision-making methods. In doing so, we argue for systematic analysis of such methods beforehand, so that, based on an investigation of characteristics of different methods, different classes of parameter settings can be distinguished. Whether, *on average* across many random problem instances, a certain method performs better or worse than alternatives is not the issue, given that the agent using the method always exists in a particular setting. We find that combining trust values using our likelihood method gives performance which is relatively robust to changes in the setting an agent may find herself in.

1 Introduction

In open multi-agent systems such as grid-based virtual organizations [1], agents typically need to rely on others for the delivery of information or resources or for the execution of tasks. Since different agents' capabilities, goals and intentions do not necessarily agree with each other, however, trust can not be taken for granted in the sense that an agent can not always be expected to be willing and able to perform optimally from a focal agent's point of view.

---

* We are grateful to the anonymous referees for helpful comments.
** Corresponding author.

K. Stølen et al. (Eds.): iTrust 2006, LNCS 3986, pp. 206–220, 2006.
© Springer-Verlag Berlin Heidelberg 2006

In many different circumstances and application settings, therefore, it turns out to be worthwhile for an agent to build up a measure of her trust in other agents in her environment, and to update it on the basis of her experiences with those other agents, or on the basis of other agents' experiences to the extent she has access to those experiences, e.g. through a centralized or decentralized reputation storage. The term 'agent,' in whose capabilities, intentions, etc. trust is being built, can be construed very broadly here, in the sense that, in previous work, it has encompassed such diverse entities as human or corporate transaction partners in online e-commerce settings [2,3,4], software agents in multi-agent systems [5,6,7,8,9], peers in peer-to-peer (P2P) systems [10], providers of web services on the semantic web [11,12], potential members of virtual organizations on the grid [1], sensors in distributed sensor networks [13], or nodes in mobile ad-hoc networks [14].

For the purpose of assessing trust, many different computational trust models have been proposed in the literature, based on a wide variety of techniques (see, e.g., [15] for an overview of trust models in e-commerce settings, or [16] for a review of computational trust models in multi-agent systems). Once an agent has established a trust or reputation value for a particular agent, resource, service, etc., the agent needs to act on the basis of that value. In some circumstances, this may involve ordering or ranking a number of alternatives, e.g. service providers or potential trade partners; in others, a decision needs to be made about whether or not the agent should interact or continue interacting with a particular other agent. In general, the value of a certain, often binary, random variable typically needs to be established, which might be the presence or absence of some environmental feature (fire, injured people, hazardous materials) in the context of incident management [7,8], or whether some other agent has good vs. bad intentions in a strategic interaction setting [17] or in a mobile ad-hoc network or a peer to peer network.

The bulk of previous work has focused on designing (computational) trust models that take direct interactions and possibly third-party (reputation) information into account in making as accurate as possible an assessment of another agent's capabilities or intentions, including, for example, making truthful reporting of reputation information incentive compatible for those third parties [18,19], or filtering out unfair reputation ratings provided by third parties [20]. In the current paper, we focus on the subsequent decisions that need to be taken by agents *based on* these trust values: if some agents are trusted (highly) and some are not and they're providing conflicting information, how should one combine these trust values with the information provided? Which of the agents are more important, and how should conflicting claims be weighted?

For simplicity, we investigate how an agent should choose between just 2 possible values of an unobservable random variable, when she receives possibly conflicting reports about the actual value of the variable from a set of observers in whom she adaptively develops different amounts of trust, based on the feedback she obtains after making her decision. We investigate the relative effectiveness of a variety of methods for combining trust values. The remainder of the paper is structured as follows. In Section 2 we present the computational model an agent uses to establish and update her trust in other agents' capabilities, based on past experiences. Section 3 introduces and discusses a number of different ways in which the agent may combine trust values to accomplish her task. A comparison among them is done using simulation experiments, results of which are reported in Section 4. Section 5 concludes.

2   The Beta Trust Model

In this paper, we look at agents establishing trust in other agents' capabilities, rather than their intentions (cf. [21]). We employ a popular trust mechanism to let an agent establish and update her trust in various other agents' capabilities [22], and focus on the way in which the agent may combine those trust values when making decisions based on possibly conflicting information provided by those other agents.

In many studies, the Beta probability density function (pdf) is used for modeling trust [13,3,22,8,23,24,4]. The Beta pdf is a probability density of a continuous random variable $\theta \in [0,1]$. In the context of trust models, θ governs an agent j's behavior, and the pdf is interpreted as another agent i's belief function over the values of that random variable. Usually then, the expected value of the Beta pdf is used as agent i's trust in agent j's capabilities or intentions: agent i's subjective probability that j is trustworthy.

Most of the popularity of the Beta pdf stems from the fact that it is convenient mathematically: in Bayesian inference, the Beta pdf is a conjugate prior for binomial likelihood functions, meaning that the posterior is from the same family as the prior (see below). Furthermore, a trust value expressed as the expected value of a Beta random variable is a very simple functional form of the parameters of the Beta pdf. Finally, it has features which capture some of the intuition of trust models, in particular, that an agent's trust in another agent gradually goes up with positive experiences and down with negative experiences, as captured by the Beta pdf's parameters.

As explained above, trust models based on the Beta distribution are typically used to estimate the parameter θ of a distribution generating binary events, such as a trading partner behaving honestly or opportunistically, or an agent delivering true or false information. In the case of such a binary event, with 'success' or 'failure' as possible outcomes, the number of successes n out of a total of N (of these so-called Bernoulli trials), is described probabilistically by the binomial distribution (see [25] for a more complete discussion):

$$p(n \mid \theta, N) = \binom{N}{n} \theta^n (1 - \theta)^{N-n}, \tag{1}$$

where θ is the 'bias,' the probability of success in each independent trial—the quantity we wish to infer the value of. Apart for the binomial coefficient (the leading factor in Eq. 1), the binomial likelihood $p(n \mid \theta, N)$ has the shape $\theta^n (1 - \theta)^{N-n}$, which has the same structure as the Beta distribution:

$$\text{Beta}(\theta \mid r, s) = \frac{1}{\beta(r, s)} \theta^{r-1}(1 - \theta)^{s-1}, \tag{2}$$

for $0 \le \theta \le 1$ and $r, s > 0$, where $\beta(r, s)$ is the beta function.

The expected value of the Beta distribution is $E(\theta) = \frac{r}{r+s}$. The fact that the Beta distribution is a conjugate prior for the binomial likelihood, means that, when it is used as a prior function in Bayesian inference problems concerning a binomial likelihood, the posterior distribution is still a Beta distribution (disregarding the normalization factor in the denominator of Bayes' rule, since it does not depend on θ):

$$\overbrace{p(\theta \mid n, N, r, s)}^{\text{posterior}} \propto \overbrace{\left[\theta^n (1 - \theta)^{N-n}\right]}^{\text{likelihood (see Eq. 1)}} \overbrace{\left[\theta^{r-1}(1 - \theta)^{s-1}\right]}^{\text{prior (see Eq. 2)}}$$

$$\propto \theta^{n+r-1}(1 - \theta)^{N-n+s-1}.$$

Defining $r' = r + n$ and $s' = s + N - n$, the expected value becomes $E(\theta) = \frac{r'}{s'+r'} = \frac{r+n}{r+s+N}$, so in effect, one simply adds the new counts of successes (n) and failures ($N - n$) to the old values of the parameters of the Beta distribution r and s, respectively, and obtains a new distribution which can be used as a prior for calculating the posterior given yet more evidence.

In the context of trust models, an agent i's trust in another agent j's capabilities or intentions, is calculated as the expected value of the current beta distribution

$$\text{trust}_i^j = \frac{r}{r + s},$$

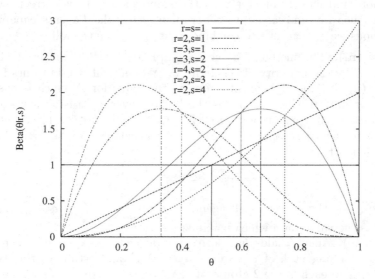

Fig. 1. The Beta pdf of θ for different values of r and s, as indicated. The expected value of θ in each case is indicated by a vertical line of the corresponding type. (Of course, the vertical line for $(r, s) = (2, 1)$ overlaps with that of $(4, 2)$.).

where r and s are the current counts of positive and negative experiences ('successes' and 'failures,' respectively) that i has had with j. In the absence of such experiences, the values $r = s = 1$ are used, yielding a uniform prior, and an expected value of 0.5 for the value governing j's behavior (random behavior). Figure 1 gives the shape of the Beta probability density function of θ given different amounts of evidence.

3   Combining Trust Values

The combination of evidence from multiple sources has received ample attention in the context of Bayesian reputation systems, which model an agent's reputation as the trust to be established in its capabilities or intentions on the basis of different agents' experiences with that agent. In this paper however, we focus on the way in which an agent j's reputation value, irrespective of the way in which it was constructed, should be used in making decisions on the basis of information received from that agent j, for which purpose it should also be combined with different other agents' reputation values.

We suggest a variety of different ways to combine trust values: when an agent receives information from a variety of source-agents or sensors, it needs to combine the information from these sources, taking into account that they have different capabilities, as witnessed by agent i's distinct individual interaction histories with each of them. Agent i needs to guess what the value $a \in \{0, 1\}$ of a binary variable A is, given that each in a set $\mathcal{J}$ of observing agents $j = 1, \ldots, J$ reports to i its (possibly incorrect) observation a_j of the value of A, where agent j's probability of a correct observation is θ_j. After having combined all this information, and chosen and reported the value she thinks is correct, agent i learns the true value and can adjust her trust in each of the J agents' capabilities. The methods we give agent i to combine trust values are the following.

Majority (m). This method lets agent i simply report the value for A which is observed by the majority of agents in $\mathcal{J}$. (We only allow odd values for J.)

Average (a). In this case, agent i reports the value for A which is observed by the group in which she holds the highest average trust: i averages her trust across all agents reporting each possible value $a \in \{0, 1\}$ and chooses the values which is reported by the group in which she places the highest average trust:

$$\overline{\text{trust}_i^{\mathcal{J}_a}} = \frac{\sum_{j \in \mathcal{J}_a} \text{trust}_i^j}{|\mathcal{J}_a|},$$

where $\mathcal{J}_a$ is the subset of all agents who observed a, for $a \in \{0, 1\}$. She chooses the value for a which maximizes $\overline{\text{trust}_i^{\mathcal{J}_a}}$.

Evidence (e). Agent i adds her positive and negative experiences across all agents claiming each of the values $a \in \{0, 1\}$ and estimates the average capability in each of the 2 groups of agents.

$$E(\theta_{\mathcal{J}_a}) = \frac{\sum_{j \in \mathcal{J}_a} \text{positive}_i^j + 1}{\sum_{j \in \mathcal{J}_a} \text{positive}_i^j + \sum_{j \in \mathcal{J}_a} \text{negative}_i^j + 2}$$

She chooses the value for a which maximizes $E(\theta_{\mathcal{J}_a})$.

Although they look similar, especially when the same number of experiences has been had with each observer, there is a difference between the 'a' and 'e' methods: the 'a' method averages across the estimates of different observers' capabilities, whereas the 'e' method estimates the observers' average capability. Both do this on the basis of the expected value of the resulting distribution, but the 'a' method takes the average of the expected values of different distributions (one per observer), while the 'e' method takes the expected value of the distribution that results when the experiences with different observers have been added together. The difference in our case (where the number of experiences with each observer is the same) is negligible, so we will not be showing results from using the 'a' method in this paper.

Likelihood (l). Using this method, agent i calculates the joint probability of the observations twice—assuming each value for A to be the correct one. The intuition is the following: each value $a \in \{0, 1\}$ will have been observed by a subset $\mathcal{J}_a$ of the set of observers $\mathcal{J}$. So, assuming each value to be correct, agent i calculates the joint probability of the observations, which is the same as the likelihood of each of the two values for a, given the observations. For each value of $a \in \{0, 1\}$ (where $\bar{a} = 1 - a$), the likelihood of it being the true value of A is equal to

$$L(A = a | \text{observations}) = p(\text{observations} | A = a) = \prod_{j \in \mathcal{J}_a} \text{trust}_i^j \prod_{j \in \mathcal{J}_{\bar{a}}} (1 - \text{trust}_i^j)$$

where $\mathcal{J}_b$ (for $b \in \{a, \bar{a}\}$) is the subset of $\mathcal{J}$ claiming $A = b$. In other words, if A is equal to a (or $\bar{a}$, respectively), then all the agents in $\mathcal{J}_a$ ($\mathcal{J}_{\bar{a}}$) are correct, which, from the perspective of i, has a joint probability of $\prod_{j \in \mathcal{J}_a} \text{trust}_i^j$, while at the same time, all agents in $\mathcal{J}_{\bar{a}}$ ($\mathcal{J}_a$) are incorrect, which has a joint probability of $\prod_{j \in \mathcal{J}_{\bar{a}}} (1 - \text{trust}_i^j)$. Since different agents' observations are conditionally independent, the joint probability is the product of these marginal probabilities. Agent i reports the value $b \in \{a, \bar{a}\}$ which maximizes the likelihood $L(A = b | \text{observations})$.

4   Simulation Experiments

4.1   Experimental Setup

In our initial experiments, each of the $j = 1, \ldots, J$ observers has a capability θ_j which determines the probability of his success in observing the true value of A.[1] In order to be able to capture the effect of dynamics of the situation, each of these θ_j has an independent probability $0 \leq \delta \leq 1$ of changing in each round of the simulation, which we vary across different experiments. The different θ_j

---

[1] Because agent i is ultimately not interested in learning the value of A directly, but just in assessing each observer's capability and, particularly, in sensibly using those assessments in choosing the value she thinks is most likely (according to the methods discussed in Section 3), we fix the true value at $A = 0$ without loss of generality.

start out at 0.5 and in the case of a change, there is an increase of ± 0.05, chosen uniformly at random, while keeping θ_j between 0 and 1.

4.2   Initial Experiments

As an illustration, Figure 2 shows the results from one run of one of our experiments. In this particular case, agent i uses the 'evidence' method to combine observations from $J = 5$ observers, whose dynamically changing capabilities are shown by the dashed lines that start at 0.5 in round 0, and that change in each round with a probability $\delta = 0.05$. Agent i updates her estimate of the true values of these θ_j as her trust in each of the J agents' capabilities. The line marked "|error|" (near the bottom of the graph) is the absolute value of the difference between agent i's assessments and the true values of these θ_j, averaged across all J agents. Finally, each '+' marks whether, in the given round, agent i ended up reporting the correct value for A: if the '+' is at 0, then i was incorrect, and if it is at 1, agent i was correct in that round.

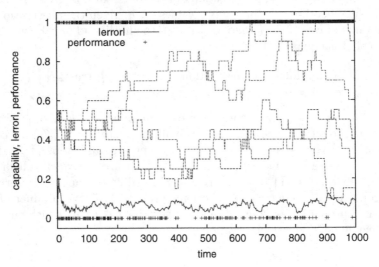

Fig. 2. Results from one run of the experiment (see the text for explanation)

4.3   Discussion

Before we turn to more systematic exploration of these different methods, we have to realize, and can analyze in advance, that the different methods have strong and weak points; in particular, each will work best under particular circumstances. Any numerical investigation can then be tuned to such circumstances, so that different settings believed to be representative of particular empirical situations can be distinguished, and conclusions can be drawn appropriately. In this section, we consider each method in turn, and analyze the circumstances in which each is expected (not) to perform.

Majority. This method does not use trust at all. If there are more observers with a low capability than with a high capability, the majority method is expected not to work well, since it will follow the majority who will be wrong in this case. In fact, in multiple replications of a randomized setup where different observers' capabilities change randomly, this method will perform like random choice, on average.

Evidence. This method estimates the average capability in each of the groups having observed each of the 2 possible values of the random variable A, by setting up a beta distribution based on the aggregated positive and negative experiences with all agents in each group, and calculating and comparing the expected values of both distributions. To the extent that positive and negative experiences with different observers accurately represent those observers' capabilities (which we can assume), this method is expected not to perform well if there isn't at least one agent with relatively high capability present. If all agents are moderately capable, then this method is unable to distinguish between them, because in each given round, they are all correct in their observation with the same probability, and since this method functions like averaging, there is no way to incorporate a comparison between the *size* of both groups, like the majority-method discussed above does. If the capabilities are favorably assigned, the majority-method can be expected to perform well. Its problem is just that it can not deal with low capabilities, which the evidence- and the likelihood-methods can (by estimating those and discounting observations using the estimated capability of the corresponding observer—basically by believing the opposite of what a low-trusted agent claims to have observed).

Likelihood. This method is the best of both worlds, in the sense that groupsize considerations are combined with estimation of capabilities. If all capabilities are equal, they are assessed as such, and when differently sized groups claim different values for A, groupsize is effectively incorporated in the likelihood calculation. The value observed for A by a relatively large group of agents with low estimated capabilities will in fact be less likely, even though the group is large, exactly because the joint probability of all those agents being correct at the same time is very small.

4.4   Further Experiments

Keeping different observers' capabilities fixed for the moment ($\delta = 0$), we now focus on investigating the consequences of the analysis in Section 4.3. The main thrust of this work is the realization that any methods proposed for combining trust values should not be investigated in a randomized environment, as is often done. Rather, the methods' performance in distinct environmental settings should be compared, which should be set up so as to resemble real-world scenarios these agents might encounter. In general, for example, in many real world multi-agent systems, agents will not have randomly assigned and randomly changing capabilities. Moreover, randomized change will yield many experimental situations which are not representative of the state of the multi-agent system as it develops through adaptation to its environment. Agents in real-world multi-agent systems operate in a particular setting, and not in a random setting, so although performance in a random environment may be low, the randomly oc-curing parameter settings that degrade performance may occur infrequently in reality, rendering them over-represented in a random simulation experiment.

To illustrate this point, we first assign $J = 7$ observing agents $j = 1, \ldots, 7$ random capability $0 \leq \theta_j \leq 1$. The results are shown in Figure 3, where each line is the average across 1000 replications. There are actually 3 lines at the bottom, which show the average absolute error between agent i's estimation of each of the observers' capabilities and their actual capabilities. As mentioned above, these capabilities are fixed in these experiments, so in the long run, a reasonably good approximation can be made (average absolute error is about 0.02). Also, the way in which this approximation is made, is independent of the method used for combining them, which is why the lines are pratically on top of each other. The other lines depict the performance in each round, averaged across 1000 replications. The majority-method performs equivalently to random choice, on average, as discussed above: when capabilities are high, the majority-method performs well, but when they are low, then, unable to use any additional information, this method suffers. The two lines near the top of the graph are the lines for the other two methods, evidence and likelihood, where the likeli-hood method can be seen to be slightly better than the evidence method. Since capabilities are assinged randomly in each run of the experiment, and will typ-ically vary quite a lot between different observers, both methods are perfectly capable of distinguishing between any two groups of observers. The likelihood method does slightly better, because, where necessary, it is even able to make a distinction based on groupsize, unlike the evidence-method (see the discussion in Section 4.3 above).

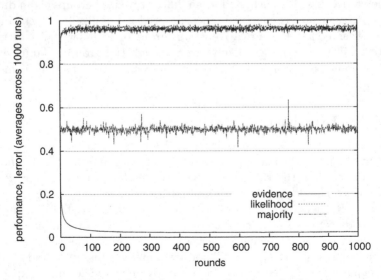

Fig. 3. Capabilities are assigned randomly

As argued above, these kinds of randomized setups are not very informative about the relative effectiveness of the methods specified here, or, more generally, about many other solutions proposed elsewhere. Figures 4 and 5 show some more detail of the relative efficacy of these methods in certain settings. All observers' capabilities are fixed at 0.4 (Fig. 4(a)), and then one observer's capability is increased to 0.45 (Fig. 4(b)), 0.65 (Fig. 4(c)), and 0.85 (Fig. 4(d)). Let's first consider the influence on the performance of the majority-method (the lowest plot in all graphs). It is barely influenced in Fig. 4(b), but starts to increase more strongly in the two lower graphs (4(c) and 4(d)). It may be expected that the group of $J = 6$ observers with their capability fixed at 0.4 typically (on average) splits in two groups of 3, each observing a different value for the random variable A. As one agent's capability starts to increase, it will join the (randomly) correct group more and more often, giving it a majority and leading to that group's observation being selected by agent i. This effect is more pronounced as the expert's capability increases more strongly, and above a value of 0.5.

When all observers' capabilities are equal to 0.4, the evidence method performs slightly better than random, since there is a pattern to be discerned in the observations of the observers: they are more often wrong than right, and

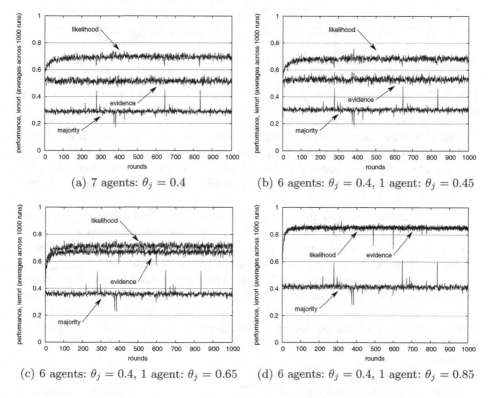

(a) 7 agents: $\theta_j = 0.4$ (b) 6 agents: $\theta_j = 0.4$, 1 agent: $\theta_j = 0.45$

(c) 6 agents: $\theta_j = 0.4$, 1 agent: $\theta_j = 0.65$ (d) 6 agents: $\theta_j = 0.4$, 1 agent: $\theta_j = 0.85$

Fig. 4. Most capabilities are fixed at a relatively low level, and 1 agent's capability is increased in steps

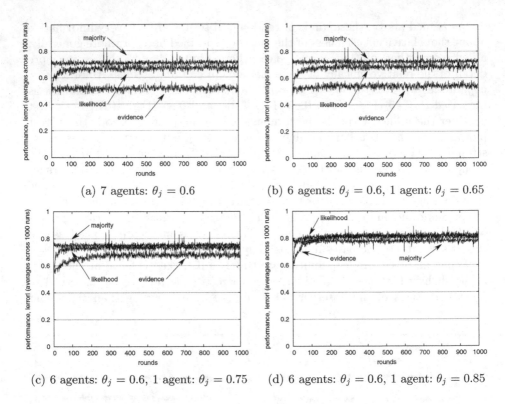

(a) 7 agents: $\theta_j = 0.6$ (b) 6 agents: $\theta_j = 0.6$, 1 agent: $\theta_j = 0.65$

(c) 6 agents: $\theta_j = 0.6$, 1 agent: $\theta_j = 0.75$ (d) 6 agents: $\theta_j = 0.6$, 1 agent: $\theta_j = 0.85$

Fig. 5. Most capabilities are fixed at a relatively high level, and 1 agent's capability is increased in steps

this information can be used to discount their reports, but the evidence method still has trouble distinguishing which group is correct and which is not, because they are basically equally reliable. Only when one agent's reports become more trustworthy, that one agent can drag the others along with him, in convincing the evidence method.

The likelihood method initially performs the best, even when all agents' capabilities are equal and quite low. This is because, as discussed above, the likelihood method can take into account groupsize, unlike the evidence-method: the larger group is more likely to be incorrect, simply because it's a large group and capabilities are smaller than 0.5. (This effect is reversed in the next experiment, where all agents' capabilities are initialized at 0.6: there, the larger group is—correctly—inferred to be correct by the likelihood method.) In Fig. 4(d), the relative advantage of the likelihood method decreases to the point where the two methods' performance is equal: the incorporation of groupsize is not necessary anymore.

Figure 5 shows what happens when all observers' capabilities are fixed at 0.6 (Fig. 5(a)), and when subsequently, one observer's capability is increased to 0.65 (Fig. 5(b)), 0.75 (Fig. 5(c)), and 0.85 (Fig. 5(d)). The majority method does relatively well here, because all agents' capabilities are higher than 0.5. The difference between the likelihood and evidence methods starts out the same as in Figure 4, and they again become equal, with both surpassing the majority method in performance as the expert agent's capability increases to 0.85.

4.5   A Versatile Approach

So, even though the initial experiment with randomized assignment showed the evidence and likelihood methods to almost perform equally well, there is obviously more going on. Different classes of parameter settings can and should be distinguished. For the agents involved, what matters is what class they are in, and not what the various methods' performance in random situations would be, or how those methods perform on average, when tested in a wide variety of randomly generated settings. In this section, we will start exploring such different classes of circumstances.

Consider Fig. 6, which compares the three methods in situations where all observers are equally capable, at different levels, ranging from $\theta = 0.05$ in Figure 6(a), via 0.35 and 0.65 in Figures 6(b) and 6(c), respectively, to $\theta = 0.95$ in Fig. 6(d). In all settings, the likelihood method performs the best, or almost

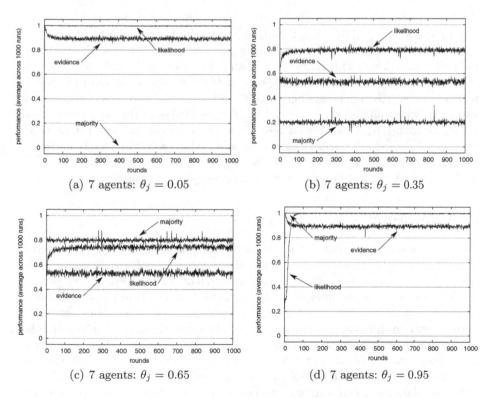

(a) 7 agents: $\theta_j = 0.05$

(b) 7 agents: $\theta_j = 0.35$

(c) 7 agents: $\theta_j = 0.65$

(d) 7 agents: $\theta_j = 0.95$

Fig. 6. Examination of the sensitivity of the different methods' performance to variations in the observers' capabilities

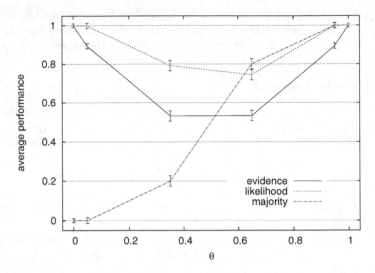

Fig. 7. Overall results

the best. Only the majority method is superior, but only when the observers' capabilities are very high, while the likelihood method is also able to attain good performance when observers' capabilities are low, in which case the majority method breaks down. This is also clear from the overall results in Figure 7, which shows the average across the last 500 rounds of the values per round in Figure 7, which are themselves averages across 1000 replications of each run. Especially in situations where all observers' capabilities are near 0.5 does the evidence method suffer, as compared to settings where observers' behavior is more pronounced. Overall, of course, an agent does not know in which environment it currently resides, so a sensible approach is clearly to go with the likelihood method, since it gives relatively good performance across a range of circumstances.

5   Conclusion

We have proposed a variety of methods for combining an agent's trust in different agents, who provide information about the value of a random variable, which might be a certain state of the environment, or the behavior of yet another agent in a reputation system. We argue for systematic analysis of different methods' characteristics, and for an investigation of these methods' expected performance in different circumstances. At the same time, randomized simulation environments for testing competing methods are considered inappropriate, since real-world agents do not inhabit random environments, but will typically find themselves in certain classes of circumstances. We suggest the use of computer simulations to investigate such classes of circumstances and illustrate this approach by systematically varying one dimension of the situation. From these experiments, we conclude that, even though an individual agent typically does not know in which circumstances it exists, the likelihood method provides a method which seems robust against changes across a wide range of values for the agents' capabilities.

References

1. Foster, I., Jennings, N.R., Kesselman, C.: Brain meets brawn: Why grid and agents need each other. In: Proc. AAMAS 2004, ACM (2004) 8–15
2. Dellarocas, C.: The digitization of word-of-mouth. Management Science (2003)
3. Jøsang, A., Hird, S., Faccer, E.: Simulating the effect of reputation systems on e-markets. In: Proc. 1st Int. Conf. on Trust Management, Crete, Greece (2003)
4. Vassileva, J., Breban, S., Horsch, M.: Agent reasoning mechanism for long-term coalitions based on decision making and trust. Computational Intelligence **18** (2002) 583–595
5. Barber, K.S., Kim, J.: Belief revision process based on trust. In Falcone, R., Singh, M.P., Tan, Y.H., eds.: Trust in Cyber-Societies. Volume 2246 of LNAI. Springer, Berlin (2001) 73–82
6. Barber, K.S., Kim, J.: Soft security: Isolating unreliable agents from society. In Falcone, R., Barber, K.S., Korba, L., Singh, M.P., eds.: Trust, Reputation and Security: Theories and Practice. Volume 2631 of LNAI. Springer, Berlin (2003) 224–233
7. Klos, T.B., La Poutré, H.: Using reputation-based trust for assessing agent reliability. In Falcone, R., Barber, K.S., Sabater-Mir, J., Singh, M.P., eds.: Proc. of the 7th Int'l. Workshop on Trust in Agent Societies at AAMAS-04, New York, NY (2004) 75–82
8. Klos, T.B., La Poutré, H.: Decentralized reputation-based trust for assessing agent reliability under aggregate feedback. In Falcone, R., Barber, K.S., Sabater-Mir, J., Singh, M.P., eds.: Trusting Agents for Trusting Electronic Societies. Volume 3577 of LNCS/LNAI. Springer, Berlin (2005) 110–128
9. Pujol, J.M., Sangüesa, R., Delgado, J.: Extracting reputation in multi-agent systems by means of social network topology. In: Proc. AAMAS'02. (2002)
10. Wang, Y., Vassileva, J.: Trust and reputation model in peer-to-peer networks. In: Proc. P2P'03. (2003)
11. Yolum, P., Singh, M.P.: An agent-based approach for trustworthy service location. In: Proc. 1st Int. Workshop on Agents and Peer-to-Peer Computing. Number 2530 in LNAI. Springer, Berlin (2002) 45–56
12. Yu, B., Singh, M.P.: Search in referral networks. In: Proc. AAMAS'02 Workshop on Regulated Agent-Based Social Systems. (2002)
13. Ganeriwal, S., Srivastava, M.B.: Reputation-based framework for high integrity sensor networks. In: Proc. SASN 2004. ACM (2004) 66–77
14. Liu, J., Issarny, V.: Enhanced reputation mechnisms for mobile ad hoc networks. In Jensen, C., Poslad, S., Dimitrakos, T., eds.: Proc. iTrust. Volume 2995 of LNCS. Springer (2004) 48–62
15. Jøsang, A., Ismail, R., Boyd, C.: A survey of trust and reputation systems for online service provision. Decision Support Systems **(to appear)** (2005)
16. Sabater-Mir, J., Sierra, C.: Review on computational trust and reputation models. AI Review **24** (2005) 33–60
17. Klos, T.B., Alkemade, F.: Trusted intermediating agents in an electronic trade network. In: Proc. AAMAS-05, Utrecht, The Netherlands (2005)

18. Jurca, R., Faltings, B.: Enforcing truthful strategies in incentive compatible reputation mechanisms. In: Internet and Network Economics. Volume 3828 of Lecture Notes in Computer Science. Springer (2005) 268–277
19. Miller, N., Resnick, P., Zeckhauser, R.: Eliciting honest feedback: The peer prediction method. Management Science **51** (2005) 1359–1373
20. Whitby, A., Jøsang, A., Indulska, J.: Filtering out unfair ratings in bayesian reputation systems. Icfain Journal of Management Research **4** (2005) 48–64
21. Liu, W., Williams, M.: Trustworthiness of information sources and information pedigrees. In Meyer, J.C., Tambe, M., eds.: Intelligent Agents VIII. Volume 2333 of Lecture Notes in Artificial Intelligence. Springer (2002) 290–306
22. Jøsang, A., Ismail, R.: The Beta reputation system. In: Proc. 15th Bled Electronic Commerce Conference, Bled, Slovenia (2002)
23. Mui, L., Mohtashemi, M., Halberstadt, A.: A computational model of trust and reputation. In: Proc. 35th Hawaii International Conference on System Science. (2002)
24. Pavlov, E., Rosenschein, J.S., Topol, Z.: Supporting privacy in decentralized additive reputation systems. In: iTrust 2004. Volume 2995 of LNCS. Springer, Berlin (2004) 108–119
25. D'Agostini, G.: Bayesian inference in processing experimental data: Principles and basic applications. Reports on Progress in Physics **66** (2003) 1383–1419

Jiminy: A Scalable Incentive-Based Architecture for Improving Rating Quality

Evangelos Kotsovinos[1], Petros Zerfos[1], Nischal M. Piratla[1],
Niall Cameron[2], and Sachin Agarwal[1]

[1] Deutsche Telekom Laboratories,
Ernst-Reuter-Platz 7, 10587 Berlin, Germany
firstname.lastname@telekom.de
[2] Pembroke College,
Cambridge CB2 1RF, UK
niall.cameron@cantab.net

Abstract. In this paper we present the design, implementation, and evaluation of Jiminy: a framework for explicitly rewarding users who participate in reputation management systems by submitting ratings. To defend against participants who submit random or malicious ratings in order to accumulate rewards, Jiminy facilitates a probabilistic mechanism to detect dishonesty and halt rewards accordingly.

Jiminy's reward model and honesty detection algorithm are presented and its cluster-based implementation is described. The proposed framework is evaluated using a large sample of real-world user ratings in order to demonstrate its effectiveness. Jiminy's performance and scalability are analysed through experimental evaluation. The system is shown to scale linearly with the on-demand addition of slave machines to the Jiminy cluster, allowing it to successfully process large problem spaces.

1 Introduction

Reputation management systems (RMSs) allow participants to report their experiences with respect to past interactions with other participants. RMSs are often provided by retailer web sites, on-line movie review databases, auction systems, and trading communities. However, as identified in [12], information within such systems may not always be reliable. Many participants opt not to submit ratings, as there is little incentive for them to spend time performing the rating task — especially if interactions are frequent and participants expect utility standards of service. Furthermore, participants tend to report mostly exceptionally good or exceptionally bad experiences as a form of reward or revenge respectively. Additionally, ratings are often reciprocal, as underlined by the observation that a seller tends to rate a buyer after the buyer rates the seller [17].

In our previous work we proposed Pinocchio [12], an incentive model where participants are explicitly *rewarded* for submitting ratings, and are *debited* when they query the RMS. Providing explicit incentives a) increases the quantity of ratings submitted and b) reduces the bias of ratings by removing implicit or hidden rewards, such as revenge or reciprocal ratings. To prevent participants from

K. Stølen et al. (Eds.): iTrust 2006, LNCS 3986, pp. 221–235, 2006.
© Springer-Verlag Berlin Heidelberg 2006

submitting arbitrary or dishonest feedback with the purpose of accumulating rewards, Pinocchio features the credible threat of halting rewards for participants who are deemed dishonest by its probabilistic *honesty estimator*.

In this paper we present *Jiminy*, a distributed architecture that employs the Pinocchio model to build a scalable system for providing participation incentives. This work makes the following contributions:

- It presents the design, implementation, and cluster deployment of Jiminy, including an algorithmic implementation of the Pinocchio mathematical model, suitable for a clustered architecture.
- It analyses a large data set (from the GroupLens[1] project) of one million movie ratings submitted by human users. It does so in order to verify the validity of the assumptions based on which our model is designed, regarding the distribution of our honesty estimator and the independence of ratings.
- It demonstrates the effectiveness of the Jiminy honesty assessment algorithm by showing that it can detect four different types of dishonest users injected into the GroupLens data set.
- It demonstrates experimentally that the Jiminy cluster can scale to process large problem spaces — i.e., large numbers of participants and ratings — at run-time, as the cluster's performance increases almost linearly with the addition of more slave machines.

The rest of the paper is organised as follows. A brief outline of the Pinocchio reward and honesty assessment scheme is provided in Section 2. The design, implementation, and deployment of Jiminy in a cluster — including an algorithmic realisation of the Pinocchio model and extensions for its efficient implementation in a distributed environment — is described in Section 3. The effectiveness of the Jiminy algorithms and the scalability of the clustered system is evaluated in Section 4. Related work in trust management and incentive schemes is presented in Section 5. Finally, our conclusions and future work are discussed in Section 6.

2   Background

The Pinocchio model provides a mechanism for the assessment of the quality of ratings that are submitted by users[2] of a reputation management system (RMS). It defines an *honesty metric* that quantifies in a probabilistic sense how honest a participant is in her ratings, and outlines a *reward model* that provides incentives for participants to submit honest ratings. In this section we provide brief background information on the Pinocchio model — a detailed description is provided in [12].

2.1   Honesty Metric

The honesty metric in the Pinocchio model is used to discourage participants from submitting random ratings in an attempt to accumulate rewards. Moreover, it

---

[1] http://www.grouplens.org
[2] We use the terms *user* and *participant* as equivalent throughout this paper.

detects participants who always submit average ratings, which convey little useful information to other users of the reputation management system. The entities that are reviewed by participants are referred to as *subjects*. When participants interact with a subject they form opinions about it and report these opinions to the RMS through a numeric score, or *rating*. The opined-about subjects comprise the set R. Sufficient number of ratings by different participants on a specific subject can be used to fit a probability distribution that corresponds to the ratings of all participants for that subject. This probability distribution can then be used to check the credibility of ratings submitted by participants for that subject.

Suppose participant u reported a rating value Q_s for subject s. We compute the log-probability of likelihood L_s of Q_s based upon the probability distribution of all ratings available for subject s. The more unlikely a rating value on a subject, the more negative L_s becomes:

$$L_s = \ln\left(\Pr(Q_s)\right) \tag{1}$$

We define a subset B, $B \subseteq R$, which contains all subjects rated by a given participant u. Summing over all subjects (elements of B) about which u has reported reviews, we obtain T_u:

$$T_u = \sum_{s \in B} \ln\left(\Pr(Q_s)\right) \tag{2}$$

These values alone are not sufficient for estimating honesty; they would be biased towards users who are continually submitting ratings with a high probability, i.e., the average opinion of the community. It is necessary to protect against this, thus the honesty estimator measures the deviation Z of random variable T_u from its mean value $\bar{T}$ (considering all participants), and standard deviation $\hat{\sigma}$:

$$Z = \frac{(T_u - \bar{T})}{\hat{\sigma}} \tag{3}$$

$|Z|$ is used as the estimator, and is referred to as the *nose-length* of the participant in the Pinocchio model.

The calculation of the nose-length $|Z|$ of a participant from Equation 3 requires the scaling of her T_u value according to the total number of rating submissions the participant has made. Without the scaling process, all users are expected to provide same number of ratings, placing a limitation on the applicability of the model to real-world data sets. In Jiminy this aspect is taken into account in the definition of honesty metric, as discussed in the following section.

2.2   Reward Model

Participants are encouraged to submit their experiences on subjects by being provided with a reward for each experience that they report. A credit balance is kept for each participant, which is credited with a reward for each rating that she contributes, and debited for each query that she makes.

Rewarding a participant for the ratings she makes is also subject to whether she is deemed honest or not. When her nose-length rises above a certain threshold (*dishonesty threshold*), she is deemed dishonest and rewards for further ratings that she submits to the RMS are halted. For her rewards to be resumed, her honesty metric has to fall below the *honesty threshold*, and remain so for a specific period of time (*probationary period*). Pinocchio seeks to ensure that there is a substantial penalty for recurring dishonest behaviour, and, at the same time avoid being too strict to first-time cheaters. To achieve this, an exponential back-off scheme is followed for the value of the probationary period, which is doubled each time a participant is considered as being dishonest.

3   Design and Implementation

In this section we present the design and implementation of Jiminy. We describe the main components and operations of the system, and discuss the approach that we followed to realise its deployment in a distributed environment. The latter is necessary in order for Jiminy to scale to a large number of participants, each of which requires computationally intensive operations and increases the system load considerably.

Jiminy is a multiprocess, multithreaded application written in Java, which interacts with a MySQL backend database for storage and retrieval of system/user data. Figure 1 shows the main components of the system, along with their interaction with the RMS. The architecture of Jiminy follows the master-slave model for server design. The goal is to distribute the processing load that is involved in the calculation of the nose-lengths $|Z|$ of participants to multiple machines, and parallelise the operation so that it scales with the number of participants and ratings. The more slave machines are added to the system, the higher the possibility of bulk processing of user honesty updates.

Without limiting the applicability of Jiminy, we assume the RMS to be distributed, running a node on each Jiminy slave. This RMS architecture is similar to that of BambooTrust [13].

Master.   Upon initialisation of the system, the main process on the master node starts a new thread that listens for incoming registration requests from slave nodes — operation 1 in Figure 1. Once several slaves have registered their presence with the master node, the latter assigns to each one of them a distinct subset of all users that participate in the ratings system, which is used to populate each slave's local database — operation 2. The user subsets that are assigned to the slave machines are disjoint to eliminate contention for any given user profile on the master, minimise the load from queries on participant information submitted by slave machines to the master node, and also reduce network traffic.

Additionally, when the master node receives a query from the RMS regarding the trustworthiness of a user — operation 3, it acts as a dispatcher and forwards the request to the appropriate slave machine for retrieving the respective value — operation 4. Queries are encoded in XML format to allow interoperability with a

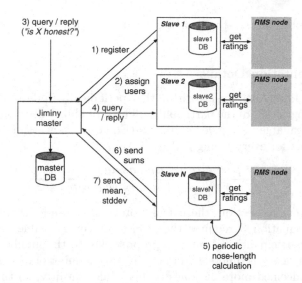

Fig. 1. An overview of the Jiminy clustered architecture

variety of reputation management systems. Dispatching of queries is also handled by a separate thread to allow the main process to maintain an acceptable level of responsiveness of the system to user input. Lastly, the master also provides a graphical user interface, through which users of the system can perform queries on the honesty of participants, and set the system parameters such as honesty and dishonesty thresholds.

Slave. The main process (*Slave i, i = 1..N* in Figure 1) that runs on a slave node initially registers itself with the master — operation 1, and receives the subset of participants this slave will be responsible for, as well as system-wide variables — operation 2. It then listens for incoming query requests from the master. Queries are of several types such as requests for the credit balance of a user, notifications of a new rating to the RMS, requests for a trust value, etc. They are parsed and processed by a pool of threads that is started by the main slave process — operation 4.

Slave nodes also update the honesty metrics for their assigned participants, and calculate a user's position with respect to the reward model. This is performed by a separate thread that runs periodically on the slave, connects to the RMS node to receive aggregate information on the ratings for use in honesty calculations, and updates the honesty values of all participants who have in the past evaluated subjects that received a new rating — operation 5.

The Jiminy system makes use of persistent storage for storing intermediate results and general statistics on the participants and the subjects that are rated. The aim is to avoid costly re-calculations upon system crash, and perform only incremental updates on the T_u values as new ratings are submitted to the RMS. System information such as honesty threshold, length of probationary period, mean and standard deviation of the T_u values, as well as histogram statistics for the rated subjects are stored in the local MySQL database on each slave machine.

3.1   Implementation Details

At the heart of Jiminy lies the algorithm that periodically updates the T_u values and the nose-lengths $|Z|$ of the participants. The probability distribution $Pr(Q_s)$ of the ratings available for a given subject s (Equation 2) is estimated using the following formula for every rating ρ:

$$Pr(Q_s) = \frac{\#\ participants\ who\ assigned\ rating\ \rho\ to\ s}{\#\ participants\ who\ rated\ s}$$

As stated in previous section, the calculation of the nose-length $|Z|$ of a participant from Equation 3 requires the scaling of her T_u value. Without this adjustment, a participant's T_u value is proportional to the number of her submissions, and in case it is different from the average number of ratings submitted per user she is deemed more dishonest. This is also intuitive in the sense that a participant with many ratings is more likely to have made dishonest ratings, however Jiminy is interested in the rate of disagreement, not the total number of its occurrences. To account for this fact, Equation 3 is modified as follows:

$$Z = \frac{\frac{T_u}{\#\ ratings\ made\ by\ u} - \bar{T}}{\hat{\sigma}} \tag{4}$$

The pseudocode for the calculation of T_u values is shown in Algorithm 1.

As new ratings get submitted to the reputation management system, users who have reviewed subjects that are rated by the new ratings need to have their T_u values updated (variable $AffectedUsers$ of Algorithm 1). For each one of these users, the algorithm finds the ratings that affect her T_u value and accordingly adjusts it based on whether the user rated the subject with the same rating as the one carried in the new rating (lines 11–15 of Algorithm 1). Since T_u values do not change dramatically from one rating to another, the algorithm runs periodically to reduce processing overhead, and waits for several new ratings to accumulate in the RMS. New ratings are determined using a timestamp that is associated with each rating that is received.

Each slave machine updates the nose-lengths of the users that have been assigned to it. To better distribute the user space to the group of slaves, the master assigns new and existing users to slaves according to the formula: $slave\_number = (userid\ \%\ n)$, when n is the number of slaves present. Failure of slave machines is handled by the master using the Java exception handling facility, however a more robust fail-over mechanism still remains part of our future work.

Last, the calculation of nose-lengths $|Z|$ requires the mean $\bar{T}$ and standard deviation $\hat{\sigma}$ of the T_u values of all the N participants. From the formulas for the mean and standard deviation we have:

$$\bar{T} = \frac{1}{N} \sum_{u=1}^{N} T_u \tag{5}$$

Algorithm 1. UpdateT_uValues()

Require: New ratings added to RMS since last update
1: $AffectedUsers \leftarrow$ Find users that have rated subjects that appear in new ratings
2: **for** (each user u in $AffectedUsers$) **do**
3:   $UserSubjects \leftarrow$ Find subjects rated by user u
4:   $NewUserRatings \leftarrow$ Find new ratings about $UserSubjects$
5:   **for** (each new user rating i in $NewUserRatings$) **do**
6:     $Subject \leftarrow$ Subject rated by i
7:     $UserRating \leftarrow$ Rating about $Subject$ by user u
8:     $NumberSame \leftarrow$ Number of ratings about $Subject$ equal to $UserRating$
9:     $TotalSubjectRatings \leftarrow$ Number of ratings that rate $Subject$
10:     $T_u \leftarrow T_u - (log(NumberSame) - log(TotalSubjectRatings))$
11:     **if** $(UserRating = $ rating of rating $i)$ **then**
12:       $T_u \leftarrow T_u + (log(NumberSame + 1) - log(TotalSubjectRatings + 1))$
13:     **else**
14:       $T_u \leftarrow T_u + (log(NumberSame) - log(TotalSubjectRatings + 1))$
15:     **end if**
16:   **end for**
17: **end for**

---

and

$$\hat{\sigma} = \sqrt{\frac{1}{N-1} \sum_{u=1}^{N} \left(T_u - \bar{T}\right)^2} \qquad (6)$$

By substituting (5) into (6) and after simple algebraic manipulations, we get:

$$\hat{\sigma} = \sqrt{\frac{1}{N(N-1)} \left(N \sum_{u=1}^{N} T_u^2 - \left(\sum_{u=1}^{N} T_u \right)^2 \right)} \qquad (7)$$

Each slave transmits the sum and the sum-of-squares of T_u values for its participant set to the master — operation 6 in Figure 1. The master then calculates the mean and standard deviation for all the participants, and disseminates the results back to the slaves for further use in estimating $|Z|$ — operation 7.

4   Evaluation

In this section we present a three-fold evaluation of our architecture. We first analyse the GroupLens data-set to ensure that the assumptions made by our model about the distribution of nose-lengths and independence of ratings hold. Furthermore, we demonstrate that our algorithm can successfully detect dishonesty. Finally, we show by means of experimental evaluation that Jiminy can scale on-demand to accommodate increasing numbers of participants and subjects.

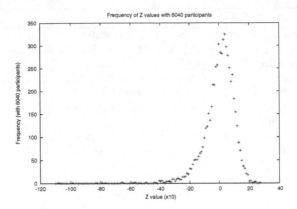

Fig. 2. Distribution of Z values (x10)

4.1   Analysis of the Data Set

Nose-Length Distribution. The ability to judge, given a set of participant ratings, whether a participant is likely to be honest is a crucial element of the system. In [12] we simulated the behavior of *nose-length* values for different users, for various subjects. We predicted that nose-length would have the form of a Gaussian random variable, with a small number of potentially dishonest users being at the far left or right parts of the distribution.

We analysed the GroupLens movie ratings data set to determine the real distribution of nose-length values inside the set, for the users it contains. The nose-length value was plotted against its frequency of occurrence. The result of this analysis is shown in Figure 2; the nose-length distribution does indeed fit the theoretically anticipated Gaussian distribution. This provides a strong indication about a relationship between one's relative frequency of disagreement and his or her probability of being honest. Section 4.2 demonstrates that this relationship holds, and that Jiminy is able to exploit it to detect dishonesty.

Distribution and Correlation of Ratings. As expected, our analysis of the chosen data set revealed that ratings given by users to films did not always have a normal distribution. Figure 3(a) shows three density plots of ratings for three different movies namely, "Toy Story", "Jumanji" and "Big Bully".

Film ratings are highly subjective. Some participants are likely to be very impressed by a film while others may consider it disappointing. This can lead to ratings exhibiting a multi-modal distribution — for example, approximately half of the participants may assign a rating of 1 or 2, and the other half a rating of 4 or 5. This type of distribution could lead to a mean value which almost no one has entered, and to a high standard deviation for ratings. Our analysis showed that this potential problem does not appear to be severe; most films did have a firm most common rating, although this value may not always be exactly reflected on the mean.

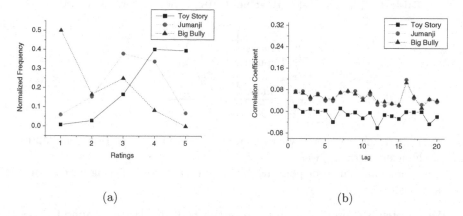

(a)   (b)

Fig. 3. a) Variation in distributions of ratings, and b) correlation among ratings for three subjects: Toy Story, Jumanji and Big Bully

In addition to the distribution of ratings, the correlation of ratings in the GroupLens set was also studied, as illustrated in Figure 3(b). Since the correlation coefficients are very low, it can be safely assumed that the ratings provided by a user are independent of the existing ratings, thus making the rating process independent and identically distributed. This observation emphasises that $\bar{T}$ and $\hat{\sigma}$ of the distributions are appropriate to capture and characterise user honesty.

4.2   Evaluation of the Algorithm

To evaluate the effectiveness of Jiminy with respect to assessing the honesty of participants we conducted the following experiment. We injected the ratings of four known dishonest users into the existing GroupLens data set, fed the resulting data set into the Jiminy cluster, and monitored the nose-length values that Jiminy assigned to the known dishonest users.

We created the following four users and subsequently injected their ratings into the data set:

- *Mr. Average.* This user periodically queries the RMS to obtain the average rating for each movie he wishes to rate, and subsequently submits the integer rating closest in value to the average rating reported for the same movie. This average rating reported is unlikely to continually be the most popular rating because of the nature of the ratings' distributions.
- *Ms. Popular.* This user periodically queries the RMS to establish the most popular rating for each movie she wishes to rate, which she then submits for the same movie.
- *Mr. Disagree.* This user periodically queries the RMS to obtain the average rating for each movie he wishes to rate, and then reports a rating that is as far from the average value as possible. For instance, he would report 1 if the

Table 1. T_u and nose-length values (x10) of the four users in question

User	T_u	Z
Mr. Average	-8.95	19.28
Ms. Popular	-7.84	24.78
Mr. Disagree	-39.35	-132.85
Ms. Random	-20.31	-37.64

average rating was 5 and vice versa, and he would report 1 or 5 (at random) if the average rating was 3.

– *Ms. Random.* This user periodically submits a random rating for each movie she wishes to rate.

We selected a subset of 43 films from the RMS for these dishonest users to rate, entered their corresponding ratings — one per movie per user, and used Jiminy to assess their honesty values. The results of this experiment are shown in Table 1.

The above shows that dishonest users do have a nose-length (Z value) quite different from that of the honest users. Mr. Average and Ms. Popular have Z values appearing at the far right side of the graph in Figure 2, as predicted. Mr. Disagree and Ms. Random both appear to the left side, with Mr. Disagree off the side of the graph. Interestingly, no users in the original data set disagreed to this extent, but at the opposite end of the scale there were users who agreed with a frequency similar to — though not quite as high as — that of Ms. Popular.

This result demonstrates that the honesty metric is effective, being able to spot our simulated dishonest users in a large data set of real ratings. It can also be used to choose appropriate honesty and dishonesty threshold values, which is discussed in the following section.

Discussion

Selection of Threshold Values. Choosing honesty and dishonesty thresholds presents a trade-off: setting the dishonesty threshold too high may allow dishonest participants to be rewarded, while setting it too low may punish honest participants who, owing to the subjective nature of the rating topic, vary in opinion a little too frequently or too infrequently. At the same time, setting the honesty threshold too low would make it difficult for a dishonest user to be deemed honest again, while setting it too high would increase fluctuation between the honest and dishonest states.

Jiminy allows for these parameters to be adjusted by the system administrator. Suitable honesty and dishonesty thresholds can be devised through inspection of the nose-lengths of known dishonest users (such as the ones in the previous section), the distribution of nose-lengths, and depending on the trustworthiness of the environment in which the system is deployed. Tuning the thresholds effectively determines the *tolerance* (or harshness) of Jiminy.

Table 2. Specifications and base time for machines in the Jiminy cluster

Machine	Specs	base time (s)
1	AMD Opteron 244, 1.8GHz, 2GB RAM	765.85
2	AMD Opteron 244, 1.8GHz, 2GB RAM	764.90
3	UltraSPARC-IIIi, 1.0GHz, 2GB RAM	1904.79
4	Intel Xeon, 3.06 GHz, 1GB RAM	2556.06
5	UltraSPARC-IIIi, 1.0GHz, 8GB RAM	1793.37

As an example, as Figure 2 shows, 89.6 % of participants are within the Z ($\times 10$) range -14.5 to 14.5, and 93.34% are within the Z range -17 to 17. Setting the honesty threshold at 14.5 and the dishonesty threshold at 17 would deem 6.66% of participants dishonest.

Rating Engineering. Let us consider a participant that submits a number of honest ratings, enough to take her well above the dishonesty threshold. She then submits a mixture of dishonest and honest ratings in varying proportions, and tests whether she is still deemed honest. She keeps increasing the proportion of dishonest ratings until she is deemed dishonest, and then reverses that trend. At some point, the user may find an equilibrium where she can be partially dishonest — but not enough for the system to halt her rewards. We term this type of attack *rating engineering*.

Jiminy has a number of countermeasures against such attacks. First, it does not make the threshold values publicly accessible. At the same time, it conceals fine-grained nose-length values, providing only a binary honest/dishonest answer when queried about a certain user. Additionally, the exponentially increasing probationary period introduces a high cost for such attacks. As credits cannot be traded for money, we believe that the incentive for determined rating engineering is reasonably low. However, as part of our future work we plan to investigate the design of an algorithm with more explicit defences against such attacks.

4.3 Scalability

Experimental Setup. To assess the performance and scalability of Jiminy we deployed the system on a cluster composed of five machines, as shown in Table 2. We deployed five slave instances, one on each machine. The master node was run on machine number one, along with one slave instance. The *base value* shown in the table represents the time needed by each machine (running the entire Jiminy system on its own) to update the nose-length of each participant in the GroupLens data set, when 5000 new ratings have been submitted. We term *new* ratings the ones submitted after the latest periodic execution of the algorithm.

The performance difference between the slaves, as indicated by the disparity of base time values, is due to both hardware differences and level of load. For instance, slave number four has been relatively heavily used by third-party applications during the time the experiments were undertaken.

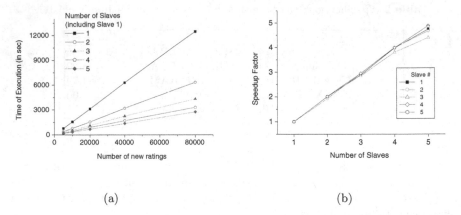

(a)   (b)

Fig. 4. a) Time taken by the periodic nose-length calculation on slave 1 for different numbers of ratings and slaves present, and b) speedup observed by increasing the number of slaves

Results. We measured the time needed by slave number one to finish the periodic calculation of nose-lengths for 5000, 10000, 20000, 40000, and 80000 new ratings, and while running in a cluster of one to five slaves. The results of this are shown in Figure 4(a). We observe that the time required increases linearly with the number of new ratings, and that adding slaves to the cluster significantly improves system performance. As an example, for 5000 ratings, slave number one completed its calculation in 161 seconds when five slaves were present, compared to 765 seconds when running on its own. For 20000 ratings the same computation took 676 seconds in a cluster of five and 3110 seconds on slave number one alone.

We also measured the *speedup*, denoted as the ratio of time required when a slave ran alone over the respective time when N slaves were participating in the cluster, to perform the same calculation. We measured the speedup achieved by each slave as new slaves were added to the cluster for 5000, 10000, 20000, 40000, and 80000 new ratings. The results of this experiment for 5000 ratings are shown in Figure 4(b). Speedup results for experiments with more ratings look nearly identical to these. As shown in the graph, each slave achieves a near-linear performance improvement for every new slave that is added to the cluster. This underlines that the cluster can be scaled *on-demand* to accommodate increasing numbers of participants and subjects. The small deviation from a precise linear performance increase is attributed to our user space partitioning scheme, assigning slightly different parts of the user space to slaves.

Also, it is worth noting that the master node was not a bottleneck in the system, presenting a very low CPU and memory utilisation compared to the slaves. Additionally, our experiment demonstrates that the performance and scalability of Jiminy allow it to be deployed in a realistic setting. By increasing its performance linearly when slave machines are added to the cluster, Jiminy can scale to calculate nose-length values at a rate equal to (or higher than) the rate at which ratings are submitted. Our modest five-machine cluster — a commercial deployment would be equipped with more and more capable high-end servers — can process approximately 31 new ratings per second, in a data set of one million ratings in total.

5   Related Work

We identify two areas of research as relevant to the work presented in this paper: reputation management systems, and incentive schemes.

Reputation Management Systems. RMSs are widely employed within a range of systems and communities. In peer-to-peer systems [2, 15] they serve as a means of reducing free-riding [3, 14] and selecting reliable peers. In ad-hoc networks, they support detecting selfish nodes [6]. In auction sites[3] and on-line marketplaces[4][7] they help buyers identify reliable sellers and vice versa.

We investigated the use of an RMS in public computing [10], and observed that requirements are different in this environment [12]. To summarise, computing resources are regarded as utility and users take good service for granted, thus ratings would tend to only be exceptionally negative and (less frequently so) exceptionally positive. Additionally, interactions happen more frequently and in short timescales, increasing the overall overhead of submitting ratings.

Another observation we make is that there is a trade-off between the *level of anonymity* of participants and their *willingness to participate*. Anonymity and the lack of a sense of permanent identity act as disincentives for active participation. This is part of the reason why files in file-sharing peer-to-peer systems are rarely rated, as well as why peers are indifferent about their reputation — they can easily escape bad ratings by re-registering using a different identity [9].

On the other hand, participants in auction sites care about their reputations more than peers in peer-to-peer systems, due to the semi-permanent, pseudony-mous nature of their identities. However, semi-permanent identities provide an incentive for submitting biased information; submitting positive feedback about others is often related to an expectation of reciprocity, while submitting negative feedback is often due to a feeling of revenge [1].

Jiminy complements RMSs, facilitating explicit participation rewards and providing information about the honesty of users. Its XML interface supports interoperability with a variety of RMSs.

Incentive Schemes. Providing incentives for participation is a fairly general research avenue. Recent studies have focused on incentives for cooperation between nodes in wireless ad hoc networks [8]. Peer-to-peer systems such as Kazaa[5] often provide incentives for providing content by linking peer ratings to download rates [4, 18, 19]. Bittorrent[6] uses a 'tit-for-tat' approach to ensure peer participation.

---

[3] http://www.ebay.com, http://auctions.yahoo.com/
[4] http://www.amazon.co.uk/exec/obidos/tg/stores/static/-/marketplace/welcome/
[5] http://www.kazaa.com
[6] http://bitconjurer.org/BitTorrent

Social means for improving collaboration within communities have been examined [5, 11, 16], suggesting that interactions should carry a notion of *visibility*, *uniqueness*, and *benefit* for the participant. In accordance to these findings, we believe that the explicit incentives that Jiminy provides can help enhance the feeling of a participant that she benefits from submitting ratings.

While incentive models have been proposed before, to the best of our knowledge there is a need for an architecture that a) provides an honesty metric to improve the quality of received feedback, and b) performs and scales well in order to accommodate realistically large data sets.

6 Conclusion

This paper presented the design, implementation, and cluster deployment of Jiminy, a distributed architecture for providing explicit incentives for participation in reputation systems. Jiminy features a reward mechanism and a probabilistic honesty metric based on the Pinocchio [12] model to encourage the submission of honest ratings.

The GroupLens data set of one million real movie ratings was employed to verify our assumptions about the distribution of nose-length values (our honesty estimator), and about the independence of ratings. Furthermore, the system's effectiveness was evaluated by showing that it is able to detect four typical types of dishonest participants whose ratings we injected into the GroupLens data set. Finally, experiments were conducted to demonstrate that Jiminy performs and scales well, increasing its performance near-linearly as slaves are added to the cluster, and being able to process ratings at run-time.

At the time of writing, we are evaluating Jiminy using different types of data sets, where rating subjectivity is higher or lower. We also plan to investigate algorithms with inherent resilience towards rating engineering, and mechanisms for the dynamic repartitioning of computation according to the performance and workload of individual slaves.

Acknowledgments

We would like to thank Prof. Sahin Albayrak, Silvan Kaiser, and the Technical University of Berlin for providing support for our experiments. We would also like to thank the anonymous reviewers for their constructive comments and suggestions.

References

1. A. Abdul-Rahman and S. Hailes. Supporting Trust in Virtual Communities. In *Proc. Hawaii Intl Conf. on Sys. Sciences (HICSS)*, January 2000.
2. K. Aberer and Z. Despotovic. Managing Trust in a Peer-2-Peer Information System. In *Proc. 10th Intl Conf. of Inf. and Knowledge Mgmt*, 2001.

3. E. Adar and B. Huberman. Free riding on gnutella. Technical report, Xerox PARC, Aug. 2000.

4. K. Anagnostakis and M. Greenwald. Exchange-based incentive mechanisms for peer-to-peer file sharing. In *Proc. 24th Intl Conf. on Dist. Comp. Sys. (ICDCS 2004)*.

5. G. Beenen, K. Ling, X. Wang, K. Chang, D. Frankowski, P. Resnick, and R. E. Kraut. Using social psychology to motivate contributions to online communities. In *Proc. ACM Conf. on Comp. supported Coop. work (CSCW '04)*, 2004.

6. S. Buchegger and J. Y. L. Boudec. A robust reputation system for p2p and mobile ad-hoc networks. In *Proc. 2nd Workshop on the Econ. of Peer-to-Peer Sys. (P2PEcon 2004)*, 2004.

7. A. Chavez and P. Maes. Kasbah: An agent marketplace for buying and selling goods. In *Proc. 1st Intl Conf. on the Practical App. of Int. Agents and Multi-Agent Tech. (PAAM'96)*. Practical Application Company, 1996.

8. J. Crowcroft, R. Gibbens, F. Kelly, and S. Ostring. Modelling incentives for collaboration in mobile ad hoc networks. In *Proc. of WiOpt'03*, 2003.

9. J. R. Douceur. The Sybil Attack. In *Proc. of the 1st Intl Workshop on Peer-to-Peer Sys.*, March 2002.

10. B. Dragovic, S. Hand, T. Harris, E. Kotsovinos, and A. Twigg. Managing trust and reputation in the XenoServer Open Platform. In *Proc. 1st Intl Conf. on Trust Mgmt*, May 2003.

11. T. Erickson, C. Halverson, W. A. Kellogg, M. Laff, and T. Wolf. Social translucence: designing social infrastructures that make collective activity visible. *Communications of the ACM*, 45(4):40–44, 2002.

12. A. Fernandes, E. Kotsovinos, S. Ostring, and B. Dragovic. Pinocchio: Incentives for honest participation in distributed trust management. In *Proc. 2nd Intl Conf. on Trust Management (iTrust 2004)*, Mar. 2004.

13. E. Kotsovinos and A. Williams. BambooTrust: Practical scalable trust management for global public computing. In *Proc. of the 21st Annual ACM Symp. on App. Comp. (SAC)*, Apr. 2006.

14. R. Krishnan, M. D. Smith, and R. Telang. The economics of peer-to-peer networks. Draft technical document, Carnegie Mellon University, 2002.

15. S. Lee, R. Sherwood, and B. Bhattacharjee. Cooperative Peer Groups in NICE. In *Proc. of IEEE INFOCOM*, 2003.

16. P. J. Ludford, D. Cosley, D. Frankowski, and L. Terveen. Think different: increasing online community participation using uniqueness and group dissimilarity. In *Proc. SIGCHI Conf. on Human Factors in Comp. Sys. (CHI '04)*, 2004.

17. P. Resnick and R. Zeckhauser. Trust among strangers in internet transactions: Empirical analysis of ebay's reputation system. In *The Econ. Internet and E-Comm.*, volume 11 of *Advances in App. Microec.* Elsevier Science, 2002.

18. Q. Sun and H. Garcia-Molina. Slic: A selfish link based incentive mechanism for unstructured peer-to-peer networks. In *Proc. Intl Conf. on Dist. Comp. Sys. (ICDCS '04)*.

19. B. Yang, T. Condie, S. Kamvar, and H. Garcia-Molina. Non-cooperation in competitive p2p networks. In *Proc. Intl Conf. on Dist. Comp. Sys. (ICDCS '04)*.

Virtual Fingerprinting as a Foundation for Reputation in Open Systems

Adam J. Lee and Marianne Winslett

Department of Computer Science,
University of Illinois at Urbana-Champaign,
Urbana, IL, 61801 USA
{adamlee, winslett}@cs.uiuc.edu

Abstract. The lack of available identity information in attribute-based trust management systems complicates the design of the audit and incident response systems, anomaly detection algorithms, collusion detection/prevention mechanisms, and reputation systems taken for granted in traditional distributed systems. In this paper, we show that as two entities in an attribute-based trust management system interact, each learns one of a limited number of *virtual fingerprints* describing their communication partner. We show that these virtual fingerprints can be disclosed to other entities in the open system without divulging any attribute or absolute-identity information, thereby forming an opaque pseudo-identity that can be used as the basis for the above-mentioned types of services. We explore the use of virtual fingerprints as the basis of Xiphos, a system that allows reputation establishment without requiring explicit knowledge of entities' civil identities. We discuss the trade-off between privacy and trust, examine the impacts of several attacks on the Xiphos system, and discuss the performance of Xiphos in a simulated grid computing system.

1 Introduction

Open systems are distributed computing systems in which resources are shared across organizational boundaries. Common examples of open systems include grid computing networks, corporate virtual organizations, disaster response networks, joint military task forces, and peer-to-peer systems. Open systems that attempt to make access control decisions based on the identities of their participants cannot be truly open, because they suffer from scalability limitations as the number of authorized users increases. Recent research has addressed this problem by proposing *attribute-based* trust management systems for use in these environments (e.g., [2, 3, 4, 5, 6, 13, 15, 20, 22]). These types of systems provide an effective and scalable means for making authorization decisions in truly open systems, but depending on their deployment model, may have the side-effect of virtually eliminating absolute identity information.

This lack of absolute identity can be a double-edged sword in that it increases system scalability but also increases user anonymity; this may not be appropriate

K. Stølen et al. (Eds.): iTrust 2006, LNCS 3986, pp. 236–251, 2006.

in all application domains. In traditional distributed computing, user identity forms the basis of audit and incident response systems, anomaly detection algorithms, collusion detection and prevention mechanisms, and reputation systems. As such, this functionality either does not exist or exists only in extremely limited forms in current attribute-based trust management systems. In this paper, we take a first step towards addressing this problem by describing a method for the linking and correlation of multiple identities used by the same entity in attribute-based trust management systems. We then show how these identities can be turned into *virtual fingerprints* which can be exchanged between entities in the system without leaking sensitive attribute or civil-identity information. Virtual fingerprints act much like fingerprints in the physical world in that they allow multiple actions initiated by an entity to be linked without knowing the civil identity of their owner, thereby forming a solid foundation upon which the types of functionality previously described can be constructed.

To illustrate the promise of virtual fingerprinting, in this paper we show how virtual fingerprints can form the basis of the Xiphos reputation system. Reputation systems will be a necessary part of the open systems of the future, as current research trends are beginning to embrace distributed theorem proving approaches to access control [1, 23]. In these systems, proof fragments and access hints are collected from various parties in the network and used to construct proofs of authorization. Accepting these items from malicious entities could have dire consequences, including unbounded searches for non-existent credentials and the risk of being denied access to a resource which one is actually authorized to access. We show how virtual fingerprinting can be used as the foundation of a reputation system that will allow entities in an open system to gain confidence in information provided by others (including proof hints) without compromising each entity's desire to protect his or her sensitive credentials or identity.

In Section 2, we describe how virtual fingerprints can be derived from the information collected during interactions in attribute-based trust management systems. Section 3 describes the design of a reputation system in which ratings are aggregated by using the virtual fingerprinting mechanism described in Section 2. We also discuss several deployment models for this reputation system, each of which allows for a different balance of privacy and completeness of available information. In Section 4, we discuss the privacy implications of Xiphos, examine the effects of several attacks against the system, summarize the results of a performance study that we have undertaken, and comment on the general applicability of virtual fingerprinting to reputation systems. We then overview related work in Section 5 and present our conclusions and directions for future work in Section 6.

2   Virtual Fingerprinting in Open Systems

Each entity, A, in an attribute-based trust management system has a finite set of credentials, $\mathcal{C}_A = \{c_1, \ldots, c_n\}$, which attest to her various attributes. Although these credentials might never explicitly reference A's civil identity (for example, they could be X.509 credentials that assert only that their owner has a given attribute), we claim that in practice, $\mathcal{C}_A$ completely describes A. In trust management systems such as PolicyMaker [5], KeyNote [4], QCM [10], Cassandra [2], and various trust negotiation proposals (e.g., [3, 13, 15, 22]), each credential is issued to exactly one owner in order to avoid the group key revocation problem. Thus, if an entity E can prove ownership of some $c \in \mathcal{C}_A$, then necessarily $E = A$.

Since entities may consider some of their credentials to be private, $\mathcal{C}_A$ is in most cases not globally available as a basis of comparison for identity establishment. However, as entities in these systems interact, they collect valuable information about one another even if no civil identity information is explicitly disclosed. Specifically, as entities A and B interact, B learns $\mathcal{D}_A^B \subseteq \mathcal{C}_A$. We will call sets such as $\mathcal{D}_A^B$ descriptions.

Definition 1. *A description is a subset of the credentials owned by one entity which is learned by another entity in the system. We will use the notation $\mathcal{D}_A^B$ to represent the description of A known by B. It is important to note that for B to accept $\mathcal{D}_A^B$ as a description of A, A must demonstrate proof of ownership of each credential $c \in \mathcal{D}_A^B$ to B.[1] The collection of all such descriptions will be denoted by $\mathbb{D}$.*

Over the course of multiple interactions, B can use previously obtained descriptions to recognize when he is communicating with a familiar entity. For this to be useful, however, the number of useful descriptions which an entity can use must be small. We assert that this is indeed the case; even though an entity can have an infinite number of self-issued or other low-value credentials, only credentials issued by *trusted* third parties will be useful in gaining access to the resources shared in an open system. It should not be possible to obtain an unlimited number of such credentials (e.g., a user should not be able to obtain two drivers licenses), which implies that the set of descriptions which can be learned about an entity will necessarily be finite.

Although descriptions are useful for allowing one entity to recognize another entity with whom she has interacted previously, privacy concerns restrict descriptions from being shared between entities. This follows from the fact that entities may consider some of their attributes to be sensitive: even though B learns some credential c which belongs to A, this does not mean that any arbitrary entity in the system has the right to learn c. To allow certain information contained within a description to be shared between entities, we introduce the notion of *virtual fingerprints*.

Definition 2. *The virtual fingerprint associated with a description $\mathcal{D}_A^B = \{c_1, \ldots, c_k\}$ is defined as $\mathcal{F}_A^B = \{h(c_1), \ldots, h(c_k)\}$, where $h(\cdot)$ is a cryptographic hash function. The collection of all such fingerprints will be referred to as $\mathbb{F}$.*

---

[1] The only exception to this rule occurs when c is a delegated credential. In this case, $\mathcal{D}_A^B$ should contain both c and the long-term credential from which c was derived. For obvious reasons, proof of ownership of the long-term credential is not required.

The collision-resistance property of hash functions allows virtual fingerprints to be used as pseudo-identifiers in the same way as descriptions. For instance, if SHA-1 is used to derive virtual fingerprints, we expect that each person on earth would need to hold 2^{47} credentials before a collision would be found, given that the current population is about 6.2 billion $< 2^{33}$ people. Therefore, if two virtual fingerprints overlap, their corresponding descriptions overlap, and thus the two virtual fingerprints both describe the same entity. Since virtual fingerprints mask out the details of a user's credentials, they are more likely candidates for allowing inferred pseudo-identity information to be shared between entities. Note that an entity may have multiple disjoint virtual fingerprints and thus even if two entities have interacted with this entity, they may not be able to agree on this fact based on virtual fingerprints alone. However, the limited number of virtual fingerprints used by an entity, A, in the system (which follows directly from the limited number of descriptions of A) implies that over time, factions of entities who known A by each of her virtual fingerprints will form. Clearly, virtual fingerprints can be used to link and correlate the actions of users in an open system without revealing their private attribute data to entities who do not know it already.

It should be noted that virtual fingerprinting cannot be used in conjunction with all types of trust management systems. For example, virtual fingerprints cannot be derived in systems that use anonymous credentials (e.g., [8, 7]) or hidden credentials [11], since the credentials belonging to an entity are never fully disclosed. In addition, the systems discussed in [8, 7] were designed to prevent actions taken at disparate points in an open system from being linked, and thus prevent any form of distributed auditing. However, there are many types of systems that could benefit from the scalability of attribute-based trust management systems, but require the ability to audit transactions in the system so that users can be held accountable for their actions. Examples include grid computing systems, critical infrastructure management networks, joint military task forces, and disaster management coordination centers. Virtual fingerprinting can pave the way for the adoption of attribute-based trust management systems in these types of high-assurance environments by increasing user accountability and auditability. In the remainder of this paper, we substantiate this claim by describing how virtual fingerprints can form the basis of a reputation system for use in systems such as those described in [2, 3, 4, 5, 6, 13, 15, 20, 22].

3   The Xiphos Reputation System

In this section, we present Xiphos, a reputation system based on the virtual fingerprints described in Section 2. The reputation update equations used by Xiphos are similar to those used in other proposals and could easily be changed as better reputation update mechanisms are proposed; in fact, many of the equations presented in this section are adaptations of those presented by Liu and Issarny in [16] altered to work within our virtual fingerprint collection and analysis framework. Thus, our primary contribution is not the reputation update equations themselves, but rather the framework though which entities can record, index, and exchange virtual fingerprints obtained during their interactions in a privacy-preserving manner to formulate reputations for entities whose identities may never be fully disclosed.

3.1   Local Information Collection

As entities in an attribute-based trust management system interact, they learn valuable information regarding one another's virtual fingerprints. Formally, as entities interact, they store tuples of the form $T = \langle \mathcal{F} \in \mathbb{F}, r \in \mathcal{R}, \tau \in \mathbb{T} \rangle$, where $\mathcal{F}$ is a virtual fingerprint, r is a rating, and τ is the timestamp of the entity's most recent interaction with the entity described by virtual fingerprint $\mathcal{F}$. We assume that the set of all possible timestamps is $\mathbb{T}$ and that reputation ratings come from some set $\mathcal{R}$ of possible values. To simplify our discussion, in this paper we use $\mathcal{R} = [-1, 1]$. However, in practice it will often be the case that ratings are vector quantities (i.e., $[-1, 1]^n$) that allow an entity to rate several aspects of her interaction with another entity (e.g., both the service quality and recommendation quality). All operations carried out on reputation ratings in this paper can be carried out on vectors, so we use $n = 1$ without loss of generality.

Over time, it is possible that some entity B will learn several non-overlapping virtual fingerprints describing another entity A. Thus, after a tuple $\langle \mathcal{F}_A^B, r, \tau \rangle$ is inserted into B's database, B must condense the set of all overlapping tuples. That is, B will remove the set of all tuples $\mathcal{T} = \{T \mid T.\mathcal{F} \cap \mathcal{F}_A^B \neq \emptyset\}$ from his database and insert a single tuple T' which is defined as follows:

$$T' = \left\langle \bigcup_{T \in \mathcal{T}} T.\mathcal{F}, \frac{\sum_{T \in \mathcal{T}} T.r * \varphi(T.\tau)}{\sum_{T \in \mathcal{T}} \varphi(T.\tau)}, \tau_{now} \right\rangle \tag{1}$$

In the above equation, τ_{now} is the current timestamp and $\varphi(\cdot)$ is a function which computes a factor in the interval $[0, 1]$ which is used to scale the impact of older ratings. One possible definition of $\varphi(\cdot)$ fades ratings linearly over some duration d, though other definitions are certainly possible:

$$\varphi(t) = \begin{cases} 1 - \frac{\tau_{now} - t}{d} & \text{when } \tau_{now} - t > 0, \\ 0 & \text{otherwise.} \end{cases} \tag{2}$$

Equations 1 and 2 form the basis of a local reputation system in which any entity can track her interaction history with any other entity in the absence of concrete identity information; this history can then be used as a predictor of future success. In the following subsections, we describe three ways in which entities can exchange portions of their local histories to form a system-wide reputation system.

3.2   A Centrally Managed Reputation System

Information Collection. The simplest types of reputation systems to reason about are systems in which a central server is responsible for storing and aggregating reputation values, such as the eBay feedback system. In a centralized deployment of Xiphos, the server will store tuples of the form $T = \langle \mathcal{F}_A \in \mathbb{F}, lc \in [0,1], \mathcal{F}_B \in \mathbb{F}, r \in \mathcal{R}, \tau \in \mathbb{T} \rangle$ where $\mathcal{F}_A$ is a virtual fingerprint of the entity reporting the rating, lc is the server's linkability coefficient for the entity whose virtual fingerprint is $\mathcal{F}_A$, $\mathcal{F}_B$ is the virtual fingerprint of the entity being rated (as observed by the rater), r is the rating, and τ is the timestamp at which this rating was logged. Prior to discussing the calculation of reputation values based on these tuples, we must first explain (1) how the server learns $\mathcal{F}_A$ and (2) the mechanism through which lc is calculated.

For several reasons discussed later in this paper, it is important that the server records one of the rater's virtual fingerprints along with each reputation rating registered in the system. One way for this to occur is for the rater to simply reveal several credentials to the server while reporting his reputation rating. Alternatively, the rater could carry out an *eager trust negotiation* [21] with the reputation server prior to submitting his reputation ratings. An eager trust negotiation begins by one party disclosing his public credentials to the other party. Subsequent rounds of the negotiation involve one party disclosing any credentials whose release policies were satisfied by the credentials that they received during previous rounds of negotiation. This process continues until neither entity can disclose more credentials to the other.

In Xiphos, linkability coefficients are used to weight the reputation rating submitted by a particular entity based on how much the rater is willing to reveal about herself. To this end, the function $\gamma : \mathbb{D} \to [0,1]$ is used to establish the linkability coefficient associated with a description (as defined in Section 2) learned about an entity. The exact definition of $\gamma(\cdot)$ will necessarily be domain-specific, but several important properties of $\gamma(\cdot)$ can be easily identified. First, low-value (e.g., self-signed) credentials should not influence the linkability coefficient associated with a description. This prevents an entity from establishing a large number of descriptions that can be used with high confidence. Second, $\gamma(\cdot)$ should be monotonic; that is, an entity should not be penalized for showing more credentials, as doing so increases the ease with which her previous interaction history can be traced. Third, to help prevent ballot-stuffing attacks, the sum of the linkability coefficients derived from any partitioning of a description should not be greater than the linkability coefficient derived from the entire description. More formally, given a description $\mathcal{D} \in \mathbb{D}, \forall P = \{p_1 \subseteq \mathcal{D}, \ldots, p_k \subseteq \mathcal{D}\}$ such that $\cap_{p \in P} p = \emptyset$, $\gamma(\mathcal{D}) \geq \sum_{p \in P} \gamma(p)$. We discuss and evaluate a particular $\gamma(\cdot)$ function which meets these criteria in the technical report version of this paper [14].

The linkability coefficient is a good metric by which to establish a "first impression" of an entity, as a high linkability coefficient implies that an entity's previous interactions can be more easily tracked. This becomes especially meaningful if the reputation system itself stores vector quantities and can look up a "rating confidence" value for a particular user (such as the $RRep$ value stored in [16]). Entities with higher linkability coefficients are more likely to have many meaningful rating confidence scores reported by other entities which could be used to weight their contributions to the system.

Given that the server stores tuples in the above mentioned format, we now discuss how reputation ratings are updated. Assume that after interacting with some entity, the server determines that the tuple $T = \langle \mathcal{F}, lc, \mathcal{F}', r, \tau \rangle$ should be inserted into the database. Prior to inserting this tuple, the database first purges all prior reputation ratings reported by the entity described by $\mathcal{F}$ regarding the entity described by $\mathcal{F}'$. That is, the set of tuples $T_{old} = \{T \mid (T.\mathcal{F}_A \cap \mathcal{F} \neq \emptyset) \wedge (T.\mathcal{F}_B \cap \mathcal{F}' \neq \emptyset)\}$ are deleted from the database.[2] At this point, T can be inserted. Note that user updates replace older reputation ratings rather than scaling them since users locally time-scale their own ratings according to Equation 1.

Query Processing. Having discussed how information is stored at the reputation server, we now describe how queries are processed. If an entity is interested in obtaining the reputation of some other entity whose virtual fingerprint is $\mathcal{F}$, he submits a query of the form $\mathcal{F}_Q \subseteq \mathcal{F}$ to the reputation server. To compute the reputation for the entity with the virtual fingerprint $\mathcal{F}_Q$, the server must first select the set of relevant tuples $T_Q = \{T \mid T.\mathcal{F}_B \cap \mathcal{F}_Q \neq \emptyset\}$. If any subset T_Q^A of the tuples in T_Q have overlapping $\mathcal{F}_A$ components, these tuples will be removed from T_Q and replaced with a summary tuple of the form:

$$\left\langle \bigcup_{T \in T_Q^A} T.\mathcal{F}_A, max(\{T.lc \mid T \in T_Q^A\}), \bigcup_{T \in T_Q^A} T.\mathcal{F}_B, \frac{\sum_{T \in T_Q^A} T.r * \varphi(T.\tau)}{\sum_{T \in T_Q^A} \varphi(T.\tau)}, \tau_{now} \right\rangle$$

$$(3)$$

This duplicate elimination prevents the server from overcounting the rating of a single entity A who knows the subject of the query by more than one disjoint virtual fingerprint, each of which overlaps $\mathcal{F}_Q$. Let T_Q' denote the results of performing this duplicate elimination process on T_Q. Given T_Q', the reputation associated with the query $\mathcal{F}_Q$ is defined by the following equation:

$$r_Q = \frac{\sum_{T \in T_Q'} (T.lc * \varphi(T.\tau) * T.r)}{\sum_{T \in T_Q'} (T.lc * \varphi(T.\tau))}$$

$$(4)$$

In short, the reputation returned by the server is the weighted average reputation rating of entities matching the virtual fingerprint $\mathcal{F}_Q$, where each reputation rating is weighted based on both the linkability coefficient of the rater (which acts as an estimator of her rating confidence value) and the age of the reputation rating.

The curious reader might wonder why the set intersection operator is used to define $T_Q = \{T_i \mid T_i.\mathcal{F}_B \cap \mathcal{F}_Q \neq \emptyset\}$ as the set of matching tuples for a query $\mathcal{F}_Q$ rather than the transitive closure of this operator. While in a network with only honest participants, the transitive closure would give more accurate reputation ratings, it would cause incorrect results to be calculated if cheaters are present in the system. As an illustration, consider a system in which some entity E (with virtual fingerprint $\mathcal{F}_E$) is known to have an excellent reputation. A malicious

---

[2] Alternatively, these tuples could be saved for historical purposes, but marked as expired.

entity M (with virtual fingerprint $\mathcal{F}_M$) could then inflate his reputation by having some third party N (with virtual fingerprint $\mathcal{F}_N$) report a rating for the "entity" whose virtual fingerprint is $\mathcal{F}_E \cup \mathcal{F}_M$, thereby causing the tuple $T = \langle \mathcal{F}_N, lc_N, \mathcal{F}_E \cup \mathcal{F}_M, r, \tau \rangle$ to be inserted into the central database. If the transitive closure of the set intersection operation was then used to define $\mathcal{T}_Q$, any searches for M's reputation would then also include all ratings for E, thereby inflating M's reputation. For this reason, we use only set intersection for query matching, as entities can submit queries derived from virtual fingerprints which they have *verified* to belong to another entity. This further justifies the use of the linkability coefficient as a first impression of another entity, since as the linkability coefficient increases towards 1.0, the information included in $\mathcal{T}_Q$ approaches completeness.

3.3   A Fully Distributed Reputation System

We now describe a fully distributed deployment of Xiphos. In this model, entities calculate reputation ratings for other entities by querying some subset of the other entities in the system and aggregating the results from their local databases. As in the centralized model, queries are of the form $\mathcal{F}_Q \in \mathbb{F}$. Each node queried selects from their local database all tuples which overlap $\mathcal{F}_Q$ (i.e., $\mathcal{T} = \{T \mid T.\mathcal{F} \cap \mathcal{F}_Q \neq \emptyset\}$) and then creates a summary tuple of the form $T = \langle r_Q, \tau \rangle$ to return to the querier. If only a single tuple T' matches the query, then its r and τ components are used to form T, otherwise Equation 1 is used to generate a tuple whose r and τ components are used.

Upon receiving each of these summary tuples, the querier then augments them by adding the linkability coefficient that she has associated with the entity which sent the result. This linkability coefficient can either be cached from a previous interaction, the result of an eager trust negotiation initiated by the querier, or calculated from a set of credentials sent by the other entity along with the summary tuple. Given this collection of augmented summary tuples, $\mathcal{T}_Q$, the querier then computes the reputation rating of the entity whose virtual fingerprint is characterized by $\mathcal{F}_Q$ as follows:

$$r_Q = \omega_{local} * r_Q^{local} + (1 - \omega_{local}) * \frac{\sum_{T \in \mathcal{T}_Q} (T.lc * \varphi(T.\tau) * T.r)}{\sum_{T \in \mathcal{T}_Q} (T.lc * \varphi(T.\tau))} \qquad (5)$$

The term $\omega_{local} \in [0, 1]$ represents a weighting factor which allows the querier to determine how much of the reputation rating that she calculates should be based on her previous interactions with the subject of a query (denoted by r_Q^{local}) versus the reputation ratings reported by other entities in the system. In addition to choosing the weight given to the reputations returned by others, users must manually balance the time they spend querying other nodes with the accuracy of the reputation rating that they hope to derive.

3.4   A Reputation System for Super-Peer Network Topologies

The final deployment model which we consider is a reputation system built on top of a super-peer network. Super-peer networks are peer-to-peer networks that leverage the heterogeneity of nodes in the network by using nodes with higher bandwidths and faster processors to act as intelligent routers which form the backbone of the network. In these networks, a small number of so-called "super nodes" act as gateways for a large number of standard peers.

In this model, each super node is assumed to have complete information regarding the virtual fingerprint to reputation bindings stored by each of its client peers; that is, each super node acts as a centralized server as described in Section 3.2. Given a query $\mathcal{F}_Q$, a super node then uses Equations 3 and 4 to compute a local reputation rating, r_Q^S, based on the ratings provided by its client peers. However, in addition to calculating this local reputation rating, the super node can also include the reputations reported by other super nodes. After reissuing the query to each other super node and obtaining $\mathcal{T}_Q$, the set of resulting summary tuples calculated using Equations 3 and 4, the super node computes the aggregate reputation in response to the query $\mathcal{F}_Q$ as follows:

$$r_Q = \omega_S * r_Q^S + (1 - \omega_S) * \frac{\sum_{T \in \mathcal{T}_Q} (T.lc * \varphi(T.\tau) * T.r)}{\sum_{T \in \mathcal{T}_Q} (T.lc * \varphi(T.\tau))} \tag{6}$$

As in the fully distributed model, ω_S is a weighting factor that determines how much the reputation rating calculated from the super node's local peer group is weighted in comparison to the reputation ratings returned by all of the other super nodes.

4   Discussion

In this section, we see that Xiphos is in fact a double-edged sword, and system architects must make explicit choices regarding balancing privacy preservation and completeness of available information when deciding which deployment model to use. We then discuss several attacks on Xiphos, summarize the results of an in-depth analysis of the Xiphos system, and comment on the use of virtual fingerprints in conjunction with other reputation systems.

4.1   Privacy Considerations

Possible Privacy Violations. We have identified three types potential privacy violations which may occur as a result of the Xiphos system: leakage of interaction history, discovery of groups of entities with similar attributes, and inference of particular attribute information. Interaction history leaks occur in the centralized and super-peer deployments of the Xiphos system any time that one entity registers a reputation rating for another. This action allows the super peer or central server to infer that the rater and the ratee have interacted in the past. In the fully distributed deployment model, anytime that A answers a query issued by B, B can infer that A has interacted with the subject of his query. However, leakage of interaction history occurs in every other reputation system that we are aware of, thus we do not discuss it further here.

The second type of privacy violation occurs as a central server or super peer collects large amounts of reputation tuples. Recall that these tuples are of the form $T = \langle \mathcal{F}_A, lc, \mathcal{F}_B, r, \tau \rangle$. After building a substantial database, a malicious server can select all tuples whose $\mathcal{F}_B$ component overlaps a given $\mathcal{F}_Q$ exactly. We now claim that the $\mathcal{F}_A$ components of these matching tuples determine a set of entities in the server's view of the open system who have similar attributes. The justification of this claim comes from the fact that each entity described by some $T_i.\mathcal{F}_A$ was able to determine the same virtual fingerprint for the entity matching $\mathcal{F}_Q$. Thus, each of these entities was able to unlock each of the credentials used to derive $\mathcal{F}_Q$, a feat which requires that each of these entities be able to satisfy the same set of credential release policies. Because these release policies are not always strict conjunctions, we cannot determine that each matching $T_i.\mathcal{F}_A$ has the *same* set of defining attributes, though we can claim that these entities are *similar* in some respects. Note that the similarity of these entities is directly correlated with the restrictiveness of the release policies protecting the credentials used to derive $\mathcal{F}_Q$; more restrictive policies lead to more related entities.

The third type of privacy violation allows certain entities in the system to infer attributes possessed by another entity in the system. In the centralized and super-peer models, this attack is an extension of the previously discussed attack. Consider the case where a server S knows the description $\mathcal{D}_A^S$ of a node A. Let us also assume that some $c \in \mathcal{D}_A^S$ is protected by a release policy, p, which is also known to S (e.g., as a result of a previous interaction). S can then form a query $\mathcal{F}_Q = \{h(c)\}$ and process it using the technique described above, thereby learning the virtual fingerprints of a group of entities who can satisfy p. Since S knows p, he then knows not only that each entity that matched his query is related *somehow*, but also that they satisfy p; that is, S can infer the attributes which cause the similarities between the nodes which match his query.

A Balancing Act. To an extent, these attacks can be mitigated by choosing an appropriate deployment model for the Xiphos system. The centralized model makes these attacks easier to carry out, as the server has complete information regarding the reputation tuples registered with the system. By using a super-peer deployment, the information flow is restricted greatly. Both the group discovery and attribute inference attacks are limited to occurring within a single peer group, since super nodes do not have access to each others' databases. Thus, if client nodes restrict their information sharing to super nodes whom they can trust (e.g., super nodes with Better Business Bureau memberships or TRUSTe-issued privacy policies), then they can have some assurance that the super node will not abuse their partial information to carry out these attacks. Limiting the size of peer groups managed by each super node further restricts these attacks. It should also be noted that using the super-peer deployment model does not sacrifice the completeness of information available, as ratings registered by every peer are still included as the contribution of each super node is folded into the reputation rating calculated using Equation 6. However, unless each super node has a roughly equivalent number of members, ratings may be biased towards the opinions of entities at super nodes with fewer members. Additionally, unless super nodes coordinate to ensure that there is no overlap between their respective peer groups, the accuracy of the reputation ratings calculated using this method may suffer, as malicious peers could register ratings at multiple super nodes.

These attacks can be further limited by using the fully distributed deployment model, as no entity in the system has any sort of complete information. Each entity is restricted to querying a limited number of other entities in the system, as querying each node in turn becomes inefficient as the size of the network grows. Additionally, when issuing the query $\mathcal{F}_Q$, an entity A cannot be sure if the responding entities have matched all of $\mathcal{F}_Q$ or simply some $\mathcal{F}' \subset \mathcal{F}_Q$. This implies that A must carry out the group discovery or attribute inference attacks by issuing queries $\mathcal{F}_Q$ where $|\mathcal{F}_Q| = 1$ to ensure that all matches returned are total matches. Note also, that A will most likely need to know c where $\mathcal{F}_Q = \{h(c)\}$, as otherwise she is simply guessing that $\mathcal{F}_Q$ is an "interesting" virtual fingerprint, which may often be a difficult task. This implies that A is very likely to know p, the release policy for c, as she satisfied p to learn c in the first place. In this respect, the group discovery attack is eliminated, as A is forced to carry out the stronger attribute inference attack. The attribute inference attack is itself no more feasible than trying to determine whether the attribute a attested to by c is possessed by each node in the network directly (e.g., by means of an eager negotiation or another resource access request protocol), thus this attack is no more feasible with Xiphos in place than it would have been without it. This implies that attacks which cause the aforementioned privacy violations can be virtually eliminated by using the fully distributed deployment model, though at the cost of losing the completeness of reputation information.

In addition to choosing an appropriate deployment model, another possible avenue for the prevention of privacy-related attacks involves the use of *obligations*. Obligations are requirements that can be attached to personal information in certain types of trust management systems. For instance, the owner of a digital medical record might attach an obligation to that record requiring that her health care provider send her an email any time this record is shared (e.g., while filing a referral to another physician). In these types of systems, it would be possible for entities to attach obligations to their credentials which limit the ways that other entities can disclose virtual fingerprints including hashes of these credentials. For example, an entity could indicate that any virtual fingerprint including a hash of her Department of Energy security clearance credential may only be released to servers operated by the U.S. government. These types of obligations allow users to reap the benefits of Xiphos while still maintaining some control over their private information. We expect that most entities will allow at least some "interesting" subset of their credential hashes to be included in virtual fingerprints because they will likely interact with other entities who require the ability to obtain their reputation rating prior to interaction.

4.2   Attacks and Defenses

One common attack against reputation systems is whitewashing, in which a user sheds a bad reputation by establishing a new identity. In some cases, this is as simple as reconnecting to the network to obtain a new node identifier, while in others it may involve establishing a new pseudonym (e.g., email address) by which one is known. In Xiphos, nodes are identified by their virtual fingerprints. As discussed in Section 2, users have a limited number of virtual fingerprints, which are uniquely determined by the set of credentials that the user possesses. Obtaining new identities thus reduces to establishing new virtual fingerprints; this requires that a user obtain *all* new credentials, as *any* overlap will link this entity to old ratings. If users are routinely required to use multiple credentials, this process becomes time consuming and involves multiple certificate authorities, thereby making whitewashing an impractical attack for *habitual* cheaters.

In many reputation systems, it is possible for an entity to "stuff the ballot box" by registering multiple ratings for a single entity. Xiphos limits this attack because entities have only a finite number of disjoint virtual fingerprints which can be used to register claims for a given entity. In addition to capping the number of ratings that an entity can register, the virtual fingerprint system also limits the benefits of registering multiple ratings. A properly designed $\gamma(\cdot)$ function will assign lower linkability coefficients to ratings associated with a small rater virtual fingerprint than it will to ratings associated with large rater virtual fingerprints. This means that given a properly designed $\gamma(\cdot)$ function, an entity's influence on the overall rating of another entity will be less if she registers multiple ratings using a large number of small virtual fingerprints than it would have been if she had registered only a single rating using the union of each smaller virtual fingerprint. Such a $\gamma(\cdot)$ function is discussed in [14].

One attack against Xiphos itself involves exploiting $\varphi(\cdot)$. Recall that $\varphi(\cdot)$ is used to weight the contribution of a single tuple to the overall reputation calculated for a query. In centralized or super-peer deployments, entities may try to increase their influence by repeatedly updating their ratings for other entities to keep them current. In the absence of certified transactions and synchronized clocks, there is little that can be done to prevent this problem. However, this attack will have little influence on the ratings calculated by a server if the majority of the users remain honest. Nonetheless, investigating mechanisms for providing certified timestamps is an important area of future work.

One last attack on which we comment occurs when a malicious party M is able to steal some set of credentials $\mathcal{C}'_A \subseteq \mathcal{C}_A$ from another entity A. If M then submits a reputation rating for some entity B described by the virtual fingerprint $\mathcal{F}_B$ while posing as A (by using the stolen credentials $\mathcal{C}'_A$), this rating will overwrite the rating previously stored by A. Though this attack is serious, it is possible in any system in which one entity is able to effectively steal the identity of another. Due to the fact that users in attribute-based trust management systems have many identities (which we have referred to as descriptions in this paper), open systems researchers must focus on making secure identity management easy for users of their systems to prevent these types of attacks.

4.3   Performance Evaluation

As mentioned in Section 3, Xiphos uses reputation update equations similar to those whose convergence behavior was studied in [16]. Rather than studying convergence, we focused on quantifying the effect of using virtual fingerprints as the basis for a reputation system, instead of more traditional identities, in a number of simulated grid computing environments. To this end, we studied the growth rates of local databases over time, evaluated the effect of these more complex local databases on query processing time, and designed and evaluated the impact of a $\gamma(\cdot)$ function for our application domain. The complete results of this study are presented in [14].

We found that when using a conservative tuple eviction policy, the average size of a local reputation database in a network with 10,000 users was approximately 1,500 tuples after 5,000 days of simulated interactions. In a network of 70,000 users, the average local database contained 4,000 tuples after 5,000 simulated days. When executing a prototype Xiphos implementation on a 1.6GHz laptop, Xiphos could process queries on databases of these sizes at throughputs of 600 and 200 queries per second, respectively, without using indexes. The use of a more aggressive, though still reasonable, tuple eviction policy resulted in query throughputs of over 2,200 queries per second on both simulated networks; it is unlikely that the network characteristics of actual grid computing systems would even allow queries to arrive at such a high rate. We also verified that a suitable $\gamma(\cdot)$ function can limit the damages caused by attackers in the system by penalizing them for maliciously using multiple identities. These observations indicate that virtual fingerprints can be used as a reasonable basis for reputation in the open systems of the future.

4.4   Virtual Fingerprinting and Reputation

Virtual fingerprints provide a general notion of pseudo-identity that can be bound to reputation scores in systems where explicit identity information may not be present. Virtual fingerprints are also difficult to change, making white-washing impractical and reducing the benefits of assuming multiple personalities. In this paper, we described the use of virtual fingerprinting as the basis for one *particular* reputation system. However, the reputation scores bound to virtual fingerprints can be aggregated according to *any* reputation calculation method, provided that the complications arising from the legitimate assumption of multiple identities (in the form of disjoint virtual fingerprints) are addressed.

In particular, systems need to mitigate the effects of malicious users assuming multiple identities to over-influence the system. Additionally, the fact that queries may overlap multiple tuples could lead to problems maintaining precomputed reputation scores at a naive server. In [14], we describe an ontology-based definition of $\gamma(\cdot)$ that prevents malicious entities from over-influencing our simulated grid computing system; similar definitions are likely to be possible in other domains. We also present a method for maintaining precomputed reputation estimates at a centralized server, though space limits prohibit its discussion here. Similar modifications could be made to other reputation systems (including those not yet developed), thereby enabling them to use virtual fingerprints and extending their applicability to attribute-based trust management systems.

5 Related Work

While the area is too broad to survey in general, papers such as [9, 12, 16, 19] address the design of general-purpose reputation systems. These types of systems assume that entities have established identities in the system and many times suffer from whitewashing and ballot-stuffing attacks. The authors of [17] recommend designing systems which require non-repudiable *evidence* of a transaction be shown in order for a reputation rating to be registered; this certainly prevents an entity from registering multiple claims, but requires that the underlying system support certified transactions. In this paper, we introduced the notion of virtual fingerprints and showed how they can be used as the basis of the Xiphos reputation system. The nature of virtual fingerprints limits the effectiveness of the aforementioned attacks without requiring non-repudiable transaction support from the underlying system.

Other authors have also addressed the privacy versus trust trade-off discussed in Section 4. Anonymous credential schemes (e.g., [8, 7]) assume that privacy is more important than history-based mechanisms such as reputation systems and allow a credential to be used under different pseudonyms; this prevents transactions carried out by a single entity from ever being linked. In [18], the authors discuss this trade-off in detail and show how entities can explicitly reveal linkages between multiple identities to establish trust when needed. Xiphos allows system designers to balance this trade-off by choosing an appropriate deployment strategy. In addition, if Xiphos is used in systems supporting obligations, users can further limit the dissemination of their personal information.

6 Conclusion

In this paper, we presented a method for the linking and correlation of multiple identities in attribute-based trust management systems. We discussed how the descriptions that one entity learns about another can be transformed into opaque virtual fingerprints which can be used as the basis of the Xiphos reputation system. We explored the privacy versus utility trade-off for three deployments of Xiphos and examined the impacts of several attacks against the system. We also highlighted the results of a performance evaluation study of Xiphos, the details of which are available in the technical report version of this paper [14].

One interesting avenue for future work involves the development of index structures for virtual fingerprints to increase the query throughput of the Xiphos system. It is also likely that virtual fingerprinting can be used as the foundation for other useful security services. To this end, we are investigating secure audit, incident response, and collusion-detection systems based on virtual fingerprints.

Acknowledgments. This research was supported by the NSF under grants IIS-0331707, CNS-0325951, and CNS-0524695. Lee was also supported by a Motorola Center for Communications graduate fellowship.

References

[1] L. Bauer, S. Garriss, and M. K. Reiter. Distributed proving in access-control systems. In *Proceedings of the 2005 IEEE Symposium on Security and Privacy*, May 2005.

[2] M. Y. Becker and P. Sewell. Cassandra: Distributed access control policies with tunable expressiveness. In *Proceedings of the 5th IEEE International Workshop on Policies for Distributed Systems and Networks (POLICY '04)*, pages 159–168, 2004.

[3] E. Bertino, E. Ferrari, and A. C. Squicciarini. Trust-X: A peer-to-peer framework for trust establishment. *IEEE Transactions on Knowledge and Data Engineering*, 16(7):827–842, Jul. 2004.

[4] M. Blaze, J. Feigenbaum, and A. D. Keromytis. KeyNote: Trust management for public-key infrastructures (position paper). *Lecture Notes in Computer Science*, 1550:59–63, 1999.

[5] M. Blaze, J. Feigenbaum, and J. Lacy. Decentralized trust management. In *IEEE Conference on Security and Privacy*, May 1996.

[6] P. Bonatti and P. Samarati. Regulating service access and information release on the web. In *7th ACM Conference on Computer and Communications Security*, pages 134–143, 2000.

[7] J. Camenisch and E. V. Herreweghen. Design and implementation of the *idemix* anonymous credential system. In *CCS '02: Proceedings of the 9th ACM Conference on Computer and Communications Security*, pages 21–30, 2002.

[8] D. Chaum and J.-H. Evertse. A secure and privacy-protecting protocol for transmitting personal information between organizations. In *CRYPTO '88*, volume 263 of *LNCS*, pages 118–167. Springer-Verlag, 1988.

[9] A. Fernandes, E. Kotsovinos, S. Östring, and B. Dragovic. Pinocchio: Incentives for honest participation in distributed trust management. In *The 2nd International Conference on Trust Management (iTrust 2004)*, pages 63–77, 2004.

[10] C. A. Gunter and T. Jim. Policy-directed certificate retrieval. *Software—Practice and Experience*, 30(15):1609–1640, 2000.

[11] J. Holt, R. Bradshaw, K. E. Seamons, and H. Orman. Hidden credentials. In *2nd ACM Workshop on Privacy in the Electronic Society*, Oct. 2003.

[12] S. D. Kamvar, M. T. Schlosser, and H. Garcia-Molina. The eigentrust algorithm for reputation management in P2P networks. In *WWW '03: Proceedings of the 12th International Conference on World Wide Web*, pages 640–651, 2003.

[13] H. Koshutanski and F. Massacci. An interactive trust management and negotiation scheme. In *2nd International Workshop on Formal Aspects in Security and Trust (FAST)*, pages 139–152, Aug. 2004.

[14] A. J. Lee and M. Winslett. Virtual fingerprinting as a foundation for reputation in open systems. Technical Report UIUCDCS-R-2006-2691, University of Illinois at Urbana-Champaign, Feb. 2006.
    Available at http://dais.cs.uiuc.edu/pubs/adamlee/xiphos_tech.pdf.

[15] N. Li and J. Mitchell. RT: A role-based trust-management framework. In *Third DARPA Information Survivability Conference and Exposition*, Apr. 2003.

[16] J. Liu and V. Issarny. Enhanced reputation mechanism for mobile ad hoc networks. In *The 2nd International Conference on Trust Management (iTrust 2004)*, pages 48–62, 2004.

[17] P. Obreiter. A case for evidence-aware distributed reputation systems. In *The 2nd International Conference on Trust Management (iTrust 2004)*, pages 33–47, 2004.

[18] J.-M. Seigneur and C. D. Jensen. Trading privacy for trust. In *The 2nd International Conference on Trust Management (iTrust 2004)*, pages 93–107, 2004.

[19] A. A. Selçuk, E. Uzun, and M. R. Pariente. A reputation-based trust management system for P2P networks. In *4th IEEE/ACM International Symposium on Cluster Computing and the Grid (CCGRID 2004)*, 2004.

[20] L. Wang, D. Wijesekera, and S. Jajodia. A logic-based framework for attribute based access control. In *2nd ACM Workshop on Formal Methods in Security Engineering (FMSE 2004)*, pages 45–55, Oct. 2004.

[21] W. H. Winsborough, K. E. Seamons, and V. E. Jones. Automated trust negotiation. In *DARPA Information Survivability Conference and Exposition*, Jan. 2000.

[22] M. Winslett, T. Yu, K. E. Seamons, A. Hess, J. Jacobson, R. Jarvis, B. Smith, and L. Yu. The TrustBuilder architecture for trust negotiation. *IEEE Internet Computing*, 6(6):30–37, Nov./Dec. 2002.

[23] M. Winslett, C. Zhang, and P. A. Bonatti. PeerAccess: A logic for distributed authorization. In *Proceedings of the 12th ACM Conference on Computer and Communications Security (CCS 2005)*, Nov. 2005.

Towards Automated Evaluation of Trust Constraints

Siani Pearson

Trusted Systems Laboratory, Hewlett Packard Research Labs,
Filton Road, Stoke Gifford, Bristol, BS34 8QZ, UK
Siani.Pearson@hp.com

Abstract. In this paper we explore a mechanism for, and the limitations of, automation of assessment of trustworthiness of systems. We have implemented a system for checking trust constraints expressed within privacy policies as part of an integrated prototype developed within the EU Framework VI Privacy and Identity Management for Europe (PRIME) project [1]. Trusted computing information [2,3] may be taken into account as part of this analysis. This is the first stage of ongoing research and development within PRIME in this area.

1 Introduction

Trust is important to enable interactions on the Internet. People quite often have to trust e-commerce sites, service providers, online services and enterprises that they will perform as expected, provide agreed services and goods and will not exploit and misuse personal and confidential information.

The trust that people have in enterprises can be built, reinforced or modified via a variety of means and tools, including personal experience, analysis of prior history, recommendations, certification and auditing by known authorities. The behaviour of an enterprise, the fact that it will fulfil agreed tasks in due time and perform as predicted are all important aspects to shape its reputation and perception of trustworthiness. Related to this, the way an enterprise handles privacy aspects has also an important impact on trust.

An open issue to address is how to provide people with more customisable and fine-grained mechanisms to allow them to make judgments about the trustworthiness and privacy compliance of the remote receiver of their Personally Identifiable Information (PII) (i.e. data that can identify the end-user). For example, users might want to get some assurance of the capabilities of an enterprise, even before engaging in any interaction or transaction with this enterprise. This includes obtaining degrees of assurance that the enterprise can actually support specific privacy policies and obligations, that their data will be processed and managed securely, that enterprises' web services, applications and data repositories are installed, run and patched according to security standards and good IT practices, and/or that secure and trusted platforms are used.

This paper addresses this issue and, more specifically, focuses on describing automation of analysis of trust constraints – conditions about the trustworthiness of a (network of) computer system(s) – within such a system. This is part of a broader

K. Stølen et al. (Eds.): iTrust 2006, LNCS 3986, pp. 252–266, 2006.

goal within the PRIME project [1] to use technology to automate delivery of privacy in enterprises in order to address increasing complexity and dynamism within service provision and to rely less on human processes (which are prone to failure, malicious attack and fraud). In addition, automation can be used to ensure that delivery of privacy is operating correctly by acting as a bridge between should happen and what is actually happening. Smart technology is needed, in the form of powerful trusted services as well as monitoring of these services, processes and resources. We have developed the first version of a component that is designed to do this.

2 Motivation for Automation of Trust Assessment

The strategic objective of the PRIME project [1] is to research and develop approaches and solutions for privacy-enhancing identity management that can empower European citizens to exercise their privacy rights, and thus enable them to gain trust and confidence in the Information Society. In order to increase user control over the release of their personal information, we wish to provide a mechanism to help the user to assess the trustworthiness of back end systems before releasing such information. This mechanism can also be used in order to allow the user to check the proof of properties contributing to trust (such as the validity of seals of approval), and not have to rely upon assertions by companies that could be deliberately or erroneously false or misleading. In addition, it can be used to help 'good willing' enterprises – that are aware of the importance of privacy as a driving factor to underpin trust, reputation and a business enabler – to ensure that their trust and security are operating as expected and to comply with legislation. The most basic starting point for building trust is just to check that the services side has a PRIME system that is operating correctly and via education enhance the user's trust in the body certifying this system. More detailed justification of our approach in line with the approach taken by PRIME is given in Section 3.1 below.

We recognise that the problem cannot be solved by deploying technologies alone: behaviour and implementation of correct process are very relevant. However, our objective is to build technical solutions that can help enterprises increase automation and give people additional support in making informed decisions about trust.

2.1 Scenarios Considered

As considered above, the main driver for this work is that it increases user trust and willingness to engage in e-commerce and e-government. Example scenarios include:

- giving consumers the ability to determine whether unknown vendors on the Web are using IT systems and processes that can be trusted to execute their stated privacy policies,
- trust-related information could be both more reliable and more open – for instance, compliance reports about enterprises could be accessible to the public, such as being available for viewing directly via a website.

Let us consider in more detail the example where a user engages for the first time with an enterprise that implements aspects of our model (presented in Section 4). In addition to other aspects that might be supported by the enterprise (such as seals and recommendations by other parties), users might require the enterprise to assure them about privacy practices, security and trustworthiness of their IT systems. Users might request the enterprise, by means of assurance policies, to provide them with fine-grained statements about their security systems and business practices and declarations of which privacy policies they support, specifically about how their data will be handled. The user could go even further by directly checking the trustworthiness of some platforms, via TCG-enabled mechanisms [2,3] if supported. The user can use their compliance checking system to verify enterprise statements and promises, remember their expectations and re-check them over time. If the user is satisfied by these initial statements, they might decide to engage in an interaction or transaction with the enterprise and potentially disclose their personal data.

A further driver for our work relates to enterprise compliance with corporate governance legislation, enterprise policies and privacy legislation. Since this is not the main focus of this paper we will not give further details here.

3 Privacy and Identity Management for Europe (PRIME) Project

The PRIME project started in March 2004; its goals have been introduced above. Further details and its architecture may be found in [1,4].

In the PRIME model, end-users formulate their (individual) privacy preferences before interacting with an organisation, and can negotiate the proofs that need to be provided to an organisation. In some situations, zero knowledge techniques could be used and the end-user could remain anonymous, although in other situations PII may need to be transferred in order for the particular type of transaction to go ahead. This negotiation is automated, although input may be given by the user in complex situations. Following W3C recommendations [5], in order to encourage adoption of this approach by service-providers, it would probably be necessary to have the service-side start the negotiation process by transmitting an initial set of requirements and options to the end-user. Several different approaches and techniques are possible:

- *Anonymous checking of service side:* End-users could check up-front the fulfilment of specified back-end (enterprise) properties or trust requirements (for example, whether the service side could support obligations or was providing a secure processing environment) before deciding whether or not to proceed with a transaction.
- *Negotiation of 'sticky' policies:* End-users could be offered a choice of trust requirements by the service provider which would then be customisable; alternatively, end-users could add new trust requirements into the negotiation process (between the end-user and service side). The resultant negotiated policies can 'stick' to personal data and as it moves around the back end these policies will be enforced; these policies can include trust requirements.
- *Compliance checking by 'good willing' enterprises:* The service side can automate checking of trust and assurance necessary conditions in access control policies.

This model where end-users formulate their (individual) privacy policies before interacting with an organisation, and then have the organisation verify that it will comply with the end-user policy, is in contrast with much current practice where at best an end-user looks at an organisation's policy and decides if it is acceptable. Thereby, this model is supporting users to maintain control over their personal spheres and thus to technically enforce informational self-determination, and hence is in accordance with the philosophy and motivation of PRIME. Informational self-determination is a core aspect of privacy and is in many countries acknowledged as a basic human or constitutional right. As an end-user it would be preferable to have the possibility (in case the user so desired) to dictate or customise some of the privacy policies, rather than passively accept whatever is dictated by the enterprise [6,7]. The desire for this is supported by various studies that highlight end-users' concerns about privacy violations. For instance, according to a study by the UK Information Commissioner [8], 40% of the UK population are classified as "the Concerned" who have proactively protected PII through withholding it. They are less likely to purchase products if they have to give away too much information, and their attitudes towards organisations are likely to be influenced by a reputation for good information handling practices. This study also classifies 13% of the UK population as "the Proactive", who prefer working with companies that excel at good personal information management.

Based on results of a meta-analysis of user surveys related to Internet privacy in Europe, social researchers within the PRIME project have derived the importance of trust assurance methods for (re)establishing trust in online relationships as an important social requirement for PRIME technologies. Besides this, the meta-analysis also indicates a preference of many users to have more transparency and better user control over the use of their online behavioural data [9]. Also, usability tests conducted on PRIME early prototypes and user interface mock-ups of identity management systems showed that many users distrusted the tested systems [10,11] and were also pointing out the users' need for trust assurance methods.

Turner has carried out various studies to assess factors that affect the perception of security and privacy of e-commerce web sites [12,13,14]. He concludes that consumers depended on recommendations from independent third parties to ensure security [12]. This supports our view that end users would find it helpful to be able to be given enterprise assurance details provided by third parties, such as privacy seals.

Note that it is not necessary for people to have to author policies, because default policies can be provided which they could use, preferably vouched for by entities that they trust (for example, consumer organisations).

3.1 The System Policy Compliance Checker (SPCC) Component

A compliance checker component has been developed as part of the PRIME architecture [4], which is used both on the services side and on the user side (as there is a mirrored design). The System Policy Compliance Check (SPCC) component in the PRIME architecture responds to requests about whether policies (and in particular trust constraints) are satisfied on the service side. Within PRIME this component is implemented as being separate from the Access Control Decision Function (ACDF) component, but it could in fact be implemented as part of ACDF and part of other components such as Identity Control (IC) (for checking trust constraints when access control is not invoked). An example of the latter case would be if someone wished to check the trustworthiness of a service-provider upfront in a 'preamble' phase before provision of any identity information (potentially in a fully anonymous manner).

4 Our Model

In this section we define what we mean by trust constraints and present our approach and generic system architecture for evaluation of such constraints.

4.1 Trust Constraints

Trust constraints are part of a broader representation of constraints within policy languages. Figure 1 illustrates how – within the context of policies and preferences – they are a subset of a broader set of constraints about data processing: assurance constraints.

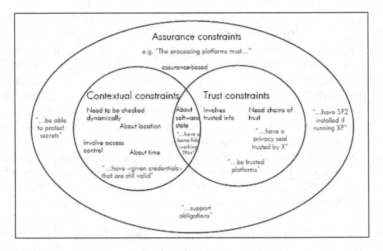

Fig. 1. Trust and assurance constraints

Assurance constraints may be contextual constraints, i.e. formulated by people to restrict the cases in which their data will be processed, according to parameters that may vary dynamically (such as time, location or platform state), and/or trust constraints. Figure 1 shows how these can be related and provides some examples. To a greater or lesser degree, all assurance constraints could be regarded as trust constraints since something must ultimately be trusted to make the assertions (and indeed the policy compliance checker must be trusted to issue compliance statements), but for convenience we may distinguish those statements that directly involve trust-related information and for whose automated evaluation a compliance checker needs to take chains of trust into account.

These constraints may be expressed within user-side preferences or policies. Such policies ('assurance policies') would then include a set of conditions and constraints formulated to obtain degrees of assurance from enterprises that their data will be processed according to peoples' expectations, such as compliance to privacy, security and IT standards. On the client side the SPCC can check their satisfaction (via information provided by the service-side SPCC) prior to disclosing any personal information or during the negotiation process (when SPCC provides input to both the local user and service-side requester). It can also be desirable to check contextual constraints on the service side after information has been disclosed. This would be through the use of sticky policies, which are negotiated using the preferences and then associated with data as it travels around, perhaps just using a weak binding, although preferably this would use a strong binding provided by cryptographic mechanisms: see for example [15]. Furthermore, such constraints may be expressed within service-side access control policies to help enterprises comply with privacy legislation, such that service side SPCC will not allow a transaction to be continued unless the constraints are fulfilled.

To clarify exactly what we mean by assurance policies (or constraints), let us consider the W3C Platform for Privacy Preferences (P3P) [5] and Enterprise Privacy Authorisation Language (EPAL) [16] schemas representation of privacy policy rules. These rules are formed of 6 elements, namely data user, data item, action, purpose, conditions and obligations. Assurance policies could be thought of as an extension to privacy policy rules in that they contain certain trust, contextual or assurance constraints which, if fulfilled, are not sufficient for the transaction to proceed: semantically, these constraints are necessary conditions. An example of an assurance policy which is an access control policy would be: `subject with subjexp can action on object with objexp if condition onlyif assurance constraint`. (Alternatively, such an assurance policy could be represented by conjoining the assurance constraint to each subcondition.) There can be other, similar, forms of assurance policy, such as a policy that is attached to data and that contains assurance constraints that must be satisfied before certain actions may be performed on the data.

Assurance constraints (including trust constraints) can also be thought of in an orthogonal sense as breaking down into subconstraints, such that there can be functional decomposition of higher-level privacy and trust goals into one or more lower-level goals, and so on recursively until 'facts' about the knowledge base (e.g. checks about the value of constraint settings, the presence of software, the availability of services for a given minimum uptime, etc.) are invoked at the lowest level. This decomposition is captured by rules within our system that hook into the ontologies used so that the meaning can be agreed across multiple parties. For example, even a fairly low level trust constraint such as that the receiving party should use tamper-resistant hardware to store key information must be defined in such as way as to make clear the manufacturers, version numbers and other ancilliary information such as degree of tamper resistance that would or alternatively would not be acceptable. In practice, a third party would define such rules in advance and then they would be viewable and/or customisable if desired at a later stage by users or administrators.

4.2 Architecture for Evaluation of Trust Constraints

This section gives an overview of our system within PRIME that handles privacy obligations and assurance policies in enterprises. This is currently being developed; although it is work in progress, an initial working version of this system is available. Figure 2 shows the core aspects of this model.

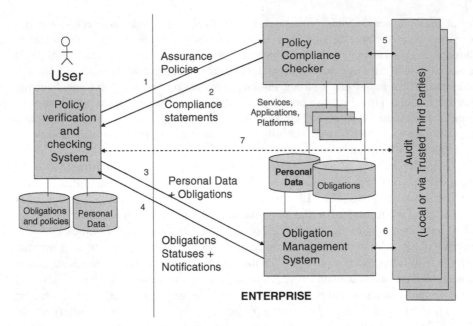

Fig. 2. Simplified architecture

The model supports the following core interactions between users and an enterprise:

- **Users ask an enterprise to demonstrate their support and compliance to a set of policies (cf. 1 of Figure 2):** This can be done by users before engaging in any interaction with the enterprise. The "policy compliance checker" module, within the enterprise, issues compliance statements and potentially it supports degrees of verifications made by users. For example, users could require that the enterprise will protect their data to a specified level of tamper resistance, that the enterprise is not running certain software that has known bugs without the requisite patches, that the enterprise can support obligation checking or that the enterprise has a certain type of privacy seal. The outcome is recorded and remembered by the "policy verification and checking system" on the user side for future reference and control. A similar mechanism can be deployed in enterprises in federated contexts where the enterprise needs to disclose data subjects' personal data to other parties (during business interactions and transactions).
- **Users disclose their personal data along with their privacy obligations (cf. 3 of Figure 2):** User can dictate the set of privacy obligations and constraints they want to be fulfilled on their personal data [17].
- **Users control and verify their expectations and compliance over time (cf. 2,4,7 of Figure 2):** The "policy verification and checking system", at the user side, remembers commitments, obligations and promises made by an enterprise. It processes them against evidence and information provided by the enterprise and potential third parties in order to verify their consistency and compliance. This module provides users with intuitive visual clues that help them to make decisions

and influence their perceptions of the trustworthiness of an enterprise in executing what has been agreed.

Figure 3 provides further technical details about the compliance checking system.

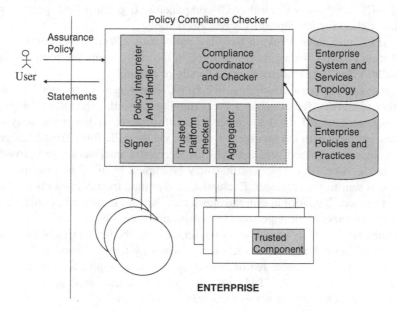

Fig. 3. High-level architecture of a policy compliance checker

This system includes the following components:

1. **Policy interpreter and handler:** The component that interprets an assurance policy and determines if it is well expressed and can be handled by the system.
2. **Compliance coordinator and checker:** This component coordinates the collection of required information to provide support to tests/requirements expressed by a user via an assurance policy. It can potentially allow remote users to directly perform tests on service side platforms.
3. **Trusted platform checker:** This interacts with and retrieves information about the status of critical platforms running enterprises' services and applications and that store and handle personal data; it analyses this information to assess the trustworthiness of those platforms with respect to the current context.
4. **Aggregator:** This component aggregates information collected from various enterprise systems, in order to provide a comprehensive result to the user; this may involve analysis to provide an overall trust assessment.
5. **Enterprise system and services topology:** Database containing information about the topology of enterprise systems and services.
6. **Enterprise policies and practices:** Database containing information about the policies and procedures supported by an enterprises.
7. **Signer:** The component responsible for signing the statements made by the policy compliance checker for integrity and non-repudiation reasons; this could be done via a trusted hardware device such as a TPM [2].

4.3 SPCC Functionality Within PRIME

Within the PRIME architecture [4], the SPCC component is in charge of handling trust and assurance constraints that cannot be directly managed by the Identity Control (IC) and Access Control (AC) components. It performs the privacy policy compliance checking concept already described above.

The SPCC may have a role in handling policies on client, server and third party sites. Within PRIME, we are most interested in the cases where the back end system that handles PII is to be evaluated, either locally or remotely.

When evaluating trust constraints, the SPCC component might need to interact with other platforms (for example, servers running a specific service or dealing with the management of PII data) to gather trust information. It has a topology of the resources, interacts with the involved IT entities via their Platform Trust Management (PTM) component, gathers measures of trust, correlates information and provides an answer in the form of a statement that may be signed by IC. The resulting signed statement is sent to the requester. Evaluation of dynamic trust constraints needs to be triggered via access control in order to check that the trust constraint is satisfied in the current circumstances before personal information is accessible.

In summary, the policy compliance checker we describe has a privacy focus. It can: model organisational resources such as database systems, firewalls, hosts, virus scanners and privacy seals; reason about system and application properties, for example host patching or TPM self test; reason about user provisioning and maintenance; check that IT controls are working as expected.

5 An Implemented System

The SPCC component has been implemented within the PRIME v1 integrated prototype. There is a component just for the services side that allows the services-side access control to check that access control policies that include trust constraints are met. In particular, this allows 'good willing' enterprises to check that the system is in a suitable state before the negotiation protocol is completed and personal information is transferred to the services side. The same mechanism forms part of the solution for allowing users to express and check trust constraints related to the services side.

As shown in Figure 4, which shows server-side interactions in PRIME directly involving the SPCC component, the SPCC component consists of internal subcomponents that handle incoming policies (or constraints), model the back-end topology, gather and aggregate service-side trust and assurance information (including trusted platform information, privacy seals and security certificates), and analyse whether the policies are currently satisfied. Analysing assurance information will often not be just a simple matter of syntax checking: not only assurance information, but also other external information including context and event information, needs to be analysed to decide whether the policies do comply with these. The Platform Trust Manager (PTM) component provides most of the trust input and support for analysis is given by the Reasoner component: this allows hierarchical and semantic web based inferences; special rules break down the semantics of the assurance constraints and an assurance ontology is used to standardise interpretation of assurance information and allow querying over (a model of) available assurance data relating to the data processing environment(s).

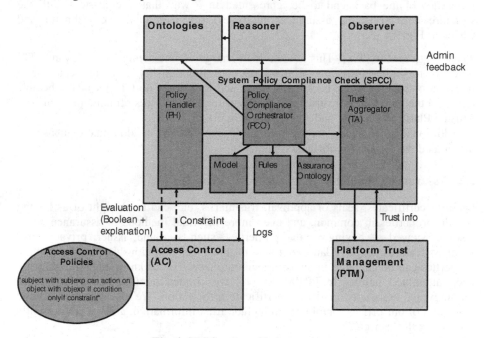

Fig. 4. SPCC server-side interactions

At present, the SPCC supports checking of the following initial list of constraints (or combinations thereof): the receiving platform must be able to protect secrets, must be a Trusted Platform, and/or must support obligations; the receiving platform's Trusted Platform Module must be bona fide and working; if the receiving platform is running XP, it must have Service Pack 2 installed; the receiving party must have a valid privacy seal.

5.1 Overview of the Architecture of the SPCC Component

The SPCC component is a specific implementation of the generic system shown in Figure 3 and is comprised of the following modules, as shown in Figure 4:

Policy Handler [PH]: This module is a policy interpreter; it parses an incoming policy, checks for its integrity and validity and dispatches it to the PCO module. It coordinates processes within the SPCC and acts as a single point of contact for other components to interact with SPCC (cf. Policy Interpreter and Handler, Fig. 3).

Policy Compliance Orchestrator [PCO]: This module interprets and executes a compliance task as dictated by the policy. It orchestrates interactions with modules specialised in checking for specific compliance requirements. In v1 two kinds of compliance check are supported: trust compliance via the TA module and assurance compliance via the Reasoner module to carry out inferences using SPCC rules that allow constraints to be analysed in terms of simpler components and references to ontologies and to locally stored models of assurance data (that allow the particular properties of the back end to be represented in a way that is consistent with the structure defined in the assurance ontologies) (cf. Compliance Coordinator and Checker, Fig. 3).

Trust Aggregator [TA]: This module is in charge of interacting with relevant PTM modules to gather measures of trust; its core functionality is to aggregate trust information relating to the back end service, and in order to do this it needs to be able to model the back end infrastructure and key enterprise services running upon this (cf. Trusted Platform Checker and Aggregator, Fig. 3).

Additional functionality shown in Figure 3 is contained in additional databases or distributed throughout the PRIME system.

5.2 Assurance Ontologies

Security certificates, seals of approval, trustmarks, etc. can be thought of as having certain properties in common, and even more informal methods of assurance could also be viewed as having similar properties, such as name, issuer, privacy/trust/ security features, expiry date, etc.: the meaning and relationships between these properties can be captured in an assurance ontology. To our knowledge, this has not been attempted before. In PRIME IP v1, we created an OWL-based assurance ontology and associated models of certificate information. We also provided a basic extension of our privacy ontologies to include trust information, and we are currently improving this aspect.

5.3 Use of Trusted Platforms

The implemented system allows information provided by trusted computing to be taken into account within the evaluation of trust constraints. A Trusted Platform (TP) is designed to create a foundation of trust for software processes; the Trusted Computing Group (TCG) has specified how it must be constructed [2,3]. Allied technologies are currently being developed [18]. Trusted computing information can be useful in assessing trust because a TP will either operate in the expected manner for a particular purpose, or else can be relied upon to signal clearly if it does not. Other mechanisms for making judgments are also required, including higher level integrity mechanisms at the OS level, vouching mechanisms provided by trusted third parties and recommendation systems. It is also possible to create trust domains that are based on multiple TPs [19].

Information about a particular TP is provided by the PTM: this could include various types of trust information including reputation information and trusted computing feedback. The SPCC component will collate and aggregate such information, and analyse it with respect to its models about the resources deployed within the system and about functional decomposition of privacy and trust information to decide whether the trust constraints are met within the current circumstances.

6   Comparison with Related Work

Our research is novel in several aspects in comparison with prior work in this area. Steps towards the provision of more assurance to people on privacy have been made by various privacy seals providers and verifiers [20]. This approach provides users with general purpose information about the conformance of a service provider or an enterprise with certified, privacy compliant processes when handling and managing PII data. However these approaches do not take into account specific, fine-grained requirements, needs and constraints dictated by individuals.

The usage of recommendation mechanisms [21,22] – based on people sharing evaluations of enterprises' behaviour – is another well-explored approach for dealing with trust matters. These mechanisms can also be used to evaluate enterprises' compliance to privacy and, as a side effect, have an impact on the perception of the trustworthiness of an organization. This approach is complementary to the problems the author wants to address. Related complementary work includes [23], which describes how a trust index of a CA may be computed.

As already discussed in Section 4 above, in our work we employ privacy practices that can be deduced from the W3C EPAL [16] and P3P [5] specifications and that implement the philosophy of recent privacy legislation. P3P specifications allow people to describe their privacy expectations and match them against the level of privacy supported by an enterprise. This helps shape people's trust in enterprises. However P3P only checks if their expectations are matched against promises made by the enterprise, and does not provide mechanisms to check and prove upfront compliance with fine-grained constraints.

KeyNote [24], PolicyMaker [25] and REFEREE [26] all suggest a programming language to define a policy based on certificates and an engine to decide access control regarding the holder of certificates, and the Trust Policy Language (TPL) [27] allows rule definition for becoming a group member. Other policy definition languages, schemes and verification tools include Trust-X (an XML-based framework for peer-to-peer trust negotiation) [28], OASIS XACML [29], and Ponder [30]. We can leverage aspects of this work, in particular [15] to provide a stronger association of assurance policies to confidential data, but we use the PRIME policy framework. There is prior work in developing trust ontologies (see for example [31,32,33]), but these are not well-developed and do not immediately suit the PRIME context.

In terms of policy compliance checking, we are not aware of products or solutions providing flexible, model-driven assurance and compliance verifications. Products such as Synomos [34] and SenSage [35] hardcode their compliance checking process and cannot model privacy processes and IT components.

In summary, our work differs from related work in particular in that it exploits much richer policy definitions including trust constraints, provides the user with feedback about the fulfilment of these policies, provides evidence for assurance claims and measures the trustworthiness of the service provider.

7   Current Status

The work presented in this paper describes providing organisations with an infrastructure for interpreting requests for checking trust-related constraints, executing the relevant checks and providing an answer to users. The current status is that a compliance check component and associated protocols have been integrated within PRIME v1 integrated prototype and associated tests are complete; this involved usage of trusted computing information. In addition, we integrated a compliance check plug-in that is able to evaluate certain trust constraints in a similar manner within an audit-focused compliance auditing and reporting system. We are currently carrying out further research and implementation for v2 of PRIME integrated prototype.

To date, we have implemented compliance checking of the constraints shown in Figure 1 by 'good willing' enterprises. However, this is a very rich research area and many interesting issues have been raised during the course of this work. Our next steps focus around addressing some of the following key issues:

- **Only partial automation is possible.** For example, manual processes currently used to check the validity e.g. of privacy seals are difficult to automate. However, we can automatically generate websites to request information for which manual process entries are necessary.
- **Complexity of back end infrastructure and of how trust constraints can be functionally decomposed.** To address this, we plan to extend the model to include justification meta-data and weighting, and to highlight areas of concern in a report to the user or the administrator, as appropriate.
- **There is some missing infrastructure at present making automation limited.** In particular, there is a need to standardise a meta-data format for machine-readable certificates: our assurance ontology could be a starting point for this.

There is an additional issue relating to the lack of a trusted infrastructure around the provision of evidence that is assessed when evaluating trust constraints. The problem is that malicious layered services could operate unknown to (our) monitoring services - there is a risk of employees compromising the system and also a risk when checking external topologies. This issue is not completely solved yet, but we plan to address this in future versions of our system. Note that this problem is generally faced by compliance monitoring and reporting systems. Approaches to solve this include:

- Authentication between components (which may be enhanced by using trusted hardware to protect private keys)
- Next generation trusted computing and infrastructure, e.g. TCG integrity checking [2,3], NGSCB [18], agents isolated in trusted compartments, etc.

Finally, whether trust constraints are satisfied or not is in general not a black and white issue – we need to provide suitable feedback to the user in order to help the user decide. We are currently in the process of iteratively defining and testing appropriate user interfaces to enable users to define trust constraints and receive feedback about results that can be 'drilled down' to a desired level of detail.

8   Conclusions

Currently, people disclose their PII to service providers, organisations (or other people) based on the assumption that the receivers will process this information in a suitable way, according to basic privacy requirements dictated by law and/or personal agreements. Today this approach is mainly based on trust: people make their decisions based on promises made by the receivers of their PII data, previous experience in interacting with them, recommendations by known people or just faith. We aim to provide a better basis for trust via automation and provision of evidence related to third party certification, configurations and status of IT resources.

To this end, we have developed a prototype that allows automated checking of trust constraints. In the short term, we have shown it is possible to automatically check basic system properties and use these in order to evaluate trust-related conditions expressed within policies. These properties include the presence, availability and properties of services, security hardware, etc. and configuration (e.g. patching). This is work in progress: in the longer term, we plan to improve the HCI associated with feedback to the user, cross check audit logs against the expected enforcement of trusted systems and use a trusted infrastructure to protect the information gathering process.

Acknowledgements. Our ideas on this topic benefited from useful input and discussions with PRIME colleagues.

References

1. PRIME, 2004. Privacy and Identity Management for Europe, European RTD Integrated Project under the FP6/IST Programme, http://www.prime-project.eu.org/.
2. TCG, 2003. TCG Main Specification, v1.1b. Available via http://www.trustedcom putinggroup.org.
3. TCG, 2003. TCG TPM Specification, v1.2. Available via http://www.trustedcomputing group.org.
4. Sommer, D (ed.), 2004. PRIME Architecture V1, D14.2b, http://www.prime-project. eu.org/.
5. Cranor, L., Langheinrich M., Marchiori, M., Presler-Marshall, M., Reagle, J., 2002. The Platform for Privacy Preferences Specification, v1.0, W3C, http://www.w3.org/TR/P3P/.
6. Kobsa, A., 2002. Personalized hypermedia and international privacy, Communications of the ACM, 45(5), pp. 64-67. http://www.ics.uci.edu/~kobsa/papers/2002-CACM-kobsa.pdf.
7. Kobsa, A, 2003. A Component Architecture for Dynamically Managing Privacy Constraints in Personalized Web-based Systems, R. Dingledine (ed.), PET 2003, Springer-Verlag, LNCS 2760, pp. 177-188.
8. UK Information Commissioner, 2003. Who Cares About Data Protection? Segmentation Research, http://www.informationcommissioner.gov.uk/cms/DocumentUploads/Segmenta tion%20Research%20Findings.pdf.
9. Leenes, R. and Lips, M., 2004. Social evaluation of early prototyoes, Fischer-Hübner, S. and Pettersson, J. S. (eds.), Evaluation of early prototypes, PRIME deliverable D6.1.b, 1. http://www.prime-project.eu.org/public/prime_products/deliverables/.
10. Fischer-Hübner, S. and Pettersson, J. S. (eds.), 2004. Evaluation of early prototypes, PRIME deliverable D6.1.b, 1. http://www.prime-project.eu.org/public/prime_products/ deliverables/.
11. Pettersson, J. S. (ed.), 2005. HCI guidance and proposals, PRIME deliverable D6.1.c, 11 February 2005. http://www.prime-project.eu.org/public/prime_products/deliverables/.

12. Turner, C.W., Zavod, M., Yurcik, W., 2001. Factors that Affect the Perception of Security and Privacy of E-Commerce Websites. Proc 4th International Conference on Electronic Commerce Research.
13. Turner, C.W., 2002. The online experience and consumers' perceptions of e-commerce security. Proc. Human Factors and Ergonomics Society 46th Annual Meeting.
14. Turner, C.W., 2003. How do consumers form their judgments of the security of e-commerce web sites? Proc. Workshop on HCI and Security Systems, CHI 2003.
15. Casassa Mont, M., Pearson, S., Bramhall, P., 2003. Towards Accountable Management of Privacy and Identity Management, Proc. ESORICS.
16. IBM, 2004. The Enterprise Privacy Authorization Language (EPAL), v1.1 specification. http://www.zurich.ibm.com/security/enterprise-privacy/epal/.
17. Casassa Mont, M., 2004. Dealing with Privacy Obligations: Important Aspects and Technical Approaches, Trust and Privacy in Digital Business, Springer, LNCS 3184, pp. 120-131.
18. Microsoft, 2006. Next-Generation Secure Computing Base home page, http://www.microsoft.com/resources/ngscb.
19. Pearson, S. (ed.), 2002. Trusted Computing Platforms, Prentice Hall.
20. Cavoukian, A., Crompton, M, 2000. Web Seals: A review of Online Privacy Programs, 22nd International Conference on Privacy and Data Protection, http://www.privacy.gov.au/publications/seals.pdf.
21. Resnik, P., Varian H.R., 1997. Recommender Systems, Communications of ACM, http://www.acm.org/pubs/cacm/MAR97/resnick.html.
22. Reputation Research Network, 2004. Online papers on reputation and reputation research, http://databases.si.umich.edu/reputations/index.html.
23. Ball, E., Chadwick, D.W., Basden, A., 2003. The Implementation of a System for Evaluating Trust in a PKI Environment, Trust in the Network Economy, Evolaris, vol 2, Eds. O. Petrovic, M. Ksela, M. Fallenbock, C. Kitti, pp. 263-279.
24. M. Blaze, J. Feigenbaum, J. Ioannidis, and A. Keromytis, 1999. The KeyNote Trust-Management System RFC 2704. http://www.cis.upenn.edu/~angelos/keynote.html.
25. M. Blaze, J. Feigenbaum, and J. Lacy, 1996. Decentralized Trust Management, Proc. 17th Symposium on Security and Privacy, pp 164-173.
26. Y.-H. Chu, J. Feigenbaum, B. LaMacchia, P. Resnick and M. Strauss, 1997. REFEREE: Trust Management for Web Applications, in World Wide Web Journal, 2, pp. 127-139.
27. A. Herzberg, Y. Mass, J. Michaeli, D. Naor, Y. Ravid, 2000. Access Control Meets Public Key Infrastructure, Security & Privacy.
28. E. Bertino, E. Ferrari, A.C. Squicciarini, 2004. Trust-X: A Peer-to-Peer Framework for Trust Establishment, IEEE Transactions on Knowledge and Data Engineering, vol. 16, no. 7, pp. 827-842.
29. OASIS, eXtensible Access Control Markup Language (XACML). See http://www.oasis-open.org/committees/tc_home.php?wg_abbrev=xacml.
30. Damianou, N., Dulay, N., Lupu, E. , Sloman, M., 2001. The Ponder Policy Specification Language. Available via http://www-dse.doc.ic.ac.uk/research/policies/index.shtml.
31. MIND SWAP Trust Ontology. http://www.trust.mindswap.org/ont/trust.owl.
32. T. Berners-Lee, 2003. Semantic Web Tutorial Using N3. http://www.w3.org/2000/10/swap/doc/Trust.
33. Web of Trust, v0.1. http://xmlns.com/wot/0.1/.
34. Synomos, 2005. Synomos Align 3.0, http://www.synomos.com/.
35. SenSage, 2005. SenSage Web site, http://www.sensage.com/.

Provision of Trusted Identity Management Using Trust Credentials

Siani Pearson and Marco Casassa Mont

Trusted Systems Laboratory, Hewlett Packard Research Labs,
Filton Road, Stoke Gifford, Bristol, BS34 8QZ, UK
{Siani.Pearson, Marco.Casassa-Mont}@hp.com

Abstract. The Trusted Computing Group (TCG) has developed specifications for computing platforms that create a foundation of trust for software processes, based on a small amount of extra hardware [1,2]. Several million commercial desktop and laptop products have been shipped based upon this technology, and there is increasing interest in deploying further products. This paper presents a mechanism for using trusted computing in the context of identity management to deal with the problem of providing migration of identity and confidential information across users' personal systems and multiple enterprise IT back-end systems in a safe and trusted way.

1 Introduction

Current identity management solutions (that enable either users or enterprises to handle identities, profiles and credentials), allow identity information to freely move across (organisational) boundaries, with consequent loss of control by the user on how this data is used. Furthermore, there might be little certification and trust in such identity information, making it hard to detect if data is changed when crossing such boundaries.

A similar issue is present in dynamic systems (adaptive enterprise, distributed data centers, etc.), when identity credentials are associated to systems and services running on platforms that might be dynamically set-up or torn-down.

Trusted Computing Group (TCG) identity mechanisms [1,2] can address the problems of certification, anonymity and 'stickiness' of credentials to a trusted system. However, it is hard to move and modify managed identities. Moreover, current forms of retail trust-related credit are tied to specific accounts or individuals, and transfer of such credit neither involves trusted identities nor allows the owners to remain anonymous.

This paper describes a secure identity management approach and solution that leverages the benefits of trusted computing to enhance privacy of managed identities and their migration across platforms.

2 Problem Statement

The central problem addressed in this paper is how to allow a secure, trusted and privacy-aware migration of credentials (stored within platforms and used by services

K. Stølen et al. (Eds.): iTrust 2006, LNCS 3986, pp. 267–282, 2006.
© Springer-Verlag Berlin Heidelberg 2006

and applications) in cases where services are dynamically reconfigured and reallocated to new platforms. Specifically, we focus on how to leverage the benefits of trusted computing to address this problem.

Trusted Computing identity mechanisms can address the problems of certification, anonymity and 'stickiness' (i.e. binding) of credentials to a trusted system. However, it is hard to move such identities around or to modify them in legitimate ways according to the demands of the environment. Within enterprises' back-end infrastructure, there is a need to migrate confidential information between machines or storage devices on demand, and yet it will not necessarily be known in advance which exact machines would be selected even though only certain machines should be trusted to hold confidential information.

3 Addressed Scenarios

In this section we briefly describe some scenarios where our solution adds value.

Users wishing to migrate trust credits between different accounts. A likely future development of trusted commerce is that users will prefer to have several identities that they use in different situations, with sensitive or credit-related information being exposed to more trusted environments only. For example, a user could use one identity when dealing with a bank, another identity when buying goods and yet another identity when posting opinions to a newsgroup - at present people often use different email accounts specifically set up to do this. A trusted identity that is used in e-commerce may gain 'credits' in the eyes of retailers of two main types:

1. copyable, such as security clearance rating, financial credit rating, "frequent flyer" status (e.g. 'gold tier'), etc.
2. non-copyable, such as outstanding balances on accounts, vouchers, loyalty points (e.g. number of air-miles), insurance no-claims bonuses.

A user may wish to set up a new identity that hides links with other identities to the retailer and yet may wish to adopt those credits from them. Alternatively, he or she may wish to transfer credits within existing identities. This has to be done in a way that is understood, accepted and trusted by all parties.

Different contexts and infrastructures. There may be a need to create an alternative representation for an identity, or an amended form of that identity in an alternative form that is more suitable for use in different circumstances or in a different environment. This might be particularly the case in a mobile environment when the same person is moving between different infrastructures that use different forms of certificate. For example, conversion between Brands' credentials [3] and X.509 certificates, or for secure email or PGP [4]. All this may need to be carried out in such a way that the different identities cannot be correlated and identified with the user, thus allowing a profile to be built up. It is likely that consumers in general will become increasingly reluctant to divulge information that may be gathered, collated and analysed without their permission, or sold. Trust management technologies such as this may be used to give consumers more control and ownership over their own spending patterns and digital profiles.

Dynamic allocation of resources within data centres spread across geographic locations. In this scenario resources (e.g. servers) are dynamically allocated to run applications and services to process data, for example, in dynamic and distributed enterprises. Workloads are spread based on the availability of such resources, to optimise their usage. However, there are privacy issues because computational resources that belong to different geographical locations, organisational boundaries and administration domains, etc. can be subject to different privacy policies. So, the "location" of the resources is an essential input to decisions about resource allocation and privacy management.

Dynamic allocation of resources over time in Consolidated Client Infrastructures (CCIs). In such infrastructures, each user is assigned different blades/resources dynamically, based on factors like security and trust requirements, time of day, department/company usage (in shared data centers), etc. , and migration of credentials is a critical issue.

Mobile employees. Employees can be dynamic, both in the sense of travelling around and using different mobile resources (devices and enterprise tools including laptops, PDAs, mobile phones, etc.) to process different types of confidential or private data used in daily work activities (such as confidential e-mails and documents, medical data, access private databases, etc). It could be desirable to ensure that such sensitive data would only be processed within well defined locations and potentially well defined types of devices (e.g. a certified laptop but not a cellular/smart phone or PDA). This is increasingly the case as ubiquitous computing spreads. Here, privacy policies could describe constraints not only on location but also type of device or resource.

4 Useful Terminology

In this section we draw a distinction between various key terms that we will use in this paper/

Identity. This is defined as "any subset of attributes of an individual which identifies this individual within any set of individuals" [5].

Identity certificate. A certificate containing one or more identity attributes. It bears a digital signature of a Certification Authority (CA) and provides assurance regarding the binding of a public key to another pseudonym.

Credential. This term is broadly used to relate to information that can demonstrate a property or properties of a subject. Thus, it could be an authorization token, a non-certified set of attributes, or a certified set of attributes that can be produced in accordance with a standard: for example X.509 certificate [6,7], SPKI certificate [8] or digitally signed XML [9].

TCG migratable key. This is a key which is not bound to a specific trusted hardware device that serves as a root of trust within a trusted platform (this is called the Trusted Platform Module, or TPM) and which, with suitable authorisation, can be used outside a TPM or moved to another TPM.

Digital pseudonym. This is a bit string which is unique as an identity (at least with very high probability) and which can authenticate the holder (e.g. a person, a system, etc.). A digital pseudonym could be realised as a public key to test digital signatures where the holder of the pseudonym can prove holdership by forming a digital signature which is created using the corresponding private key.

TCG identity credential. TCG describes mechanisms [1,2] for creating for each computer platform a *TPM endorsement certificate* (shipped with the platform and certifying that the TPM operates correctly), a *platform certificate* (generated by the platform manufacturer – referring to the TPM endorsement certificate and certifying that the platform is a genuine trusted platform) and *multiple platform identity certificates* (that can be used as platform identities, each with a different pseudonym). These TCG credentials are bound to the associated platform.

5 Trusted Computing Technology

TCG technology [1,2] provides mechanisms and tools to check the integrity of computer programs while providing protected storage and pseudonymous attestation identities (see above). Although the technology is at least initially targeted at corporate environments, the introduction of trusted computing has been the focus for an open debate about whether or not this technology will be beneficial for ordinary people – for discussion of some of the issues, see [10,11] as further consideration of that issue is out of the scope of this paper.

TCG currently supports key migration between platforms for certain types of TPM-protected keys, but not the migration of user credentials. Both are needed: this paper focuses on how to use TCG technology to protect user credentials, manage them and migrate them across platforms.

Transfers of any type of credential fundamentally requires integrity, validation of target properties and (in some cases) confidentiality. Standard security techniques of certification, cryptographic hashing and encryption can help provide such properties. Trusted computing can provide additional value: for example, hardware protection of keys and cryptographic functionality is provided, and TCG platform identity and software integrity checking mechanisms can be used within the decision making process about whether or not to migrate and subsequently allow use of such information. In essence, by leveraging TCG technology we can decrease the potential threats of having unsecured access to secret material during migration (using encryption keys and secured protocols) and before and after migration by providing hardware-based protection of the migratable keys; and in addition, greater trust can be provided in the integrity of both the migration service and the involved platforms, and in the platform identities.

6 Our Solution

Figure 1 illustrates how groups of machines (for example within an enterprise) – where a given identity is known – can form 'identity trust domains' in which credentials can be created, issued and shared (processes illustrated by the arrows in the diagram). Such scenarios can be *persistent* (for example, between an employee's laptop and office desktop machines), *mobile* (for example, between fixed machines temporarily used such as a server, printer and computer in roaming user environments) or *shared* (for example, across enterprises when subcontracting work to a partner where this involves shared access to machines).

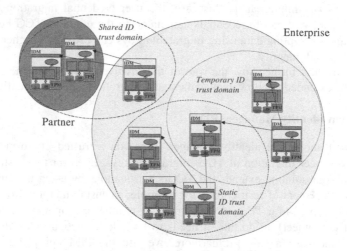

Fig. 1. Identity trust domains within enterprises

Our solution aims at allowing these scenarios by addressing the migration of "high-level" user credentials between platforms, and leveraging TCG technology. TCG technology currently supports the migration of TCG keys [12]. So, Figure 1 can be implemented right now but only for the case of TCG key migration. To do this, an identity manager on the user's TCG-compliant Trusted Platform (TP) can control the migration of these keys. TCG protocols are available that can be used to directly migrate keys between platforms, or alternatively via an intermediary [12].

However we want to enable the scenario shown in Figure 1 for migration of high-level credentials. This is where we focus in our solution. To implement it we leverage TCG key migration capabilities. Our solution involves having a Platform Identity Manager (PIM) on each trusted platform (TP), that is able to provide a local TCG migration service and is also extended to deal with other types of credential management. We also introduce the notion of a Trusted Credential Management Service (TCMS) – a Certification Authority (CA) offering 'classic' CA functionalities along with extra functionalities, such as platform validation – that performs the role of the TCG Migration Authority (MA) and/or the TCG Migration Selection Authority (MSA) (the intermediaries involved in TCG key migration) [12], as well as potentially other types of credential management as discussed further below. A variety of entities may function as the TCMS: for example, the IT Organisation within enterprises, or recognised and trusted service providers in the consumer market.

We can leverage this TCG key migration in order to migrate user credentials. At the identity management level, we are interested in higher level information structures that need to be signed, encrypted and sent across the network. These structures would include attribute and identity certificates. For example, these would be public key certificates that bear the digital signature of the TCMS and provide assurance regarding the binding of a public key to a pseudonym that relates to a user. The public key could be the public key corresponding to the private key migrated during a TCG key migration. In this case, the user credential migration procedure needs to include creation of credentials associated to the migrated TCG keys. Using TPM keys and encrypting data using migratable keys can provide a higher degree of confidentiality and integrity.

We now discuss further how the role of the involved parties and the underlying model can be extended to allow management and migration of user credentials.

6.1   Platform Identity Manager (PIM)

As mentioned above, the identity manager (PIM) on a trusted platform (TP) may govern peer-to-peer migration of TCG migratable keys. Even for this restricted type of credential, our solution extends the TCG specifications by using the PIM to give automatic enforcement of restrictions (for example, to ensure that a migratable TPM key object is copied to a TP, and to restrict the number of duplicate copies of any given TPM key object): to do this, it needs to be able to recognise TPMs, interpret credentials, and trust a CA. Furthermore, we use the PIM not just to constrain migration of TCG credentials but also to manage and create identities in a broader sense. The PIM can control modification of existing trusted identities, help create new identities and constrain migration of user credentials. PIMs may work together in a peer-to-peer manner, or else in conjunction with a TCMS as considered further in Section 6.2. The trustworthiness of the PIM can be assessed using Trusted Computing Group (TCG) software verification [1,2]. Further details follow.

The PIM allows a user to control a combination or subset of personal credentials associated with different trusted identities of the user to create a new identity that may be used by the user to entitle him or her to access or obtain a third party service. Trust values (such as bank balances or loyalty points) can be copied/transferred and certificate format changed without requiring underlying CAs to know the real identity of the user, nor be able to derive it. As considered further in Subsection 6.3, policies can be associated to credentials, governing how these may be utilised within a given domain.

The architecture of the system is shown in Figure 2. The PIM acts as a trusted component accessible by different applications, such as web browsing, e-commerce and tasks related to e-government. The PIM deployed on a client system creates or modifies credentials and associated policies on behalf of the user that are then presented to a relying party (RP), which could for example be an e-commerce site, an e-government server, an application service provider or even another user. Optionally, those parts of the credential modification service carried out within the client PIM could instead be provided by a third party specified by the user. Analogous mechanisms within the RP's PIM can allow administrators to manipulate identities.

The user selects via the PIM an appropriate type of credential to be created (for instance, reflecting a desired level of anonymity), and specifies how that credential may be exported to other machines. The RP then makes a (business) decision based on the credentials, typically whether or not to allow a request or access. In order to do this, the RP will have a PIM to authenticate the user and provide the properties needed for the transaction, etc.

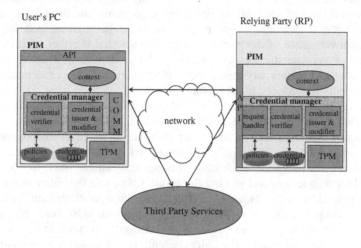

Fig. 2. Our architectural model for e-commerce

Whenever a new identity is to be created on the client machine, the PIM instructs the TPM to create a new public key pair based on random sources comprising a new public key and a new private key. For security, the private key is never revealed outside the TPM, and the PIM will request the TPM to form any operations involving it. Depending upon the circumstances, either the PIM or a CA (or other third party with enhanced CA functionality) creates an attribute certificate that certifies that the holder has certain attributes (or is authorised to perform certain specified actions). This attribute certificate includes the new public key. The CA will then need to send the attribute certificate to the user's TP, in which case the TP may decrypt messages using the new private key as evidence that it has received the certificate legitimately. Preferably this process would be a direct extension of one of the TCG identity creation protocols; if desired, a protocol may be used to generate identity certificates via a CA such that neither the CA nor other external parties need be able to correlate identities issued [2]. By analogous means it is possible to use a previously certified identity to create another representation of that identity, possibly with additional attribute values, for use in different circumstances. See [13] for details of different certificate options. An alternative solution for this is described in [14].

Key features of such trusted identity management within a TP include:

- The capabilities of the PIM module to issue or translate credentials would be certified by an external party such as a competent organisation within the enterprise.
- Secret trust management-related information could be protected via the TPM, such that the credentials will not be revealed if the machine is tampered with.

If modification just involves application of logical rules (e.g. copying or subdividing information, or changing representational form) rather than finding and incorporating new information, the PIM itself could form new credentials or modify existing ones based on these; otherwise, the PIM could use outside identities or credentials to form new credentials. For many credentials, the digital signature of a TPM is sufficient to convince a third party of its authenticity (if desired, information about the software state of the platform could be included together with this signed data to further validate the trustworthiness of the credentials); however, in certain circumstances third parties may regard the resulting certificates or credentials as being more trustworthy if produced by an established CA.

Although certificates are usually signed and not modifiable, modification of credentials would be possible if desired: Corporate IT would revoke current credential and issue a new one. However, if multiple parties are involved in issuing credentials, it may be useful to amend a credential issued by another party by attaching an amendment to the original credential, linking this amendment to the original credential in a unique way and signing the result. Of course the entity that consumes these "augmented" credentials needs to understand the overall semantic and trust all the issuers involved in the chain. An alternative approach is to create new amended credentials from older ones and preserve the integrity by referring to the unique identity of the older credentials. The older credentials will however be invalidated.

The PIM module in Figure 2 can be implemented as a module at the kernel level or can sit on top of the kernel and provide an API for communication. The credential manager contains a credential verifier (for judging who the other party is and whether they can be trusted – this may involve carrying out TCG integrity checking and analysis of the results) as well as a credential modifier, which will take into account appropriate policies and context before carrying out any credential issuance, modification or transfer. For example, certain trust properties are non-copyable.

Moreover, if a user has multiple platforms (e.g. a work PC, a PDA and a home PC) and wants to transfer trust credits across the identities he or she uses on these machines, this same mechanism used in conjunction with authentication between the TPMs within each client platform can allow the user to do so.

In the following section we consider an alternative model in which a Trusted Credential Management Service (TCMS) works in conjunction with the PIM and the TPM.

6.1.1 Example: Peer-to-Peer Migration of Personal Credentials

In this case, a person wishes to migrate a personal credential from his/her laptop to a mobile phone. The PIMs on both devices are involved in providing this service in an appropriate manner. Up-front, this person must define various policies that are associated with their credentials to avoid disclosure of certain types of data. In particular, the person has specified a policy never to decrypt their credit card data in a mobile phone. The credential is an identity that would authorise usage of the credit card data together with certain other personal information associated to the user. However, if the personal credential is migrated to the mobile phone then the PIM running on the mobile phone will ensure that the encrypted credit card information may not be decrypted and used on that platform.

6.2 Trusted Credential Management Service (TCMS)

We can have a Trusted Credential Management Service (TCMS) fulfill the role of the TCG intermediary for the type of TCG migration involving an intermediary, and also perform a broader range of functionalities as considered further below. This is an example of the "Third Party Services" shown in Figure 2. The advantage of using a TCMS rather than the direct method considered above would be that the TCMS could backup credentials if they were to be deleted from the initial machine, and generally it would be more suitable in a very dynamic environment in which credentials were moved between multiple machines. It would also allow centralised accountability and control over user credentials, and help maintain confidentiality where appropriate since the TCMS cannot obtain the plain-text contents of a migrated key object without the help of the key object's owner. In addition, the platform owner must authorise migration of keys to begin with, so delegating to a service that is trusted is a good solution.

Migration requires external software support, not only to organise and manage the wrapped objects, but also to associate additional data such as Platform Configuration Register (PCR) values (that indicates desired software state) with these objects. This external data minimises TPM complexity by enabling actions to be performed outside the TPM when those actions do not need to be trusted. Such functionality could either be provided by the PIM or by the TCMS, dependent upon the desired model for a given scenario.

6.2.1 Enterprise Scenarios

In an enterprise scenario, we may put corporate IT ultimately in control of generating the original user credentials, by asking the TPM to create a key pair, the public part of which is then sent to the TCMS (probably part of the enterprise itself) to create a credential in the form of a certificate binding the public key to time expiry and possibly additional attributes and then signed by the TCMS, which can then be used for user authentication.

In practice, corporate IT should store in a directory some user credentials together with other information such as machine serial numbers and user identity. To enhance the privacy of such a system, access would be restricted to this information based on need. Furthermore, in certain cases, users may be able to create other credentials that they may use pseudonymously, conformant to company policy. To address certificate revocation, time-dependent information could be included within the credentials and corporate IT could list Certificate Revocation Lists (CRLs) in a directory and identity managers (PIMs) on the local machines could link in and check for credential validity before usage.

6.3 Associating Policies to Credentials

We can strengthen this approach by associating policies to credentials to govern their use. In general, the policies specify conditions on the usage and migration of identity information, and thereby over access to services and resources. They could require the involvement of third parties, for example in order to provide mechanisms to refine, deploy and enforce such policies at the right level of abstraction.

Potentially, policies could be associated to various different types of credential. For example, a credential could be bound to a policy governing how that credential may be migrated and used subsequently, (encrypted) data could be bound to a policy governing its use (with reference to a credential that authorises its use), and so on. Note that the data could be accessed in some other way and need not be encrypted by the credential and bound to a policy to form a package that is then transferred, but that is one approach. Policies could also be applied to migratable keys.

To make sense of the attached policies, we need an engine that can interpret them: the TPM alone cannot do this as this is an additional logical level. The protocols that are required would vary depending on whether trusted third parties are used or not. For example, an extended PIM could be used to manage credentials, interpret policies and enforce control, or else an external entity such as a Database Controller, Corporate IT or outsourced service provider could do this.

When migration of credentials is needed, the PIM (or TCMS, depending upon whether local or centralised authorization is preferred) must ensure the policy is satisfied before allowing migration. For example, the policy could specify that credentials may only be migrated within a given set of platforms and authentication required before release, or within a given network (when the query would expect a specific network access key). The data (encrypted by another symmetric key) and that symmetric key (encrypted by a migratable key) can be moved or stored separately as they are in a protected form, and it is rather the transfer of the migratable key itself here that needs to be restricted. In the case of a more dynamic environment, the check could be made by a third party agent within the system (for example, within the controller of a virtual IT environment or by a service provided by corporate IT).

This technique could be used for resource allocation and also for hot-desking and other forms of user roaming. If combined with checks to remotely verify the software state and identify the target platform as a TP belonging to a known partner, it can be applied to platforms not under a company's direct control, such as within a public area or on a partner site.

6.3.1 Binding Privacy Policies to Credentials

Cryptographic mechanisms based on public key cryptography could be used to bind privacy policies to credentials. For example, PIM could use the TPM to encrypt a migratable key with a public key bound to a destination trusted platform via TCG migration functionality, and then wrap the output (using a convenient public key) with an external layer containing a symmetric key; in addition, the policy would be hashed and encrypted with the symmetric key.

As an alternative, Identifier Based Encryption (IBE) technology [15,16] could be used to ensure that privacy policies "stick" to the credentials (and/or data) as it is transferred. In the case of IBE, the policies could be used directly as IBE encryption keys to encrypt the transferred material. To achieve this we exploit the following core properties of IBE technology: ability to use any kind of string (i.e., sequence of bytes) as an IBE encryption key (publicly available); possibility to postpone in time the generation of IBE decryption key; reliance on at least a trusted third party, called in this approach a trust authority (TA), for the generation of IBE decryption keys. In our case, it is likely that the TA would be the same entity as the TCMS.

6.3.2 Example: Migration of Credentials Between Resources

In this example trusted software operating in conjunction with the TPM on each TP interacts with a centralised Identity Management service (the TCMS).

As shown in Figure 3, a PIM, installed on resources, manages credentials locally and is aware of local contextual information: it is a trusted software layer that interacts with the local TPM.

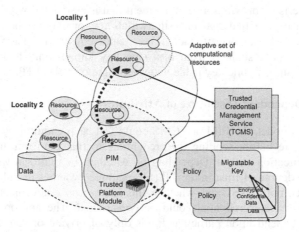

Fig. 3. Trusted Credential Management Service

When credentials (possibly together with confidential data) need to be moved (or a copy transmitted) from one resource to another, the confidential data is obfuscated and strictly associated to a policy referring to the credential or some subpart of the credential, by using traditional cryptographic techniques like RSA public key cryptography or IBE. The policy is enforced based on a variety of contextual information–for example the type of platform. This controls how credentials can be migrated and how the confidential data can be used on a given resource.

Resources require access to data and need to interact with one or more TCMSs (via their PIM) in order to access the content of the obfuscated confidential data, or to allow credential migration to other resources. The TCMS is a secured Web Service that checks for policy compliance and audit interactions. Resources are equipped with TPMs to provide higher assurance and trust about the contextual statements. The "third party" component, the TCMS, mainly interacts with resources to grant or deny them access to data (via disclosing decryption keys) based on their compliance to policies associated to data. As shown above, resources' TPMs are directly involved in this process.

6.4 Verification of Attributes

Verification allows an enquirer to place a relatively high degree of trust in the accuracy of the attribute. Two key ways in which this can happen are:

1. **Attributes may already be certified in existing certificates;** a TCMS can create new identities or update existing identities based on this information. Alternatively, in certain circumstances this can be done by trusted software within the

user's platform that can directly certify information that it has generated *as a logical consequence* from existing information it knows to be correct and there is no need for an external TTP to do this, so long as the trust chain is clear within the resulting representation.

2. **Other types of attribute can be verified by a TTP** (for example, a local registration authority or the TCMS). The TTP, if satisfied with the accuracy of the characteristic, provides an endorsement that is associated with a characteristic value to form a verified characteristic, which may or may not be in the form of a standardised digital certificate. The endorsement is suitably generated cryptographically, such as from a private key known only to the TTP and is verifiable using a public key made widely available by the TTP.

6.5 Context-Dependant Disclosure of Attributes

To enhance this model, the PIM or TCMS could test each enquirer by issuing a TCG integrity challenge before sending the credentials to that platform and engaging in further communication with it. Depending on whether the platform was a TP or not, and also on the degree of trust in the TP (for example, whether its software state was known to be compromised and whether this state was conformant to the user's policy), an appropriate credential could be constructed. The appropriateness of the identity would depend upon particular fields only of private or sensitive data being included, perhaps also subject to an according degree of generalisation. The TPM could certify such ranges and generalizations within the identity. In addition, associated policies could be altered or customised dependent upon the results of the integrity check.

7 Comparison with Related Work

For the time being trusted platforms are mainly used to protect keys and other platform secrets and to execute secure cryptography operations, via the TPM; Wave Systems also currently sell a product for migration of TPM keys [17]. Allied protected computing environments under development by certain manufacturers and open source operating systems such as Linux can support TCG facilities further: Intel's Vanderpool Technology (VT), LaGrande (LT) hardware and chipset modifications [18]; Microsoft's Next-Generation Secure Computing Base (NGSCB) [19] and leverage of TPMs within their forthcoming Vista and Longhorn OSs.

Emerging standards that are relevant to our work include Liberty Alliance's [20] and signed and encrypted XML [21]. Policy specification, modelling and verification tools include EPAL [22], OASIS XACML [23], W3C P3P [24] and Ponder [25]. Association of policies to data is considered in [26].

Work on management of attribute credentials linked to identity certificates has been done by the IETF PKIX Working Group [7], but that solution is complex in terms of reliance on multiple trusted third parties without fully addressing privacy and anonymity issues. Conversion of credentials has already been considered in [27]. Various anonymous credential schemes have been proposed, most notably those of Chaum and Brands [3,28]. Chaum's credentials [29] are digitally signed random messages that do not include a public key. Reconstruction of the user attributes needs to be carried out by mathematical analysis and with reference to published information giving correspondence between numeric values and attribute values. They are therefore particularly appropriate for less complex attribute or credential structures, such as a single issue number for a pseudonymous electronic payment credit or demonstration of a small number of attributes. In particular, the approach described in Section 5 includes an alternative to Chaum's method for subdividing credentials [30]; it lends itself well to utilizing current standardization initiatives and/or if the protocols and business scenarios are likely to involve complex representational structures.

TCG attestation certificates will not be usable if the TPM is tampered with, since the TPM is designed to zero keys in that case and authentication using these certificates would fail. The problem of revocation of attribute certificates based on these certificates (and particularly involving a chain of trust) is still an open question that has not been addressed in this paper. This method therefore needs more work to equal the applicability of systems such as Lsysanskaya's [31] that have provided a solution to this problem.

Our approach is complementary to many other approaches in the area of trust management (in particular PolicyMaker [32] and Herzberg and Mass's Credential Manager [14]) and federated identity management environments. In [32] improved certificate formats are suggested, and policy based tools for the RP to make a decision based upon the certificates. Herzberg and Mass [14] describe a Credential Manager that provides all credential management functions. Their approach could be viewed as complementary to our work in that they focus on the RP's PIM, and the mechanisms within this for converting different types of credentials into a common interface format (which is neither a certificate nor signed). We are unique in focusing on trusted mechanisms within an IDM for creating credentials and defining how these may be migrated under users' control; our approach uses trusted hardware to ensure and certify that this process is carried out correctly while providing privacy for users' credentials across trust boundaries.

8 Current Status

At HP Labs we have already implemented key sub-system modules and components that underpin the construction of our overall solution. For example, a proof of concept that encrypted data can be associated to policies has been provided by our exploitation of Identifier-based Encryption (IBE) schemas [33,34]. In addition, TPMs and HP ProtectTools already support aspects of migratable keys that we might extend with such a sticky policy capability.

We are currently collaboratively developing an identity management system within the EU Framework VI project PRIME (Privacy and Identity Management for Europe) [35]. We plan to use this as a test bed for the techniques described above. We are currently exploring extending an existing Credential Management system to provide users with greater control over creation of pseudonyms and the circumstances in which their credentials may be shared (i.e. defining the credential trust domain). We are also looking at extensions to the role of a Controller System within the adaptive enterprise - preferably that uses a hardware security module - to provide a mediation service that checks constraints associated with credentials so that data are migrated within groups of servers, storage devices, blades, etc. only within an appropriate identity trust domain.

9 Conclusions

The problem of enhancing trust in e-commerce while maintaining privacy is an important one, not least because lack of such trust is a key inhibitor to the growth of e-commerce. This paper has suggested trustworthy mechanisms for trusted credit transference, credential combination and subdivision and certificate structure change that can be carried out without infringement of user privacy. These methods are particularly appropriate if X.509 certificates or text-based credential representations rather than single numeric representations of credentials are preferred and if a Trusted Computing infrastructure is already available, and so may be readily exploited. This may be the case even in the short term.

Our method provides security and flexibility whilst enhancing privacy. Trust domains may be created via users and/or corporate IT using such mechanisms. In addition we can strengthen this approach by associating policies to credentials to govern their use. Our mechanisms can be applied in a variety of domains including within enterprises and for electronic business (for which identity management has become a key enabler).

Acknowledgements. The authors acknowledge the helpful input of Manny Novoa and various anonymous referees.

References

1. S. Pearson (ed.), Trusted Computing Platforms, Prentice Hall, 2002.
2. TCG, TCG Main Specification, v1.1b, 2003. Available via http://www.trustedcomputin ggroup.org.
3. S. Brands, "A Semi-Technical Overview of Digital Credentials", International Journal on Information Security, August 2002. Available via http://www.credentica.com.
4. Pretty Good Privacy, see http://www.pgpi.org.
5. A. Pfitzmann, M. Köhntopp, "Anonymity, unobservability, and pseudeonymity – a proposal for terminology". International Workshop on Designing Privacy Enhancing Technologies: Design Issues in Anonymity and Unobservability. H. Federrath (ed.), Springer-Verlag New York, NY, pp. 1-9, 2001.
6. S. Farrell, R. Housley, "An Internet Attribute Certificate Profile for Authorization", IETF, 1999.
7. IETF, IETF PKIX Working Group, http://www.ietf.org/html.charters/pkix-charter.html, 2005.

8. C. Ellison, B. Frantz, B. Lampson, R. Rivest, B. Thomas, T.Ylonen, "SPKI Certificate Theory", RFC 2693, IETF, 1999.
9. W3C, XML Signature WG, http://www.w3.org/Signature/, 2003.
10. W. Arbaugh, "Improving the TCPA specification", IEEE Computer, August 2002.
11. Pearson, S., "Trusted Computing: Strengths, Weaknesses and Further Opportunities for Enhancing Privacy", LNCS, Proceedings of iTrust 2005, ed. P. Herrmann, V. Issarny and S. Shiu, France, May 2005.
12. TCG, "Interoperability Specification for Backup and Migration Services", v1.0, June 2005. Available via www.trustedcomputinggroup.org.
13. J. Hughes, "Certificate inter-operability – White Paper", Computers and Security, International Journal devoted to the study of technical and financial aspects of computer security, NL, Elsevier Science publishers, Amsterdam, vol. 18, no. 3, p. 221-230, 1999.
14. A. Herzberg, Y. Mass, "Relying Party Credentials Framework", Proceedings of CT-RSA 2001, Springer-Verlag, LNCS 2020, p. 328-343, 2001.
15. D. Boneh, M. Franklin, "Identity-based Encryption from the Weil Pairing", Crypto 2001, 2001.
16. C. Cocks, "An Identity Based Encryption Scheme based on Quadratic Residues", Communications Electronics Security Group (CESG), UK, 2001. Available via http://www.cesg.gov.uk/technology/id-pkc/media/ciren.pdf.
17. Wave System, Embassy Key Management Server, http://www.wave.com/products/ktmes.html, 2006.
18. Intel, "LaGrande Technology Architectural Overview", September 2003. Available via http://www.intel.com/technology/security/downloads/LT_Arch_Overview.pdf.
19. Microsoft, Next-Generation Secure Computing Base home page, http://www.microsoft.com/resources/ngscb, 2006.
20. Liberty Alliance Project, http://www.projectliberty.org/, 2006.
21. W3C, XML Key Management Specification (XKMS), http://www.w3.org/TR/xkms/, 2003.
22. IBM, The Enterprise Privacy Authorization Language (EPAL), EPAL 1.2 specification. http://www.zurich.ibm.com/security/enterprise-privacy/epal/, IBM, 2004.
23. OASIS, eXtensible Access Control Markup Language (XACML). See http://www.oasis-open.org/committees/tc_home.php?wg_abbrev=xacml.
24. W3C, The Platform for Privacy Preferences 1.0, http://www.w3.org/TR/P3P/, 2002.
25. N. Damianou, N. Dulay, E. Lupu, M. Sloman, The Ponder Policy Specification Language, 2001, Available via http://www-dse.doc.ic.ac.uk/research/policies/index.shtml
26. M. Casassa Mont, S. Pearson, P. Bramhall, "Towards Accountable Management of Privacy and Identity Information", ESORICS, 2003.
27. J. Biskup, Y. Karabulut, "A hybrid PKI model with an application for secure mediation", 16th Annual IFIP WG 11.3 Working Conference on Data and Application Security, Cambridge, England, July 2002.
28. D. Chaum, "Untraceable electronic mail, return addresses and digital pseudonyms", Communications of the ACM, vol 24, no 2, February 1981.
29. D. Chaum, "Achieving Electronic Privacy", Scientific American, pp. 96-101, August 1992.
30. D. Chaum, "Showing credentials without identification. Signatures transferred between unconditionally unlinkable pseudonyms", F. Pichler (ed.), Advances in Cryptology – EUROCRYPT '85, LNCS 219, Springer, Heidelberg, pp. 241-244, 1986.
31. J. Camenisch, A. Lysyanskaya, "An efficient system for non-transferable anonymous credentials with optional anonymity revocation", pp. 93-118, EUROCRYPT 2001.

32. M. Blaze, J. Feigenbaum, J. Lacy, "Decentralized Trust Management", Proceedings 17th Symposium on Security and Privacy, IEEE Computer Society Press, pp. 164-173, 1996.
33. M. Casassa Mont, P. Bramhall, C. R. Dalton, K. Harrison, "A Flexible Role-based Secure Messaging Service: Exploiting IBE in a Health Care Trial", HPL-2003-21, 2003.
34. M. Casassa Mont, K. Harrison, M. Sadler, "The HP Time Vault Service: Exploiting IBE for Timed Release of Confidential Information", WWW2003, 2003.
35. PRIME Project: Privacy and Identity Management for Europe, European RTD Integrated Project under the FP6/IST Programme, http://www.prime-project.eu.org/, 2005.

Acceptance of Voting Technology:
Between Confidence and Trust*

Wolter Pieters

Institute for Computing and Information Sciences, Radboud University Nijmegen,
P.O. Box 9010, 6500 GL Nijmegen, The Netherlands
wolterp@cs.ru.nl

Abstract. Social aspects of security of information systems are often
discussed in terms of "actual security" and "perceived security". This may
lead to the hypothesis that e-voting is controversial because in paper
voting, actual and perceived security coincide, whereas they do not in
electronic systems. In this paper, we argue that the distinction between
actual and perceived security is problematic from a philosophical perspective, and we develop an alternative approach, based on the notion of trust.
We investigate the different meanings of this notion in computer science,
and link these to the philosophical work of Luhmann, who distinguishes
between familiarity, confidence and trust. This analysis yields several useful distinctions for discussing trust relations with respect to information
technology. We apply our framework to electronic voting, and propose
some hypotheses that can possibly explain the smooth introduction of
electronic voting machines in the Netherlands in the early nineties.

1 Introduction

Electronic voting is one of the most interesting examples of the application
of security-sensitive information technology in society. Democracy is one of
the foundations on which western culture is built, and it is no wonder that
the introduction of new technology into this domain has raised a considerable
amount of discussion. Controversies are strengthened by the media coverage
of security leaks and viruses in many different information technology applications, and by the advent of Internet voting as the future election platform.
Many scientific papers have appeared covering the security of e-voting systems
[1, 4, 10, 12, 13, 15, 27], but yet, there is no consensus over which aspects to take
into account in such an analysis.

There is some agreement, however, about the fact that both technical and social aspects of security should be covered [8, 21, 22, 25, 30]. The social aspects are
then often labelled "trust", and the implementation of these aspects in concrete

* This work is supported by a Pionier grant from NWO, the Netherlands Organisation
  for Scientific Research. The author wishes to thank (in alphabetical order) Marcel
  Becker, Iwan Bos, Bart Jacobs, Erik Poll, Sanne van der Ven and Martijn Warnier for
  useful comments on drafts of this paper, and Gerard Alberts for inspiring brainstorm
  sessions on the topic.

K. Stølen et al. (Eds.): iTrust 2006, LNCS 3986, pp. 283–297, 2006.

systems is delegated to user interface experts and communication departments. They are assigned the task of transforming "trustworthiness", created by the technical experts, into "trust".

Although the distinction between the trustworthiness established by the technical experts and the trust established by the user interface and marketing experts seems a very business-oriented way to think about these matters, the scientific literature – to the best of our knowledge – takes this distinction for granted as well. In fact, all of the papers that we consulted about social aspects of security reflect this view by using a distinction between "actual security" and "perceived security" in their analyses of security-sensitive systems [8, 21, 22, 25, 30].

In this paper, we provide an alternative analysis of the issue of trust in information systems, with emphasis on the case of electronic voting. First of all, we explain why we are not satisfied with the prevailing distinction between actual and perceived security. Then, we develop a new model of trust, based on literature in both computer science and philosophy. In section 4, we describe the role of technology in the trust relation, focused on information technology. In the final section, we combine the results in an analysis of trust in electronic voting. The paper ends with conclusions.

2   Actual and Perceived Security

In the prevailing approach to social aspects of information system security, the notions of "actual security" and "perceived security" are used. "Actual security" can be assessed by technical experts, and "perceived security" is a more or less distorted version of this in the mind of a member of the non-technical community. From this point of view, trust is based on "perceived security", as opposed to "actual security". It can easily be determined to be either justified or unjustified depending on the agreement between the perceived and actual security of the system.

This distinction can also be applied to election systems. Xenakis and Macintosh [30] argue that "[s]ince procedural security is *evident and understandable* to voters, it has a comparative advantage when it comes to developing and supporting the social acceptance for the new e-processes" [our italics]. In the case of procedural security (as opposed to technical security), the actual security of the system can apparently be perceived by the voters, such that trust can easily be established and justified.[1] This yields the hypothesis that resistance to electronic voting is explained by the fact that the paper system is evident and understandable to voters and electronic systems are not.

---

[1] There is a remarkable resemblance here to Descartes conceiving certain ideas as "clear and distinct". It is supposed, in both cases, that there are certain things that are understandable by just common sense, as opposed to derived or expert knowledge. These things can be directly extracted from experience, such that "perceived" and "actual" coincide. However, many researchers after Descartes' time have confirmed that there is much more "constructed" about our experience of even common sense issues than people in the Enlightenment age would have admitted. The appar-

We have two main objections against this approach. First of all, the idea that some people have access to the actual security of a system and others do not is problematic. Science and technology studies have been showing for a long time that scientific research and technological development are full of matters of perception and acceptance themselves,[2] and we think that it is essential for understanding the issues to provide a more integrated perspective.

Moreover, the "actual security" of a system is often verified in terms of a model of security that has its own limitations. It is well known in the field of information security that even small security protocols may contain major flaws that go unnoticed for decades, precisely because verification is done using a limited model of security.[3] Also, security assessment of systems involves looking into the future, trying to guess what attackers will be up to. Thus, the tools available for assessing "actual security" are inherently fallible.

Next to the general objections, we also think that this approach does not reach the core of the matter in the case of electronic elections. Although there is a difference in degree of complexity between the paper system and electronic systems, that does not mean that, in the paper case, everyone just knows what is happening and what the risks are. The paper system is complex enough in itself to reach beyond the understanding of the average citizen, and not to be "evident and understandable". Instead, the security sensitivities of the traditional procedural voting system have been "black-boxed"[4] in our experience of democracy. Only when something goes wrong in an election, the black box of the "evident and understandable" paper election system is opened, and risks are exposed. Meanwhile, electronic election systems have not been black-boxed yet, and their vulnerabilities are out there for everyone to discuss. The whole phenomenon of the traditional system being black-boxed, and therefore being "evident and understandable", is already based on trust. Trust is not a derivative of "actual security" here, but it *defines* "actual security". And this actual security is perceived as well.

These are the main arguments supporting our view that there is no meaningful distinction between "actual security" and "perceived security". Security is always perceived security. Of course, the perception of the security of a system, and the reasons why the system is believed to be or not to be secure, may differ from person to person based on the tools[5] of analysis that are available, which are different for an expert than for a layman. However, there is no such thing

---

ent clear-and-distinctness of certain things is nothing more than our self-initiated reduction of complexity.

[2] Cf. [14], p. 7: "Modern technology studies have opened up the "black box" of technological development and revealed the intimate intertwinement of technology and society. Both scientific facts and technological artifacts appear to be the outcome of negotiations, in which many diverse actors are involved."

[3] For example, the Needham-Schroeder protocol was thought to be correct for 17 years, until it was eventually broken [16].

[4] Cf. the actor-network theory of Bruno Latour, as explained in [29]: ch. 6.

[5] Tools are meant in a pragmatist way here; these include all that people have at their disposal for problem solving purposes.

as "actual security" to be considered apart from the tools that were used to determine it. Just as "actual intelligence" is not an objective property measured by an IQ-test, but rather defined in terms of the test, security is defined in terms of the available tools for analysis.

As philosophers, we conclude that the distinction between actual and perceived security gives a too naive realist account of the matter.[6] Instead, we start from the observation that people *experience* an environment as more or less secure. This can be seen as a phenomenological approach to the issue [11, 29]. Based on this perspective, we argue that trust is the primary factor in the relations between humans and systems when it comes to security, and not a derivative of an objective kind of security. We will develop this approach further in the following sections.

3   Trust

First of all, we need to make sure that the reader is familiar with the distinction between *safety* and *security*. Safety refers to limited effects of the possible failure of a system under normal circumstances. Security refers to limited effects of an attacker deliberately trying to make the system fail in the worst possible way. In scientific research into technological systems, the first property is estimated by verifying the *correctness* of the design. Security is assessed by verifying the *tamper-resistance* of the design. In computer science, these two branches of research can be distinguished easily.[7]

In society, trust relations with respect to systems are characterised by being concerned with either safety or security. In the first case, the trust relation involves trust in the limited effects of failure; in the second case, it involves trust in the limited effects of attack. For example, trust in a nuclear power plant is composed of trust in the *safety* of the plant (e.g. it does not explode under normal circumstances) and trust in the *security* of the plant (e.g. it does not explode under terrorist bombing).

A second distinction that we wish to draw here is connected to the scope of the effects of failure or attack. These effects may be either *private* or *public*. When I drive a car, I trust in the limited effects of failure of the car for my own health. When I vote, I trust in the limited effects of failure of the election system for the whole country. The same holds for the effects of attack: an attack on a nuclear power plant may have private effects (if I or some of my friends live near it) and public effects (changes in politics due to the attack).

Having set this general background, we now investigate the concept of trust itself a bit further. One of the most confusing things that emerges from the lit-

---

[6] Recent attempts to derive a taxonomy for dependability and security of information systems suggest a realist view as well [2]. We do not doubt the value of such approaches as a tool for analysis. We do think, however, that a philosophical approach may shed more light on the origin of the concepts used in such a taxonomy.

[7] Note that we do not consider correctness and tamper-resistance as objective properties apart from the (scientific) tools that were used to determine them.

erature is the existence of two different conceptions of trust. On occasion, they even appear in the same article [8]. Although the analysis of trust in voting systems that is presented there covers many concrete risks involved in using these systems, the conception of trust that is used is apparently not completely coherent. In a section named "*Increasing* trust" [our italics], the following sentence is found: "One way to *decrease* the trust voters must place in voting machine software is to let voters physically verify that their intent is recorded correctly." [our italics] But was the intent not to *increase* trust? Do we want to increase and decrease trust at the same time? What is happening here?

Apparently, computer scientists stem from a tradition in which minimising trust is the standard. "In computer security literature in general, the term is used to denote that something must be trusted [...]. That is, something trusted is something that the users are necessarily dependent on." [21] Because we *must* trust certain parts of the system for the whole system to be verifiably correct according to the computer science models, we want to minimise the size of the parts we have to trust, thus minimising trust itself. However, from a psychological perspective, or even a marketing perspective, it is desirable that users trust the *whole* system. Maximising trust seems to lead to more fluent interaction between the user and the system, and is therefore desirable. In [20], Matt Blaze says: "I've always wanted trust, as a security person, to be a very simple thing: I trust something if it's allowed to violate my security; something that's trusted is something that I don't have to worry about and if it is broken, I am broken. So I want as little trust in the system as possible, and so security people are worried about minimising trust and now suddenly we have this new set of semantics that are concerned with maximising trust, and I'm terribly confused."

In the following, we try to alleviate this confusion by explicating the assumptions found in both approaches to trust, and placing them within a larger (philosophical) context. Apparently, two different definitions of trust have to be distinguished (cf. [21]):

- trust as something that is *bad*, something that people establish because they *have to*, *not* because the system is trustworthy;
- trust as something that is *good*, something that people establish because they *want to*, because the system *is* trustworthy.

How can we conceptualise this difference? In political science, there is a well-known distinction between *negative freedom* and *positive freedom*. Negative freedom means the absence of interference by others; positive freedom means the opportunity for people to pursue their own goals in a meaningful way.[8] We see a parallel here with two possible concepts of safety and security, namely a negative and a positive one:

- negative safety/security: absence of everything that is unsafe/insecure;
- positive safety/security: opportunity to engage in meaningful trust relations.

---

[8] Cf. [6], pp. 36-39. The notion was originally introduced by Isaiah Berlin [3].

When people use a negative concept of security, trust has to be minimised, since it denotes a dependence on (possibly) insecure systems. By removing everything that is insecure, trust defined in this way can indeed be minimised. In a setting where security is defined positively, however, trust suddenly forms an essential precondition for security, because security then requires the possibility to engage in trust relations. This is precisely the approach that comes from psychology, as opposed to the dominantly negative approach of computer science (remove all insecurities).

We will label these two conceptions of trust *bad trust* and *good trust*, respectively. We deliberately avoid the terms negative and positive in our distinction of trust, because these are used in the definitions of both freedom and security as indicators of how the concepts are defined (certain things *not* being there vs. certain things *being* there), not of their desirability. Bad and good instead indicate whether we should try to minimise or maximise the associated appearance of trust. Thus, we linked the two different interpretations of trust to two different conceptions of security. Bad trust is linked to a negative conception of safety and security, and good trust to a positive conception. In philosophy, distinctions between different modes of trust have been drawn before. We will use such a distinction to further clarify the differences.

Luhmann [17] provides an extensive model of trust, based on the view of systems theory. According to Luhmann, trust is a mechanism that helps us to reduce social complexity.[9] Without reducing complexity, we cannot properly function in a complex social environment. Luhmann distinguishes several types of trust relations. First of all, he distinguishes between *familiarity* and *trust*. Familiarity reduces complexity by an orientation towards the past. Things that we see as familiar, because "it has always been like that", are accepted – we do engage in relations with those – and things that we see as unfamiliar are rejected – we do not engage in relations with those. For example, especially elderly people often refuse to use ATM's or ticket vending machines, precisely because they are not used to them.[10]

Trust, on the contrary, has an orientation towards the future: it involves expectations. We trust in something because we expect something. For example, we use ATM's because we expect these machines to provide us with money faster than a bank employee behind the counter. Luhmann distinguishes personal trust, i.e. trust in interpersonal relations, from system trust, i.e. trust in the general functioning of a non-personal system. We may expect something from a person, or we may expect something from society as a whole or from a machine. Since we are interested in technological systems here, trust in this paper is always system trust.

---

[9] The function of trust as a means for reduction of complexity seems to be known in computer science. For example, Nikander and Karvonen [21] mention this aspect. However, this paper does not refer to the work on trust by Luhmann.

[10] One may argue instead that the reason is not that they are not used to them, but rather the fact that it is harder for them to learn new things. Yet this is precisely one of the conditions that invites relying on familiarity rather than trust.

In later work [18], Luhmann also draws a distinction between *trust* and *confidence*. Both confidence and trust involve the formation of expectations with respect to contingent events. But there is a difference. According to Luhmann, trust is always based on assessment of risks, and a decision whether or not to accept those. Confidence differs from trust in the sense that it does not presuppose a situation of risk. Confidence, instead, neglects the possibility of disappointment, not only because this case is rare, but also because there is not really a choice. Examples of confidence that Luhmann gives are expectations about politicians trying to avoid war, and of cars not suddenly breaking down and hitting you. In these cases, you cannot decide for yourself whether or not to take the risk.

When there *is* a choice, trust takes over the function of confidence. Here, the risky situation is evaluated, and a decision is made about whether or not to take the risk: "If you do not consider alternatives [...] you are in a situation of confidence. If you choose one action in preference to others [...], you define the situation as one of trust." [18] If you choose to drive a car by evaluating the risks and accepting them, this is a form of trust.

Apparently, Luhmann ascribes the same negative characteristics to confidence that are ascribed to bad trust from a computer science perspective, in the sense that people do not have a choice. People *have to* have confidence in "trusted" parts of the system. Moreover, what Luhmann calls trust has the positive connotation of our good trust, in the sense that people can decide for themselves whether they want to trust something. Trust is then necessary for a system to be successful. We have to note, however, that Luhmann does not regard confidence as a bad thing in general; it is even necessary for society to function. Still, with respect to information systems, confidence means accepting a system without knowing its risks, and computer scientists are generally not willing to do this.

Thus, Luhmann distinguishes between two kinds of relations of self-assurance, based on whether people engage in these relations because they have to or because they want to. Luhmann calls these two relations confidence and trust, respectively. These observations also cover the situation we described in computer science. This means that the distinction we made is not something that characterises social aspects of security in information systems only, but something that can be considered a general characteristic of trust relations.

From now on, we will use *relations of self-assurance* as a general notion. Confidence and trust will only be used in Luhmann's sense. We describe relations of self-assurance based on three distinctions:

- self-assurance with respect to safety vs. self-assurance with respect to security;
- self-assurance with respect to private effects vs. self-assurance with respect to public effects;
- confidence vs. trust.

Computer scientists generally try to replace confidence with trust, i.e. exchange unconscious dependence on a system for explicit evaluation of the risks, and minimising the parts in which we still have to have confidence.[11] Philosophers (and social scientists), instead, recognise the positive aspects of confidence, and may evaluate positively people having a relation of self-assurance with the system without exactly knowing its risks (i.e. confidence). Our point of view in this discussion is that, because society is too complex for everyone to understand all the risks, there should be a balance between the trust experts have in the system, based on their analysis of the risks, and the confidence the users have in the system. This ensures that there *is* knowledge of the detailed workings and risks of the system within the *social* system in which it is embedded, but there is no need for everyone in the social system to know exactly what these risks are, precisely because there is a relation between expert trust and public confidence. How to establish such a relation is a question that we do not discuss further here.

Based on the distinctions we discussed in this section, we will now turn our attention to trust in technology.

4   Trust in Technology

When discussing security aspects of technology, reliability and trustworthiness are often mentioned. First of all, we propose a distinction between reliability and trustworthiness. A system acquires *confidence* if it is *reliable*, and it acquires *trust* if it is *trustworthy*.[12] A reliable system is a system that people can use confidently without having to worry about the details. A trustworthy system is a system that people can assess the risks of and that they still want to use.

There is a fairly subtle relation between reliability and trustworthiness. On the one hand, trustworthiness is a stronger notion than reliability. Before they give their trust to a system, people will perform a risk analysis. People who establish confidence in a system do not do this. In this sense, it is harder for a system to *acquire* trust than to *acquire* confidence. However, *maintaining* trust is easier than *maintaining* confidence. When people trust a certain system, they are already conscious of the risks and decide to use it anyway. This means that trust is not necessarily broken if something fails. In the case of reliability, however, people have put their confidence in a system because they do not see alternatives, and they will probably not accept any failures. Trustworthiness is therefore the stronger notion for the short term, and reliability is the stronger notion for the long term.

How are reliability and trustworthiness established? As we have made clear in the introduction, we argue that they are not objective properties of a system that are reflected in subjective confidence and trust. Instead, we take a phenomenological point of view, i.e. we conceive the relation between persons

---

[11] This general approach is not without exceptions; cf. [20].

[12] Reliability is used in the more limited sense of continuity of correct service in [2]. Our notion of reliability roughly corresponds to the "alternate definition of dependability" in their taxonomy, whereas trustworthiness corresponds to the "original definition of dependability".

and a system as primary to the objective and subjective aspects [11, 29]. The objective aspects of reliability and trustworthiness and the subjective aspects of confidence and trust emerge from the relation between people and the system. The way in which they are established depends on the analytic tools that are available to the person. If a person is just using the system, the outcome will probably be different than in case an expert performs a full security audit based on her expertise.

The relations that different people have with the system make the objective aspects of reliability and trustworthiness converge into different images of the system. These images then become "objective" properties of the system. The relations that experts have with the system determine what is often called the "actual" security of the system, but this "actual" security is still based on perception and relations of self-assurance, and therefore we rather avoid the term "actual".

How does this analysis of trust in technology apply to computer systems? Computer systems can be characterised as congealed procedures. Such procedures are typically more rigid than human-managed procedures. They are less easy to circumvent, but also less robust. Humans are easy to persuade to abandon the rules, computers are not. Humans can easily find solutions for problems that do not exactly match the rules, computers cannot. Because computers are not flexible, congealed procedures must be specified in more detail than human procedures. Every possible situation should be covered. This, and the fact that most people do not have expert knowledge about computers, makes congealed procedures hard to understand.

As we have seen before, trust in a system requires understanding of the risks involved in using a system. This is usually relatively easy to achieve in human procedures, not necessarily because the systems are less complex, but because we have a good understanding (or at least we think we have a good understanding) of how humans function. Understanding the risks of using a computer system is typically much harder. On the other hand, precisely because congealed procedures are more rigid, the associated systems are generally more reliable, in the sense that they produce fewer errors. This makes them more suitable for being reliable and acquiring confidence, while less suitable for being trustworthy and acquiring trust. Thus, automation implies a transition from public trust to public confidence. This makes it all the more important that a balance is established between expert trust and public confidence, in order to have public confidence still reflect a risk analysis in some way.

Luhmann observes the same tendency of replacing trust by confidence in functional differentiation of society. Because people in a functionally differentiated environment have knowledge of only a very small part of the complex structures that surround them, establishing trust is hard, and confidence is extremely important. This also requires procedures to be increasingly rigid, precisely because they need to maintain confidence. This may be seen as a first step in the freezing of procedures; automation is then a continuation of this process, by entering these semi-frozen procedures into machines, and thereby fixing all the details even further.[13]

The concepts of reliability and trustworthiness extend the conceptual framework we introduced in the previous section. We will now investigate whether this framework yields new results when we apply it to voting technology.

5   Trust in Voting Systems

Voting is a way to surrender oneself to a representational body in a democracy. It is at the same time a reconfirmation of the social contract between the rulers and the ruled, and a reconfirmation of the autonomous individual that engages in this contract. In this act, the Enlightenment ideals are established over and over again. The reconfirmation of the social contract and the autonomous individual has the character of a ritual. The associated relation of self-assurance is primarily based on familiarity, for a ritual always has an orientation towards the past.

But this ritual dimension is not the only relation of self-assurance in democratic politics. There are also expectations involved about the functionality of the political system, for example the expectation that the desires of the public are accurately represented in policy by this system. Engaging in political activities such as voting requires confidence or trust that these expectations will be fulfilled. Finally, there is also a need for trust and confidence in the present government, which represents the people based on expectations not about the political system in general, but about the current policy.

Thus, elections involve at least three different relations of self-assurance: the familiarity with democracy that is established by means of a ritual, the confidence or trust that people have in the government and confidence or trust in the political system.[14]

However, trust and confidence in the election procedures themselves are also necessary. These in turn co-evolve with the relation of self-assurance that people have with the government and the political system. This means that a lack of trust or confidence in election procedures may reduce trust or confidence in the government or the political system, but also the other way around. The specific

---

[13] Interestingly, this transformation of trust in human procedures into confidence in congealed procedures goes against the tendency that Luhmann observes in liberalism. According to Luhmann, "liberalism focuses on the individual responsibility for deciding between trust and distrust [...]. And it neglects the problems of attribution and the large amount of confidence required for participation in the system" [18]. From this point of view, either information technology is a threat to liberalism, or liberalism should revise its goals.

[14] Generally, people have confidence with regard to politics rather than trust, in Luhmann's sense. It is precisely the phenomenon of elections that may turn political confidence into trust: "A relation of confidence may turn into one of trust if it becomes possible (or is seen to be possible) to avoid that relation. Thus elections may to some extent convert political confidence into political trust, at least if your party wins. Conversely, trust can revert to mere confidence when the opinion spreads that you cannot really influence political behaviour through the ballot." [18].

characteristics of this relation are a topic for further research. In this section, we will focus on trust and confidence in the election system. We will primarily discuss the differences that can be observed from this point of view between the traditional paper systems and electronic variants.

Why do we want electronic voting? The rigidness of technology is often an argument. Errors with paper ballots, as in the Florida presidential elections in 2000, may be a reason to switch to the supposedly more reliable Direct Recording Electronic (DRE) machines. Indeed, electronic machines may be more reliable and trustworthy with respect to *safety* than paper systems are, because possibilities for error, both in casting and in counting, are reduced.

However, reliability and trustworthiness with respect to *security* are not as straightforward, especially when there is little transparency in the design, e.g. when the source code is kept secret. Acquiring trust in security, as opposed to trust in safety, is hard when things are secret. Insider attacks against security, e.g. an employee of the manufacturer changing something in the software, are indeed pretty easy in such a case, and experts evaluating the risks will at some point notice this. This not only includes possibilities for altering the results, but also the possibility to deduce a relation between a voter and a vote.[15] This lack of transparency may make it hard as well to maintain public confidence in the long run, since this confidence is often influenced by expert trust.

Besides the distinction between security and safety, we also proposed a distinction between private effects and public effects. Self-assurance with respect to private effects in voting amounts to trust or confidence that one's own vote is handled correctly, e.g. kept confidential. Self-assurance with respect to public effects means trust or confidence that the results are calculated correctly. *Both* kinds need to be acquired by an election system. People may have confidence in electronic systems in the sense that they calculate the results correctly in general, but if they are not sure what happens to their own vote – e.g. doubt the secrecy of their vote – the whole system may not acquire confidence anyway.

In the previous section, we argued that congealed procedures are more suitable for confidence, whereas human procedures are more suitable for trust. Still, because the paper system has been the only option for a long time, the relation of self-assurance people had with the paper system was largely based on confidence. Confidence in the election system, confidence in the government and confidence in the political system supported each other. Now, what happens when electronic voting comes into play?

First of all, electronic voting systems *may* be seen as alternatives to the existing system. Whether this is indeed the case depends on the situation. If they are seen as alternatives, people suddenly get the option to *choose* a voting system. This invites actively assessing the risks of the different systems, and basing the decision on an analysis of these risks. This means that *trust* now becomes the dominant form of self-assurance, as opposed to confidence. This has as a consequence that voting systems are required to be *trustworthy* rather than reliable

---

[15] We do not discuss vote buying and vote coercion in this paper; see e.g. [23] for discussions on this issue for the case of Internet elections.

only. This, again, leads to the traditional paper system becoming *more* attractive, because it is based on human procedures, and human procedures more easily acquire trust than congealed procedures. On the other hand, if the new technologies are not seen as an alternative, but as an improvement of existing procedures, electronic devices are more attractive, because they are more reliable and thus more easily acquire confidence.

If various alternatives are available, and citizens cannot assess the risks themselves, it can be desirable to establish a balance between expert trust and public confidence, in order to establish a relation of self-assurance between citizens and the election system again. This is important for maintaining people's confidence in the government and the political system. However, if people do not see these options as alternatives, risk analysis may instead break their confidence in the existing system by exposing the risks, and thereby destroy confidence. Thus, the role of the expert in these matters is extremely important. This role will be a topic of ongoing research.

As an example of the value of our approach for the analysis of concrete developments, we propose some hypotheses as explanations for the fact that in the Netherlands, electronic voting machines have been introduced in the early nineties without much discussion about their security. It was not regarded a serious problem that the design was secret, and only the independent voting system licenser TNO knew the details. Most of the concern was about whether all citizens would be able to operate the machines. Possible hypotheses for the smooth and uncontroversial introduction are:

- the ritual of going to the polling station, identifying oneself and casting a vote remained fairly stable (as opposed to online voting), maintaining familiarity;[16] also, the Dutch machines have a layout that is very similar to the paper ballots used before;[17]
- confidence in the government was relatively high, which led to confidence in the election systems proposed by the government as well;
- trust and confidence in information systems were more related to safety than to security at the time; people knew that calculators were reliable, and probably no one had ever attacked a calculator;
- voters paid more attention to the election outcome (public effects) than to what happened to their own vote (private effects); they knew that computers were able to calculate reliably, and therefore had confidence in the computers with respect to the public effects; focusing instead on the private effects of a machine "stealing" or revealing one's vote will expose the lack of transparency and probably undermine confidence;

---

[16] In relatively new democracies, such as Estonia, tradition (and thus familiarity) are less important. This may explain why Estonia already implemented Internet voting. See e.g. http://www.euractiv.com/Article?tcmuri=tcm:29-145735-16&type=News, consulted November 17, 2005.

[17] This means, among other things, that all candidates have their own button on the machine, as opposed to PC software in which one first chooses a party and then a candidate.

– the electronic systems were not seen as *alternatives* to the existing procedures, but rather as automated versions of existing procedures; this made it easy to transfer confidence to the new systems; nowadays, trust *is* an issue in other countries: e-voting is really seen as an *alternative*, instead of just automating a known process;

– risk evaluation of computer systems was not as mature at the time as it is now; this made it harder for computer scientists to transform confidence into trust by making explicit the risks involved.

Each of these possible causes, which are based on the philosophical analysis in this paper, can serve as a hypothesis for empirical research. Also, the fact that voting machines are now under discussion in the Netherlands as well may be explained by a change in situation with respect to these hypotheses. For example, international developments may have changed the image of voting machines from a simple automation of existing procedures to a real alternative. These hypotheses show the relevance of our conceptual framework for voting system sciences in general. Of course, some of them are related, and further research, both theoretical and empirical, would be useful to determine these interdependencies.

6   Conclusions

In this paper, we described a framework for discussing trust in relation to voting procedures. Instead of distinguishing between actual and perceived security, we took a more phenomenological approach, in which subjective and objective aspects of security are seen as constituted from the relation between the people and systems involved. The main concepts were discussed both from a computer science point of view and from a philosophical perspective. Luhmann was the primary source for the latter.

Based on the theory of Luhmann, we distinguished between familiarity, confidence and trust. Luhmann understands these concepts as means for the reduction of social complexity. Familiarity has an orientation towards the past, whereas confidence and trust are based on expectations and thus oriented towards the future. People trust because they want to, based on risk evaluation. People have confidence because they have to, not because they understand the risks. The concepts of confidence and trust are related to the different views on trust that can be found in the computer science literature, namely bad and good trust. These are again related to negative and positive conceptions of security, respectively. Computer scientists generally try to replace confidence with trust by making explicit the risks involved in using the system. This, again, allows the public to base their confidence on expert trust.

The "objective" aspects related to the "subjective" aspects of confidence and trust were labelled reliability and trustworthiness. Human procedures are typically good at being trustworthy (and thus at acquiring trust), whereas the congealed procedures of computers are good at being reliable (and thus at acquiring confidence).

In elections, the traditional election system, whatever it may be, always invites confidence, precisely because it is the established system, and people are not conscious of alternatives. When new technologies for elections are presented, these may be seen as alternatives. Then, election systems suddenly have to be trustworthy instead of reliable only. This is one of the reasons why the demands posed on new election technologies are often more severe than those posed on existing systems. However, the fact that alternatives are now available may also undermine confidence in the existing system, and require this system to earn trust as well.

In this situation, an interdisciplinary approach to matters of trust in election systems is indispensable. The hypotheses we offered for the smooth introduction of voting machines in the Netherlands serve as a modest attempt at illustrating possible results. We hope to have justified trust in the benefits of such an approach here.

References

1. R.M. Alvarez and T.E. Hall. *Point, click & vote: the future of Internet voting.* Brookings Institution Press, Washington D.C., 2004.
2. A. Avižienis, J.C. Laprie, B. Randell, and C. Landwehr. Basic concepts and taxonomy of dependable and secure computing. *IEEE transactions on dependable and secure computing*, 1(1):11–33, 2004.
3. I. Berlin. *Four concepts of liberty.* Oxford University Press, Oxford, 1969 [1958].
4. D. Chaum. Secret-ballot receipts: true voter-verifiable elections. *IEEE Security & Privacy*, 2(1):38–47, 2004.
5. K. Chopra and W.A. Wallace. Trust in electronic environments. In *Proceedings of the 36th Hawaii International Conference on System Sciences (HICSS'03)*, 2002.
6. F. Cunningham. *Theories of democracy: a critical introduction.* Routledge, London, 2002.
7. J. Dewey. *The public and its problems.* Swallow Press / Ohio University Press, Athens, 1991 [1927].
8. D. Evans and N. Paul. Election security: perception and reality. *IEEE Security & Privacy*, 2(1):24–31, January/February 2004.
9. D. Fahrenholtz and A. Bartelt. Towards a sociological view of trust in computer science. In M. Schoop and R. Walczuch, editors, *Proceedings of the eighth research symposium on emerging electronic markets (RSEEM 01)*, 2001.
10. E.-M.G.M. Hubbers, B.P.F. Jacobs, and W. Pieters. RIES – Internet voting in action. In R. Bilof, editor, *Proc. 29th Annual International Computer Software and Applications Conference, COMPSAC'05*, pages 417–424. IEEE Computer Society, July 2005.
11. D. Ihde. *Technology and the lifeworld.* Indiana University Press, Bloomington, 1990.
12. D. Jefferson, A.D. Rubin, B. Simons, and D. Wagner. Analyzing internet voting security. *Communications of the ACM*, 47(10):59–64, 2004.
13. C. Karlof, N. Sastry, and D. Wagner. Cryptographic voting protocols: a systems perspective. In *Proceedings of the 14th USENIX Security Symposium*, pages 33–50, 2005.

14. J. Keulartz, M. Korthals, M. Schermer, and T. Swierstra. Ethics in a technological culture: A proposal for a pragmatist approach. In J. Keulartz, M. Korthals, M. Schermer, and T. Swierstra, editors, *Pragmatist ethics for a technological culture*, chapter 1, pages 3–21. Kluwer Academic Publishers, 2002.

15. T. Kohno, A. Stubblefield, A. D. Rubin, and D. S. Wallach. Analysis of an electronic voting system. In *Proceedings of the 2004 IEEE Symposium on Security and Privacy*, 2004.

16. G. Lowe. Breaking and fixing the Needham-Schroeder public key protocol using FDR. In *Tools and algorithms for the contruction and analysis of systems*, volume 1055 of *Lecture notes in computer science*, pages 147–166. Springer, 1996.

17. N. Luhmann. *Trust and power: two works by Niklas Luhmann*. Wiley, Chichester, 1979.

18. N. Luhmann. Familiarity, confidence, trust: problems and alternatives. In D. Gambetta, editor, *Trust: Making and breaking of cooperative relations*. Basil Blackwell, Oxford, 1988.

19. D.P. Moynihan. Building secure elections: E-voting, security and systems theory. *Public administration review*, 64(5), 2004.

20. P. Nikander. Users and trust in cyberspace (transcript of discussion). In B. Christianson, B. Crispo, J.A. Malcolm, and M. Roe, editors, *Security Protocols: 8th International Workshop, Cambridge, UK, April 3-5, 2000, Revised Papers*, number 2133 in Lecture Notes in Computer Science, pages 36–42. Springer, 2001.

21. P. Nikander and K. Karvonen. Users and trust in cyberspace. In B. Christianson, B. Crispo, J.A. Malcolm, and M. Roe, editors, *Security Protocols: 8th International Workshop, Cambridge, UK, April 3-5, 2000, Revised Papers*, number 2133 in Lecture Notes in Computer Science, pages 24–35. Springer, 2001.

22. A.M. Oostveen and P. Van den Besselaar. Security as belief: user's perceptions on the security of electronic voting systems. In A. Prosser and R. Krimmer, editors, *Electronic Voting in Europe: Technology, Law, Politics and Society*, volume P-47 of *Lecture Notes in Informatics*, pages 73–82. Gesellschaft für Informatik, Bonn, 2004.

23. W. Pieters and M. Becker. Ethics of e-voting: An essay on requirements and values in Internet elections. In P. Brey, F. Grodzinsky, and L. Introna, editors, *Ethics of New Information Technology: Proc. Sixth International Conference on Computer Ethics: Philosophical Enquiry (CEPE'05)*, pages 307–318, Enschede, 2005. Center for Telematics and Information Technology.

24. B. Randell and P.Y.A. Ryan. Voting technologies and trust. Technical Report CS-TR-911, School of Computing Science, University of Newcastle upon Tyne, 2005.

25. R. Riedl. Rethinking trust and confidence in european e-government: Linking the public sector with post-modern society. In *Proceedings of I3E 2004*, 2004.

26. A. Riera and P. Brown. Bringing confidence to electronic voting. *Electronic Journal of e-Government*, 1(1):43–50, 2003.

27. A.D. Rubin. Security considerations for remote electronic voting. *Communications of the ACM*, 45(12):39–44, 2002.

28. B. Shneiderman. Designing trust into online experiences. *Communications of the ACM*, 43(12):57–59, 2000.

29. P.P.C.C. Verbeek. *What things do: Philosophical Reflections on Technology, Agency, and Design*. Pennsylvania State University Press, 2005.

30. A. Xenakis and A. Macintosh. Procedural security and social acceptance in e-voting. In *Proceedings of the 38th Hawaii International Conference on System Sciences (HICSS'05)*, 2005.

B-Trust: Bayesian Trust Framework
for Pervasive Computing

Daniele Quercia, Stephen Hailes, and Licia Capra

Department of Computer Science, University College London,
London, WC1E 6BT, UK
{D.Quercia, S.Hailes, L.Capra}@cs.ucl.ac.uk

Abstract. Without trust, pervasive devices cannot collaborate effectively, and without collaboration, the pervasive computing vision cannot be made a reality. Distributed trust frameworks may support trust and thus foster collaboration in an hostile pervasive computing environment. Existing frameworks deal with foundational properties of computational trust. We here propose a distributed trust framework that satisfies a broader range of properties. Our framework: (i) evolves trust based on a Bayesian formalization, whose trust metric is expressive, yet tractable; (ii) is lightweight; (iii) protects user anonymity, whilst being resistant to "Sybil attacks" (and enhancing detection of two collusion attacks); (iv) integrates a risk-aware decision module. We evaluate the framework through four experiments.

1 Introduction

Significant commercial benefits are predicted from the deployment of new services that pervasive computing will enable. These benefits are, however, theoretical in the absence of appropriate security. Fundamental to the creation of security are mechanisms for assigning trust to different pervasive devices. Also, it is in the nature of such devices that security mechanisms must be automatic - they must operate without the need for users to intervene. To make commercial benefits true, distributed trust frameworks may be employed as they provide security by automatically managing trust among pervasive devices.

To design a general distributed trust framework, one needs to identify its desirable properties first. From literature (e.g., see work by Liu and Issarny [9], and by Suryanarayana and Taylo [17]), those properties are: (i) be distributed; (ii) protect user anonymity, whilst providing accountability; (iii) be lightweight in terms of both required storage and scalability; (iv) minimize bandwidth demand; (v) be robust to common attacks; (vi) evolve (social) trust as humans do (e.g., trust evolves based on reputation information); (vii) support both types of recommendations (good and bad ones); (viii) incorporate the three classical dimensions of computational trust: context, subjectiveness, and time; (ix) be integrated with a decision module; (x) have a trust metric that is expressive, yet tractable.

A common limitation to many existing trust frameworks is that they deal with only a very narrow subsets of these properties. Abdul-Rahman and Hailes [1] were the first to propose the use of recommendations. Carbone *et al.* [5] then integrated more advanced

K. Stølen et al. (Eds.): iTrust 2006, LNCS 3986, pp. 298–312, 2006.

aspects in a formal trust model. More recently, Liu and Issarny [9] focused on designing a (reputation-based) trust framework that integrates additional trust aspects, including robustness to some attacks.

Our contribution lies in designing and evaluating a distributed trust framework with the above ten properties in mind. Our framework: (i) uses a generic n-level discrete trust metric that is expressive (more than existing 2-level Bayesian solutions), yet tractable; (ii) incorporates the trust dimensions of subjectiveness, time and context; (iii) is lightweight in terms of required storage and bandwidth: as the number of its peering devices increases, its data structures grow linearly, and the computation and bandwidth demand remain flat; (iv) supports anonymous authentication, whilst being resistant to "Sybil attacks" [7]; (v) enhances detection of two collusion attacks; (vi) evolves trust embedding social aspects, in that : trust evolves from both direct experiences and (positive and negative) recommendations; evaluation of recommendations depends on their originator's trustworthiness and ontology view; finally, the trust metric embeds the distinction between trust levels and trust confidence; (vii) integrates a well-founded decision module. We have evaluated the framework through four experiments.

We structure the paper as follows. Section 2 introduces existing research and how our framework enhances it. As our trust evolution process is based on reputation information, section 3 defines trust and reputation. Section 4 then dwells on describing the whole trust management framework. Section 5 presents an experimental study. Section 6 concludes.

2 Related Work

The body of work in distributed computational trust is littered with frameworks that are often based on social (human) considerations, sometimes attack-resistant, rarely integrated with well-founded decision modules.

Foundational distributed trust frameworks were already based on social trust considerations, in that they evolved trust based on direct experiences and recommendations, and they integrated the classical trust dimensions of context, subjectiveness, and (only later) time. Abdul-Rahman and Hailes first proposed the use of recommendations for managing context-dependent and subjective trust [1]. Although foundational, the previous approach suffered from, for example, the lack of a process for trust evolution. To fill the gap, Mui *et al.* [10] proposed a Bayesian formalization for a distributed rating process. However, two issues remained unsolved: they considered only binary ratings and did not discount them over time. Buchegger and Le Boudec [4] tackled the latter issue, but not the former: they proposed a Bayesian reputation mechanism in which each node isolates malicious nodes, ages its reputation data (i.e., weights past reputation less), but can only evaluate encounters with a binary value (i.e., encounters are either good or bad). Using a generic n-level discrete trust metric, our Bayesian framework addresses the issue. Furthermore, it discounts its trust beliefs over time (i.e., it decreases the confidence level it has in its trust beliefs). This avoids excessive capitalization on past good behavior and allows discarding old reputation information (contributing to make the framework lightweight).

Recent frameworks account for advanced social trust aspects. For example, Carbone *et al.* [5] have proposed a *formal* model for trust formation, evolution, and propagation based on a policy language. They also have thrown light on a previously unexplored aspect: the distinction between trust levels and trust confidence. We regard such distinction as fundamental and, thus, preserve it in our Bayesian formalization of trust evolution.

The design of frameworks resistant to attacks is not a common occurrence in literature. The most felicitous example we find in Liu and Issarny's work [9]. They proposed a model robust to both defamation and collusion attacks. Although foundational, their work suffers from other attacks, such as privacy breaching (the lack of user anonymity protection). Of the relatively small body of academic work published in anonymity protection, Seigneur and Jensen [16] proposed the use of disposable pseudonyms. Such approach facilitate anonymity, yet hinder cooperation in the absence of a central authority due to "Sybil-attacks" [7] (attacks resulting from users who maliciously use multiple identities). Our framework enhances the detection of defamation and collusion attacks, and it tackles "Sybil attacks" (we will name the first two attacks as bad mouthing and ballot stuffing collusion attacks, respectively).

Trust frameworks' integration with decision-making mechanisms, though fundamental, is rare. Within the SECURE project, a trust model's output feeds a decision-making mechanism [6]. More recently, Quercia and Hailes [11, 12] proposed a decision model for trust-informed interactions that, on input of trust assessments, estimates the probability of potential risks associated with an action, based on which it decides whether to carry out the action. Our framework combines trust assessments in a way that such model is easily integrable.

3   Trust Definition, Trust Properties, and Reputation

We now define the concept of trust and highlight some of its properties. We will then stress trust dependence on reputation. Let us first define trust with a commonly accepted definition [8]: " *[Trust] (or, symmetrically, distrust) is a particular level of the subjective probability with which an agent will perform a particular action, both before [we] can monitor such action (or independently of his capacity of ever be able to monitor it) and in a context in which it affects [our] own action"*.

From this definition, three properties of trust emerge: subjectiveness, context-dependence, and dynamism. The same behavior may lead to different trust levels in different trusting entities, hence *subjectiveness* qualifies trust. As trust (e.g., in giving good advices) in one context (e.g., academia) does not necessarily transfer to another context (e.g., industry), we add *context-dependence* to the list of trust properties. Finally, the fact that trust increases after successful observations, while it decays over time exemplifies its *dynamism*. As a result, trust evolution must embed the notion of *time*.

Reputation relates to trust, as the following definition suggests [10]: *"Reputation [is the] perception that an agent creates through past actions about its intentions and norms"*. Actions build up reputation (the perception about intensions and norms). Direct experiences and recommendations about one entity describe the entity's past actions, which, thus, create the entity's reputation (i.e., the perception about entity's intentions and norms).

Reputation is not to be confused with trust: the former only partly affects the latter. Other factors affect trust, and they include disposition to rely more on personal experiences rather than on recommendations, disposition to forget past experiences, risk, and motivation.

4 Trust Management Framework

We now present our distributed trust management framework. We first provide a general overview. We discuss authentication support. We then introduce the data structures containing reputation information. After that, we describe the processes of trust evolution (i.e., updating the reputation data structures), trust formation (i.e., trustworthiness assessment), and trust decision (i.e., contemplating whether to carry out an action based on the trust formation process and on local policies).

4.1 General Description of the Framework

Here, we describe our framework's main processes: trust formation and trust evolution. In so doing, we resort to an abstract situation: a *trustor* p_x (trusting peer) interacts with both a *trustee* p_y (trusted peer) and a *recommender* p_r. We finally describe our trust metric.

First, p_x forms its trust in p_y by: (i) assessing the part of trust, also called *direct trust*, stemming from evaluations of its past direct experiences with p_y ; (ii) assessing the part of trust, also called *recommended trust*, from others' recommendations about p_y; (iii) combining the previous assessments to obtain the *overall trust*. We keep separated direct trust and recommended trust so that two types of collusion attacks can be detected, as we will describe in this section. Note that when p_x assesses trust (as it does in the first two steps), it just retrieves reputation data and process it.

Second, p_x evolves its trust in p_y upon obtaining new reputation information, which consists of direct experience's evaluations and recommendations. After a direct experience with p_y, p_x evaluates the corresponding outcome, and consequently evolves its direct trust in p_y. After receiving a recommendation about p_y from p_r, p_x assesses recommendation reliability, and it consequently evolves its recommended trust in p_y.

Finally, consider our trust metric. The random variables of direct trust, direct experience evaluation, recommendation and recommended trust are *discrete*: they can assume any of the following n levels $\{l_1, ..., l_n\}$. For example, with four levels ($n = 4$), we may have the following semantics for the different levels: l_1 means *'very untrustworthy'*, l_2 means *'untrustworthy'*, l_3 means *'trustworthy'* , and l_4 means *'very trustworthy'*. Since the random variables describing direct trust, recommended trust, and overall trust are discrete (i.e., they assume one of n discrete values $\{l_1, \ldots, l_n\}$), our framework has numerous advantages: (i) the random variable distributions emerge as a consequence of updates and are not fixed *a priori*, as existing models impose; (ii) a generic n-level metric is more *fine-grained* than a binary metric (for which an entity is either completely trustworthy or completely untrustworthy), as existing models impose;

(iii) discrete metrics are more computationally *tractable* than continuous metrics (e.g., they do not involve the computation of integrals).

Throughout this section, we will use the following notation. $DT_{x,y}$ is a random variable expressing p_x's direct trust in p_y (($DT_{x,y} = l_\alpha$) is the event 'p_x *deems* p_y *deserves a level* l_α *of direct trust*'). $DE_{x,y}$ is a random variable expressing p_x's evaluations of direct experiences with p_y (($DE_{x,y} = l_\beta$) is the event 'p_x *evaluates the direct experience with* p_y *at a* l_β *satisfaction level*'). $RT_{x,y}$ is a variable expressing p_x's recommended trust in p_y (($RT_{x,y} = l_\alpha$) is the event 'p_x *deems* p_y *deserves level* l_α *of recommended trust*'). Finally, $SR_{r,x}$ is a variable expressing the recommendations p_r sent p_x (($SR_{r,x} = l_\beta$) is the event 'p_r *sent* p_x *a recommendation whose level is* l_β').

4.2 Authentication Support

We consider that peers using our framework authenticate themselves by means of once in a lifetime anonymous pseudonyms.

To support anonymous authentication resistant to Sybil attacks, we propose the use of distributed blind threshold signature. Consider the situation in which p_x has to authenticate p_y. To protect p_y's user anonymity, the piece of information used to authenticate p_y has to be anonymous. Generally, such piece is a public key randomly generated by p_y. However, to protect against Sybil attacks, p_y has to have the limitation of possessing one and only one valid public key. We enforce such a limitation with public key certification that is both distributed (to match the distributed nature of our framework) and blinded (to protect anonymity). We propose a detailed scheme in [14].

4.3 Reputation Data Structures

The peer p_x stores reputation evidences locally: p_x solely relies on its local data structures to produce *subjective* trust assessments, thus being suitable for pervasive computing environments, in which peers frequently enter, leave, or simply disconnect from network domains. p_x maintains reputation-related evidence in the following sets:

C $= (c_1, \ldots, c_q)$ is the set of contexts known to p_x.

P $= (p_a, \ldots, p_z)$ is the set of peers that p_x has interacted with.

Direct Trust Set (DTS) stores direct trust levels. It contains p_x's direct trust levels in other peers. For each context c_k and peer p_y, an n-tuple $d = (d_1, \cdots, d_n)$ exists, where d_j is the probability that p_x has a l_j direct trust level in p_y (i.e., $p(DT_{x,y}) = l_j$). The relation DTS is defined as $DTS \subseteq C \times P \times D$, where $D = \{(d_1, \cdots, d_n)\}$.

Direct Experience Set (DES) stores data from which p_x assesses one of its direct trust prior beliefs. From it, p_x computes the probability $p(DE_{x,y} = l_\beta | DT_{x,y} = l_\alpha)$ for all $\beta = 1, \ldots, n$ and $\alpha = (1, \ldots, n)$, as Subsection 4.5 will discuss. DES is defined as $DES \subseteq C \times P \times EC$, where $EC = \{(EC_1, \ldots, EC_n)\}$. For each context c_k and peer p_y, n ordered sets of n-tuple exist: $EC_\beta = (ec_{1\beta}, \ldots, ec_{n\beta})$. To see what a single member $ec_{\alpha\beta}$ means, consider p_x deciding whether to interact with p_y. p_x has direct trust in p_y exclusively at level l_α; it decides to interact; it then evaluates the just completed direct experience with p_y at level l_β; it records such an experience by just increasing one of the member in EC: as it acted upon a

l_α direct trust level and then experienced a level l_β, p_x increases the counter $ec_{\alpha\beta}$. Therefore, after each interaction with p_y, p_x does not store the interaction outcome, but it simply increases one of the counter associated with p_y. For example, if $n = 4$, p_x aggregates into 16 counters all the direct experiences with p_y.

Recommended Trust Set (RTS) stores recommended trust levels. This contains trust levels solely based on other peers' recommendations. For each context c_k and peer p_y, an n-tuple $r = (r_1, \cdots, r_n)$ exists, where r_j is the probability that p_x has l_j recommended trust in p_y (i.e., $p(RT_{x,y} = l_j)$). $RTS \subseteq C \times P \times R$, where $R = \{(r_1, \cdots, r_n)\}$.

Sent Recommendation Set (SRS) stores data from which p_x assesses one of its recommended trust prior beliefs. From it, p_x computes the probability $p(SR_{r,x} = l_\beta | RT_{x,y} = l_\alpha)$, as subsection 4.5 on trust evolution will discuss. $SRS \subseteq C \times P \times RC$, where $RC = \{(RC_1, \ldots, RC_n)\}$. For each context c_k and recommender peer p_r, n ordered sets of $n-$tuple exist: $RC_\beta = (rc_{1\beta}, \ldots, rc_{n\beta})$. To clarify the meaning of a single member $rc_{\alpha\beta}$, consider that p_x has built up a recommended trust in p_y at level l_α from all the recommendations received. It then receives an additional recommendation about p_y from p_r, which recommends a trust level l_β. p_x records how far p_r's recommendation is from other peers' recommendations by increasing one member in RC: as it had a l_α recommended trust level and received a l_β recommendation level, p_x increases $rc_{\alpha\beta}$. Thus, after receiving a recommendation from p_r, p_x does not store it, but increases one of the n counters corresponding to p_r.

The data structure design minimizes the overhead imposed on p_x, thus leading to a *lightweight* framework. All of these data structures increase linearly with the number of peers with which p_x has interacted with or with the number of contexts p_x has experienced. We thus do not require large amounts of data to be processed as we aggregate reputation-related information each time p_x either carries out a new direct experience or processes a new recommendation.

Data Structure Bootstrapping. If peer p_x meets p_y for the first time, p_x's beliefs about p_y distributes uniformly. That is, for the peer p_y and the context c_k, p_x has: $D = (\frac{1}{n}, \ldots, \frac{1}{n})$; $R = (\frac{1}{n}, \ldots, \frac{1}{n})$; $ec_{\alpha\beta} = \Delta_d$, for $\alpha \in [1, n]$ and $\beta \in [1, n]$; and $rc_{\alpha\beta} = \Delta_r$, for $\alpha \in [1, n]$ and $\beta \in [1, n]$. In other words, to express maximum uncertainty in the initialization phase, p_x's prior beliefs equal a uniform distribution. The counter of direct experiences (recommendations) equals a constant Δ_d (Δ_r). The choice for the constant should consider that the greater its value is, the more the bootstrapping phase persist over time.

4.4   Trust Formation

Whenever the trustor p_x contemplates whether to interact with a trustee, it has to assess the trustee's trustworthiness, i.e., it has to carry out the process of *trust formation*. As our model considers three types of trust, p_x carries trust formation out in three steps: (i) direct trust formation; (ii) recommended trust formation; (iii) overall trust formation.

Direct Trust Formation. To determine its direct trust in p_y in the context c_k, p_x obtains the relation (c_k, p_y, d) from DTS. The jth member of $d = (d_1, \ldots, d_n)$ is the probability that p_x has a l_j direct trust level in p_y: $p(DT_{x,y} = l_j) = d_j$.

The tuple d describes the distribution of p_x's direct trust in p_y in context c_k. For example, assuming both $n = 4$ and the semantics in subsection 4.1 on trust metric, a tuple $d = (0.8, 0.2, 0, 0)$ suggests that p_x deems p_y 'very untrustworthy', whereas with a tuple $d = (0.1, 0.1, 0.2, 0.6)$, p_x places more trust in p_y.

As a trustor can only have a partial knowledge about a trustee, trustor's assessments contain a level of uncertainty and have, consequently, a confidence level. In particular, the confidence level that p_x places in its direct trust assessment equals d's variance: $dtc_{x,y} = \frac{\sum_{j=1}^{n}(d_j - \mu)^2}{n-1}$, where the mean $\mu = \frac{\sum_{j=1}^{n} d_j}{n}$. As $\sum_{j=1}^{n} d_j = 1$ (i.e., the probabilities sum up to 1), then $\mu = \frac{1}{n}$. The confidence level ranges from 0 to $(1 - \frac{1}{n})$. Note that we compute the confidence level (the variance) dividing by $(n - 1)$ (and not by n) because the variance we are estimating is of an unknown distribution (and not of a known one) - in general, dividing by $(n - 1)$ provides an unbiased estimation of the variance of an unknown distribution.

As d's variance decreases, direct trust levels tend to become equally probable, and p_x hence places less and less confidence in its direct trust assessment. For example, assuming $n = 4$, the uncertainty of $d = (0.25, 0.25, 0.25, 0.25)$ is maximum, its variance zero, and, thus, the associated confidence level has to be minimum.

Recommended Trust Formation. To determine its recommended trust in p_y in context c_k, p_x first obtains the relation (c_k, p_y, r) from RTS. The jth member of $r = (r_1, \ldots, r_n)$ represents the probability p_x has a l_j recommended trust level in p_y: $p(RT_{x,y} = l_j) = d_j$.

For instance, assuming both $n = 4$ and the semantics in subsection 4.1 on trust metric, $r = (0, 0, 0, 1)$ suggests that the recommenders (that p_x considered so far) deem p_y totally trustworthy.

Similarly to direct trust, p_x associates a confidence level with its recommended trust: $rtc_{x,y} = \frac{\sum_{j=1}^{n}(r_j - \mu)^2}{n-1}$, where the mean $\mu = \frac{1}{n}$ and the confidence level ranges from 0 to $(1 - \frac{1}{n})$.

Overall Trust Formation. The overall trust combines direct trust and recommended trust. For example, the probability p_x totals its overall trust in p_y at a level l_j is the weighted sum of the probabilities that p_x values both its direct trust and recommended trust in p_y at a level l_j.

Hence, to determine its overall trust in p_y in context c_k, p_x obtains both the relation (c_k, p_y, d) from DTS and the relation (c_k, p_y, r) from RTS, where $d = (d_1, \ldots, d_n)$ and $r = (r_1, \ldots, r_n)$. It then computes $\forall j \in [1, n] : p(T_{x,y} = l_j) = \sigma \cdot d_j + (1 - \sigma) \cdot r_j$, where the weighting factor σ holds the importance p_x places on direct experiences over others' recommendations. This increases as two factors increase: (i) the confidence level $dtc_{x,y}$ over $rtc_{x,y}$; (ii) p_x's subjective reliance on its own personal experiences rather than on on others' recommendations.

Similarly to direct and recommended trust, the confidence level p_x associates with its overall trust is: $tcl_{x,y} = \frac{\sum_{j=1}^{n}(p(T_{x,y}=l_j) - \mu)^2}{n-1}$, where $\mu = \frac{1}{n}$ and the confidence level ranges from 0 to $(1 - \frac{1}{n})$.

4.5   Trust Evolution

The process of trust evolution updates both direct trust and recommended trust. In so doing, it incorporates social aspects of trust. Recommended trust evolves based on both good and bad recommendations that are weighted according to recommenders' trustworthiness and recommenders' subjective opinion - to account for honest and dishonest recommenders and to resolve the different ontological views of the world honestly held by different peers. Both direct and recommended trust evolutions: (i) incorporate the time dimension both to prevent peers from capitalizing excessively on good past behavior and to discard old reputation from data structures; (ii) and are based on Bayes' theorem which has "far-reaching ... implications about scientific inference and how people process information" [2].

Trust Evolution Through Direct Experience Evaluation. Consider p_x contemplating whether to have a direct experience with p_y in context c_k. *Before* the direct experience, p_x has the following prior beliefs (probabilities):

1. p_x has a direct trust belief in p_y. For context c_k and peer p_y, p_x finds the relation (c_k, p_y, d) from DTS, where $d = (d_1, \ldots, d_n)$ expresses p_x's direct trust belief distribution;

2. p_x has a belief that a direct experience will show a certain level of satisfaction. More formally, for context c_k and peer p_y, p_x finds the relation (c_k, p_y, EC) from DES, where $EC = (EC_1, \ldots, EC_n)$.

   From $EC_\beta = (ec_{1\beta}, \ldots, ec_{\alpha\beta}, \ldots, ec_{n\beta})$, p_x computes, for all $\beta = 1, \ldots, n$, the probability which the first row of figure 1 shows.

After interacting, p_x evaluates the direct experience with a, say, l_β satisfaction level. Based on that:

1. p_x updates its Direct Experience Set (DES). It updates EC_β (i.e., the experience counter of a l_β direct experience level) as follows: $\forall \alpha \in [1, n] : ec_{\alpha\beta} = ec_{\alpha\beta} + d_\alpha$;

2. p_x evolves its direct trust according to Bayes' Theorem as the second row of figure 1 shows.

$$p(DE_{x,y} = l_\beta | DT_{x,y} = l_\alpha) = \frac{\#\text{events } DE_{x,y} = l_\beta \text{ given } DT_{x,y} = l_\alpha \text{ took place}}{\#\text{events } DT_{x,y} = l_\alpha} = \frac{ec_{\alpha\beta}}{\sum_{\gamma=1}^n ec_{\alpha\gamma}}$$

$$d_\alpha^t = \frac{d_\alpha^{(t-1)} \cdot p(DE_{x,y} = l_\beta | DT_{x,y} = l_\alpha)}{\sum_{\gamma=1}^n d_\gamma^{(t-1)} \cdot p(DE_{x,y} = l_\beta | DT_{x,y} = l_\gamma)}$$

$$p(SR_{r,x} = l_\beta | RT_{x,y} = l_\alpha) = \frac{\#\text{events } SR_{r,x} = l_\beta \text{ given } RT_{x,y} = l_\alpha \text{ took place}}{\#\text{events } RT_{x,y} = l_\alpha} = \frac{rc_{\alpha\beta}}{\sum_{\gamma=1}^n rc_{\alpha\gamma}}$$

$$r_\alpha^t = \frac{r_\alpha^{(t-1)} \cdot p(SR_{r,x} = l_\beta | RT_{x,y} = l_\alpha)}{\sum_{\gamma=1}^n r_\gamma^{(t-1)} \cdot p(SR_{r,x} = l_\beta | RT_{x,y} = l_\gamma)}$$

Fig. 1. Formulae that evolve prior and posterior beliefs about both direct trust and recommended trust

Trust Evolution Through Recommendation Evaluation. Consider now that p_x gets a recommendation from p_r about a peer p_y in context c_k and that the recommendation level is l_β. *Before* receiving the recommendation, p_x has the following prior beliefs (probabilities):

1. p_x has a recommended trust belief in p_y. For context c_k and peer p_y, p_x finds the relation (c_k, p_y, r) from RTS, where $r = (r_1, \ldots, r_n)$ and expresses p_x's recommended trust belief distribution;
2. p_x has beliefs that p_r will send certain recommendation levels. More formally, for context c_k and recommender peer p_r, p_x finds the relation (c, p_r, RC) from SRS, where $RC = (RC_1, \ldots, RC_n)$.

   From $RC_\beta = (rc_{1\beta}, \ldots, rc_{\alpha\beta}, \ldots, rc_{n\beta})$, p_x computes, for all $\beta = (1, \ldots, n)$, the probability which the third row of figure 1 shows.

After receiving a recommendation whose level is l_β:

1. p_x updates its Sent Recommendation Set (SRS). It updates RC_β (i.e., the recommendation counter associated with a recommendation level equal to l_β) as follows: $\forall \alpha \in [1, n] : rc_{\alpha\beta} = rc_{\alpha\beta} + r_\alpha$;
2. p_x evolves its recommended trust according to Bayes' Theorem as the forth row of figure 1 shows.

In the forth row, the portion $p(SR_{r,x} = l_\beta | RT_{x,y} = l_\gamma)$ weights p_r's recommendations according to either p_r's reliability as recommender or p_r's ontological view.

Trust Evolution Over Time. As time goes by, direct trust' and recommended trust' confidence levels decrease.

Let us first see how direct trust evolves over time. As we said, the tuple $d = (d_1, \ldots, d_n)$ shows p_x's direct trust in p_y. Let t be the time elapsed from the last d's update. If $t \to \infty$ (i.e., a very long time goes by before a new update), d converges to a uniform distribution (i.e., to its bootstrapping values). To age its direct trust values, p_x decreases some of d's members while it increases others over time, so that all members sum to 1. In particular, it increases the members below $\frac{1}{n}$ (d's mean when uniformly distributed), whilst increasing the members above. More formally, let I be the indicator function, $n_d = I(d_\alpha > \mu)$ be the number of members p_x decreases, and $n_i = I(d_\alpha < \mu)$ be the number of members p_x increases. If $d_\alpha < \mu$, $d_\alpha = (d_\alpha + \delta)$. If $d_\alpha > \mu$, $d_\alpha = d_\alpha - (\frac{n_d \cdot \delta}{n_i})$.

Same considerations apply for recommended trust. The tuple $r = (r_1, \ldots, r_n)$ represents p_x's recommended trust in p_y. To age its information, p_x increases some of r's members (those below $\frac{1}{n}$), while decreasing others (those above $\frac{1}{n}$).

If some tuples, as a consequence of evolution over time, converge to the bootstrapping value, then we delete them. This saves storage space without any reputation information loss.

Trust Evolution and Attack Detection. We here expose how our framework protects against two types of collusion in certain cases, whilst enhancing their detection in the rest of the cases.

Let us first describe the two types of collusion. The first is the *bad mouthing collusion* attack. A collection of attackers colludes in that each of them spreads negative recommendations about the same benevolent entity. After evaluating those unanimous recommendations, recipients build a negative trust in the benevolent entity. Hence, the attackers lower the benevolent entity's reputation without harming their own. For example, some peers decide to team up against peer p_y: they start spreading negative recommendations about p_y (e.g., p_y is a bad packet forwarder) so to damage its reputation. The second type of attack is the *ballot stuffing collusion* attack. Here we have a collection of colluding attackers: some offer services and others increase the remaining attackers' reputations as recommenders. The last subset of attackers (the good recommenders) send positive recommendations about those in the subset of service providers. Based on the positive opinions, a victim selects the providers. They then offer a low quality of service. The victim lowers its trust level in the abusing service providers only, whereas it still deems trustworthy the remaining attackers. To clarify, consider a peer p_y boosting its own reputation by means of colluding with three other peers p_{c1}, p_{c2}, and p_{c3}. p_{c1} sends positive recommendations about p_{c2}'s and p_{c3}'s trustworthiness as recommenders. p_{c2} and p_{c3} then send positive recommendations about p_y. Based on those, the victim (p_x) chooses as packet forwarder p_y, which drops all the packets.

The rule for re-evaluating trust assessments based on recommendations protects against both collusion types. To clarify, let us see how p_x evolves its recommended trust in p_y from a set of recommendations. p_x uses a Bayesian evolution rule that weights similar recommendations more, whilst filtering out extreme ones. If the number of false recommendations (i.e., those received from any of the collusions above) are less than honest recommendations, then the evolution rule protects against those collusion attacks.

However, if p_x receives recommendations mainly from colluding sources, the evolution rule is no more collusion-resistant.

In such cases, separating direct trust from recommended trust helps detecting both collusion attacks. In the presence of either collusion, p_x's direct trust in p_y significantly differs from its recommended trust in p_y. In particular, direct trust depicts a more trustworthy p_y than does recommended trust in case of bad-mouthing (p_y offers good direct experiences and is just subject to bad mouthing), whereas the reverse is true in case of ballot stuffing (p_y offers bad experiences, even though colluding recommenders assures p_x to the contrary).

4.6 Trust Decision

To take better-informed decisions, a peer has to be able to integrate a well-founded decision module with its distributed trust framework. The trust framework produces trust assessments. p_x then uses such assessments to decide the best action to be carried out (e.g., to decide whether to forward a packet). We thus integrate our framework with a decision module that Quercia and Hailes recently proposed [12]. Such a model, local to a peer p_x, selects an action that maximizes p_x's utility. User-specified local policies influence p_x's utility.

For integration purposes, any trust framework has to adapt its output to what the decision module takes on input. Quercia and Hailes's module takes on input a single trust value and the value's confidence. On the other hand, the trust framework produces a single confidence value, but not a single trust value: it produces a distribution of trust levels (represented with the random variable T). We thus extract one single value from the distribution by means of a weighted sum of the values of each trust levels. Weighting factors increase as the corresponding trust levels increase. The condensed trust value $t_{x,y}$ (that p_x has in p_y) hence takes the form: $t_{x,y} = (\sum_{j \in [1,n]} p(T_{x,y} = l_j) \cdot \frac{j}{n})$. For example, with $n = 4$, the weighting factor for level l_1 (very untrustworthy) is $\frac{1}{4}$, while the factor for level l_4 (very trustworthy) is 1.

5 Experiments

We here describe the experimental setup and the four experiments we have conducted.

Goal: The objective of this set of experiments is to determine the impact of our trust management framework on successful packet delivery in a network configuration where part of the peers act maliciously. Such a configuration refers to a scenario in which a set of peers pool their resources so to share their Internet connectivity [13]. Benevolent peers share their connectivity, whereas malevolent ones exploit others' connectivity without actually sharing their own.

Simulated Configuration: As we are interested in analyzing the local impact of our framework at a peer level, we simulate a configuration consisting of a peer p_x and a set of corresponding next-hops. These are connected directly to Internet. We consider p_x forwarding packets to its next-hops, which make available their connectivity. p_x selects a next-hop either randomly or through two types of trust-informed decisions (discussed later). The next-hop acts according to the behavioral model to which it belongs.

Next-Hop Behavioral Models: A next-hop belongs to one of the following four behavioral models: fully malicious, malicious, benevolent, and fully benevolent. Depending on its behavioral model, a next-hop offers the following packet loss ratios if it was selected for the whole simulation duration: 100% for a fully malicious next-hop, 70% for a malicious one, 30% for a benevolent one, and 15% for a fully benevolent one. Both fully malicious and malicious next-hops drop packets randomly, whereas both benevolent and fully benevolent do it according to a *Gilbert model* [3]. To understand why, consider that the next-hops are connected directly to Internet. As a consequence, packet losses through (fully) benevolent next-hops depend on Internet congestion, which is bursty. A Gilbert model reproduces such burstiness. We have thus implemented the model whose parameters varied according to packet loss ratios it simulated (either 30% or 15%).

Next-Hop Selection Methods: A peer p_x chooses its next-hops in three different ways. The first is *random* selection, i.e., it selects each of its next-hops with equal probability. The second is *pure trust-informed* selection, i.e., it selects the most trustworthy next-hop. The third is *probabilistic trust-informed* selection, i.e., p_x selects its next-hop p_y with a probability P_y that is directly proportional to p_x's trust in p_y: $P_y = \frac{t_{x,y}}{\sum_j t_{x,j}}$, where j represents each of p_x's next-hops. As we will see, we introduce the latter selection method as a better load balancing alternative to the pure trust-informed method.

Simulation Execution: A simulation consists of several executions of an experiment. An experiment duration is of 100 time units. At each time unit, p_x selects one of its next-hops and sends it a stream whose size is 10 packets. Based on the number of packet losses, p_x computes its satisfaction and consequently evolves its trust. We collect the overall number of packet losses at each time unit. We run each experiment 10 times and the results of all runs are averaged.

Experiment Metrics: We consider two metrics. The first is p_x's average fraction of successfully sent packets. The second is the load distribution among p_x's next-hops.

We now describe four different experiments. For each, we describe goal, setup, and results.

Experiment A.

Goal: To understand whether a more-fine grained trust metric gives a greater average fraction of successfully sent packets.

Setup: We simulate p_x with four next-hops, one for each next-hop behavioral model. p_x first uses a framework whose trust metric is binary ($n = 2$). It then uses a more fine-grained metric, i.e., $n = 4$. The next-hop selection method is pure trust-informed.

Results: Switching from the binary trust metric ($n = 2$) to one that is more fine-grained ($n = 4$), p_x improves its average fraction of successfully sent packets from 67% to 83%. Figure 2 shows that the more fine-grained trust metric outperforms the binomial one.

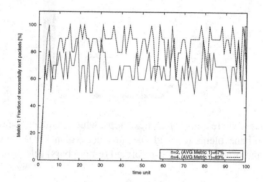

Fig. 2. Experiment A. Fraction of successfully sent packets in the case of p_x using a framework based on pure trust-informed selection with a binomial trust metric $n = 2$ (continuous line) and with a more fine-grained one $n = 4$ (dashed line).

Experiment B.

Goal: To understand whether pure trust-informed selection gives a greater average fraction of successfully sent packets than random selection.

Setup: We simulate a peer p_x with four next-hops, one for each next-hop behavioral model. We first consider p_x using random next-hop selection. We then consider p_x using pure trust-informed selection. For both cases, $n = 4$.

Results: When using pure trust-informed selection, p_x successfully sent 84% of the packets on average, in contrast to 42% when using random selection.

Experiment C.

Goal: To understand whether probabilistic trust-informed selection gives a better load distribution than pure trust-informed selection, whilst showing a greater fraction of successfully sent packets than random selection.

Setup: We simulate a peer p_x with five next-hops, one for each next-hop behavioral model plus an additional benevolent next-hop. The additional next-hop may lead to more interesting results for the discussion about load balancing. With a constant $n = 4$, p_x applies in turn the three next-hop selection methods.

Results: From figure 3, we note that (i) pure trust-informed selection shows an unbalanced load share: the fully benevolent next-hop (fb) has a 96% of such a share; (ii) probabilistic trust-informed selection shows a better load share, whilst penalizing malicious next-hops: the fully malicious (fm) one has received 9% of the traffic in contrast to 29% of a fully benevolent (fb). However, probabilistic selection leads to an average fraction of successfully sent packets of 60%, that is worse than pure trust-informed selection (83%), but better than random selection (47%).

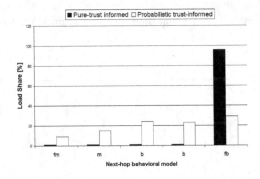

Fig. 3. Experiment C. Load share among p_x's next-hops, which include: one fully malicious (fm), one malicious (m), two benevolents (b), and one fully benevolent (fb). p_x uses both pure trust-informed (filled bars) and probabilistic trust-informed (empty bars) selections.

Experiment D.

Goal: To understand which factors have an effect on the average fraction of successfully sent packets. We consider two factors, each with two extreme levels. The first factor is n whose levels are 2 and 4. The second factor is the next-hop selection method p_x uses: its levels are probabilistic and pure trust-informed.

Setup: We simulate a peer p_x with four next-hops, one for each next-hop behavioral model. We set $n = 2$. We first consider p_x using random selection. We then consider p_x using pure trust-informed selection. We then set $n = 4$ and repeat what we did before after setting $n = 2$.

Results: Figure 4 shows that the change of trust metric (from n=2 to n=4) has a positive impact (16%) on the average fraction of successfully sent packets. It also confirms the intuition that the use of the trust framework has the most significant impact (68%).

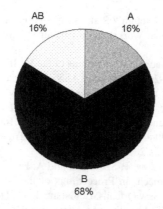

Fig. 4. Experiment D. The impact on the average fraction of successfully sent packets of: (i) the change of trust metric (factor A); (ii) whether the trust framework is used (factor B); (iii) the combination of both (factor AB).

6   Conclusion

We have presented a distributed framework that produces trust assessments based on direct experience evaluations and on (both good and bad) recommendations. All of this is based on a Bayesian formalization, whose generic n-level trust metric improves on existing Bayesian solutions (which use binary metrics). The framework is lightweight and integrates a well-founded decision module. Furthermore, it supports user anonymity by means of pseudonyms, whilst being robust to "Sybil attacks". It also enhances detection of two types of collusion attacks. Finally, we have conducted four experiments which shows that the use of our framework and a more fine-grained trust metric have a considerable positive impact on packet delivery in a network where part of the peers act maliciously.

As part of future work, we plan to design mechanisms for trust bootstrapping (i.e., how to set the initial trust in an unknown entity).

References

[1] A. Abdul-Rahman and S. Hailes. Using Recommendations for Managing Trust in Distributed Systems. In Proceedings of IEEE Malaysia International Conference on Communication, Kuala Lumpur, Malaysia, November 1997.

[2] Amir D Aczel. Chance. High Stakes, London, 2005.

[3] M. Arai, A. Chiba, K. Iwasaki. Measurement and modeling of burst packet losses in Internetend-to-end communications. In Proceedings of the IEEE International Symposium on Dependable Computing, pages 260-267, Hong Kong, 1999.

[4] Buchegger and J.-Y. L. Boudec. A robust reputation system for p2p and mobile ad-hoc networks. In Proceedings of the 2nd Workshop on the Economics of Peer-to-Peer Systems, Cambridge, MA, USA, June 2004.

[5] M. Carbone, M. Nielsen, and V. Sassone. A Formal Model for Trust in Dynamic Networks. In Proceedings of the 1st IEEE International Conference on Software Engineering and Formal Methods, pages 54-63, Brisbane, Australia, September 2003.

[6] N. Dimmock. How much is 'enough'? Risk in Trust-based Access Control. In Proceedings of the 12th IEEE International Workshop on Enabling Technologies, page 281, Washington, DC, USA, June 2003.

[7] J. R. Douceur. The Sybil Attack. In Proceedings of the 1st International Workshop on Peer-to-Peer Systems, pages 251-260, Cambridge, U.S., March 2002. Springer-Verlag.

[8] D. Gambetta. Can we trust trust? . In D. Gambetta, editor, Trust, Making and Breaking Cooperative Relations, pages 213237. Basil Blackwell, Oxford, 1998.

[9] J. Liu and V. Issarny. Enhanced Reputation Mechanism for Mobile Ad Hoc Networks. In Proceedings of the 2nd International Conference on Trust Management, volume 2995, pages 4862, Oxford, UK, Mar. 2004. LNCS.

[10] L. Mui, M. Mohtsahemi, C. Ang, P. Szolovits, and A. Halberstadt. Ratings in Distributed Systems: A Bayesian Approach. In Proceedings of the 11th Workshop on Information Technologies and Systems, New Orleans, Louisiana, USA, December 2001.

[11] D. Quercia, S. Hailes. MATE: Mobility and Adaptation with Trust and Expected-utility. To appear in the International Journal of Internet Technology and Secured Transactions.

[12] D. Quercia and S. Hailes. Risk Aware Decision Framework for Trusted Mobile Interactions. In Proceedings of the 1st IEEE/CreateNet International Workshop on The Value of Security through Collaboration, Athens, Greece, September 2005.

[13] D. Quercia, M. Lad, S. Hailes, L. Capra, S. Bhatti. STRUDEL: Supporting Trust in the Dynamic Establishment of peering coaLitions. Proceedings of the 21st ACM Symposium on Applied Computing. April 2006. Dijon, France.

[14] D. Quercia, L. Capra, S. Hailes. TATA: Towards Anonymous Trusted Authentication. In Proceedings of the 4th International Conference on Trust Management, Lecture Notes in Computer Science, Pisa, Italy, May 2006. Springer-Verlag.

[15] S. Ross. A first course in probability. Macmillan College Pub. Co., 1994.

[16] J.-M. Seigneur and C. D. Jensen. Trading Privacy for Trust. In Proceedings of the 2nd International Conference on Trust Management, volume 2995, pages 93107, 2004. Springer-Verlag.

[17] G. Suryanarayana and R. N. Taylo. A Survey of Trust Management and Resource Discovery Technologies in Peer-to-Peer Applications. ISR Technical Report number UCI-ISR-04-6, University of California, 2004.

TATA: Towards Anonymous Trusted Authentication

Daniele Quercia, Stephen Hailes, and Licia Capra

Department of Computer Science, University College London, London, WC1E 6BT, UK
{D.Quercia, S.Hailes, L.Capra}@cs.ucl.ac.uk

Abstract. Mobile devices may share resources even in the presence of untrustworthy devices. To do so, each device may use a computational model that on input of reputation information produces trust assessments. Based on such assessments, the device then decides with whom to share: it will likely end up sharing only with the most trustworthy devices, thus isolating the untrustworthy ones. All of this is, however, theoretical in the absence of a general and distributed authentication mechanism. Currently, distributed trust frameworks do not offer an authentication mechanism that supports user privacy, whilst being resistant to "Sybil attacks". To fill the gap, we first analyze the general attack space that relates to anonymous authentication as it applies to distributed trust models. We then put forward a scheme that is based on blinded threshold signature: collections of devices certify pseudonyms without seeing them and without relying on a central authority. We finally discuss how the scheme tackles the authentication attacks.

1 Introduction

To produce reliable assessments, distributed trust frameworks must be able *uniquely* to authenticate their users. To see why, consider the following example. Samantha's and Cathy's devices exchange recommendations about shops in their local area. After the exchange, as they know (have authenticated) each other, Samantha's device values Cathy's recommendations based on Cathy's reputation as recommender (i.e., whether her past recommendations have been useful), and vice versa. If it was able to easily generate a new pseudonym, Cathy's device could produce fake recommendations without being traceable. In general, to trace past misbehavior, users should not be able easily to change their pseudonyms - ideally, each user should have one and only one pseudonym.

On the other hand, to protect their privacy, users should *anonymously* authenticate each other, i.e., authenticate without revealing real identities. For example, Samantha may wish to buy kinky boots. She thus uses her mobile device to collect the most useful recommendations from the most trustworthy sources. The recommendation sharing service requires devices to use trust models that, in turn, require users to authenticate. Thus, Samantha's device has to authenticate in order to ask for recommendations; as the subject (kinky boots) is sensitive, the device authenticates itself without revealing Samantha's identity (anonymously).

Existing research in distributed reputation-based trust models does not offer any general solution for *unique* and *anonymous* authentication without relying on a central authority. Some distributed trust models [1] allow the use of anonymous pseudonyms

K. Stølen et al. (Eds.): iTrust 2006, LNCS 3986, pp. 313–323, 2006.

that, however, suffer from "Sybil attacks" [7]. Others tackle such attacks, but mostly with either centralized solutions [15] or approaches that only apply to limited scenarios [11] [12] [13] [17].

Our contribution lies in: firstly, systematically analyzing the general attack space that relates to anonymous authentication as it applies to distributed trust models; secondly, proposing a scheme that is decentralized, yet general enough to be applied to most of the existing trust models. More specifically, the scheme meets appropriate security requirements and supports desirable features. Security requirements include: (i) *anonymity* to prevent privacy breaches; (ii) *non-repudiation* to prevent false accusation; (iii) *unique identification* to avoid attacks caused by disposable pseudonyms; (iv) *pseudonym revocation* to cope with stolen pseudonyms. Desirable features include: (i) *general applicability*, in that our scheme is general-purpose so that any reputation-based system benefits from it; (ii) *off-line authentication* between two users without relying on anyone else; (iii) *distributed pseudonym issuing*, in that valid pseudonyms are issued without relying on a central authority.

The remainder of the paper is structured as follows. Section 2 discusses related work. Section 3 introduces a scenario that we will use to exemplify our model. Section 4 describes the attacks that relate to anonymous authentication. Starting from both those attacks and the general problem space, section 5 draws security requirements and desirable features for a protection scheme. Section 6 details our proposition and section 7 critically analyzes how it meets the security requirements and supports the desirable features. Section 8 concludes.

2   Related Work

Over the course of nearly five years, cooperation and authentication have begun to diverge: authentication has relied on central authorities, while cooperation has migrated to decentralized solutions. Only recently, authentication for cooperative mechanisms started to be decentralized.

Disposable pseudonyms facilitate anonymity, yet hinder cooperation in the absence of a central authority. To see why, consider a collection of actors cooperating. If each actor authenticates himself with an anonymous pseudonym, then he does not have to disclose his real identity and, thus, he can remain anonymous. However, an actor may profit from ease of creating pseudonyms. For example, an actor may authenticate himself with a pseudonym, misbehave, create a new pseudonym, authenticate himself with the new pseudonym (pretending to be new actor), and misbehave again. As a result, the actor misbehaves without being traceable. Resnick and Friedman [15] formally laid down such a problem, presenting a game theoretical model for analyzing the social cost of allowing actors to freely change identities. They concluded that, if actors generate pseudonyms by themselves, all unknown actors should be regarded as malicious. To avoid mistreating all unknown actors, they proposed the use of free but unreplaceable (once in a lifetime) pseudonyms, which a *central* authority certifies through blind signature. A couple of years later, Doucer put similar ideas to test in P2P networks. He discussed the attacks resulting from P2P users who could use multiple identities and named them "Sybil attacks" [7]. He concluded with a critical take on decentralized authentication support: in the absence of a trusted central identification authority, Sybil attacks undermine trust relationships and, thus, cooperation.

At the same time as centralized solutions were used to support authentication, distributed trust models were aiming at promoting cooperation in the absence of a central authority, whilst supporting users' anonymity. For example, EigenTrust [9] is a distributed trust model that suffers from "Sybil attacks" in the absence of a central entity. It uses reputation to decrease the number of downloads of inauthentic files in a P2P file sharing network. In such a network, pseudonyms are used to authenticate peers, thus enabling both peer anonymity and, at the same time, Sybil attacks. EigenTrust partly tackles such attacks, but assumes the presence of a central entity: to get a new identity, a user must perform an entry test (e.g., must read a text off a JPEG) and must send the result to a central authority. As such, it will be costly for a simple adversary to create thousands of users.

Recently, doubts about central authentication solutions for decentralized trust models have surfaced. The SECURE [5] project marks the introduction of a decentralized trust management model with a fully decentralized anonymity support. Within that project, Nielsen et al. [6] presented a formal decentralized trust model, and Seigneur and Jensen [16] proposed the use of context-dependent pseudonyms: a user can have more than one pseudonym depending on his/her context of interaction. However, their approach suffers from "Sybil attacks". They thus recently enhanced the original trust model so that trust updates internalize the costs of Sybil attacks [17]. However, such a solution applies only to a specific representation of trust values (as counts of outcomes). More recently, Bussard et al. [4] proposed a general distributed privacy-enhancing scheme for trust establishment. However, their work focuses on making users' *recommendations* anonymous and untraceable.

We propose a *general-purpose* scheme based on threshold blind signatures. A user is free to choose his own pseudonym depending on the context he interacts in, although he has only one pseudonym per context. Pseudonyms are certified in a *distributed* fashion through threshold signatures, thus tackling "Sybil attacks". Furthermore, during the certification process, the threshold signature is blinded to ensure *anonymity*.

3   Scenario of Mobile Recommenders

Here, we introduce an application scenario that we will use throughout the paper to illustrate our scheme.

The scenario features electronic communities of mobile recommenders. A group of people found a community around the shops in Oxford Street: their breakthrough idea consists of customers sharing their shopping experiences through their mobile devices. The initial community starts to grow and lead to the creation of several *communities* around different shop types such as "bookshops", "beauty shops", and "music shops".

Recommendation sharing is automatic and *distributed*, that is, customers store experiences on their mobile devices that they will then automatically share in the form of recommendations, without relying on a central server.

As an incentive for contributions, recommenders remain anonymous so that both their shopping behavior is not associated with their identities and they do not fear retaliation from poorly-rated shops. As such, a *unique* and *anonymous* pseudonym authenticates each recommender.

To distinguish good recommendations from bad ones, each mobile device uses a *trust model*: it weights contributions from highly trusted recommenders more than those from untrustworthy recommenders. Most of the distributed trust models (e.g., [1], [10], and [14]) may be used for that. They generally evaluate a recommendation depending on the quality of its originator's past recommendations. Such quality varies: for example, it may be low because the recommender misbehaves (i.e., sends false recommendations).

All of this recommendation sharing service aims to improve and speed up shopping experience: based on the recommendations that their devices have collected, customers may better short-list the most useful shops for their current needs.

4 Attacker Model

In order to devise a robust protocol scheme, we must identify possible attacks first. In this section we focus on the possible attacks from which we wish to protect ourselves.

Privacy breaching: A user (attacker) knows the identity of a victim and keeps track of all her interactions. As such, the attacker infers the victim's habits (privacy breaching). For example, the server at a corner shop may log recommendation exchanges among people happening to be in a certain area. Based on these logs, the server may profile people's habits (and, eventually, spending behavior).

False accusation: A user unjustly accuses another user of misbehaving. In our scenario, Cathy's device requests a recommendation Samantha's. The latter device sends the recommendation. The protocol for exchanging recommendations now requires that Cathy's device pays a fee. However, Cathy's device unjustly denies having either requested or received the recommendation.

Sybil-like attacks: A user can manage a set of pseudonyms and, thus, can carry out masquerading attacks (i.e., he masquerades as different entities through its pseudonyms). We categorize such attacks based on whether the attacked target is a single entity or a group of entities:

   1. Attacks against a *single entity*. We can identify the following cases:

      Self collusion for ballot stuffing: Here we have a collection of colluding pseudonyms that the same attacker owns. These pseudonyms can be grouped into three categories: pseudonyms used to offer services; pseudonyms used to increase the remaining pseudonyms' reputations as recommenders; pseudonyms used to send positive recommendations about those in the subset of service providers. The attack unfolds as follows. A victim selects service providers based on faked positive opinions. The service providers then offer a low quality of service. The victim lowers its trust level in the abusing service providers. The attacker, which has orchestrated all of this, will never again use the service providers' pseudonyms because it can create other pseudonyms at will. As a consequence, the victim has been deceived and the attacker has profited without repercussions. Transposing this situation into our scenario, it may happen that Cathy's device (the victim) gets and pays for fake opinions coming from Samantha's. Consider that Samantha's device manages three pseudonyms: S_1, S_2, and S_3. S_1 says to Cathy's device: "S_2 is good at suggesting good recommenders". Cathy's device queries S_2's, which says: "S_3 is good at sharing opinions about shops". Cathy's device then pays S_3's for its opinions. S_3's device shares fake opinions while gaining money. At that point, Samanantha will never again use her pseudonym S_3; she will instead replace it with a newly created pseudonym, S_4.

Self collusion for bad mouthing: A collection of pseudonyms corresponding to the same attacker colludes in that each of them spreads negative recommendations about the same benevolent user. After evaluating those unanimous recommendations, recipients build negative trust in the benevolent user. Hence, the attacker lowers the benevolent user's reputation without harming his own. For example, Samantha does not like Cathy and, thus, her device bad mouths Cathy under the pseudonyms S_1, S_2, and S_3. Upon receiving such opinions, other devices wrongly deduce that four other different devices (persons) dislike Cathy.

2. Attacks against a *group of entities*. We can identify the following cases:

Insider attack: The attacker chooses one pseudonym under which he joins the target group. It then externally misbehaves towards users of *other* groups. They consequently lower the trust in the target group. As such, the attacker lowers the target group's reputation at the price of lowering the reputation of his pseudonym, which he will never use again. For example, some members of the "bookshops" community and others from the "music shops" community look for recommendations about good beauty shops. Being a member of the "beauty shops" community, Samantha's device (under the pseudonym S_1) provides them recommendations about those shops, but fake ones. After experiencing the suggested beauty shops, the recommendation recipients lower the reputation both of S_1 and of the "beauty shops" community (to a certain extent). Samantha's device drops S_1 and will thus not suffer any repercussion in the future.

Outsider attack: Under one pseudonym, the attacker joins some groups *other* than the target group. Within each joint group, it builds up a good reputation in being a reliable recommender and, once reaching the planned reputation level, starts spreading negative recommendations about the target group. As a consequence, the attacker lowers the target group's reputation without harming its own. For instance, Samantha's device joins both "bookshops" and "music shops" communities under one pseudonym. It builds up a good reputation as recommender and then starts to bad mouth about the "beauty shops" community.

Stolen pseudonyms: A user (attacker) steals a victim's pseudonym so as to be able to use it in future interactions. For example, Samantha's device steals Cathy's pseudonym. It then misbehaves under the new pseudonym. Cathy will unjustly suffer from such a theft.

5   Security Requirements and Desirable Features

In the previous section, we described some attacks. As we aim at designing a scheme robust to those attacks, we now infer from them the *security requirements* that our scheme should meet: *anonymity* (a pseudonym does not reveal any information about the real identity of its owner thus preventing privacy breaching); *non-repudiation* (in a reputation-based interaction, each user is prevented from denying previous commitments or actions, thus avoiding false accusation); *unique identification* (a user possesses a unique, valid identifier thus hindering attacks caused by disposable pseudonyms); and *revocation* (once a pseudonym gets stolen, its owner should get a new one at the price of revoking the old one).

Our scheme should also support the following desirable features: *general applicability* (any type of distributed reputation systems benefits from the proposed scheme); *off-line authentication* (users authenticate each other without needing to involve anyone else); *distributed issuing of pseudonyms* (issuing of pseudonyms does not rely on a central authority).

6   The 2-Protocol Scheme

The scheme consists of two protocols: an induction protocol and an authentication protocol. During a one-shot *induction* protocol, a user obtains his pseudonym (i.e., a public key (anonymous) and corresponding signature). Each time two users wish to authenticate each other, they run through an *authentication* protocol, i.e., they exchange their pseudonyms and then verify their validity. After that, they will use the public key in each other's pseudonyms to encrypt their communication (thus avoiding main-in-the-middle and false accusation attacks).

In this section, we describe these protocols. We first briefly introduce the blind threshold primitives we will use. We then show the bootstrapping procedure. Finally, we describe the protocols in details.

6.1   Blind Threshold Signature Algorithms and Protocols

The scheme borrows the protocols and algorithms below from the blind threshold signature literature (see [2] [8] [18]). Blind (t, n) threshold signatures allow n parties to share the ability to blindly sign messages (i.e., sign messages without seeing them), so that any t parties can generate signatures jointly, whereas it is infeasible for at most $(t - 1)$ parties to do so.

SETUP: A protocol that generates a public key K_C and n secrets.
Blinding : An algorithm that on input of a message, a random blinding factor r, and the public key K_C, produces a blinded version of the message.
DISTRSIGN: A protocol used by any subset of t parties that on input of t secrets, t randomizing factors, a blinded message and the public key K_C, produces the blind signature of the message.
Unblinding: An algorithm that on input of a blinded message and the random blinding factor r, extracts the message (i.e., removes the blinding factor).

Verify: An algorithm that on input of a message and corresponding signature, determines whether the signature is valid for the message.

PARTIAL: A protocol used by any subset of t parties that on input of t secrets produces t partial secrets.

Secret: An algorithm that on input of t partial secrets determines one single secret.

REFRESHING: A protocol used by $n\prime$ parties that on input of $n\prime$ old secrets produces $n\prime$ new secrets.

6.2   Community Bootstrapping

The authentication scheme is based on pseudonyms and on threshold signature. When it is issued, each pseudonym needs to be *certified*, and when it is used, it has to be *verified* (i.e., its certification needs to be checked). This is to ensure that each user has only one pseudonym. Certifying a pseudonym means signing it: in a (t, n)-threshold scheme, the private key used for signatures is built up from t secrets, each owned each by a different party. Verifying a pseudonym means checking its signature; in a threshold scheme, there is a shared and unique public key for such a purpose. Therefore, to certify and verify a pseudonym, a collection of parties (community) needs jointly to create a common public key and a secret for each party. This is done in what we call the community bootstrapping phase.

To clarify, consider n community members (potential signers) and denote them by the set $(signer_1, \ldots, signer_n)$. Each ith member $signer_i$ chooses a random string rs_i. All members submit their strings to the *SETUP* protocol. This produces both the community public key KU_C as public output to all members, plus a $secret_i$ as private output to each member.

6.3   The Induction Protocol

To avoid attacks caused by disposable pseudonyms, each community member must have no more than one pseudonym. To achieve this, pseudonyms are issued only for *prospective* community members (and not for already certified ones).

A prospective community member has to run through a 5-step *induction* protocol, after which he obtains his pseudonym (to anonymously authenticate himself) and his own secret (to take part in future inductions). To tackle replay and interleaving attacks, each of the following messages includes a timestamp and a signature, which the recipient checks.

Step 1. The prospective member P broadcasts an induction request, that includes the prospective member's certificate $Cert_P$ (i.e., the certified pair of his identity ID_P and public key KU_P). The recipients must know ID_P to verify whether it corresponds to an already certified member or to someone new. Furthermore, to ensure that the request has been generated by a member with that identity, P signs the request ($Signature_{KR_P}$) with his public key KU_P. The use of public key certificates is limited to the induction protocol and does not require to contact any central authority as the certification authority's public key is available in the community.

$$P \rightarrow: \{Cert_P, Timestamp_P, Signature_{KR_P}\}$$

Step 2. Each member who wishes to participate in the induction (denoted by $signer_j$) sends a positive response. The response contains the member's public key KU_j and the threshold t because, to reply back, the prospective member has to know both the public key of the responder and the current t (number of members needed to proceed with an induction; note that t may change as the community size changes). The response also contains a hash value of a randomizing factor $h(rf_j)$ and the community public key KU_C because, after selecting the responses, the prospective member has to generate a public key and blind it, and to do so, it needs KU_C and a set of hash values of randomizing factors. The response is then encrypted with the prospective member's public key.

$$signer_j \rightarrow P : KU_P\{KU_j, t, h(rf_j), KU_C, Timestamp_j, Signature_{KR_j}\}$$

Step 3. Once enough responses (at least t) have been collected, a quorum of t members must have decided to admit the prospective member. At this point, the prospective member chooses t responders and sends them a blinded pseudonym (a blinded public key) and a list containing the chosen responders' public keys and identities. From the list, all the selected responders will know each other's identities and will thus be able jointly to sign the blinded public key. Let us now focus on the composition of the message for this step. Without loss of generality, we indicate the t members with the set $(signer_1, \ldots, signer_t)$. The prospective member randomly creates a key pair (public key AKU_P and private key AKR_P) and submits that public key together with a random number r (blinding factor), the community public key KU_C, and the set $(h(rf_1), \ldots, h(rf_k))$ to the *Blinding* algorithm. From that, it obtains the blinded anonymous public key AKU'_P, encrypts it along with the list with each responder's public key, and sends the encrypted bits to the respective responders. For $j \in [1, t]$:

$$P \rightarrow signer_j : KU_j \ \{AKU'_P, (KU_1, ID_1, \ldots, KU_t, ID_t), Timestamp_P,$$
$$Signature_{KR_P}\}$$

Step 4. At the end of the induction, the prospective member has to obtain the signature of its anonymous public key and a secret (to participate in future inductions). Thus, in this second-last step, the t-group of members jointly computes and sends the signature of the anonymous public key and a set of partial secrets (from which a secret can be computed). The group does so only if the requesting member has never received a pseudonym before (i.e., if he is actually a new community member and not an old one). More specifically, from the list of responders that the prospective member sent, a group forms. From the initial prospective member's request (step 1), the just-formed group knows the prospective member's identity. It thus checks with up to $(n - 2t + 1)$ community members (external to the group) whether they already released a pseudonym for that identity. If not, the prospective member is entitled to receive its pseudonym and additional information to generate a secret. The group submits AKU'_P, their secrets $(secret_1, \ldots, secret_t)$ and their randomizing factors $(rf_1, \ldots, rf_t)$ to the distributed signing protocol *DISTRSIGN*. This produces the blinded signature s'_P of AKU'_P. As the anonymous public key is *blinded*, the group signed without seeing it. Using the *PARTIAL* protocol, the group then computes a set of partial secrets $(secret_1^P, \ldots, secret_t^P)$ from which the prospective member will be able to compute its own secret. Each group member $(signer_j)$ encrypts and sends both s_P' and $secret_j^P$ to the prospective member. For $j \in [1, t]$:

$$signer_j \rightarrow P : KU_P\{s_P', secret_j^P, Timestamp_j, Signature_{KR_j}\}$$

Step 5. The prospective member first removes from s_P' the random blinding string r through the *Unblinding* algorithm $(s_P = Unblinding(s_P', r))$. It then submits the received partial secrets to the *Secret* algorithm that computes the single secret $secret^P$.

Now the member has its own valid pseudonym, which consists of its anonymous public key (no one knows it) along with corresponding signature, and its secret so that it can participate in future inductions.

6.4 The Authentication Protocol

To decide whether to interact, two community members have to authenticate each other (running the authentication protocol) first, then retrieve reputation information associated with each other's pseudonyms and finally evaluate whether each other's reputations are promising enough for embarking on an interaction.

During the *authentication* protocol, two members send their anonymous public keys and associated signatures, verify whether the counterpart's pseudonym is valid and, if so, use the counterpart's anonymous public key (part of the pseudonym) to retrieve reputation information. To clarify, consider that Cathy's device wishes to interact with Samantha's. It thus sends Samantha's device its pseudonym (its anonymous public key and corresponding signature), and so does Samantha's device. They then check the validity of each other's pseudonyms through the *Verify* algorithm. More specifically, Samantha's device submits Cathy's anonymous public key AKU_{Ca}, the corresponding signature s_{Ca}, and the community public key KU_C to the *Verify* algorithm. This returns *true* if s_{Ca} is a *valid* signature for the anonymous public key (i.e., if a group of at least t members generated it). Cathy's device does the same.

If both verifications run positively, the members involved have each other's valid anonymous public keys and use them to encrypt their subsequent communication, thus avoiding man-in-the-middle attacks and false accusation.

Periodically, a community needs to refresh its members' secrets as some of them may get compromised or the community size changes. To do so, n' members team up $(n' < n)$ and submit their secrets to the *REFRESHING* protocol, which generates n' new secrets. Note that the community public key does not change.

7 Analysis of the Security Requirements and Desirable Features

Having presented our scheme, we now discuss how it meets the security requirements and the desirable features previously pointed out.

Anonymity: A user pseudonym includes an anonymous public key, i.e., a public key that a group of users certified while knowing the corresponding user identity, but without seeing the key itself. Thus, users are authenticated through their pseudonyms, which do not link to real users' identities.

Non-repudiation: After authenticating, two users encrypt their communication with each other public keys, which are part of their corresponding pseudonyms. As they encrypt the communication, the users cannot repudiate any of the message exchanged.

Unique identification: As we use a (t, n) threshold scheme, we can only have one pseudonym for each context, unless we collude with more than t devices. By properly setting t, we have increased the probability that this will not happen.

Revocation: A user can revoke its pseudonym, e.g., if it is stolen. For that, the user should broadcast its anonymous public and private keys so that he can run the induction protocol once again.

Off-line authentication: A user locally verifies the pseudonyms of his interacting parties through a community public key. As he stores such key, he does not need to contact anyone else for authentication purpose.

Distributed pseudonym issuing: We conceived pseudonym certification to be highly available in that it does not rely on the availability of a unique identification authority, but rather just needs that any t users team up.

General applicability: Most of the existing distributed trust frameworks perform the same steps, i.e., they: authenticate the interacting party, retrieve reputation information about that party, compute trust assessments from the reputation information, make a decision whether to interact and eventually interact. Our scheme is general as it applies to these steps. More precisely, it enhances the first and the last steps: it ensures off-line, anonymous, unique authentication; and it then provides non-repudiation support when interacting.

8   Conclusion

We have proposed a general and distributed authentication scheme (as opposed to existing solutions that rely either on a central entity or on a specific trust framework). The scheme supports user anonymity, whilst being resistant to a wide range of attacks, including "Sybil-like" ones. Most of the existing distributed trust frameworks could make use of it to offer flexible (off-line) authentication without relying on a central service.

The scheme shows one relevant limitation though: that of *weak identification*. If a new person joins (a new anonymous identity appears), and that is the only recent joining, one can link the anonymous identity with the real one. As part of future work, we will investigate whether introducing delays into the scheme will address the problem, whilst not affecting usability.

Acknowledgements

The authors gratefully acknowledge the support of the European Commission through the SEINIT and RUNES projects.

References

[1] A. Abdul-Rahman and S. Hailes. Supporting Trust in Virtual Communities. In Proceedings of the 33rd IEEE Hawaii International Conference on System Sciences, volume 6, page 6007, Washington DC, USA, 2000.

[2] D. Boneh and M. Franklin. Efficient generation of shared RSA keys. Journal of the ACM, pages 702–722, Volume 48(4), 2001.

[3] D. Boneh and M. Franklin. Identity-Based Encryption from the Weil Pairing. In Proceedings of Advances in Cryptology, volume 2139, pages 213-229, August 2001. LNCS.

[4] L. Bussard, Y. Roudier, R. Molva. Untraceable Secret Credentials: Trust Establishment with Privacy. In Proceedings of the 2nd IEEE Annual Conference on Pervasive Computing and Communications Workshops, page 122, Orlando, USA, March 2004.

[5] V. Cahill, E. Gray, J.-M. Seigneur, C. Jensen, Y. Chen, B. Shand, N. Dimmock, A. Twigg, J. Bacon, C. English, W. Wagealla, S. Terzis, P. Nixon, G. Serugendo, C. Bryce, M. Carbone, K. Krukow, and M. Nielsen. Using Trust for Secure Collaboration in Uncertain Environments. IEEE Pervasive Computing Mobile and Ubiquitous Computing, 2(3):5261, August 2003.

[6] M. Carbone, M. Nielsen, and V. Sassone. A Formal Model for Trust in Dynamic Networks. In Proceedings of the 1st International Conference on Software Engineering and Formal Methods, pages 5463, Brisbane, Australia, September 2003. IEEE.

[7] J. R. Douceur. The Sybil Attack. In Proceedings of the 1st International Workshop on Peer-to-Peer Systems, pages 251-260, Cambridge, U.S., March 2002. Springer-Verlag.

[8] R. Gennaro, S. Jarecki, H. Krawczyk, T. Rabin. Robust and Efficient Sharing of RSA Functions. In Proceedings of the 16th Annual International Cryptology Conference on Advances in Cryptology, pages 157-172, volume 1109, London, UK, 1996.

[9] S. D. Kamvar, M. T. Schlosser, H. Garcia-Molina. The Eigentrust algorithm for reputation management in P2P networks. In Proceedings of 12th Conference World Wide Web. Budapest, Hungary, pages 640651, 2003. ACM.

[10] J. Liu and V. Issarny. Enhanced Reputation Mechanism for Mobile Ad Hoc Networks. In Proceedings of the 2nd International Conference on Trust Management, volume 2995, pages 4862, Oxford, UK, March 2004. LNCS.

[11] D. Quercia, S. Hailes. MATE: Mobility and Adaptation with Trust and Expected-utility. To appear in the International Journal of Internet Technology and Secured Transactions.

[12] D. Quercia and S. Hailes. Risk Aware Decision Framework for Trusted Mobile Interactions. In Proceedings of the 1st IEEE/CreateNet International Workshop on The Value of Security through Collaboration, Athens, Greece, September 2005.

[13] D. Quercia, M.Lad, S. Hailes, L. Capra, S. Bhatti. STRUDEL: Supporting Trust in the Dynamic Establishment of peering coaLitions. In Proceedings of the 21st ACM Symposium on Applied Computing, Dijon, France, April 2006.

[14] D. Quercia and S. Hailes and L. Capra. B-trust: Bayesian Trust Framework for Pervasive Computing. In Proceedings of the 4th International Conference on Trust Management, Pisa, Italy, May 2006. LNCS.

[15] Resnick, P.: The Social Cost of Cheap Pseudonyms. Journal of Economics and Management Strategy 10(2): 173-199, June 2001.

[16] J.-M. Seigneur and C. D. Jensen. Trading Privacy for Trust. In Proceedings of the 2nd International Conference on Trust Management, volume 2995, pages 93107, 2004. Springer-Verlag. J.-M.

[17] J.-M. Seigneur, A. Gray, and C. D. Jensen. Trust Transfer: Encouraging Self-Recommendations without Sybil Attack. In Proceedings of the 3rd International Conference on Trust Management, volume 3477, pages pages 321-337, 2005. Springer-Verlag.

[18] V. Shoup. Practical Threshold Signatures. In Proceedings of Eurocrypt, LNCS, Volume 1807, pp. 207-220, 2000.

The Design, Generation, and Utilisation of a Semantically Rich Personalised Model of Trust

Karl Quinn, Declan O' Sullivan, Dave Lewis,
and Vincent P. Wade

Knowledge & Data Engineering Group, Department of Computer Science,
Trinity College Dublin, Dublin 2, Ireland
Firstname.Lastname@cs.tcd.ie
http://kdeg.cs.tcd.ie/

Abstract. "Trust is a fashionable but overloaded term with lots of intertwined meanings" [1] and it has therefore been argued that trust is bad for security. We have designed, developed and evaluated a rich, semantic, human-centric model of trust that can handle the myriad of terms and intertwined meanings that defining trust has. This model of trust can be personalised on a per user basis and specialised on per domain basis. In this paper we present this model with accompanying experimental evaluation to support it and introduce a mechanism for the generation of personalised models of trust. Furthermore, we describe how this model has been utilised through the combination of a policy and trust sharing mechanism to empower trust based access control.

1 Introduction

Trust is a difficult issue to define and contemplate as it is a human idea with a myriad of general meanings, uses, and associated issues such as risk and privacy. In defining trust many synonyms of trust or trust inspiring terms such as "Belief" [2], "Credibility or Reliability" [3], "Confidence or Faith" [4], "Reputation" [5], and "Competence and Honesty" [6] are often quoted. These definitions generally try to convey that trust has a quantitative value associated with it, that trust is multidirectional, and that trust can be made specific (e.g. to medical procedures). We believe that trust is not just a single, easily definable idea but it is a dynamic entity that is dependent on a point of view and relates multiple trust characteristics to determine an overall idea of trust. Therefore, for our purpose, trust is a combination of the above definitions, or trust concepts, encoded in a rich ontology and bound together with varying relationships, personalised on a per user basis. Ontologies are suited for our purpose as they endeavour to encode conceptual models, such as a user's conceptual model of trust, in a format that is usable by software applications. This approach can be related, or specialised, towards multiple domains such as Web Services [7] or Instant Messaging (IM) [8].

In calculating trust values much research [3], [9], [10] concentrates on calculations that render a simple single trust value; we too aim for simplicity to allow for easy comparison and decision making by applications. However, we arrive at this trust

K. Stølen et al. (Eds.): iTrust 2006, LNCS 3986, pp. 324–338, 2006.
© Springer-Verlag Berlin Heidelberg 2006

value via a personalised model of trust combined with trust evidence and/or trust opinion collected on a collaborative basis.

In this paper, section 2 explores related research work. Section 3 presents our model of trust and what it means to specialise that model. In section 4 we report an experiment that evaluated the model of trust in terms of its trust concepts, relationships, and requirement for personalisation. Section 5 introduces a mechanism to generate personalised models of trust and illustrates how trust calculations are rendered using it. In section 6 we describe an application that utilises the model of trust and supporting framework. Section 7 provides a summary and future work.

2 Related Work

The related work section is scoped into two broad areas; semantic representation of trust and systems that utilise trust.

There are a limited number of ontologies that are already defined for trust, and reputation, a sub-element of trust. In [5] an extension is made to the Friend-Of-A-Friend [11] ontology that allows for the assignment of a reputation value to a person. This extension to allow for the reputation value is similar to Golbeck's earlier work [3] where the value assigned was for trust. Both [3] and [5] describe how trust/reputation relationships can be applied to a person for a specific subject area by such a degree. The levels of trust used by Golbeck are defined in [12] where the trust values are measured on a scale from one to ten, one being absolute distrust and ten being absolute trust. Golbeck's ontology does not currently describe the myriad of properties, relationships, relationships and concepts that the domain of trust can provide. In our model of trust the final value uses a similar range format to Golbeck's but the calculation used to arrive at the final value uses the semantic richness of the properties and relationships found in the model of trust.

The TRELLIS [13] project enables users to express their trust in a source so that many individual trust values can be combined into an overall assessment of trust. It is presented as an information analysis tool that enables users to annotate how they analyse and use information when making some decision. In our research we also enable such expressions of trust through the use of a personalised model of trust and the ability to annotate a source with trust data. This annotation data can be shared on a collaborative basis in order to calculate what Marsh refers to as general trust in [14].

OpenPrivacy [15] allows a trustor to describe their trust in a trustee by use of a real value held within a certificate along with a confidence value for the trustor. Our research has the ability to weight specific sources of trust information to enable that source to have a greater say in the determination of a final trust value.

The Advogato [9] project automatically calculates trust using group assertions. Interestingly, the Advogato metric for calculating trust is highly attack resistant. This allows the system to cut out portions of the network that are subsequently identified as 'bad' or disingenuous. Our research can calculate trust values using trust data collaboratively provided by a group of individuals and it is possible to block/remove untrustworthy collaborators.

SULTAN's [10] logical approach enables the user to designate an action and trust condition to a trustee by a trustor. The policy approach in this research enables us to create such event, condition, action rules that can be used by a trustor to represent trust based conditions that a trustee must meet before an action can proceed.

We enable users to share trust data without the need for a central or infrastructure based approach. This is done in a collaborative, peer to peer manner that is similar to PGP's [16] Web of Trust approach.

3   Semantic Model of Trust

The semantic model of trust that we present aims to reflect the individual user's ideas of trust. It can be used at runtime by applications to determine the trustworthiness of resources with which the user, or application acting on the user's behalf, would like to interact with. The model can be specialised on a per domain basis, and personalised on a per user basis. Specialisation refers to the ability of a general upper ontology to be applied to domain specific models of trust, such as Web Services and Instant Messaging. This paper only explains specialisation and provides examples to illustrate the point. Please see [7], [17], and [18] for more information on specialisation. Personalisation refers to a flexible and dynamic model of trust with the ability to capture an individual's ideas of trust and the relationships that may exist. We represent our model of trust as a rich semantic model that has the ability to provide this necessary functionality. To our knowledge there is as yet no other research published which relates to personalised and flexible models of trust. This paper focuses on personalisation in its illustration, evaluation, generation, and use.

We have used the Web Ontology Language (OWL) [19] as the representation format for the model of trust as it provides extendibility, reusability, mapping, and semantics. An ontological approach provides an accurate reflection of the trust concepts and relationships in a sharable, reasonable, and understandable format. We believe that an ontological approach therefore provides the support needed to realise the model of trust. However, an ontological approach is only one format in which this model can be realised.

We now present a detailed overview of the model of trust including how it is specialised and personalised.

3.1   Model of Trust Overview

Our model of trust mirrors the complex myriad of human notions of trust and its relationships. Our approach to modelling trust can be viewed as having four levels;

  (i)   Meta-model,
  (ii)   Upper ontology,
  (iii)   Domain specific model,
  (iv)   Personalised model of trust.

(i)   Different strength relationships exist between trust concepts as it is our hypothesis that people have different ideas as to how strongly one trust concept leverages another trust concept when determining trust. This is why we created three different strength relationships to link concepts. As per figure 1 the relationships are *derivedFrom*, *informedBy*, and *affectedBy*. The strongest relationship is *derivedFrom* and implies a measured bond between concrete concepts only. The second strongest relationship is *informedBy* and it can be formed between any abstract and concrete concept. The weakest relationship is *affectedBy* and it provides a less tangible relationship between abstract concepts. We created the relationships system in an effort to ensure that influences that the user assigns between various concepts are more accurately represented.

Fig. 1. Meta-model

(ii) The OWL based upper ontology, figure 2, is made up of trust concepts and trust relationships. The trust concepts are split into two groups; concrete (full line circles) and abstract (dot-dashed circles). It is a generic and reusable ontology that forms the basis for the generation of personalised models of trust and for the creation of generations of disparate domain specific models. In section 4 we present experimental evaluation to support it.

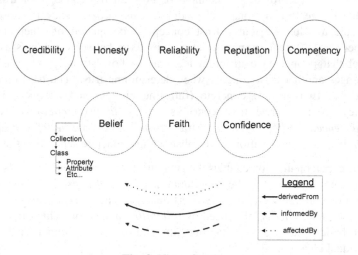

Fig. 2. Upper Ontology

(iii) In our initial work, [7], we created a domain specific model that described each trust concept in terms of domain specific classes and properties. As per figure 3, *reliability* is made up of the following classes; *assurance*, *availability*, *performance*, and *msgDelivery*. These are in turn made up of a set of properties.

For example, *availability* has a set of properties that includes *downtime* and *meanTimeBetweenFailure*. The selection criteria for these classes and attributes were based on a rapid prototyping of a specialised service and are by no means empirical. Each of the trust concepts is engineered in this way, which enables the set of eight trust concepts to be aligned with a personalised model of trust. More recently, we have developed a domain specific model that is applicable to modelling trust in the domain of Instant Messaging [8].

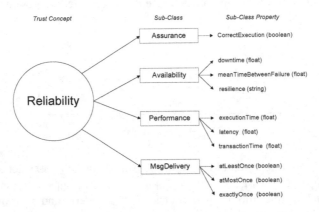

Fig. 3. Service Specific Model (Reliability Only)

(iv)   In figure 4, we provide an example of how all the concepts of trust can be related to create a personalised model of trust. *Competency* is chosen as the example to illustrate that a trust concept is comprised of other classes and properties. Different strength relationships exist between concepts as it is our belief that people have different ideas as to how strongly one trust concept leverages another trust concept when determining trust. The trust concepts are split into two groups; concrete (full line circles) and abstract (dot-dashed circles). The concrete trust concepts are *credibility*, *reliability*, *reputation*, *competence*, and *honesty*. The abstract trust concepts are *belief, confidence* and *faith*. For more information on the abstract and concrete separation see [17, 18].

In essence, personalisation enables the generation of personalised models, based on the upper ontology, to suit the individual needs of the user. As per figure 4, personalisation can allow one user to assert that the concept *reputation* is influenced by *honesty*, or that *belief* is influenced by *reliability*, and so on. This can be repeated in order to build up a model of trust that suits the user's requirement and to reflects their individual idea of trust.

We used Stanford's Protégé Ontology Editor [20] and OWL plug-in to create the upper ontology. Personalised models of trust are instances of the upper ontology. The ontology itself is encoded in OWL Description-Logic (OWL-DL), a sub-language of OWL. It provides the maximum expressiveness of OWL while also retaining computational completeness (all conclusions are guaranteed to be computed) and decidability (all computations will finish in finite time).

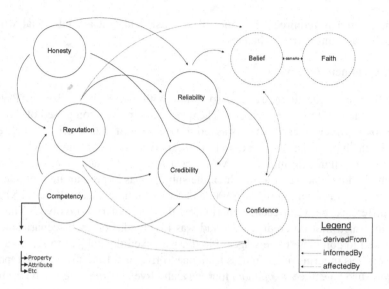

Fig. 4. Personalised Model of Trust

An application utilises the personalised model of trust in conjunction with the domain specific models. For example, when the Web Services application developed in [7] attempts to recommend a trustworthy service the application requests the user's personalised model of trust and the service specific domain model. The application will then use the personalised model with respect to the domain model. This is partially illustrated in figure 3, where we presented the *reliability* concept from figure 4 in terms of *reliability's* service classes (i.e. *availability*) and properties (i.e. *meanTimeBetweenFailure*).

Section 5 presents a mechanism for generating personalised models of trust and illustrates how calculations can render personalised trust values.

4   Experiment Based Evaluation

The goals for the evaluation were to (i) evaluate the upper ontology, (ii) evaluate the meta-model, (iii) evaluate the need for personalisation, and (iv) examine whether individual personalised models of trust alter as context changes, and if so how it changes over varying contexts.

4.1   Hypotheses

We had several hypotheses that directly related to each of the evaluation goals. From the first goal it was our hypothesis that the trust concepts found in the upper ontology were (a) useful to subjects and (b) that subsets of these concepts were either abstract or concrete. From goal two the hypothesis to be tested was that the model of trust had different strength relationships that linked, and interlinked, abstract and concrete concepts. From goal three and four we wanted to investigate our hypothesis that personalisation is required when modelling trust, and that an individual's model of trust alters as context (risk) changes.

4.2 Experiment Overview

We designed a questionnaire in association with Dr. Deirdre Bonini, Psychology Department, Trinity College Dublin. The questionnaire was comprised of three simple scenarios in which the subject was asked to rate a set of characteristics that related to trust. Each characteristic was rated on the basis of how useful the subject thought the concept was when determining a level of trust specific to each scenario. Scenario one presented a low risk scenario in which the subject was buying an item online for $10, scenario two was medium risk at $100, and scenario three was high risk at $1000. The only difference between each scenario was the level of risk involved. The subjects were informed that no credit card fraud was involved. For each scenario the subject was asked to complete three stages. Firstly, we asked the subject to scale each of the trust concepts in terms of usefulness from one to five on a Likert scale; one representing *very low*, two *low*, three *no opinion*, four *high*, and five *very high*. Secondly, we presented the full set of trust concepts and the subject was asked to rank the three concepts they considered most important in relation to determining how much the subject trusted the seller. Finally, the subject was asked to choose a trust concept that most influenced each of their chosen top three concepts.

The subjects were offered the opportunity to take part in a competition to win tickets to a U2 concert in Dublin, Ireland. We advertised via email to a wide range of faculties within Trinity College Dublin, including Computer Science, Psychology, Dentistry, Zoology, and Arts at undergraduate, postgraduate, and staff levels. We also emailed Ericsson Research Group in Dublin, Ireland, and posted notes on forums such as trustcomp.org and U2.com. We received 279 fully completed questionnaires, which we analysed with the Statistical Package for Social Sciences (SPSS).

4.3 Results and Analysis

When evaluating the upper ontology we found that, as per figure 5, 78.5% of the subjects viewed these trust concepts as *no opinion*, *high*, or *very high* in terms of usefulness in determining trust in the $10 scenario. However, when the risk increased to $100 this figure rose to almost 89%, and at $1000 the figure rose even further to 91%. This is significant evidence to support the usefulness of the trust concepts of the upper ontology to the user, and illustrates how the model alters as risk changes.

Furthermore, from the analysis of the data we found the following observations that are key to evaluating the meta-model.

(i)   The concepts with the lowest frequencies across all three ranking scores are *faith* (3.7%), *confidence* (7%), and *belief* (8.8%),

(ii)   The concepts with the highest amount of *very low* and *low* Likert scores across all three scenarios are *belief* (19%) and *faith* (16.5%), and

(iii) The least influential concepts at every risk level are *faith* (3.8%), *belief* (7.2%), and *confidence* (7.9%).

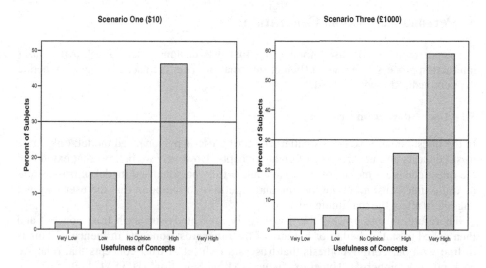

Fig. 5. Likert Scales for all Concepts for Scenario One and Scenario Two

These observations regarding the rankings, Likert scores, and influence scores can be explained by the use of the terms 'concrete' and 'abstract'. We believe that the subjects do not see abstract concepts as well-defined and measured and they therefore attribute low scale scores, low ranking, and low influence to them. Conversely, concrete concepts, such as *reputation, reliability,* and *credibility* scored highest in rank, influence, and on the Likert scale. This supports our original meta-model hypothesis. The influence of abstract concepts (3.8%, 7.2%, and 7.9%) falls far below the random influence average (12.5%), whereas concrete concepts meet, or surpass, this average. This significant data result combined with the high Likert-scales received for the usefulness of concrete concepts leads us to conclude that concrete concepts have a greater impact on overall trust than abstract concepts.

With regards evaluating personalisation we found that 55% of subjects altered their view of the usefulness of the trust concepts as the risk increased. The (i) differences in weight that an individual assigns to certain trust concepts, (ii) range of various model of trust that can exist, and (iii) statistical probability of a user altering their personalised model as risk increases supports the hypothesis that personalisation is required.

An SPSS analysis of the data found a positive correlation, 0.318 at the 0.01 level of significance, between increasing risk and the increasing Likert values the subjects provided for the trust concepts. From this it can be said, with confidence, that the data suggests that as risk increases so too does the subjects reliance on the trust concepts rise. This is evident in figure 5, where (i) the trend for low Likert scores reduces as risk rises and (ii) where the peak scales shift from *high* to *very high* as risk increases. Further detail of the results and analysis from this experiment is the subject of another paper which is under preparation.

5   Personalised Model Generation

To generate a personalised model of trust we designed and developed a user interaction process to garner sufficient information from the user in order to generate the personalised model of trust.

5.1   User Interaction Process

In the questionnaire we got a smaller subset of a user's personalised model; only three trust concepts and not the core of eight concepts. However, we believe that extending the questionnaire's methodology to generate a fully personalised model of trust would be quite time consuming, inefficient, and repetitive to the point that the user may not engage to affect the maximum benefit.

Therefore, in this process the user is only presented with each trust concept and then asked to state whether or not any of the other trust concepts influence it. This is in line with our core hypothesis that trust is a rich set of trust concepts that relate to each other. Kleinberg's 'Hypertext Induced Topic Selection' (HITS) [21] was chosen as the personalisation algorithm as the notions of 'hub' and 'authority' that it presents are applicable to our trust concepts. In our model of trust a concept can be viewed as an authority if it influences many other concepts, and a hub if it is influenced by other concepts. The system can apply the HITS algorithm to a users influence data to rank and weight the individual concepts in respect to each other.

5.2   Personalised Model Example

In figure 7 a user has provided what she believes the influences are between trust concepts. We have taken this data and used the HITS algorithm to calculate the weights (illustrated at the centre of each concept in figure 7). The algorithm assigns a weight to the outgoing relationships that each concept has. A concept that is an authority (see *credibility*) will have greater weight assigned to its relationships than

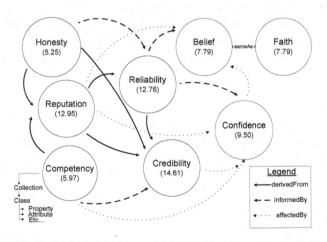

Fig. 6. Personalised Model of trust with HITS Algorithm Calculated Weights

the relationship weights found in hub concepts (see *honesty*). We have implemented a process whereby each concept then receives its final weight value when the weights of the relationships that apply to it are summed. It is important to state that a user can state that no relationships exist between the various concepts. In this case the algorithm assigns equal final weight values to each concept.

In figure 7, *credibility* is influential to many other concepts, whereas *honesty* is only influenced by many other concepts. It is for these reasons that the algorithm has issued *credibility* with a relatively high score and *honesty* a relatively low score.

The user interaction process that generates the personalised models of trust is available via a web page, but it could also be integrated in an application or as part of an interview process. The final weights provide us with an introspective weighting between the models that enable us to rank all the concepts and scale them relative to each other. This personalised model can be used in conjunction with collaboratively received trust data in order to calculate trust values as shown in the next section.

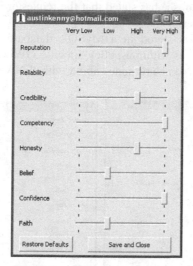

Fig. 7. Semantic Annotation GUI

6   Application Utilisation

We have applied the model of trust to two distinct domains; Web Services and Instant Messaging (IM). In the first instance [7] the model of trust was used in conjunction with trust data and provided the user with service recommendations based on trust. In our more recent work we have developed an IM application [8] that is trust enabled. The IM application has most of the basic functions of a commercial IM system such as Microsoft Corporation's Instant Messenger; add and remove contacts and chat online. However, we have added the ability to annotate other users with opinion based trust data. The user is also empowered with the ability to create specific policies that allow the user to regulate access to location information that has been embedded in the IM application. The combination of personalised trust model, trust data, calculations, and policies provides a flexible form of trust based access control.

6.1 Semantic Annotation & Policy Specification

Once a user has added another user to her list of contacts, also known as the 'buddy list', the user can provide trust data for that user. This is done via a graphical user interface as per figure 8. The user can set a desired default level that can be applied to every member of the buddy list when they are first added. The user can then alter this default set as necessary. In figure 8, *austinkenny@hotmail.com* has been annotated with trust information, which has been persistently stored.

The policy specification GUI, as illustrated in figure 9, enables the user to create event, condition, action policy specification. The condition is a minimum overall trust requirement; *very low*, *low*, *high*, or *very high*. However, it is possible to add minimum trust requirements for specific trust concepts. In figure 9, the user has specified that she will allow access (the action) to her location information (the event), so long as the requesting user has a minimum overall trust value of *very high* (the condition). In addition, she has stated that the requestor must also have *very high reputation* and *belief* values.

The policy GUI data is stored in a MySQL database, which is automatically converted to OWL instances within a policy specific OWL ontology. Therefore, the data is open, portable, and can be reasoned about with JENA [22] technology.

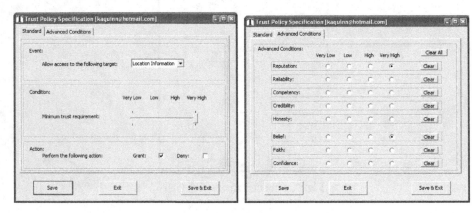

Fig. 8. Policy Specification GUI

	Example 1	Example 2
userSource	karl.quinn@cs.tcd.ie	karl.quinn@cs.tcd.ie
belief	4	3
faith	3	4
confidence	4	4
credibility	4	3
reputation	4	4
reliability	4	3
honesty	4	4
competency	4	4
userDestination	dave.lewis@cs.tcd.ie	Austin@cs.tcd.ie

Fig. 9. Example Trust Data

6.2 Calculating Trust

By way of explanation we have created three users in an IM scenario; Karl, Dave, and Austin. As per figure 10 the 'userSource' (Karl) has integer data for each trust concept for the 'userDestination' (Dave and Austin). The integer data representation spans from 1 to 4 where 1 is *very low*, 2 is *low*, 3 is *high*, and is four is *very high*. In this instance the data is considered primary data as it originates from the user herself. It is possible for the users within the IM network to collaboratively share their trust data when queried; the resulting data is considered secondary data.

Trust calculations are methodologies that are used in conjunction with the personalised model of trust (figure 7) and the trust data (figure 10) in order to render a final trust value. We designed the methodology described below but it is possible to substitute different methodologies to render final trust values.

In the IM scenario we place the average weight of the top three concepts in to a 'gold band', the average weight of the concepts ranked four to six into a 'silver band', and the average weight of the bottom two concepts into a 'bronze band'. This renders a gold band value of ~13, a silver band value of ~8, and a bronze band value of ~5 for the concepts in figure 2.

We now average the trust data for Dave based on the three bands. As per figure 2 the gold band has *credibility*, *reputation*, and *reliability* each of which has a trust value of 4. Therefore, the average value, 4, is assigned to the gold band. We do the same for the concepts in the silver and bronze bands, which assigns 3.66 to the silver band and 4 to the bronze.

As per figure 11 we can see that the gold band has significantly more weight in relation to the silver band, and in turn the silver band has significantly more weight that the bronze band. The band value in the highly weighted gold band will be used as the final, overall, trust value. Therefore, we can say that Dave is *very highly* trusted. In this example Dave meets the policies minimum overall trust requirement and also the concept specific policy requirements (*reputation* and *belief* are *very high*).

Band	Band Weight	Band Value
Gold	13	4
Silver	8	3.66
Bronze	5	4

Fig. 10. Dave's Band Weights and Values

Band	Band Weight	Band Value
Gold	13	3.3
Silver	8	3.66
Bronze	5	4

Fig. 11. Austin's Band Weights and Values

Austin's values are shown in figure 12. The three bands have the same weight as the same personalised model is used. However, the band values now reflect the trust data associated with Austin. The gold band value for Austin is rounded to 3, or *highly* trusted. In this example Austin does not meet the policies minimum overall trust requirement. In addition Austin does not meet the concept specific requirements.

It may be suggested that sharing trust data (therefore secondary data) is highly susceptible to subjective conditions. There may be a semantic difference between what people say and what other people think that they say. This difference has been handled in [7] by implementing the Abdul-Rahman-Hailes [23] algorithm. This algorithm has the effect of weighting secondary information with respect to the requestor's previous encounters with the secondary data provider.

7 Summary and Future Work

In this paper we have presented our semantically rich, flexible model of trust and have provided evidence that has been gathered through experimentation, which supports our view that our model has the characteristics necessary to support the generation of personalised trust models. This experimental evaluation found that (i) the trust concepts were considered useful by people, (ii) captured the relationships between the concepts appropriately, and (iii) confirmed the need for personalisation of the trust model on a per user basis. In addition, through our initial application of the trust models in different domains, we have found that the ontological approach taken provides the support necessary to realise personalised and specialised models of trust.

Furthermore, we introduced a mechanism for generating personalised models of trust based on Kleinber's HITS algorithm and have shown how a calculation methodology can render final trust values that can be used to make trust comparisons and decisions. We plan to evaluate the HITS algorithm as a tool for generating personalised models of trust. The model of trust was integrated into an Instant Messaging application that enables users to annotate resources with trust data and to create policies that impose their will on the systems that they use.

Our future research will concentrate on producing several evaluation experiments. We need to assess the true value of a personalised approach versus a non-personalised approach. This requires the HITS approach to generating personalised models of trust to be explicitly evaluated. It will also require the research and development of a wide range of calculation methodologies. These methodologies will be analysed in order to find the approaches that yield the best results for the user. The model and supporting framework was developed for sharing trust data with scalability in mind. However, we will need to critically analyse and evaluate its operation on larger scales. We believe that this future evaluation will reinforce our belief in personalised models of trust.

Acknowledgements

This work was partially funded by the Irish Higher Education Authority under the M-Zones programme. Karl Quinn receives a scholarship for his research from IRCSET. The initial part of this work was carried out in the Ericsson Ireland Research

Department as part of an Internship by the Author, Karl Quinn, during 2004. We would also like to thank Dr. Deirdre Bonini, Psychology, TCD for her valuable input in designing the evaluation questionnaire. Finally, we would like to thank Professor Padraig Cunningham, Computer Science, TCD for his valuable input.

References

[1] Gollmann, D., 'Why Trust is Bad for Security', Keynote Speech, IEEE 6th International Workshop on Policies for Distributed Systems and Networks (POLICY 2005), Stockholm, Sweden, 6-8 June, 2005.

[2] McKnight, H.D., Chervany, N.L., 'The Meanings of Trust; Technical Report 94-04, Carlson School of Management, University of Minnesota', 1996.

[3] Golbeck, J., Hendler, J., Parsia, B. 'Trust Networks on the Semantic Web', 12th International Web Conference (WWW03), Budapest, Hungary, May 2003.

[4] Shadbolt, N., 'A Matter of Trust', IEEE Intelligent Systems, pp. 2-3 January/February 2002.

[5] Golbeck, J., Hendler, J., 'Inferring Reputation on the Semantic Web', 13th International Web Conference (WWW2004), New York, NY, USA, May 2004.

[6] Grandison, T., Sloman, M., 'A Survey of Trust in Internet Applications', IEEE Communications Surveys, 3, pp. 2-16, Fourth Quarter 2000.

[7] Quinn, K., O'Sullivan, D., Lewis, Wade, V.P., 'Composition of Trustworthy Web Services', Information Technology & Telecommunications Conference (IT&T 2004), Limerick, Ireland, October 2004.

[8] Quinn, K., Kenny, A., Feeney, K., Lewis, D, O'Sullivan, D., Wade, V.P., 'Flexible Relationship-driven Management in the Decentralisation of Collaborative, Context Aware Systems', 10th IEEE/IFIP Network Operations and Management Symposium (NOMS 2006), Vancouver, Canada, April 3-7, 2006.

[9] Levien, R., Aiken, A., 'Attack resistant trust metrics for public key certification.', 7th USENIX Security Symposium, San Antonio, Texas, January 1998.

[10] Grandison, T., Sloman, M., 'SULTAN - A Language for Trust Specification and Analysis', Proceedings of the 8th Annual Workshop HP OpenView University Association (HP-OVUA), Berlin, Germany, June 24-27, 2001.

[11] RDFWeb: FOAF: 'the friend of a friend vocabulary', http://rdfweb.org/foaf/

[12] Golbeck, J., 'Trust Ontology', http://trust.mindswap.org/ont/trust.owl.

[13] Gil, Y., Ratnakar, V., 'Trusting Information Sources One Citizen at a Time.', Proceedings of the First International Semantic Web Conference (ISWC), Sardinia, Italy, June 2002.

[14] Marsh, S.: Formalising Trust as a Computational Concept. PhD thesis, University of Stirling, Department of Computer Science and Mathematics (1994)

[15] Labalme, F., and Burton, K., 'Enhancing the Internet with Reputations. An OpenPrivacy White Paper', March 2001.

[16] Zimmerman, P.R., 'The Official PGP Users Guide', MIT Press, Cambridge, MA, USA, 1995.

[17] Quinn, K., O'Sullivan, D., Lewis, D., Brennan, R., Wade, V.P., 'deepTrust Management Application for Discovery, Selection, and Composition of Trustworthy Services.' Proceedings of IDIP/IEEE 9th International Symposium on Integrated Network Management (IM 2005), Nice, France, May 2005.

[18] Feeney, K., Quinn, K., O'Sullivan, D., Lewis, D., Wade, V.P., 'Relationship-Driven Policy Engineering for Autonomic Organisations', IEEE 6th International Workshop on Policies for Distributed Systems and Networks (POLICY 2005), Stockholm, Sweden, 6-8 June, 2005.

[19] McGuinness, D.L., van Harmelen, F., 'OWL Web Ontology Language Overview', W3C Proposed Recommendation, 15th Dec 2003.

[20] Musen, M. A. , Tu, S. W. , Eriksson, H., Gennari, J. H. , and Puerta, A. R., 'PROTEGE-II: An Environment for Reusable Problem-Solving Methods and Domain Ontologies', International Joint Conference on Artificial Intelligence, Chambery, Savoie, France, . 1993.

[21] J. Kleinberg. Authoritative sources in a hyperlinked environment. Proc. 9th ACM-SIAM Symposium on Discrete Algorithms, 1998.

[22] Hewlett Packard, http://www.hpl.hp.com/semweb/jena.htm.

[23] Abdul-Rahman, A., Hailes, S., 'Supporting Trust in Virtual Communities', In Proceedings Hawaii International Conference on System Sciences 33, Maui, Hawaii, 4-7 January 2000.

A Trust Assignment Model Based on Alternate Actions Payoff[1]

Vidyaraman Sankaranarayanan and Shambhu Upadhyaya

Computer Science and Engineering, University at Buffalo,
Buffalo, NY 14260
Phone: 716-645-3180, Fax: 716-645-3464
{vs28, shambhu}@cse.buffalo.edu

Abstract. The human component is a determining factor in the success of the security subsystem. While security policies dictate the set of permissible actions of a user, best practices dictate the efficient mode of execution for these actions. Unfortunately, this efficient mode of execution is not always the easiest to carry out. Users, unaware of the implications of their actions, seek to carry out the easier mode of execution rather than the efficient one, thereby introducing a certain level of uncertainty unacceptable in high assurance information systems. In this paper, we present a dynamic trust assignment model that evaluates the system's trust on user actions over time. We first discuss the interpretation of trust in the context of the statement "the system trusts the users' actions" as opposed to "the system trusts the user." We then derive the intuition of our trust assignment framework from a game-theoretic model, where trust updates are performed through "compensatory transfer." For each efficient action by a user, we assign a trust value equal to the "best claim for compensation", defined as the maximum difference between the benefits of an alternate action and the selected efficient action by the user. The users' initial trust and recent actions are both taken into account and the user is appropriately rewarded or penalized through trust updates. The utility of such a model is two-fold: It helps the system to identify and educate users who consistently avoid (or are unaware of) implementing the organization's best practices and secondly, in the face of an action whose conformance to the organizational policies is contentious, it provides the system or a monitoring agent with a basis, viz. the trust level, to allow or disallow the action. Finally we demonstrate the application of this model in a Document Management System.

Keywords: Compensatory Transfers, Document Management Systems, Trust Metrics.

1 Introduction

In recent times, it has been observed that human factor is a critical aspect to the success of a security system in any architecture. Any system, with its requirements and

[1] Research supported in part by Advanced Research and Development Activity (ARDA), contract no. NBCHC030062 and by DARPA, under contract no. F30602-00-10507.

K. Stølen et al. (Eds.): iTrust 2006, LNCS 3986, pp. 339–353, 2006.

corresponding security schemes, is often besotted with its own set of unique problems that, more often than not, require and rely on human intervention. Right from the act of choosing strong passwords to the application of the latest security patches, the human in the security loop is often the determining component in the success of the security system. Security policies are a first step towards defining the set of permissible actions by the user in a given role. Among these permissible actions, there is an efficient mode of execution and an easy mode, e.g., choosing a strong password that is difficult to remember vs. choosing a weak password that is easy to remember [14]. If the user adheres to the best practices stipulated by the organization, (and even adapts them depending on the situation), there is a higher probability of the system remaining secure and resistant against most attacks. However, determining if the actions of the user are in conformance with the systems overall functioning is a difficult task, particularly since not all user actions over time are black-and-white as choosing a strong password vs. a weak one. Additionally, actions initiated by users can be evaluated differently depending on the current security state at which the system resides. Since each system has its own problems, user actions are usually varied and as a result, it is not always possible for a monitoring mechanism to decide if the action taken by the user is in the interests of the system.

In this work, we present a system independent trust model called the Compensatory Trust Model (CTM) to dynamically evaluate the trust level of users based on their actions. This measure is representative of the systems trust in the users' actions. This Trust Model can be applied to evaluate the trustworthiness of users and the efficiency of their actions towards maintaining the security level of the system. The parameters can be assigned such that the trust level updates are as granular or as coarse as required by the system. This model evaluates the users' actions continuously and provides the monitoring mechanism with a basis to allow or disallow an action, which, while permitted by the security policies in the system, is not clearly favorable or detrimental to the system. To illustrate our point, consider the scenario: A security patch has been released for protection against a virus that propagates on the Internet through port 4444. However, the system administrator for some system finds that installation of the patch cripples the core business engine necessary for the survival of the organization. Until the issue has been resolved with the vendors, the administrator decides to block all incoming connections on port 4444 through an external firewall and delays the application of the security patch. Such compound actions have a cause and effect relationship that is not immediately apparent to the monitoring engine. The question arises: Should the administrator be allowed to delay the installation of the patch? Should an alarm be raised so that another system administrator can audit this action? In such situations, we argue that the monitoring mechanism is at an advantage by making a decision based on the users trust level. On a parallel track, the trust model progressively lowers the trust level of the user so that periodic peer reviews can determine individual users' adherence to the organizational best policies, and educate/reprimand them or even update the best practices. One such example in the real world is the delayed application of Microsoft Windows XP Service Pack 2 in some organizations due to VPN connectivity problems. These organizations applied the Service pack after Microsoft released an update [1] to address the issue.

Traditionally, trust metrics [4],[10],[6] have been developed for systems where the delegation of certain rights on a system to an (un)known third-party is thought necessary for proper functioning or in situations where certain actions need to be taken based on a unverifiable statement by a third party. These models have found great utility in architectures like Recommender Systems (RS) where the trust of a subject is evaluated based on past history [12]. Still other approaches to trust assignment involve public-key certification chains [5] with provisions for incorporating revocation status [9] in the trust metrics. The work by Kemal *et al.* [9] gives a good overview of Trust Metrics. Most of the systems where these trust assignment models are applied are distributed systems or virtual organizations [13], where some form of extranet can be said to exist. These models are not appropriate for situations (nor were they designed to be) where trust assignments are based on user actions and need to be dynamic. The work in this paper is significantly different from all these aforementioned works in that the primary utility of the trust model is to evaluate and judge the efficacy of the human factor in the security system. We derive the intuition for our framework from a game-theoretic model by Green [7] called "Compensatory Transfers." The user in our scenario is authenticated and assumed to be under continuous monitoring.

The important question from a research perspective is how we can improve the human factor in the security subsystem in a continuous and technically meaningful manner (as opposed to only educating users about best practices in the system). The line of reasoning of this paper is that we can approach such a goal by constantly monitoring the users' actions and assigning a measure to the user which is representative of the systems trust in the users' *actions* (as opposed to the systems trust on the users). At periodic intervals, the system can derive and generate a *trust report* from the model that states the trust level of the user and the reason for the same. Over a period of time, users with low trust levels can review these *trust reports* and through peer-review sessions, learn the unintended consequences of their actions on the system. In this manner the system can better judge and allow/disallow user actions and users are constantly cautioned about the effects of their actions on the system.

The contributions of this paper are as follows: (1) We present a dynamic trust assignment and evaluation model that is used to evaluate the adherence of users actions to system policies and best practices. (2) We argue how this model helps in improving the human factor component in information systems by generating *trust reports* that provide a feedback to users on their actions. (3) We present the application of this model in a Document Management System that is adequately representative of a typical application scenario, viz. a system with a unique set of problems, with an inbuilt monitoring mechanism that has a need to evaluate the users' actions at each step. The rest of the paper is organized as follows. Section 2 describes the Compensatory Trust Assignment model. Section 3 addresses the issues involved in the translation of the model to a feasible implementation. Section 4 describes the application of our model on a Document Management System. We discuss some technical aspects of the model in Section 5. Finally, we summarize and present concluding remarks in Section 6.

2 Compensatory Trust Model (CTM)

We derive the intuition for our trust-assignment framework from a game-theoretic formulation by Green [7] where the user and the system are modeled as playing a virtual game. Each user is assigned an initial trust score which is updated dynamically on every action. The initial trust scores are assigned depending on the context of the application domain. Trust updates are performed through a model called "compensatory transfer" where for each efficient action by a user, we assign a trust value equal to the "best claim for compensation" [7]. A claim of compensation is the difference between the benefits of the alternate action and the selected efficient action by the user. The users' initial trust and his recent actions are both taken into consideration and the user is appropriately rewarded or penalized. We demonstrate the application of this model in a Document Management System.

2.1 Interpretation of Trust

Before we progress towards the trust model, we first discuss the interpretation of trust in this work. Trust, according to [16] is interpreted differently in different contexts. It is usually a process, with the final trust value representing the current state of the process. Reconciling trust with security, however, is not a straightforward task. Recall the basic assumption for this model, viz. the user is authenticated and assumed to be under constant monitoring, *even* when he is deemed as completely trustworthy. In that sense, the view of trust in this work may be construed as somewhat cynical. It may usually be expected that when a user is trusted, not only is the user allowed to perform *any* action, but is subjected to *lesser or practically zero* surveillance. That is usually the essence of trust. But this reasoning does not fit in with the security side of things, particularly in this work, where the central goal is to improve the human factor by monitoring actions. In this context it is instructive to consider the view of Nissenbaum [11] who argues that the level of security does not affect trust; instead, she says it exists only to reduce risk and not increase trustworthiness. As a counterargument, Pearson *et al.*, [16] think that security may increase, decrease or maintain the trust level, depending on the system. We argue that increased security reduces risk and hence increases trust. And in the context in which this work is applicable, this reduced risk is extracted by addressing the weak human factor. There is an additional notion in this paper of what exactly we are trusting; it is the users' *actions*, not the user, that we are trusting. Effectively, the question we attempt to answer is, "Are the users' actions conforming to the best practices of the system?" and not, "Is the user a malicious user?" which is another area by itself. Hence the well known trust paradigms like "Trust is gained slowly and lost swiftly" may not always apply; such philosophies can be applied in this model depending on the system under consideration – they effectively depend on the context in which this model is applied.

2.2 Preliminaries

First we define some general terms and symbols that are required for the development of the model.

$\mathbf{U}$	:	The set of all users in a system where $u_i \in \mathbf{U}$
$\mathbf{A}$	:	The set of all actions in the system where $a_k \in \mathbf{A}$
$\mathbf{R}$	:	The set of all resources in the system where $r_j \in \mathbf{R}$
$u_i{\rightarrow}(a_k, r_j)$	:	User u_i performs an action a_k on the resource r_j
$\alpha(u_i)$	:	The initial trust level of the user u_i

$\tau(u_i)$	:	The current trust level of the user u_i ; $\tau^k(u_i)$ represents the value of $\tau(u_i)$ for the kth iteration
t	:	A Trust update parameter; t^i represents the value of t for the ith iteration
$A(r_j,u_i)$	:	The set of *permissible actions* on the resource r_j by the user u_i. By *permissible actions*, we mean those actions that are allowed by the security policy that is in place.
$P_u(a_k,r_j)$	:	The payoff for user u performing action a_k on resource r_j : $a_k \in A(r_j,u)$

The payoff is representative of the efficiency level of the users' action. Note that the definition of $A(r_j,u_i)$ is set to implicitly cover the security policies in the system, thereby eliminating the need to factor in security policies in the model. We can explicitly include the notion of security policies and their satisfiability in the model if the system is expected to derive a feedback from this model to change the policies themselves. However, in this paper, we limit our discussion to a system with well defined policies and best practices.

2.3 Trust Update

We describe the trust update process for this model as follows. For a given system state, a user u is assigned an initial trust level given by $\alpha(u)$. The user performs some action a_k on a resource r_j, i.e., $u \rightarrow (a_k,r_j)$, where $a_k \in A(r_j,u)$. This action a_k has a payoff that is given by $P_u(a_k,r_j)$. Now for all possible actions in $A(r_j,u)$, compute the maximum payoff difference between each action in $A(r_j,u)$ and the selected action, normalize the difference and update the trust level according to the parameter t. The intuition behind this model is that this updated trust value is the 'compensation' that the user receives (or pays) for choosing the action. The model proposed by Green [7]

```
1.  Fix α(u) and Start the Session
2.  Assign τ⁰(u)=α(u)
        /* τⁱ(u) is τ(u) for the iᵗʰ iteration */
3.  Start Actions by user u
4.  Let the user choose an action aₖ for some re-
    source rⱼ ∈ R: aₖ ∈ A(rⱼ,u)
5.  u→(aₖ,rⱼ)
6.  For all aₘ ∈ A(rⱼ,u): aₘ ≠ aₖ compute the user's
    compensation c:
```

$$c = sign[P_u(a_k,r_j) - P_u(a_m,r_j)]max \left| \frac{P_u(a_k,r_j)-P_u(a_m,r_j)}{P_u(a_k,r_j)} \right|$$

```
7.  Update the current trust value
    if ((τ⁽ⁱ⁻¹⁾(u) < 1) || (c < 0))
    then τⁱ(u)= τ⁽ⁱ⁻¹⁾(u)+ct
8.  Perform User Action - GOTO Step 4
9.  End Session
```

Fig. 1. Compensatory Trust Model Algorithm

involves a notion of a combined payoff for two players which we ignore, since the other player (the system in our case) is completely trusted. The model is described in Figure 1. The compensatory trust model, when implemented, needs the payoff values for the actions (on different resources) as input. Typically, $\tau(u_i) \in [0,1]$. The trust update parameter t should also be dynamically updated so that $\tau(u_i)$ approaches 1 slowly. The updates *increment* will stop if $\tau(u_i) = 1$. Lastly there is an issue of updating t. Trust models follow different paradigms while assigning and updating trust. They adopt either a pessimistic approach where trust is assigned slowly and dropped at a faster rate or an optimistic approach where every subject is assigned complete trust to start with, and a corresponding (negative) update rate. Hence the parameter t can be constant, or decreasing slowly as $\tau(u_i)$ increases, or updated according to the system update policy.

3 Implementation Issues

In this section, we catalog the steps for translating the model to a feasible implementation. We also bring out some implementation specific issues for the trust model. For clarity, we would like to emphasize that the application of the model will involve an extensive knowledge of the system internals and a deep insight into the actions that are (a) critical to the functioning of the system and, (b) have the potential to cause a slow, but eventual destabilizing effect on the security level of the system. Understanding the Threat Model for which the system has been designed is crucial to identifying the actions and assigning their payoffs. Broadly, the steps for implementing this model are as follows:

- The first step is to list the resources in the organization. Resources can mean anything from computers, mobile devices, printers, file servers or documents containing information (proprietary or otherwise).
- For each user $u_i \in \mathbf{U}$, list the permissible actions $A(r_j, u_i)$ for all resources $r_j \in \mathbf{R}$.
- For each of these actions, either assign a payoff $P_u(a_k, r_j)$ or calculate the payoffs depending on the system state.

The important issue to note during implementation is the scope for a state explosion. The number of users in an organization may be very high. Still, since each user is assigned a computation device, monitoring users' actions may not be an issue. But setting a payoff for each of the permissible actions on a resource may be difficult due to two reasons. First, the number of actions possible on all resources may be hard to enumerate. Secondly, even if they were enumerated and payoffs assigned to them, calculating c in step 6 would be computationally intensive, especially since this computation is performed for every alternate action of the user. This is equivalent to the statement that the value of:

$$\sum_{\forall r \in R} A(r, u_i) \tag{1}$$

for a particular user u_i would be very large. To circumvent this, only the important actions on a resource could be enumerated, thereby reducing the number of payoff functions. Finally, deciding the important actions is a system dependent task. We wish to point out that although all actions of a user may not be enumerable, it is still possible to implement this model by enumerating only those actions that are critical. Setting appropriate payoff values for actions, however, is a system specific issue that may require extensive manual input. It is a one time process that must be performed before the deployment of the model. Finally, the trust update parameter t can be updated for every n actions depending on the paradigm (pessimistic or optimistic updates) or a system dependent policy.

A Sample Update Policy. We illustrate a sample update policy for t updated for every action ($n = 1$). This update policy relies heavily on the first few actions performed by the user, but can be modified depending on the system under consideration. The policy, while simple, has two desired characteristics: First, this strategy ensures that the trust update rate is self limiting. Secondly, it ensures that users gain trust slowly and also lose it slowly. While this may run contrary to the maxim "Trust is hard to gain and easy to lose", this approach is appropriate for our purpose, since this model is intended to measure the users' conformance to the best practices of the organization (which can also be interpreted as the extent of user cooperation with the security mechanism), *not whether the user is malicious or not* (in which case we should stop trusting the user even if a single malicious action was observed). We have mentioned and discussed this in detail in the section titled "Interpretation of Trust". The update policy may also be changed if the system requirements are different. We initialize and update t as follows:

- $t^1 = 0.1$
- $t^i = | \tau^{(i-1)}(u) - \tau^{(i-2)}(u) | \ \forall \ i \geq 2$

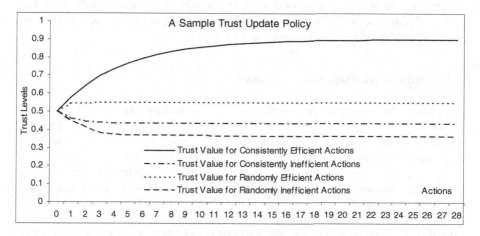

Fig. 2. A Sample Update Policy for t

Note that $\tau^0(u) = \alpha(u)$ and $\tau^1(u)$ is evaluated from t^1 and c. The graph in Figure 2 shows the trend of the trust levels in the face of consistent and random actions that are efficient (and inefficient respectively). We arbitrarily chose $\alpha(u) = 0.5$ and $c = 0.8$ for consistently efficient actions (and -0.4 for consistently inefficient actions). We observe in Figure 2 that a user with consistently efficient actions slowly approaches a trust level of 1 (0.9 in the graph), whereas a user with randomly efficient actions (c = 0.9 to 0.1), although above the initial trust level, is stagnant at a level below 0.6. Similar trends are observed for inefficient actions. For this particular update policy, the trust levels are heavily dependent on the initial values and actions and will stabilize very soon.

After a peer-review session, the core trust evaluation engine must be started again with $\alpha(u) = \tau(u)$ and $t^1 = 0.1$. Users with a higher gradient/value of $\tau(u)$ (as the action number goes high) must be suitably rewarded with a greater t^1 value. Having fixed initial values of the model and the update policy, an organization can correlate the trust levels to the types of users it represents. Table 1 lists the effective actions allowed for a user with a given range of $\tau(u)$.

Table 1. Effective actions allowed for a user based on $\tau(u)$

$\tau(u)$	Effective Actions Allowed
Between 0.8 – 1	Trustworthy – allow user to perform any action
Between 0.7 – 0.8	Trustworthy – allow user to perform any action; Reduce $\tau(u)$ in next iteration if action is not efficient
Between 0.6 – 0.7	Trustworthy – allow user to perform certain actions; Reduce $\tau(u)$ in next iteration if action is not efficient and reset $t = 0.1$
Between 0.5 – 0.6	Allow only efficient actions
Below 0.5	Depends on system. Can either disallow all actions until peer-review or allow only efficient and safe actions with some restrictions

Over a period of time, peer-review sessions could be held for users with a low trust level, while users with a high trust level can be safely expected (and allowed) to perform actions in the interest of the systems security.

4 Document Management System

A Document Management System (DMS) is a proprietary system that enables an organization to create, store and work with documents in a secure manner. The main resource in a DMS is digital documents; they can contain proprietary information like organizational blueprints or financial information or can even be emails and public memos. Documents in a DMS have two levels of protection: The first level of protection is document encryption so that mere compromise of the file server or possession of the digital file cannot reveal the contents of the file. The second level of protection involves the application of Digital Rights Management (DRM) technology to documents. Each protected document can be opened by a viewer that is specific to the format of the document. For example, files with .doc extension can be opened by Microsoft Word. These viewers, apart from word editing functionalities, have additional capabilities built into them that allow for the authentication of users and enforcement of security policies on the document. These policies dictate the rights of a user on a document. For example, for a document MergerDetails.doc, a developer would have no access, a secretary of the CEO might have read and write permissions, while a **Board Member** would have complete permissions, viz. read, write and print permissions. These policies are enforced by the document viewers/editors. The basic architecture of a DMS with the constituent action sequence is shown in Figure 3.

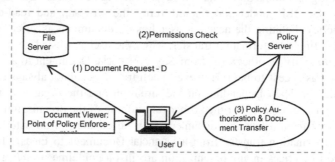

Fig. 3. Document Management System Architecture

Some implementation specific differences between vendors do exist. For example, the File Server and Policy Server may be merged into one single unit and in some cases, the document policies may be embedded into the documents themselves. The whitepaper [2] by Microsoft presents an overview of the threat model and the solutions in a DMS. Although their solution of "Information Rights Management" is specific to the Office 2003 product line, the basic architecture, as shown in Figure 3, is the same for all vendors.

4.1 The BLP Policy Model

All documents in a DMS are classified. The classification labels depend on the organizations. For example, an IT organization may have the labels Software Documentation, Blueprints, Patents, Email, Public Memos, Financial Accounts, etc., while a military organization may classify documents as Unclassified, Confidential, Secret, Top-Secret, etc. Security policy models are constructed based on these labels and organizational requirements. In this paper, we will restrict our attention to the Bell-La Padula [3] policy model, although any other policy model can be used. The Bell-La Padula (BLP) model was originally designed for the military. The idea behind the model was that officers were allowed to contribute information only to other officers at the same level or above, and they were allowed to assimilate information from officers of the same level or below. By 'officers of the same level', we mean officers with the same level of security clearance. This is formalized by a 'write-up' rule and a 'read-down' rule where information can be transferred, for example, from an Unclassified document to any level above (Confidential, Secret, Top-Secret), but information from a Secret document cannot be transferred to any document of a lower classification (Unclassified, Confidential). The equivalent of information transfer in a DMS is a cut/copy and paste operation from one document to another. This model assumes that users with a lower security clearance will not introduce inaccurate information into the system, i.e., it does not assure information integrity. Further information about the BLP model can be found in [3] in greater depth.

4.2 The DMS Policy Problem

Consider a DMS in a commercial organization with a set of document classifiers. Commercial organizations do not have a strict ordering of the classifications which is required for the BLP model and for enforcing the write-up and read-down rules. While the policy dictating the access a user has on documents is strict, there are no clear rules relating to information transfer. Thus the user is trusted not to leak information (intentionally or otherwise) from, say a Financial Document to a Public Memo, given that he has access to both. However, such transfers cannot always be construed as an information leak. Depending on the situation and the organizational requirements, they may be required for the proper functioning of the organization. For example, a summary from a Financial document may be emailed to an external financial consultant (information transfer from a Financial Document to Email). This goes to show that best practices in any organization are just a guideline, *which is what separates them from policies*. But consistent transfers, depending on their severity, may eventually lead to unintended consequences. For this situation, we show how the application of the Compensatory Trust Model can help evaluate users in a DMS on a constant basis, and assign appropriate trust levels based on their actions. A sample of the trust report that can be generated by our implementation is also shown.

4.3 Application of the CTM

In this section, we follow the basic steps outlined in Section 3. For purposes of this illustration, we regard only the digital documents in a DMS as the primary resource for protection. Every user, depending on his role (or group), is assigned rights on different document classifications. For example, a Developer will have complete access to Software Documentation a read-only access to Blueprints, while the Project Manager will have read, write and print permissions on Blueprints. Neither of them will have any access to Financial Documents, while Board members will have complete access on Financial Documents. Thus the security policy defines the list of permissible actions of a user on a document. This is enforced by the document viewer, like Microsoft Word, Adobe Acrobat, etc. Next we describe the intuition for setting payoffs for the actions. Let us impose a partial ordering on the document classifications and the actions on them. For example, Email can be placed very high on the list since information transfer occurs to someone outside the organization. Financial documents, Blueprints and patents can be placed next. Similarly, a read action is innocuous while an editing action is rated higher and a print action still higher. We now define payoffs as follows: Payoffs for information transfer between two documents with the same classification are rated highest. Payoffs for information transfer between two documents of different classifications are rated proportionately, depending on the partial ordering of the document classifications. We formalize this as below:

$\mathbf{C}$:   The set of document classifiers where $c_i \in \mathbf{C}$

$\mathbf{D}$:   The set of documents, where $d_{\mathrm{ci}} \in \mathbf{D}$ represents a document with classification c_i

L	:	The set of user levels (or user roles) where $l_j \in$ **L**. $l(u)$ represents the level of user u.
A	:	The set of actions in the system – read, edit, transfer-edit and print {r,e,te,p}
$A(d_{ci},u)$	:	The set of permissible actions (decided by the security policy)

Although word editors like Microsoft Word provides a rich set of functionalities, the set of actions has been limited for this illustration. We define a transfer-edit operation as a compound action of cut or copy from one document and a paste in another document.

Finally, the payoff function is defined as:

$$P_u(a_k,d_{ci}) = \begin{cases} l(u){\cdot}a_k{\cdot}c_i & \text{if } a_k \neq \text{te} \\ l(u){\cdot}a_k{\cdot}[\min(c_i,c_j)]^2/\max(c_i,c_j) & \text{if } a_k = \text{te} \end{cases} \quad (2)$$

where ci and cj are the classifications of the two documents involved in the transfer-edit operation. In this manner, the payoffs (and the trust level) can be calculated dynamically for every action performed by the user. Since the document viewer in a DMS knows the user credentials and the document classification when the document is loaded, evaluating the payoffs and the trust levels are not computationally intensive. Further, defining payoffs in a functional manner based on a lumped metric (the document classification) reduces the search space for evaluating c in step 6 (in Figure 1), since only ak and cj are the variables in Eq. (2).

4.4 Implementation of the DMS Prototype

To validate our model, we developed a plug-in for Microsoft Word [18] that is capable of creating and enforcing custom policies and monitoring the user's actions on Microsoft Word 2003. The plug-in, built on the .NET platform and written in C#, records all editing actions including information transfers from one document to another, in the form of any object (text, pictures, ClipArt's, etc.) and dynamically updates the users trust levels. It can be downloaded and installed from http://www.cse.buffalo.edu/DRM/prototype/Secure%20Viewer.htm. Using the plug-in, we created documents with custom policies and classifications. Our first observation was that the plug-in did not introduce any performance degradation in Microsoft Word. It was also able to dynamically update the users trust level and record the information transfers. With this information, we were able to generate trust reports that listed the users' history of information transfers and the systems opinion on them.

We now present an overview of the steps to generate a trust report. The components of the trust report are also described here. After installing the plug-in and creating sample documents, we classified and set custom policies on them using the "UB Document Control" Menu bar. More details on these custom policies can be found in [17]. After starting Trust Monitoring, we transferred information between different document types (and security levels). Finally, we generated a trust report that lists the following information:

1. Date and Time of Information Transfers
2. The Document Type (Financial, Merger, Public Memo, etc.) and the security level (Low, Medium or High Priority)

3. **Critical:** If the information transfer was from a high security level to a lower security level document, the transfer was deemed to be critical; otherwise the transfer was not critical

4. **Advised:** If the information transfer was between the same document types, it is advised, else it was deemed inadvisable to affect such transfers.

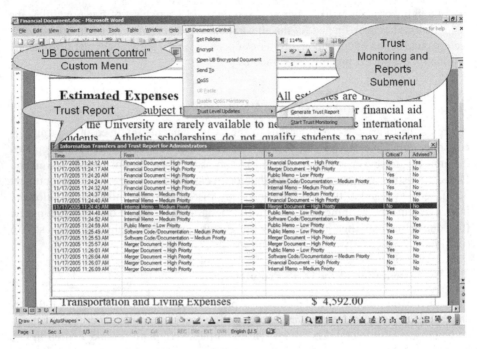

Fig. 4. A Sample Trust Report

A sample trust report for the Administrator is shown in Figure 4. For illustration purposes, the role and user name have been merged as "Administrators". The user is assumed to have unrestricted access to all documents in the DMS. The highlighted row in Figure 4, for example, shows a transfer from an Internal Memo to a Merger Document. Since the transfer is from a Medium Priority to a High Priority document, it is not deemed critical. But it is also not deemed advisable since the document types are different. The decision on criticality and advisability of information transfers is based on the ad-hoc policy (shown in 3 and 4 above) formulated for illustration purposes. The actual decision on whether an information transfer is Advised or Critical will depend on the organizational policies and best practices. We are currently working towards an automated suggestion engine which will present an alternate action for users with low trust levels. For example, if the user decides to transfer information from d_{ci} to d_{cj} where $c_i >> c_j$, it will prompt the user to create a new document with level c_i and merge the relevant information. In this manner, an organization that has a Document Management System is benefited in two ways. The first benefit, one of immediate consequence, is the utility of this model in increasing the security level of a DMS by detecting and eventually preventing accidental information leak across documents of different categories and security levels. The second benefit is broad and has far reaching consequences. We hope that the periodic peer reviews of the users with low trust levels, with an explanation of the same through trust reports, will instill a 'culture of security' [8] in users. This is the final goal that will strengthen the weak human factor.

5 Discussion

The greatest risk in any information system, according to Schneier [15] is the very interaction between users and the system. This interaction is also the lowest common denominator for all systems, including advanced information systems. The trust model proposed in this paper attempts to quantify this system-user interaction and eventually improve the weak human factor inherent in it. In this section, we attempt to address the similarities of the model with the game structure and explain the basis for our intuition. Firstly, game theory usually has an information structure. The information structure in our model corresponds to the payoffs and the choices available to the users in terms of choosing the actions corresponding to the payoffs. These payoffs are not predefined, nor are their corresponding actions known before the application domain (context) is fixed. As a consequence, no strategies, or equilibrium analysis is possible here as in regular game theory. Secondly, there is an issue of rationality in game-theory, i.e., players in a game are assumed to be rational and choose their strategies in a rational manner. Since all users are not always fully trusted (which translates to their implementation of inefficient actions), this begs the question in our model: "Why are users irrational?" The answer to this question lies in the nature of the human factor. Indeed, it is the human factor that is irrational, that makes mistakes as simple as choosing easy passwords, or delays applying critical security patches, either due to inherent laziness or due to ignorance, or more often due to a combination of both. Lastly there is an issue of assigning initial trust values. While the sample update policy has used an arbitrary value, the initial values have to be decided based on the application domain. For example, in the Document Management System, administrators and developers can be assigned high trust values, for they may be expected to know the systems functioning and hence act according to the best practices, while secretaries may be assigned low initial trust values. However, we would like to stress that such ad-hoc initial assignments are highly subjective and depend on the context where the model is applied.

6 Summary and Conclusion

The central theme of this paper has been to improve the weak human factor in systems. Educating users on the best practices of a system is a first step towards achieving this goal. The trust evaluation model presented in this paper goes a step further by constantly monitoring the users' actions and assigning a trust level based on those actions. Our task has been compounded by the fact that not all actions of the user have a straightforward cause and effect relationship and hence, at times when the effects of an action is not determinable, the system monitoring agent uses the trust level to make a decision whether to allow the action to proceed or not. Over a given pre-determined time period, the system can generate trust reports that states the trust level of a user as well as the actions that were not in the interests of the systems security. Peer review process based on these trust reports can help in educating users about the best practices of the organization and in some cases, may even update obsolete best practices and erroneous policies. In this manner, users whose actions do not conform to the organizational best practices are made aware of the unintended consequences of their actions. The application of this model is extremely system dependent and context specific, as the interpretation of trust in this paper is somewhat cynical and is more in tune with the security side of trust rather than the 'human' interpretation. Our future work will concentrate on gathering user feedback on the performance of this model under controlled situations in our lab. We also intend to investigate the application of this model in wireless ad-hoc domains, where continuous monitoring and authentication are not always assured.

According to Hassell and Wiedenbeck [8], users of advanced information systems need to "adopt a culture of security" for any security scheme to be effective. The goal is to eventually inculcate a culture of security in users so that the weak link in the chain, viz. the human factor, can be strengthened. Whether the application of this model will *really* instill a culture of security is debatable, but we hope the selective reviews of users with a low trust level will go a long way towards improving the human factor in the security loop.

References

[1] *Microsoft Knowledge Base Article 884020*, Microsoft Corporation, 2005.
[2] *Microsoft Office 2003 Editions Security Whitepaper, http://www.microsoft.com/technet/ prodtechnol/office/office2003/operate/o3secdet.mspx*, Microsoft Corporation, 2003.
[3] D. E. Bell and L. J. L. Padula, *Secure computer systems: Mathematical foundations and model*, The MITRE Corporation, 1973.
[4] Z. Cai-Nicolas and L. Georg, *Spreading Activation Models for Trust Propagation, Proceedings of the 2004 IEEE International Conference on e-Technology, e-Commerce and e-Service (EEE'04)*, IEEE Computer Society, 2004.
[5] C. Davis, *A localized trust management scheme for ad hoc networks*, 3rd International Conference on Networking (ICN'04), 2004.
[6] J. Golbeck, J. Hendler and B. Parsia, *Trust networks on the Semantic Web, Cooperative Intelligent Agents*, 2003.
[7] J. Green, *Compensatory transfers in two-player decision problems*, International Journal of Game Theory, Springer, 33(2) (2005), pp. 159-180.
[8] L. Hassel. and S. Wiedenbeck., *Human factors and information security, http://clam. rutgers.edu/~birget/grPssw/hasselSue.pdf*, 2004.
[9] B. Kemal, C. Bruno and S. T. Andrew, *How to incorporate revocation status information into the trust metrics for public-key certification, Proceedings of the 2005 ACM symposium on Applied computing*, ACM Press, Santa Fe, New Mexico, 2005.
[10] R. Levien., *Advogato Trust Metric*, UC Berkeley, 2003.
[11] H. Nissenbaum, *Can Trust be Secured Online? A theoretical perspective*, Etica e Politica, no. 2 (1999).

[12] A. Paolo, M. Paolo and T. Roberto, *A trust-enhanced recommender system application: Moleskiing, Proceedings of the 2005 ACM symposium on Applied computing*, ACM Press, Santa Fe, New Mexico, 2005.

[13] A. Richard, L. Mark and A. Paul, *Automated cross-organisational trust establishment on extranets, Proceedings of the workshop on Information technology for virtual enterprises*, IEEE Computer Society, Queensland, Australia, 2001.

[14] M. Robert and T. Ken, *Password security: a case history*, Commun. ACM, 22 (1979), pp. 594-597.

[15] B. Schneier, *Secrets and Lies: Digital Security in a Networked World*, John Wiley & Sons, Inc., New York, 2000.

[16] M. C. M. Siani Pearson, Stephen Crane, *Persistent and Dynamic Trust: Analysis and the Related Impact of Trusted Platforms, Trust Management: Third International Conference, iTrust*, Springer-Verlag GmbH, Paris, France, 2005.

[17] P. Suranjan, S. Vidyaraman and S. Upadhyaya, *Security Policies to Mitigate Insider Threat in the Document Control Domain, Proceedings of the 20th Annual Computer Security Applications Conference (ACSAC'04) - Volume 00*, IEEE Computer Society, 2004.

[18] S. Vidyaraman, P. Suranjan and S. Upadhyaya, *UB Secure Viewer: http://www.cse.buffalo.edu/DRM/prototype/Secure%20Viewer.htm*, 2004.

Privacy, Reputation, and Trust: Some Implications for Data Protection

Giovanni Sartor

Department of Law, European University Institute, Florence
giovanni.sartor@iue.it
http://www.iue.it/LAW/People/Faculty/CVs/sartor.shtml

Abstract. The present contribution analyses the connection between privacy and trust, with regard to data protection. In particular, it shows how the need to facilitate trust-based relationships may justify some limitations of privacy (in the sense of a right to self-determination over personal data), but may also provide some grounds for the protection of privacy.

1 Privacy as Self-determination Over One's Personal Data

It has often been remarked that the right to privacy has greatly changed in the last decades, in connection with the development of information technologies: information privacy[1] can no longer be viewed as a legal barrier protecting the intimate space from unwanted intrusions; it has become a power of decision over one's own information (personal data),[2] the right to informational self-determination.[3] Such a right to informational self-determination seems to include one's power to:

- determine whether a personal datum can be collected (control over data collection);
- determine whether the datum can be transmitted (control over data circulation);
- determine the ways in which the datum can be used (control over data usage).

---

[1] I shall limit my analysis to information privacy, namely, privacy concerning personal information, without addressing the broader and much controversial idea of privacy as freedom of action in the private sphere, an idea which can be found in some US judicial decisions (like the famous abortion case Roe v. Wade, of 1973).

[2] For our purposes, we do not need to distinguish between information and data (though this distinction is important in some domains, like knowledge management). We shall rather use these terms interchangeably, as loosely synonymous.

[3] *Informationelle Selbstbestimmung*, in the words used by the German Constitutional Court in a famous decision of 1983, which upheld this right with regard to information gathered and processed by government agencies for a national census.

K. Stølen et al. (Eds.): iTrust 2006, LNCS 3986, pp. 354–366, 2006.

Moreover, even after agreeing to the treatment of one's own information, one has the power to:

- view the data (right of access);
- obtain the rectification of an incorrect datum or the integration of an incomplete datum (control over the adequacy of the data);
- obtain the deletion of a datum (control over the persistence of the data, right to oblivion).

Obviously, the regulation of data protection is not limited to the statement of the powers just listed. First of all, the right to informational self-determination is limited by legal provisions establishing that certain kinds of personal data can legitimately be processed—by certain subjects and for certain purposes—even without the consent of the person concerned.[4] Moreover, certain forms or contents may be required for consent to be legally valid (for instance, the declaration of consent may need to be in writing, or to concern a sufficiently delimited domain and purpose). Finally, even consent may be insufficient to make processing permissible, under certain conditions, for certain types of data, or for certain types of uses (for instance, an official authorisation may be required for processing sensitive data, and such processing may in any case be limited to specific aims).[5]

However, for our purposes it is useful to abstract from such limitations and qualifications—as well from the many issues concerning the foundations and the characterisation of the right to privacy in the information society[6]— and present the right to privacy as an absolute right, with regard to both its counterparts (as a right towards any other subject) and its content (as a right concerning any type of personal data). On the basis of an absolute protection of the right to informational self-determination, any treatment (collection, processing, communication, etc.) of a personal datum would be allowed only under the condition that the concerned person freely consents to the treatment.

2   Trust

By *trust* in a very generic sense, we usually mean one's expectation that another will act in a way that is advantageous to oneself, supplemented by

---

[4] As indicated in art. 8, par. 2, of Directive 95/46/EC of the European Parliament and of the Council of 24 October 1995 on the protection of individuals with regard to the processing of personal data and on the free movement of such data.

[5] See art. 8, par. 2 (a), of Directive 95/46/EC, which enables national states to establish that the prohibition to process sensitive data may not be lifted by the data subject's consent.

[6] To do that we would need to examine the evolution of the debate on data protection, in connection with technological development, from the beginnings of informatisation (see for instance Westin [1]), to the diffusion of personal computing (see for instance Bing [2]), to the Internet age (see for instance Lessig [3, Chap. 13]).

one's availability to act upon such expectation, accepting the corresponding risks.[7]

In the last years attention has been devoted to the notion of trust, and its importance has often been stressed with regard to the conditions of the information society. Trust appears indeed to be the precondition of many social relations: without trust one would not enter into any risky relationship (namely, any relationship such that the potential risks are greater that the possible gains), and thus one would avoid most meaningful social contacts, both in the economical and in the personal dimension. How could we face social life if we did not trust our fellows, if we did not expect, up to a certain extent, that they will behave properly, in line with our expectations (that doctors will cure us, that sellers will deliver their merchandise, and so on). Similarly, we would not make use of technological systems and of the corresponding socio-technical infrastructures unless we had some trust in their proper functioning, and in the correctness and loyalty of their administrators.[8]

For our purposes it is useful to refer to the distinction, originally proposed by Luhmann [10], between two species of trust, which we may call *confiding* and *active trust*.[9] According to Luhmann, confiding is a merely passive attitude

---

[7] Many different notions of trust exist in the literature, but we do not need to commit ourselves to any one of such notions. Some authors have proposed strong concepts of trust, like Fukuyama [4, 26], according to whom: "Trust is the expectation that arises within a community of regular, honest, and cooperative behaviour, based on commonly shared norms, on the part of other members of the community." A normative concept of trust is also defended, for instance, by Herzberg[5, 319], according to whom "unlike reliance, the grammar of trust involves a perspective of justice: trust can only concern that which one person can rightfully demand of another." The idea that trust relationship have a component which is irreducible to rational expectation is also developed by Baier [6], who views trust (as opposed to mere reliance) as based upon the (truster's belief in the) trustee's good will towards the truster. Others have proposed more neutral ideas. For instance, a notion of trust as encapsulated interest is proposed by Harding [7] (who views the truster's expectation as being based upon the assumption that it is in the trustee's interest to take care of the truster's interest, such trustee's interest not necessarily having a moral or altruistic nature). Another non-normative view of trust is developed by Castelfranchi and Falcone [8], according to whom there is trust whenever all of the following conditions obtain: (a) the truster has a certain goal, (b) the truster believes that the trustee is both capable and willing to achieve this goal, (c) the truster depends upon the trustee for the achievement of the goal, and (d) the truster believes that the goal will be achieved thanks to the cooperation of the trustee. For instance, according to the latter view, I trust my contractual counterpart when I believe that he or she is capable and available to perform, I depend on him or her for such performance (after the execution of the contract, making a new one, with a different partner, would be difficult and costly), and finally I believe that the counterpart will actually accomplish the performance.

[8] For an interdisciplinary discussion of trust, see Gambetta [9].

[9] To distinguish these two attitudes, Luhmann uses the words "confidence" and "trust" tout court. We speak of *active trust* to denote the second attitude, in order to avoid terminological confusion, while continuing to use term "trust" to subsume both ideas.

(we conduct our lives in the expectation that certain negative events will not take place: that a certain level of public security will be maintained, that the judiciary will decide cases with some rationality and impartiality, that money will not suddenly loose all its worth). Active trust, instead, presupposes a decision, namely, the choice to expose oneself to a risk toward the counterpart, in the expectation that the counterpart will not profit of the situation.[10] Such a choice happens for instance when a client enters a contract (in the expectation that the chosen provider will perform) or when partners establish a commercial company (each one expecting that each other will be both able and willing to contribute to the company, having a loyal and cooperative attitude), but also when one enters into a friendly or even an affectionate relationship, or when one confers (or contributes to confer) political representation. The preservation of confidence is certainly an important objective: confidence is the psychological counterpart of security and a necessary precondition of well being within any social framework. However, active trust (in the sense just specified) is even more important, since the decision to rely upon is an necessary precondition of many kinds of cooperative social action.[11] If we were to abstain from relying on others, we would need to renounce many social contacts: economical exchanges, communications, social relationships would dwindle.

It has been observed that trust can emerge in various ways: it may depend on the special history of one's interaction with one's counterpart, it may be connected to the fact that such a counterpart plays a certain professional role

---

[10] Luhmann [10] characterises as follows the distinction between confidence and active trust: "The normal case is that of confidence. You are confident that your expectations will not be disappointed: that politicians will try to avoid war, that cars will not break down or suddenly leave the street and hit you on your Sunday afternoon walk. You cannot live without forming expectations with respect to contingent events and you have to neglect, more or less, the possibility of disappointment. ... Trust, on the other hand, requires a previous engagement on your part. It presupposes a situation of risk. You may or may not buy a used car which turns out to be a 'lemon'. ... You can avoid taking the risk, but only if you are willing to waive the associated advantages. ... The distinction between confidence and trust thus depends on perception and attribution. If you do not consider alternatives (every morning you leave the house without a weapon!), you are in a situation of confidence. If you choose one action in preference to others in spite of the possibility of being disappointed by the action of others, you define the situation as one of trust. ... Moreover, trust is only possible in a situation where the possible damage may be greater than the advantage you seek . ... Trust is only required if a bad outcome would make you regret your action."

[11] Loss of confidence and loss of trust are distinguished as follows by Luhmann [10]: "The lack of confidence will lead to feelings of alienation, and eventually to retreat into smaller worlds of purely local importance to new forms of "ethnogenesis", to a fashionable longing for an independent if modest living, to fundamentalist attitudes or other forms of retotalizing milieux and "life-worlds". ... The lack of trust, on the other hand, simply withdraws activities. It reduces the range of possibilities for rational action. It prevents, for example, early medication. It prevents, above all, capital investment under conditions of uncertainty and risk."

(consider for instance trust toward a doctor, a lawyer, or an accountant), that he or she belongs to a particular group or organisation. In any case, trusted expectations must not be disappointed too much: those who are too often let down, with consequences too negative, will less likely give trust in the future.

In this regard the connection between law and reliance becomes particularly relevant (see Memmo, Sartor and Quadri [11]), a connection which can take different shapes. Sometimes the law can provide an alternative to trust: legal protection is required because trust is lacking, there being no chance of obtaining spontaneous cooperation.[12] Moreover a heavily regulated environment may hinder the formation of trust-based relationships: I (being, for instance, a contractor, or a client of a public administration) do not expect that you (the other contractor, or the public official) will provide an adequate solution to my problem, taking into account my interests and needs; I know that I cannot delegate to you the care of such interests and needs, since you are focused only on complying with a set of detailed regulations, and I cannot expect anything more from you.

However, the thesis that there is a necessary conflict between law and trust can be contested by considering that in various circumstances the law can provide us with reasons for relying upon others (whatever further reasons, moral or not, we have for such a reliance). In fact, even if we endorsed a strongly normative notion of trust—namely, if we required, for an expectation to be qualified as trust, that it have a moral component, or that it assume an altruistic attitude by the trustee—it would remain true that the truster must also: (a) predict that the trustee will behave according to truster's expectation and (b) accept the risk of being disappointed. In both regards, the law can contribute to the rational formation of a trust attitude. On the one hand, legal penalties increases the chance that the trustee behave according to the truster's expectations (by adding the threat of punishment to the internal motivations of the trustee and possibly also by appealing to an additional internal motivation of hers, namely, her endorsement of the obligation to comply with the law). On the other hand the law may diminish the expected losses of the disappointed truster (for instance, by providing the truster with compensation, or by enabling him to withdraw from a contract, as is the case in on-line sales, or by ensuring him the same result which he would have obtained if the trusted-to-happn situation had obtained).

In conclusion, the law can facilitate the choice to rely on one's counterpart, both by increasing the chance that reliance-based expectations are complied with and by diminishing the negative consequences of the violation of such expectations: by protecting the truster's expectations the law favours reliance (and thus it facilitates the formation of trust-based interactions).

---

[12] For the thesis that trust and law are mutually alternative, see for instance Fukuyama [4], 27, according to whom in invidualistic societies the legal system—that is, "a system of formal rules and regulations, which have to be negotiated, agreed to, litigated, and enforced, sometimes by coercive means"—substitutes trust, but this substitution entails high "transaction costs" (like the cost of drafting very detailed contracts, and of litigating them).

3   Reputation

Though trust can be based upon many different sources (social conventions, legal rules, professional ethics, the history of personal relationships, and so on), such sources are often unable to provide sufficient warrant: social rules are weak, especially between parties who are distant in space and culture (as in Internet contracts); legal proceedings are uncertain and costly, and they can entail negative consequences for those who start them; professional ethics give dubious indications, which are not always complied with; personal contacts may be superficial and unlikely to be repeated. In such cases rational reliance seems to require information about the individual counterpart one is interacting with, and in particular it may require reference to his or her social consideration, that is, to reputation. Such information may be useful, for instance, when we have to make an important purchase, of objects which are not familiar to us (a car, a financial product ...), to entrust a professional (a doctor, a lawyer ...) with a difficult and risky task, or to choose the counterpart with whom to execute an important contract.

By *reputation* we mean both the evaluative opinion that people (the public in general or certain sections of it) have of a particular person, and the social mechanism which produces such an opinion. One's reputation usually refers to specific attitudes and capacities, which may concern both one's capacity to adequately perform certain actions (for instance, the technical competence of a professional) and one's propensity to act thus, and to do so in an appropriate way (through cooperation, reciprocity, respect of existing conventions and of other people's interests). Reputation results from shared beliefs, which spread in a society as a consequence of complex social interactions: individuals form opinions concerning a certain person (on the basis of personal experience or of certain indexes), they convey such opinions (person X is ...) or their beliefs about others' opinions (it is said that person X is ...), these opinions and beliefs are adopted by others and further conveyed (see for instance Conte and Paolucci [12]).

The mechanism of reputation has a double social relevance.

Firstly, it provides a cognitive basis for our decisions to trust: we often choose to rely upon a certain person (and thus to face the risks which are entailed by our reliance and by our subsequent determinations), based on the positive reputation of this person. To the extent that reputation provides useful indications (to the extent that people having a good reputation actually tend to behave competently and properly), it appears to be an important mechanism of social cognition: as the invisible hand of the market assigns prices to things (beyond the usage-value they have for particular individuals), so the invisible judge of reputation confers its evaluation upon persons (beyond the view that the concerned person has of himself or herself, and beyond the opinion that any specific individual has of that person). The link between reputation and trust is particularly important in the global space of the Internet: in deciding whether to trust, for example, commercial partners with whom we never had contacts in the past (and with whom we are unlikely to have contacts in the future), we cannot rely on personal experience, but we must count on other people's experience or on the reputation which our partners enjoy. And we can perceive reputation through the judgments and evaluations of others, but also though computer technologies combining such judgments and evaluations. For instance, many e-commerce sites not only allow individual buyers to express their evaluations on products and vendors, but also combine individual evaluations in global ratings.

The second function of reputation we need to mention here is its ability to elicit certain actions, namely, those actions whose perception (by others) may determine the kind of reputation one desires (obviously, this my only happen when such actions can be detected by others, and when such detection, or the conclusions which are derived from it, can be communicated). In particular, a person having a positive reputation can be the object of others' reliance, and thus can be invited to enter those relationships (for instance, contracts) which are based upon reliance, and can obtain the benefits which ensue from such relationships. Thus one, in order to foster one's own positive reputation—namely, the reputation of being a subject capable and willing to behave in appropriate ways—may be induced to behave in such ways, and to do so consistently.

4   Privacy Versus Reputation-Based Trust

Privacy, as self-determination over one's own personal data, seems to conflict with reliance based upon reputation. In fact, an absolute right to self-determination over one's own data—enabling one to determine, according to one's own interests and choices, what information others can collect and process—seems to impair the correct formation of reputation: if one is the master of one's own personal information, one can block the circulation of all negative information regarding oneself. And if reliable reputation is not available, others will tend not to develop trust in the individuals concerned.[13]

The consideration of the connection between privacy, reliance, and reputation has led some authors to a very negative view of privacy. For instance, Richard Posner has affirmed that privacy does not deserve a specific legal protection:

> All that privacy means in the information context . . . is that people want to control what is known about them by other people. They want to conceal facts about themselves that are embarrassing or discreditable . . . Often this involves concealing information that would cause potential

---

[13] Enabling the circulation of relevant information not only is in the interest of candidate trusters, but is also in the interest of candidate trustees, since potential trusters will be more likely to trust when they believe to have sufficient information about their counterparts. Thus, allowing candidate trusters to access adequate information (or at least putatively adequate information) about candidate trustees is an advantage for all candidate trustees beforehand, as a prerequisite for being trusted upon, and thus as a prerequisite for doing business, though this can determine a disadvantage for some of them in retrospect, when a piece of negative personal information is propagated.

transacting partners to refuse to transact with them or to demand better terms as a condition of doing so. Such concealment is a species of fraud (Posner's blog 8 may 2005, see also Posner [13]).

According to this view, privacy—and in particular, the right to informational self-determination—gives a legal protection to deception (through selective disclosure). Non only is one allowed to abstain from communicating relevant facts about oneself (at least up to the point where silence violates good faith), but data protection prohibits others from collecting, processing and communicating such data, even if the data were obtained without the activity of the person concerned. Thus, privacy gives one the possibility to manipulate one's social image and consequently one's reputation, by blocking the circulation of negative data, even when such data are true.

The subject of the connection between privacy, deception and reputation is viewed in a similar way by Nock [14], who observes that trust is often based upon reputation, and that privacy impedes the formation of trust since it makes it more difficult to know the reputation of others, which is a precondition for relying upon strangers.[14]

On the view just presented, the right to information self-determination would impair the formation of a reliable reputation, and thus would impair the formation of reputation-based trust. Moreover, the legal protection of privacy would represent a paternalistic intervention which (as public intervention in the markets) threatens to impair the autonomous functioning of an impersonal social mechanism. Thus, privacy protection would have a double noxious effect: on the one had it would enable the individual to manipulate his or her social image, and on the other hand it would impede the autonomous formation of social opinions, on the basis of all available data.

The views which we have just presented can be countered with various objections (as presented, for instance, by Solove [16]).

First of all, as many authors have observed (like Rodotà [17]), privacy protection contributes to certain important legal values, which can outweigh the need to favour reliance: protecting freedom, intimacy, and dignity; ensuring the possibility to change and improve; preventing discriminations, and so on.

Secondly, we need to consider that the mechanism of reputation, despite having in principle a cognitive value, does not always work correctly. The legal issues we need to address with regard to the function of reputation are similar to the legal issues we have to face with regard to markets (and different lawyers will take very different attitudes according to their ideology and personal opinions): how to ensure the best functioning of a fundamental instrument of social cognition,[15] while avoiding that this mechanism, abandoned to itself, endangers individuals and communities, and also calls into question its own functioning.

---

[14] For further considerations on the costs of privacy, see for instance Walker [15].

[15] The market can indeed be viewed as a cognitive mechanism clustering into prices information about needs and production costs, thus ensuring an efficient deployment of resources (see for example Hayek [18]).

Just as monopolies, but also fraud and information distortion can impair the functioning of markets, so monopolies on the provision and circulation of information (for instance, in the media), but also the manipulation of information, can disturb the functioning of reputation.[16]

Moreover, reputation can often result from irrational attitudes. This happens when prejudice (stigmatisation) is present: from certain features of a person (belonging to an ethnic or racial group, having certain sexual orientations, having had certain diseases, holding certain religious or political views) we erroneously draw certain negative conclusions concerning other aspects of that person (capacity to work, competence, honesty, and so on), and thus we make choices which damage that person (for instance, denying him or her a job). Negative evaluations, then, spread in society exactly according to the mechanism of reputation (given that others have a negative opinion about a certain person, I too adopt such a negative opinion, and thus I contribute to creating the basis for other people to form a negative opinion about the same person). When prejudice and stigmatisation are present, reputation can fail as a cognitive mechanism. To prevent such failure or to diminish its impact, legal limitations on the free circulation of personal information may be opportune.

Also when prejudice is not at issue, the rationality of reputation can be endangered by the scarcity of the available time and by the necessity of forming opinions on the basis of limited data. The right to control one's personal data enables one to prevent misunderstandings that can be determined by access to partial information about oneself: one can limit access to one's data to those people who are able to put such data in context, thanks to a sufficient knowledge of oneself, or one can impose adequate ways of providing context for the data.

This problem is particularly pressing today, in the era of the so-called information overload.[17] Being unable to process all the information that is accessible to us, we end up evaluating others according to a casual or even biased selection of such information, for instance, according to a few top ranked documents we retrieve through a search engine. This may lead us to negative judgments (and consequent decisions) which would be unjustified on the basis of a larger body

---

[16] Posner's unconditioned acceptance of the mechanism of reputation is indeed related to his faith in the market. He rebuts the argument that the communication of certain private information (for instance, about ethnicity, political opinions, or sexual preferences) may determine odious discrimination, by observing that "in a diverse, decentralised and competitive society, irrational shunning will be weeded out over time" (Posner [13, 235]). This can be expected to happen because when one (for instance, an employer) discriminates one's counterpart (a potential employee) on the basis of aspects which are irrelevant to the counterpart's performance, one would sustain higher costs than one's competitors and would be pushed out of the market. For similar observations, see Von Mises [19].

[17] This aspect is emphasised by Rosen [20], who says that "[p]rivacy protects us from being misdefined and judged out of context in a world of short attention spans, a world in which information can easily be confused with knowledge."

of information.[18] Moreover, our inability to check the correctness of most of the information we retrieve may lead us to form our judgments on a certain person on the basis of erroneous or outdated information.

Thus, in some cases here is no conflict, but rather a useful synergy between informational self-determination and correct formation of reputation: the data subject—by correcting his or her data, supplementing them with further information, requiring an adequate form for their communication, or even excluding those who would be unable to understand the data (by putting the data in context)—can contribute to the correctness of his or her social image, and thus to the cognitive function of the process through which reputation is formed. In these cases, the individual interest in a positive reputation converges with the social interest in a reputation corresponding to fact.

However, in other cases, the individual interest in a positive reputation and the social interest in a cognitively correct reputation do not coincide: one tries to obtain positive reputation by giving false or partial information about oneself and by blocking the circulation of true information which would impair one's social image. Under such circumstances, the balancing of the conflicting interests can lead us to subordinate the individual interest to the social one (or rather to subordinate the interest of the data subject to the individual interests of his or her counterparts). In particular, the need to enable the correct formation of a reputation so as to favour reputation-based reliance plays a fundamental role both in the economy (when we need to rely on contractual counterparts) and in politics (where we need to rely on the persons who are entrusted with public tasks, and in particular on our political representatives).

Accordingly, the circulation of personal information has a significance that goes beyond those who need particular pieces of information, being involved in specific economic transactions or political debates. For instance, the circulation of information about politicians also advantages people who do not directly take part in debates and are unaware of specific facts, but only perceive the aggregate results (the reputation) that are associated with a certain politician. The same holds in the economic domain, with regard to professional abilities or financial conditions. Thus, there is a justification for collecting and circulating certain

---

[18] The Italian data-protection Authority (Garante per la la protezione dei dati) has recently decided a case related to information overload (see Newsletter 21-27 march 2005). The Italian Authority on competition and on markets (Autorità garante della concorrenza e del mercato) had made accessible on the Internet (where it was indexed by search engines) two old decisions where a particular company was punished for misleading advertising. That company claimed that its reputation had seriously, and unduly, been damaged, since such decisions were the first documents to come up whenever one made an Internet search using the name of the company. The data-protection Authority recognised that claim, ordering that old decisions of the Authority for competition and markets should be made publicly accessibly only through queries initiated within the site of that authority (not through general search engines).

kinds of personal data (besides concerns for freedom of speech),[19] namely, the need that informed evaluations be accomplished, and that a widespread social opinion (a reputation) emerge. The emergence of such an opinion can support reliance by individuals, but also may elicit the competent and correct behaviour of the person concerned, so as to prevent the formation of a negative reputation.

Obviously, our arguments supporting the circulation of certain personal data only apply to data which are relevant for determining whether to rely upon somebody in a specific domain, namely, data which are relevant for the assessment of the risks inhering in a particular relationship (information on the competence and financial solidity of a businessperson, the prudence and the honesty of a politician, and so on); such arguments cannot be extended to personal information having no possible impact on such risks.[20]

In other domains of human life, like those pertaining to affective relationship, sexual preferences, ethnic origins, political opinions (of a person who does not have, nor aims to have any public function) the protection of personal data is not limited by the need to enable the formation of reliance based upon reputation (or in any case based upon the knowledge of personal information which was not provided by the concerned person, nor directly obtained through interaction with such person or with people belonging to his or her milieu). In such domains, the right to informational self-determination can find a broader recognition and restrain others from processing, communicating and distributing one's personal data (at least when such operations take place in the framework of professional activities, or anyway in a large scale, for instance, through publication on a web site).

It seems that considerations pertaining to reputation and trust can contribute to provide a rationale for some aspects of data protection, offering some indications on how to explain, justify, and circumscribe the limitations of the right to informational self-determination.

No man is an island (as the poet John Donne said): on the one hand one interacts with the others, and decides whom to rely upon according to one's own personal experience, but also according to the social image and reputation of the others; on the other hand one develops one's own personality and morality by confronting one's social image, by matching one's actions with shared rules

---

[19] For reasons of space, and in order to focus on the idea of trust, I shall not address here the very important issue of the conflict between privacy and freedom of speech. This has the advantage of allowing me to avoid addressing the vast literature on freedom of speech (see for instance Sadurski [21]).

[20] According to Nagel [22], privacy protection should also include people having a public role, in particular through active involvement in politics. The fact that the public "feels entitled to know the most intimate details of the life of any public figure" impairs participation in the public sphere, since "[m]any people cannot take that kind of exposure": the fear of exposure to the public can induce a person having the best skills and qualities for a public office, but having held in the past some minor deviant behaviour (or even just presenting some eccentric trait), to withdraw in the private sphere, renouncing to engage in active politics. For a discussion of this thesis, and for bibliographical reference, see Solove [16, par. 4].

and judgments, and by linking one's views of oneself with one's reputation.[21] This is, however, a very delicate dialectical interaction between individual and community, an interaction that usually works properly only within the restricted circle of the persons having frequent and direct contacts with the individual in question. Within this circle one can effectively contribute to the formation of one's social image, though not having the power of unilaterally determining it (not even by imposing silence over the aspects of one's personality which could have a negative impact on one's reputation): the person in question by correcting possible misunderstanding, or offering his or her reasons, has a fair chance to induce his or her partners to reconsider their opinions. Beyond such circle, on the contrary, the burden to take care of one's social image, in all its aspects, even the most intimate ones, risks becoming unbearable, especially when one does not have the means for intervening efficaciously. Such a burden is much heavier today, when each personal datum can be eternally preserved in electronic memories and can be made accessible to everybody over the World Wide Web.

Finally, we need to observe that informational self-determination, while being an obstacle to reputation-based trust, can favour reliance in a different respect, that is, by diminishing the risks which are related to certain social contacts. If one has no control over one's personal data, one must add to the risks inherent in a certain social relationship (for instance, the risk that a physician should behave negligently or incompetently) a further risk: the possible damage deriving from the improper use or transmission of personal data. An effective protection of privacy reduces such risks and thus facilitates reliance by the person who must provide personal data in order to start a certain interaction. Consequently, it may facilitate the choice to establish such an interaction (for instance, the choice to let oneself be cured for a illness which carries a serious social stigma).

5 Conclusion

In the present paper I have only sketched some provisional ideas on the connection between privacy (as informational self-determination). on the one hand, and trust and reputation, on the other hand. It seems to me that this line of inquiry deserves to be developed further, in order that we can better understand the impact of data protection on social relationships, and can provide legal solutions duly taking into account all the interests at stake.

---

[21] From this viewpoint, gossip seems to play a positive social function (though individual freedom may be impaired by social sanctions against deviating behaviour, an aspect stressed already by Mill [23]). More generally, gossip may be beneficial to individual autonomy since it provides us with information on the "experiments of living" of others (to use an expression of Mill [23]), from which we can draw indications for our own choices. For some considerations on the value of gossip, see Zimmw[24], who argues against upholding the "public disclosure" tort in US law, a tort, which, following the suggestion of [25], gives one a cause of action when another widely discloses one's private matter that is "highly offensive to a reasonable person" and "is not of legitimate concern to the public." On the merit of gossip, as pertaining to the exercise of freedom of speech, see recently [26].

References

1. Westin, A.: Privacy and Freedom. Athenaum, New York (1967)
2. Bing, J.: Data protection in a time of change. In Altes, W.F.K., Dommering, E.J., Hugenholtz, P.B., Kabel, J.J.C., eds.: Data Protection. Kluwer, Dordrecht (1992) 247–59
3. Lessig, L.: Code and Other Laws of Cyberspace. Basic, New York, N. Y. (1999)
4. Fukuyama, F.: Trust. Free Press, New York (1995)
5. Herzberg, L.: On the attitude of trust. Inquiry **31** (1988) 307–22
6. Baier, A.: Trust and antitrust. Ethics **96** (1986) 131–60
7. Harding, R.: Trusting persons, trusting institutions. In: Strategy and Choice. Cambridge, Mass., Cambridge, Mass. (1991) 185–209
8. Castelfranchi, C., Falcone, R.: Socio-cognitive theory of trust. In Pitt, J., ed.: Open Agent Societies: Normative Specifications in Multi-Agent Systems. Wiley, London (2005)
9. Gambetta, D.: Trust. Basil Blackwell, Oxford (1990)
10. Luhmann, N.: Familiarity, confidence, trust: Problems and alternatives. In: Trust: Making and Breaking Cooperative Relations. Oxford University Press, Oxford (1988) 4–107
11. Memmo, D., Sartor, G., Quadri, G.: Trust, reliance, good faith and the law. In Nixon, P., Terzis, S., eds.: Trust Management and the law: Proceedings of the First International Conference on Trust Management. Springer, Berlin (2003) 150–64
12. Conte, R., Paolucci, M.: Reputation in Artificial Societies: Social Beliefs for Social Order. Kluwer, Dordrecht (2003)
13. Posner, R.A.: Privacy and related interests. In: The Economics of Justice. Harvard University Press, Cambridge, Mass. (1983) 229–347
14. Nock, S.L.: The Costs of Privacy: Surveillance and Reputation in America. Aldine, New York (1993)
15. Walker, K.: Where everybody knows your name: A pragmatic look at the costs of privacy and the benefits of information exchange. Stanford Technology Law Review (2000) (http://stlr.stanford.edu/STLR/Articles/00_STLR_2)
16. Solove, D.J.: The virtues of knowing less: Justifying privacy protections against disclosure. Duke Law Journal **53** (2004) 967
17. Rodotà, S.: Tecnologie e diritti. Il Mulino, Bologna (1995)
18. Hayek, F.A.: Law, Legislation and Liberty. Volume I: Rules and Order. Routledge, London (1973)
19. Von Mises, L.: Liberalism: In the Classical Tradition. Cobden, San Francisco, Cal. (1985) (1st Ed. 1927).
20. Rosen, J.: The Unwanted Gaze: The Destruction of Privacy in America. Random House, New York, N. Y. (2000)
21. Sadurski, W.: Freedom of Speach and Its Limits. Kluwer, Dordrecht (1999)
22. Nagel, T.: Concealment and exposure. Philosophy & Public Affairs **27** (1998) 3–30
23. Mill, J.S.: On Liberty. Penguin, Harmondsworth (1974) (1st ed. 1859.).
24. Zimmerman, D.L.: Requiem for a heavyweight: A farewell to warren and brandeis's privacy tort. Conrnell Law Review **68** (1983) 291
25. Warren, S., Brandeis, L.: The right to privacy. Harvard Law Review **4** (1890) 193–220
26. Baker, C.E.: Autonomy and informational privacy, or gossip: The central meaning of the first amendment. Social Philosophy and Public Policy **21** (2004) 215–68

A Reputation-Based System for Confidentiality Modeling in Peer-to-Peer Networks

Christoph Sorge and Martina Zitterbart

Institute of Telematics, Universität Karlsruhe (TH),
Karlsruhe, Germany
{sorge, zit}@tm.uka.de

Abstract. The secure transmission of messages via computer networks is, in many scenarios, considered to be a solved problem. However, a related problem, being almost as crucial, has been widely ignored: To whom to entrust information? We argue that confidentiality modeling is a question of trust. Therefore, the article at hand addresses this problem based on a reputation system. We consider a Peer-to-Peer network whose participants decide on whether or not to make information available to other nodes based on the author's trust relationships. Documents are only forwarded to another node if, according to the sender's local view, the recipient is considered to be sufficiently trustworthy. In contrast to most existing reputation systems, trust relationships are considered only with respect to a specific domain. Privacy is preserved by limiting the revelation of trust relationships.

1 Introduction

Peer-to-Peer networks are widely used for the exchange of all kinds of information. In networks like Gnutella [17] and Kazaa [13], every user can potentially access any file or document available. Even without security mechanisms in the P2P network, it is still possible to distribute documents securely, i.e. to make them accessible for their authorized readers only by simply encrypting the documents themselves.

In general, we can assume this problem—securely transmitting information to a known entity—to be solved by cryptography. A different problem, however, remains: How does Alice know which information she wants to entrust to Bob? This is not a problem of security, but of trust. There is a number of scenarios in which the answer is not obvious. For example, Alice wants to ask for advice about an illness she has, but she does not want her boss to know about this illness. Or Alice might be looking for a restaurant recommendation, which could be greatly improved if she provided information about her food preferences. But she might not be willing to provide that information to everyone. She has to trust the person she gives the information to.

In peer-to-peer networks, the situation can get even worse. Alice may submit a document to the network without even knowing who the recipient will be. At

K. Stølen et al. (Eds.): iTrust 2006, LNCS 3986, pp. 367–381, 2006.

the time someone wants to access the information, Alice may not be connected to the network. Therefore, other (trusted) entities must be able to decide on Alice's behalf. This article gives a model that could facilitate this decision, while preserving the privacy of Alice's trust relationships when possible. We call the resulting approach the REBCON (*R*eputation-*B*ased *Con*fidentiality Modeling) system.

1.1 Trust and Reputation Systems

Trust has been defined as a "generalized expectation that an advance effort is not exploited" [5, p. 73. Translation by the author.]. Trust is a three place relationship: A(lice) trusts B(ob) to do Z. [10, p. 15918] This means that trust depends on the kind of the "advance effort", or, speaking more generally, on the domain[1] of the relationship. You might, for example, trust your doctor with respect to health questions, but not financial issues.

Trust is established over time; in case of a one-time or first-time contact, there is (at first glance) no reason to trust. *Reputation* can solve this problem by allowing the interpersonal transfer of trust. Abdul-Rahman and Hailes [2] define reputation as "an expectation about an agent's behaviour based on information about or observations of its past behaviour." These observations can be made by the person considering to establish a trust relationship or (considered in the following) by third parties.

A common way of establishing trust on the internet is to use *reputation systems*. They can be defined as systems which provide information used to enable the assessment of an entity's trustworthiness, or reputation. By sharing views on a person's reputation, reputation systems enable the transfer of trust in a decentralized manner. The term "decentralized" only refers to the trust model (there is not just one single trust anchor). The storage and management of reputation can still be done on a central server.

Resnick et al. [16] state that "a reputation system collects, distributes, and aggregates feedback about participants' past behavior." In summary, reputation systems serve to the creation of trust in their participants and other entities, based on the asumption that entities who behaved well in the past will also do so in the future.

While most reputation systems try to compute a global reputation value for each entity, this would be inappropriate for the task at hand: The decision with whom to share information is highly personal and subjective. Even if a large part of the community believes someone to be trustworthy, you may have good reasons not to do so. While this is not a problem e.g. in the file-sharing scenario, in which most people agree on the properties desirable for a transaction partner, you may not want to give someone an information because many other people (most of which you do not know) trust that person. Moreover, the decision is domain-dependent: Though you may be willing to share your reading preferences with your bookseller, you might not want to entrust him medical information about yourself.

---

[1] Also referred to as *context*.

Why could you be willing to entrust information to someone else? Firstly, you could have own experience with that other person. Secondly, you may have friends (i.e. persons you trust) who have told you that they trust that person. Systems that model these properties of trust already exist, the most prominent one being the PGP web of trust [1]. Its scope is, however, quite limited: The purpose is to create trust in the authenticity of public keys.

This article suggests to use a reputation system based on the web of trust as a confidentiality model. In comparison to the PGP web of trust, several adaptations are necessary to model the domain-dependence of trust. Additionally, transitivity of trust (which is defined in the PGP trust model, but hardly used in practice) is modeled differently.

1.2 The Need for Privacy

The aim of data privacy regulations worldwide is the protection of informational self-determination. This term is especially used referring to German constitutional law, in which informational self-determination is a base right; however, the concept is a general one. It has been described in [20]: "Privacy is the claim of individuals, groups or institutions to determine for themselves when, how, and to what extent information about them is communicated to others".

In other words, privacy means that an individual can decide which information he or she is willing to reveal to others, and who these others are. The REBCON system gives technical support for this decision by implementing a simple trust model.

1.3 Outline

The next section gives an overview on related work. Measurements of trust and confidentiality, being a precondition for the proposed system, are briefly discussed in section 3. Section 4 describes the basic idea of a confidentiality-modeling reputation system, including requirements and assumptions needed for the system to work. In section 5, the system design is presented. Section 6 analyzes to what extent the requirements are fulfilled. The article is concluded in section 7.

2 Related Work

While peer-to-peer reputation systems have only been discussed in the recent years, the topic of trust is older. From a sociological perspective, it has been discussed (among others) in [6]. In [14], the formalization of trust is dealt with from a computer science point of view.

Existing reputation systems, including their flaws, have been described in a number of articles. Good introductions to the topic are given in [16] and, including a survey on other factors influencing trust, in [3].

Systems like the eBay reputation system [15] are based on a central server that manages the trust ratings given by their users. Yet, the centralized approach is vulnerable to manipulation by the server's operator, and it is less robust than a decentralized system can potentially be.

The different quality of contents distributed in peer-to-peer networks has been a major motivation for systems enabling distributed reputation management. The Credence system [19] is an example of such a system, specifically designed for filesharing networks. [11] describes the EigenTrust algorithm used to securely compute a unique global trust value for an entity in a distributed fashion. Similarly, [9] suggests an architecture for a partially distributed reputation system.

Most reputation systems do not model transitive trust.[2] Limited transitive trust has, however, been implemented in the PGP web of trust [1]. Yet, the scope of the PGP system is restricted to one application: It is only used to establish the authenticity of a public key used in asymmetric cryptography. Attempts to generalize the web of trust idea, using transitive trust in reputation systems, can be found in [8] and [2].

Only few reputation systems do, however, attempt to model the domain-dependence of trust, among them [2]. [21], too, describes a reputation system whose scope is not limited to a single domain like file-sharing or electronic commerce, but does not model domain-dependence explicitly.

While a number of applications for peer-to-peer reputation systems have been discussed in literature, the authors are not aware of an approach that uses trust or reputation for confidentiality modeling in peer-to-peer systems, as it is done in this article.

3   Measurements of Trust and Confidentiality

In order to assign trust values to other entities, some kind of trust measurement is required. However, measuring trust is not a trivial task. One approach is to use a monetary measurement: The level of trust you have in a person is given by the amount of money you are willing to entrust to that person. This measurement has been used in empirical research [7]. However, monetary equivalents cannot be used in all trust domains, as their determination will often be difficult.

An alternative is to use a trust scale without a concrete meaning or real-world equivalent. This approach has been used in the PGP trust model: A person can be trusted "fully" or "marginally" or considered "untrustworthy", but no explicit meaning is assigned to these terms [1]. The same is true for a number of reputation systems, often using a scale from 0 to 1 [12], [11]. This approach does not seem to be satisfactory, as the semantics of a certain trust assessment may differ between users. However, there is no better solution available. The problem may be reduced by assigning labels to certain values of the numerical range. For example, the label "completely untrusted" may be assigned to *0*; *0.3* might mean "only unimportant information may be entrusted to this person", and so forth. This approach provides an orientation for assigning trust values. In [14, section 2.3], the use of numerical values as a trust scale is discussed in greater depth.

---

[2] Still, transitive trust can exist implicitly.

For the article at hand, the relationship of trust and confidentiality plays an important role: We focus on determining who should have access to certain types of confidential information. In other words, we define a model that helps to decide whether to entrust confidential information to others, based on a measurement of confidentiality. But is there such a measurement?

In the network security community, confidentiality has been defined as "the protection of transmitted data from passive attacks" [18]. This definition does not leave room for a measurement of confidentiality. However, such a measurement is necessary: There is information that you would not give to anybody. But there is also information that you entrust to some close friends—or even to your colleagues at work. Still, the information can be confidential, as you would not like to read it in a newspaper. To explain this differentiation, a notion of "more confidential" or "less confidential" can be helpful. The concept of trust can help to come to such a notion: Entrusting information to someone usually means that you trust this person—there are exceptions (you may be forced to give the information away, or may feel obliged to do so), but in general, that relation between trust and confidentiality holds. The more confidential an information is, the more trust in the recipient must the author have if he or she entrusts that information to the recipient.

The confidentiality level of a piece of information can therefore be defined as the extent of trust the author must have in another person before willing to entrust the information to that person. This way, confidentiality can be measured on the same scale as trust.

4   Basic Idea of a Confidentiality-Modeling Reputation System

The aim of REBCON system is to protect the confidentiality of information (represented in documents); only persons who are sufficiently trustworthy should be able to access a document. For this purpose, each user classifies his documents into distinct domains (this can be done semi-automatically) and rates their confidentiality. Similarly to the PGP web of trust, the reputation system requires a user to perform two trust assessments with respect to at least one other person. A user A has to decide to which degree he or she trusts another user B both with respect to a certain domain, i.e. up to which confidentiality level he or she is willing to send documents to B, and as a trust introducer (transitive trust).

4.1   Terminology and Concepts Used

The following notation is used to describe the local view on a trust relationship. The term *node* instead of *user* is used in order to clarify that decisions are made by a network participant, but not necessarily by a human user:

$T_A^D(B, C)$ Node B's trust in node C with respect to domain D, as seen by node A.
$I^D(B, C)$ Node B's trust in node C as a trust introducer, i.e. the extent to which B trusts C to assess other users' trustworthiness, in the domain D.

$Conf(Z)$ Confidentiality level of document Z. Each document belongs to a certain domain D.

All values T, I, and $Conf$ must be in the interval $[0; 1]$.

Depending on the confidentiality level of a document Z and the trust its author has in a potential recipient B, each participant can decide whether or not to send the document Z to B.

Assigning different trust introducer ratings for each domain may be a complex task for a user. As a simplification, node B could assign a general trust introducer rating $I(B, C)$ to node C. The domain-specific value $I^D(B, C)$ would then be computed by multiplying the general trust introducer rating with the domain-specific trust in C: $I^D(B, C) = I(B, C) \cdot T_B^D(B, C)$. However, this is a local decision, and B could choose to determine trust introducer ratings in a different way.

Note that the confidentiality of a document is not modeled as being domain-dependent. As a consequence, a piece of information may only be assigned one domain. In reality, information can belong to several domains. For example, the amount of money you spend on pharmaceuticals is an information that belongs to the financial as well as the medical domain. Maybe you are reluctant to give this information to your financial advisors (high confidentiality rating in the finance domain), but do not care whether your doctor gets the information (low confidentiality rating in the medical domain). The REBCON system could easily be extended to allow for information that belongs to multiple domains. Yet, in the interest of a clear presentation of the protocol, we omit this extension.

The idea of the REBCON system is to give each node in the network as much information on trust relationships as necessary in order to decide whether it can forward a piece of information (i.e. whether the author of the information trusts the intended recipient sufficiently). Forwarding a document belonging to a domain D is only allowed if the document's confidentiality rating is below the author's trust in the intended recipient. The author is not necessarily available for this decision; therefore, a trust model must allow other nodes to decide for him or her. However, information about the author's (and other nodes') trust relationships should not be revealed unless necessary for this decision. Section 5 explains in greater detail how this is done.

4.2 Requirements

Taking the basic idea (pointed out above) as a starting point, we have identified a number of requirements:

- *(R1) A document may only be forwarded to a node B, if (from the forwarding node A's point of view) the trust of the document's author C in B (with respect to the domain D of the document Z) is at least equal to the confidentiality rating of the document:* $T_A^D(C, B) \geq Conf(Z)$.
  The first requirement describes the foundation of the protocol.
- *(R2) For privacy reasons, it should not be possible to find out to what extent other people trust a node without prior contact to that node.*

In most existing reputation systems and related approaches, including the PGP web of trust, trust relations are visible to the public. Therefore, one might argue that hiding trust relations is unnecessary. However, in a protocol whose main target is to preserve privacy, it makes sense to also hide this information, when possible. For example, you may not want your boss to find out that you trust your co-workers more than her.

- *(R3) A node M cannot choose $T_M^D(B, C)$ higher than allowed by B without being detected.*

  Otherwise, a malicious node M could forward B's documents to the not sufficiently trusted node C and also convince other (even obedient) nodes to do so without having to fear any sanctions.

- *(R4) Multiple identities do not lead to an advantage for a malicious node.*

  This means the system is immune to the Sybil attack (the increase of a reputation value by creating multiple identities [4]).

- *(R5) A node can change its trust assessments with respect to other nodes at any time.*

  Trust relations change over time; particularly, trust may be lost quickly.

- *(R6) The system should not require constant availability of its participants.*

  In typical Peer-to-Peer networks, it is not realistic to assume all nodes to be available at all times.

With these requirements, we have focused on privacy and security aspects. Other properties may be desirable, but are not the focus of this work. The list of requirements should not be considered to be complete; instead, it represents the aspects considered most relevant by the authors.

4.3   Assumptions

The REBCON system relies on several assumptions:

- (A1) Indirect trust relationships are built upon direct ones. This requires at least a certain extent of transitive trust.
- (A2) There must be a way to create the above-mentioned direct trust relationships. This requires long-living identities of the system participants. These identities need not be mapped to real-world identities.
- (A3) No positive direct trust values may be assigned to newcomers in the system, or it must be difficult to create new identities (e.g. by mapping them to real-world identities using pseudonyms that can be uncovered by a trusted entity). This means that there is no direct trust in new participants at all, or they have to make an effort to gain trust. This assumption is necessary to fulfill requirement R4.
- (A4) A public key infrastructure is needed to enable asymmetric encryption of documents. The design of this public key infrastructure may also be the basis for fulfilling the assumptions A2 and A3.

5   System Design

We begin our explanation of the REBCON system by giving a simple example of (transitive) trust relationships. Afterwards, the protocol is described in more detail.

5.1   Example

This section gives an example of the results of trust assessments in the REBCON system (see figure 1).

Alice gives Bob a trust value of 0.3 in the domain "nutrition" (N) and a general trust introducer rating of 0.7. From this, Alice computes a domain-specific trust introducer rating of 0.21 for Bob.

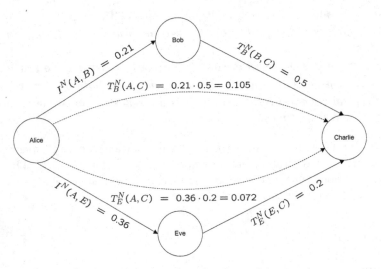

Fig. 1. A simple example of transitive trust

$$I^N(A, B) = 0.21$$

Bob gives Charlie a trust value of 0.5 in the domain "nutrition".

$$T_B^N(B, C) = 0.5$$

From Bob's point of view, this means that

$$T_B^N(A, C) = I^N(A, B) \cdot T_B^N(B, C) = 0.21 \cdot 0.5 = 0.105$$

In the next step, Alice gives Eve a trust value of 0.4 in the domain "nutrition" (N) and a general trust introducer rating of 0.9, leading to a trust value of 0.36 as a trust introducer in the "nutrition" domain.

$$I^N(A, E) = 0.36$$

Eve trusts Charlie in the domain "nutrition" with 0.2.

$$T_E^N(E, C) = 0.2$$

That means that from Eve's point of view, the following holds:

$$T_E^N(A, C) = I^N(A, E) \cdot T_E^N(E, C) = 0.36 \cdot 0.2 = 0.072$$

Therefore, Eve could forward a document in the "nutrition" domain created by Alice to Charlie only if its confidentiality rating is below 0.072. Given Bob's assessment, the document could be forwarded to Charlie up to a confidentiality rating of 0.105. This could even be done by Eve, if she is aware of Bob's assessment.

The example makes clear that a precondition for the REBCON system design is the existence of some direct trust relationship among its participants. On the one hand, this refers to the trust domain itself, on the other hand, it concerns the trust in an entity as a trust introducer.

Whenever a document is sent to another node, the information about the author's trust relationships to other nodes—as depicted in the example—is attached to it. The recipient gets to know his or her rating as a trust introducer I. Any further information about trust assessments is encrypted with the public key of the entities assessed. Therefore, the sender is not required to reveal more about his trust relationships than necessary for checking whether a recipient is sufficiently trusted; not even the node receiving the document can read the information.

5.2   Trust Formation

As a first step, it is important for each node A to choose and locally save the values $T_A^D(A, B)$ and $I^D(A, B)$ for at least one node B. There may be various reasons for trusting a node. Personal acquaintances are not necessary. For example, you may assign a positive initial trust value to all nodes whose IP addresses belong to the company you work at, or (using certificates) to all nodes whose identity has been checked by a trusted third party. Moreover, an existing reputation system can serve as a basis for assigning initial trust values.

5.3   Transmission of a Document

This section describes the protocol to be followed when transmitting a document. At first, we consider the transmission by the author himself. As a second step, we describe the determination of trust values by other entities forwarding a document.

Submission by the Author. When creating a document Z, user A assesses its confidentiality Conf(Z), with $0 \leq Conf(Z) \leq 1$. Besides, he or she chooses a domain D to which the document belongs.

If a document created by A is to be sent by user A to another user B, node A will check whether $T_A^D(A, B) \geq Conf(Z)$. If this is not the case, the transmission must not take place.

If the transmission is possible, A sends the following information to B ($E_B(X)$ means X, encrypted with B's public key; $S_A(X)$ means X, signed by A. All signatures include a timestamp; for clarity, timestamps are not listed separately in the following sections.):

- $S_A(Z, Conf(Z))$
  i.e. the signed document and its confidentiality rating.
- $S_A(I^D(A, B))$
  i.e. the extent to which A trusts B as a trust introducer. This enables A to adjust the degree of transitivity of trust.
- For each user U, for whom $T_A^D(A, U) \geq Conf(Z)$ (this includes B) :
  - $E_U(S_A(T_A^D(A, U)))$
    Sending A's trust relationships along allows other nodes to compute trust levels on behalf of A. However, they are encrypted with the respective trusted node's public key. This means that B cannot reveal to what extent A trusts another node without participation of that node: B can only read one entry of this vector. Though sending this information along causes considerable protocol overhead, we have chosen not to store it on a central server, as this would violate the Peer-to-Peer paradigm and introduce a single point of failure. Considering the typical number of trust relations in other trust networks (like the PGP web of trust), it seems reasonable to assume that A will have a few dozen trust relations per domain at maximum. We believe the resulting message size to still be tractable.

Additionally, all the information sent to B is encrypted with B's public key.

Forwarding a Document: The Second Step. If B now wants to forward the document Z to user F, he also has to check whether F is sufficiently trusted, i.e. whether $T_B^D(A, F) \geq Conf(Z)$. B determines $T_B^D(A, F)$ in one of the following ways:

- The value may be cached from previous contacts.
- Given $I^D(A, B)$ and $T_B^D(B, F)$, B sets $T_B^D(A, F) = I^D(A, B) \cdot T_B^D(B, F)$.
- If B has information about trust assessments performed by other nodes, B can compute a trust path from A to F, using the assumption that $\forall X, Y, Z$: $T_X^D(Y, Z) = I^D(Y, X) \cdot T_X^D(X, Z)$, i.e. X's trust in Z is discounted due to Y's limited trust in X as a trust introducer. If more than one trust path is found, the maximum trust value is used.

Querying for Higher Trust Values. However, if B does not yet trust F sufficiently, i.e. if $T_B^D(A, F) < Conf(Z)$, B must first get to know whether part of the encrypted trust information (not readable by him) he received justifies a different assessment:

B sends the vector $(E_U(S_A(T_A^D(A,U))))$ (where U represents the entities assessed, who are not known to B) received by A to F *prior* to forwarding the document Z.

If one of the entries can be decrypted with F's private key (i.e. it contains a trust assessment of F), F decrypts this entry $S_A(T_A^D(A,F))$ and sends it back to B, encrypted with B's public key.[3] This proves to what extent A trusts F.

B saves $T_A^D(A,F)$. B repeats the determination of $T_B^D(A,F)$. If this value is now greater than Conf(Z), the further transmission can be done in the same manner as if B had been able to establish the trust relationship to F himself.

Information Sent by B. Additional to his own trust assessments, B has to prove that his possession of the document is justified: If it was not, F could uncover B as a malicious node and forbear from distributing the document any further. Therefore, B sends to F:

- $S_B(S_A(Z,Conf(Z))$
  i.e. the signed document and its confidentiality rating.
- $S_B(S_A(I^D(A,B)))$
  i.e. A's trust in B as a trust introducer.
- $S_B(S_A(T_A^D(A,B)))$
  i.e. A's trust in B with respect to the domain D.
- For each user U (with the exception of B), for whom B has received a trust assessment from A:
  - $E_U(S_A(T_A^D(A,U)))$
- For each user U for whom $I^D(A,B)\cdot T_B^D(A,U) \geq Conf(Z)$ (this includes F) :
  - $E_U(S_B(T_B^D(A,U)))$

Additionally, all the information sent to F is encrypted with F's public key.

The second and the third item make traceable why B is entitled to possess and to forward the document Z.

Further Steps. Any further communication steps can be performed analogously: Every time a document is supposed to be forwarded, the sender checks if the trust information he or she has justifies that. If it does not, the sender asks the recipient to decrypt encrypted trust information that possibly refers to the recipient. In case the document can be sent, the sender also proves that his or her own possession of the document was justified.

In general, each forwarding of a document by a user includes

- The document and its confidentiality assessment, signed by the original author.
- The chain of all trust introducer assessments from the original author to the node forwarding the document, including the signatures of all nodes being part of that chain.

---

[3] Alternatively, F could choose not to answer, e.g. if F does not want to reveal to what extent A trusts him.

- The chain of all domain-specific trust assessments from the original author to the node forwarding the document, including the signatures of all nodes being part of that chain.
- All trust assessments received by the forwarding node, encrypted with the assessed nodes' public keys.
- The forwarding node's own trust assessments, encrypted with the assessed nodes' public keys.

5.4   Changing Trust Assessments

If the trust by one node in another node changes or a pre-defined time span after their creation has passed, cached trust values have to be overwritten. When the first document after the change is sent, message contents remain the same. In the vector $E_U(S_A(T_A^D(A,U)))$, as sent by node A, the respective entry is marked as updated. The new trust value, however, will not be uncovered. All trust assessments made by A are cleared from the cache of all users who receive the updated vector. If a node F receives the vector $E_U(S_A(T_A^D(A,U)))$ and is asked to uncover the trust value $T_A^D(A,U)$, it may still reply with the old value. However, as the signatures used include timestamps, this fraud can be detected.

Note that this procedure will not securely prevent the further distribution of old documents to now untrusted entities: There is a chance that the updated trust information does not reach a node in time before it forwards a document.

6   Security Analysis and Fulfillment of Requirements

This section explains to what extent the requirements described in section 4.2 are fulfilled by the system.

- (R1) A document may only be forwarded to a node B, if (from the forwarding node A's point of view) the trust of the document's author C in B (with respect to the domain D of the document Z) is at least equal to the confidentiality rating of the document: $T_A^D(C,B) \geq Conf(Z)$.

   If the forwarding node is obedient, the fulfillment of this requirement is granted: The protocol makes all information available which is necessary to check the condition. Depending on the application scenario, inadvertent disclosure may occur—this is the case if the information is to be read by a human user and not just to be processed by his computer system. User interface design can help reminding a user of the confidentiality of an information; e.g. the accidental creation of digital copies can be prevented.

   If the forwarding node is malicious, the system can only make sure that the recipient can detect the protocol violation. The recipient can check the signature of the document's confidentiality rating and reconstruct his or her own trust rating. Yet, if a malicious node pretends to be the author of the protected document, replacing the original signature with its own, unauthorized forwarding cannot be detected. However, the existence of two identical documents from different authors may lead to uncovering of the malicious behavior. Watermarking may also be helpful, but is not considered in this article.

Note that one single node receiving a confidential document turns out not to be trustworthy, the out-of-band disclosure of information cannot be prevented; therefore, the underlying trust relations have to be reliable.

– *(R2) For privacy reasons, it should not be possible to find out to what extent other people trust a node without prior contact to that node.*

This is achieved by encryption of the trust assessments; only the trusted person can decrypt them. An attacker M could attempt to deceive the trusted node C by requesting the decryption of trust assessments using the identity of a different node B. However, C will encrypt these trust assessments with B's public key; therefore, even M's active attack will fail.

– *(R3) A node M cannot choose $T_M^D(B, C)$ higher than allowed by B without being detected.*

To achieve this, M must make available to the recipient all (signed) information which allow to reconstruct why he or she is entitled to possess the document and to forward it to the recipient.

– *(R4) Multiple identities do not lead to an advantage for a malicious node.*

As long as no participant from outside the group generated by the malicious node trusts a member of this group, no documents will be sent to the group. Multiple identities allow for the creation of longer trust paths, and of more trust paths. However, longer trust paths only lead to reduced trust; additional trust paths have no effect, as only the one leading to maximal trust will be considered. While the protocol design does not give users with multiple identities an advantage concerning the transitive trust relations, assumption A3 is needed to ensure the same for the underlying direct trust relations.

– *(R5) A node can change its trust assessments with respect to other nodes at any time.*

The procedure for the change of trust assessments is described in section 5.4.

– *(R6) The system should not require constant availability of its participants.*

The system does not require longer-lasting communication connections than necessary for the document distribution itself: All communication is performed only directly prior to the transfer of a document.

7   Conclusion

This article describes the REBCON system used for confidentiality modeling. It allows users in a Peer-to-Peer network to limit the distribution of documents to nodes considered trustworthy. The system cannot prevent trusted nodes from distributing the documents over channels outside the systems. Even inside the system, this unauthorized forwarding is detectable (as long as the original author information is not removed), but cannot be prevented.

However, the system can make information available that allows obedient nodes to judge the trustworthiness of other nodes, and to decide whether the creator of a document would agree to its distribution to certain nodes. Privacy is preserved by revealing trust relationships only with the consent of the entities whose trustworthiness is assessed.

Acknowledgements

This article has been made possible by funding from the *Graduate School Information Management and Market Engineering* of the Deutsche Forschungsgemeinschaft (German Research Foundation). The authors would also like to thank Lars Völker and Artus Krohn-Grimberghe for proofreading previous versions of this article, and their anonymous reviewers for valuable suggestions.

References

1. A. Abdul-Rahman. The PGP Trust Model. *EDI Forum: The Journal of Electronic Commerce*, April 1997.
2. A. Abdul-Rahman and S. Hailes. Supporting trust in virtual communities. In *HICSS '00: Proceedings of the 33rd Hawaii International Conference on System Sciences-Volume 6*, page 6007, Washington, DC, USA, 2000. IEEE Computer Society.
3. M. Daignault, M. Shepherd, S. Marche, and CarolynWatters. Enabling trust online. In *Proceedings of the 3rd International Symposium on Electronic Commerce*, pages 3–12. IEEE, 2002.
4. J. R. Douceur. The sybil attack. In P. Druschel, F. Kaashoek, and A. Rowstron, editors, *Peer-to-Peer Systems: First International Workshop. Revised Papers.*, volume 2429 of *Lecture Notes in Computer Science*, 2002.
5. H. Esser. *Institutionen*, volume 5 of *Soziologie: Spezielle Grundlagen*. Campus Verlag, Frankfurt/New York, 2000.
6. D. Gambetta, editor. *Can We Trust Trust?* Basil Blackwell, 1988.
7. E. L. Glaeser, D. I. Laibson, J. A. Scheinkman, and C. L. Soutter. Measuring trust. *The Quarterly Journal of Economics*, 115(3):811–846, 2000.
8. R. Guha, R. Kumar, P. Raghavan, and A. Tomkins. Propagation of trust and distrust. In *WWW '04: Proceedings of the 13th international conference on WorldWide Web*, pages 403–412, New York, NY, USA, 2004. ACM Press.
9. M. Gupta, P. Judge, and M. Ammar. A reputation system for peer-to-peer networks. In *NOSSDAV '03: Proceedings of the 13th international workshop on Networkand operating systems support for digital audio and video*, pages 144–152, New York, NY, USA, 2003. ACM Press.
10. K. Jones. *International Encyclopedia of the Social and Behavioral Sciences*, volume 23, chapter Trust: Philosophical Aspects, pages 15917–15922. Elsevier, Amsterdam, Paris, New York, 2001.
11. S. D. Kamvar, M. T. Schlosser, and H. Garcia-Molina. The Eigentrust algorithm for reputation management in P2P networks. In *WWW '03: Proceedings of the 12th international conference on WorldWide Web*, pages 640–651, New York, NY, USA, 2003. ACM Press.

12. M. Kinateder and S. Pearson. A Privacy-Enhanced Peer-to-Peer Reputation System. In K. Bauknecht, A. M. Tjoa, and G. Quirchmayr, editors, *Proceedings of the 4th International Conference on Electronic Commerce and Web Technologies (EC-Web 2003)*, volume 2738 of *LNCS*, pages 206–215, Prague, Czech Republic, Sept. 2003. Springer-Verlag.

13. N. Leibowitz, M. Ripeanu, and A. Wierzbicki. Deconstructing the kazaa network. In *WIAPP '03: Proceedings of the The Third IEEE Workshop on Internet Applications*, page 112, Washington, DC, USA, 2003. IEEE Computer Society.

14. S. P. Marsh. *Formalising Trust as a Computational Concept*. PhD thesis, University of Stirling, 1994.

15. P. Resnick and R. Zeckhauser. Trust among strangers in internet transactions: Empirical analysis of ebay's reputation system. In M. Baye, editor, *The Economics of The Internet and E-Commerce*, volume 11 of *Advances in Applied Microeconomics*. Elsevier, 2002.

16. P. Resnick, R. Zeckhauser, E. Friedman, and K. Kuwabara. Reputation systems. *Commun. ACM*, 43(12):45–48, 2000.

17. M. Ripeanu. Peer-to-peer architecture case study: Gnutella network. In *P2P '01: Proceedings of the First International Conference on Peer-to-Peer Computing (P2P'01)*, page 99, Washington, DC, USA, 2001. IEEE Computer Society.

18. W. Stallings. *Cryptography and Network Security: Principles and Practices*. Prentice Hall, 3rd edition, 2003.

19. K. Walsh and E. G. Sirer. Fighting peer-to-peer spam and decoys with object reputation. In *P2PECON '05: Proceeding of the 2005 ACM SIGCOMM workshop on Economics of peer-to-peer systems*, pages 138–143, New York, NY, USA, 2005. ACM Press.

20. A. F. Westin. *Privacy and freedom*. Atheneum, 1967.

21. B. Yu and M. P. Singh. A social mechanism of reputation management in electronic communities. In *Cooperative Information Agents*, pages 154–165, 2000.

Robust Reputations for Peer-to-Peer Marketplaces*

Jonathan Traupman and Robert Wilensky

U.C. Berkeley, Computer Science Division,
Berkeley, CA 94720-1176
jont@cs.berkeley.edu, wilensky@cs.berkeley.edu

Abstract. We have developed a suite of algorithms to address two problems confronting reputation systems for large peer-to-peer markets: data sparseness and inaccurate feedback. To mitigate the effect of inaccurate feedback – particularly retaliatory negative feedback – we propose EM-trust, which uses a latent variable statistical model of the feedback process. To handle sparse data, we propose Bayesian versions of both EM-trust and the well-known Percent Positive Feedback system. Using a marketplace simulator, we demonstrate that these algorithms provide more accurate reputations than standard Percent Positive Feedback.

1 Introduction

Reputation systems allow users of distributed and peer-to-peer systems to make trust decisions regarding potential partners about which they are unlikely to have firsthand knowledge. In the past several years, many novel reputation algorithms have been proposed for applications such as email filtering [1], multi-agent and grid computing [2], and electronic markets [3, 4], among others.

Large peer-to-peer online marketplaces present particular challenges for reputation system research because the interaction patterns among their users prevent the use of many existing algorithms. Users rarely interact more than once with a trading partner, rendering ineffective algorithms that use past interactions to predict future performance. Unlike pure peer-to-peer systems, trading partners in existing large markets are typically matched via a global search facility, which yields an interaction graph that is unlikely to have much "small world" structure, reducing the effectiveness of reputation systems designed to exploit such information. Furthermore, information about user behavior in these markets is typically very sparse: the 1.4 billion items listed last year on eBay represents less than .00005% of the possible interactions between active users.

Reputation systems for large-scale markets must also be able to intelligently handle inaccurate feedback. Of particular concern is retaliatory negative feedback, where a user that receives a negative feedback responds with a negative, even if his or her partner did nothing wrong aside from complain. It is difficult to ascertain which negative is accurate, and should thus count against the user's reputation, and which is merely retaliation and should be ignored or discounted. A further effect of retaliatory negatives is the overall chilling effect they have on participation in the feedback process. A single negative

---

* This research supported in part by the Digital Libraries Initiative under grant NSF CA98-17353.

K. Stølen et al. (Eds.): iTrust 2006, LNCS 3986, pp. 382–396, 2006.

feedback will have a large effect on the reputation of a user who has participated in only a few transactions, while it will have scarcely any effect on users with long histories. Experienced users exploit this asymmetry by rarely leaving feedback first and always retaliating for received negatives, even ones that are justified. Users aware of this tactic often will not leave negative feedback except in the case of outright fraud out of fear of damage to their reputation. Negative feedback is thus discouraged and underreported [5], a phenomenon that some researchers believe eBay ignores because a marketplace with abundant positive feedback appears safer and more inviting to new customers [6].

In this report, we present several techniques for building reputation systems that are robust with respect to the sparse and inaccurate data that will be encountered in real marketplaces. To mitigate the effect of retaliatory negative feedback, we propose EM-trust, an algorithm that uses a latent variable model of the feedback process to estimate reputations using Expectation-Maximization. EM-trust essentially assumes away the problem of retaliation by distributing fault for a failed transaction in a statistically fair manner. To address the problem of data sparseness, we propose Bayesian variants of both EM-trust and eBay's Percent Positive Feedback (PPF). Since the prior distribution of user reliability needed for a Bayesian estimator is not immediately available, we also demonstrate how a workable prior distribution can be estimated on-line from feedback data.

Using a marketplace simulator, we show that EM-trust estimates users' true reliability more accurately than PPF, even in the absence of retaliatory negative feedbacks. We further demonstrate that the relative performance of EM-trust improves at high rates of retaliation. We also demonstrate the advantages of using Bayesian estimates in both EM-trust and PPF in a realistically sparse dataset. The Bayesian EM-trust reputation system, which effectively manages both missing and inaccurate feedback data, produces the most accurate estimates of users' true reliability.

2   Related Work

Reputation systems grew out of earlier work on soft security, the problem of determining whether online services should be trusted [7]. The concept of reputation has been studied in some depth by the economics community; for example, Kennes and Schiff [8] present a theoretical analysis of the value of reputation, and Tadelis [9] models reputation as an asset that can be traded. Marsh [10] is among the early work that combines notions of trust and reputation from philosophy, psychology, and economics and applies them to multi-agent systems.

Many existing reputation systems can be broadly divided into those that primarily use one's previous experience with a user to estimate its reliability [11] and those that use small-world phenomena to build chains of acquaintance to find other users who can vouch for the reputation of a potential trading partner [1, 12, 3]. Some systems, like Kasbah's Histos and Sporas system, use a combination of both mechanisms [4]. As mentioned above, we feel that these techniques have limited applicability to large markets.

The problem of fraud in online markets and in the feedback system has recently attracted considerable attention both from researchers and the mainstream press. Dellarocas [13] discusses the problem of making robust evaluations of reputation despite unreliable feedback. The Pinocchio system [14] tries to detect and discourage inaccurate feedback using a combination of economic incentives and fraud detection.

Online marketplaces, and particularly eBay, have been widely studied by the economics and business communities. For example, Lucking-Reiley et al. [15] look at online auctions of rare coins to determine what features drive pricing differences among similar items on eBay. Bajari and Hortacsu [16] also look at pricing and compare eBay users' behavior to theoretically ideal auction behavior. Calkins [6] analyzes the eBay reputation system from a legal standpoint and finds it lacking. Resnick and Zeckhauser performed a major empirical study [5] of eBay user behavior, including participation rates, bidding behavior and feedback. Resnick, Zeckhauser, and other collaborators also authored a comparison of various reputation systems [17] that analyzed their strengths and weakness.

3   Algorithm Design

We begin by defining a user i's reliability, λ_i, as the probability that the user will perform acceptably in a transaction. As suggested by [18], we currently do not try to assess motivation — poor performance caused by deception or malice is indistinguishable from mere incompetence. Since the end result is the same, we do not think it is necessary to treat the sources of unacceptable performance separately.

The job of the reputation system, then, is to accurately estimate λ_i from users' (possibly unreliable) feedback. When user i interacts with user j in a transaction, we observe two feedback variables, F_{ij} and F_{ji}, indicating the feedback left by user i for user j and vice versa. These variables are can take values from the set $\{-1, 1, 0\}$ indicating negative, positive, and no feedback respectively. We do not currently model neutral feedback, since it is both infrequently given and is considered by most to be merely a weak negative.

Also associated with each transaction are two latent Bernoulli random variables, T_{ij} and T_{ji}. T_{ij} indicates whether user i performed acceptably in the transaction with user j, and T_{ji} represents user j's performance in the same transaction. We assume independence between transactions, so the distribution of these Bernoulli random variables is characterized by the users' reliability parameters, λ_i and λ_j.

In general, the feedback variables can depend on the individual performance variables as well as on each other. These dependencies are complex and difficult to quantify, so we do not attempt to model them explicitly. However, we do make some assumptions about the way rational users leave feedback. Our first assumption is that all transactions are legitimate transactions between real users. While reputation fraud, such as ballot stuffing and badmouthing, perpetrated by fake transactions and Sybil users is an interesting problem in its own right, it is beyond the scope of this paper.

Second, we assume that positive feedback always indicates that the recipient behaved acceptably in the transaction. While users may leave positive feedback despite small faults (e.g. slow shipping) in the hope of encouraging a reciprocal positive, it seems unlikely that a user would leave positive feedback for a grossly under-performing partner just to get a positive in return. In any case, we cannot discern a false positive from a true positive feedback, so we consider them all to be legitimate.

Finally, we assume that a negative feedback by itself does not indicate poor performance, unless the recipient of the negative feedback has left a positive for his or her partner. We know that the process of retaliation creates false negatives, and we also hypothesize that nefarious users may leave pre-emptive false negatives to try to disguise bad behavior.

3.1 The EM-Trust Algorithm

If we could observe the T_{ij} and T_{ji} variables, estimating λ_i would be trivial. Since these variables are latent, we proceed by using an Expectation-Maximization algorithm to iteratively refine our estimates of these parameters. We start with initial estimates $\lambda_i^{(0)}$ for each user's reliability parameter. These starting values do not have a great effect in our application, so we start with $\lambda_i^{(0)} = 0.5$ for all i.

Expectation Step. For each transaction involving user i, we calculate the conditional expectation that i performed acceptably given the observed feedback:[1]

$$\mathbb{E}[T_{ij}|F_{ij} = 1, F_{ji} = 1] = 1$$
$$\mathbb{E}[T_{ij}|F_{ij} = 0, F_{ji} = 1] = 1$$
$$\mathbb{E}[T_{ij}|F_{ij} = -1, F_{ji} = 1] = 1$$
$$\mathbb{E}[T_{ij}|F_{ij} = 1, F_{ji} = -1] = 0$$
$$\mathbb{E}[T_{ij}|F_{ij} = 0, F_{ji} = -1] = \mathbb{E}[T_{ij}|T_{ij}T_{ji} = 0]$$
$$\mathbb{E}[T_{ij}|F_{ij} = -1, F_{ji} = 0] = \mathbb{E}[T_{ij}|T_{ij}T_{ji} = 0]$$
$$\mathbb{E}[T_{ij}|F_{ij} = -1, F_{ji} = -1] = \mathbb{E}[T_{ij}|T_{ij}T_{ji} = 0]$$

We do not compute the expectation for the two unlisted cases ($F_{ij} = 1, F_{ji} = 0$ and $F_{ij} = F_{ji} = 0$) and instead treat these transactions as missing data. The calculations for $\mathbb{E}[T_{ji}|F_{ij}, F_{ji}]$ are the same with the subscripts reversed.

When at least one negative and no positive feedback is given, all we know is that someone behaved unacceptably. We cannot rely on the feedback being accurate in these cases, so we use the more fundamental expectation $\mathbb{E}[T_{ij}|T_{ij}T_{ji} = 0]$. To compute this expectation, we look at the joint distribution, $\mathbb{P}\{T_{ij}T_{ji}, T_{ij}, T_{ji}\}$, marginalize over T_{ji}, condition on $T_{ij}T_{ji} = 0$, and take the expectation to obtain the expression:

$$\mathbb{E}[T_{ij}|T_{ij}T_{ji} = 0] = \frac{\lambda_i^{(t)} - \lambda_i^{(t)}\lambda_j^{(t)}}{1 - \lambda_i^{(t)}\lambda_j^{(t)}} \tag{1}$$

---

[1] We observe a slight increase in accuracy if we let $\mathbb{E}[T_{ij}|F_{ij} = 0, F_{ji} = -1] = 0$ and treat $\mathbb{E}[T_{ij}|F_{ij} = -1, F_{ji} = 0]$ as missing data. However, doing so creates an incentive for retaliation beyond the social incentives that already exist. Thus, rational users will always retaliate, so performance with this modification should converge to that of the version presented in the body of this report. Since our simulated users do not adapt to the system being tested, we feel any performance gains from this modification are due to simulation biases rather than a true improvement in accuracy. However, when deploying EM-trust in a real market, it may be worthwhile to reconsider this modification.

This estimation process is the key to the EM-trust algorithm. We assume that negative feedback is mostly unreliable and so we penalize both parties in such a transaction. The amount of "blame" given to each is based on the current reputations of the two parties in a transaction, with more blame given to the lower reputation user. The aim of this technique is to render retaliatory feedback irrelevant. If a user has received a negative feedback, it does not matter whether he or she leaves a retaliatory negative or not: the reputations of both parties will be computed in the same fashion regardless of whether the user retaliates.

The only way in which the recipient of a negative feedback can change the outcome of the reputation process is by leaving a positive for its partner, which will have the effect of shifting *all* blame for the transaction failure onto itself, lowering its reputation even further. On its face, it is not desirable for the reputation system to discourage users from leaving honest feedback. However, users rarely leave positive feedback for others that gave them negative feedback, even when such behavior will not result in a lower reputation: Resnick and Zeckhauser [5] report that none of the buyers and only 13% of sellers who received negative feedback respond with a positive feedback. Therefore we feel that making slightly more optimal the pre-existing strategy of not praising those who criticize you is a worthwhile tradeoff for mitigating the effect of the far more damaging tactic of retaliation.

Maximization Step. For the maximization step, we use the above conditional expected values as the sufficient statistics needed to update estimates of the parameters λ_i. Let $\langle T_{ij} \rangle^{(t)} = \mathbb{E}[T_{ij}|F_{ij}, F_{ji}]$ be the conditional expectation of user i's behavior in a transaction with user j computed in the expectation step of iteration t. Let A be the set of users with which user i has interacted and for whom we have computed $\langle T_{ij} \rangle^{(t)}$. We estimate the updated value of user i's reliability parameter as

$$\lambda_i^{(t+1)} = \frac{1}{|A|} \sum_{j \in A} \langle T_{ij} \rangle^{(t)} \tag{2}$$

We then use these updated parameter estimates in the next estimation step and repeat the whole process until convergence.

Currently, if a pair of users have had multiple transactions together, EM-trust behaves like PPF and only counts the most recent transaction, making it more difficult for malicious users to create bogus reputations by leaving multiple positive feedbacks for sales of non-existent items. If it should become desirable to include all transactions between two users, the modifications to EM-trust would be trivial.

As an iterative algorithm, EM-trust is naturally more expensive to run than PPF. Each iteration, though, is linear in the number of transactions, and convergence is fast in practice. We are also developing an incremental version of EM-trust that recalculates reputations only as needed for user queries that will permit scaling to realistically sized marketplaces.

3.2 Bayesian Algorithms

To help manage data sparseness, we developed Bayesian versions of PPF and EM-Trust that use a prior distribution of user behavior as well as the observed data to estimate the user's actual behavior distribution. For a prior we use a mixture of Beta distributions:

$$\gamma \text{Beta}(\alpha_1, \beta_1) + (1 - \gamma)\text{Beta}(\alpha_2, \beta_2) \tag{3}$$

where the α_1 and β_1 parameters describe the probability distribution of acceptable performance among users that are mostly honest and competent (i.e., the reliable users) and α_2 and β_2 describe the distribution of acceptable performance among mostly dishonest or incompetent (i.e. unreliable) users. The γ parameter describes the proportion of reliable users in the market. As with all Bayesian methods, estimating these parameter values is one of the main challenges for a successful implementation.

For EM-trust, the estimation step remains the same, but the maximization step replaces the simple maximum likelihood estimate with the mean of the posterior distribution:

$$\lambda_i^{(t+1)} = \gamma' \frac{\alpha_1'}{\alpha_1' + \beta_1'} + (1 - \gamma')\frac{\alpha_2'}{\alpha_2' + \beta_2'} \tag{4}$$

where

$$\gamma' = \frac{\gamma B(\alpha_1', \beta_1')B(\alpha_2, \beta_2)}{\gamma B(\alpha_1', \beta_1')B(\alpha_2, \beta_2) + (1 - \gamma)B(\alpha_2', \beta_2')B(\alpha_1, \beta_1)}$$

$$\begin{aligned} \alpha_1' = \alpha_1 + \sum_{j \in A}\langle T_{ij}\rangle^{(t)} \qquad \beta_1' = \beta_1 + |A| - \sum_{j \in A}\langle T_{ij}\rangle^{(t)} \\ \alpha_2' = \alpha_2 + \sum_{j \in A}\langle T_{ij}\rangle^{(t)} \qquad \beta_2' = \beta_2 + |A| - \sum_{j \in A}\langle T_{ij}\rangle^{(t)} \end{aligned} \tag{5}$$

and $B(\alpha, \beta)$ is the Beta function, $\int_0^1 x^{\alpha-1}(1-x)^{\beta-1}dx$. This same formula is used to create a Bayesian version of PPF. However, instead of the sufficient statistics, $\langle T_{ij}\rangle$, Bayesian PPF uses the observed feedbacks F_{ji} directly.

3.3 Estimating the Bayesian Prior

The Bayesian versions of EM-trust and PPF realize all of their advantages by incorporating knowledge of the prior distribution of user reliability during the estimation process. Without information about this prior distribution, these techniques are useless: using a non-informative (uniform) prior resulted in lower performance than the non-Bayesian versions of the algorithms.

We have developed a method for estimating the prior that uses nothing but the observed feedback. This method exploits the fact that non-Bayesian EM-trust and PPF both calculate acceptably accurate estimates of user reliability. We can use these estimates along with one of several well-known techniques to estimate the density of the reliability distribution. Essentially, we bootstrap the Bayesian versions of EM-trust and PPF by using the results of their non-Bayesian counterparts to estimate the prior distribution. During simulation, we periodically (every 10,000–25,000 transactions) re-estimate the prior by running the non-Bayesian reputation algorithm to generate reliability values and fitting a density to this data.

4 Testing Methodology

Because testing reputation systems in a real market is not feasible, we developed a simulator to evaluate our algorithms. While simulated results are at best an approximation of what can be expected in a real marketplace, we believe it is a better demonstration of a reputation system's characteristics than the simple test cases or theoretical bounds that are prevalent in the literature. Simulation also permits us to test algorithms in multiple markets with varied characteristics in order to examine robustness across a range of plausible scenarios.

For simplicity, our simulator assumes that all users are trading in a single commodity at a fixed price. Since none of the algorithms we test currently use price, commodity type, or bidding behavior when calculating reputations, it was unnecessary to simulate the full auction process.

Users created by our simulator have a number of parameters, including the frequency with which they buy and sell, the probability of successfully completing a transaction (reliability), the probability of leaving the first feedback, and conditions under which they will leave positive and negative feedback. All of these parameters can be modified in order to simulate different marketplace behaviors.

To simulate a single transaction, the simulator chooses a seller and a buyer according to Poisson rate parameters that govern how often each user buys or sells. The seller and buyer then decide whether they want to interact with each other based on their reputations. The probability that a user will interact is given by applying a sigmoidal function to its partner's reputation. Two parameters, the interaction threshold and interaction width, control the location and steepness of the sigmoid's inflection point. If a user cannot find a partner willing to trade within a set period of time, the buy or sell offer expires and the user has to try again later.

Once a buyer/seller pair agrees to interact, the simulator determines their performance in the transaction according to the users' reliability parameters (λ_i). They then leave feedback for each other based on their performance in the transaction. The user that leaves feedback second may also use the feedback he or she received to determine what type of feedback to leave.

Both for efficiency reasons and because feedback is not usually left immediately after completion of a transaction, we do not recalculate reputations after each transaction. Instead, the simulator pauses and recalculates the reputation of all users in the system after a set number of transactions (the *epoch*, currently 1000 transactions). All the simulations in this report were run for 500 epochs, or 500,000 transactions.

At the start of each epoch, users may find that their new reputation is low enough that they will have a greater chance of interacting as a new user with no reputation than with their current identity. These users will either discard their accounts and start anew with a fresh identity or will leave the market. In addition, the simulator adds new users in order to model marketplace growth over time.

We believe that the simulator achieves our desiderata: its assumptions appear to us to be realistic, at least to a first approximation; it seems to model observed behavior well enough, and robustly enough, so that the results are plausible proxies for what would happen in real marketplaces. Moreover, as far as we can tell, it does not incorporate any biases designed to favor (or disfavor) our models. The robustness of the simulation results suggests that further complications are unwarranted, at least for our purposes. Of course, various improvements, such as more accurately and automatically determining model parameters, are possible. We refer the interested reader to [19] for more detailed descriptions of the simulator and our methods of choosing realistic simulation parameters.

4.1 Marketplace Characteristics

In order to demonstrate the effect of different marketplace characteristics on the reputation systems we test, we developed two different simulated marketplaces. The parameters of our first marketplace — henceforth called *Marketplace A* — were chosen such that certain statistics, such as the rates of different types of feedback and the distribution of number of transactions per user, have values after 500,000 transactions that are close to the values reported by [5] in their study of eBay. The market begins with 8000 buyers and 1000 sellers. Of these users, 1% are "bad," with a mean reliability of 0.01. The remaining 99% are "good" and have mean reliability 0.99. The overall mean reliability in this market is thus 0.9802. New users are added at the rate of 1.15% per simulated day and have the same reliability distribution as the original set of users. Users that leave due to a low reputation return to the market 60% of the time, and their new user identity keeps the reliability and other characteristics of their old identity.

While the reliability values in Marketplace A may seem remarkably high, they do agree with observations that the vast majority of users at eBay behave correctly essentially all the time. However, some researchers believe that the extremely high reliability at eBay is due to systematic underreporting of minor faults in the Feedback Forum. To show how the reputation systems perform in a market with less than perfect users, we created *Marketplace B*. Marketplace B is slightly smaller (1350 sellers and 4000 buyers) and does not grow as fast (0.25% per day). However, the main difference is the distribution of user reliability. In Marketplace B, 98% of the users are "good," but the mean of good user reliability is only 0.9. Likewise, the bad users' mean reliability is 0.1, so the overall user mean is 0.884. This market models users that have higher variance around their mean behavior. By showing results in both of these marketplaces, we obtain some indication of how sensitive various reputation systems might be to the actual distribution of user reliability.

5   Experimental Results

In order to test EM-trust, we ran a series of simulations and used several metrics to compare PPF, EM-trust, and their Bayesian variants. Our first test measures how accurately the four reputation systems can estimate the true underlying performance parameters for the users in a marketplace. In the second test, we evaluate how well the algorithms detect and eliminate low performance users. The final test measures the influence they have on the liquidity of the simulated market.

The Bayesian results presented in this section use priors estimated using the methods discussed in Sect. 3.3. We used an EM density estimation method with five random restarts per run to avoid local maxima, a technique that had the best balance of accuracy and speed in our tests. The resulting distributions have a mean Kullback-Liebler divergence from the true prior of 2.6 in Market A and 1.1 in Market B, while the noninformative prior's divergence from the true prior in these markets is 5.3 and 1.9, respectively. As we show below, even this simple prior estimation method offers significant advantages over not using prior information. However, that there are still differences between the true priors and these estimates suggest that there are opportunities to further improve reputation system performance by simply refining prior estimation techniques. The performance when using the true prior gives an upper bound on these potential gains of about 25-35% in Market A and 35-45% in Market B.

5.1   Predicting Reliability

Our first experiment measures the reputation systems' abilities to learn the actual reliability of a set of users. For each reputation system, we ran simulations at three different levels of retaliation. The 0% level simulates a marketplace where all feedback is completely accurate. At the 50% level, good users leave retaliatory negative feedback for about half of the negative feedbacks they receive, while bad users always retaliate. At the 100% level, all users always retaliate for negative feedback. From the data in [5] and assuming that simultaneous failure of both the buyer and seller is rare, the 50% retaliation level represents our best estimate of the rate of retaliation at eBay.

After each epoch of 1000 transactions, we computed the mean absolute error between the reputations returned by the reputation systems and the known ground truth reliability of the users in the system. The results of this test are shown in Fig. 1.

With no retaliation, PPF and EM-trust performed roughly equally. In Market B, EM-trust was slightly more accurate, while in Market A, PPF was better, at least during the early stages of simulation. However, the advantages of EM-trust become apparent as the level of retaliation is increased. While both algorithms become less accurate with more retaliation, PPF's performance decreases more than EM-trust. This experiment demonstrates that both EM-trust variants accomplish the goal we set for them: they perform at least as well as PPF in the zero retaliation case, and are much less influenced by inaccurate feedback data introduced by retaliatory negatives.

These results also demonstrate the power of incorporating prior information in the estimation process. The worse of the two Bayesian algorithms outperformed both of the non-Bayesian ones. The Bayesian algorithms were also less susceptible to errors caused by retaliation than their non-Bayesian counterparts.

5.2   Classification Performance

While more accurate evaluations of users' performance is certainly a desirable feature in reputation systems, the fundamental problem they aim to solve is one of classification. A participant in a peer-to-peer marketplace hopes to use the information returned by the reputation system to make a choice about whether to interact or not with a potential trading partner.

To test the algorithms' ability to distinguish good users from bad ones, we looked at two statistics: the transaction success rate and the precision of user deactivations. The transaction success rate is simply the percentage of transactions where both parties behaved correctly. The deactivation precision is the percentage of deactivated users (users who leave the system because of a low reputation) whose true reliability is less than the overall mean reliability. In other words, deactivation precision is the percentage of users removed from the system who actually deserved to be removed. The former statistic can

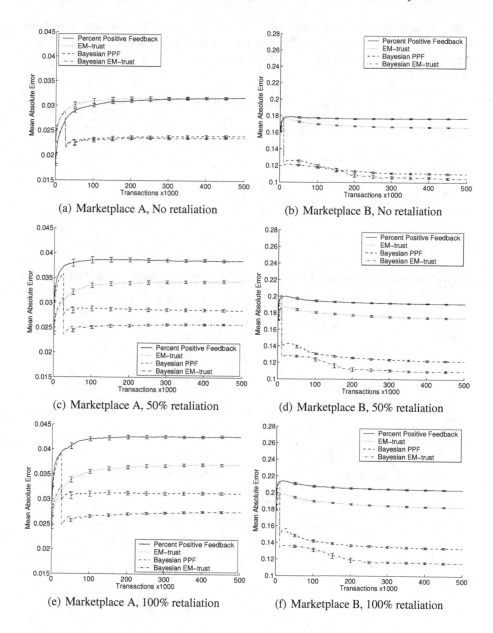

Fig. 1. Reputation system mean absolute error with (a)(b) no retaliation, (c)(d) 50% retaliation, and (e)(f) 100% retaliation in Marketplace A (a)(c)(e) and Marketplace B (b)(d)(e). Error bars indicate 95% confidence intervals.

be intuitively interpreted as a form of recall and the latter as type of precision. An ideal reputation system would score 1.0 on both metrics. We also present an overall performance metric that combines these two results by taking their harmonic mean.

We evaluated the algorithms over a range of interaction thresholds to show how these two statistics change with the selectivity of the marketplace's participants. In Marketplace A, with a mean reliability of 0.9802, we vary the threshold from 0.9 to 1.0. For

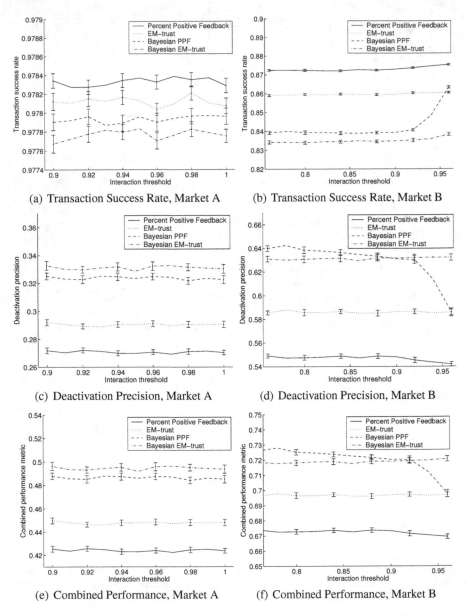

(a) Transaction Success Rate, Market A   (b) Transaction Success Rate, Market B

(c) Deactivation Precision, Market A   (d) Deactivation Precision, Market B

(e) Combined Performance, Market A   (f) Combined Performance, Market B

Fig. 2. Effect of the interaction threshold on the (a)(b) transaction success rate, (c)(d) deactivation precision, and (e)(f) combined performance in Marketplaces A and B. Error bars indicate 95% confidence intervals.

Marketplace B, with a mean reliability of 0.884, we vary the threshold from 0.76 to 0.96. With thresholds higher than 0.96 in this market, users are so reluctant to interact with all but a tiny subset of their peers that the simulation becomes impractically slow. All tests were conducted with the retaliation rate set to 50% for good users and 100% for bad users. The results are shown in Fig. 2.

In both marketplaces, PPF had the highest transaction success rate, followed by EM-trust, then Bayesian PPF, and finally Bayesian EM-trust. By and large, the transaction success rates are not greatly affected by the interaction threshold, with the notable exception of Bayesian PPF, whose performance in Marketplace B rises rapidly at very high threshold values and exceeds EM-trust's performance at 0.96.

That lower error rates should result in lower transaction success rates may seem counterintuitive. However, we must keep in mind that the MAE metric aggregates both over- and underestimates of users' true performance. PPF, because it does not account for retaliatory negatives, is pessimistic and tends to underestimate true performance. Thus, it effectively detects bad behavior, but at the price of lower estimates for all users. The other algorithms are significantly less pessimistic, but their more accurate estimates fail to detect a small number of the bad transactions found by PPF. However, the differences between the four algorithms on this test are very small: in Marketplace B, the best performance is less than 5% better than the worst performance. In Marketplace A, the algorithms are even closer in performance, with the observed differences being practically insignificant.

In Marketplace A, the interaction threshold has little effect on the transaction success rate. This is likely an artifact of the fact that the distribution of user reliability in this market has a very high mean (0.9802) and very low variance (5×10^{-5}). In such a market, users are likely to be nearly always reliable or nearly always unreliable, so to filter out the bad users, it really doesn't matter whether the interaction threshold is set to 90% or 99%.

The interaction threshold does affect all four algorithms to some degree in Marketplace B, with the greatest effect on Bayesian PPF and the least effect on EM-trust. The non-Bayesian algorithms start to show a slightly increase in transaction success around 0.88, while the Bayesian algorithms are nearly unaffected by the interaction threshold until around 0.9-0.91, at which point they start to rise more rapidly.

The deactivation precision reveals greater differences among the four systems in both markets. The algorithms that do better in the transaction success rate test tend to be the worse performers on this test, suggesting that there is a tradeoff between precision and recall. In Marketplace A, all of the algorithms show a slight decrease in precision as the interaction threshold increases, but the amount of change is not practically significant. Bayesian EM-trust has the highest precision in this market, followed by Bayesian PPF, then non-Bayesian EM-trust, and finally non-Bayesian PPF.

In Marketplace B, Bayesian PPF performs best at low interaction thresholds, but drops off quickly as the interaction threshold increases. Next comes Bayesian EM-trust, then standard EM-trust, neither of which is strongly affected by the interaction threshold. Finally, non-Bayesian PPF performs the worst, with its precision declining slightly more as the interaction threshold is increased.

The ranking of algorithms and overall trends in the combined metric results look very much like the precision results because of the much greater differences among the algorithms' precisions than among their transaction success rates. If we accept the assumption that both precision and recall are equally important for this task, these results imply that EM-trust and the Bayesian algorithms provide significant improvements to the reputation system precision while giving up only negligible transaction success compared to the baseline PPF system. We also conjecture that this increased precision may in fact have other benefits. Because users are less likely to get unfairly low reputations, they may be more inclined to participate in the reputation system, thus further increasing accuracy.

5.3   Market Liquidity

While preventing failed transactions is the obvious first priority of a reputation system, it must be balanced against other marketplace concerns. One of a reputation system's ancillary effects is the influence it has on the liquidity of the market. A reputation system that prevents all but the best users from buying and selling would likely be very safe, but it would also create a market where it is very hard to find a buyer or seller willing to trade.

To measure the effect of the reputation algorithms and the users' interaction thresholds on market liquidity, we look at the average number of transactions per user per simulated day. A higher number of transactions per day indicate a market where it is easier for a user to buy or sell his or her goods. These results are given in Fig. 3.

In both simulated markets, the liquidity results are similar to the deactivation precision results. This is not surprising, because a market that deactivates fewer good users will likely have more buyers and sellers available at any given time. In Marketplace A, all three of our algorithms have similar liquidity, with the Bayesian systems outperforming standard EM-trust by a small margin. All three are significantly better than the baseline PPF rate.

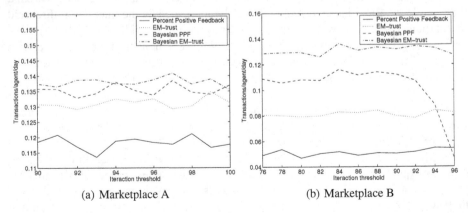

(a) Marketplace A   (b) Marketplace B

Fig. 3. Effect of the interaction threshold and reputation system choice on market liquidity in (a) Marketplace A and (b) Marketplace B

Once again, there are greater differences among the systems in Marketplace B. Bayesian EM-trust gives the highest liquidity with Bayesian PPF having the next highest at low interaction thresholds. However, the liquidity of the market when using Bayesian PPF drops off dramatically above 0.90 and by 0.96, it has the lowest liquidity of the four. This sudden drop is the main reason we are only able to present results through 0.96 for marketplace B: as the liquidity decreases the time needed to run the simulation grows to the point where we cannot finish 500,000 transactions in a reasonable length of time. Standard PPF has the lowest liquidity of the four systems, with standard EM-trust roughly splitting the difference between PPF and Bayesian PPF.

6 Conclusion

Accurate reputation systems are a requirement for a successful peer-to-peer marketplace. If a reputation system does not provide accurate reputations, it will discourage participation, running the risk of entering a vicious cycle where declining feedback rates cause even less accurate reputations. This problem is particularly serious for reputation systems that give unfairly poor reputations to reliable users, who we most likely expect to provide accurate feedback.

The EM-trust and Bayesian algorithms we present in this report make improvements to the simple eBay averaging approach that we believe will help make reputation systems more accurate and useful. All three of our algorithms estimated true user reliability more accurately than the PPF algorithm used by eBay. While they did permit a negligibly small increase in failed transactions, they gave many fewer good users unfairly poor reputations. Additionally, the EM-trust algorithms are far less prone to errors caused by retaliatory negative feedback than their PPF counterparts. We hope that by decreasing the effect of retaliation, we can eliminate some of the hesitation users feel about giving honest negative evaluations. Finally, under most circumstances, all three of our algorithms result in a more liquid market, where users are more willing to trade.

In addition to the measurable benefits of these algorithms, we believe that their more accurate reputations will encourage more users to trust and thus participate in the feedback process. It is our hope that this increased participation will further increase feedback accuracy, creating instead a virtuous cycle that improves both the participation in and the accuracy of the reputation system.

References

1. Golbeck, J., Hendler, J.: Reputation network analysis for email filtering. In: Proc. CEAS. (2004)
2. Patel, J., Teacy, W.L., Jennings, N.R., Luck, M.: A probabilistic trust model for handling inaccurate reputation sources. In: Proc. iTrust. (2005) 193–209
3. Yu, B., Singh, M.: A social mechanism for reputation management in electronic communities. In: Proc. CIA Workshop. (2000)
4. Zacharia, G., Moukas, A., Maes, P.: Collaborative reputation mechanisms in electronic markets. In: Proc. of the 32nd Hawaii International Conference on System Sciences. (1999)

5. Resnick, P., Zeckhauser, R.: Trust among strangers in internet transactions: Empirical analysis of ebay's reputation system. In Baye, M.R., ed.: The Economics of the Internet and E-Commerce. Elsevier Science (2002) Volume 11 of Advances in Applied Microeconomics.

6. Calkins, M.M.: My reputation always had more fun than me: The failure of ebay's feedback model to effectively prevent online auction fraud. The Richmond Journal of Law and Technology 7(4) (2001) http://law.richmond.edu/jolt/v7i4/note1.html.

7. Khare, R., Rifkin, A.: Weaving a web of trust. World Wide Web Journal 2(3) (1997) 77–112

8. Kennes, J., Schiff, A.:   The value of a reputation system.   Technical Report 0301011, Economics Working Paper Archive at WUSTL (2003) available at http://ideas.repec.org/p/wpa/wuwpio/0301011.html.

9. Tadelis, S.: What's in a name? reputation as a tradeable asset. The American Economic Review 89(3) (1999) 548–563

10. Marsh, S.: Formalising Trust as a Computational Concept. PhD thesis, University of Stirling (1994)

11. Josang, A., Ismail, R.: The beta reputation system. In: Proc. of the 15th Bled Conference on Electronic Commerce. (2002)

12. Venkatraman, M., Yu, B., Singh, M.P.: Trust and reputation management in a small-world network. In: Proc. ICMAS, Washington, DC, USA, IEEE Computer Society (2000) 449

13. Dellarocas, C.: Building trust online: The design of robust reputation reporting mechanisms in online trading communties. In Doukidis, G., Mylonopoulos, N., Pouloudi, N., eds.: Information Society or Information Economy? A combined perspective on the digital era. Idea Book Publishing (2003)

14. Fernandes, A., Kotsovinos, E., Östring, S., Dragovic, B.: Pinocchio: Incentives for honest participation in distributed trust management. In: Proc. iTrust. (2004)

15. Bryan, D., Lucking-Reiley, D., Prasad, N., Reeves, D.: Pennies from ebay: the determinants of price in online auctions. Papers 00-w03, Vanderbilt - Economic and Business Administration (2000) available at http://ideas.repec.org/p/fth/vander/00-w03.html.

16. Bajari, P., Hortaçsu, A.: The winner's curse,reserve prices and endogenous entry: Empirical insights from ebay. RAND Journal of Economics (2003) 329–355

17. Resnick, P., Zeckhauser, R., Friedman, E., Kuwabara, K.: Reputation systems: Facilitating trust in internet interactions. Communications of the ACM 43(12) (2000) 45–48

18. Barber, K.S., Fullam, K., Kim, J.: Challenges for trust, fraud and deception research in multi-agent systems. Trust, Reputation, and Security: Theories and Practice (2003) 8–14

19. Traupman, J., Wilensky, R.: EM-trust: A robust reputation algorithm for peer-to-peer marketplaces. Technical Report UCB/CSD-05-1400, University of California, Berkeley, Computer Science Division (2005)

From Theory to Practice: Forgiveness as a Mechanism to Repair Conflicts in CMC

Asimina Vasalou, Jeremy Pitt, and Guillaume Piolle

Intelligent Systems & Networks Group, Dept. of Electrical & Electronic Engineering,
Imperial College London, London, SW7 2BT, UK

Abstract. In computer-mediated communication (CMC) online members often behave in undesirable ways, therefore creating a need for an active regulating force. Trust and reputation mechanisms have been adopted to address this problem and in doing so have eliminated the high costs of employing a human moderator. However, these systems have emphasized the need to 'punish' a given offender, while neglecting to account for alternative ways to repair the offence e.g. by forgiveness. In this paper, we define a theoretical model of forgiveness which is operationalized using a fuzzy logic inference system and then applied in a particular scenario. It is argued that forgiveness in CMC may work as a possible prosocial mechanism, which in the short-term can help resolve a given conflict and in the long-term can add to an increasingly prosocial and homeostatic environment.

1 Introduction

In human societies, when violating a norm, the offender is usually 'punished' both emotionally (e.g. experiencing embarrassment) and practically (e.g. by prosecution). The threat of these two sanctions is persistently evoked by physical markers, (e.g. people watching, the presence of law enforcement officials) and works preventively so that a sense of general social order is maintained within the community. Online societies differ from physical societies, in how both the emotional and practical implications are perceived. To begin with, anonymity and the absence of a physical self weaken the impact of the emotional consequences (e.g. shame or embarrassment) that an offender experiences as a result of his/her offence. To add to this, the presence of an active policing force is not visible until the member's behaviour has reached what is considered to be illegal according to law. Therefore, one of the problems identified through these two points is the need for an intermediate mechanism that will signal the offender early on and that will also inform the community about milder offences where punitive legal action against the offender is perhaps inappropriate.

Trust and reputation mechanisms have been widely adopted in addressing this issue [15]. These mechanisms have empowered members of online communities by allowing them to appraise and capture the granularity of their fellow members' actions (e.g. through ratings). However, in doing so, the designers of those

K. Stølen et al. (Eds.): iTrust 2006, LNCS 3986, pp. 397–411, 2006.
© Springer-Verlag Berlin Heidelberg 2006

systems have placed emphasis and value on the quantitative appraisal that usually follows an offence while neglecting to account for the qualitative appraisal that often makes repair between two members possible [19]. In human-human interactions, a violation of norms is unavoidable but not necessarily unforgivable.

In this article, we address this issue by proposing forgiveness as a repair mechanism that is instantiated during a given conflict, possibly facilitating a resolution between online members. In previous work, we have described the conceptual framework of the forgiveness proposal [19]. We now reify this proposal by developing a stand-alone operational model of forgiveness that is straightforward to automate, and can be integrated into any platform or configured for any application domain.

This article is divided into 5 main sections. Section 2 gives an overview of the motivations for considering forgiveness in CMC. Section 3 presents a theoretical model of human forgiveness collectively investigated in the field of psychology. In Section 4, we describe the forgiveness model implemented as a fuzzy inference system driven by the theory described in Section 3. Section 5 integrates the model into a collaborative distance learning scenario. Finally, this paper concludes in Section 6 with a summary and a discussion of further work.

2   Motivation

There are strong incentives for considering forgiveness as a possible reparative mechanism in online communities. For example, issuing forgiveness is known to stimulate the offender into voluntary actions of repair [7]. Moreover, punishing the offender for an action they did not intentionally perform (e.g. bad ratings for accidentally delivering the wrong product) often results in emotions of anger and low-compliancy behaviors [7]. This could possibly motivate a member to withdraw from the online community due to the unjust treatment. Even more, one's judgment can be sometimes misguided and construed on false information. In this situation, a system that supports irreversible judgments is both unfair and unethical. Finally, although forgiveness does not necessarily mean that trust is automatically regained [3], it often provides closure, which may alleviate the aggression created from a disrupted interaction. This point is further demonstrated by the physical well-being of those who tend to issue forgiveness more frequently [21].

To summarize, forgiveness promises short-term benefits in CMC such as giving the offender an outlet through which to apologize or pacifying the victim of the offence, so that both victim-offender can resolve the conflict. At the same time, the short term benefits ultimately have the potential to increase the overall equilibrium of the online community.

3   Theoretical Model

Forgiveness results from a number of prosocial motivational changes which reverse one's initial desire to adopt negative strategies towards the offender (i.e. revenge, avoidance). In this sense, forgiveness replaces malevolent motivations towards the offender with constructive and positive behaviors which work to reverse the initial censure [10]. The forgiveness process, as described in psychology, is further depicted in Figure 1, where the offender, member x, violates a rule with action A. Following victim y's negative predisposition towards offending action A, four positive motivations collectively add up to possibly formulate forgiveness. The positive motivations we consider are empathy, actions of repair, the beneficial historical relationship of victim-offender and an appraisal-judgment of the offence.

The definition used here employs a degree of freedom in long-term relationships as the victim may forgive a single offence without explicitly reversing their attitude as a whole [10]. Likewise, while a certain violation may be forgiven, other past behaviors may still impede one's trust towards another. Despite popular definitions of forgiveness forgetting, condoning, trusting or removing accountability are not necessarily considered to be a part of forgiveness [3].

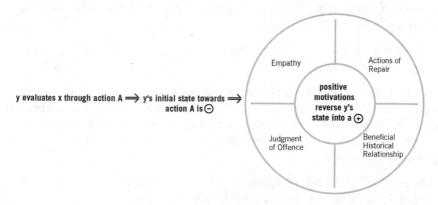

Fig. 1. A motivation-driven conceptualization of forgiveness where positive motivations add up to increase forgiveness

On the basis of the forgiveness definition given here, we propose the following:

> *Premise 1 – x* violates rule *A*. Initially *y*, the observer/victim of *x*'s offence is inclined negatively towards *x*. *y* assesses all the factors surrounding *x*'s action-violation *A* and decides to issue forgiveness by applying a series of (+) positive motivations to his initial (−) negative state.

Next, we discuss the four central positive motivations of the theoretical forgiveness model which are the judgment of offence, actions of repair, beneficial historical relationship and empathy. The four positive motivations are described by eleven constituent parts which are the offence severity, offence frequency, intent, apology, reparative actions, prior interactions, utility of benefits, and frequency of benefits, visible acknowledgment, similarity and propensity to embarrassment.

Judgment of Offence. Observers/victims of one's offence make attributions by accounting for a number of factors surrounding the offence. First, the severity of the current act is assessed. More severe violations lead to harsher judgments [1, 2]. Furthermore, a historical trail of one's past behaviors is compared against the current violation. Together, frequency and severity of past acts impact one's inclination to forgive [2]. Additionally, apparent intent leads towards more negative attributions with low intent actions supporting more positive attributions [1, 8]. Given this, we state:

> *Premise 2 − y* assesses *x*'s action by (severity) AND (frequency/severity of *x*'s historical actions) AND (*x*'s intent)

Actions of Repair. A truthful apology or a good deed [2] that reverses the offence can pacify the observer or victim of the offence. In fact, apology and restitution, together constitute a strong partnership facilitating and even predicting forgiveness [20]. However, reversing one's violation with a reparative action brings up an important issue. Inevitably the weight of a good deed against a severe and frequently performed violation will have to be formulated or accounted for. As a result, we state:

> *Premise 3 − y* issues forgiveness if *x* offers (an apology) AND (reparative action $B \geq$ action A)

Beneficial Historical Relationship. Prior familiarity and a relationship of commitment with the offender positively predispose the victim and increase the likelihood of forgiveness [11]. Good friends or successful business partners rely on a longer, richer and mutually-rewarding history fostering a propensity towards forgiveness. Therefore:

> *Premise 4 − y* will issue forgiveness if (the utility of *x*'s actions has been high) AND (*x* has been frequently beneficial to *y*)

Empathy. Empathy, one's emotional response towards another's affect [5] is regarded as a mediator, appeasing the victim and facilitating forgiveness. Empathy is evoked by offender's apologies among others, is a predictor of forgiveness and its intensity has been found to positively correlate to the extent of forgiveness the victim issues for the offender [12]. Empathy also manifests in embarrassment to form 'empathic embarrassment', a milder form of embarrassment 'incurred' by imagining oneself in another's place. Empathic embarrassment has four determinants. First, the salience of the offender's embarrassment controls the degree of felt empathic embarrassment. Visibly embarrassed offenders elicit more empathic embarrassment from others. Second, the emotion intensifies when the victim is somewhat familiar to the offender. Third, we foster stronger feelings of empathy towards those who are most similar to us in terms of personality or characteristics (e.g. a colleague or a cultural compatriot). Similarly, one will be more empathic towards an offender with whom s/he shares a similar history of offences. Finally, the observer's propensity to embarrassment determines to a great degree the empathic embarrassment s/he may experience. A highly 'embarrasable' observer will experience increased empathic embarrassment (see [9, 13] for a detailed account. On the basis of the previous discussion we propose the following:

> *Premise 5* – The extent of y's forgiveness will vary by the (degrees of empathy/empathic embarrassment y feels for x) which increases IF (x's embarrassment is visibly intense) AND (if y has some prior familiarity with x) AND (if y shares similar characteristics with x) AND (if y's propensity to embarrassment is high) AND (if x apologises for the offence)

This completes the theoretical basis for forgiveness as formulated in the field of psychology and specified in [10]. We have extracted five premises encapsulating the overall forgiveness decision and identified the four motivations for forgiveness, composed of eleven constituent parts. The objective of Section 4 is to propose a generic computational model built on the basis of this theory which can be then implemented and adapted into any domain.

4   Computational Model of Forgiveness

In this section, we develop a computational model that reifies the theoretical basis of forgiveness and is built using fuzzy inference systems (FIS). We first justify our reasoning for using FIS and outline FIS. We then describe the implementation of the decision maker. Finally, we give examples of the fuzzy rules which are used by the decision maker to make its inference.

4.1   Fuzzy Inference Systems as the Operational Basis

The theoretical work we have discussed so far, with the exception of a study conducted by Boon and Sulsky [1], has isolated and then measured the constituents (e.g. intent) of each motivation (e.g. judgment of offence) separately. Boon and Sulsky's study clearly demonstrates the independent rater 'disagreement' on how the different constituents weigh on the decision to forgive. Therefore, in operationalizing the theory, there is a need to define a more concrete model that describes the ranges, weights and interactions of all four motivations and their eleven constituent parts.

To address this issue we implemented the forgiveness decision maker by using the Takagi-Sugeno fuzzy inference system (FIS) [17], as fuzzy logic satisfied these three important aspects. (1) Ranges: FIS allowed for each motivation constituent to be stored in ranges, from high to low, which was particularly important as for example, an offence 1 may be considered 80% severe whereas an offence 2 is regarded as 20% severe. (2) Weights: The violation appraisal captured by the judgment of the offence motivation is the most powerful motivation of forgiveness. FIS allowed us to attribute more weight to the judgment of the offence over the remaining three motivations of actions of repair, beneficial historical interactions and empathy. (3) Interactions: The decision maker closely followed the structure of the five premises so that each motivation was separately computed on the basis of its own constituents and then passed onto the final decision maker.

FIS Overview. Fuzzy Logic, as developed by Takagi-Sugeno [17] is a formalism which facilitates reasoning about imprecise facts, uncertainties, and value judgments – in other words, all the human factors that might inform a forgiveness decision. Fuzzy Logic is the basis of fuzzy inference systems, although there are different types of fuzzy systems as there are various different ways in which outputs can be determined.

In general, to build a fuzzy system, an engineer might start with a set of application-dependent fuzzy rules as specified by a domain expert. In our case, the fuzzy rules for the operational model are derived from the theoretical model described in Section 3. Fuzzy rules are expressed in the form "*if ... then ...*" that convert inputs to outputs, where both inputs and outputs are members of fuzzy sets (a fuzzy set is a set in which objects are members to some degree). So, for example, we might have a rule of the form:

> *If* the offender apologizes *and* does not repair the offence
> *then* the forgiveness value is increased by 10%

Similarly:

> *If* the offender apologizes *and* repairs the offence
> *then* the forgiveness value is increased by 30%

Given a set of such rules, it may be that a particular range of inputs fire (activate) any given subset of those rules. The rules which are fired then contribute proportionally to the fuzzy output: this is calculated by applying the implication method of fuzzy logic to the activated rules and aggregating all the results. The process of defuzzification converts the aggregated output into a 'crisp' value (the usual method is a centroid calculation, i.e. finding the centre of an area under a curve).

This entire process, called fuzzy inference, thus converts quantitative inputs into a precise output using qualitative statements: in our case, this precise output is a yes-no decision on whether to forgive or not.

FIS of Forgiveness. The FIS decision maker that we implemented (see Fig. 2) receives numerical values of the eleven constituent motivations as its input in order to make a yes-no forgiveness decision (d) as its output.

The forgiveness decision maker goes into effect only when an offence occurs i.e. a user has violated a norm. At that time, the eleven constituent motivation signals of forgiveness are computed. They are then input into FIS2 through FIS5. The outputs of FIS2 through FIS5 represent the weights of the four forgiveness motivations which are input to FIS1 to compute a final output value d. FIS1 is the operationalization of premise 1 in Section 3 and the final value d constitutes the forgiveness recommendation (*if* $d > 0.5$, *then* forgiveness = true). We note that the weight of the judgment of offence motivation on the overall forgiveness decision (d) is 0.5 while actions of repair, beneficial historical relationship and empathy are each weighted 0.166.

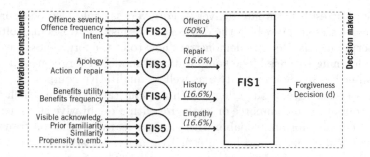

Fig. 2. The Forgiveness Decision Maker

4.2 Examples of Fuzzy Rules of Forgiveness

The fuzzy inference systems FIS1-5 are based on a set of rules that follow the structure, form and theory of premises 1 through 5 of Section 3. The full set of rules can be found at [18]. Here, we give representative examples of two fuzzy sets, the fuzzy set for judgment of offence and the fuzzy set for the overall forgiveness decision.

The judgment of offence as expressed in premise 2 is reliant on the three constituents of severity, frequency and intent. As each increases so does the probability of a low forgiveness rating. An example of two rules follows that demonstrates this difference in granularity:

> *If* severity is low *and* frequency is low *and* intent is high
> *then* the judgment of offence motivation is 0.4

In contrast:

> *If* severity is low *and* frequency is high *and* intent is high
> *then* the judgment of offence motivation is 0.2

Following the calculation of each individual motivation, its value is input in the fifth FIS and a crisp value of forgiveness is computed on the basis of its own rules. For example:

> *If* judgment of offence is high *and* actions of repair is high
> *and* beneficial historical interactions is low *and* empathy is high
> *then* forgiveness is 0.83

5 Application Domain and Integration of the Model

In the previous section, our aim was to create a generic forgiveness model whose integration and input values are ultimately determined by the domain it is fit into. The objective of this section is to integrate the forgiveness model into a specific CMC scenario.

Arguably, the mechanism could be integrated into an e-commerce platform such as eBay where a seller may be unjustly rated due to unforeseen factors (e.g. slow post resulting in late delivery). Forgiveness could also be appropriate in an e-health scenario in which the discussion of sensitive topics may often lead to misinterpretations. Here we demonstrate how to fit the forgiveness mechanism into an e-learning scenario. The computational model of forgiveness developed in this paper has many quantitative as well as qualitative components. For example, a user can reverse the offence with a quantitative action which may be most appropriate in e-commerce or apologize with a qualitative statement, relevant to an e-health forum. Collaborative distance learning relies on transactions (e.g. assignments) but it also has a social capacity, i.e. students may use the tools available to communicate before transacting. Therefore, the transactional and social elements of e-learning permit us to test both the quantitative and qualitative aspects of the forgiveness model.

In this section, we first outline a collaborative distance learning domain into which we customized the forgiveness model. Next, we describe the collection and then the computation of the eleven constituent parts of the four motivations which as illustrated in the previous section, are used by the FIS as inputs (see Figure 2). Finally, we demonstrate how the constituent motivations and decision maker integrate into a complete comprehensive architecture.

5.1   Overview

The forgiveness tool is integrated in a collaborative distance-learning environment. The workflow of this environment supports two-party interactions at a given time, where team tasks are broken down into segments and executed sequentially. The term 'collaboration' in this domain, constitutes the successful delivery of an assignment and can be contingent on a number of factors such as timeliness, good communication skills, quality of work etc.

When signing up to participate in the community, a member is requested to fill out a short survey reporting two successful and two unsuccessful past teamwork experiences. The first signifies a benefit gained as a result of the team collaboration, while the second represents an offence executed during the collaboration. These reports are in turn processed by a human moderator, who checks them in terms of quality (e.g. grammar, clarity of articulation). The moderator then posts the reports online so that the distance-learning community can collectively rate them. The final output of this process is a list of successful and unsuccessful collaboration incidents, each of which has a corresponding 'utility' or 'severity' rating derived from the mean of all ratings. These ratings represent an objective measure of severity or utility. The collaboration reports and their corresponding ratings are updated annually when new users sign up. This way the knowledge base is constantly updated.

Upon collaborating with another member, a user selects the benefit or offence which most closely characterizes his/her experience from the knowledge base. This report is stored, and over time builds up a member's history. In the event of an offence report, two sequential events happen. At first, the offender is offered reparative tools e.g. enabling him/her to reverse or apologize for the action-violation. The intelligent component executed with fuzzy inference systems is instantiated and assesses whether the particular offender should be granted forgiveness. The victim of the offence is then informed of this decision and is presented via the interface with relevant-to-the offence information (e.g. the offender's past history and all the other factors used by the FIS to compute value d). The act of forgiveness is ultimately the user's decision as his/her personal judgment may differ from the one inferred by the FIS.

5.2   Collection and Computation of the Constituent Motivation Signals

Earlier, eleven forgiveness constituent motivations were mentioned, each of which impact on one's decision to forgive. In face-to-face interactions these constituents may be collected by memory, perception or interaction. For example, the offender's visible acknowledgment is immediately perceived through his/her face. Similarly, the offender has immediacy of contact, therefore making it possible to apologize for an offence. In this forgiveness application, we constructed new ways for collecting this kind of data. We now detail the computation and/or collection method for each motivation individually.

j_0: The **severity** of an offence is a value that is assigned to each type of offence automatically and is measured from 0 to 0.5. Rating values higher than 0.5 are classified as beneficial collaborations. As described in the previous section, the severity value is the mean of ratings for each offence as given by users of the community upon signing up.

j_1: The **frequency** of a particular offence is computed by:

$$j_1 = \frac{\left(\frac{n_{offencekind}}{n_{offences}} + \frac{n_{offences}}{n_{collaborations}}\right)}{2} \tag{1}$$

where $n_{offencekind}$ denotes the number of the offender's offences of the current kind, $n_{offences}$ is the offender's total number of offences across time and $n_{collaborations}$ is the offender's total collaborations within the community. Two aspects of frequency are encapsulated in this formula: the frequency of the current offence is computed with the first division and the frequency of the offender's total past offences is computed with the second division. Among other possibilities, this equation intends to capture the instances where a user has infrequently violated a particular norm but at the same time frequently violates many others.

j_2: A judgment on the offender's **intent** is reported both by the offender and the victim via a user interface which activates upon the offence. The report values range from 0 to 1 (i.e. $[0, 1]$). Each user's intent-report is given a different weight depending on his/her credibility which is computed on the basis of past offence frequency and severity. Specifically, a user's credibility C_u is:

$$C_u = \frac{\sum_{i=1}^{n} R_i}{n} \tag{2}$$

where n is the number of the total collaborations that the user has had within the community and R_i $(1 \leq i \leq n)$ is the rating of each collaboration. As previously mentioned, ratings between 0 and 0.5 are considered offences, whereas ratings greater than 0.5 and less than 1 are categorized as benefits. The following formula then encapsulates intent:

$$j_2 = \frac{(I_o \times C_o) + (I_v \times C_v)}{2} \tag{3}$$

In this formula C_o denotes the offender's credibility, C_v is the victim's credibility, and I_o and I_v signify the offender's and victim's intent report rating.

j_3: **Apology** from an offender is reported via a user interface and is then offered to the victim of the offence. A_o is a binary value where 1 indicates that the offender has apologised to the victim and 0 indicates the absence of an apology offer. The credibility and honesty of the offender's report is then given a rating A_v by the victim, ranging from 0 to 1. This rating is weighed into the overall apology value. Similar to computing intent, the offender's and victim's credibility C_o and C_v are taken into account and weighted into the overall apology value. Therefore, apology is given by:

$$j_3 = \frac{(A_o \times C_o) + (A_v \times C_v)}{2} \tag{4}$$

j_4: The offender may offer a **reparative action** RA_o to the victim by either reversing the offence or by completing a new task. This process is facilitated by a user interface. The value for RA_o is binary. When the action of repair has been completed, the victim rates it with RA_v, ranging from 0 to 1. RA_v is then weighed into the total reparative action value. The offender's and victim's credibility is also computed into the final reparative action value. The formula for reparative action is:

$$j_4 = \frac{(RA_o \times C_o) + (RA_v \times C_v)}{2} \tag{5}$$

j_5: The **utility of benefits** is a value that is assigned to each type of benefit automatically and is more than 0.5 and less than 1. As described in Section 5.1, this value is the mean of ratings for each benefit as given by users of the community upon signing up.

j_6: The value of **benefits frequency** between two members is calculated by dividing the number of benefits $n_{benefits}$ that the victim has experienced while collaborating with the offender, by the total number of collaborations between the victim and the offender $n_{collaborations}$. As such, beneficial historical relationship is:

$$j_6 = \frac{n_{benefits}}{n_{collaborations}} \tag{6}$$

j_7: The offender's **visible acknowledgement** (e.g. the blush) value is controlled by the degrees of the offence frequency formula j_1. That is, if the offender has rarely performed the action in question, the visible acknowledgment value will be high and the victim of the offence will be signaled of the offender's emotional display.

j_8: **Prior familiarity** between two members is defined by the formula:

$$j_8 = min\left(1, \frac{|n_{collaborations}|t}{f}\right) \tag{7}$$

where $n_{collaborations}$ denotes the number of collaborations between victim and offender in time interval t. Both t and f values are application specific. In our scenario, is set to the 3-month academic quarter during which the student-users will be using this system. We intuitively consider familiarity to be gained after collaborating for at least 3 times, so that f equals 3. This formula then tracks the number of total collaborations between the victim and offender during the 3-month time interval and considers familiarity to be achieved following three or more collaborations.

j_9: **Similarity** between two members is given by:

$$j_9 = match(\mathbf{d}_o, \mathbf{d}_v) \tag{8}$$

where $\mathbf{d}_v$ is the victim's set of all past forgiveness decisions (d), each containing the eleven constituent motivations $j_0 - j_{10}$. For each element of $\mathbf{d}_v$, the *match* function finds the closest set of constituent signals to those of the offender's in the set of $\mathbf{d}_o$. It then goes on to compare the final forgiveness decision (d) of those sets. Similarity is the sum of all identical decisions divided by the victim's total number of forgiveness decisions.

j_{10}: Finally, **propensity to embarrassment** is collected with a short self-report questionnaire [14] that all members fill out when first signing up. The propensity value is registered and stored in the input conversion layer hereafter.

5.3   System Architecture

The overall framework integrating both the eleven constituent motivations and the forgiveness decision maker is depicted in Figure 3. It consists of two main modules:

- An *input conversion layer* which stores and computes the values of the eleven signals $j_0 - j_{10}$.
- The *decision maker* that outputs the final forgiveness decision (d).

The input conversion layer of the system, stores a member's successful (beneficial) or unsuccessful (offensive) collaborations as two separate objects. Those objects are labeled the *Collaboration Report* object and the *Offence Appraisal* object respectively. Following a collaboration with another member, a user reports on his/her experience. If the experience was positive, then the user's report is stored in a Collaboration Report object. The Collaboration Report object captures the identity of the user, a timestamp, and a measure of the benefit of the collaboration. In contrast, if the collaboration experience was negative, the user's report is stored into an Offence Appraisal object. The Offence Appraisal object captures the type of offence, the identity of the offender, a timestamp, measure of the offence severity and parameter values which are used to compute some of

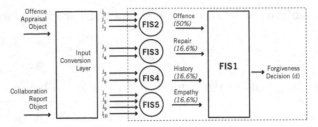

Fig. 3. System architecture integrating the eleven constituent motivations and the FIS decision makers

the constituent motivation values. These include the intent, apology and reparative actions offered by the offender. The embarrassment propensity constituent motivation is a constant value that has been stored in the input conversion layer. The motivations that rely on historical data, such as offence frequency, historical relationship, similarity and prior familiarity between the offender-victim and visible acknowledgement are computed separately in the input conversion layer to be later passed as signals to the decision maker. Upon completing the interaction, both the Collaboration Report and the Offence Appraisal objects are stored so that each user builds up a history over time.

6   Conclusions

This article presented forgiveness in light of the prosocial and healing benefits it brings to human societies. We proposed the inclusion of forgiveness online as a way to encourage prosocial behaviors both in the victim and offender. The motivation behind our work is the reparative nature of forgiveness in some cases, while the destructive consequences of its absence in others. We went on to discuss the formation of forgiveness by the collective 'accumulation' of four positive motivations. Resulting from this definition, we designed an operational model additively shaped by the motivations' interactions, implemented with fuzzy inference systems. In doing this, our guiding principle was to create a model that is straightforward to automate, and can be integrated into any platform e.g. multi-agent systems or configured for any application domain e.g. e-commerce. The fuzzy sets that FIS uses as a basis to make an inference are written in a natural processing language which is both comprehensive and replicable by a wider audience ranging from social scientists to computer scientists. Even more, fuzzy rules offer flexibility in changing the weights of the motivations to reflect any expert's judgment.

6.1   Raised Issues

The objective of this article was to bring forward the neglected but yet significant topic of forgiveness while at the same time creating an operational model that can be easily adapted in a number of domains. Although psychology offers positive prospects for forgiveness applications, we cannot neglect the possible challenges we may face when integrating and evaluating such a model in a computer-mediated environment:

Vulnerability: Forgiveness may encourage harmful behaviors by withdrawing well-deserved punishment [6]. As in many applications, users may 'hijack' the system and find ways to manipulate it to their advantage. Therefore, a responsible and careful facilitation is vital.

Semantics: Human actors' expectations, perception and understanding of forgiveness often exceed the actual function of forgiveness as formally given in psychology [3]. For example, despite colloquial beliefs, forgetting or trusting is not part of forgiveness. We intend to address this point with the design of clear and communicative language during the forgiveness facilitation. It should be emphasised that forgiveness does not automatically repair trust. Even more, given the disparity between lay understanding and formal definitions of forgiveness, it is argued that the word 'forgiveness' should not be displayed directly during the users interaction.

Training and Incentives: A well-known problem in reputation mechanisms is that users are not inclined to report their experiences unless they are negative. In order for the forgiveness model to work properly, this issue has to be resolved. It is therefore vital that users are trained on why this mechanism is important, what information it requires to work efficiently, and given incentives to report equally on their positive and negative experiences. This issue should be also considered when designing the reporting interfaces so that the information input required is minimal.

Promotion of inhibition: The 'collection' and presentation of judgment factors may enhance prosocial decisions during offences that warrant forgiveness but they may have the opposite effect during severe offences that are well-deserving of punishment. Often, online users are more uninhibited (e.g. [16]) compared to their offline conduct. One could clearly argue that due to this online disposition, higher severity offences emphasized in the interface, may support unjustifiably severe punishments. It is therefore proposed that the forgiveness facilitation takes place only in the event of positive forgiveness decisions, while users can rely on 'traditional' trust and reputation mechanisms during negative forgiveness decisions.

The offender's privacy: In presenting the relevant constituent motivations to the victim of the offence, it could be argued that the offender's privacy is compromised. Although we do not address this issue directly, it is recommended that users are first trained on the purpose of the tools and also given the choice to turn off the forgiveness component if desired.

Objective Ratings: The severity and utility ratings for each offence and collaboration are provided by the overall community. Therefore, the ratings used by the model to make its inference are objective and representative of the collective opinion. To that effect, studies have shown weak correlations between subjective and objective judgments [4]. In arguing for personalization rather than objectivity, we choose objectivity as we believe it is important to promote a collective view rather than to allow for individuals skewed judgments. While we believe that objective assessments of this kind are important, users autonomy should be respected. In that sense, the interface will output the eleven constituent motivations so that users' decisions can be informed both by their own judgment but also by the FIS inference.

6.2   Further Work

Further work on forgiveness will focus on four separate lines of investigation: refining the constituent motivation formulas, evaluating the fuzzy rules, designing the presentation of the facilitation tool and exploring the impact of the forgiveness mechanism on human behaviour. Specifically, we intend to address the first point with the design of more sophisticated formulas for the eleven constituents. For instance, the victim's beneficial history with the offender can be seen in light of the utility and frequency of benefits, while it is also possible to measure utility in terms of relative utility. An offender of medium utility may be considered a good partner in a community of overall low beneficial transactions. Secondly, although the fuzzy rules were tailored around the theory of forgiveness, there is still a need to evaluate the forgiveness mechanism to determine whether the inference is accurate. This will be done through a series of questionnaires correlating users' judgments to the ones generated by the system. Thirdly, as discussed earlier, the word forgiveness is loaded with different meaning, depending on who the speaker is. In designing an intelligent interface which will facilitate forgiveness, it is important to convey the constituent motivations and the final forgiveness decision in the appropriate language. Finally, the most important point of interest is whether the forgiveness mechanism offers the benefits hypothesized. Some open research questions on this topic are whether people will follow the forgiveness recommendation and if the act of forgiving via this form of facilitation will alleviate anger resulting from a disrupted interaction.

Acknowledgements

Special thanks to Paolo Petta, Maria Chli and Jens Riegelsberger for their valuable input. Theodore Georgas is gratefully acknowledged for his assistance. The reviewers' comments were especially helpful. This research was funded by the HUMAINE IST Framework VI Network of Excellence.

References

1. S. Boon and L. Sulsky. Attributions of blame and forgiveness in romantic relationships: A policy-capturing study. *Journal of Social Behavior and Personality*, 12:19–26, 1997.
2. A. Buss. *Self-consciousness and social anxiety*. W. H. Freeman: San Francisco, CA, 1980.
3. J. Exline, E. Worthington, P. Hill, and M. McCullough. Forgiveness and justice: A research agenda for social and personality psychology. *Personality and Social Psychology Review*, 7:337–348, 2003.

4. F. Fincham, H. Jackson, and S. Beach. Transgression severity and forgiveness: Different moderators for objective and subjective severity. *Journal of Social and Clinical Psychology*, (in press).
5. R. Gruen and G. Mendelsohn. Emotional responses to affective displays in others: The distinction between empathy and sympathy. *Journal of Personality and Social Psychology*, 51:609–614, 1986.
6. M. Holmgren. Forgiveness and the intrinsic value of persons. *American Philosophical Quarterly*, 30(4):341–451, 1993.
7. B. Kelln and J. Ellard. An equity theory analysis of the impact of forgiveness and retribution on transgressor compliance. *Personality and Social Psychology Bulletin*, 25:864–872, 1999.
8. A. Manstead and G. Semin. Social transgression, social perspectives, and social emotionality. *Motivation and Emotion*, 5:249–261, 1981.
9. D. Marcus, J. Wilson, and R. Miller. Are perceptions of emotion in the eye of the beholder? a social relations analysis of judgments of embarrassment. *Personality and Social Psychology Bulletin*, 22:1220–1228, 1996.
10. M. McCullough. Forgiveness who does it and how do they do it. *Psychological Science*, 10(6):194–197, 2001.
11. M. McCullough, K. Rachal, S. Sandage, E. Worthington, S. Brown, and T. Hight. Interpersonal forgiving in close relationships: Ii. theoretical elaboration and measurement. *Journal of Personality and Social Psychology*, 75:1586–1603, 1998.
12. M. McCullough, E. Worthington, and K. Rachal. Interpersonal forgiving in close relationships. *Journal of Personality and Social Psychology*, 73(2):321–336, 1997.
13. R. Miller. Empathic embarrassment: Situational and personal determinants of reactions to the embarrassment of another. *Journal of Personality and Social Psychology*, 53:1061–1069, 1987.
14. A. Modigliani. Embarrassability scale. In *Measures of personality and social psychological attitudes*, pages 173–176. Academic Press: San Diego, CA, 1991.
15. P. Resnick, R. Zeckhauser, E. Friedman, and K. Kuwabara. Reputation systems. *Communications of the ACM*, 43(12):45–48, 2000.
16. W. Stritzke, A. Nguyen, and K. Durkin. Shyness and computer-mediated communication: A self-presentational theory perspective. *Media Psychology*, 6(1):1–22, 2004.
17. M. Sugeno. *Industrial Application of Fuzzy Control*. Elsevier, 1985.
18. A. Vasalou and G. Piolle. Fuzzy rules of forgiveness. http://www.luminainteractive.com/research/frules.pdf, 2005.
19. A. Vasalou and J. Pitt. Reinventing forgiveness: A formal investigation of moral facilitation. In *Trust Management, Third International Conference, iTrust 2005*, volume LNCS3477, pages 146–160. Springer, 2005.
20. C. Witvliet, E. Worthington, N. Wade, and J. Berry. Justice and forgiveness: Three experimental studies. Presentation at the Christian Association of Psychological Studies, Arlington Heights, IL, 2002.
21. E. Worthington and M. Scherer. Forgiveness is an emotion-focused coping strategy that can reduce health risks and promote health resilience: Theory, review, and hypotheses. *Psychology and Health*, 19:385–405, 2004.

A Novel Protocol for Communicating Reputation in P2P Networks

Kouki Yonezawa

Knowledge Media Laboratory,
Graduate School of Engineering,
Hokkaido University,
Sapporo, Hokkaido, Japan
yonezawa@meme.hokudai.ac.jp

Abstract. Many reputation systems mainly concentrate on avoiding untrustworthy agents by communicating reputation. Here arises the problem that when an agent does not know another agent very much then there is no way to notice such ambiguity. This paper shows a new protocol in which an agent can notice that ambiguity using the notion of statistics, and illustrates the facility of designing agents' algorithms as well as existing reputation systems.

1 Introduction

In P2P networks, agents can communicate their own opinions for collaboration in order to avoid other agents that are not so trustworthy among strangers. Here it occurs that an agent is unconfident about its opinions to others. It would be better that other agents that received an opinion of another agent take the ambiguity into account. In the existing systems, however, such ambiguity has rarely been considered.

This paper gives a novel protocol for communication of their opinions. It uses the notion of statistics, that is, in this protocol reputation is considered as a tuple that consists of the average and the variance. The average and the variance of reputation correspond to the level of trustworthiness and the expected fluctuation, respectively.

This approach is quite different from researches [13, 16, 17] that use the beta function to represent trust and reputation. In their researches, reputation is considered as a probabilistic distribution by each agent but only the alternative evaluation, say, "cooperate" or "defect", is used, and so agents do not communicate the parameters of their probabilistic distributions themselves. On the other hand, we assume that the degree of the performance is defined as a real number in $[0, 1]$, which we will mention later, and agents need to communicate the parameters themselves.

In our protocol there are two kinds of reputation, reputation as a recommender and that as a participant, as well as in [12, 14]. Higher reputation as a recommender means that its opinions to other agents as a participant seem

K. Stølen et al. (Eds.): iTrust 2006, LNCS 3986, pp. 412–422, 2006.

closer to their actual performance. Reputation is updated after knowing agents' actual performances. Here, it should be noted that the variance of reputation that the agent had sent together with the average should be taken into account in updating its reputation.

We do not think that showing the way to design algorithms or to evaluate them is so important. Thus in this paper, we show the facility of designing efficient algorithms of agents as well as the existing protocols through several simulations instead. In our simulations, we consider several typical malicious agents that may be harmful for others, and we show the examples of designing efficient algorithms against such attacks.

The remainder of this paper is organized as follows. Section 2 describes reputation in P2P networks. Section 3 gives the formal model and several definitions. Section 4 explains our idea and our representation for reputation. Section 5 shows our result for appealing the facility of designing strategies. In Section 6 we mention several related papers. Finally, Section 7 concludes this paper.

2   Reputation in P2P Networks

In P2P networks, each agent can be a participant, which has several files and allows to download them, and can be a recommender, which has opinions to other agents and tells them to others. In [12, 14], trust or reputation as a participant and that as a recommender are defined as the different types and we follow their definition.

2.1   Reputation as a Participant

Reputation as a participant of agent A represents the degree of trustworthiness about A's performance, for example, downloading speed or the number of files A treats. It should be calculated with the performance of A, and its reputation in the eyes of other agents, and their opinions as a recommender to A. In the following discussion, this is denoted by Rep^{P}.

2.2   Reputation as a Recommender

Reputation as a recommender of agent A represents how trustworthy A's opinions about others are. It should be calculated with performances of agents whose reputation has been sent by A. We should note that there may be agents that are trustworthy as a recommender but untrustworthy as a participant. In the following, this reputation is denoted by Rep^{R}.

3   Formal Model

In this section, we give the definition for modeling P2P networks. Suppose that there are n agents each of which acts independently on others. These agents

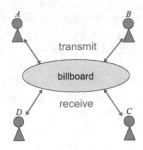

Fig. 1. Communication between agents with a billboard

communicate their own opinions through a billboard, where each agent can know all the opinions of others[1] (see Fig. 1).

3.1   Performance of Agents

In [12], performances of agents are distinguished according to the contexts and thus reputation is also distinguished. In P2P networks, the contexts are a downloading speed, the number of files an agent treats, security, and so on. We define agent A's performance as a *service vector* $s_A = (s_A^1, \ldots, s_A^k)$, where k is the number of contexts and $s_A^i \in [0, 1]$ for $i = 1, \ldots, k$.

3.2   Satisfaction

Next, we define the satisfaction of an agent with the performance of another agent. It may occur that two agents have different satisfactions with the same performance of the other agent. Namely, suppose that there are two agents one of which prefers a downloading speed and another emphasizes security. Then their their opinions to others would differ. Thus we assume that each agent has a *preference vector*. A preference vector of agent A is denoted by $p_A = (p_A^1, \ldots, p_A^k)$, where p_A^i corresponds to how much A emphasizes the ith item and $p_A^i \in [0, 1]$ for $i = 1, \ldots, k$.

The satisfaction of agent A with agent B, $S_A(B)$, is defined as an inner product of B's service vector s_B and A's preference vector p_A, that is,

$$S_A(B) = \sum_{i=1}^{k} s_B^i \cdot p_A^i.$$

Note that by the definition $S_A(B) \in [0, 1]$ holds.

3.3   Flow at Each Round

In our settings, we have T rounds at which each agent gives its performance. At the beginning of one round, each agent performs and knows its satisfactions

---

[1] In [7], Douceur called such a structure a *communication cloud*.

with others. After that, it updates the opinions to others as a recommender with such satisfactions. Then it updates the opinions as a participant with such satisfaction and the opinions as a recommender that are already updated. After all agents decide their opinions, they send those to a billboard and they know opinions of other agents, which are updated at the current round. (Note that in [12], the opinions as a participant are first updated. However, we do not follow because the error of evaluating them would cause worse results in reality.)

In the settings aforementioned, we execute several simulations where an agent tries to protect itself against malicious attacks. We assume that there are αn agents that execute our method, which we call *honest* agents, and each honest agent does not know even which agents are honest.

4   Protocol with Statistics

As we mentioned above, we introduce the notion of statistics for representing reputation. In our protocol, reputation is defined as a tuple that consists of two elements, the average and the variance.

Our idea is as follows: suppose that the performance of an agent is extreme, i.e., it gives the performance of 0 or 1 alternatively. Then the average of the performance is 0.5, but it does not seem so useful for other agents because its performance is either completely good or completely bad. Thus we consider that introducing variance enables us to represent such the performance more precisely.

As we told in Section 1, the average of reputation means its level and the variance means the degree of the fluctuation. In the above case, other agents would have higher variances for the agent.

In the following discussion, reputation of B in the eyes of A is denoted by $\mathrm{Rep}_A(B) = (\mathrm{E}_A(B), \mathrm{Var}_A(B))$, where $\mathrm{E}_A(B)$ and $\mathrm{Var}_A(B)$ denote the *average* and the *variance* of B's reputation, respectively. It should be noted that there may be agents that report only an average or ones that do not report their opinions at some round.

5   Experiments

In this section, we show the results of several experiments. Before we mention the result, we need to explain our strategy that each agent executes independently. Note that as we mention in Section 1, it is not so important to design algorithms themselves but it is important to show the facility of designing algorithms. Thus, our algorithm looks kind of simple.

5.1   Our Strategy

Our strategy decides the opinion of an agent together with the current performance of the target agent and opinions of other agents. When agent A calculates $\mathrm{Rep}_A^{\mathrm{R}}(B)$, the reputation of B in the eyes of A as a recommender, the strategy decides that using the difference of S_C and $\mathrm{Rep}_B^{\mathrm{P}}(C)$, where C is in set $\mathcal{C}$, which denotes the subset of agents which has Rep_B^{P}, the reputation in the eyes of B, that is, the subset of agents that are observed by B.

Before we mention the method, we define a useful function $g_A(B,t)$. We define $g_A'(B,C,i,t) = \frac{1}{t}(S_A(C,i) - E_B^{\text{P}}(C,t))^2 / \{\text{Var}_B^{\text{P}}(C,t)\}^{1/2}$, where $S_A(C,i)$ denotes the satisfaction of A with C at round i. Intuitively, g_A' means the ratio between the variance of the difference between S_A and the average of an other's opinion as a participant, and its standard deviation, the square root of the variance. So we define $g_A(B,t)$ as follows:

$$g_A(B,t) = \frac{1}{(t+1)|\mathcal{C}|} \sum_{C \in \mathcal{C}} \sum_{i=1}^{t+1} \min\{g_A'(B,C,i,t), 1/g_A'(B,C,i,t)\}.$$

$g_A(B,t+1)$ gets larger when the difference between S_A and E_B^{P} is similar to $\text{Var}_B^{\text{P}\,1/2}$. Note that by the definition, it holds that $g_A(B,i) \in [0,1]$ for any A, B and i. Next, we give the definition of $h_A(B,t)$ for representing the normalized difference between S_A and E_B^{P}, namely,

$$h_A(B,t) = \frac{1}{(t+1)|\mathcal{C}|} \sum_{C \in \mathcal{C}} \sum_{i=1}^{t+1} \{1 - \text{norm}(|S_A(C,i) - E_B^{\text{P}}(C,t)|, E_B^{\text{P}}(C,t))\},$$

where $\text{norm}(x,y)$ means that for $x, y \in [0,1]$, if $y < 0.5$ then $\text{norm}(x,y) = x/(1-y)$ and otherwise then $\text{norm}(x,y) = x/y$. By the definition, $\text{norm}(|x-y|,y) \in [0,1]$ for any $x, y \in [0,1]$ and thus $h_A(B,i) \in [0,1]$ for any A, B and i. $h_A(B)$ gets larger when $S_A - E_B^{\text{P}}$ is relatively small at each round.

Here, $\text{Rep}_A^{\text{R}}(B,t+1) = (E_A^{\text{R}}(B,t+1), \text{Var}_A^{\text{R}}(B,t+1))$, $\text{Rep}_A^{\text{R}}(B)$ at round $t+1$, is calculated as follows:

$$E_A^{\text{R}}(B,t+1) = \beta \cdot g_A(B,t) + (1-\beta) \cdot h_A(B,t),$$

$$\text{Var}_A^{\text{R}}(B,t+1) = \frac{1}{(t+1)|\mathcal{C}|}$$

$$\times \sum_{C \in \mathcal{C}} \sum_{i=1}^{t+1} \{\beta \cdot g_A(B,t) + (1-\beta) \cdot h_A(B,t) - E_A^{\text{R}}(B,t+1)\}^2,$$

where β is a constant between 0 and 1 for weighting $g_A(B,t)$ and $h_A(B,t)$. In our simulations, β is fixed 0.5, i.e., we consider g_A as well as h_A.

After that, we calculate $\text{Rep}_A^{\text{P}}(B,t+1)$, B's reputation as a participant in the eyes of A at round $t+1$, with $\text{Rep}_D^{\text{P}}(B)$ and $S_A(B)$, where D is in $\mathcal{D}$ that is the subset of all agents that observe agent B. So, $\text{Rep}_A^{\text{P}}(B,t+1)$ is calculated as follows:

$$E_A^{\text{P}}(B,t+1) = \gamma \cdot \frac{1}{t+1} \sum_{i=1}^{t+1} S_A(B,i)$$

$$+ (1-\gamma) \cdot \sum_{D \in \mathcal{D}} \frac{E_A^{\text{R}}(D,t+1) \cdot E_D^{\text{P}}(B,t)}{E_A^{\text{R}}(D,t+1)},$$

$$\text{Var}^{\text{P}}_A(B, t+1) = \gamma \cdot \frac{1}{t+1} \sum_{i=1}^{t+1} (S_A(B,i) - \bar{S}_A(B))^2$$

$$+(1-\gamma) \cdot \sum_{D \in \mathcal{D}} \frac{\text{E}^{\text{R}}_A(D, t+1) \cdot \text{Var}^{\text{P}}_D(B, t)}{\text{E}^{\text{R}}_A(D, t+1)},$$

where γ is a constant in $[0, 1]$ for weighting and $\bar{S}_A(B)$ denotes the average of $S_A(B, i)$ for $i = 1, \ldots, t+1$. The second terms of these two formulas mean the weighted average of $\text{E}^{\text{P}}_D(B)$ and $\text{Var}^{\text{P}}_D(B)$ by $\text{E}^{\text{R}}_A(D)$, respectively, which means the average taking into account the degree of the recommenders' trustworthiness (c.f., see [12]). In our simulations, we set $\gamma = 0$, namely, we consider only other agents' opinions, to show the importance of them like [12].

In the following, we consider two typical kinds of agents that do not execute the algorithm above. One of those uses the simpler algorithm to calculate reputation and another does not report variance or take variances of reputation into account. What we need to do is to show that reputation of such malicious agents in the eyes of honest agents as a recommender becomes lower than that of other honest agents. We will show in the following sections that the algorithm above can perform better than such agents. Here, our setting is as follows:

- the number of agents: 100
- the ratio between the number of honest agents and that of all agents $\alpha = 0.1$
- the total number of rounds $T = 100$
- the initial values of average: values in $[0, 1]$ are assigned at random
- the initial values of variance: values in $[0, 0.1]$ are assigned at random
- preference vectors: each element is assigned a value in $[0, 1]$ randomly
- service performance: values in $[0, 1]$ are assigned at random, that is, the average is 0.5 and the variance is $1/12$.

5.2   Against Superficial Agents

We consider the agents that emphasize only the difference between the opinions of others and the actual performance, which we call *superficial* agents. Formally, a superficial agent A_{sf} calculates reputation as a recommender as follows:

$$\text{E}^{\text{R}}_{A_{\text{sf}}}(B, t+1) = \frac{1}{(t+1)|\mathcal{C}|} \sum_{C \in \mathcal{C}} \sum_{i=1}^{t+1} |S_{A_{\text{sf}}}(B, i) - \text{Rep}^{\text{P}}_C(B, t)|,$$

$$\text{Var}^{\text{R}}_{A_{\text{sf}}}(B, t+1) = \frac{1}{(t+1)|\mathcal{C}|}$$

$$\times \sum_{C \in \mathcal{C}} \sum_{i=1}^{t+1} (|S_{A_{\text{sf}}}(B, i) - \text{Rep}^{\text{P}}_C(B, t)| - \text{E}^{\text{R}}_{A_{\text{sf}}}(B, t+1))^2,$$

and reputation as a participant as follows:

$$\text{E}^{\text{P}}_{A_{\text{sf}}}(B, t+1) = \frac{1}{t+1} \sum_{i=1}^{t+1} S_{A_{\text{sf}}}(B, i),$$

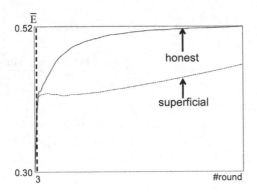

Fig. 2. Comparing $\bar{\mathrm{E}}^{\mathrm{R}}$ between honest agents and superficial agents

$$\mathrm{Var}^{\mathrm{P}}_{A_{\mathrm{sf}}}(B, t+1) = \frac{1}{t+1} \sum_{i=1}^{t+1} (S_{A_{\mathrm{sf}}}(B, i) - \mathrm{E}^{\mathrm{P}}_{A_{\mathrm{sf}}}(B, t+1))^2.$$

We compare $\bar{\mathrm{E}}^{\mathrm{R}}_{A_{\mathrm{honest}}}$, the average of $\mathrm{E}^{\mathrm{R}}_{A_{\mathrm{honest}}}$, over other honest agents and that over superficial agents. See Fig. 2. You can see that after the third round $\bar{\mathrm{E}}^{\mathrm{R}}$ over honest agents gets greater than that over superficial agents. Thus we succeed to get the reputation of superficial agents in the eyes of honest agents lower than that of other honest ones.

5.3   Against Lazy Agents

Next, we consider the *lazy* agents, which report only the average of reputation and at each round they do not calculate the variance at all. Namely, lazy agent A_{lazy} calculates the reputation as a recommender as follows:

$$\mathrm{E}^{\mathrm{R}}_{A_{\mathrm{lazy}}}(B, t+1) = \frac{1}{(t+1)|\mathcal{C}|} \sum_{C \in \mathcal{C}} \sum_{i=1}^{t+1} \mathrm{norm}(|S_{A_{\mathrm{lazy}}}(B, i) - \mathrm{E}^{\mathrm{P}}_C(B, t)|, \mathrm{E}^{\mathrm{P}}_C(B, t)),$$

where $\mathrm{norm}(x, y)$ is defined in Section 5.1, and that as a participant as follow:

$$\mathrm{E}^{\mathrm{P}}_{A_{\mathrm{lazy}}}(B, t+1) = \frac{1}{t+1} \sum_{i=1}^{t+1} S_{A_{\mathrm{lazy}}}(B, i).$$

In this case, honest agents have to speculate the variance of a lazy agent's reputation because it does not calculate the variance at all. Here, they speculate that from the history of $\mathrm{E}^{\mathrm{R}}_{A_{\mathrm{honest}}}(B_{\mathrm{lazy}})$. More precisely, they use the difference between $\mathrm{E}^{R}_{A_{\mathrm{honest}}}(B_{\mathrm{lazy}}, i)$ and $\bar{\mathrm{E}}^{R}_{A_{\mathrm{honest}}}(B_{\mathrm{lazy}})$, the average of $\mathrm{E}^{R}_{A_{\mathrm{honest}}}(B_{\mathrm{lazy}}, i)$ over the whole rounds. The speculated variance of lazy agent B_{lazy}'s reputation in the eyes of A_{honest}, which is an honest agent, is calculated as follows:

$$\mathrm{Var}^{\mathrm{R}}_{A_{\mathrm{honest}}}(B_{\mathrm{lazy}}, t+1) = \frac{1}{(t+1)|\mathcal{C}|}$$

$$\times \sum_{C \in \mathcal{C}} \sum_{i=1}^{t+1} (\mathrm{E}^{\mathrm{R}}_{A_{\mathrm{honest}}}(B_{\mathrm{lazy}}, i) - \bar{\mathrm{E}}^{\mathrm{R}}_{A_{\mathrm{honest}}}(B_{\mathrm{lazy}}))^2,$$

$$\mathrm{Var}^{\mathrm{P}}_{A_{\mathrm{honest}}}(B_{\mathrm{lazy}}, t+1) = \frac{\sum_{C \in \mathcal{C}} \mathrm{E}^{\mathrm{R}}_{A_{\mathrm{honest}}}(C, t+1) \cdot \bar{\mathrm{E}}^{\mathrm{R}}_{A_{\mathrm{honest}}}(C)}{\sum_{C \in \mathcal{C}} \mathrm{E}^{\mathrm{R}}_{A_{\mathrm{honest}}}(C, t+1)},$$

where $\bar{\mathrm{E}}^{\mathrm{R}}_{A_{\mathrm{honest}}}(B_{\mathrm{lazy}})$ and $\bar{\mathrm{E}}^{\mathrm{R}}_{A_{\mathrm{honest}}}(C)$ denote the average of $\mathrm{E}^{\mathrm{R}}_{A_{\mathrm{honest}}}(B_{\mathrm{lazy}}, i)$ for agent B_{lazy} and that for agent C according for round, respectively.

In the same way as Section 5.2, we compare $\bar{\mathrm{E}}^{\mathrm{R}}_{A_{\mathrm{honest}}}$ over other honest agents and that over lazy agents at each round. The result is shown in Fig. 3. You can see that $\mathrm{E}^{\mathrm{R}}_{A_{\mathrm{honest}}}(B_{\mathrm{lazy}})$ gets lower than $\mathrm{E}^{\mathrm{R}}_{A_{\mathrm{honest}}}(B_{\mathrm{honest}})$.

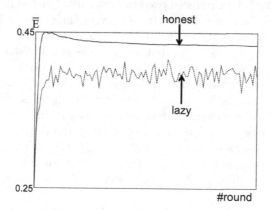

Fig. 3. Comparing $\bar{\mathrm{E}}^{\mathrm{R}}$ between honest agents and lazy agents

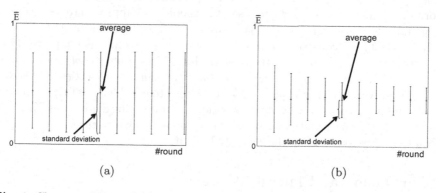

(a)   (b)

Fig. 4. Changes of Rep of (a) other honest agents and (b) lazy agents in the eyes of an honest agent

Here we show another interesting feature. Fig. 4(a) and (b) show the changes of Rep, at every 10 rounds, of (a) other honest agents and (b) lazy agents in the eyes of an honest agent, respectively, considering their standard deviations together. One can see that the averaged standard deviation of lazy agents' reputation gets smaller gradually as the round goes by. It should be noted that in the previous simulation we could not find such a feature.

6   Related Work

There are many researches on trust and reputation systems. Policymaker [5] and KeyNote [6] proposed the protocols of trust networks without a decentralized server, namely, they work in networks where each agent has to decide its own action independently. However, they considered only one type of trust and in order to tackle with actual problems several kinds of trust and reputation are required.

Moreton and Twigg [14] introduced two kinds of trust, trust as a recommender and that as a participant, and showed the safety of their system by using two different layers of networks. Their measure of trust is represented with logic symbols, and so we are just not sure that using those is useful for more precise representation of trust and reputation. Liu and Issarny [12] considered the similar structure in ad hoc networks and showed the results of several simulations. They considered reputation as a degree of how trustworthy an agent is, but we consider that it is not enough for representing reputation as we mentioned in Section 4.

Mui *et al.* [13] proposed the formal model of trust and reputation, and there are several advanced results using their model (see [16, 17], for example). In their research, those are considered as a probabilistic distribution but they considered satisfaction of agents as 0 or 1. We think it may less useful to represent trust and reputation.

Recently, on the other hand, theoretical researches on trust and reputation have been done for several years. On collaborative filtering, where agents try to avoid untrustworthy peers without having knowledge in advance if an agent is trustworthy or not, Kumar *et al.* [9] first proposed the theoretical approach to recommendation and there are several noticeable results [1, 2, 3, 4, 10]. Drineas *et al.* showed that it is possible to construct recommendation systems which is guaranteed on the performance by the theoretical analysis. Moreover, Kamvar *et al.* pointed out that reputation networks in P2P networks have the similar properties as PageRank [15]. However, in either paper, it is kind of hard to consider what the measure means, namely, what we can achieve as a benefit by improving algorithms. Now we consider to model our framework to a theoretical model in which the metric we aim to achieve is easy to represent the concrete benefit.

7   Conclusion and Future Work

In this paper we show a novel protocol for communicating reputation using the notion of statistics and the facility of designing algorithm against typical malicious attacks. Our protocol enables to give more precise representation of reputation and we are sure that it can be applied into other systems. Comparing to existing systems, our protocol only requires one more parameter and it gives more flexible representation of reputation.

Here we consider two points to do in the future; one is to give a theoretical analysis. There are several theoretical analyses that shows the efficient algorithm for reputation system. Thus we consider to model this framework and analyze the efficiency. Another one is to implement our protocol into P2P networks. It is also important to show the advantage of our protocol in real networks as well as execution of simulations.

References

1. B. Awerbuch, Y. Azar, Z. Lotker, B. Patt-Shamir, and M.R. Tuttle. Collaborate With Strangers To Find Own Preferences. Proc. 17th Annual Symposium on Parallelism on Algorithms and Architectures (SPAA '04), 2004.
2. B. Awerbuch and R.D. Kleinberg. Competitive Collaborative Learning. Proc. 18th Annual Conference on Learning Theory (COLT '05), 2005.
3. B. Awerbuch, B. Patt-Shamir, D. Peleg, and M. Tuttle. Improved Recommendation Systems. Proc. ACM-SIAM Symposium on Discrete Algorithms (SODA), 2005.
4. B. Awerbuch, B. Patt-Shamir, D. Peleg, and M. Tuttle. Collaboration of Untrusting Peers with Changing Interests. Proc. 5th ACM Conference on Electric Commerce (EC), 2004.
5. M. Blaze, J. Feigenbaum, and J. Lacy. Decentralized Trust Management, Proc. 1996 IEEE Symposium on Security and Privacy, 164-173, 1996.
6. M. Blaze, J. Feigenbaum, and A.D. Keromytis. KeyNote: Trust management for public-key infrastructure, Proc. Security Protocols: 6th International Workshop, 59-63, 1999.
7. J.R. Douceur. The Sybil Attack. Proc. 1st International Workshop on Peer-to-Peer Systems (IPTPS), 251-260, 2002.
8. P. Drineas, I. Kerenidis, and P. Raghavan. Competitive Recommendation Systems. Proc. Annual ACM Symposium on Theory of Computing, 2002.
9. R. Kumar, P. Raghavan, S. Rajagopalan, and A. Tomkins. Recommendation Systems: A Probabilistic Analysis. Proc. 39th Annual Symposium on Foundations of Computer Science (FOCS), 664-681, 1998.
10. J. Kleinburg and M. Sandler. Using Mixture Models for Collaborative Filtering. Proc. Thirty-sixth Annual ACM Symposium on Theory of Computing (STOC), 2004.
11. S.D. Kamvar, M.T. Schlosser, and H. Garcia-Molina. The EigenTrust Algorithm for Reputation Management in P2P Networks. Proc. Twelfth International World Wide Web Conference (WWW2003), 640-651, 2003.
12. J. Liu and V. Issarny. Enhanced Reputation Mechanism for Mobile Ad Hoc Networks. Proc. Trust Management 2004 (iTrust 2004), 48-62, 2004.
13. L. Mui, M. Mohtashemi, and A. Halberstadt. A Computational Model of Trust and Reputation. Proc. 35th Annual Hawaii International Conference on System Science (HICSS '02), 2002.
14. T. Moreton and A. Twigg. Enforcing Collaboration in Peer-to-Peer Routing Services. Proc. Trust Management 2003 (iTrust 2003), 255-270, 2003.

15. L. Page, S. Brin, R. Motwani, and T. Winograd. The PageRank Citation Ranking: Bringing Order to the Web. Technical report, Stanford Digital Library Technologies Project, 1998.
16. J. Patel, W.T.L. Teacy, N.R. Jennings, and M. Luck. A Probabilistic Trust Model for Handling Inaccurate Reputation Sources. Proc. Trust Management 2005 (iTrust 2005), 193-209, 2005.
17. A. Whitby, A. Jøsang, and J. Indulska, Filtering Out Unfair Ratings in Bayesian Reputation Systems. Proc. Workshop on Trust in Agent Societies (AAMAS 2004), 2004.

A Scalable Probabilistic Approach to Trust Evaluation

Xiaoqing Zheng, Zhaohui Wu, Huajun Chen, and Yuxin Mao

College of Computer Science, Zhejiang University, Hangzhou 310027, China
{zxqingcn, wzh, huajunsir, maoyx}@zju.edu.cn

Abstract. The Semantic Web will only achieve its full potential when users have trust in its operations and in the quality of services and information provided, so trust is inevitably a high-level and crucial issue. Modeling trust properly and exploring techniques for establishing computational trust is at the heart of the Semantic Web to realize its vision. We propose a scalable probabilistic approach to trust evaluation which combines a variety of sources of information and takes four types of costs (operational, opportunity, service charge and consultant fee) and utility into consider during the process of trust evaluation. Our approach gives trust a strict probabilistic interpretation which can assist users with making better decisions in choosing the appropriate service providers according to their preferences. A formal robust analysis has been made to examine the performance of our method.

1 Introduction

Just as the Internet is shifting its focus from information and communication to a knowledge delivery infrastructure, the Semantic Web extends the current Web to enable Web entities (software agents, users and programs) to work in cooperation in which information and services are given well-defined meaning. The philosophy of the Semantic Web is that anybody can produce information or provide services or consume and enjoy anyone else's information and services on open environment full of uncertainty and dynamic. There is likely to be a service-rich environment, necessitating the selection between similar services being offered by different providers. The Semantic Web, conceived as a collection of agents, brings new opportunities and challenges to trust research. One of these challenges is modeling trust properly and exploring techniques for establishing computational trust and determining the provenance and quality of content and services. We need to face this important issue of how to decide how trustworthy each information source is and which service we should choose according to these trustworthiness. Trust is a response to uncertainty and uncertainty can be considered as the lack of adequate information to make a decision. Uncertainty is problem because it may prevent us from making the best decision and may even cause a bad decision to be made. Some fundamental questions should be answered before trying to find the best way of modeling trust. These are: what is the exact meaning of trust from the Semantic Web point of view, what information is relevant when evaluating trust, and how to combine information from various sources to produce final trust value. Scalable

K. Stølen et al. (Eds.): iTrust 2006, LNCS 3986, pp. 423–438, 2006.

probabilistic approximation seems a direction for future research to deal with this uncertainty. In this paper, we try to answer these questions and propose a composite trust model based on Bayesian sequential analysis which gives trust a formal probabilistic interpretation. Our model combines prior and reputation information to produce a composite assessment of an agent's likely quality and balances the costs (operational, opportunity service charge and consultant fee) and benefits (utility) when communicating or dealing with other agents.

Consider a scenario in which a user (*initiator* agent) want to find a service provider (*provider* agent) to fulfill a special task on the Semantic Web, and his problem is which provider may be the most suitable for him. Assuming that he maintains a list of acquaintances or neighbors (*consultant* agents), and gives each acquaintance a *reliability* factor that denotes what degree this acquaintance's statements can be believed. Each agent also has such a set of acquaintances. During the process of his evaluating the qualities of different providers and making the decision in selecting the best one among them, he can "gossip" with his acquaintances by exchanging information about their opinions on providers' qualities, termed *statements*. This process can be described as using the strategy of exploiting *transitivity*. The idea of this strategy is that an agent sends a message out to request opinions on the quality of the agent who can provide given service. The network of acquaintances of that agent will then either send back an opinion based on experience, or pass the message onto its acquaintances, many of which will be unknown to the first agent. The aim is to enhance the scope of an agent's knowledge by exploring the network feature of agent communities to bring in information from other, unknown, agents. We call it *reputation* of a given provider agent that integrates a number of opinions from acquaintances and acquaintances of acquaintances. Besides reputation information, we also consider initiator agent's *prior information* that is direct experience from history interactions with the provider agent and the various relationships that may exist between them (e.g. owned by the same organization, relationships derived from relationships between the agents' owners in the real life such as friendship or relatives). And then, the *trust* can be generated by incorporating prior and reputation information in our opinion.

The remainder of this paper is organized as follows. In Section 2, a brief overview of research on trust is presented and Section 3 proposes our closed and open trust models based on Bayesian sequential analysis. Then, in Section 4, we give experimental results that show how our models work across a wide variation of the number of agents, the quality of agent population and the accuracy of the survey in terms of precision and the corresponding costs. The conclusions and future work are summarized in Section 5.

2   Related Work

Given its importance, a number of computational models of trust have been developed in security, e-commerce and multi-agents systems. Probably the most widely used trust models are those on *eBay* and *Amazon* Auctions. Both of these are implemented as a centralized rating system so that their users can rate and learn about each other's reputation. For example, in *eBay*, sellers receive feedback (+1, 0, −1) for their reliability in each auction and their trust is calculated as the sum of those ratings over the last six months. Both approaches are completely centralized and require users to explicitly make and reveal their ratings of others. However, it is questionable if the ratings reflect the trustworthy behavior of sellers, since in the online marketplaces, it is very likely for users to misbehave or trick with malice. The worse is that these systems are not convenient for users to receive a personalized set of trusts according to their preferences.

Social network analysis techniques are used in [J. Golbeck et al., 2003] to measure trust over a Friend of a Friend (FOAF) network, extended with trust relations. This work describes the applicability of social network analysis to the Semantic Web, particularly discussing the multi-dimensional networks that evolve from ontological trust specifications. But this work uses simply function to calculate trust and does not consider more in depth investigation of algorithms for calculating trust. So, it is nearly impossible for application in real world. Moreover, the algorithm for evaluating trust in this method is just heuristic and no reasonable explanation in terms of mathematics.

[S. D. Ramchurn et al., 2003] develops a trust model, based on confidence and reputation, and shows how it can be concretely applied, using fuzzy sets, to guide agents in evaluating past interactions and in establishing new contracts with one another. But this model is rather complex and cannot be easily used in today's electronic communities. The main problem with their approach is that every agent must keep rather complex data structures, which can be laborious and time-consuming. Also, it is not clear how the agents get needed information and how well the model will scale when the number of agents grows.

[E.M. Maximilien and M.P. Singh, 2003] proposes a centralized agent to measure the reputation of Web services by monitoring and collecting client feedback, and making this information available to other agents. Relying on centralized institutions to measure trust takes the burden off the interactive agents when deciding which agents to trust. However, such systems raise the question of how trustworthy is the sources of their trust information in the first place, and why such trust warehouses should be trusted at all. We argue against these centralized units for measuring trust because of their scalability limitations and the implicit trust measurement mechanisms they adopt.

[Dong Huynh, 2004] presents FIRE, a trust and reputation model that integrates interaction trust, role-based trust, witness reputation and certified reputation to generate a comprehensive assessment of an agent's likely performance. But this work assumes that all agents are honest in exchanging information, uses static parametric model that can not dynamically adjust themselves to the change of environment, and has no learning abilities, so, it can not be used in real open environment.

[Yao Wang and Julita Vassileva, 2003] proposes a Bayesian network-based trust model for a file sharing peer-to-peer application which enables an agent consider its trust in a specific aspect of another agent's capability or in a combination of multiple aspects. According to this model, peers make recommendations to each other, by exchanging and comparing their Bayesian networks. After this comparison, the agents update their trust ratings of each other, depending on whether they share similar preferences, on the assumption that an agent with similar preferences is more likely to give suitable recommendations than others. However, the model's mathematical formulation for the calculation of trust can at best be described as intuitive—without justifications and their experiments just use a very simple naïve Bayesian network, which cannot represent complex relationships. Furthermore, this model is applicable in small-size network and does not scales well to any social network size because maintaining and comparing more complex Bayesian network for each agent will be computationally intractable.

3 Trust Model

The main point of a trust model is to provide a way to operate under uncertainty, not taking too many risks, not missing too many opportunities, not deliberating too long before making commitments. Therefore, before presenting our trust model it is necessary to understand the risks and benefits associated with the trust evaluation. There are many different kinds of costs and benefits an agent might incur when communicating or dealing with other agents and the trust model should balance these costs and benefits. We begin by extending the viewpoint of [K. O'Hara et at., 2004] and discussing four types of costs: operational, opportunity, service charge and consultant fee and continue by introducing utility function that is used to reflect the preferences of agent's owner.

Operational Cost. Operational cost is the expenses of computing trust value. In other words, this is the cost of setting up and operating the whole trust plan. Therefore, the more complex the algorithm is, the higher this cost is expected to be.

Opportunity Cost. Opportunity cost is the lost of missing some possibility of making better decision via further investigation. Generally, the more observations, the lower the opportunity costs.

Service Charge. Service providers differ from each other not only in their qualities but also in their charges of services. Service charge is that will be paid to the selected provider agent who provides fee-based services.

Consultant fee. Consultant fee is incurred when an agent asks the opinions of other agents who (may be professional in given domain) charge for their opinions.

Utility Function. To work mathematically with ideas of "preferences", it will be necessary to assign numbers indicating how much something is valued. Such numbers are called *utilities*, and *utility theory* deals with the development of such numbers. *Utility function* can be constructed to state preferences and will be used to estimate possible consequences of the decisions.

3.1 Closed Trust Model

In our model, the quality of provider agent can be considered to be an unknown numerical quantity, and will represent it by θ (possibly a vector) and it is possible to treat θ as a random quantity with a probability distribution. Consider the situation of an agent A try to make an estimate of agent B's trust value. A holds a prior information (subjective) of B, represented by distribution $\pi(\theta)$ (for either the continuous or discrete case), and request A's acquaintance to give opinions on B's quality. After A receives the assessments of B's quality from its acquaintances, A takes these statements as sample about θ. Outcome of these sample is a random variable and will be denoted X (Often X will be a vector). A particular realization of X will be denoted x and X will be assumed to be either a continuous or a discrete random variable, with density $f(x|\theta)$. Then, we can compute "posterior distribution" of θ given x, denoted $\pi(\theta|x)$. Just as the prior distribution reflects beliefs about θ prior to investigation in B's reputation, so $\pi(\theta|x)$ reflects the update beliefs about θ after (posterior to) observing the sample x. In other words, the posterior distribution combines the prior beliefs about θ with the information about θ contained in the sample, x, to give a composite picture of the final beliefs about θ. We take the posterior distribution of θ, $\pi(\theta|x)$, as the estimate of B's trust. If we want to take another investigation on B's quality for more accuracy, $\pi(\theta|x)$ will be used as prior distribution for the next investigation instead of original $\pi(\theta)$.

When several similar provider agents exist, A need to decide which one should be selected. At that time, the preferences of agent A's owner should be considered properly to make this decision. Therefore, *utility function* should be constructed for agent A's owner, which represented by $U_A(r)$, to express his preferences, where r represents rewards of the consequences of a decision. Supposing that $\pi(\theta|x)$ is the posterior distribution of provider agent B, the expected utility of function $U_A(r)$ over $\pi(\theta|x)$, denoted $E^{\pi(\theta|x)}[U_A(r)]$, is possible gain of consequence of selecting B. If there are several provider agents can be considered, we simply select one that will result in the most expected utility as decision.

By treating an agent as a node, the "knows" relationship as an edge and remember that trust is an asymmetric relation, a directed graph emerges. To facilitate the model description, agents and their environment are to be defined. To clarify the idea of our trust model, we begin with a simple illustration. Consider the scenario that agent A is evaluating trust value of B and C for being business. The set of all consultant agents that A requests for this evaluation as well as A, B, C can be considered to be a unique society of agents N. In our example (see Figure 1), N is $\{A, B, C, D, E, F, G, H, I, J, K\}$ and is called a "closed society of agents" with respect to A.

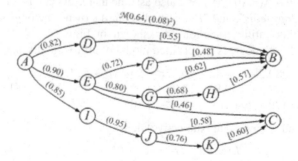

Fig. 1. A "closed society of agents" with respect to agent A

Decisions are more commonly called *actions* and the set of all possible actions under consideration will be denoted $\mathcal{A}$. In our example, initiator agent A is trying to decide whether to select agent B (action b) or C (action c) as business partner

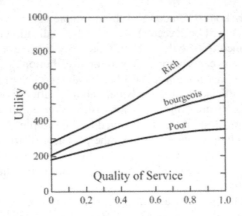

Fig. 2. Utility function

($\mathcal{A} = \{b, c\}$). Service charges of B and C are 250 and 210 units respectively ($SC_B = 250$, $SC_C = 210$, where SC denotes service charge). We will treat the quality of service, θ, as a continuous variable here, and the unknown quantity θ that affects the decision process is commonly called the *state of nature*. See Figure 1, a notion on an edge between initiator and consultant agent or between the two consultant agents represents reliability factor, that between consultant and provider agent is the assessment of service quality and that between initiator and provider agent is prior information. According to Figure 1, the agent A feels that θ_B, the service quality of B, has a normal prior density, $\mathcal{N}(0.64, (0.08)^2)$ (subscript denotes which an provider agent is being taken consideration). We also suppose that the prior density of θ_C is $\mathcal{N}(0.5, (0.15)^2)$ here[1]. The probability distribution of X that represents the assessments of service quality from consultant agents will, of course, depend upon the unknown state of nature θ. Therefore, we assume that X is another continuous random variable with density $f(x|\theta) \sim \mathcal{N}(\theta, (0.05)^2)$. We also assume that users can be divided into three types, "*Rich*", "*Bourgeois*", and "*Poor*", and agent A's owner belongs to "*Bourgeois*". The curves of their utility functions are shown in Figure 2. We use polynomial regression up to fourth degrees to get fitted model of utility curves and we have

$$
\begin{aligned}
U_{Rich}(r) &= 280.2 + 334.1r + 705.7r^2 - 944.1r^3 + 524.5r^4 \\
U_{Bourgeois}(r) &= 208.4 + 459.8r - 17.95r^2 - 99.84r^3 \\
U_{Poor}(r) &= 179 + 294.1r - 77.62r^2 - 80.03r^3 + 34.97r^4
\end{aligned}
$$

Note that θ and X have joint (subjective) density

$$
h(x, \theta) = f(x \mid \theta)\pi(\theta) \tag{1}
$$

and in making decision it is clearly important to consider what the possible states of nature are. The symbol Θ will be used to denote the set of all possible states of nature. So, X has marginal (unconditional) density.

---

[1] Here, we use simple noninformative prior, [James O. Berger, 1985] discussed other methods to construct prior distribution, such as histogram, relative likelihood, maximum entropy, moment, marginal distribution and ML- II approaches.

$$m(x) = \int_{\Theta} f(x \mid \theta)\pi(\theta)d\theta \qquad (2)$$

it is clear that (providing $m(x) \neq 0$)

$$\pi(\theta \mid x) = \frac{h(x,\theta)}{m(x)} \qquad (3)$$

In discrete situations, the formula for $\pi(\theta|x)$ is commonly known as Bayes's theorem.

Assume a sample $X = (X_1, X_2, \ldots, X_n)$ from a $\mathcal{N}(\theta, \sigma^2)$ distribution is to be taken (σ^2 known), and Let be prior information, $\pi(\theta)$, a $\mathcal{N}(\mu, \tau^2)$ density, where μ and τ^2 are known. Since $\overline{X}$ is sufficient for θ and noting that $\overline{X} \sim \mathcal{N}(\theta, \sigma^2/n)$. Therefore, the posterior distribution θ of give $x = (x_1, x_2, \ldots, x_n)$ is $\mathcal{N}(\mu(x), \rho)$, where

$$\mu(x) = \frac{\sigma^2/n}{(\tau^2 + \sigma^2/n)}\mu + \frac{\tau^2}{(\tau^2 + \sigma^2/n)}\overline{x} \qquad (4)$$

$$\rho = \frac{\tau^2\sigma^2}{(n\tau^2 + \sigma^2)} \qquad (5)$$

we also need to understand how to calculate the value of n and $\overline{x}$ in the Formula 4 and 5. Following formulas are used to get n and $\overline{x}$, where m represents how much opinions from a variety of sources (sample information) are used to evaluate the trust value. r_i and s_i denote the reliability factor and the statement of service quality for given provider on path i respectively.

$$n = \sum_{i=1}^{m} r_i \qquad (6)$$

$$\overline{x} = \sum_{i=1}^{m} \frac{s_i \times r_i}{n} \qquad (7)$$

Now, we can evaluate trust value of B for A by using above formulas and information. We take the assessments of B's quality from consultant agents as sample about θ_B and combine these sample information (x) and prior information into posterior distribution of θ_B given x. As shown in Table 1, n_B and $\overline{x}_B$ are:

$$n_B = 0.82 + 0.72 + 0.648 + 0.4896 = 2.6776$$
$$\overline{x}_B = \frac{0.55 \times 0.82 + 0.62 \times 0.72 + 0.48 \times 0.648 + 0.57 \times 0.4896}{2.6776} = 0.5555$$

Table 1. Calculating n and $\overline{x}$ of Agent B

No.	Path	Statement	Reliability Factor
1	A→D→B	0.55	0.8200
2	A→E→G→B	0.62	0.7200
3	A→E→F→B	0.48	0.6480
4	A→E→G→H→B	0.57	0.4896
	Total	–	2.6776

Table 2. Calculating n and $\overline{x}$ of Agent C

No.	Path	Statement	Reliability Factor
1	A→E→C	0.46	0.9000
2	A→I→J→C	0.58	0.8075
3	A→I→J→K→C	0.60	0.6137
	Total	–	2.3212

hence, $\pi_B(\theta|x) \sim \mathcal{N}(\mu_B(x), \rho_B)$, where

$$\mu_B(x) = \frac{0.05^2/2.6776}{0.08^2 + 0.05^2/2.6776} \times 0.64 + \frac{0.08^2}{0.08^2 + 0.05^2/2.6776} \times 0.5555 = 0.5663$$

$$\rho_B = \frac{0.08^2 \times 0.05^2}{2.6776 \times 0.08^2 + 0.05^2} = 0.0285^2$$

Note that we employ multiplying to merge two or more than two reliability factors. For example, the reliability factor of the edge $A{\to}E$ is 0.9 and that of $E{\to}G$ is 0.8, then the value of reliability factor on the path $A{\to}G$ is 0.72 (0.9 × 0.8). The reason behind using multiplying is that if the statement is true only if the agents that propagate this statement all tell the truth and it is considered to be independent for any two agents to lie or not to lie. Like B, agent C has a posterior distribution of $\pi_C(\theta|x) \sim \mathcal{N}(0.5370, 0.0321^2)$. After obtaining the final posterior distribution of B and C, we can compare the result of the expectation of $U_A(r)$ over $\pi_B(\theta|x)$ minus SC_B with that of the expectation of $U_A(r)$ over $\pi_C(\theta|x)$ minus SC_C, and simply select the agent that possibly will produce more utility. Expected utility of B and C are (Simpson method is used to solve definite integral):

$$\text{Utility of } B = \int_{-\infty}^{+\infty} U_A(r)\pi_B(\theta \mid x)d\theta - SC_B$$

$$= \int_{-\infty}^{+\infty} (208.4 + 459.8\theta - 17.95\theta^2 - 99.84\theta^3) \times$$

$$\frac{1}{\sqrt{2\pi} \times 0.0285} e^{-\frac{(\theta - 0.5663)^2}{2 \times 0.0285^2}} d\theta - 250$$

$$= 194.72$$

$$\text{Utility of } C = \int_{-\infty}^{+\infty} U_A(r)\pi_C(\theta \mid x)d\theta - SC_C$$

$$= \int_{-\infty}^{+\infty} (208.4 + 459.8\theta - 17.95\theta^2 - 99.84\theta^3) \times$$

$$\frac{1}{\sqrt{2\pi} \times 0.0321} e^{-\frac{(\theta - 0.5370)^2}{2 \times 0.0321^2}} d\theta - 210$$

$$= 224.46$$

hence (224.46 > 194.72), action c should be performed which means that C is more appropriate than B in the eyes of A.

3.2 Open Trust Model

Above discussion is under the condition that the "closed society of agents" must be defined at first, but it is nearly impossible for inherent open and dynamic Web. Our idea is that at every stage of the procedure (i.e., after every given observation) one should compare the (posterior) utility of making an immediate decision with the "expected" (preposterior) utility that will be obtained if more observations are taken. If it is cheaper to stop and make a decision, that is what should be done. To clarify

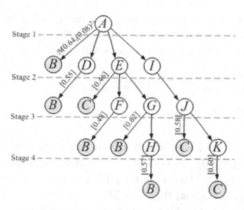

Fig. 3. The process of trust evaluating

this idea, we transform Figure 1 to the structure of tree, shown in Figure 3. The root of tree is an initiator agent, a no leaf node represents a consultant agent (a provider agent also is allowed in real application) and a leaf node represents a provider agent.

The goal of preposterior analysis is to choose the way of investigation which minimizes overall cost. This overall cost consists of the decision loss (opportunity cost) and the cost of conducting observation (consultant fee). Note that these two quantities are in opposition to each other. To lower the decision loss it will generally be necessary to carry out a larger observation, whereby the cost of consultant fee will be increased. In this section, we propose an approach to balance these two costs.

We continue above example used in the illustration of the closed trust model. As shown in Figure 3, we begin at the stage 1 when A only hold the prior information of B and has no any information about C (even the existence of C, but it is more likely that an agent with the prior distribution of $\mathcal{N}(0.5, (0.15)^2)$ and the expected service charge of 210 is near in the network). Agent A either can make an immediate decision (to select B) or can send request to its acquaintances for their opinions by extending the tree of Figure 3 down to the next layer.

Suppose that the cost of consultant service is determined by how much agents will be requested at the next stage and consultant fee is the constant of 1 for each times (for example, at the stage 1, agent A can ask Agent D, E and I for their opinions, therefore the cost of consultant fee at stage 1 will be 3). When preposterior and Bayesian sequential analysis are performed in our sample, we use the 1-step look ahead procedure for simplicity.

The utility of an immediate decision is the larger of

$$\int_{-\infty}^{+\infty} U_A(r)\pi_B(\theta)d\theta - SC_B = 217.78$$

here, $\pi_B(\theta) \sim \mathcal{N}(0.64, (0.08)^2)$.

And $\int_{-\infty}^{+\infty} U_A(r)\pi_C(\theta)d\theta - SC_C = 207.54$

here, $\pi_C(\theta) \sim \mathcal{N}(0.5, (0.15)^2)$.

(note that C is not known at this stage, we use subscript of C in above equation just for convenience). Hence the utility of an immediate decision is 217.78. If the request message is sent and x observed, the posterior density $\pi_B(\theta|x)$, is $\mathcal{N}(\mu_B(x), \rho_B)$, where

$$\mu_B(x) = \frac{0.05^2}{0.08^2 + 0.05^2} \times (0.64) + \frac{0.08^2}{0.08^2 + 0.05^2}(x) \cong 0.1798 + (0.7191)x$$

$$\rho_B = \frac{0.08^2 \times 0.05^2}{0.08^2 + 0.05^2} \cong 0.0018$$

However, that we do not know which x will occur, but we know the marginal distribution of X, $m(x)$, is $\mathcal{N}(\mu, \sigma^2 + \tau^2)$ and the "predictive" distribution, $m_B(x)$, which in this situation is $\mathcal{N}(0.64, (0.08)^2 + (0.05)^2)$. Note that if $x < 0.5914$ is observed, the expected utility of $\pi_B(\theta|x)$ is less than 207.54, so we prefer to select C instead of B. Hence expected utility of not making immediate decision is

$$\int_{-\infty}^{0.5914} 207.54\, m_B(x)\,dx +$$

$$\int_{0.5914}^{+\infty} (\int_{-\infty}^{+\infty} U_A(r)\pi_B(\theta\,|\,x)d\theta - SC_B)m_B(x)dx - 3$$

$$= 219.24$$

This is no other than the opportunity cost (3 is consultant fee in above equation). Because 219.24 > 217.78, and then further investigation would be well worth the money, in other words, A should send request to its acquaintances for their opinions. In order to answer the question of which sample information should be used with higher priority, we prescribe that the sample from the agent with shorter referral distance should be used first.

Remember that the further exploiting should be terminated immediately along the path on which a cycle is detected. Table 3 and 4 show the each stage of the process for agent B and C respectively and the residual process of Bayesian sequential analysis are shown in Table 5.

Table 3. The process of evaluating B's trust

No.	Sources of Opinions	$\mu_B(x)$	ρ_B	Utility
1	None	0.6400	0.0800	217.78
2	D	0.5790	0.0454	198.80
3	D, G, F	0.5656	0.0311	194.45
4	D, G, F, H	0.5663	0.0285	194.72

Table 4. The process of evaluating C's trust

No.	Sources of Opinions	$\mu_C(x)$	ρ_C	Utility
1	None	0.5000	0.1500	207.54
2	E	0.4644	0.0497	197.65
3	E, J	0.5157	0.0371	216.79
4	E, J, K	0.5370	0.0321	224.46

See Table 5, at the stage 3, the expected utility of C begins to larger than that of B, and because 216.79 > 214.78, making an immediate decision is more profitable (There is no need for the opinions of agent H and K). Therefore, A should stop investigating and select C as a decision. The advantage of sequential analysis should be clear now. It allows one to gather exactly the correct amount of data needed for a decision of the desired accuracy.

Table 5. The process of Bayesian sequential analysis

Stage	Agent B				Agent C				Consultant Fee	Utility		Decision
	Prior Distribution		Marginal Distribution		Prior Distribution		Marginal Distribution			Immediate Decision	Further Investigation	
	μ_B	τ_B	μ_{xlB}	σ_{xlB}	μ_C	τ_C	μ_{xlC}	σ_{xlC}				
1	0.6400	0.0800	0.6400	0.0943	0.5000	0.1500	–	–	3	217.78	219.24	Continue
2	0.5790	0.0454	0.5790	0.0675	0.4644	0.0497	–	–	3	198.80	199.36	Continue
3	0.5656	0.0311	–	–	0.5157	0.0371	0.5157	0.0623	2	216.79	214.78	Stop

4 Experiments

In this section, we developed a simulation system to measure some properties of our trust models. We present three sets of experiments. The goal of the first experiment is to see if our trust models help users to select the appropriate providers that match better their preferences. We compared the performance of the closed and open models in terms of precision and consultant fee. The second experiment is to examine the effect that varying the accuracy of the survey has on the overall performance of the system, and finally, we want to see what quality of agent population is necessary for the system to work well.

For the sake of simplicity, each agent in our system played only one role at a time, either the role of service provider or the role of consumer (including initiator and consultant agents). The numbers of provider and consumer agent were equal and had half each. Every consumer agent kept two lists. One was the list of "neighbor" that recorded its all acquaintances to each of which a reliability factor was attached. The other was the provider list that recorded the known providers and the corresponding prior information. The number of total items in above two lists is defined as "the degree of outgoing" and in our experiments the degree of outgoing is set to 5.

Following [M. Richardson et al., 2003], we expected the information on the Semantic Web to be of varying quality, so we assigned to each consumer agent i a quality $\gamma_i \in [0, 1]$. A consumer's quality determined what degree that a statement passed or issued by the consumer was true. Unless otherwise specified, the quality of consumers was chosen from a Gaussian distribution with $\mu = 0.8$ and $\sigma = 0.15$. For any pair of consumer i and j where i trust j:

$$t_{ij} = \text{uniformly chosen from } [max(\gamma_j - \delta, 0), min(\gamma_j + \delta, 1)]$$

Where γ_j is the quality of consumer j and δ is a noise parameter that determines how accurate consumers were at estimating the qualities of other consumers, and for these experiments we let $\delta = 0.2$. We also generated randomly each provider agent's quality that was represented by distribution $\pi(\theta)$ (the mean of θ was chosen from a Gaussian distribution $\mathcal{N}(0.5, (0.20)^2)$ and the variant of θ was chosen from a Gaussian distribution $\mathcal{N}(0.08, (0.02)^2)$, see Section 3 for more detail) and its corresponding service charge, and assumed that consultant fee was the constant of 1 for each times. Unless otherwise specified, the probability distribution of X that represents the assessments of service quality from consultant agents (the accuracy of the survey) was $\mathcal{N}(\theta, (0.05)^2)$.

As above mentioned, we assumed that the consumers are divided into three types, "*Rich*", "*Bourgeois*" and "*Poor*", and which type a consumer belong to was decided randomly during the experiments. The curves of the consumers' utility functions are shown in Figure 2.

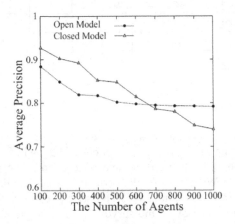

Fig. 4. Effect of the number of agents on the precision

Let G be the set of all provider agents in an experiment. The symbol M_i is used to denote the maximum utility that a provider in G can bring consumer i and let O_i be the utility that is produced by a provider selected by i using certain trust model, so *precision*$_i$ can be defined as O_i / M_i. The maximum path length was 10 in our experiments. The program would terminate and generate the results when reaching this maximum. We run each configuration for 10 times and use the means for the final experimental results.

Varying the Number of Agents. We explored the effect of varying the number of agents for the closed and open trust models introduced earlier. As shown in Figure 4, we found that the precision differed only slightly between the closed and open models. We also did the experiment for 10000 agents and the average precisions of closed and open models are 0.6147 and 0.7745 respectively. To our surprise, the open model began to outperform the closed model when the number of agents reached to 700. Through careful investigation, we believe this is because the closed model will meet with more noise in the network than the open model when the number of agents grows. We also found that the average precision of the open model decreased slightly when the number of agents grew from 100 to 10000. Therefore, the results show that the open trust model is robust to the population of agents.

As shown in Table 6 and Figure 4, we found that the average consultant fee of the open trust model was significantly lower than that of the closed trust model, though two models differed only slightly in terms of precision. This also meant that the open model had less runtime for trust evaluation. Furthermore, the average consultant fee of the closed model dramatically went up after 200 agents, otherwise, that of the open model increased comparatively smoothly (since the maximum path length was set to 10, the average consultant fee of the closed model did not increase significantly after

300 agents. If the experiments were not restricted to this maximum, it would larger than the numerical value shown in Table 6). This is because that if more investigation is not profitable, the open model will terminate exploration and make an immediate decision. Therefore, the open model is computational scalability that may not the case for the closed model.

Table 6. Average consultant fee of closed model vs. open model during the process of trust evaluation

Number of Agents	Average Consultant Fee		Number of Agents	Average Consultant Fee	
	Closed Model	Open Model		Closed Model	Open Model
100	1048.36	11.23	600	2044.53	13.23
200	1948.54	12.85	700	2034.93	13.08
300	2075.07	13.61	800	2267.41	13.38
400	2062.19	13.27	900	2287.80	13.57
500	2302.92	13.14	1000	2581.62	13.31

Varying the Accuracy of the Survey. It is necessary to know the effect that the accuracy of consultant agents' assessments of service quality has on the average precision of the system. We explored this by varying the variant of X (the accuracy of the survey) from 0.02 to 0.12. We set the number of agents to 100 here. As shown in Figure 5, we found that the more accurate the assessment, the more exactly we estimated value of trust. So, the closed and open trust models all depended on the accuracy of the survey. Also the high correlation between the precision of the open model and the accuracy of the survey was observed.

Varying the Population Quality. It is important to understand how the average precision is affected by the quality of agent population. We explored this by the varying the mean quality of agents and set the number of agents to 100 too. To measure the robustness of the models to bad agents, we selected agent qualities from six Gaussian distribution, with means from 0.4 to 0.9 and the same variant of 0.15. We varied the fraction of agents drawn from each distribution. Overall, as shown in Figure 6, we found that the system using the closed and open models differed only slightly in terms of precision, and the better the agent population, the higher the average precision was, which makes sense because in this case, the agent should get a more accurate estimate of provider's quality.

The results show that the closed and open trust models are robust to the quality of agent population and the accuracy of the survey generally, and the open trust model is robust to the number of agents. Also, the open model outperforms the closed model in terms of precision and consultant fee after the number of agents exceeds 700. We believe the reason underlies these results is: the closed model uses the transitivity strategy to prune its searches and is affected by the length of a chain of recommendations, falling as the chain gets longer. This pruning is likely to result in the loss of too much investigation. However, the idea of the open model is that at every stage of the procedure (after every given observation) one should compare the posterior Bayesian risk (or utility) of making an immediate decision with the "expected" posterior Bayesian risk (or utility) that will be obtained if more elaborate observations are taken. If it is cheaper to stop and make a decision, that is what should be done. Experimental results also show that the open model will stop mostly before pruning its all searches and its precision is not bad than the close model. Furthermore, the open model scales well to any social network size, as only tiny subsets of relatively constant size are visited and is computational scalability.

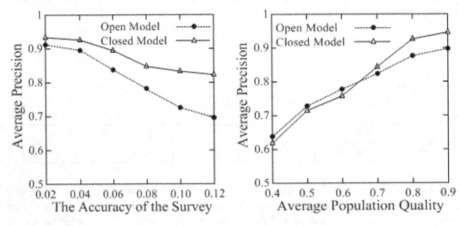

Fig. 5. Average precision for various accuracy of the survey

Fig. 6. Average precision for various qualities of agent population

5   Conclusions and Future Work

To achieve a pervasive, worldwide Semantic Web, an enhancement of computational trust model should be designed to support and enable computers and people to acquire, represent, exchange and integrate data and information available efficiently and conveniently. The Semantic Web is full of heterogeneous, dynamic and uncertain. If it is to succeed, trust will inevitably be an issue. After the cost and utility associated with the trust evaluation are discussed, two trust models have been formalized. We extend our trust models from discrete case of previous work to continuous case and improve the performance and precision of the system in this paper. Our work's contributions are: (1) The closed and open trust models have been proposed based on Bayesian sequential analysis. These models give trust a strict mathematical interpretation in terms of probability theory and lay the foundation for trust evaluation; (2) The utility and four types of costs: operational, opportunity service charge and consultant fee incurred during the process of trust evaluation have been considered sufficiently and an approach is proposed to balances these cost and utility; (3) Our approach enables users to combine a variety of sources of information to cope with the inherent uncertainties within the open Web environment and each user receives a personalized set of trusts, which may vary widely from person to person. (4) Experiments and some formal robust analyses have been made to examine the performance of our trust models. However, our proposed approach goes beyond other approaches in the kinds of representations of trust, the algorithms of trust evaluation and the formal analysis. Experimental results show that our open trust model is computational scalability and able to select the appropriate service providers for users effectively and efficiently according to their preferences.

For the future more robust analysis should be made properly, but we can mention that robustness can be dealt with more easily in Bayesian analysis. Service quality is multi-faceted. For instance, the file providers' capability can be presented in various aspects, such as the download speed, file quality and file type. We would like to consider multi-valued trust in the future.

Acknowledgment

The work is supported by the Subprogram of China 973 Project under Grant No. 2003CB317006, the National Science Fund for Distinguished Young Scholars of China NSF Program under Grant No. NSFC60533040, the Program for New Century Excellent Talents of China under Grant No. NCET-04-0545, and also the China NSF Program under Grant No. NSFC60503018.

References

1. B. Yu, M. P. Singh. Trust and reputation management in a small-world network. In Proc. 4th Int. MultiAgent Systems, 2000, pp.449-450.
2. Dong Huynh, Nicholas R. Jennings, Nigel R. Shadbolt. Developing an integrated trust and reputation model for open multi-agent systems. In Proc. 7th Int. Workshop on Trust in Agent Societies, 2004, pp.65-74.
3. D. J. Watts, S. H. Strogatz. Collective dynamics of "small-world" networks. *Nature*, June, 1998, 393: 440-442.
4. E. M. Maximilien, M. P. Singh. An ontology for Web service ratings and reputations. Workshop on Ontologies in Agent Systems, 2nd Int. Joint Conference on Autonomous Agents and Multi-Agent Systems (AAMAS), Melbourne, Australia, 2003.
5. James O.Berger. Statistical decision theory and Bayesian analysis (second edition). Springer-Verlag, New York Inc, 1985.
6. J. Golbeck, Bijan Parsia, James Hendler. Trust networks on the Semantic Web. Lecture Notes in Computer Science, September, 2003, pp.238-249.
7. K. O'Hara, Harith Alani, Yannis Kalfoglou, Nigel Shadbolt. Trust strategies for the Semantic Web. Workshop on Trust, Security, and Reputation on the Semantic Web, 3rd Int. Semantic Web (ISWC), Hiroshima, Japan, 2004.
8. Li Ding, Lina Zhou, Timothy Finin. Trust based knowledge outsourcing for Semantic Web agents. In Proc. 2003 Int. Web Intelligence, October, 2003, pp.379-387.
9. Lik Mui, Mojdeh Mogtashemi, Ari Halberstadt. A computational model of trust and reputation. In Proc. 35th Int. System Sciences (HICSS), January 7-10, 2002, pp.2431-2439.
10. S. Majithia, A. S. Ali, O. F. Rana, D. W. Walker. Reputation-based semantic service discovery. 13th IEEE International Workshops on Enabling Technologies: Infrastructure for Collaborative Enterprises, 2004, pp. 297-302.
11. M. Richardson, Rakesh Agrawal, Pedro Domingos. Trust management for the Semantic Web. In Proc. 2nd Int. Semantic Web, Sanibel Island, Florida, 2003.

12. M. Winslett, T. Yu, K. E. Seamons, A. Hess, J. Jacobson, R. Jarvis, B. Smith, L. Yu Negotiating trust on the web. *IEEE Internet Computing*, 2002, 6(6): 30-37.
13. N. R. Jennings, An agent-based approach for building complex software systems. *Communications of the ACM*, 2001, 44(4): 35-41.
14. S. D. Ramchurn, Nicholas R. Jennings, Carles Sierra, Lluis Godo. A computational trust model for multi-agent interactions based on confidence and reputation. Workshop on Deception, Fraud and Trust in Agent Societies, 2nd Int. Joint Conference on Autonomous Agents and Multi-Agent Systems (AAMAS), Melbourne, Australia, July, 2003.
15. S. Milgram. The small world problem. *Psychology Today*, 1967.
16. S. P. Marsh. Formalising trust as a computational concept. Ph.D. dissertation, University of Stirling, 1994.
17. Xiaoqing Zheng, Huajun Cheng, Zhaohui Wu, Yu Zhang. A computational trust model for Semantic Web based on Bayesian decision theory. In Proc. 8th Int. Asia Pacific Web Conference, January 16-18, 2006, pp.745-750.
18. Yao Wang, Julita Vassileva. Bayesian network-based trust model. In Proc. 2003 Int. Web Intelligence, October 13-17, 2003, pp.372-378.
19. Y. Gil, V. Ratnakar. Trusting information sources one citizen at a time. In Proc. 1st Int. Semantic Web (ISWC), Sardinia, Italy, June 9-12, 2002, pp.162-176.

The Agent Reputation and Trust (ART) Testbed

Karen K. Fullam[1], Tomas Klos[2,*], Guillaume Muller[3], Jordi Sabater-Mir[4],
K. Suzanne Barber[1], and Laurent Vercouter[3]

[1] The University of Texas at Austin, USA
{kfullam, barber}@lips.utexas.edu
[2] Center for Mathematics and Computer Science (CWI),
Amsterdam, The Netherlands
tomas.klos@cwi.nl
[3] École Nationale Supérieure des Mines,
Saint-Étienne, France
{muller, Laurent.Vercouter}@emse.fr
[4] Artificial Intelligence Research Institute (IIIA-CSIC),
Barcelona, Spain
jsabater@iiia.csic.es

Abstract. The Agent Reputation and Trust (ART) Testbed initiative
has been launched with the goal of establishing a testbed for agent
reputation- and trust-related technologies. The ART Testbed serves in
two roles: (1) as a competition forum in which researchers can compare
their technologies against objective metrics, and (2) as a suite of tools
with flexible parameters, allowing researchers to perform customizable,
easily-repeatable experiments. In the Testbed's artwork appraisal domain, agents, who valuate paintings for clients, may purchase opinions
and reputation information from other agents to produce accurate appraisals. The ART Testbed features useful data collection tools for storing,
downloading, and replaying game data for experimental analysis.

1 Introduction

The Agent Reputation and Trust (ART) Testbed [1] serves two roles: (1) as a competition forum for comparing technologies against objective metrics, independent
from participating researchers, and (2) as an environment for performing customizable, easily-repeatable experiments. In the testbed's art appraisal domain,
agents valuate paintings for clients and gather opinions from other agents to produce accurate appraisals. As a versatile, universal experimentation site, the ART
Testbed scopes relevant trust research problems and unites researchers toward
solutions via unified experimentation methods. Through objective, well-defined
metrics, the testbed provides researchers with tools for comparing and validating
their approaches. The testbed also serves as an objective means of presenting
technology features—both advantages and disadvantages—to the community. In
addition, the ART Testbed places trust research in the public spotlight, improving
confidence in the technology and highlighting relevant applications.

---

* Corresponding author.

K. Stølen et al. (Eds.): iTrust 2006, LNCS 3986, pp. 439–442, 2006.

2 Testbed Domain Problem

The ART Testbed provides functionality for researchers of trust and reputation in multi-agent systems. As such, it operates in two modes: competition and experimentation. In competition mode, each participating researcher controls a single agent, which works in competition against every other agent in the system. At the 2006 iTrust conference, we will demonstrate the ART Testbed with a variety of agents (e.g., participants in the First ART Testbed Competition, at AAMAS 2006). To utilize the testbed's experimentation mode, the Testbed is downloadable for researcher use independent of the competition [5]: results may be compared among researchers for benchmarking purposes, since the testbed provides a well-established environment for easily-repeatable experimentation.

The testbed operates in an art appraisal domain (see [2] for a detailed justification), where researchers' agents function as painting appraisers with varying levels of expertise in different artistic eras. Clients request appraisals for paintings from different eras; if an appraiser does not have the expertise to complete the appraisal, it may purchase opinions from other appraisers. Other appraisers estimate the accuracy of opinions they send by the cost they choose to invest in generating an opinion, and opinion providers may lie about the estimated accuracy of their opinions. Appraisers produce appraisals using their own opinion and opinions received from other appraisers, receiving more clients, and thus more profit, for producing more accurate appraisals. They may also purchase reputation information from each other about third-party agents. Appraisers attempt to accurately valuate their assigned paintings; their decisions about which opinion providers to trust directly impact the accuracy of their final appraisals. In competition mode, the winning agent is selected as the appraiser with the highest bank account balance.

3 Testbed Architecture

As shown in Figure 1, the testbed architecture, implemented in Java, consists of several components (see [3] for a detailed description of the ART Testbed architecture). The Testbed Server manages the initiation of all games by starting a Simulation Engine for each game. The Simulation Engine is responsible for controlling the simulation environment by enforcing chosen parameters. In each timestep, the Simulation Engine assigns clients with paintings to each appraiser. Then appraisers conduct reputation and opinion transactions with each other as described above. Finally, the Simulation Engine assesses each appraiser's accuracy based on the opinions the appraiser purchases and the 'weights' the appraiser places on those opinions. Weights are real values between zero and one that an appraiser assigns, based on its trust model, to another's opinion.

Through the Simulation Engine, the Database collects environment and agent data, such as true painting values, opinions, transaction messages, calculated final appraisals, client share allocations, and bank balances. With access tools for navigating, downloading/uploading, and replaying Database logs, data sets

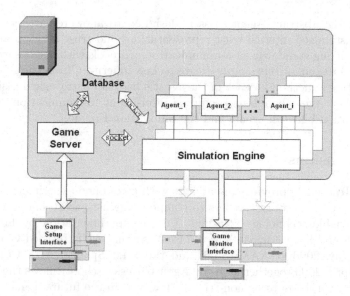

Fig. 1. The ART Testbed architecture

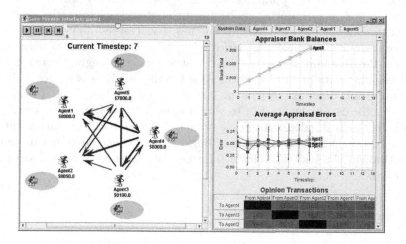

Fig. 2. The Game Monitor Interface for viewing game data

are made available to researchers after each game session for game re-creation and experimental analysis.

User Interfaces permit researchers to observe games in progress and access information collected in the Database by graphically displaying details. Figure 2 shows the Game Monitor Interface, by which observers can view opinion and reputation transactions between agents on the left and detailed statistics, such as bank balance, about each appraiser agent on the right. The Game Monitor Interface's play-pause buttons permit games to be played and replayed, regardless of whether the game is in progress or completed.

Finally, the abstract Agent class is designed to allow researchers to easily implant customized internal trust representations and trust revision algorithms while permitting standardized communication protocols with entities external to the appraiser agent. Users simply create a class inheriting from the Agent class, implementing a method for each of the agent's necessary strategic decisions. The abstract class Agent handles all required inter-agent communication, as well as communication between agents and the Simulation Engine.

4   Conclusions

The ART Testbed 1) provides researchers with a common experimentation environment and 2) allows researchers to compete against each other to determine the most viable technology solutions. Initial experimentation by Fullam and Barber [4] and by participants in the First Annual ART Testbed Competition (held in May, 2006 at AAMAS-06) and the First Spanish ART Competition (held in April, 2006 together with the AgentCities.es school) shows the testbed's art appraisal problem to be non-trivial. However, in the future, game rules may be changed to keep the competition challenging (for example, not revealing actual painting values to appraisers, changing the format by which reputations are represented or introducing multi-dimensional trust characteristics, such as quality, timeliness, and availability). Further, the Testbed may be expanded to incorporate multiple problem scenarios relevant to a wider range of trust-related research. Possible improvements to the Testbed include logging additional data and developing data processing utilities for forensic analysis of games and wrappers to permit designing agents in languages other than Java. In addition, organizing the development effort to permit contributions from the research community via the Testbed's SourceForge webpage [5] will speed the implementation of these features and the correction of bugs. Development progress can be monitored through the testbed website [1], where updates to testbed development are posted.

References

1. ART Testbed Team. *Agent Reputation and Trust Testbed Website.*
   http://www.art-testbed.net/, 2006.
2. K. Fullam, T. Klos, G. Muller, J. Sabater-Mir, A. Schlosser, Z. Topol, K. S. Barber, J. S. Rosenschein, L. Vercouter, and M. Voss. A Specification of the Agent Reputation and Trust (ART) Testbed In *Proc. AAMAS*, 2005, pp. 512–518.
3. K. Fullam, T. Klos, G. Muller, J. Sabater-Mir, Z. Topol, K. S. Barber, J. S. Rosenschein, and L. Vercouter. The Agent Reputation and Trust (ART) Testbed Architecture In *Proc. Trust Workshop at AAMAS*, 2005, pp. 50–62.
4. K. Fullam, and K. S. Barber. Learning Trust Strategies in Reputation Exchange Networks In *Proc. AAMAS*, 2006.
5. ART Testbed Team. ART *Testbed SourceForge project page.*
   https://sourceforge.net/projects/art-testbed, 2006.

Trust Establishment in Emergency Case

Laurent Gomez and Ulrich Jansen

SAP Corporate Research - SAP Lab France,
805 Avenue du Docteur Maurice Donat,
06250 Mougins, France
laurent.gomez, ulrich.jansen@sap.com

Abstract. Access to medical information, e.g. current medication, blood group, and allergies, is often vital, especially in case of emergency. An emergency physician has to know medication incompatibilities and to access to the patient's treatment history. It raises the issue of patient's privacy. Thus a patient grants access to his medical information to his physician because he has a pre-established trust relationship with this physician. But he wants to prevent any other physician to gain access to his medical information. In emergency case, due to the patient's unconsciousness, it is difficult to establish a trust relationship between patient and emergency physician. In our demonstration, we show how to exploit context information to address the problem of granting access to medical information without a pre-established trust relationship between an emergency physician and a patient.

1 Motivation

Today, management of data-flow within health care systems is still mostly paper-based. Severals projects [1], [2], [3] try to address this by introducing an electronic infrastructure for health insurances, physicians and patients. The vision is to create an electronic health record for patients containing among others personal data, treatment history, X-ray pictures or current medication. In emergency case, for example, physicians know patient's allergies and are able to choose the most appropriate treatment.

This approach raises a major privacy issue with respect to patient's medical information. In order to cope with this privacy issue, the project Gesundheit-skarte [3] introduces mechanisms for authentication and authorisation, requiring patient's interaction, therefore not adapted to emergency cases.

In our demonstrator, we propose a solution using contextual information (e.g. user's location and health condition), as a part of access control policies. This demonstrator shows the feasibility of such extended access control mechanisms. After a short description of the demonstrator scenario in section 2, we give an overview of existing context-aware access control solutions in section 3. In section 4, we describe the demonstration infrastructure.

Moreover, we raise the issue of trustworthiness of context information. As our access control exploits context information, it implies that acquired context information have to trustworthy enough to be exploited.

K. Stølen et al. (Eds.): iTrust 2006, LNCS 3986, pp. 443–448, 2006.
© Springer-Verlag Berlin Heidelberg 2006

2   Scenario

The demonstrator adresses one of the use cases defined within the MOSQUITO project [4]. MOSQUITO aims at enabling secure and trusted collaboration between mobile workers in ubiquitous environment. MOSQUITO's vision is that mobile workers have secure, trusted and ubiquitous access to business applications. The project provides the required technical infrastructure so that workers and their clients can perform daily business processes collaboratively and safely according to determined security policies. Networks have tremendously evolved in terms of wireless technology and mobility, but business application and service support have lagged behind.

In this scenario, a patient, Bob, carries a health monitor device containing his medical information and health sensors (e.g heart rate, body temperature or blood pressure sensors). Bob's medical information are protected by means of a context-aware access control mechanism, defined by the following rules:

- *If Bob is unconscious, any physician, close to Bob, can get access to any Bob's medical information.*

The statement "*Bob is unconscious*" or "*Bob is healthy*" is evaluated using his pulse, whereas the statement "*Physician is close to Bob*" is evaluated from the physical distance between Bob and physician. This scenario clearly demonstrates context-aware access control.

3   Context-Aware Access Control

In this section, we discuss related work on context-aware access control solutions. Context-aware access control can be defined as any kind of access control mechanism, which exploits context information. Several architectures have been developed for context-aware access control:

- **Gaia**
  Roman et al. [5] defined a generic context-based software architecture for physical spaces, so-called Gaia. A physical space is a geographic region with limited and well defined boundaries, containing physical objects, heterogeneous networked devices, and users performing a range of activities. Derived from the physical space, an Active Space provides to the user a computing representation of physical space.
- **Authorisation mechanisms for Intranet**
  This context-aware authorisation architecture, based on Kerberos authentication, enables to activate or deactivate roles assigned to a user depending on his context [6]. For example, if a user is not in a secure place such as airport terminal, the access to sensitive data is denied whereas in the corporate building of the user, he has access to confidential data.
- **Environmental Roles**
  Covington et al. [7] propose a uniform access control framework for environmental roles. It is an extension to the Role-Based Access Control

(RBAC) model. In the RBAC model, permissions are associated with roles. In an administrative domain, a role can be a developer or a manager. An environmental role is a role that captures environmental conditions. Environmental roles are based on General Role Based Access Control. As opposed to the RBAC model which is only subject-oriented, GRBAC allows defining access control policies based on subject but also on object and environment.

In the scope of our demonstration, Gaia enable us to represent the patient and physician and their proximity. But it is too restricted to physical environment. it does not permit us to take into account the patient's health condition. With respect to authorization mechanims for intranet, we believe that the Kerberos infrastructure is not appropriate for mobile application in an ubiquitous environment.

We believe that GRBAC is the most suitable approach for our demonstration. We define the following environment-based role: "*physician close to unconscious patient*". This role implies physician's authentication (e.g. role), patient's and physician's proximity and patient's health condition evaluation. It implies a reasoning about low-level context information (e.g. users' location, patient's pulse or body temperature) to derive high-level context information (e.g. users' proximity, patient's health condition).

4   Demonstration Infrastructure

Figure 1 depictes the three main element of our demonstration: the patient, the physician and the Medical Information Portal (MIP). The patient carries a pulse sensor, a GPS receiver and a health monitor. Based on the acquired pulse, the health monitor delivers the patient's health condition. The physician carries a Web-browser enabled mobile device and his mobile phone. The only requirement

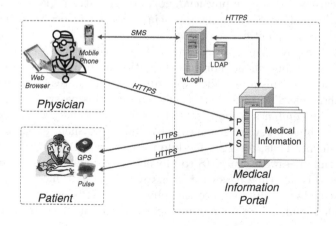

Fig. 1. Infrastructure Overview

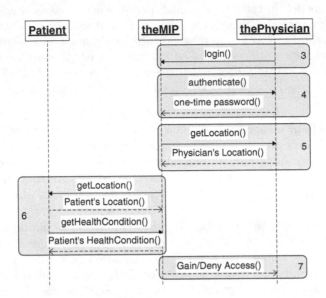

Fig. 2. Sequence Diagram

regarding the mobile Web-browser enabled mobile device is the support of SSL connection to the MIP. Finally, the MIP delivers patient's medical information. The MIP is a Web-based application hosted by SAP Netweaver server. Our context-aware access control policy is enforced at the Pluggable Authentication Service (PAS) on the SAP Netweaver server.

An overview of the data-flow between the main elements of the demonstrator is described in figure 2. In our demonstration, we suppose that (1) the nearest physician to the unconscious patient received an emergency notification with the patient's location and (2) the physician goes to the patient's location. The notification can be sent via SMS to the physician's mobile device with the patient's location and unique identifier to the MIP.

When (3) the physician logins to the MIP, the physician has to authenticate himself with his mobile phone. For authentication of the physician, we use a one-time password mechanism, so called wLogin [8]. It generates random passwords and sends them via SMS to the client, who can use this password to get authenticated. wLogin combines a good level of security, especially when compared to standard username/password schemes, with low deployment effort and no additional equipment. Thus, the PAS module uses the wLogin (4.a-4.b) solution to send a one-time password via SMS to physician's mobile device. The physician has to enter this one-time password to his web browser. Once the physician is authenticated, PAS module acquires the physician's GPS location from the GSM operator (5). Finally, the PAS module acquires patient's health condition and position (6).

According the physician's authentication, location and patient's health condition and location, the PAS grants or denies access to the patient's medical information. The physician get access to the MIP via an SSL connection (7).

To allow modularity within the architecture and platform independency, we choose Web Services as interface between the different entities where applicable.

Further enhancements concern physician notification via SMS and evaluation of the proximity between the physician and the patient. Regarding physician's notification, we aim at trigerring emergency alert from the patient's health monitor either to an emergency center or by broadcasting notification to the closest physician to the health monitor. With respect to proximity evaluation, we focus on combination of WiFi-based, GPRS-based and GPS location service.

For gaining confidence in the proximity between the physician and the patient, we reason about different context information. We evaluate the distance between the physician and the patient based on their GPS and WLAN locations. We compare also cell ID of their respective mobile phones. Even if those three measurements do not have the same accuracy, they support us for gaining confidence in the proximity between the physician and the patient.

5 Conclusion

In the scope of MOSQUITO, this demonstrator is considered as a proof of concept regarding context-aware access control. Moreover, we demonstrate the need of adapting trust relationship establishment depending on the context.

In our demonstration, we have two pre-established trust relationships: between the MIP and the physician and the patient and the MIP. The physician-MIP trust relationship permits the MIP to authenticate the physician, and trust his location. Moreover, with the MIP-patient trust relationship, patient's context information are considered as trusted by the MIP.

We do not require any pre-established trust relationship between the patient and the physician. In our demonstrator, we propose a combination of physician's authentication, proof of proximity between the patient and the physician and the patient's health condition support us for building this trust relationship.

The exploitation of context information raises the issue of trust in this context information. Even if the patient and the physician are trusted, it does not implies that the context information is trustworthy. Trust evaluation of context information is a subject of our ongoing research work. Our goal is to provide metric and operators to combine trust evaluation about context information in ubiquitous environment.

6 Disclaimer

IST-Directorate General / Integrating and strengthening the ERA: the project MOSQUITO [4] is supported by the European Community. This document does not represent the opinion of the European Community. It is also the sole responsibility of the author and not the responsibility of the European Community using any data that might appear therein.

References

1. IST Project FP6 IST-1-508015: (Knowledge Sharing and Decision Support for Healthcare Professionals (DOCHAND))
2. IST Project FP6 IST-1-507760: (A Diagnosis Collaborative Environment for Medical relevant Situations (DICOEMS))
3. Bundesministerium fur Gesundheit: (Die gesundheitskarte.)
4. IST Project FP6 - IST-004636: MOSQUITO - Mobile Workers secure business applications in ubiquitous environment (2004)
5. J. Al-Muhtadi, A. Ranganathan, R.C., Mickunas, M.D.: Cerberus: A context-aware security scheme for smart spaces. (2003)
6. Wullems Chris, M.L., Clark, A.: Toward context-aware security: an authorization architecture for intranet environments (2004)
7. Michael J. Covington Prahlad Fogla Z.Z., Ahamad, M.: A context-aware security architecture for emerging applications. In: Proceedings of the Annual Computer Security Applications Conference (ACSAC), Las Vegas, Nevada, USA (2002)
8. Siltanet: (wLogin)

Evaluating Trust and Authenticity with CAUTION

Jacek Jonczy

University of Berne,
Institute of Computer Science and Applied Mathematics,
CH-3012 Berne, Switzerland
jonczy@iam.unibe.ch
http://www.iam.unibe.ch/~run

Abstract. The purpose of this paper is to show how to use CAUTION, a tool for the specification and evaluation of credential networks. The resulting degrees of support and possibility allow to make decisions concerning the authenticity and/or trustworthiness of an unknown entity in an open network. The specification of a credential network and the subsequent computations will be illustrated by examples.[1]

1 Introduction

The recently introduced notion of *credential networks* is a new generic approach for handling trust and authenticity in a distributed environment [1]. Its main concept are *credentials*, which are digitally signed statements about an unknown entity's trustworthiness and/or authenticity. Authenticity relates to the entity's public key, which is an indispensable requirement for verifying digital signatures.

In a completely decentralized environment any network user is allowed to issue credentials. The set of users and involved credentials forms a *credential network*. Such a network is always considered from the viewpoint of a particular user, called the *owner* X_0 of the network.

The problem is, from the perspective of the owner, to judge another network user Y in two ways, namely with respect to Y's general *trustworthiness* (i.e. w.r.t. any possible trust matter), denoted by $Trust_Y$, and the authenticity of Y's public key, denoted by Aut_Y. In most cases, Y will be unknown to X_0. Consequently, X_0 has to rely upen credentials issued by third parties in order to prove the truth or falsity of $Trust_Y$ or Aut_Y.

There is a distinction between two classes of credentials, depending on whether the credential contains a statement about the trustworthiness or authenticity of the recipient. Furthermore, credentials may be *positive* (certificates and recommendations), *negative* (revocations and discredits), and *mixed* (authenticity and trust ratings), resulting in six different credential types.

For a more detailed definition of credentials and credential networks, as well as the exact semantics of the various credential types, we refer to [1, 2].

---

[1] This research is supported by the Swiss National Science Foundation, project no. PP002–102652, and the Hasler Foundation, project no. 2042.

K. Stølen et al. (Eds.): iTrust 2006, LNCS 3986, pp. 449–453, 2006.

2   CAUTION

The CAUTION (*Credential-based Authenticity and Trust In Open Networks*) system is both a specification language and an evaluation tool for credential networks. Its user interface is a simple macro language. The following list gives a short overview of the CAUTION language, for more details see [3].

(users <X_1> ... <X_n>) ::= Creates n new users $X_1, ..., X_n$.

(owner <X>) ::= Specifies the owner of the network.

(cert <X> <Y> [<π>]) ::= Specifies a certificate issued by X for Y with (optional) weight π.

(rec <X> <Y> [<π>]) ::= Analogous for recommendations.

(rev <X> <Y> [<π>]) ::= Analogous for revocations.

(dis <X> <Y> [<π>]) ::= Analogous for discredits.

(a-rate <X> <Y> [<π>]) ::= Analogous for authenticity ratings.

(t-rate <Y> <Y> [<π>]) ::= Analogous for trust ratings.

(aut <Y> [<π>]) ::= Specifies a certificate issued by the owner for Y.

(trust <Y> [<π>]) ::= Analogous for recommendations.

(negaut <Y> [<π>]) ::= Analogous for revocations.

(distrust <Y> [<π>]) ::= Analogous for discredits.

(show-args [<X_1> ... <X_n>]) ::= Starts the evaluation and outputs the sets of arguments for each specified user $X_1, ..., X_n$.

(show-counter-args [<X_1> ... <X_n>]) ::= Analogous for counter-arguments.

(show-dsp [<x_1> ... <x_n>]) ::= Starts the evaluation and outputs the degrees of support for each specified user $X_1, ..., X_n$.

(show-dps [<x_1> ... <x_n>]) ::= Analogous for degrees of possibility.

Using the above commands, one can specify a credential network, compute arguments supporting or defeating respective hypotheses Aut_X and $Trust_X$, and compute corresponding *degrees of support* (*dsp*) and *degrees of possibility* (*dps*). These metrics allow the owner to judge another user with respect to his or her trustworthiness and public key authenticity [1, 3].

3   Examples

Example 1. The first example shows how to model a *PGP Web of Trust* as a credential network. Suppose that the owner A signs directly the public keys of B, C, and D, as shown in Fig. 1(a). In our language, this corresponds to *absolute* certificates of weight $\pi = 1.0$. In PGP's web of trust, all certificates are absolute (the explicit labels +1.0 are omitted in the picture). Furthermore, the trust values *full*, *marginal*, and *none* are assigned solely by the owner (we omit *ultimate* trust in this example for the sake of simplicity). We translate them here into recommendations of weight $\pi_{full} = 1.0$, $\pi_{marginal} = 0.5$, and $\pi_{none} = 0$, respectively. By doing so, issuing a recommendation of weight 0 is like not issuing a recommendation at all, like in the case of User E, H, and I. Consequently, certificates issued by those entities will have no further impact, which corresponds

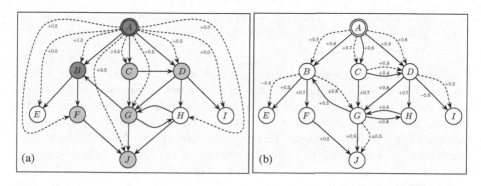

Fig. 1. Two credential networks: The nodes represent users, the owner is doublecircled, and arrows represent credentials. (a) A network with absolute certificates and owner-assigned trust. *Full, marginal,* and *no* trust is emphasized with dark-grey, light-grey, and white circles, respectively. (b) A network with different types of credentials and varying weights, issued by various users.

to the behavior of the PGP trust model. The network in Fig. 1(a) is the result of evaluating the following CAUTION commands:

```
> (users a b c d e f g h i j)    > (trust i 0.0)      > (cert d g)
> (owner a)                      > (trust j 0.5)      > (cert d h)
> (trust b 1.0)                  > (cert a b)         > (cert d i)
> (trust c 0.5)                  > (cert a c)         > (cert f j)
> (trust d 0.5)                  > (cert a d)         > (cert g j)
> (trust e 0.0)                  > (cert b e)         > (cert g h)
> (trust f 0.5)                  > (cert b f)         > (cert h g)
> (trust g 0.5)                  > (cert c d)         > (cert h j)
> (trust h 0.0)                  > (cert c g)
```

Assume now we want to evaluate the network and we are interested in User J. The results of the evaluation are shown below: there are three minimal arguments for Aut_J and one minimal argument for $Trust_J$. The *dsp* for Aut_J is 0.68 and for $Trust_J$ it is 0.5. But the *dps* for both Aut_J and $Trust_J$ is 1.0, since there are no counter-arguments which would decrease the *dps*.

```
> (show-args j)               > (show-dsp j)           > (show-dps j)
USER: J                       USER: J                  USER: J
args(Aut_J):                  dsp(Aut_J) = 0.69        dps(Aut_J) = 1.00
 0: ((REC A D)(REC A G))      dsp(Trust_J) = 0.50      dps(Trust_J) = 1.00
 1: ((REC A C)(REC A G))
 2: ((REC A F))
args(Trust_J):
 0: ((REC A J))
```

These results allow the owner to consider User J as being trustworthy to a degree of 0.5, whereas concerning the authenticity, a higher support of 0.69 has been computed. In both cases, however, collecting more evidence may be appropriate since the *dsp* are not very high and the *dps* are still maximal, as apparent from the output above.

Example 2. In the second example, trust is not only assigned by the owner, but also by other users, and by means of recommendations and trust ratings. Furthermore, certificates are no longer necessarily absolute, but have varying weights. The network is shown in Fig. 1(b) and can be specified in an analogous manner as in the first example. Due to restricted space, this is omitted here. For the evaluation we use the same commands as before. For example, the arguments and counter-arguments, as well as *dsp* and *dps* for User G are shown in the output box below:

```
> (show-args g)                                          > (show-dsp g)
USER: G                                                  USER: G
 args(Aut_G):                                             dsp(Aut_G) = 0.72
  0: ((REC A D)(CERT A D)(CERT D G))                      dsp(Trust_G) = 0.58
  1: ((REC A C)(CERT A C)(CERT C G))                     > (show-dps g)
  2: ((REC A C)(REC A D)(CERT A C)(CERT C D)(CERT D G))  USER: G
  3: ((REC A C)(REC C D)(CERT A C)(CERT A D)(CERT D G))   dps(Aut_G) = 1.00
  4: ((REC A C)(REC C D)(CERT A C)(CERT C D)(CERT D G))   dps(Trust_G) = 0.86
 args(Trust_G):
  0: ((REC A B) (REC B G) (CERT A B))
> (show-counter-args g)
USER: G
 counter-args(Trust_G):
  0: ((REC A B) (CERT A B) (DIS B G))
```

The hypothesis Aut_G has a relatively high degree of support and a maximal degree of possibilty. Thus Aut_G might be accepted. On the other hand, $Trust_G$ has still a high possibility, but a relatively low support. As a consequence, the owner will probably leave it open whether to trust User G or not.

4   Conclusion

This short article describes how credential networks are described and evaluated by means of the CAUTION language. Complex networks can be described conveniently in an intuitive manner. The measures *dsp* and *dps* serve as authenticity and trust metrics, which are used to judge and decide on a user's trustworthiness and authenticity. This decision process allows many possible strategies (e.g. the use of thresholds), depending on the context and application. But this is a separate issue and beyond the scope of this paper.

References

1. Jonczy, J., Haenni, R.: Credential networks: a general model for distributed trust and authenticity management. In Ghorbani, A., Marsh, S., eds.: PST'05: 3rd Annual Conference on Privacy, Security and Trust, St. Andrews, Canada (2005) 101–112

2. Haenni, R., Jonczy, J., Kohlas, R.: Two-layer models for managing authenticity and trust (accepted). In Song, R., Korba, L., Yee, G., eds.: Trust in E-Services: Technologies, Practices and Challenges. (2006)
3. Jonczy, J., Haenni, R.: Implementing credential networks (accepted). In: iTrust'06: 4rd International Conference on Trust Management, Pisa, Italy (2006)

Using Jiminy for Run-Time User Classification Based on Rating Behaviour

Evangelos Kotsovinos[1], Petros Zerfos[1], Nischal M. Piratla[1],
and Niall Cameron[2]

[1] Deutsche Telekom Laboratories
`firstname.lastname@telekom.de`
[2] Pembroke College, Cambridge
`niall.cameron@cantab.net`

1   Introduction

This paper describes an application of our prototype implementation of *Jiminy*, a scalable distributed architecture for providing participation incentives in on-line rating schemes. Jiminy is based on an incentive model where participants are explicitly *rewarded* for submitting ratings, and are *debited* when they query a participating reputation management system (RMS). Providing explicit incentives increases the quantity of ratings submitted and reduces their bias by removing implicit or hidden rewards, such as those gained through revenge or reciprocal ratings. To prevent participants from submitting arbitrary or dishonest feedback for the purpose of accumulating rewards, Jiminy halts rewards for participants who are deemed dishonest by its probabilistic *honesty estimator*. Using this estimator, Jiminy can also perform *classification* of users based on their rating behaviour, which can be further used as criteria for filtering the rating information that users obtain from the RMS.

More background on the theoretical foundations of Jiminy can be found in [1], while [2] provides details on the system design, implementation and performance evaluation.

2   Application Scenario

Jiminy follows a cluster-based architecture and is deployed on a number of computers, for real-time computation of the statistical analysis of ratings. This allows online monitoring and classification of the rating behaviour of users. Jiminy operates in the following steps:

Bootstrapping. Jiminy starts its operation by connecting to the ratings database, discovering the available slaves, and deciding how to partition the problem space — we use the Grouplens[1] ratings data set — among the slaves, based on the number of slaves available. It then communicates to each slave the part of the problem space it is assigned, and starts a network daemon listening to requests from the reputation management system (RMS).

---

[1] `http://www.grouplens.org`

K. Stølen et al. (Eds.): iTrust 2006, LNCS 3986, pp. 454–457, 2006.

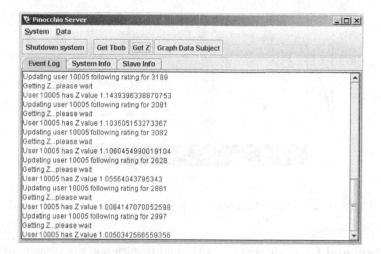

Fig. 1. Interface of the Jiminy master during periodic Noselength updates

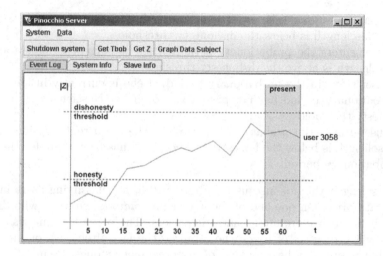

Fig. 2. Run-time monitoring of a user's Noselength, and classifications

Periodic Honesty Recalculation. Jiminy periodically runs the algorithm that calculates and updates the *Noselength* value for each user — our honesty metric, as described in [2]. The Jiminy GUI provides a log of honesty recalculation events — as shown in Figure 1. It also displays a certain user's Noselength value by producing a graph of his Noselength in real time, as shown in Figure 2. Submitting dishonest ratings will have a negative effect on the Noselength of the user who submitted them, which can be reversed by submitting honest ratings.

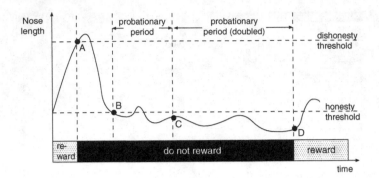

Fig. 3. Honesty and dishonesty thresholds, and probationary period

Probation and Classification. At the end of each honesty recalculation iteration, Jiminy identifies whether each user is to be considered honest or dishonest, and whether she is to face a probationary no-rewards period, as follows:

- A user stays outside the probationary period, if she is currently outside and her Noselength is below the dishonesty threshold
- A user enters the probationary period, if she is currently outside and her Noselength is above the dishonesty threshold
- A user stays in the probationary period, if she is currently inside and the probationary period has not passed yet, or if her Noselength is above the honesty threshold
- A user leaves the probationary period, if she is currently inside and her Noselength is below the honesty threshold and has been there for the whole probationary period

The Noselength value is also used by the system for classifying users into different categories. On one end of the spectrum, *radicals* are users who disagree with others much more often that other users. The other extreme class is *followers*, which consists of users who disagree the less often with others. Those users that maintain a healthy level of disagreement amongst them fall into the *average* class.

Consultation to the RMS. The reputation management system contacts Jiminy to query the trustworthiness of a certain user, in order to determine whether to reward her for submitting statements. A trustworthy user receives a credit amount for each statement she has submitted since the last query. The RMS interface during a query to Jiminy and the result returned by Jiminy are shown in Figure 4.

Use of Classification Information. The class in which a user resides — in terms of rating behaviour — can be obtained from Jiminy. This can be used to, for instance, transparently filter ratings taken into account for a given user. As

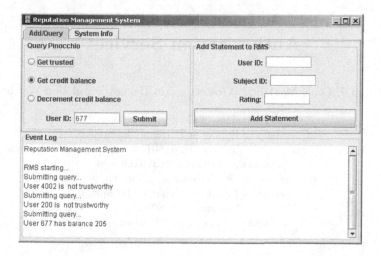

Fig. 4. Interface of the RMS for querying Jiminy

an example, a retailer web site linked to Jiminy could automatically calculate the average rating of a product based on the ratings of users in the same class as the user who is viewing the product. A radical user is likely to prefer seeing the ratings of other radical users, rather than those of sheep users.

References

1. A. Fernandes, E. Kotsovinos, S. Ostring, and B. Dragovic. Pinocchio: Incentives for honest participation in distributed trust management. In *Proc. 2nd Intl Conf. on Trust Management (iTrust 2004)*, Mar. 2004.
2. E. Kotsovinos, P. Zerfos, N. Piratla, N. Cameron, and S. Agarwal. Jiminy: A Scalable Incentive-Based Architecture for Improving Rating Quality. In *Proc. 4th Intl. Conf. on Trust Mgmt (iTrust '06)*, May 2006.

Traust: A Trust Negotiation Based Authorization Service*

Adam J. Lee[1], Marianne Winslett[1], Jim Basney[2], and Von Welch[2]

[1] Department of Computer Science,
University of Illinois at Urbana-Champaign,
Urbana, IL 61801
{adamlee, winslett}@cs.uiuc.edu
[2] National Center for Supercomputing Applications,
University of Illinois at Urbana-Champaign,
Urbana, IL 61801
{jbasney, vwelch}@ncsa.uiuc.edu

Abstract. In this demonstration, we present Traust, a flexible authorization service for open systems. Traust uses the technique of trust negotiation to map globally meaningful assertions regarding a previously unknown client into security tokens that are meaningful to resources deployed in the Traust service's security domain. This system helps preserve the privacy of both users and the service, while at the same time automating interactions between security domains that would previously have required human intervention (e.g., the establishment of local accounts). We will demonstrate how the Traust service enables the use of trust negotiation to broker access to resources in open systems without requiring changes to protocol standards or applications software.

1 Introduction

Making intelligent authorization decisions in large computer systems is a nontrivial task. Traditional authorization systems require some explicit notion of the users accessing the resources provided by the system; this knowledge is usually in the form of a user account protected by a password or some other digital credential. While systems such as Kerberos [5] and hierarchical PKIs [4] help reduce the overhead of managing these systems on a per-organization basis, it is widely accepted that they do not scale well in large-scale open systems where information and resources are shared across organizational boundaries.

The increasing popularity of the Internet has led to a surge in the number of resources provided through open environments such as the world wide web, peer-to-peer networks, virtual organizations, disaster response networks, joint task forces, and grid computing environments. In these systems, it is unreasonable to

---

* This work was supported by the NSF under grants IIS-0331707, CNS-0325951, and CNS-0524695 and by NCSA. Lee was also supported by a Motorola Center for Communications Graduate Fellowship.

assume that entities will have—or even need to have—explicit knowledge of the peers that they are communicating with. For instance, can users of a peer-to-peer network reasonably be expected to enforce access controls on their shared resources based on the identities of the thousands of other peers in the system? We argue that in the context of large-scale open systems, authorization decisions are best made based on the attributes of the users in the system, as this allows for better scalability as the number of users continues to increase.

Trust negotiation [10] is a technique developed to allow peers to conduct bilateral and iterative exchanges of digital credentials to bootstrap trust relationships in open systems. Current work in trust negotiation has focused on the development of languages and strategies for trust negotiation [6, 7, 12], or the embedding of trust negotiation into commonly used protocols [3, 9]. In fact, little attention has been focused on designing a general-purpose authorization system based on trust negotiation. In this demonstration, we present Traust, a general purpose authorization service based on trust negotiation. Traust provides a uniform interface for clients to obtain the credentials necessary to access resources provided by systems in a different security domain and acts as a viable migration path for the adoption of trust negotiation research into existing open systems.

2   Goals

The design of Traust embodies five major design goals. These goals build on the strengths of trust negotiation techniques developed in the past and help Traust act as a scalable and flexible authorization service for large-scale open systems.

Bilateral trust establishment. It is important not only for a service provider to trust the clients requesting its services, but for clients to trust the services that they choose to interact with. Before disclosing any requests or credentials to the Traust service, clients may conduct a content-triggered trust negotiation session [2] to protect their potentially sensitive requests.

Run time access policy discovery. In open systems, clients cannot be expected to know the access requirements of services of interest a priori. Traust supports the discovery of these policies during the authorization process.

Privacy preserving. An interaction between a client and the Traust service should not reveal any extraneous information about either the client or the service. Trust should be established iteratively, each entity providing more sensitive credentials in response to the disclosures of the other entity.

Support for legacy and trust-aware applications. Incorporating   the Traust service into existing open systems should not involve completely redesigning deployed applications or protocols. Traust should support tight interaction with trust-aware applications via the use of a public API, but also remain accessible to clients who wish to access legacy applications.

Light-weight, yet robust. The Traust service should be light-weight enough for a single user (e.g., a peer-to-peer client) to deploy on her local machine, yet robust enough to meet the demands of a large security domain.

3   Design and Implementation

The Traust service was designed to provide a mechanism through which trust negotiation can bridge the security gap that exists between security domains in large-scale open systems without requiring widespread protocol or application software updates. Traust servers act as authorization brokers that distribute access tokens for certain services deployed within their security domain to *qualified* outsiders. Traust client software allows users to carry out a number of trust negotiations with the Traust server; these negotiations allow both the client and server to establish some degree of trust in one another.

Traust relies on SSL to protect the confidentiality and integrity of connections between clients and the service. Upon connecting to the Traust service, clients have the opportunity to conduct a content-triggered trust negotiation with the service to gain some level of trust before disclosing a potentially sensitive resource request. If this negotiation succeeds, the client then discloses its resource request to the Traust server. Resources can be as specific as a particular RPC method call or as broad as a request for access to a system-wide role. When the Traust service receives such a request, it locates the policies protecting the requested resource and initiates a trust negotiation with the client to determine if the client is a qualified outsider. If this negotiation succeeds, the Traust service issues the client any credentials needed to access the requested service. The server can obtain these tokens through either accessing static tokens in its credential repository, referencing files in its file system, or interfacing with external processes (e.g., one-time password generators, Kerberos servers, or MyProxy servers [8]). There are no fundamental limits on the types of credentials that can be issued.

Our implementation of the Traust service is written in Java and leverages the TrustBuilder framework and protocol for trust negotiation [11]. TrustBuilder has been successfully incorporated into several protocols [3, 9] and currently supports the use of X.509 attribute certificates as its native form of credentials and the IBM Trust Establishment language [1] for trust negotiation. Our implementation of the Traust service currently supports the issuance of username/password pairs and X.509 proxy certificates. We have developed both a stand-alone client application that can be used to obtain credentials to access legacy services and a client API that can be incorporated into the design of trust-aware applications.

4   Demonstration

In our demonstration, we show how the Traust service can enable the use of trust negotiation to grant qualified users access to a legacy resource without requiring any changes to the underlying resource or applications used. We illustrate how a volunteer search and rescue dog handler can use Traust to gain access to a web-based information portal used to coordinate the recovery effort for an earthquake, despite having no pre-existing trust relationship with the portal. The user first browses to this web site and is presented with a login form and resource descriptor to pass into her Traust client. She then uses

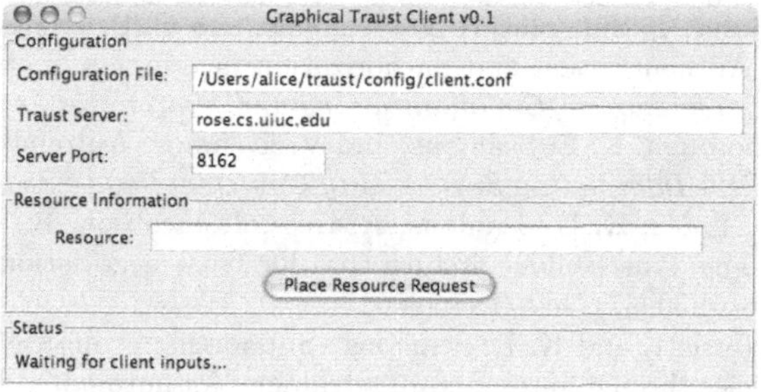

Fig. 1. Screenshot of the graphical Traust client

our graphical Traust client to initiate an interaction with the Traust server responsible for protecting access to this site (see Fig. 1). This interaction allows the client to establish trust in the server (by verifying that the server can demonstrate proof-of-ownership of a state-issued disaster response coordinator credential) and allows the server to gain trust in the user (by verifying that she can demonstrate proof-of-ownership of trusted credentials which indicate that he is a certified rescue dog handler with up-to-date vaccinations). The Traust server then returns a one-time-use password for the web site. Further information regarding our demonstration can be found at the following URL: `http://dais.cs.uiuc.edu/~adamlee/research/traust/demo/disaster_demo.html`.

References

[1] A. Herzberg, J. Mihaeli, Y. Mass, D. Naor, and Y. Ravid. Access control meets public key infrastructure, or: Assigning roles to strangers. In *IEEE Symposium on Security and Privacy*, May 2000.

[2] A. Hess, J. Holt, J. Jacobson, and K. E. Seamons. Content-triggered trust negotiation. *ACM Transactions on Information System Security*, 7(3), Aug. 2004.

[3] A. Hess, J. Jacobson, H. Mills, R. Wamsley, K. E. Seamons, and B. Smith. Advanced client/server authentication in TLS. In *Network and Distributed Systems Security Symposium*, Feb. 2002.

[4] R. Housely, W. Ford, W. Polk, and D. Solo. Internet X.509 public key infrastructure certificate and CRL profile. RFC 2459, Jan. 1999.

[5] J. Kohl and C. Neuman. The Kerberos network authentication service (V5). RFC 1510, Sep. 1993.

[6] H. Koshutanski and F. Massacci. Interactive trust management and negotiation scheme. In *2nd International Workshop on Formal Aspects in Security and Trust (FAST)*, pages 139–152, Aug. 2004.

[7] N. Li and J. Mitchell. RT: A role-based trust-management framework. In *Third DARPA Information Survivability Conference and Exposition*, Apr. 2003.

[8] J. Novotny, S. Tuecke, and V. Welch. An online credential repository for the grid: MyProxy. In *Tenth International Symposium on High Performance Distributed Computing (HPDC-10)*, Aug. 2001.

[9] T. van der Horst, T. Sundelin, K. E. Seamons, and C. D. Knutson. Mobile trust negotiation: Authentication and authorization in dynamic mobile networks. In *Eigth IFIP Conference on Communications and Multimedia Security*, Sep. 2004.

[10] W. H. Winsborough, K. E. Seamons, and V. E. Jones. Automated trust negotiation. In *DARPA Information Survivability Conference and Exposition*, Jan. 2000.

[11] M. Winslett, T. Yu, K. E. Seamons, A. Hess, J. Jacobson, R. Jarvis, B. Smith, and L. Yu. The TrustBuilder architecture for trust negotiation. *IEEE Internet Computing*, 6(6):30–37, Nov./Dec. 2002.

[12] T. Yu, M. Winslett, and K. E. Seamons. Supporting structured credentials and sensitive policies through interoperable strategies for automated trust negotiation. *ACM Transactions on Information and System Security*, 6(1), Feb. 2003.

The Interactive Cooperation Tournament

How to Identify Opportunities for Selfish Behavior of Computational Entities*

Philipp Obreiter[1] and Birgitta König-Ries[2]

[1] Institute for Program Structures and Data Organization,
Universität Karlsruhe (TH), 76128 Karlsruhe, Germany
obreiter@ipd.uni-karlsruhe.de
[2] Institute of Computer Science,
Friedrich-Schiller-Universität Jena, 07743 Jena, Germany
koenig@informatik.uni-jena.de

Abstract. Distributed reputation systems are a self-organizing means of supporting trusting decisions. In general, the robustness of distributed reputation systems
to misbehavior is evaluated by the means of computer based simulation. However,
the fundamental issue arises of how to anticipate kinds of successful misbehavior.
Existing work in this field approaches this issue in an ad-hoc manner. Therefore,
in this paper, we propose a methodology that is based on interactive simulation
with human subjects. The requirements for such interaction are discussed. We
show how they are met by the Interactive Cooperation Tournament, a simulation
environment for identifying promising counter-strategies to the distributed reputation system EviDirs which is showcased in our demo.

1 Introduction

In this paper, we propose a demo of our Interactive Cooperation Tournament (ICT).
ICT is a simulation environment that provides realistic evaluations of the robustness of
our distributed reputation system. We describe *why* systems like ICT are needed and
what functionality they need to provide in order to facilitate the engineering of robust
distributed reputation systems.

Context. If you look at computer systems, there is a clear trend away from closed mono-
lithic systems towards self-organizing artificial societies composed of autonomous entities with no central control and no commonly trusted unit. Examples are peer-to-peer
systems, open multi-agent systems, and ad hoc networks. All these systems have a
number of characteristics in common: In order to achieve their individual goal, it is
necessary for the entities in the system to cooperate. However, due to their autonomy,
on the one hand, entities will only cooperate, if it is beneficial to them, but on the other
hand, entities are able to cheat in the course of a cooperation. In order to avoid being
cheated on, an entity will only cooperate with entities it trusts. Yet, trusting decisions

---

* The work done for this paper is funded by the German Research Community (DFG) in the
context of the priority program (SPP) no. 1140.

K. Stølen et al. (Eds.): iTrust 2006, LNCS 3986, pp. 463–466, 2006.

can only be taken by an entity if it has formed its beliefs regarding the other entities based on prior experiences. The means of doing so are prescribed by the algorithms of the *distributed reputation system*. Several of such systems have been proposed in the past (e.g. [1, 2, 3]). The distributed reputation system of [3] (*EviDirs*) exhibits several desirable properties and, thus, builds the foundation of the remainder of this work. We distinguish between two types of computational entities. *Normative entities* adhere to the prescriptions of the distributed reputation system. In an application scenario, these entities are found on the devices of those human principals who make use of the original system software, as it has been distributed by system's initiator. On the other hand, *strategic entities* are not compelled to comply to the prescriptions and, thus, exhibit selfish behavior. This situation arises whenever human principals are able to tamper the original system software.

Problem. Analytic proofs are a viable means of displaying core properties of a distributed reputation system. Yet, their application is restricted to specific behavior within the overall system. This becomes apparent in their idealizing assumptions that have to be made in order to apply the methodology of game theory. Thus, they fail to capture and consider every opportunity of misbehavior by strategic entities. Consequently, a means of testing the robustness of the distributed reputation system is required. In analogy to the methods applied in evolutionary game theory, computer based *simulation* appears as a natural solution to both problems [4]. Even though this approach is viable, it poses a fundamental question to the designer and evaluator of distributed reputation systems: *Is it possible to anticipate how the system software is tampered and, if yes, what kind of tampering has to be anticipated?*

The state of the art regarding this question is as follows: The evaluator defines the counter-strategies to the system design according to his intuition. This approach suffers from two considerable drawbacks. First, the evaluator may overlook more intricate means of misbehavior. The existence of such means is probable due to the complexity of common distributed reputation systems. Second, the evaluator is, in general, also the designer of the distributed reputation system. Consequently, he might be induced to consider only those counter-strategies that his design is able to cope with. As a result of these drawbacks, we require a means of reliably identifying counter-strategies that should be included in the system's simulative evaluation.

Outline. In order to solve this problem, we propose the following approach: The simulation environment is made *interactive* such that human subjects may assume the role of certain entities. The simulation environment is built such that the human subjects are both able and motivated to find promising counter-strategies. In Section 2 the ensuing requirements and its implementation example for EviDirs is discussed. The obtained simulation environment ICT. It will be showcased in our demo.

2   The Interactive Cooperation Tournament (ICT)

In this section, we discuss the requirements that arise from our approach of interactively identifying promising counter-strategies. For each requirement, we point out how it can be implemented. In this regard, the ICT acts as a point of reference.

Fig. 1. The user interface of the Interactive Cooperation Tournament

As a basic requirement, the human subjects have to be *informed* about the incidents that happen in the overall system. Furthermore, mere information is not enough since it has to be presented in a user-friendly manner. Only if this is achieved, the human subjects are able to intuitively grasp the context of their behavioral decisions and choose their respective strategies accordingly. Figure 1 illustrates how the ICT implements this requirement. Each participating entity is assigned an avatar so that the human subjects are more likely to recognize them and remember their prior behavior. The avatars and the labeling of the entities are assigned randomly for each tournament so that the human subjects do not know which entity is controlled by the simulation environment and which are not. This corresponds to the situation in real system in which the entities do not know who is normative and who is strategic. Each human subject is able to access the complete record of the experiences his entity has made. That information is aggregated and displayed by additional icons nearby the avatars.

A further requirement consists of the *accessibility* of the simulation environment. The human subjects do not have to be experts of the distributed reputation system Ev-iDirs in order to participate. Only by this means, the number of potential human subjects is not restricted and, hence, a wide range of counter-strategies can be obtained. The ICT takes this requirement into account by providing a tutorial, a glossary and a forum in which system-specific questions are debated. As a further assistance for the human subjects, the simulation environment may control behavioral aspects (e.g., the more intricate recommendation behavior) that novice subjects are not able to cope with.

The third requirement refers to the *motivation* of the human subjects. In real application scenarios, tampered system software is used in order to reduce one's own costs or enhance one's own benefits of participating to the system. As a consequence, we have to anticipate counter-strategies that aim at maximizing the individual utility of the entities that follow them. The ICT makes use calories as the metaphor of individual utility. On the one hand, the cost category of transactions is illustrated by adequate food icons (a pizza has more calories than an apple...). On the other hand, one's own individual utility is visualized by a guy on the lower left corner: the fatter he is the more successful the human subject has performed. A further source of motivation is the policy to contact the most successful subject after termination of the tournament and to ask for the counter-strategy he has followed. By this means, the evaluator obtains information about the kind of counter-strategies that are most successful and, thus, have to be anticipated. According to our experiences, the human subjects are able to express the basic principles of the strategy (or strategies) they followed. By additionally consulting the simulation log, the evaluator is able to define and parameterize the identified counter-strategies.

For the demo, we run an instance of the tournament and allow visitors to explore themselves how it works and find out how good the strategies are that they follow.

3   Conclusion

Distributed reputation systems are a self-organizing means of supporting trusting decisions. In order to simulate such systems, we have to be able to anticipate successful (and thus likely) counter-strategies that could be pursued by misbehaving entities. In this paper, we have proposed a methodology that is based on interactive simulation with human subjects. The requirements for such interaction are threefold: The simulation environment has to inform the human subjects appropriately about the system's incidents, it has to be accessible to a wide range of potential subjects and, finally, the human subjects have to be motivated to maximize the individual utility of the respective entity they control. Furthermore, we have shown how these requirements are met by the ICT, an interactive simulation environment of the distributed reputation system EviDirs. As a result of meeting the requirements, the participating human subjects have identified promising counter-strategies to EviDirs in a hands-on manner.

In the future, similar interactive simulation environments have to be developed for other distributed reputation systems. This necessity arises from the fundamental problem of anticipating realistic means of misbehavior. Even though the development of adequate simulation environments or, if possible, of a generic simulation environment is an intricate task, it provides the only means of solving this problem and, thus, credibly testing the robustness of arbitrary distributed reputation systems. The discussion of this paper provides the basis for such future work.

References

1. Despotovic, Z., Aberer, K.: A probabilistic approach to predict peers' performance in P2P networks. In: 8th Intl Workshop on Cooperative Information Agents (CIA'04). (2004)
2. Liu, J., Issarny, V.: Enhanced reputation mechanism for mobile ad hoc networks. In: Second International Conference on Trust Management (iTrust'04), Oxford, UK, Springer LNCS 2995 (2004) 48–62
3. Obreiter, P., König-Ries, B.: A new view on normativeness in distributed reputation systems – beyond behavioral beliefs. In: Fourth Workshop on Agents and Peer-to-Peer Computing (AP2PC'05), Utrecht, Niederlande (2005)
4. Axelrod, R.: The Evolution of Cooperation. Basic Books (1984)

eTVRA, a Threat, Vulnerability and Risk Assessment Tool for eEurope*

Judith E. Y. Rossebø[1,2], Scott Cadzow[3,4], and Paul Sijben[4,5]

[1] The Norwegian University of Science and Technology
[2] Telenor R&D, Norway
judith.rossebo@telenor.com
[3] Cadzow Communications, UK
scott@cadzow.com
[4] ETSI STF 292
stf292@etsi.org
[5] Eem Valley Technology, The Netherlands
sijben@eemvalley.com

Abstract. Securing the evolving telecommunications environment and establishing trust in its services and infrastructure is crucial for enabling the development of modern public services. The security of the underlying network and services environment for eBusiness is addressed as a crucial area in the eEurope action plan [2]. In response to this Specialist Task Force (STF) 292 associated with the European Telecommunication Standardisation Institute (ETSI) TISPAN [3] under contract from eEurope, has developed a threat, vulnerability and risk assessment (eTVRA) method and tool for use in standardisation. Using the eTVRA method and tool, the threats to a next generation network (NGN) can be analyzed and a set of recommended countermeasures identified that when implemented will reduce the overall risk to users of NGNs. In this paper we present the eTVRA method and tool along with the results of using the eTVRA for an analysis of a Voice over IP (VoIP) scenario of the NGN.

1   Introduction

During the past decade in Europe we have seen the evolution from single, nationally owned and operated networks featuring voice services to the situation of today with numerous network operators, and service providers featuring a wide range of different types of services. There is a trend for fixed and mobile networks to converge, sharing a single IP-based core in the emerging next generation network (NGN). Standardisation plays an important role in enabling operators to deliver services to the users and ensure that the regulatory, interconnection and interoperability requirements are met.

---

* This work is supported by the eEurope initiative [1] and by the Research Council of Norway project SARDAS (152952/431).

K. Stølen et al. (Eds.): iTrust 2006, LNCS 3986, pp. 467–471, 2006.

Standardisation also applies to provision of security mechanism as an important means for achieving and establishing trust between the operators and the parties they serve. The emerging NGN is destined to become the platform for eBusiness and eGovernment, both of which require an assurance of the level of security that the NGN will provide. ETSI is in the process of developing standards for the NGN and as part of that process is also preparing guidance on methods of developing security standards.

Fundamentally providers and users of systems such as the NGN need some assurance that their use of the NGN will not give rise to unwanted incidents. The probability of such incidents arising is inherent in the system design and the role of standards bodies is to ensure that the likelihood of such incidents arising is low and the impact of their occurrence is also low, and to ensure that the standards do not contribute to the risk. This can be achieved by providing a systematic method for security design from conducting a threat, vulnerability and risk analysis through to specification of an appropriate set of security countermeasures within a standards context, and by integrating systematic methods in standards development. The route adopted in ETSI for the first of these areas has been to develop a method for eTVRA based on the common criteria for security evaluation [4], the ETSI standard for threat analysis and risk assessment [5] and CORAS [6]. The eTVRA has been adapted to meet the needs of the current and future standardisation environment. This paper presents both the eTVRA method and the tools created to support it within the context of the NGN.

2   eTVRA Method

The eTVRA method involves a systematic identification of the unwanted incidents to be prevented in the system, and for the system itself, identifying the assets it is composed of and their associated weaknesses, the threats and the threat agents that will attack the system, before determining the risk to the system by modelling the likelihood and impact of attacks on the systems vulnerabilities. Although in this sense, the eTVRA method builds on existing risk assessment methods (e.g. CORAS [6]), it is different in detail from such existing methods that are primarily designed for assessment of commercial products or systems, often in isolation, and often to determine commercial risk for purposes of financing a venture.

This is because the purpose of risk assessment in a standards environment is different and intended to address the concerns of a broad set of stakeholders including consumers, service providers, network operators, vendors, and regulatory authorities. The concerns of the different stakeholders must be weighed and taken into account by the analysis. Indeed, these stakeholders may own or control different assets in different parts of the NGN, each of which is exposed to threats, and which may pose threats to each other. The outcome of a standards based eTVRA is intended to drive subsequent standards decisions, i.e. to find those vulnerabilities common to a set of stakeholders where common development and deployment of a countermeasure is warranted. The documen-

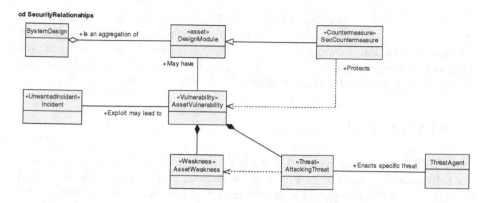

Fig. 1. The system relationships

tation resulting from applying the *e*TVRA may also be incorporated in a Protection Profile (PP), as described in [7].

The *e*TVRA method uses a model as shown in Fig. 1. The *e*TVRA models a system consisting of *Assets*. An *Asset* may be physical, human or logical. *Assets* in the model may have *Weaknesses* that may be attacked by *Threats*. A *Threat* is enacted by a *Threat Agent*, and may lead to an *Unwanted Incident* breaking certain pre-defined security objectives. A *Vulnerability*, consistent with the definition given in [8], is modelled as the combination of a *Weakness* that can be exploited by one or more *Threats*. When applied, *Countermeasures* protect against *Threats* to *Vulnerabilities* and reduce the risk. The *e*TVRA method process consists of the following steps:

1. *Identification of the objectives.*
2. *Identification of the requirements, derived from the objectives from step 1.*
3. *Inventory of the assets.*
4. *Identification and classification of the vulnerabilities in the system, the threats that can exploit them, and the unwanted incidents that may result.*
5. *Quantifying the occurance likelihood and impact of the threats.*
6. *Establishment of the risks.*
7. *Identification of countermeasures framework (architecture).*

Each step in the method has guidance attached to lead the analyst. In particular for step 5, which involves detailed calculations of the likelihood and impact values, the use of repeatable metrics is essential to the repeatability of the analysis over time. The metrics used in step 5 are developed from the guidance given in [5] and [4]. One characteristic of the method is to include an evaluation of whether an attack exploiting a vulnerability can be automated thereby offering an additional metric to be used in assessing risk. The product of occurrence likelihood and impact values from step 5 gives a measure of the risk to the asset. A countermeasure will reduce the likelihood of the threat being successful and/or reduces its impact. This step results in a set of countermeasures to protect the vulnerabilities against threats. Note that countermeasures may create new vulnerabilities, indicating that the eTVRA will need to be executed again, and the method should be repeated until all the risks have been reduced to an acceptable level. Furthermore, by allowing the analysis to be rerun when attack likelihood changes, the risk to the system may be re-evaluated as knowledge of new or revised attacks becomes available.

3   eTVRA Tool

The eTVRA has been developed as a database structure. The database accepts the full model represented in Fig. 1 to be entered and produces the likelihood weighting, and the computation of the impact of automated threat agents and countermeasures as well as the resulting risk values. We are using the eTVRA method and the eTVRA tool to conduct a Threat Vulnerability and Risk Analysis of a Voice over IP (VoIP) deployment using the session initiation protocol (SIP) [9] and the telephone number resolution system called Enhanced Number (ENUM) [10]. Using the current database version of the tool we have demonstrated the eTVRA method and tool on a test-case of a typical SIP and ENUM system.

Table 1. Some critical risks found by the VoIP eTVRA

Asset	Vulnerability	Threat	Threat Family	Likeli-hood	impact	Unwanted Incidents
call state IN SIP or other session server	illegal message content	closing of sessions	Denial of service	likely	High	Loss of service availability
call state IN SIP or other session server	illegal message format	overload of communication	Denial of service	likely	High	Loss of service availability
data in transit IN link to ENUM leaf server	limited transport/processing capacity	overload of communication	Denial of service	likely	High	Loss of service availability
ENUM query IN SIP or other session server	limited transport/processing capacity	overload of communication	Denial of service	possible	High	Loss of service availability
server keys IN Leaf server	accessible credentials	credential manipulation	Manipulation	possible	High	1. Loss of service availability 2. Data security breaches

A summary of some of the critical risks found in this case is given in Table 1. The table shows the assets (logical assets in physical assets), the type of vulnerability the risk applies to, the threat that may impact this vulnerability, the likelihood, the impact, and the resulting unwanted incidents. The computed likelihood is calculated taking into account the expertise level necessary to execute the threat, the level of access that is required, and the time needed to mount the attack. Each of the threats listed in Table 1 can lead to partial or total loss of service availability. The threats involving manipulation of credentials also can lead to consumer data security breaches. The resulting major unwanted incidents for the service provider are Loss of reputation, Loss of revenue, and in the case of consumer data security breaches, legal issues.

4   Conclusions

In this paper we have described the eTVRA method and tool as developed by STF292 in ETSI/TISPAN under contract from eEurope. The model has been validated in a case study carried out on SIP and ENUM which has demonstrated the usability of the eTVRA. The model has been implemented in a database and a web-front-end is being constructed allowing the wider community to use the tool. While the work is ongoing the results are being applied to the development of standards for the NGN. In particular, it is demonstrating that one of the major challenges for the NGN is ensuring availability of the network and services, demonstrated by the eTVRA of SIP and ENUM, for which the unwanted incident of loss availability is associated with a large number of critical threats and vulnerabilities.

References

1. eEurope: Supporting the eEurope initiative. http://portal.etsi.org/eeurope (2005)
2. Council of the European Union: Council Resolution on the implementation of the eEurope 2005 Action Plan. (2003)
3. European Telecommunication Standardisation Institute: Telecommunications and Internet converged Services and Protocols for Advanced Networking (TISPAN). http://portal.etsi.org/tispan/TISPAN_ToR.asp (2006)
4. International Standards Organization: ISO/IEC 15408, Information technology – Security techniques – Evaluation criteria for IT security. (1999)
5. European Telecommunication Standardisation Institute: ETSI ETR 332, Security techniques advisory group (STAG)– Security Requirements Capture. (1996)
6. Vraalsen, F., den Braber I. Hogganvik, F., Stølen, K.: The CORAS tool-supported methodology for UML-based security analysis. Technical report STF90 A04015, SINTEF ICT (2004)
7. European Telecommunication Standardisation Institute: ETSI ES 202 382, Telecommunications and Internet converged Services and Protocols for Advanced Networking (TISPAN); Security Design Guide; Method and proforma for defining Protection Profiles. (2005)
8. International Standards Organization: ISO/IEC 13335, Information technology – Security techniques – Guidelines for the management of IT security. (2001)
9. Rosenberg, J., Schulzrinne, H., Camarillo, G., Johnston, A., Peterson, J., Sparks, R., Handley, M., Schooler, E.: SIP: Session initiation protocol. RFC 3261 (2002)
10. Faltstrom, P., Mealling, M.: The E.164 to uniform resource identifiers (URI) dynamic delegation discovery system (DDDS) application (ENUM). RFC 3761 (2004)

Author Index

Agarwal, Sachin 221
Ahsant, Mehran 3

Barber, K. Suzanne 439
Basney, Jim 458

Cadzow, Scott 467
Cameron, Niall 221, 454
Capra, Licia 298, 313
Casassa Mont, Marco 267
Castelfranchi, Cristiano 1, 19
Chandran, Suroop Mohan 33
Chen, Huajun 423

Elgesem, Dag 48
English, Colin 62

Falcone, Rino 19
Foukia, Noria 77
Fullam, Karen K. 439

Golbeck, Jennifer 93
Gomez, Laurent 443

Haenni, Rolf 164
Hailes, Stephen 298, 313
Haller, Jochen 193
Herrmann, Peter 105
Hofstede, Gert Jan 120
Houmb, Siv Hilde 135

Jansen, Ulrich 443
Jensen, Christian D. 150
Jonczy, Jacek 164, 449
Jonker, Catholijn M. 120
Jøsang, Audun 179
Joshi, James B.D. 33

Karabulut, Yücel 193
Kerschbaum, Florian 193
Klos, Tomas 206, 439

König-Ries, Birgitta 463
Kotsovinos, Evangelos 221, 454
Krishna, Ananth 3

La Poutré, Han 206
Lee, Adam J. 236, 458
Leonard, Thomas 3
Lewis, Dave 324

Mao, Yuxin 423
Marsh, Stephen 179
Marzo, Francesca 19
Meijer, Sebastiaan 120
Muller, Guillaume 439
Mulmo, Olle 3

Neuman, Clifford 77

Obreiter, Philipp 463
O Connell, Paul 150
O'Sullivan, Declan 324

Panyim, Korporn 33
Pearson, Siani 252, 267
Pieters, Wolter 283
Piolle, Guillaume 397
Piratla, Nischal M. 221, 454
Pitt, Jeremy 397
Pope, Simon 179

Quercia, Daniele 298, 313
Quinn, Karl 324

Ray, Indrajit 135
Ray, Indrakshi 135
Robinson, Philip 193
Rossebø, Judith E.Y. 467

Sabater-Mir, Jordi 439
Sartor, Giovanni 354

Sijben, Paul   467
Sorge, Christoph   367
Surridge, Mike   3

Terzis, Sotirios   62
Traupman, Jonathan   382

Upadhyaya, Shambhu   339

Vasalou, Asimina   397
Vercouter, Laurent   439
Verwaart, Tim   120
Vidyaraman, Sankaranarayanan   339

Wade, Vincent P.   324
Welch, Von   458
Wilensky, Robert   382
Winslett, Marianne   236, 458
Wu, Zhaohui   423

Yonezawa, Kouki   412

Zerfos, Petros   221, 454
Zheng, Xiaoqing   423
Zhou, Li   77
Zitterbart, Martina   367

Lecture Notes in Computer Science

For information about Vols. 1–3883

please contact your bookseller or Springer

Vol. 3987: M. Hazas, J. Krumm, T. Strang (Eds.), Location- and Context-Awareness. X, 289 pages. 2006.

Vol. 3986: K. Stølen, W.H. Winsborough, F. Martinelli, F. Massacci (Eds.), Trust Management. XIV, 474 pages. 2006.

Vol. 3984: M. Gavrilova, O. Gervasi, V. Kumar, C.J. K. Tan, D. Taniar, A. Laganà, Y. Mun, H. Choo (Eds.), Computational Science and Its Applications - ICCSA 2006, Part V. XXV, 1045 pages. 2006.

Vol. 3983: M. Gavrilova, O. Gervasi, V. Kumar, C.J. K. Tan, D. Taniar, A. Laganà, Y. Mun, H. Choo (Eds.), Computational Science and Its Applications - ICCSA 2006, Part IV. XXVI, 1191 pages. 2006.

Vol. 3982: M. Gavrilova, O. Gervasi, V. Kumar, C.J. K. Tan, D. Taniar, A. Laganà, Y. Mun, H. Choo (Eds.), Computational Science and Its Applications - ICCSA 2006, Part III. XXV, 1243 pages. 2006.

Vol. 3981: M. Gavrilova, O. Gervasi, V. Kumar, C.J. K. Tan, D. Taniar, A. Laganà, Y. Mun, H. Choo (Eds.), Computational Science and Its Applications - ICCSA 2006, Part II. XXVI, 1255 pages. 2006.

Vol. 3980: M. Gavrilova, O. Gervasi, V. Kumar, C.J. K. Tan, D. Taniar, A. Laganà, Y. Mun, H. Choo (Eds.), Computational Science and Its Applications - ICCSA 2006, Part I. LXXV, 1199 pages. 2006.

Vol. 3979: T.S. Huang, N. Sebe, M.S. Lew, V. Pavlović, T. Kölsch, A. Galata, B. Kisačanin (Eds.), Computer Vision in Human-Computer Interaction. XII, 121 pages. 2006.

Vol. 3978: B. Hnich, M. Carlsson, F. Fages, F. Rossi (Eds.), Recent Advances in Constraints. VIII, 179 pages. 2006. (Sublibrary LNAI).

Vol. 3970: T. Braun, G. Carle, S. Fahmy, Y. Kocheryavy (Eds.), Wired/Wireless Internet Communications. XIV, 350 pages. 2006.

Vol. 3968: K.P. Fishkin, B. Schiele, P. Nixon, A. Quigley (Eds.), Pervasive Computing. XV, 402 pages. 2006.

Vol. 3967: D. Grigoriev, J. Harrison, E.A. Hirsch (Eds.), Computer Science – Theory and Applications. XVI, 684 pages. 2006.

Vol. 3964: M. Ü. Uyar, A.Y. Duale, M.A. Fecko (Eds.), Testing of Communicating Systems. XI, 373 pages. 2006.

Vol. 3960: R. Vieira, P. Quaresma, M.d.G.V. Nunes, N.J. Mamede, C. Oliveira, M.C. Dias (Eds.), Computational Processing of the Portuguese Language. XII, 274 pages. 2006. (Sublibrary LNAI).

Vol. 3959: J.-Y. Cai, S. B. Cooper, A. Li (Eds.), Theory and Applications of Models of Computation. XV, 794 pages. 2006.

Vol. 3958: M. Yung, Y. Dodis, A. Kiayias, T. Malkin (Eds.), Public Key Cryptography - PKC 2006. XIV, 543 pages. 2006.

Vol. 3956: G. Barthe, B. Gregoire, M. Huisman, J.-L. Lanet (Eds.), Construction and Analysis of Safe, Secure, and Interoperable Smart Devices. IX, 175 pages. 2006.

Vol. 3955: G. Antoniou, G. Potamias, C. Spyropoulos, D. Plexousakis (Eds.), Advances in Artificial Intelligence. XVII, 611 pages. 2006. (Sublibrary LNAI).

Vol. 3954: A. Leonardis, H. Bischof, A. Pinz (Eds.), Computer Vision – ECCV 2006, Part IV. XVII, 613 pages. 2006.

Vol. 3953: A. Leonardis, H. Bischof, A. Pinz (Eds.), Computer Vision – ECCV 2006, Part III. XVII, 649 pages. 2006.

Vol. 3952: A. Leonardis, H. Bischof, A. Pinz (Eds.), Computer Vision – ECCV 2006, Part II. XVII, 661 pages. 2006.

Vol. 3951: A. Leonardis, H. Bischof, A. Pinz (Eds.), Computer Vision – ECCV 2006, Part I. XXXV, 639 pages. 2006.

Vol. 3950: J.P. Müller, F. Zambonelli (Eds.), Agent-Oriented Software Engineering VI. XVI, 249 pages. 2006.

Vol. 3947: Y.-C. Chung, J.E. Moreira (Eds.), Advances in Grid and Pervasive Computing. XXI, 667 pages. 2006.

Vol. 3946: T.R. Roth-Berghofer, S. Schulz, D.B. Leake (Eds.), Modeling and Retrieval of Context. XI, 149 pages. 2006. (Sublibrary LNAI).

Vol. 3945: M. Hagiya, P. Wadler (Eds.), Functional and Logic Programming. X, 295 pages. 2006.

Vol. 3944: J. Quiñonero-Candela, I. Dagan, B. Magnini, F. d'Alché-Buc (Eds.), Machine Learning Challenges. XIII, 462 pages. 2006. (Sublibrary LNAI).

Vol. 3943: N. Guelfi, A. Savidis (Eds.), Rapid Integration of Software Engineering Techniques. X, 289 pages. 2006.

Vol. 3942: Z. Pan, R. Aylett, H. Diener, X. Jin, S. Göbel, L. Li (Eds.), Technologies for E-Learning and Digital Entertainment. XXV, 1396 pages. 2006.

Vol. 3939: C. Priami, L. Cardelli, S. Emmott (Eds.), Transactions on Computational Systems Biology IV. VII, 141 pages. 2006. (Sublibrary LNBI).

Vol. 3936: M. Lalmas, A. MacFarlane, S. Rüger, A. Tombros, T. Tsikrika, A. Yavlinsky (Eds.), Advances in Information Retrieval. XIX, 584 pages. 2006.

Vol. 3935: D. Won, S. Kim (Eds.), Information Security and Cryptology - ICISC 2005. XIV, 458 pages. 2006.

Vol. 3934: J.A. Clark, R.F. Paige, F.A. C. Polack, P.J. Brooke (Eds.), Security in Pervasive Computing. X, 243 pages. 2006.

Vol. 3933: F. Bonchi, J.-F. Boulicaut (Eds.), Knowledge Discovery in Inductive Databases. VIII, 251 pages. 2006.

Vol. 3931: B. Apolloni, M. Marinaro, G. Nicosia, R. Tagliaferri (Eds.), Neural Nets. XIII, 370 pages. 2006.

Vol. 3930: D.S. Yeung, Z.-Q. Liu, X.-Z. Wang, H. Yan (Eds.), Advances in Machine Learning and Cybernetics. XXI, 1110 pages. 2006. (Sublibrary LNAI).

Vol. 3929: W. MacCaull, M. Winter, I. Düntsch (Eds.), Relational Methods in Computer Science. VIII, 263 pages. 2006.

Vol. 3928: J. Domingo-Ferrer, J. Posegga, D. Schreckling (Eds.), Smart Card Research and Advanced Applications. XI, 359 pages. 2006.

Vol. 3927: J. Hespanha, A. Tiwari (Eds.), Hybrid Systems: Computation and Control. XII, 584 pages. 2006.

Vol. 3925: A. Valmari (Ed.), Model Checking Software. X, 307 pages. 2006.

Vol. 3924: P. Sestoft (Ed.), Programming Languages and Systems. XII, 343 pages. 2006.

Vol. 3923: A. Mycroft, A. Zeller (Eds.), Compiler Construction. XIII, 277 pages. 2006.

Vol. 3922: L. Baresi, R. Heckel (Eds.), Fundamental Approaches to Software Engineering. XIII, 427 pages. 2006.

Vol. 3921: L. Aceto, A. Ingólfsdóttir (Eds.), Foundations of Software Science and Computation Structures. XV, 447 pages. 2006.

Vol. 3920: H. Hermanns, J. Palsberg (Eds.), Tools and Algorithms for the Construction and Analysis of Systems. XIV, 506 pages. 2006.

Vol. 3918: W.K. Ng, M. Kitsuregawa, J. Li, K. Chang (Eds.), Advances in Knowledge Discovery and Data Mining. XXIV, 879 pages. 2006. (Sublibrary LNAI).

Vol. 3917: H. Chen, F.Y. Wang, C.C. Yang, D. Zeng, M. Chau, K. Chang (Eds.), Intelligence and Security Informatics. XII, 186 pages. 2006.

Vol. 3916: J. Li, Q. Yang, A.-H. Tan (Eds.), Data Mining for Biomedical Applications. VIII, 155 pages. 2006. (Sublibrary LNBI).

Vol. 3915: R. Nayak, M.J. Zaki (Eds.), Knowledge Discovery from XML Documents. VIII, 105 pages. 2006.

Vol. 3914: A. Garcia, R. Choren, C. Lucena, P. Giorgini, T. Holvoet, A. Romanovsky (Eds.), Software Engineering for Multi-Agent Systems IV. XIV, 255 pages. 2006.

Vol. 3910: S.A. Brueckner, G.D.M. Serugendo, D. Hales, F. Zambonelli (Eds.), Engineering Self-Organising Systems. XII, 245 pages. 2006. (Sublibrary LNAI).

Vol. 3909: A. Apostolico, C. Guerra, S. Istrail, P. Pevzner, M. Waterman (Eds.), Research in Computational Molecular Biology. XVII, 612 pages. 2006. (Sublibrary LNBI).

Vol. 3908: A. Bui, M. Bui, T. Böhme, H. Unger (Eds.), Innovative Internet Community Systems. VIII, 207 pages. 2006.

Vol. 3907: F. Rothlauf, J. Branke, S. Cagnoni, E. Costa, C. Cotta, R. Drechsler, E. Lutton, P. Machado, J.H. Moore, J. Romero, G.D. Smith, G. Squillero, H. Takagi (Eds.), Applications of Evolutionary Computing. XXIV, 813 pages. 2006.

Vol. 3906: J. Gottlieb, G.R. Raidl (Eds.), Evolutionary Computation in Combinatorial Optimization. XI, 293 pages. 2006.

Vol. 3905: P. Collet, M. Tomassini, M. Ebner, S. Gustafson, A. Ekárt (Eds.), Genetic Programming. XI, 361 pages. 2006.

Vol. 3904: M. Baldoni, U. Endriss, A. Omicini, P. Torroni (Eds.), Declarative Agent Languages and Technologies III. XII, 245 pages. 2006. (Sublibrary LNAI).

Vol. 3903: K. Chen, R. Deng, X. Lai, J. Zhou (Eds.), Information Security Practice and Experience. XIV, 392 pages. 2006.

Vol. 3902: R. Kronland-Martinet, T. Voinier, S. Ystad (Eds.), Computer Music Modeling and Retrieval. XI, 275 pages. 2006.

Vol. 3901: P.M. Hill (Ed.), Logic Based Program Synthesis and Transformation. X, 179 pages. 2006.

Vol. 3900: F. Toni, P. Torroni (Eds.), Computational Logic in Multi-Agent Systems. XVII, 427 pages. 2006. (Sublibrary LNAI).

Vol. 3899: S. Frintrop, VOCUS: A Visual Attention System for Object Detection and Goal-Directed Search. XIV, 216 pages. 2006. (Sublibrary LNAI).

Vol. 3898: K. Tuyls, P.J. 't Hoen, K. Verbeeck, S. Sen (Eds.), Learning and Adaption in Multi-Agent Systems. X, 217 pages. 2006. (Sublibrary LNAI).

Vol. 3897: B. Preneel, S. Tavares (Eds.), Selected Areas in Cryptography. XI, 371 pages. 2006.

Vol. 3896: Y. Ioannidis, M.H. Scholl, J.W. Schmidt, F. Matthes, M. Hatzopoulos, K. Boehm, A. Kemper, T. Grust, C. Boehm (Eds.), Advances in Database Technology - EDBT 2006. XIV, 1208 pages. 2006.

Vol. 3895: O. Goldreich, A.L. Rosenberg, A.L. Selman (Eds.), Theoretical Computer Science. XII, 399 pages. 2006.

Vol. 3894: W. Grass, B. Sick, K. Waldschmidt (Eds.), Architecture of Computing Systems - ARCS 2006. XII, 496 pages. 2006.

Vol. 3893: L. Atzori, D.D. Giusto, R. Leonardi, F. Pereira (Eds.), Visual Content Processing and Representation. IX, 224 pages. 2006.

Vol. 3892: A. Carbone, N.A. Pierce (Eds.), DNA Computing. XI, 440 pages. 2006.

Vol. 3891: J.S. Sichman, L. Antunes (Eds.), Multi-Agent-Based Simulation VI. X, 191 pages. 2006. (Sublibrary LNAI).

Vol. 3890: S.G. Thompson, R. Ghanea-Hercock (Eds.), Defence Applications of Multi-Agent Systems. XII, 141 pages. 2006. (Sublibrary LNAI).

Vol. 3889: J. Rosca, D. Erdogmus, J.C. Príncipe, S. Haykin (Eds.), Independent Component Analysis and Blind Signal Separation. XXI, 980 pages. 2006.

Vol. 3888: D. Draheim, G. Weber (Eds.), Trends in Enterprise Application Architecture. IX, 145 pages. 2006.

Vol. 3887: J.R. Correa, A. Hevia, M. Kiwi (Eds.), LATIN 2006: Theoretical Informatics. XVI, 814 pages. 2006.

Vol. 3886: E.G. Bremer, J. Hakenberg, E.-H.(S.) Han, D. Berrar, W. Dubitzky (Eds.), Knowledge Discovery in Life Science Literature. XIV, 147 pages. 2006. (Sublibrary LNBI).

Vol. 3885: V. Torra, Y. Narukawa, A. Valls, J. Domingo-Ferrer (Eds.), Modeling Decisions for Artificial Intelligence. XII, 374 pages. 2006. (Sublibrary LNAI).

Vol. 3884: B. Durand, W. Thomas (Eds.), STACS 2006. XIV, 714 pages. 2006.